Wissenschaftliche Untersuchungen
zum Neuen Testament · 2. Reihe

Herausgeber / Editor
Jörg Frey (Zürich)

Mitherausgeber / Associate Editors
Friedrich Avemarie (Marburg)
Markus Bockmuehl (Oxford)
Hans-Josef Klauck (Chicago, IL)

289

Meira Z. Kensky

# Trying Man, Trying God

The Divine Courtroom in Early Jewish
and Christian Literature

Mohr Siebeck

MEIRA Z. KENSKY, born 1978; 1999 B.A. in Liberal Arts from Sarah Lawrence College; 2001 M.A. from the University of Chicago; 2009 Ph.D. from the University of Chicago; currently Assistant Professor of Religion at Coe College in Cedar Rapids, IA.

ISBN 978-3-16-150409-9

ISSN 0340-9570 (Wissenschaftliche Untersuchungen zum Neuen Testament, 2. Reihe)

Die Deutsche Nationalbibliothek lists this publication in the Deutsche Nationalbibliographie; detailed bibliographic data are available on the Internet at *http://dnb.d-nb.de*.

The book was published with HelveticaU and NewJerusalemU fonts courtesy of Linguist's Software, printed by Laupp & Göbel in Nehren on non-aging paper and bound by Buchbinderei Nädele in Nehren.

Printed in Germany.

"A court of law has a curious attraction, hasn't it?"
Franz Kafka, *The Trial*

*In memory of my mother, Tikva Frymer-Kensky*
*In honor of my father, Rabbi Allan Kensky*
*And even my brother, Eitan Lev Kensky*

# Preface

This monograph is a revised version of my 2009 dissertation at the University of Chicago, over which I spilt much blood, sweat, and tears. At the first I would like to express my gratitude to Hans-Josef Klauck, whose expertise, advice, generosity of spirit, and commitment to excellence has made me the scholar I am today, and whom I am proud to call my Doktorvater. Next to Michael Fishbane, whose innovation and insight is legend, and without whom I would be a paltry reader of texts. I would like to thank also Gregory Sterling, who has provided me not only with precise critique and review, but with an excess of kindness and support.

Several other professors deserve special thanks, particularly Margaret M. Mitchell for her guidance throughout my graduate career. At Sarah Lawrence I was initiated into the study of the New Testament by Cameron Afzal, who infused the study of texts with pure joy and a sense of discovery. At Sarah Lawrence also I was privileged to study under Elfie S. Raymond, who captivated me with her attention to detail and her Yoda-like ability to capture wisdom and profundity in a simple movement. I would also like to thank Lyde Cullen Sizer, David Bernstein, and Ilja Wachs of Sarah Lawrence College; Benedicta Ward, O.P., of the University of Oxford; Roger Griffin of Oxford Brooks University; and, at the University of Chicago, W. Clark Gilpin, David Martinez, Jim Robinson, Richard Rosengarten, and William Schweiker. I would also like to thank Robin Jensen of Vanderbilt University and Patrick Alexander of Penn State Press.

As Klauck often repeated to me, *first live, then study philosophy:* At the University of Chicago I was fortunate to receive a Martin Marty Dissertation Fellowship that enabled me to focus on my writing and research for a sustained period of time. Dominic Colonna and Clare K. Rothschild at Lewis University offered me continuous employment and a supportive and collegial environment in which to participate. Thank you to my new colleagues at Coe College, particularly John Lemos, Jeff Hoover, and Peter McCormick, for inviting me to join them in Cedar Rapids and for welcoming me with great enthusiasm into the Department of Philosophy and Religion. Special thanks to Marie Baehr, Dean of the Faculty at Coe, for supporting my research and allowing me to hire an assistant in the formatting and indexing of this manuscript.

My friends and colleagues are the bedrocks of this study as well as my sanity. In particular I would like to thank Janet Spittler, Emily Brunner,

Robert Matthew Calhoun, Gabrielle Novacek, Edward Silver, Annette Borland Huizinga, Joel Dries, Matthew Baldwin, James Kelhoffer, Clare Rothschild, and Edward Upton for their friendship and support over the years. Thanks also to my new friends and colleagues Mónica Fuertes-Arboix, Melissa Sodeman, Gina Hausknecht, and Julie Fairbanks, as well as the entire Coe faculty who have made this transition such a pleasure. I would also like to thank all of the wonderful students I have had over the years, especially the participants in my Fall 2006 Studies in Paul Seminar at Lewis University, whose questions and blunt comments shaped my thinking on Paul just as much as any piece of secondary literature.

This manuscript could not have been completed without the able and noble assistance of my research assistant Vaclav Shatillo. I was fortunate to meet someone at Coe with such fluency both in classical languages and the modern languages of computer programs. He will be sorely missed at Coe, but leaves us for a promising career in classics that he will begin at University of Arizona. I am so thankful for the many hours he put in to this text, and for not bringing technical problems to me until after they were already solved. I thank also Anna Krüger at Mohr Siebeck for being so patient and helpful over the course of this past year. Also I would like to thank Jörg Frey and Henning Ziebritzki of Mohr Siebeck for having confidence in me and believing in the publication of this manuscript.

Ultimately one owes their very self to their family. I am blessed to have a great one, full of wisdom and eye-rolling. My mother, Tikva Frymer-Kensky, did not live to see this finished project, but she was here for its genesis and has remained a constant presence throughout its pages. I would like to thank my father, Rabbi Allan Kensky, whom I love dearly and stuff, and my brother Eitan Lev Kensky, the consummate renaissance man. We have also been privileged to add Adina Kleiman and Jennifer Broxmeyer to our family, who have only made it stronger and more interesting. Thank you to my aunt Susan Kensky and my uncle Samuel Goldman, and to my grandparents of blessed memory, Dr. Berl and Elyse Frymer, and Samuel and Ada Kensky. Special shout out and thank you to my surrogate family John and Faye Chaplin, Nancy Kisel, Jody Ann Joseph, Joshua Chaplin, and Diana Mogilevsky for making life truly wonderful.

Finally, I would not even be able to get up in the morning without knowing that my partner Geoff Chaplin is in the other room. Geoff, I love you with all my heart. You are the craziest and grumpiest man I know, and yes, courtrooms are a major part of the Christian tradition even though they are not in Dante. Est quod est! I cannot wait to experience my life with you; thank you for loving me and bearing with me all these years, and bringing me countless glasses of Diet Coke and ice.

Iowa, June 2010                                        Meira Z. Kensky

# Table of Contents

Chapter 1

# Introduction

In the Albert Brooks comedy *Defending Your Life*, Daniel Miller wakes up dead in an afterlife which bears a striking resemblance to 1991 Los Angeles. He discovers that he is in Judgment City, a way-station where he will go through a forensic process to determine whether he shall proceed to the next stage of existence or return to earth to go through human life again. In this process, he is represented by Bob Diamond (Rip Torn), an advocate charged with the responsibility of persuading the panel of judges that Daniel should be allowed to go forward. Unfortunately for Daniel, he is being prosecuted by a dragon-lady attorney against whom his advocate has a poor record, and his judges seem predisposed not to like him. This is a result, he learns, of the fact that he has been through this process before, many many times. Daniel seems doomed to a harsh verdict. This impression is reinforced when, on a day when his advocate is unavailable, his substitute defense counsel seems totally unconcerned and indifferent to providing good advocacy, cowtowing to the prosecution on every given point.

While in Judgment City, Daniel meets and falls in love with Julia (Meryl Streep), a woman whose trial is proceeding in absolute divergence from Daniel's. Julia is enjoying her trial, calling her advocate by his first name and taking advantage of all the amenities Judgment City has to offer. Though Julia does not divulge too many details about her earthly life, Daniel realizes that her trial is totally different than his own. When he peeks in to her trial, he sees why: on the giant screen where scenes from the defendant's life are played for evidence, he sees Julia rescuing children from a blazing house fire, and if that wasn't enough, after ensuring her children's safety, going back for the dog. When the scene stops playing and the lights go up, everyone in the room is in tears, and one of the judges apologizes: she knows that the day is running late, but she just needed to see that scene again.

Over the course of the movie, Daniel and the viewer realizes that the criteria by which he is being judged is not whether he lived a morally upright life, but whether or not he lived a life free from fear. Julia is brave and courageous; Daniel, on the other hand, is shown to have lived his life too scared to make decisions that would have benefited him both financially and emotionally. The culmination of the prosecution's case against him is when she shows a scene not from his life but from his time in Judgment City, in which Daniel admits to Julia that he is terrified of what lies ahead. Though Diamond objects vigorously to the acceptability of the evidence, it is admitted into the trial, and seals Daniel's fate. Daniel gets the word – he is going back to earth. Julia, on the other hand, is headed towards "points beyond," and the love that has developed between them seems to be over.

Throughout all of this, the audience has been watching from Daniel's perspective, learning things when he learns them, viewing his trial as he views it, and thinking about the process with his character. Daniel is not shy about expressing his opinions, especially when he thinks elements of his trial are unfair and that he is getting a raw deal in Judgment City. When Diamond is absent from his trial, and his substitute attorney does not provide vigorous advocacy, Daniel expresses frustration and anger, a position which the viewer may well be expected to share. When Daniel objects to the fact that the prosecutor and his advocate seem to have some sort of relationship separate from the trial, and the judges dismiss his objections, the viewer is expected to think about the equity of the situation and whether the judges are judging his trial fairly. Most importantly, when Daniel learns that he is being judged on the criteria of fear, the viewer is asked, along with Daniel, to think about whether this is a fair and proper criteria for adjudication. Daniel expresses shock at this discovery, asserting that humans are taught to admit to their fears and to be honest about them. The viewer is expected to take a position on this issue, as it is this that ultimately seals the verdict against Daniel.

Throughout the course of this movie, the viewer is expected not to sit as mere passive spectator on the trial, but to act as the real judge, evaluating and adjudicating the system in which the two protagonists find themselves, especially since so many decisions that drastically affected their trials were decided before they even entered the room. Julia's actions in life, before she even stepped foot in the courtroom, guaranteed her a sympathetic and friendly panel of judges, prosecutor, and advocate. Daniel's actions, however, led to a hostile and adversarial courtroom situation. How impartial can the verdict be if the deck was already stacked against the defendant? And is it fair to use the very criteria at issue in the courtroom to set up the courtroom itself? What about the evidence presented, especially the scene from Judgment City? This was highly unusual and seemingly inappropriate evidence. Were the judges right to allow it? Did the panel issue a just verdict?

Luckily for Daniel, this is a comedy, and so at the very end of the movie he is united with Julia and the system is ultimately exonerated. When Daniel commits a truly brave and heroic act at the end of the film, the camera pans back to reveal that the scene is playing out on the evidence screen before Daniel's panel, prosecutor, and advocate. The judges give the word and Daniel's verdict is overturned. He is reunited with Julia. The viewer is allowed to leave the theatre feeling like ultimately, the bureaucracy of Judgment City was able to secure a positive verdict, and though at times its methods seemed partial and inequitable, in the end the system functioned successfully. Though it was Daniel who was ostensibly the defendant, ultimately it was the system itself which was on trial, and the viewers were truly the judges of Judgment City.

*Defending Your Life* participates in a long trajectory of texts that depict the adjudication of one's post-mortem destiny using courtroom and trial imagery. From the literature of ancient Egypt, which could imagine death itself as a vindicatory lawsuit between Osiris and Seth,[1] to the recent film *Wristcutters*, based on the short story by the Israeli author Edgar Keret, scenes of post-mortem courtroom procedures pepper Western literature, drama, art, and film.[2] In addition to these depictions of the courtroom in the afterlife, which usually involve either God or heavenly functionaries, we also find depictions of divine decision-making imagined as the result of courtroom proceedings, whether that courtroom is located in the past, in a simultaneous present, or in the future, as at the end of days. Something about the trial and the courtroom has held our attention for thousands of years as a consistent way of imagining the way God or gods make decisions of the utmost importance. The courtrooms, of course, have changed, and this is reflected in the literature. In the Hebrew Bible trials are conducted in throneroom settings, reflecting the earthly associations of trials with kings and royal adjudication, while under Roman imperial rule trials were elaborate and bureaucratic, and this imagery was transferred to the divine courtroom by authors such as Seneca, Lucian of Samosata, and Tertullian. But there remains this consistent creative move to use this situation familiar from our earthly landscape to imagine how decisions are made beyond earth.

In many ways, this is not surprising, due to the dual nature of the courtroom. On the one hand, the courtroom is a familiar and recognizable aspect of the daily life of Western culture. It is a place where arguments are presented, evidence is weighed, and decisions are handed down everyday.

---

[1] See the discussion in Jan Assman, *Death and Salvation in Ancient Egypt* (Ithaca: Cornell University Press, 2001), 70ff.

[2] For an overview of some of the more prominent scenes in religious literature, see S. G. F. Brandon, *The Judgment of the Dead: The Idea of Life After Death in the Major Religions* (New York: Charles Scribner's Sons, 1967); More recently Alan Segel, *Life after Death: A History of the Afterlife in the Religions of the West* (New York: Doubleday, 2004). I am told that these scenes occur also in Eastern literature and art, though this is beyond the scope of this study.

It is, in other words, ordinary, and to a certain degree omnipresent. Most people in the modern world have had some experience with courtrooms and are familiar with their set up, rules, and cast of characters. Courtroom scenes appear throughout the classics of Western literature and film, from the trial of Socrates to *To Kill a Mockingbird* to *Legally Blonde*. Just like in the ancient world, forensic rhetoric has entered the educational system, as Mock Trial teams have become part of American high school extracurriculars. Lawyer jokes have been around since at least the time of Shakespeare. Nothing could be more familiar, so much a part of the everyday experience of society, than the courtroom.

On the other hand, courtrooms are also deeply unfamiliar and scary places, places of increased formality and solemnity. Courtrooms are places in which no less than life and death decisions are handed down, places infused with the enormous power of the state, places in which people's lives can literally hang in the balance. Courtrooms are also passionate locations, places of great emotions like fear, anger, grief, and relief. Nothing could be more extraordinary than the courtroom. Courtrooms are places that lift people out of the ordinary and put them into the extraordinary. They are infused with the ideals of justice and equity, dispassion, and reason, and yet they are also places which can provoke suspicion, anxiety, and great fear.

This dual nature of the courtroom is one of the reasons why courtrooms have become such a standard part of our conception of the afterlife. Courtrooms manage to simultaneously capture both human ideals and human realities. Part of the argument of this study is that the courtroom functions powerfully as a symbol or microcosm of anxiety over the afterlife, as it perfectly captures both the ideal and the reality: the ideal, that one's life will be fairly and impartially judged, and the reality: that in truth, we just do not know how impartial that assessment is going to be. Since the earliest depictions of the divine courtroom in the Hebrew Bible and the literature of Ancient Egypt and Greece, these scenes have been infused with the very real fears and worries of their creators and their audiences. This is reflected also in the literature of nascent Judaism and Christianity, the primary focus of this study.

But as in *Defending Your Life*, the audiences and readers are not passive spectators in the divine courtroom. Instead, the trial scenarios ask the readers to take on a different rôle, that of judges. The audiences of these scenes are asked to be critics in the truest sense of the word – judges of what is put before them, including the system itself and the verdict handed down. This is crucial for understanding what is truly taking place in these scenes of the divine courtroom, even in those that date from the ancient world.

This manuscript is a full-length study of the divine courtroom in the formative literature of early Judaism and early Christianity. The central argument of this study is that these courtroom scenes, though fanciful in nature and often remarkably entertaining, are part of a serious inquiry taking place throughout the Mediterranean as to the nature of divine justice. These scenes can contain explicit criticism about the adequacy and equity of God's justice, or can attempt to vindicate God from charges of injustice and inequity. What is important is that this amounts to a rotation of the courtroom scene: the courtroom, rather than simply functioning on the narrative level with the reader as an additional spectator, is rotated so that the reader is in the judicial position, and it is the judge and the process itself which are being adjudicated. When man is tried, it is truly God who is on trial.

A secondary but related argument of this study is that courtroom imagery is not benign. Throughout every culture and time period surveyed in this manuscript, people express wariness and anxiety regarding courtrooms and the judicial process. Courtrooms in the ancient Mediterranean, Antique, and Late Antique worlds were not necessarily places associated with justice. People were wary of going to court and regarded courtrooms with fear and suspicion. Courtrooms were places which were associated with the failure of justice as often if not more often than the opposite. The use of courtroom scenes to depict the operation of divine justice is not necessarily an endeavor meant to be consoling or optimistic. Often authors deliberately play on their audiences' anxieties and fears about courtrooms in general, regarding the divine courtroom as a place to be feared even if one believes they are innocent and should be acquitted or vindicated therein.

Scenes of the divine courtroom vary from text to text, but several points remain consistent. God is pictured as the ultimate judge, holding court (often in a throneroom) on matters ranging from the lives of individuals on earth to the destination of souls after death. He is often flanked by ministering angels, who perform the roles of prosecutor and defender for the matter at hand. Judgments are recorded for posterity, either on scrolls or tablets, and the case is closed. The most prominent example of this scene in biblical literature occurs as the framing narrative to the poetry of Job, in which God, holding court, brags about his servant Job to the Accuser (*hasatan*), whose role it is apparently to roam around the earth and find examples of human impropriety. However, the Accuser's role in Job is actually more subversive – these examples of human impropriety are used to impeach *God*, and while the matter at hand is ostensibly the piety of Job, the true challenge presented is whether or not God's conception of justice holds up to intense scrutiny and trial. The actions of man thus have direct implications for the question of God's ultimate justice and propriety. The

trial setting and the legal questions and scenarios it invokes is a key motif
in the theology of the wisdom literature, and is the center of an ongoing
and eternal question: is God's justice actually just?

Each chapter in this manuscript examines the way this imagery of the
divine courtroom appears in a corpus of literature. Chapter two examines
the way the divine courtroom appears in the Hebrew Bible, particularly in
the way biblical texts imagine God's judicial process. The legal relationship between God and Israel is invoked time and again throughout the Bible by the prophets and psalmists, in various ways for various purposes.
This includes use of a genre of literature referred to as the *riv*-pattern, or
'covenantal lawsuit.' Normally this genre is understood as God indicting
Israel for breach of contract, with God acting as both judge and prosecutor.
However, I will argue that the prophetic use of this genre actually begs the
question of God's justice, inviting the reader to sit in judgment on God's
actions. Because of the centrality of the legal relationship between God
and Israel, pictures of the heavenly courtroom and God's judgment therein
are especially potent mediums for expression of anguish, consolation, and
philosophical investigation.

Chapter three examines scenes of the divine courtroom in Greek and
Roman literature from Homer to Seneca and Lucian, texts that are very
much part of the cultural backdrop of the early Jewish and Christian texts
which are the focus of this study. Not only do we have comparable scenes
of the god(s) administering justice from Homer to Lucian, but in addition
we have an equally important literary tradition that posed the philosophical
questions of justice, civic obligation, morality, violence, religion, ethics,
etc. to an audience of judges – Greek tragedy. Greek drama put these questions, including questions of the justice of divine activity, on stage to be
judged – literally – before a large audience, the same audience who regularly attended trials and lawsuits, the audience of the city. In this chapter I
demonstrate that over time, the portrayal of the divine courtroom by Greek
and Roman authors became more and more critical. While the earliest texts
only allude to questions of the justice of Zeus and his ability faithfully and
justly to administrate the cosmos, the later texts put this question front and
center, using scenes of the divine courtroom not to present a post-mortem
world that functions orderly and judiciously, but instead a post-mortem
world that is incapable of ensuring justice and incompetent in judicial matters. In this way the Greek and Roman literature, though having different
characters and settings than those of the Hebrew Bible, finds itself running
a slightly parallel course in terms of the way this literary motif is employed in both cultures.

Chapters four through six represent the heart of the study, as I turn my
attention to the way the divine courtroom appears in Second Temple Jew-

ish literature, the letters of Paul, and New Testament narrative. The influence of Greco-Roman culture becomes immediately apparent as the location of the divine courtroom moves from an atemporal, eternal address to a more permanent residence either at the end of days, as God acts as ultimate judge of Israel and the nations, or to the immediate afterlife, as God sits in judgment on the fate of individual souls. Scenes of the divine courtroom are often found in apocalyptic literature such as 1 Enoch and 4 Ezra, and in otherworldly journeys undertaken by biblical patriarchs, most prominent of these being the possibly parodic and definitely entertaining *Testament of Abraham*. Often these scenes are used to provoke a number of attitudes on the part of the reader, such as humor, consolation, fear, or a reaffirmation of personal piety and commitment to God. However, these scenes are also part of an ongoing conversation that began in the Hebrew Bible: the question of God's ultimate justice in the universe and the issue of theodicy. These scenes become opportunities for authors to work out their visions of ultimate justice, often attempting to vindicate God of charges of injustice, impropriety, or abandonment. In particular, Second Temple literature deals with the complicated relationship between justice and mercy. I will demonstrate in this chapter that throughout the Second Temple period there is a consistent concern by authors to prove to their readers that God is justified in his actions. Forensic scenarios become the carriers of these conversations. The courtroom scenes serve as vehicles in these authors's attempts literally to vindicate God, affording them the opportunity to show God's judicial activity firsthand. What is exceptional is that this does not go unnoticed even by contemporary (or slightly later) authors. I will argue that in the most elaborate of these courtroom scenes, the longer recension of the *Testament of Abraham*, the author actually parodies these very attempts to vindicate God, forcing the reader to take a step back and look at what they are doing in these courtroom scenes.

Chapters five and six examine the literature of the New Testament first with an analysis of the way the divine courtroom is found and functions in the letters of Paul (chapter five), and then in New Testament narrative (chapter six), particularly the Gospels of Matthew and John, and the book of Revelation. I argue in chapter five that there is significant tension in the way Paul utilizes the imagery of the divine courtroom. Ultimately, I demonstrate that Paul finds himself within the long-standing tradition of using the language of the divine courtroom as an opportunity to acquit God of perceived injustices. However, this stands in some tension with another aspect of Paul's thought, his *rejection* of the legal metaphor as an appropriate way to imagine the relationship between God and the new Israel, the *ekklesia*. If the period of the law is over, as Paul argues in Galatians 3-4, then so to are the protections that the law offers for humanity. People no longer have recourse to the law as a means for argumentation and complaint against God, nor can they use the contractual arrangements of the covenant as arguments in their own defense. Paul's understanding of the anthropological nature of man *vis-à-vis* that of God strongly hampers the ability of mankind successfully to stand trial before God. It would seem that the divine courtroom no longer would carry the same currency for Paul as a medium for picturing man's destiny, and yet Paul continues to use the forensic metaphor to picture what will come at the end of days (cf. 1 Cor 3), as well as the scene of the courtroom to shame the Corinthians, who think that they – not God – should be Paul's judge and jury (2 Cor 10-12). The forensic metaphor continues to be a part of Pauline discourse, but it now stands in a tension previously not present.

In chapter six, I examine the way the divine courtroom appears in the gospels of Matthew and John, and the book of Revelation. First I discuss the way Matthew uses the divine courtroom, demonstrating that his use of the divine courtroom is designed to provoke fear and repentance. Following that discussion, I examine the unique innovations of the Gospel of John and its "lawsuit motif," engaging especially with the important work of Andrew Lincoln on this matter. Finally, I will turn to the presentation of the divine courtroom at the end of days that appears in Revelation. In all three of these cases, I will demonstrate that far from simple dioramas of the courtroom, the authors paint a picture of the divine courtroom that expects the reader to take an active and judicial role in the proceedings, and use this knowledge as part of their compositional strategies. Though this is most evident in John and Revelation, it is also part of the way Matthew has structured and presented his Gospel.

Chapters seven and eight take as their objects of study the divine courtroom in early Christian literature and rabbinic literature. In chapter seven I examine the extensive courtroom scenes found in the *Apocalypse of Peter* and the *Visio Pauli*, demonstrating that the authors used these courtroom scenes to answer criticisms regarding God's justice, fully intending the reader to play the true judicial rôle in the proceedings. Following this examination, I then demonstrate that at least one very vocal early Christian reader – Marcion of Sinope – did exactly what the courtroom scenario expected him to do, act as judge on the proceedings. Marcion, however, came to the conclusion as some modern readers: that the god of these scenes was entirely unjust and not truly God. God was truly on trial for Marcion, and Marcion pronounced him guilty. In the latter half of the chapter I examine Marcion's critique and the response of Tertullian, who attempts to demonstrate, using the exact forensic criteria that Marcion interrogated, that the judicial attributes are entirely appropriate to God's justice and, indeed, appropriate to God. In chapter eight I provide a broad survey of the way the divine courtroom appears in the wide corpus of rabbinic literature. I demonstrate that within this corpus we have several examples of this same use of the divine courtroom as a means of calling into question or answering accusations regarding God's justice.

This manuscript demonstrates that throughout the formative literature of Judaism and Christianity, the use of the courtroom imagery for figuring God and the process of divine decision making carried with it a challenge to the reader to think critically and judicially about God. These ancient authors took seriously the distinct judicial rôle for the reader in the imagined and narrated courtroom. Ancient authors used the imagery of the divine courtroom with the full knowledge and expectation that their readers would take a significant role in the proceedings. Though most modern scholars have neglected this aspect of the literature, ancient writers knew all too well that all audiences sat in judgment on what was presented before them.[3] Aristotle, in his handbook on rhetoric, writes that "the object of rhetoric is judgment – for they judge the deliberations and the verdict is a judgment" (Ars. *Rhet.* 2.1.2). According to Aristotle, it was necessary not only to consider how to make the speech convincing, but that the speaker also needs to know how to prepare the judge and how to put the judge into a particular frame of mind.

Aristotle insists that this is true whether the rhetoric is deliberately, epideictic, or forensic (2.18.1). Ancient orators were fully aware that their audiences were passing judgments on their words, and even on themselves, and they used this knowledge in the preparation of their speeches and other rhetorical compositions. If the reader is to be addressed as a judge even in epideictic rhetoric,[4] how much the more so is the reader invited to take a judicial position when the rhetoric is specifically forensic?

Not only was judgment a significant aspect of audience response, readers and audiences were more than familiar with courtroom scenes. Courtroom scenes were popular features of ancient literature, tragedy, and comedy. Saundra Schwartz has analyzed the way courtroom scenes function particularly in the Greco-Roman novels and what leads these type of scenes to be so popular. Schwartz argues that "the courtroom scene is a particularly apt formula for the dramatization of ideology. At the center of the drama is a contest, an *agōn*, between two opponents representing opposed moral positions, with the expectation that, at a predetermined end-

---

[3] David Rod has demonstrated that judgment plays a significant role in Aristotle's theory of drama and the audience of drama in the *Poetics*. Cf. David Rod, "Judgment as an Element of Audience Response in Aristotle's *Poetics*," *Theatre Annual* 36 (1981), 1-19.

[4] For a discussion of the role of judgment in epideictic rhetoric, see Christine Oravec, 'Observation' in Aristotle's Theory of Epideictic," *Philosophy and Rhetoric* 9 (1976), 162-174.

point (the verdict), one contestant will win. The trial scene, therefore, is a formula not only for the exposition of competing ideas but also for the valorization of the moral position implicitly supported by the text's ideology."[5] In addition, placing the legal system front and center before the reader invites the reader to make judgments on the *process itself*, judging whether or not it is capable of reaching a just verdict. The explicitly evaluative and judicial context draws the reader into the process as a judge more so than other scenarios.

Schwartz recognizes something of import about the courtroom scenes in the ancient novels: "The moral universe of the novels tends to be painted in black and white, and the reader is rarely in doubt as to the guilt or innocence of the parties involved in the trial scenes. Despite this, trials often result in verdicts which are contrary to what the reader knows is right. Indeed, they often confound or subvert justice, and thereby perpetuate the dramatic conflict. The novelists make great use of the dramatic device of irony in order to heighten the pathos of the wrongly accused defendant."[6] In other words, according to Schwartz the novelists counted on the audience making critical judicial decisions on the scenes before them, and used that knowledge of the inevitable activity of the audience to dramatic effect. Ancient Jewish and Christian authors were no less concerned with this aspect of literary production when they composed and presented their courtroom scenes, both human and divine.

Ancient readers were also accustomed, as I demonstrate throughout the study, to thinking critically and judicially about their gods. Prophets like Isaiah explicitly ask their readers to play this rôle when they invoke the rîv-pattern. In Isaiah 5, for example, God, in the "Song of the Vineyard," asks the people of Judah to "judge between me and my vineyard" (Isa 5:3). God in this song willingly takes on the role of defendant in order successfully to demonstrate to the people of Israel that they have no case against him. This type of maneuver is found throughout the prophetic and psalmic traditions, as I demonstrate in chapter two. In chapter three, I discuss a similar dynamic at play in Greek theatre, in which audiences were asked to form judgments on their gods.

Likewise, ancient audiences were sometimes explicitly admonished to take judicial roles both on others and even on their own selves. The Attic orator (and logographer) Isocrates adopted the fiction of a courtroom suit brought against him by a sycophant in order most advantageously to defend his teaching, treating his audience as his judges and asking them to sit in judgment upon him (Isoc. *Ant.* 8). Augustine of Hippo repeatedly en-

---

[5] Schwartz, "The Trial Scene in the Greek Novels and in Acts," 110.

[6] Schwartz, *Courtroom Scenes in the Ancient Greek Novels* (Phd. Diss. Columbia, 1998), 28.

couraged his listeners to judge themselves, using the terrifying imagery of the Roman imperial trial, exhorting his audience to sit in trial on themselves:

...first, for your own sake, sit as a judge on your own case. First judge yourself so that from the innermost recesses of your conscience you may advance with a clear mind against another person. Return into yourself, arrest yourself, debate with yourself. I want you to clear yourself in the court of an honest judge where you will require no witness.... I would like to know what sort of sentence you have pronounced. If you have conducted this hearing well, if you have conducted it honestly, if you have been just in conducting it, if you have climbed onto the judicial tribunal of your mind, if you have suspended yourself on the torture rack of your heart before you own eyes, if you have applied to yourself the tortures of fear, then you have heard the case well – if that is how you held it. And beyond any doubt, you have punished sin with repentance. So, you see: you have held a judicial examination, you have conducted the hearing, you have passed the sentence, and you have inflicted the punishment.[7]

Here Augustine explicitly asks his readers to imagine themselves sitting as judges and to conduct, as it were, their own trial, complete with torture rack, interrogation, passing of sentence. Augustine understands this internal judicial activity to be an essential prerequisite for those Christians who would consider sitting in judgment on others. A similar though far less explicit sentiment was voiced earlier by Paul, who exhorted the Corinthians that they must examine themselves to see whether they are in the faith (2 Cor 13:5) if they want to pass judgment on Paul and his colleagues.

Audiences's capacity and propensity to judge were taken seriously by ancient authors, yet this aspect of courtroom scenes is often overlooked by modern scholars, as I will demonstrate throughout this study. Though there are many excellent studies of courtroom motifs in the literature under discussion, all too often the reader is not taken into account as an active participant in the action. Only by recognizing the role of the reader, and the way that role was taken into account by the author, can we have a full appreciation of the discursive dynamic of these courtroom scenes. The theological import of this narrative strategy is evident when this dynamic is recognized in the scenes of the divine courtroom.

C. S. Lewis, in his seminal essay "God in the Dock," writes about the difference between ancient and modern people in terms of what they require from God.[8] Lewis asserts that those who live in the modern world

---

[7] Aug, *Serm.* 13.7. Translation and discussion by Brent Shaw, "Judicial Nightmares and Christian Memory," *JECS* 11 (2003), 533-563, 550. Shaw also points to other examples where Augustine uses this type of imagery in his exhortations, such as *En. in Ps.* 96.17; *En. in Ps.* 74.9; *Serm.* 16A.7; *Serm.* 49.5.

[8] Originally published as "Difficulties in Presenting the Christian Faith to Modern Unbelievers," [*Lumen Vitae* 3 (1948) 421-26], the title was given by the editor, Walter Hooper, in

demand an accounting from God, expecting God to have to justify himself to us, and that this represents a fundamental shift from what ancient people believed, which is that we have to justify ourselves to God. Lewis writes:

> The ancient man approached God (or even the gods) as the accused person approaches his judge. Fcr the modern man, the roles are reversed. He is the judge; God is in the dock. He is quite a kindly judge: If God should have a reasonable defense for being the god who permits war, poverty, and disease, he is ready to listen to it. The trial may even end in God's acquittal. But the important thing is that Man is on the bench, and God in the Dock.[9]

What this study argues, though, is that by putting man in the dock, ancient people *were* putting God in the dock, that by imagining and describing Man's trial, readers were asked to interrogate and try God.

---

the collection *Undeceptions: Essay on Theology and Ethics* (London: Blies, 1971), and has been known by that title ever since.

[9] Lewis, "God in the Dock," *Undeceptions,* 200-201.

Chapter 2

# "Shall Not the Judge of all the Earth Execute Justice?": The Divine Courtroom in the Hebrew Bible

## A. Introduction

Throughout the Hebrew Bible there are images of God holding trial and acting in a judicial capacity. Sometimes these images appear in a narrative presentation, such as the visions of Micaiah bar Imlah (1 Kgs 22), Zechariah 3, and the prologue to Job. At other points, as in Psalm 50, the framework is poetic, leaving the reader to fill out the narrative setting. Still other texts are legal in nature, and imagine God's courtroom not only as occurring in some heavenly realm, but as intersecting with the human courtroom on the ground. All these texts bear witness to the flexibility of this scene for different rhetorical and religious purposes. Sometimes the courtroom imagery is found for purposes of consolation, comfort, hope. At other points the courtroom framework is used to provoke shame, regret, and repentance. Often these reasons coincide, as more than one is intended at any given moment.

The divine courtroom in the Hebrew Bible is not always visible to the naked eye. Often the texts which become most central to later interpreters, even later interpreters within the canon itself, are not *prima facie* instances of the divine courtroom. Only an understanding of the divine courtroom as a deeply ingrained feature of the religious imagination of ancient Israel can reveal the importance of these texts. One such example occurs on Mount Sinai. Having displayed extraordinary boldness before God, advocating for Israel after the Golden Calf, Moses insists that God show him his ways, so that he may know him (Ex 33:13). The request to know "your ways" is nothing less than a desire to penetrate the workings of the divine mind, to understand the process of divine decision making, to perceive how God functions. After some negotiation, God acquiesces, and makes the following proclamation to Moses: "YHWH, YHWH, a God merciful and gracious, slow to anger, full of *hesed* and truth. Bearing *hesed* for thousands, bearing iniquity, and transgression, and sin. But he shall surely not wipe clean, visiting the iniquity of the fathers upon the children, and upon the children's children, to the third and fourth generation" (Ex 34:6-7). These attributes become central in later rabbinic depictions of the divine courtroom, as they are figured as full fledged beings, the Attribute(s) of Mercy and the Attribute(s) of Justice, arguing it out for preeminence before God in the divine judicial system.

It is not an accident that Moses has the two tablets of stone when he receives this revelation. The attributes are intricately bound up with the covenant, taken as representing a promise from God that he will continue to function in this manner with relation to the people of Israel. The attributes are, in a sense, part of the covenant, imprinted on the stone tablets as much as the legal prescriptions. This is the way they continue to appear in the biblical texts. When Moses has his next great moment for intercessory arguments before God, he uses the divine attributes as part of his petition, reminding God that he is bound by his own attributes to act in a certain manner (Num 14:11-20). They appear in arguments before God in the Psalms (e.g., Psalm 86), and participate in the deep way in which biblical authors understand the workings of God (e.g., Jonah 4:2). When the attributes appear in petitionary prayer – which often feels more like forensic argumentation than pleas for mercy – they represent an argument before God to act in accordance with his stated ways, to behave according to his own character, to live up to his own words, to administer justice *with* mercy, not to allow his wrath to overshadow his reason.

This chapter explores some of the ways in which the divine courtroom manifests itself in Hebrew Bible literature. I will demonstrate that the vocabulary and imagery of the divine courtroom are not entirely benign. Courtrooms across the ancient Mediterranean world were not known for being places of strict equity and justice. The Hebrew Bible itself bears witness to the possibility of courtrooms acting entirely opposite to the ideals of justice, truth, and fairness. The imagery of the divine courtroom captures much of this anxiety over courtroom justice. In particular, the divine courtroom is both hoped for and feared. In the depictions of God in a courtroom setting in the Hebrew Bible, there is the undercurrent of worry and fear that God will not act as a just judge, will not abide by his stated attributes, and will instead act in pure wrath with no one to check him. The divine courtroom thus becomes a carrier both for the ideals of pure justice, and the reality that justice is not always pure, even divine justice.

After discussing what is entailed in the figuration of God as a judge, I will turn to my central argument, which is that part of the way in which courtroom dramas operate, including those found in the Hebrew Bible, is by inviting the audience to judge what is taking place in front of them. The very genre of the courtroom provokes an aspect of judgment in the reader/hearer that is more explicit than with regard to other genres. In depictions of God holding court, therefore, the author has, in a sense, put *God* on trial for the reader. Often, when doing so, he intends to *vindicate* God, to participate in a theodicy in its purest form. But not always. Sometimes the author intends to *condemn* God, or at least to invite the possibility that God cannot always be vindicated, to beg the question of the justice of God as it is understood to operate. I will analyze this literary use of the divine courtroom as it appears throughout the *rîb*-pattern of the prophetic literature and culminates in the book of Job.

## B. God as Judge

Images of gods administrating justice in a courtroom-like setting can be found throughout the ancient Mediterranean world. The characteristic picture of El in Canaanite mythology was of a seated judge, handing down divine decisions.[1] Mesopotamian psalm literature, such as the Hymn to Shamash, prays to the god using forensic techniques and terminology.[2] The imagery of YHWH as presiding over the divine courtroom certainly draws upon this rich cultural heritage. But what makes an even greater impact on the way in which biblical authors use this imagery, and imagine their monotheistic divine courtroom, is their understanding of the covenant between God and Israel as constituting a binding, legal relationship. Once law is established as the dominant framework for conceiving of Israel's special relationship to the deity, courtroom imagery logically follows.

In his pioneering work *Law and Covenant in Israel and the Ancient Near East*,[3] George E. Mendenhall argued that the Israelite concept of "covenant" had a parallel in the Ancient Near East, that of Hittite contractual literature, particularly in the realm of "international relations."[4] Because of the difficulty of securing binding oaths between autonomous entities, Ancient Near Eastern nations developed legal contracts for negotiating such treaties and agreements, most notably the two Hittite types of contracts/covenants: the suzerain-vassal treaty, in which one party is significantly more powerful than the other, and the parity treaty, in which the two parties are of equal status.[5] This formal Hittite suzerainty treaty had enormous impact on the way in which Israel imagined its relationship to YHWH: Israel imagined itself as having entered into a covenant with YHWH that resembled a suzerain-vassal

---

[1] This is the case both in textual imagery, for example in the *KRT* epic or the *Aqhat* epic, and in the visual iconography of the ancient Mediterranean world. Cf. Frank Moore Cross, *Canaanite Myth and Hebrew Epic* (Cambridge: Harvard University Press, 1973), 177ff.

[2] *ANET* V. 387.

[3] Pittsburgh: The Biblical Colloquium, 1955.

[4] Mendenhall, *Law and Covenant*, 26.

[5] Mendenhall articulated the basic formal criteria of the suzerainty treaty: the preamble, historical prologue, stipulations, depositional instructions, witnesses, and curses and blessings. Mendenhall, 32-34.

treaty, in which it was YHWH's vassal.[6] This understanding of the relationship between YHWH and Israel as a binding, legal treaty had significant impact on the way the divine courtroom figures in biblical texts.

One of the most persistent ways of imaging God in the Hebrew Bible is as
a judge (שופט), an image with is intimately tied up that of God as King, as
kings across the ancient Mediterranean world had ultimate judicial power and
were responsible for ensuring justice for their subjects.[7] Nowhere in the Hebrew Bible is the connection between God's royal sovereignty and judicial
authority more explicit than in the Psalms. These two images are intertwined
throughout various different types of Psalms. For example, in Psalm 96, the
unnamed Psalmist cries out "Say among the nations, YHWH is King; The
world is firmly established; it will not be moved; He will judge the nations
with equity (ידין עמים במישרים)" (Ps 96:10). Psalm 96, one of the "enthronement psalms," celebrates God's majesty and sovereignty not only over the
people of Israel, but over all the nations, and insists that "He is coming to
judge (לשפט) the land; he will judge the world with justice, and the nations
with his truth" (96:13). This image of God's impending judgment is meant to
console, comfort, and excite, promising not only judgment, but God's *equity*
in judgment.[8] The psalmist emphasizes that not only is God a king/judge, but
the *ultimate* king/judge, who judges by just principles.[9]

---

[6] More than just a conceptual parallel, the entire book of Deuteronomy can be understood as
having been modeled on this treaty form. In this understanding, chapters 1-4 act as the pream-
ble/historical review; 5-26 the stipulations; instructions for deposition at 27:1-8 and twice in chapter 31; curses and blessings in chs. 27-28; and two sets of witnesses: the song of Moses, explicitly
marked as a witness against the people (31:16-22) and book of the law (31:24-29) and heaven and
earth (32:1ff).

[7] Hence the dictum of Proverbs 29:4: "A king upholds the land by justice; a man who takes
bribes overthrows it." For a complete discussion, see Moshe Weinfeld, *Social Justice in Ancient
Israel* (Minneapolis: Fortress, 1995). Images of kings exercising their judicial authority are found
throughout the Deuteronomistic History, most obviously in the pericopes regarding King Solomon's wisdom in judicial matters (1 Kgs 3:16-28). It was standard practice for people to bring
their grievances to the king for redress, and this forms the background of the treachery of Absalom in 2 Sam 15:1-6. By asserting his desire to execute justice wisely (2 Sam 15:4), and insinuat-
ing that King David does not intend to perform this judicial function (2 Sam 15:3), Absalom gains
the loyalty of the people and sets up his challenge to David.

[8] This connection between God's judgment and the principle of equity is also made in Psalm
99:4: "The might of the king loves justice; you have established equity; you enacted justice and
righteousness in Jacob." A complete discussion of the hendiadys משפט וצדקה is found in Weinfeld,
*Social Justice in Ancient Israel*, particularly ch. 1.

[9] Weinfeld convincingly argues that the "judgment" anticipated and expressed by these Psalms
does not refer *only* to courtroom judgment, but to a wide range of activities associated with equitable and just sovereignty, particularly with regard to the poor (cf. Weinfeld, *Social Justice*, especially 35ff). Weinfeld insists that the proper understanding of judgment is *salvation*, and that it is
metaphorically presented as a divine court decision, paralleled also in Mesopotamian literature
(42). This metaphorical usage is precisely the issue presented here.

This is an important distinction because courtroom justice in antiquity was not always equitable. The Code of Hammurabi reveals that there was concern over what could take place in a courtroom, whether it be false (or unproven) charges (§1, §2), false testimony (§ 3, §4), lack of witnesses (§11, §13, §127) or improper action by the judge (§ 5). Though these laws are designed to protect against this type of judicial misconduct, the very fact that there are laws against this is evidence of the reality of judicial misconduct.[10] Throughout the Bible itself we see examples of how judgment was lacking, manipulated, or unjust. One of the reasons the Bible gives for the failure of the system of judges and the advent of the monarchy is the failure of the pre-monarchic judicial system to execute justice, culminating in Samuel's sons Joel and Abijah, who "turned aside after profit; they took bribes, they perverted justice" (1 Sam 8:3).[11] Yet the monarchy did not bring with it perfect justice; one need not look further than the stories of 2 Sam 11-13 to see that King David, far from executing justice, behaves unjustly, committing adultery, murder, and turning a blind eye to his daughter's rape.

One of the most glaring examples of the failure of the king to act properly in a legal matter is that of Naboth's vineyard (1 Kgs 21:1-16). While the villain in this case is most certainly Queen Jezebel, she acts in King Ahab's name, sealing letters in his seal (21:8). In the letters, Jezebel calls for the establishment of a kangaroo court in which Naboth, who has refused to give up his vineyard to the king, is falsely accused of blasphemy and treason and then stoned to death (21:9), allowing King Ahab to take possession of the vineyard (21:16). This pericope, illustrating the corruption and tyranny that was the reign of Ahab and Jezebel, shows that the royal family could completely exploit courtroom "justice." Here the judicial system was manipulated as a vehicle for injustice, for murder. This, then, is part of the biblical understanding of the courtroom under the royal family.

The image of King/Judge, then, is not totally benign, and does not provoke *only* expectations of just and equitable judgments. When this image is applied to God, it becomes clear why the psalmist goes out of his way to insist on God's equity in executing justice. The nature of the king as having seemingly unchecked power is all the more applicable to God. While ultimately Elijah rebuked Ahab, and Jezebel was eaten by dogs, God as the ultimate

---

[10] Several first-person accounts from Egypt include statements that the speaker has performed justice properly and not participated in popular types of judicial misconduct. One example is from the autobiography of Rekh-Mi-Re: "When I judged the petitioner, I was not partial. I did not turn my brow for the sake of reward. I was not angry [at *him who came*] as [a petitioner], nor did I *rebuff* him, I tolerated him in his moment of outburst." Trans. John A. Wilson, *ANET* 213.

[11] The book of Judges graphically illustrates the lack of justice in the tribal confederacy with the brutal rape, torture, and murder of the Levite's concubine that leads to civil war (Judges 19-21).

King/Judge stands above everyone. No one can punish God; there is no one to check God's power. This did not go unnoticed by biblical authors. "You indeed are terrifying; who can stand before you when you are angry?" asks Psalm 76:8. Even the earth, according to this Psalm, was terrified when God rose up for judgment (76:9-10). One of the central Psalms that exploits this dual resonance of God the King/Judge is Psalm 89. On the one hand, the Psalmist asserts that "Justice and Judgment are the foundations of your throne; *hesed* and truth go before you" (Ps 89:15 [English: 89:14]). The Psalm narrates the anointing of David and the establishment of the covenant (89:19-38). The throne of David is said to be "a faithful witness in the clouds, *selah*" (89:38). However, in the very next section of the Psalm, God is said to have spurned and rejected the anointed, and renounced that covenant (89:39-46). Since God's might and power have been extolled throughout the Psalm (cf. 89:6-14), this reversal and invalidation of the covenant is another reminder of just how fragile that covenant is – even though it was supposed to be a true witness. Though God is not explicitly indicted by this Psalm for injustice, or for behaving inappropriately with regard to the covenant, the Psalmist pleads with God to remember the mortality of humans (89:48-49), accusing God of creating humans for nothing (89:48), and asking where God's *hesed* has gone (89:50). Implicitly, the Psalm points to the possibility that God will disregard his witness, not temper his wrath, and forego his covenant. The sheer power of God enables him to do so.

Throughout the Hebrew Bible God is presented as judge both in the divine assembly and on more mundane human matters. In Psalm 82, God takes his place in the divine council (עדת-אל) and holds judgment "in the midst of the gods" (בקרב אלהים; 82:1). This vision also occurs in narrative form. One important instance is in regard to the prophet Micaiah bar Imlah (1 Kgs 22). King Jehoshaphat of Judah, seeking to know whether he should join with King Ahab in a joint battle against Aram, instructs Ahab to "Inquire today for the word of YHWH" (1 Kgs 22:6).[12] Ahab assembles about 400 prophets to give a positive verdict on this alliance. Jehoshaphat, not yet convinced, inquires if there is anyone else, and Ahab reluctantly produces Micaiah bar Imlah, even though Micaiah is known for giving Ahab bad news (1 Kgs 22:8). Micaiah certainly lives up to his reputation, at first lying to Ahab about the potential for success (22:15-18). He then gives an account of his vision:

---

[12] The expression "לדרש את-ה'" usually means to consult a seer, and is found elsewhere in the Hebrew Bible in this capacity. See, for example, Ex 18:15, with Moses acting as the medium; and Gen 25:22, as Rebecca goes to "Inquire/seek out YHWH" in fertility matters, usually taken to refer to consulting an oracle. Cf. Tikva Frymer-Kensky, *Reading the Women of the Bible* (New York: Schocken, 2002), 16-17. A discussion of this expression and the ways it is transformed with regard to later phenomena is found in Michael Fishbane, *Biblical Interpretation in Ancient Israel* (Oxford: Clarendon Press, 1985), 245.

I saw YHWH seated on his throne and all the host of heaven were standing beside him to the left and to the right. And YHWH said, 'Who will entice Ahab so that he goes up and falls and Ramoth-Gilead?" And one said this, and the other that. And the spirit came forward and stood before YHWH and said "I will entice him," and YHWH said to him, "how?" And it said, "I will go out and be a lying spirit in the mouth of all his prophets." And He said "You will entice him, and you will succeed; Go and do thus." And now look! YHWH has put a lying spirit in the mouths of all these prophets, and YHWH has decreed calamity upon you. (1 Kgs 22:19-23)

This vision of the divine assembly is fundamentally similar to the image of the divine council found in the Psalms. The decision that Ahab is to fall at Ramoth-Gilead has already been decided, and the issue up for debate at the council is who will entice Ahab to do so. Different possibilities are entertained (intimated at verse 20), and God authorizes the lying spirit. Micaiah's summary that "YHWH has decreed calamity upon you (דבר עליך רעה)" (22:23) carries with it the resonances of an official legal decision. Though this is not a trial, per se – more like a sentencing hearing – God is presented here as an active judge, administrating sentence with deliberation and authority.

In several passages throughout the Bible, it appears that God is additionally expected to act as a judge in specific, human legal situations. One such example in biblical law occurs in the Covenant Code, when final arbitration is left up to God (אלהים) in cases involving robbery and disputed ownership (Ex 22:7-9). In part because it is not immediately apparent how God was expected to adjudicate these disputes, many translations translate "judges" for the Hebrew אלהים.[13] The LXX, however, has "ἐνώπιον τοῦ θεοῦ," suggesting at least that the earliest translators understood God to be indicated by the Hebrew. How was God supposed to act as judge in this type of legal scenario? Within the Pentateuch, Moses is presented as acting as a judicial medium between God and the people, sitting as judge all day long while people bring their disputes to him (Ex 18:13ff), and then bringing specific cases before God.[14] However, only Moses is presented as having this kind of immediate access to God in legal matters. The question is still open as to how rulers *other than Moses* can bring the cases before God, as instructed to do in the Covenant Code.[15]

Moses' successor Joshua will not have unmediated access to God's will. Instead, Moses is told that Joshua will stand before the priest Eleazar, "who

---

[13] This is also the case in Psalm 82, as some of the earliest interpreters (the Targum and the Midrash Tehillim, for example) translate "judges" for אלהים, though this is rejected by modern scholars. Cf. Cyrus Gordon, "'*Elohim* in its Reputed Meaning of *Rulers, Judges*" *JBL* 54 (1935), 139-144.

[14] Such as that of the daughters of Zelophehad (Num 27:1-11).

[15] Cf. also Leviticus 24:10-23; Num 9:6-14; and Num 15:32-6, as discussed by Fishbane, *Biblical Interpretation*, 98-104.

will inquire for him by the judgment of the Urim (משפט האורים) before YHWH" (Num 27:21).[16] It appears that the Urim and Thummim are used by the high priest in some form of divination ritual, an impression which is confirmed by other biblical pericopes from across the timeline.[17] The Urim and Thummim are one way by which people other than Moses can have access to God's judicial authority and relevant decisions in legal matters on the ground. The presence of the Urim and Thummim, therefore, indicate an understanding that human legal matters are not entirely separate from the divine courtroom; proper judicial decision-making has recourse to God as the ultimate authority not only by appeal to his laws and statutes, but by indirect consultation through divination.

This understanding of God's continuing role as a judge in matters relating to the human courtroom is illuminated by Mesopotamian literature and religion, in particular with regard to divination and the judicial ordeal. According to Tikva Frymer-Kensky, trials by ordeal are widely attested in nearly every society in the Ancient Near East, and were "an appeal to the supernatural to resolve legal cases."[18] The ordeal was part of the legal system with regard to many different crimes, but the most commonly attested are those of sorcery and adultery.[19] Frymer-Kensky's analysis reveals that, contrary to popular belief, the ordeal does not precede a sophisticated judicial system, but rather is used even in societies that have developed such procedures.[20] What emerges from her analysis is that the judicial ordeal in the Ancient Near

---

[16] That the Urim and Thummim are associated with judgment is indicated by their presence on Aaron's "breastpiece of judgment (חשן המשפט)" that he wears when he goes in before YHWH (Ex 28:29-30).

[17] For example, 1 Sam 28:6: "And Saul inquired (ישאל) YHWH, and YHWH did not answer him, neither by dreams, nor by Urim, nor by prophets." That the Urim and Thummim continued to be used even after the exile is confirmed by Ezra 2:63. A complete discussion of the Urim and Thummim is found in Cornelius van Dam, *The Urim and Thummim: A Means of Revelation in Ancient Israel* (Winona Lake, IN: Eisenbrauns, 1997).

[18] Tikva Frymer-Kensky, *The Judicial Ordeal in the Ancient Near East* (Phd. Diss, Yale University, 1978), i. According to Frymer-Kensky, only ancient Egyptian society shows no usage of the ordeal system. Frymer-Kensky's analysis reveals that the river ordeal was most widely practiced, but that a drinking ordeal was also frequent.

[19] Cf., Codex Hammurabi §2, §132, par.

[20] Frymer-Kensky, *The Judicial Ordeal*, 23-24., Frymer-Kensky differentiates between the use of divination and the ordeal in the judicial process, demonstrating that divination is used in the early stages of judicial procedure, while the ordeal is used to establish guilt or innocence. The reason this is so is because of the inherent unreliability of the procedure; ordeal is somehow seen as less fallible because of the immediacy of the verdict (Frymer-Kensky, *The Judicial Ordeal*, 42). Both divination and ordeal are attested throughout the Ancient Mediterranean world and in the Hebrew Bible. A possible example of the drink ordeal in the Hebrew Bible is in the case of the suspected adulteress at Numbers 5:11-32. Cf. *The Judicial Ordeal*, 474-479; cf. also Frymer-Kensky, "The Strange Case of the Suspected Sotah (Num 5:11-31)" *VT* 34 (1984), 11-26.

East was understood as reflecting the will of the divine and participating within the overarching framework of the divine courtroom. The use of divination and ordeal within sophisticated legal procedure suggests an expectation that divine beings were intimately concerned with the realities of human existence and could be relied on to sit in judgment over individuals when called. This is essential background for providing a plausible explanation for how God could be expected to decide legal disputes as prescribed in the Covenant Code and throughout biblical law. The human courtroom and the divine courtroom are understood to be closely interconnected. The image of the Israelite god YHWH as judge over the cosmos that we find, for example, in the Psalms and throughout the book of Isaiah, is not entirely separate from the image of God as acting in a judicial manner in basic legal disputes.[21]

But divination (and, by extension, the ordeal) is a deeply fallible process, and is not the most *reliable* way for determining guilt or innocence. It is not inappropriate to assume that people approached the ordeal with trepidation and anxiety, even people who were convinced of their own innocence and expected to be vindicated.[22] This goes along with an overwhelming feeling, from examining the ancient literature, that people approached trials in general with fear, mistrust, and apprehension. One example of this is found in a papyrus from Egypt ca. 1230 BCE, a prayer of an individual to the god Amon to assist him in his upcoming trial:

O Amon, give thy ear to one who is alone in the law court, who is poor; *he is* [*not*] rich. The court cheats him (of) silver and gold for the scribes of the mat and clothing for the attendants. May it be found that Amon assumes his form as the vizier, in order to permit [the] poor man to get off. May it be found that the poor man is vindicated. May the poor man surpass the rich."[23]

Here the petitioner is worried about his upcoming trial because of his lack of wealth, putting him at a great disadvantage. Ancient Near Eastern legal codes, such as the Codex Hammurabi and the Middle Assyrian Laws, display a concern for classic judicial problems such as partiality in judgment and the possibility of false witnesses, forbidding such practices. Such concern and prescriptions against partiality in judgment and against bearing false witness are evidence that this type of activity was commonplace and feared.

---

[21] The fact that God is expected to take an active role in human judicial matters is also the reason why so many of the Psalms are individual petitions for divine assistance, addressing God in his proper role as ultimate judge.

[22] A Hittite law suggests one reason to be fearful of indictment: "If men are implicated in a lawsuit and an avenger comes for them, (if) then the defendants get enraged and (one of them) strikes the avenger so that he dies, there will be no compensation." Hittite Laws §38, trans. Albrecht Goetze, *ANET* 190.

[23] Trans. John A. Wilson, *ANET* 380.

In the Hebrew Bible we find repeated prohibitions against taking sides and showing partiality in judgment. These prescriptions are found in all of the biblical legal corpora (e.g., Ex 23:1-8, Lev 19:15, Deut 16:19), as well as in the books of Chronicles (2 Chr 19:7). It is safe to say, therefore, that this concern for partiality in judgment is not confined to one era of biblical history. All of these passages connect the necessity of impartiality in judgment with the nature of God as impartial judge, charging the appointed human judges not to take this action because God will not "acquit the guilty" (Ex 23:7), God "does not show partiality, and does not take a bribe" (Deut 10:17), and "with YHWH there is no injustice, showing partiality, and taking bribes" (2 Chr 19:7). All of these references to God's impartiality and refusal to take sides are supposed to provoke fear in the judges, that God will not show impartiality to *them* if they pervert the judicial system. In addition, the repeated references to God's impartiality in judgment urges the judges to align themselves with the judicial ideal, here ascribed to God.

The fact that these prohibitions are repeated is evidence that bribery, judicial favoritism, and false charges are widely feared perversions of courtroom justice in the biblical period. Biblical authors are trying to convince the people that they should follow certain ideals because God does. But the fact that these authors repeat the assertion that God is impartial is important; it does not seem to have been a given. I believe there was real concern and expectation that God would *not* be impartial in judgment. On the one hand, this is a negative assertion – that God, the judge of all the world, could act unjustly, showing partiality in judgment, favoring one side over another. On the other hand, this is a positive assertion, what people desire in a judge, to show *them* partiality even when it is not deserved. The biblical texts bear this out. Throughout the Hebrew Bible there is the *hope* that God will *not be impartial*: that God will favor Israel over other nations, or the individual over his adversaries, because of their special relationship, and that he will act mercifully and graciously even when punishment might be due, because of his *hesed* and his long-suffering nature. The imagery of God as judge carries with it both the hope and desire for true and equitable judgment, and the very real hope and anxiety that this may not be what happens. This is what makes the imagery of God as judge so powerful, provoking both consolation and fear at the same time.

## C. Approaching the Judge: The cases of Abraham and Moses

Since God is portrayed throughout the Hebrew Bible as taking an active judicial role, sitting as judge not only over the cosmos but over specific legal matters on the ground, attention is paid to the kind of arguments that provoke a successful divine verdict. Arguments often take the form of legal petitions in which God is not *prayed to* for assistance, but *convinced* to take one position over another. While there are many related biblical texts, two specific pericopes are of the utmost importance to the understanding of how God can be approached successfully in the divine courtroom. The first is the complex negotiation between God and Abraham relating to the fate of Sodom and Gomorrah (Genesis 18:17-33), and the second is the intercession of Moses at the Golden Calf incident (Exodus 32:11-14). Both pericopes receive extensive attention by later interpreters, and are taken as fundamental clues to the nature of the divine.

The portrait of Abraham as extreme intercessor that appears in the *Testament of Abraham* has its roots in Abraham's intercession before God regarding the people of Sodom and Gomorrah. The pericope begins with God deciding not to hide his plans from Abraham because of Abraham's role as patriarch, particularly with regard to Abraham's responsibility to teach his offspring to "guard the path of YHWH, to do justice and righteousness" (Gen 18:19). In this way, as Timothy Lytton states, "God seeks to model judicial behavior for Abraham."[24] Instead of destroying Sodom and Gomorrah without warning, and then explaining his action to Abraham, God instead lets Abraham in on the plan, including him in the process of "divine decision making."[25]

Abraham is not happy with God's plan to destroy "the righteous with the wicked" (Gen 18:23), and accuses God of behaving in an unjust manner, unfit for his role as judge of all the earth: "Far be it from you to do this thing, to slay the righteous with the wicked, so that the righteous is like the wicked; Far be it from you! Will the judge of all the earth not execute justice ( השפט כל-הארץ לא יעשה משפט)?" (Gen 18:25). This is perhaps the one place in the Hebrew Bible where the question of the justice of God's actions is put so starkly. Even Job, when faced with the voice from the whirlwind, does not confront God in this manner.[26] Here Abraham, in the form of a question, tells God that his intended actions are incompatible with justice.

God tells Abraham that if he is correct in his assertion that there might be fifty righteous people in the city, not only will he spare those people, but he

---

[24] Timothy Lytton, "'Shall Not the Judge of the Earth Deal Justly?' Accountability, Compassion, and Judicial Authority in the Story of Sodom and Gomorrah," *Journal of Law and Religion* 18 (2002), 31-55, 35.

[25] Lytton, 35.

[26] The boldness of the inquiry, and the intimacy it presupposes with God, is quite shocking given the meek behavior of Abraham so far in the Genesis narratives (especially with regard to Hagar and Ishmael), and given what will happen in Genesis 22, when Abraham does not utter a word when told to offer his son as a burnt offering. The willingness of Abraham to intercede and advocate for the hypothetical righteous people of Sodom and Gomorrah, when he fails to advocate for his own family, will haunt later interpreters.

will indeed spare the entire city "for their sake" (Gen 18:26). Perhaps realizing that he has spoken too boldly to God, the tone of Abraham's next request – to get that number down to forty-five – is much more humble, emphasizing that he is "dust and ashes" (18:27). Abraham succeeds, in a series of negotiations, to which God acquiesces immediately, to reduce the number of required righteous people to ten. The story that follows illustrates the ultimate depravity of Sodom and Gomorrah and the mercy of God to save Lot and his family before raining down fire and brimstone on the city. Though we are never explicitly informed that there are not ten righteous men in the city, we are supposed to infer it from the narrative: chapter 19 is designed to illustrate conclusively that the city is beyond saving. James K. Bruckner has developed a holistic reading of Genesis 18:16-19:29 that sees the narrative as following "a fully developed court-like process".[27] He sees the negotiations between Abraham and God as representing "pre-trial hearings" before chapter 19 places the city of Sodom and Gomorrah on trial. Bruckner's close reading of this entire section leads him to the conclusion that the readers are part of the jury in this case, who will decide whether or not the citizens of Sodom and Gomorrah are guilty of wickedness.[28] Bruckner is correct in noting that the "reader is seated as a member of the jury by means of the narrative style and through hearing the *prima facie* evidence without any added value-judgments by the narrator (19.1-11)."[29] However, what Bruckner has not fully understood is that the way this story is narrated invites the reader not only to sit as jury on the citizens of Sodom and Gomorrah, but also to sit as judge and jury *over God*, as it is the justice of God's judicial decisions that is at stake here.

This story demonstrates that at the time of its composition there was concern over the justice of God's actions, and a desire on the part of the author to illustrate just how far YHWH would go to avoid destroying a city, to avoid taking such drastic measures.[30] The author desires to acquit God of the charge of acting unjustly. This is accomplished not only by showing that God is willing to save the whole city for the sake of ten righteous people, but by showing that God will intervene to save the righteous few even if the city

---

[27] James K. Bruckner, *Implied Law in the Abraham Narrative* (JSOT Supp Series 335; Sheffield: Sheffield Academic, 2001), 124, part of chapter 4, "A Close Narrative Reading of Legal Referents in Genesis 18.16-19.29: From the Inquest of the Cry Against the Sodomites to the Sentence that Follows God's Findings."

[28] See especially Bruckner's outline on pp. 157-158.

[29] Bruckner, *Implied Law*, 158.

[30] Cf. James L. Crenshaw, "Popular Questioning of the Justice of God in Ancient Israel" *ZAW* 82 (1970), 380-395, 385.

cannot be spared as a whole.[31] By having Abraham put the question to God in such strong juridical terms[32] and presenting the conversation between God and Abraham in a forensic manner, the author is in effect putting God's justice on trial for the reader/hearer. The author fully expects the reader to come out on the side of God, with a new understanding of both God's justice and mercy, and to acquit God of Abraham's implied charge of unjust behavior. The actions of the people of Sodom and Gommorah, while they condemn themselves, also bear witness to God's ultimate justice in deciding to destroy the cities in the first place. In addition, by showing God engaged in this debate with Abraham, the author portrays God as being willing to be accountable for his decisions. As Lytton argues, "By initiating the conversation, God willingly places Himself in a position to be held accountable. Accountability is a kind of reciprocity between a superior and his subordinates. In the case of judicial accountability, judging subjects the judge to the judgment of others."[33] In this case, God is held accountable not only by Abraham, but also by the reader, the ultimate judge of whether or not God's actions pass the test of strict courtroom scrutiny.

This is important because, as we shall see, applying the courtroom framework to God is problematic, since there is a concern that God's power places him, perhaps, above the law. This ultimately is the objection of Job, that there is no arbiter above God to appeal to (Job 9:33), because no one can stop God (Job 9:12). Here, however, there *is* someone to stop God – Abraham. As Lytton notes, in a monotheistic world, there is no check on God's judicial authority from above, since there is no appellate court. However, "Abraham's challenge nevertheless constitutes a check on divine judicial power from below. Abraham demands that God provide a principled accounting of His decision.... Abraham indicates that providing legal grounds for decisions is an essential responsibility of the judicial role."[34] By having God provide those grounds, the author invites the reader to realize that despite the inherent power inequality, and the potential abuse of authority that could arise from it, God is willing to be held accountable for his actions and decisions, and thus is just even by the standards of strict legal scrutiny. Genesis 18 invites the

---

[31] The concern here for the fate of the individual may reflect the new understanding of God put forth during the Babylonian Exile, that only the one who sins will perish, and God will no longer charge children with the iniquities of their parents (Ezk 18:1-32). This is a new understanding of imputed guilt as inherently unfair and not compatible with an image of a just God. Ezekiel insists that "I will judge every man according to his own path (איש כדרכיו אשפט)" (Ezk 18:30). The exchange between Abraham and God may reflect a desire on the part of the author to demonstrate that even when subject to this new understanding of justice, God is unimpeachable.

[32] For a review of the juridical usage of *spt* in the Hebrew Bible, see Sylvia H. Scholnick, "The Meaning of *Mišpat* in the Book of Job" *JBL* 101 (1982), 521-529.

[33] Lytton, 46.

[34] Lytton, 43.

reader to hold God accountable for his actions not only in this specific instance, but as a whole, and is an ultimate theodicy, a vindication of God.[35] By having God provide an accounting and engage in dialogue, the author argues that God does not act indiscriminately and without rational reflection, but acts deliberately and logically. This is similar to what we will see in the prophetic *rîb*-pattern; by presenting God as engaged in a legal process, the author mitigates the potential of God's wrath to overcome God's good judgment, and thus provides a way to imagine God's attributes of justice and mercy working in tandem with one another.[36]

Another pericope of extreme import for later interpreters in understanding how one is to approach God in his judicial role is Exodus 32:11-14, when Moses successfully advocates for the people on Mt. Sinai. When Moses hears of God's plan to allow his wrath to burn against the people (Ex 32:10), he does not fall on his face and supplicate, begging God for mercy. Instead, he attempts to convince God to turn away from his wrath, using logical argumentation (Ex 32:11-13). Moses convinces God to change his mind using three basic arguments: (1) While God had asserted that these people had been *Moses'*, whom *Moses* brought out of the land of Egypt (Ex 32:7), Moses reminds God that the people are *God's*, whom *God* brought out of Egypt (32:11). This reminds God of his connection to these people, that God cannot simply divert responsibility for them to Moses. (2) Moses reminds God that a decision to kill them now will cause his reputation to be impeded among the Egyptians, and therefore destroying the people will only harm *God* in the long run (32:12). (3) Moses reminds God that he swore by his own name to the patriarchs to bring their children into the promised land (Ex 32:13). By substituting the name "Israel" for Jacob, changing the triad from the more common "Abraham, Isaac, and Jacob" to "Abraham, Isaac, and Israel," Moses reminds God that these people are the direct descendants to which God had promised the land by oath. Moses reminds God that his own name, his own constancy and reputation is at stake. If an oath that God swore by Himself is not valid, what oath will be valid in the future, and what will this say about God?

---

[35] Lytton also notes that the exchange between God and Abraham becomes less hostile as it ensues, and that Abraham becomes more conciliatory as he realizes that God is willing to engage with his objections. This is good legal strategy for an advocate: "Abraham's role demands that he display a variety of attitudes towards judicial power. Like battle, advocacy must at times be confrontational; like conciliation, it often involves seeking an amicable resolution; and like prayer, it requires respect for authority. A talented advocate learns how to project these different attitudes depending upon the demands of the moment." Not only does this passage model proper attitudes on behalf of God the judge, it also models proper attitudes on behalf of Abraham the advocate. Lytton, 44.

[36] Lytton quotes Shalom Spiegel: "Justice cools the fierce glow of moral passion by making it pass through reflection." Lytton, 45.

Moses succeeds in convincing God to hold back his wrath and refrain from destroying the people. This action is held up as the intercession *par excellence* by later interpreters and even within biblical literature. Psalm 106, narrating these events, assigns to Moses the responsibility for God's change of heart: "And he said he would destroy them – had not Moses, his chosen one, stood in the breach before him, to turn his wrath from the destruction" (Ps 106:23).[37] Moses again has to stand in the breach when God threatens to destroy the people on account of the spies. Moses uses very similar arguments to persuade God to turn from his wrath (Num 14:11-20), but this time makes use of the divine attributes (revealed to him after the Golden Calf incident) within his petition: "And now, therefore, let the strength of the Lord be magnified as you spoke, saying: YHWH, slow to anger, abounding in *hesed*, bearing iniquity and transgression, by no means clearing the guilty, visiting the sins of the fathers on the children to the third and fourth generation. Forgive the sins of this nation according to the greatness of your *hesed*, and as you have borne for this nation from Egypt until now." (Num 14:17-19). Paramount in this petition is Moses' repeated attention to God's *hesed*, usually translated "steadfast love," or "grace." But more than that, as Sheldon Blank has articulated, "it amounts to a technical term for the divine commitment".[38] Moses asserts that God has promised his loyalty and commitment to the people of Israel, has sworn to them by his own name, has sworn to the patriarchs to bring their offspring into the land. Without saying so explicitly, the subtext is clear: Moses is telling God that "having not only pledged his word (the חסד) but also embarked upon a matching course of action, God is not now at liberty to depart from that course, for in him caprice would be intolerable."[39] Moses' petitions remind God that he has committed himself. By appealing to God to "remember," Moses is making a legal argument, showing God that according to the covenantal framework – the legal framework – which God himself established, it would amount to a breach of covenant should God act now according to his wrath.[40]

---

[37] The Psalms bear witness to the special place of Moses in negotiating the boundaries between God's wrath and God's mercy. Psalm 90, attributed in the tradition to Moses himself, entirely revolves around the nature of God's wrath, ending with a plea to God to have compassion on his servants.

[38] Sheldon Blank, "Men Against God: The Promethean Element in Biblical Prayer" *JBL* 72 (1953), 1-13, 7.

[39] Blank, "Men against God," 8. Blank sees this same argumentation at work in many Psalms, e.g., Ps 22:4-7, Ps 44:1-10; Ps. 80:9-13.

[40] Though the forensic nature of these Mosaic arguments is here only implied, only subtext, Moses' intercessions in these two instances form the background for the extensive treatment of legal argumentation before God in rabbinic literature, what will later be called the "law-court pattern in prayer." Joseph Heinemann, *Prayer in the Talmud* (Studia Judaica IX; Berlin and New York: de Gruyter, 1997), cf. Chapter 8, "Law-court patterns in prayer," 193-207.

There are important theological arguments here that should not go unnoticed. These biblical passages are putting forth a vision of God as not unreasonable and able to be convinced by means of logical argumentation. God is not, as it were, a victim of his own wrath, his own temper, his own *reactions*. Instead, by telling Abraham and Moses what he is about to do, God in a sense invites the possibility of being convinced to do otherwise. God is thus portrayed not as a static persona, but as a dynamic being, engaged and open to the appeals of humanity. Whilesome later biblical texts lament the hiddenness of God, the *Deus absconditus*, these texts instead put forth a vision of God as – at least in the past – being a sitting judge, *present and accounted for in his judicial action.*[41]

## D. God as Prosecutor and Judge: the *Rîb*-Pattern

One of the most important ways in which the divine courtroom appears in the Hebrew Bible is through its invocation in the so-called "prophetic lawsuit," or "*rîb*-pattern" form of prophetic speech. Throughout the prophetic literature, the prophets indict the people of Israel for various crimes against God, all of which ultimately lead up to the breach of covenant. For the prophets, this justifies God's intention to punish the people for their misdeeds. This form of prophetic address, therefore, is an explanation of why God's actions are just. The prophets use the legal language as a means of expressing God's formal complaints and rights as a litigant, an injured party, and show through the mechanisms of human justice how God's actions are themselves functions of divine justice, even though on the surface they may not seem so.

A classic example of the *rîb*-pattern is found at Micah 6:1-8, where Micah indicts the Southern Kingdom of Judah for social injustice and ethical improprieties:

Hear what YHWH is saying,
Arise, contend with the mountains (ריב את-ההרים), and let the hills hear your voice.
Hear, mountains, the case (ריב) of YHWH, and everlasting foundations of the earth.
For YHWH has a case against his people (ריב עם-עמו), and he will reprove his people.
My people, what have I done to you, and with what have I wearied you – answer me.
For I brought you out from the land of Egypt, and from the house of slavery I redeemed you.
And I sent before you Moses, Aaron, and Miriam.

---

[41] Additionally, the appeal of Moses to the divine attributes as a means of petitioning God to take certain juridical action becomes an archetype for later understanding of the place of the divine attributes in the divine courtroom. Not only do later authors begin to utilize the divine attributes in their own appeals (or presentation of appeals) to the divine, but it proves paramount in their understanding both of the way God functions *as a whole*, and in particular in the way God's courtroom operates, in the way God functions *judicially*.

My people, remember what Balak, the King of Moab devised, and what Balaam son of Beor
  answered him,
From Shittim to Gilgal, in order to know the justices of YHWH.
How shall I come before YHWH, bow down before the God of heights?
Shall I come before him with burnt offerings, with year-old calves?
Will YHWH be pleased with thousands of rams, with tens of thousands of rivers of oil?
Shall I give my first born for my transgressions, the fruit of my belly for the sin of my soul?
He has told you, Man, what is good, and what does YHWH seek from you but to do justice,
  to love *hesed*, and humbly to walk with your God?

In this passage, Micah lays out God's *rîb* against the people, echoing themes
from throughout Micah, such as the corruption of the leaders (e.g., Micah
3:1-11) and Judah's unethical behavior in all walks of life (Micah 6:9-16).

Much has been written about the nature of the *rîb*-pattern. Herman Gunkel
is usually credited as being the first to attempt to identify a set of formal criteria operative and characteristic of this type of prophetic speech, which he
called the *Gerichtsrede* (lawsuit). According to Gunkel, the lawsuit-pattern
consisted of two main parts: the description of the judgment scene, and the
plaintiff's address. The plaintiff's address, by far the more substantial aspect
of the form, had specific literary features, such as the summoning of heaven
and earth as witnesses or judges, the exhortation to listen or "give ear", an
outline of the charges, and an anticipation and refutation of possible defenses.[42] Though these particular *topoi* may vary from *rîb* to *rîb* in terms of
their inclusion and placement, the overall genre remains remarkably consistent in Israelite literature from early prophets such as Hosea and Amos to the
work of Deutero-Isaiah and other post-exilic texts.[43] As part of Gunkel's
overall project, identifying the formal criteria was only the first step in an
analysis of the genre, as he then attempted to identify the *Sitz im Leben* of the
*Gerichtsrede*. Gunkel believed that the *Sitz im Leben* was to be found in the
secular law-court, particularly in the administration of justice at the city-
gate.[44]

---

[42] Cf. Herman Gunkel and J. Begrich, *Einleitung in die Psalmen: Die Gattungen der religiösen Lyrik Israels* (Göttingen: Vandenhoeck and Ruprecht, 1933), 364-366. Herbert Huffmon
provides a helpful outline of Gunkel's analysis of the form in Herbert Huffmon, "The Covenant
Lawsuit in the Prophets" *JBL* 78 (1959), 285-295.

[43] Gunkel identified the following texts as examples of this form: Isaiah 3:13-15; 1:18-20;
41:1ff; 41:21ff; 43:9ff; Micah 6:1ff; Jeremiah 2:4-9; Hosea 2:4ff; Psalms 82; 50:7-13.

[44] Gunkel believed that the prophets took this speech-form from that which was commonly
practiced in Israelite society, and adapted it to their own purposes. Gunkel's influence can be seen
in contemporary discussions of particular instances of the *Rîb*-Pattern which begin by elucidating
instances of other *rîbs* in the Hebrew Bible and then analyzing the prophet's use of the *rîb*-pattern
alongside. So, for example, James Limburg, "The Root ריב and the prophetic lawsuit speeches,"
*JBL* 88 (1969) 291-304.

Gunkel's theory was challenged as scholars raised other possibilities for the *Sitz im Leben*. Ernst Würthwein proposed that this prophetic genre originated within cultic law, and that these prophetic speeches were examples of a formal ritual of the cultic-lawsuit within ancient Israel.[45] The most successful challenge to Gunkel was the result of Mendenhall, whose synthesis had near-immediate impact on research relating to the *rîb*-pattern. Two scholars in particular applied Mendenhall's conclusions in important ways. First, Herbert Huffmon recognized that one of Gunkel's formal elements, the appeal to third-parties (such as heaven and earth) to judge the dispute, had a direct parallel in the suzerain-vassal treaty, where the list of *witnesses* did not just include the gods of both nations, but also elements of nature such as rivers, mountains, and heaven and earth.[46] Huffmon thus explicitly related this formal element of the *rîb* to the covenant, and hence gave the *rîb* the title "Covenant Lawsuit."[47] This laid the groundwork for understanding the *rîb* as a particular feature of Israel's concept of their covenant with God, and in particular, for reminding us that the idea of God "suing" Israel for breach of contract was part of an overall worldview and cosmology, and not just an odd feature of the prophetic literature.[48]

Huffmon's conclusions were significantly buttressed by Julien Harvey, whose analysis of the Hittite texts led him to the conclusion that a suzerain could undertake two courses of action when a vassal breached their covenant: either the suzerain could send a warning, or a declaration of war.[49] Looking

---

[45] Ernst Würthwein, "Der Ursprung der prophetischen Gerichsrede," *Wort und Existenz: Studien zum Alten Testament* (Göttingen: Vandenhoeck & Ruprecht, 1970), 120-24. Würthwein pointed to the central role of the decalogue in the lawsuits and suggested that this type of indictment may have been part of the oral reading of the Law and to a covenant-renewal ceremony at the temple.Würthwein also included several other biblical texts under the heading of Gerichstrede: Hosea 4:1ff; 12:3ff; Jeremiah 25:30ff; and Malachi 3:5.

[46] Huffmon, "The Covenant Lawsuit in the Prophets," 291.

[47] Huffmon is primarily concerned in this article with countering the view of Frank Cross that the lawsuit "undoubtedly has its origins in the conceptions of the role of Yawheh's heavenly assembly as a court," and that therefore the appeal to heaven and earth, et cetera, would suggest that they were conceived of as physical inhabitants of the divine assembly. Cf. Cross, "The Council of Yahweh in Second Isaiah," *JNES* 12 (1953), 274 n.3, and Huffmon, 290-291.

[48] The second author to build on Mendenhall's work in this way was G.E. Wright, who expanded the corpus of literature generally included under the "lawsuit" heading to include Deuteronomy 32, the beginning of the Song of Moses. Like Huffmon, Wright took issue with Gunkel's understanding of the appeal to heaven and earth within the *rîb*. Wright argued that Gunkel was mistaken in assuming that heaven and earth (e.g., Deut 32:1) were being called upon as judges. Instead, Wright argued that the natural phenomena were being called in to "testify that they had been witnesses to the original oath which the vassal has now broken." G. E. Wright, "The Lawsuit of God: A Form-Critical Study of Deuteronomy 32," in Bernhard Anderson and Walter Harrelson, eds. *Israel's Prophetic Heritage* (New York: Harper & Brothers, 1962), 26-67, 47.

[49] Julien Harvey, *Le plaidoyer prophétique contre Israël après la rupture de l'alliance* (Paris: Desclee de Brouwer, 1967).

at the biblical materials in this light, Harvey found examples of both options, and proposed a new formal structure for the *rîb*-pattern that took into account these two options:

*a)* un *Prooimion* solennel, parfois précédé de la description de la scène du jugement; *b)* un adresse du juge-plaignant à l'accusé, généralement sous forme interrogative, contenant des reproches et une déclaration de son incapacité à réfuter l'accusation; *c)* un réquisitoire, généralement historique, résumant les bienfaits du plaignant et les ingratitudes de l'accusé; *d)* une déclaration constituant une sentence ou, en certains cas, un avertissement.[50]

By analyzing the *rîb* alongside the Hittite materials, Harvey has not only provided a nice corrective to Gunkel,[51] but also illuminated some of the purpose behind the prophetic use of this speech-pattern. Harvey argued that the prophets, in their role as messengers or oracles, communicate messages analogous to the suzerain's. Sometimes the message is that of war, or impending doom, with no possibility for repentance. But much more often in the prophetic literature the message is that of an *avertissement* or, in Harvey's words, an *ultimatum* – either you change your ways, *or* you are faced with certain doom. The *rîb*-pattern, therefore, is a *persuasive technique* by the prophet, a paraenetic strategy to convince the intended audience to amend their ways. According to Harvey, then, the prophets employed this lawsuit form to lay out God's actions in such a way that they "could be seen to be both juridically and morally correct,"[52] and thus force the people to realize their own culpability and change their actions.[53]

One of the most important and provocative aspects of Harvey's analysis is his recognition that, for the suzerain, the vassal has no answer and is not expected to have an answer to the charges laid out before him. This has significant repercussions for thinking about the way the prophets employ this pattern in their own works. Even though the prophets employ the lawsuit form, presenting God's charges against the people, the people are not expected – or allowed – to reply. The lawsuit is not a full lawsuit, it is more like a summary of the charges against the accused, presented in such a way that the accused has no choice but to accept their own guilt and to agree to sentence. If this is a lawsuit, it is not a very fair one. Instead, the *rîb*-pattern highlights the im-

---

[50] Harvey laid these out in an earlier article, "Le «Rîb-Pattern», réquisitoire prophétique sur la rupture de l'alliance," *Biblica* 43 (1962) 172-196, 177.

[51] Not only in terms of the Gattung, but also in terms of the *Sitz im Leben*, which he, like Huffmon, finds within international law.

[52] Nielsen, *Yahweh as Prosecutor and Judge*, 18.

[53] A good example of how Harvey's analysis has influenced not only overall discussions of the *rîb*-pattern but also (and perhaps more importantly) the interpretation of specific biblical texts can be seen in Marjorie O'Rourke Boyle's meticulous examination of Amos 3:1-4:13: "The Covenant Lawsuit of the Prophet Amos: III 1 -IV 13," *VT* 21 (1971) 338-362.

mense *inequity* of the situation, and the imbalanced power dynamic that exists between the two parties.

The realization that this pattern is dependent on that of the suzerain-vassal treaty, then, raises as many questions as it answers. The main problem with the *rîb* as a metaphor for what is going on between God and Israel is that in the *rîb*, as Kirsten Nielsen has well elucidated, God is acting both as prosecutor and as judge. A good example of this double-role of God during the *rîb* can be found in Psalm 50:3-7:

> Our God comes and does not keep silent.
> The fire before him is consuming, and around him is a great storm.
> He calls to the heavens above, and to the earth to judge his people.
> Gather to me my faithful; those who cut my covenant with me by sacrifice.
> And the heavens declare his justice, for God is the judge, *Selah*.
> Hear, my people, and I will speak; Israel, and I will testify against you,
> God, your God, am I.

Though verse 4 seems to suggest that the heavens and earth will judge the case, it is clear from verse 6 that only God will play this role.[54] In a monotheistic cosmology, there can be no other way for this courtroom scenario to play itself out, if God is one of the injured parties. To add a third party to the dispute would be to give power over God to someone who is not God, and thus compromise monotheistic principles.[55]

This imagining of the mechanisms of the divine courtroom, in which YHWH is both prosecutor and judge, directly contradicts the way in which human courtrooms are presented in the Hebrew Bible, which are as three-party systems. Narrative presentations of adjudications in the Hebrew Bible involve two parties coming to a third party to arbitrate or hear a dispute. The most famous example is that of Solomon judging between the two prostitutes who claim maternity over the same child (1 Kgs 4:16-28). Regardless of the historicity of this account, according to the narrative logic, which seeks to present Solomon as wise and fair in judgment, both women present their cases before a judge who has no bias or partiality, who then pronounces sentence. This type of third-party arbitration is commonly presented throughout the Hebrew Bible (cf. Deut 17:8-10), and conforms to what we know about individual disputation in the Ancient Near East generally.

Moreover, these legal contestations are usually designated in the Hebrew Bible by the word *rîb*. In the Hebrew Bible, the word *rîb* is used in the context of the administration of justice at the city-gate.[56] For example, the word

---

[54] Indeed, in the rest of the Psalm (8-23), the only speaker is God himself, laying out the charges against the people and pronouncing the verdict/ultimatum in verses 22-23.

[55] Hence Huffmon's corrective to Gunkel is a good one, theologically, in terms of how to understand the appeal to the mountains and other natural phenomena within the formal *rîb*.

[56] Hence Gunkel's original designation of this sphere as the *Sitz im Leben* of the prophetic *rîb*.

*rîb* is used several times in 2 Samuel 15:1-6 to describe the cases brought before the king for judgment.[57] The prophets' use of the word *rîb* signifies a legal case, analogous to those on the ground. And yet, it is *not* one that accords with human standards. By using this metaphor to describe what is going on between God and Israel, the prophets highlight the *inequity* of the situation and how it does not correspond to Israelite and Judean notions of how justice should be administered. The three-party system has been reduced to only two.

The most significant attempt to come to terms with this inequitous situation is that of Nielsen, who argues that this double-role played by God is inherently related to Israel's understanding of the nature of God. Nielsen recognizes that in the Old Testament, the function of a judge is not only to arbitrate disputes and to "rule on the facts which have been laid before him," but also to "secure the rights of the needier in society, where 'rights' broadly signifies 'help.'"[58] Thus, argues Nielsen, "when the OT speaks of Yahweh as both prosecutor and judge, this tension is reflected as an element of the Israelite understanding of God: the righteousness of Yahweh demands that the people's apostasy be made the object of condemnation, while his love for the Chosen People leads him to forgiveness and to the restoration of the original relationship."[59] Nielsen here recognizes something that will prove crucial in later interpretations of the divine courtroom: that God's role in the courtroom is somehow directly related to his nature, which is understood as having seemingly conflicting attributes that may push and pull God in opposite directions. YHWH's nature both as the God of mercy and the God of justice, attributes so clearly elucidated in Exodus 34 and elsewhere in the Hebrew Bible, directly lead to this tension felt in the *rîb* scenario.

If, then, the lawsuit is a problematic way for the suzerain to pronounce charges against the vassal, why then do the prophets utilize this particular form, which has clear juridical and legal resonances, for God to pronounce charges against Israel? Would not the use of this form point to the *tensions* of the divine courtroom – that God is acting as both plaintiff and judge, and Israel is "standing trial" without a trial at all – and thus seemingly subvert the reasons for using this form? In other words, does not the use of this lawsuit form point to the inequity of the situation and thus fail in its theodical motives – to explain why God's actions are just? Does not this instead point to the inherent injustice of the whole situation? And moreover, do not the prophets, by employing this metaphor, invite the hearer/reader to come to the same conclusion, in effect *to judge the inequity of the situation*?

---

[57] In 2 Sam 15:4, Absalom muses "who will place me as judge in the land, so that everyone who has a case (ריב) would come before me for judgment, and I would justify him (והצדקתיו)."

[58] Nielsen, *Yahweh as Prosecutor and Judge*, 76.

[59] Nielsen, *Yahweh as Prosecutor and Judge*, 76.

That the hearers are supposed to act as the judges in this situation is the effect of Harvey's understanding of the *rîb*-pattern as having a paraenetic purpose. If the ultimate goal, in most instances, is for the people to change their action, in order to do that they have to pronounce judgment on themselves: to evaluate their own actions in relation to what is required of them by the covenant.[60] But it is not only the case that they have to pronounce judgment upon themselves. In addition, they have to pronounce judgment *on God* – to see that what YHWH intends to do (or, in some instances, has done already), is action warranted by the situation. The hearers of the *rîb*, therefore, *are the people*. The people have to hear YHWH's *rîb* against them and pronounce judgment on it.[61]

What we have, then, in the prophetic employment of the *rîb*-pattern, is a sophisticated literary strategy that operates on multiple levels. First, by presenting YHWH's *rîb* with his people, the prophets employ a technique designed to demonstrate Israel's breach of covenant by presenting a logical and straightforward case, to which Israel can have no reply. In this view, God is acting as both prosecutor and judge, with Israel as the accused, left without a defense. However, this very imbalanced scenario also sets up a situation in which Israel acts as both the accused and the judge – judge of their own actions, and judge of the entire situation. This then, finally, has the effect of turning the tables on God, so that *God then becomes the accused*, as the hearer/reader examines God's actions to see whether or not they are justified, and in turn whether God himself has a defense. The very nature of the prophetic *rîb*, then, provides a view of the divine courtroom with multiple lenses, and is an innovative way of examining the tensions of the God-Israel relationship, bringing the hearers into the courtroom with their own special perspective.

Further development of the *rîb*-pattern highlights this situation. At a certain point in Israelite and Judean history, certain prophets realized that if the *rîb*-pattern were an appropriate way for God to present his case against Israel, then it was also an appropriate way for them to present their case against God, rotating the courtroom once more. We have significant examples of this twist on the courtroom scenario from the book of Jeremiah and from Deutero-Isaiah.

Jeremiah (or his redactors) is familiar with the classic articulation of the *rîb* pattern, utilizing it in Jeremiah 2:4ff, where he presents YHWH indicting the people for breaking the covenant. The specific charge here is idolatry, in

---

[60] This is made especially clear in Hosea 4:1, where the people are explicitly called upon to listen to the *rîb*.

[61] This is spelled out explicitly in Isaiah 5, the Song of the Vineyard, where God asks the people to judge between him and his vineyard (Isa 5:3).

turning to worship other gods (even though they are not gods, Jer 2:11).[62] In verse 9, Jeremiah specifically states that what is going on here is a *rîb*: "Therefore again I contend with you (אריב אתכם), an oracle of YHWH, and I will contend with your children's children (את-בני בניכם אריב)."[63]

However, this is not the only way that Jeremiah employs the concept and the form of the *rîb* within his writing. One of the striking and innovative aspects of Jeremiah's prophecy is the human voice that often breaks through in his writing, in which he, the prophet, does not only proclaim the word of God but also his own words, words of anguish and despair at the struggles and suffering he has experienced due to his prophetic office. In the "confessions" of Jeremiah, found within chapters 11-20, Jeremiah bears witness to his own suffering on the part of his adversaries. The suffering is so great that he wishes out loud that his mother had never born him, a "man of strife" (איש ריב) (Jer 15:10). Jeremiah properly diagnoses that it is because of God that he suffers so, calling on God to remember that as well (Jer 15:15). In these interwoven laments, the reader experiences a push and pull between Jeremiah's words of trust and praise and personal anguish and complaint.

At some point in his prophetic career Jeremiah decided to take his strife to God himself, to bring the *rîb* to God. According to William Holladay, Jeremiah understood that as recompense for his prophetic activity, God would "deliver" him from his enemies. However, as Jeremiah became (in his own view, at least) more and more persecuted, and his enemies seemed to be getting the better of him, "the thought crosses Jeremiah's mind that Yahweh is open to suit for breach of contract."[64] For Holladay, the key verse is Jeremiah 12:1, which he translates as follows: "Thou art innocent, O LORD, when I lodge a complaint with thee (צדיק אתה ה' כי אריב אליך); yet I would pass judgment upon thee."[65] The Hebrew very clearly signals Jeremiah's use of the formal *rîb*. Jeremiah knows that YHWH will be declared innocent (צדיק), yet he will lay out the charges against God, and he, in turn *will pass judgment on God.* This is a nice bit of irony from Jeremiah, the recognition that the *rîb* is totally skewed against him by the very nature of the institution. Jeremiah

---

[62] This is of course the classic charge laid against the people by the Deuteronomistic theology, in which the Book of Jeremiah participates.

[63] The use of the preposition "with" (את) here indicates that the people and their offspring are the accused in the *rîb*. For a discussion of the different prepositions used, see Limburg, "The Root ריב and the Prophetic Lawsuit Speeches."

[64] William L. Holladay, "Jeremiah's Lawsuit with God: A Study in Suffering and Meaning" *Interpretation* 17 (1963), 280-287, 285. The precise nature of Jeremiah's *rîb* is what he views around him: the seeming prosperity of the guilty while he himself suffers.

[65] This translation departs slightly from the RSV and other English translations, which in Holladay's view fail to bring out the real oomph behind the statement.

knows that God will be acquitted (צדיק, which in a legal context means "not guilty"), but this does not stop him from speaking judgment against him.[66]

Jeremiah takes the prophetic vehicle of the legal demonstration of God's justice and reframes the courtroom so that this time, Jeremiah is prosecutor and judge, while God sits in the dock. Jeremiah receives no answer from God. In public, Jeremiah is unwavering in his commitment, even when that commitment leads him to mocking and even temporary imprisonment (Jer 20:2). Yet in private, Jeremiah conducts a *rîb* with God, a *rîb* he knows he cannot win, a *rîb* that the *reader* watches, and *judges*, in the background.

Another development in the use of the *rîb* is found in Second Isaiah. In 1923 Ludwig Köhler designated nine passages in Second Isaiah as *Streitgespräch* (Disputation): Is 40:12-16, 40:17-20, 40:21-26, 41:1-5, 41:21-24, 42:18-25, 43:8-13, 48:14-16, and 49:14-21.[67] Köhler's analysis led him to the conclusion that the architectonic of Deutero-Isaiah was that of two trials, one between YHWH and the foreign gods (and the nations that worship them), and one between YHWH and the people. While in the first trial YHWH takes the accusatorial role, in the second it is YHWH who defends himself – successfully -- from the charges brought against him by the people. In Second Isaiah 41:21-22, for example, God issues a challenge to bring their case against him. "Present your case" (קרבו ריבכם), says God, "bring forth your proofs" (הגישו עצמותיכם). Likewise in Isaiah 43:22-28:

Yet you did not call upon me, O Jacob; but you have been weary of me, O Israel!
You have not brought me your sheep for burnt offerings, or honored me with your sacrifices.
I have not burdened you with offerings, or weakened you with frankincense.
You have not bought me sweet cane with money, or satisfied me with the fat of your sacrifices.
But you have burdened me with your sins; you have weakened me with your iniquities.
I, I am He who blots out your transgressions for my own sake, and I will not remember your sins.
Accuse me, let us go to trial; set forth your case, so that you may be proved just.
Your first ancestor sinned, and your interpreters transgressed against me.
Therefore I profaned the princes of the sanctuary, I delivered Jacob to utter destruction, and Israel to reviling.[68]

This use of the *rîb*-pattern is almost *less subversive* than classical use. By having God allow himself to be put on trial, and having God emerge the victor, Second Isaiah shows that even by the standards of human justice, God

---

[66] To provide evidence for his translation of *dibber mishpatim 'et*, Holladay points to Jeremiah 39:5, where Nebuchadnezzar does this action against Zedekiah. Cf. Holladay, 281.

[67] Ludwig Köhler, *Deuterojesaja (Jesaja 40-55) stilkritisch untersucht* (BZAW 37; Giessen: A. Töpelmann, 1923). This list of trial speeches was modified slightly by Antoon Schoors in 1973, who had a slightly different list of passages but nevertheless maintained the importance of this genre to Second Isaiah as a whole.

[68] Translation NRSV.

emerges in the right. Even when God is put in the dock, when the people themselves formally act as judge, and not just in the background, God's actions are proven correct and he is able to stand a successful defense. This is very similar to the narrative strategy of Genesis 18. In all of Second Isaiah's trials, God emerges victorious. This represents a real development in the prophetic use of the *rîb*-pattern, away from the open-endedness of Hosea, Amos, Micah, and even First Isaiah, to a much more closed circle of judgment. While earlier use of the *rîb*-pattern laid bare the inequity of the very institution being utilized, here the institution is upheld and God not only emerges not-guilty but, indeed, irreproachable – beyond human judgment. In fact, the people of Israel are repeatedly reminded that they are God's witnesses (e.g., Isa 44:8). Allowing the people to try God, Second Isaiah shows that this role is inappropriate for them. After all, they are only a "worm" and an "insect" (Isa 41:14), and are not "the first and the last" (44:6).

Despite the fact that this use of the *rîb*-pattern is more of a closed circle than that of previous prophetic authors, Second Isaiah represents a significant development in the use of the *rîb*-pattern because it is the first time that this genre is used as the overall schematic for an entire series of oracles. In Second Isaiah, despite the fact that scholars such as Köhler and Schoors have separated these pericopes into two types of trials, one between God and the foreign nations and one between God and Israel, Nielsen has correctly noted that all of them are, in essence, parts of the same trial, in which Second Isaiah has God defending his past actions in destroying the land and sending Judah into exile. This is no longer the type of *rîb* in which we might expect an *avertissement* or a declaration of war – it is a *rîb* regarding the justice of God's past actions. Second Isaiah's lawsuits attempt to demonstrate, through the use of courtroom procedures, God's absolute justice both in sending the people into exile and, ultimately, in bringing forth Cyrus as a deliverer. This marks an important development in the use of the *rîb*-pattern as an overarching narrative framework, even within a series of oracles that are not narrative in nature. This, in turn, sets the stage for what is perhaps the greatest use of the *rîb*-mentality in the Hebrew Bible, the book of Job.

At the very end of her extensive investigation of the *rîb*-pattern, Nielsen makes an important claim about the reasons why prophets employed this pattern. She, like other scholars before her, believes strongly that this pattern is employed for purposes of theodicy, so as to present the justice of God's actions or intended actions in ways unimpeachable by the audience. In her conclusion, Nielsen expands on her overall explanation of how the double role of Yahweh in the trial is intimately related to his special role as guarantor of the covenant: "the Covenant between Yahweh and Israel gives an assurance of protection for the people, but it also demands that the people keep to the way of Yahweh and subordinate themselves to his commandments. As god of the

Covenant, then, Yahweh is at one and the same time both the protector of the people and the one who must intervene if they overstep themselves. This 'doubleness' is most clearly expressed when the prophets depict Yahweh as both prosecutor and judge."[69] Nielsen clearly recognizes that this depiction of the divine courtroom has a tension within it that cannot be resolved according to the mechanisms of human justice, but is related to the nature of God's relationship with Israel and therefore a function of the special identity of the Israelite God, both with regard to his covenant with Israel and also with regard to his unique role in the cosmos.

But it is what Nielsen says next that represents a profound insight into what benefit the use of the divine courtroom has for the prophetic authors who employ it. Almost as an afterthought, Nielsen suggests that the use of the courtroom as a metaphor for illustrating God's judicial activity presents an image of God as participating in an "entire sequence of action."[70] According to Nielsen, the prophets used the form of the lawsuit "because they wished to make it clear that when Yahweh punished his people, it was not merely an expression of arbitrary anger. It is not the violence of the tyrant, but the punishment of their covenant-lord which strikes the Israelites down; in this sense, the lawsuit contributes to an understanding of Yahweh's righteousness."[71] For Nielsen, the fact that God engages in a series of predicted actions helps to mitigate what might otherwise be seen as pure and unpredictable wrath on the part of God.

Building on Nielsen's insight, I would argue that the courtroom metaphor attempts to mediate the powerful violence of God's punishment through a series of actions that channel that wrath through the legal administration of justice, presenting any penal decision as one upon which there has been proper deliberation and analysis. By using the courtroom metaphor explicit in the *rîb*-pattern, the authors are not only emphasizing that no decision by God is arbitrary and capricious, but they are also suggesting that God has engaged in a particular process that seeks to channel his understandable anger appropriately. René Girard has convincingly argued that the western judicial system acts as a conduit, a "curative procedure," for irruptions of vengeance and violence that might otherwise be uncontained.[72] Danielle Allen has argued that this understanding of the judicial system is also at work in ancient Athe-

---

[69] Nielsen, *Yahweh as Prosecutor and Judge*, 74,

[70] Nielsen, *Yahweh as Prosecutor and Judge*, 76.

[71] Nielsen, *Yahweh as Prosecutor and Judge*, 76.

[72] As Girard argues, "the judicial system never hesitates to confront violence head on, because it possesses a monopoly on the means of revenge." René Girard, *Violence and the Sacred* (Baltimore: Johns Hopkins, 1977), 21.

nian law.[73] The prophets of the Hebrew Bible, by employing the courtroom metaphor, may also recognize that it is a useful set of criteria for explaining how God channels his own potential for wrath and violence into appropriate action.

In this framework I refer back once again to the biblical understanding of the nature of God as expressed in the divine attributes of Exodus 34. Those attributes reflect an understanding of God that is rooted in both an understanding of God as merciful, steadfast, and long-suffering, as well as a God of ultimate retributive justice which works itself out through history. The use of the courtroom metaphor may be an early attempt to mediate the seemingly vast gulf between these two sets of attributes. Indeed, later interpretation of the attributes explicitly connects them with judicial functions and with the divine courtroom. The seeds for this later move are already in place in the conceptual framework of the divine courtroom as it manifests itself in the *rîb*-pattern of the Hebrew prophets.

## E. God as Prosecutor, Judge, and Defendant: the Book of Job

The most extended and profound view of the divine courtroom in the Hebrew Bible is found in the book of Job. The book of Job is a highly innovative and mature investigation of the possibility (and limits) of the courtroom as a vehicle for confronting God, and it has left an indelible footprint on the way future authors have employed and continue to employ this imagery and metaphorical framework.[74] So many permutations and rotations of the divine courtroom are found within its forty-two chapters that the reader is almost left spinning by the end. What starts (and ends) with a folktale-like presentation of God's court and administration of the universe, turns into an extended poetic dialogue in which Job, on the defensive, confronts the issue of the very equity of the divine judicial system, and in so doing, the nature of God himself. And when God finally makes his presence known, the result is so unexpected and in some ways disappointing, that the ultimate judge, the true arbiter of the Jobian courtroom, can only be the reader, who is left to deliberate on all that has been presented before him. It is in this way that Job has his closest colleague in Prometheus. As the audience judges the issue of Prome-

---

[73] Danielle Allen, *The World of Prometheus: The Politics of Punishing in Democratic Athens* (Princeton: Princeton University Press, 2000).

[74] It is, as B. Gemser insists, "the apex and consummation of genuine Israelite individual religious consciousness, and of a mentality and phraseology deeply stamped with the *rib*-pattern so inherent in the Hebrew mind." B. Gemser, "The *Rib*-or Controversy-Pattern in Hebrew Mentality," in A. van Selms and A. S. van der Woude, eds., *Adhuc Loquitor* (Leiden: Brill, 1968), 116-137, 135.

theus' sentence and the justice of Zeus, it is ultimately left up to Job's readers to deliver a verdict not only on Job's sentence and suffering, but on the equity of YHWH.

Even from the very beginning of Job, the polyvalent nature of the courtroom is present. The book begins with a brief introduction to the person of Job that emphasizes his moral uprightness, calling him " תם וישר וירא אלהים וסר מרע" (1:1).[75] We learn that Job is exceedingly prosperous and "the greatest of all the people of the East" (1:3), reflecting a Deuteronomistic concept of retributive justice and indicating that Job was aptly rewarded for his righteousness. Job is portrayed in these first five verses as a true patriarch, upright with respect not only to his moral and liturgical attitudes but also taking responsibility for those of his children (1:5). The ultimate goal of this first scene is clearly to portray Job as unassailable, conscientious, and perhaps practically perfect in every way. But the narrative here immediately shifts from a scene involving Job (and his sons) on Earth to a heavenly court, in which YHWH sits as king over the "Sons of God" (בני אלהים).

While the prologue has been describing nothing but scenes of calm and contentment, the Accuser (השׂתן) enters the narrative at this point (1:6), calling upon YHWH alongside the other heavenly beings. When YHWH questions the Accuser as to whence he has come, the Accuser replies "from roving and roaming about the world" (1:7).[76] Though we are not sure of the exact role of the Accuser – and who he is accusing – Marvin Pope has suggested that this portrayal of the Accuser derives from the Persian secret service, commonly known as "the eye of the king," which was charged with the responsibility of roaming about the land and reporting back.[77] In this light, the Accuser's role is apparently to roam around the earth and find examples of human impropriety.

God then provocatively singles out Job as someone to whom the Accuser should devote particular attention: "Have you considered my servant Job? There is no one like him on the earth, innocent, upright, and God-fearing, and turning away from evil" (1:8). God is here bragging about Job, which is the catalyst for Job's imminent trial. In response, the Accuser calls Job's piety into question as to being caused by self-interest (1:9-10). God has blessed Job and his family, sheltering him from all trouble and suffering. The Accuser

---

[75] The phrase "תם וישר" (innocent and upright) is used in Psalms to indicate a state of moral perfections, while the phrase "God-fearing and turning away from evil' is found repeatedly in Proverbs (3:7; 9:10; 14:16; 15:33).

[76] George Rutler has written of this response, "it is not an evasive reply indeed. Its precision is devastating, making it the most dangerous line in the Bible." George Rutler, *The Impatience of Job* (Illinois: Sherwood Sudgen & Co., 1981), 14.

[77] Marvin Pope, *Job* (AB; New York: Doubleday, 1965); cf. Raymond Scheindlin, *The Book of Job* (New York: W.W. Norton & Co, 1998), 163.

questions whether Job's piety will last if he is directly tested by suffering; whether piety is even possible in the human realm if all comfort is removed. But the question is more than just that of disinterested piety. By questioning and provoking God here, the Accuser is really questioning the *reasoning and justice of God*, the basis for the plan of the cosmos. The Accuser's role in Job is actually more subversive than at first glance – these examples of human impropriety are used to impeach *God*, and while the matter at hand is ostensibly the piety of Job, the true challenge presented is whether or not God's concept of justice holds up to intense scrutiny and trial. The Accuser's task in this test is not to accuse man – it is to accuse God. The actions of man – the outcome of Job's trial – thus have direct implications for the question of God's ultimate justice and propriety. While Job is tried, it is truly God who is on trial.

Though the heavenly court is not pictured as a formal courtroom by using legal images and vocabulary in its description, there can be no doubt that this is the impression that hangs over the scene. This impression is confirmed to a certain degree by the way in which legal language and vocabulary *is* used throughout the rest of the book. Chronicling the precise instances of juridical terms and forms throughout the book of Job has become a well-trodden field in scholarship.[78] The quantity of juridical vocabulary and metaphor throughout the book of Job only serves further to color the heavenly court of the prologue as a courtroom, and thus God and the Accuser as having particular rôles within it.

At first Job does not turn to the judicial system as a means for redressing his grievances. At the end of the prologue, when Job has been swiftly deprived of his possessions, prosperity, family, and bodily health in a whirlwind series of events, he still seems ready to accept his situation. When his wife tells him to "curse God and die" (2:9), Job chides her for being a foolish woman, asking "shall we receive the good from God, and not the bad?" (2:10). The folktale seems to be ending with an affirmation both of Job's in-

---

[78] The literature is expansive. Among the most important works are: C. H. Gordon, "The Legal Background of Hebrew Thought and Literature" (M.A. thesis, University of Pennsylvania, 1928); S. H. Scholnick, 'Lawsuit Drama in the Book of Job' (PhD dissertation, Brandeis 1975); M. Dick, "The Legal Metaphor in Job 31," *CBQ* 41 (1979), 37-50; J. B. Frye, "Legal Language and the Book of Job" (PhD dissertation, University of London, 1973); J.J.M. Roberts, "Yahweh's Summons to Job: The Exploitation of a Legal Metaphor," *Restoration Quarterly* 16 (1973), 159-65; N. Habel, "The Role of Elihu in the Design of the Book of Job," in W. Boyd Barrick and John R. Spencer, eds, *In the Shelter of Elyon* (JSOT Supp 31; Sheffield: Sheffield Academic, 1984) 81-98; S. H. Scholnick, "Poetry in the Courtroom: Job 38-41," in Elaine R. Follis, ed. *Directions in Biblical Hebrew Poetry* (JSOT Supp 40; Sheffield: University of Sheffield, 1987), 185-204; S. H. Scholnick, "The Meaning of *Mišpat* in the Book of Job," *JBL* 101 (1982), 521-529; and, most recently, F. Rachel Magdalene, *On the Scales of Righteousness: Neo-Babylonian Trial Law and the Book of Job* (Brown Judaic Studies 348; Providence, RI: Brown University, 2007).

herent righteousness and disinterested piety, and of God's correct and just administration of the universe. One almost expects the story to end here, with God restoring Job's fortunes and the Accuser slinking off, defeated.[79]

It is the very genre of the prose-tale that provokes the reader to such expectations. Carol Newsom has presented a remarkable interpretation of the book of Job as being a "contest of moral imaginations."[80] Newsom argues that the prose tale operates within a set of didactic and generic conventions that have a perspective of the operations of the universe that are smooth and sunny. In this genre, "the focal point of such patterns in the Hebrew didactic narratives is the character of the individual enacted in moments of decision. These moments are constructed as starkly binary choices between one action that would embody a virtue and another action that would repudiate it. In the moral vision of these stories, for an action to be truly good, it must be undertaken without regard to circumstances."[81] Here Job is faced with a decision, and he acts accordingly, refusing to curse God and "sin with his lips" (2:10). If this were a standard didactic narrative, following the conventions Newsom outlines, the story should end here. Obviously, it does not. And as Newsom explains, "the book does not present the prose tale on its own but fragments it and juxtaposes it to the poetic materials. This act of juxtaposition will have effects on perception. Just as red surrounded by other colors looks different from red by itself, so the prose tale is perceived differently because of its juxtaposition to the dialogues."[82] Newsom thus argues that the contrast of genres within the book of the Job itself is an authorial strategy to provoke the reader to deliberate on the adequacy of the worldview presented in the prose narrative.[83] This, then, puts the reader in the seat of ultimate judgment: judging the friends, judging Job, and ultimately judging God.

This forensic/deliberative stance of the reader is all the more confirmed by the explicitly juridical vocabulary that appears time and again throughout the book. At first it is not even the protagonist who introduces the judicial system into the dialogue, or even brings up the guilty/not guilty question. Rather, it is Eliphaz who, responding to Job's cries of lamentation and of mourning in chapter 3, brings this question to the fore. Though ostensibly the three friends are there to "comfort and console" Job (2:11), Eliphaz's words do not comfort but rather confront. Eliphaz claims to have heard a voice in a dream asking him "Can a man be more just than God (האנוש מאלוה יצדק)? Can a man be more pure than his maker?" (4:17). While Eliphaz clearly expects a negative answer to this question, the question is provocative both for Job and for the

---

[79] Certainly, the book *will* end that way, albeit with no mention of the Accuser at all.

[80] Carol Newsom, *The Book of Job: A Contest of Moral Imaginations* (Oxford: OUP, 2003).

[81] Newsom, *The Book of Job*, 50.

[82] Newsom, *The Book of Job*, 37.

[83] Newsom, *The Book of Job*, 71.

reader, who, unlike Job, is aware of the cosmic scenario that has instigated his traumas. Asking this question provokes deliberation as to the nature of God's צדק in the first place. Was God justified in allowing Job to be so harmed? If not, what does this say about God's overall צדק, and the צדק of the universe so administered?

Eliphaz's question is followed by his insistence to Job that he should put his trust in God (5:8ff), and that God will eventually restore all of Job's fortunes (5:18-27). We hear the foreshadowings of the lawsuit motif once again in 5:17, when Eliphaz exclaims "fortunate is he whom God reproves ( יוכחנו אלוה); do not despise Shaddai's discipline." The verb יכח ("reprove," "decide," "judge") will appear again in Job, with decisively legal connotations, as Job calls for an arbiter, מוכיח, to referee his case (9:33; cf. 32:12), desires to argue with God (13:3), and present legal arguments before him (תוכחות, 23:4). Though sometimes scholars assign the first appearance of legal vocabulary to Bildad (8:1-3), Eliphaz sounds the opening tones. Job immediately picks up on the legal vocabulary, though he has not yet fully explored its possibilities. This begins in 6:2, when Job cries out "Oh, that my anger were weighed, and my calamities laid together in the balances!" Job is confident that those scales would show that the anguish and torment he has experienced so outweighs any transgression that he would be acquitted and his punishment overturned. This is explicit courtroom imagery, as scales are intimately associated with the administration of justice across the Mediterranean.[84]

Eliphaz's "consolation" provokes Job, who responds angrily to Eliphaz' lack of *hesed* (6:14), calling his friends a treacherous wadi (6:15ff) and accusing them of being people who would "refuse an orphan and trade their neighbor" (6:27). Though Job had not at first diagnosed the issue as being that of his integrity and righteousness, Eliphaz has placed that issue right before him, and he advises his friends to back away from this argument, realizing that his צדק is at stake (6:29). The reader, of course, knows that it is really *God's* צדק which is at stake, and Job's own actions are merely standing as evidence in an odd and somewhat disturbing divine trial. The justice of using a human to prove a point in heaven is called into question in Job 7:17-21, though of course Job has no knowledge that this is occurring:

What is man, that you exalt him, set your mind on him, visit him in the mornings,
try him (תוכחנו) in moments?
Why won't you look away from me, not leave me alone until I swallow my spit?

---

[84] See chapter 4 for a complete discussion of the importance of scales in envisioning the divine courtroom. Later, near the end of the dialogues, as Job becomes more and more angry and virulent, coming closer and closer to assaulting God and calling God unjust, the tone of this plea changes dramatically, much closer to a challenge than a prayer: "Let him weigh me in *honest* scales and he will know that I am blameless" (Job 31:6).

Have I sinned? What have I done to you, watcher of man? Why have you made me your
mark, so that I am a burden to myself?
And why wor.'t you pardon my transgression and remove my iniquity?
For now I will lie in the dust, you will seek me, and I am not.

In this, Job confronts God directly for the first time, seeing God here as the
cause of his suffering and torment. In particular 7:17, which sounds like an
ironic reversal of Psalm 8:4, reminds us of the immense gulf between God
and humanity.[85] What *is* man, that he should be tested like this? The reader
knows that Job is being tormented precisely because he is unimpeachable –
the narrator has made that perfectly clear – and while the "moral imagination" of the prose tale might have lulled the reader into a sense that this trial
would come to a quick resolution and the world would ultimately be righted,
the dialogues have already moved in a different direction, making us feel the
pain and suffering through Job's poetic cries.

These words provoke Bildad to state the ultimate question in 8:3: "Does El
pervert judgment? Does Shaddai pervert justice?" This question is not just
before Job, it is before the reader. And while Bildad, like Eliphaz, expects a
negative answer, neither the protagonist nor the audience is prepared to give
one. This is one of the most subversive moments in all of biblical literature.
For while theologically the answer should be a resounding no, according to
the narrative logic of Job the waters are muddied. It is not that the poet tells
us that God is or is not capable of such an action, it is precisely that he leaves
the question unanswered. The reader is explicitly provoked to think about
the question with reference to this specific torment of Job, the ultimate test.

After so starkly stating the question, Bildad suggests in 8:4 that Job's sons
must have done something wrong in order for Job to merit such punishment.
This is perfectly in line with standard understandings of God's justice as retributive. However, such a suggestion puts Job in a very unfortunate position,
as Kemplar Fullerton articulates:

If the doctrine of retribution is accepted as the touchstone of God's justice, as Bildad's
statements in 8:2-7 clearly imply, then, on the basis of that doctrine, Job must either be untrue to himself and acknowledge himself as a sinner against the protests of his own conscience, or he must be untrue to God in denying the justice of the Almighty's dealings with
him, since the actions of God in his case do not correspond with the requirements of the retributive theory of suffering.[86]

Bildad's great faith in the retributive system of justice leads him also to faith
that Job's fortunes will ultimately be restored (8:21-22). In his perspective,
Job's suffering is temporary, and though he might not understand it now, it is
because of his limited view of the situation. Like Job, Bildad also points to

---

[85] On the relationship between Job 7 and Psalm 8, see Michael Fishbane, *Biblical Interpretation in Ancient Israel* (Oxford: Clarendon, 1985), 285-286.
[86] Kemplar Fullerton, "On Job, chapters 9 and 10," *JBL* 53 (1934) 321-349, 329.

the great gulf between God and humanity, using this gulf instead to remind Job that "we are of yesterday, and know nothing, because our days on earth are a shadow" (8:9). Indeed, Bildad here seems to anticipate what God will himself say when he emerges at the end of the book, that Job "darkens counsel by words without knowledge" (38:2). This answer is not satisfactory for Job in chapter eight, and it will not be satisfying for the reader in chapter thirty-eight.[87]

Bildad's assertions provoke the great poem of Job 9-10, where the courtroom imagery and metaphor begins fully to take shape. In his opening response to Bildad, Job seems to acquiesce to Bildad's understanding of the way God's justice operates: "Indeed I know this is so; and can a mortal be vindicated with God (ומה יצדק אנוש עם-אל)? If one wished to contend with him (לריב עמו), one in a thousand could not respond to him" (9:2). Fullerton has clearly demonstrated that this seemingly acquiescent response is laced with irony.[88] Job here begins to use the technical vocabulary involved in the administration of justice to explore the inequity of his suffering, and indeed, the inequity of the whole situation. Job knows that a *rîb* between man and God can only go one way, because of the sheer force and ferocity of God, evidenced by his work in creation (9:4-10). The force of the verb צדק in 9:2 is more than just whether a mortal can "*be just* before God" (NRSV), but whether or not, in a forensic context, a person could *be vindicated* against God – and Job knows that the answer is certainly not. But the problem is that this answer is *preordained* simply because of the nature of the situation. No matter what, says Job, a mortal cannot be vindicated against God – and therein lies the inherent problem. The divine courtroom is simply inequitable; God is unanswerable and accountable to no one. "Who can stop him? Who will say to him, 'what are you doing?'" asks Job (9:12).

The inability of man to answer God is a central theme of this section. Job probes the legal metaphor to hit this point, as one of the main activities of a courtroom is questioning and answering, responding to charges, justifying

---

[87] It also does not make sense with Bildad's overall understanding of the situation. If Bildad truly believed that humans cannot fully understand God's work, then why would he be so confident that God works according to the principle of retributive justice? Should he not leave room for the possibility that God does *not* operate so? Bildad's statement in 8:9 seems really superficial, as if he is saying to Job that *Job* cannot fully understand what is going on, though *he* (Bildad) has a better purchase on the situation.

[88] Cf. Fullerton, "On Job," 330, on whether a mortal can be in the right before God: "Of course he cannot be. But why not? Not because God is really in the right, but (and here the ironical note begins to sound more distinctly) because, if man were to plead in court against Him, God could break him down in cross-examination. For God is at once – a very wise person, say you? Rather, a very knowing person, shrewd and crafty, and also strong as iron! No one could oppose Him and come off whole. Might makes right."

one's activities and decisions. The power of God that Job described in verses 4-12 leads him to acknowledge his limits in the face of this divine nature:

How, indeed, can I answer him, choosing my words with him?
Whom, even if I was just, I could not answer; I could only implore my judge.
If I called out and he answered me, I do not believe he would listen to my voice.
Who crushes me with a tempest, and multiplies my wounds for no reason.
He will not allow me to get my breath, for he fills me with bitterness.
If strength – he is mighty! If judgment, who will testify for me (ואם-למשפט מי יועידני)?
Even if I am in the right, my mouth would condemn me;
I am blameless, and he will make me crooked.
I am blameless; I do not know my soul, I despise my life.
It is all one, that is why I say "he consumes the blameless and the guilty."
If a disaster suddenly brings death, he mocks at the despair of the innocent.
The land is given over to the hand of the guilty –
He covers the faces of its judges, if not he, then who? (9:14-24)

Job here cries out in despair over the total unfairness of his situation. No one can answer God; no one is going to stand up to God for Job. No one will testify for Job at court – not even his own mouth, which will condemn him (9:19-20). Whether in a contest of brute strength or in a legal *agon*, God wins.[89] The balance of power in the courtroom is completely skewed. Job is completely powerless and has no legal redress of his grievances available to him. He can only appeal for mercy (9:15), but "to appeal for mercy when justice is due is shameful."[90] Job believes he should not have to throw himself at the mercy of the court, but the situation he is faced with leaves him with no other options.

The legal metaphor only provides Job with more ammunition, more evidence that he is in the right, and that something is fundamentally wrong with the cosmic judicial system. This situation leads him to anger and despair:

If I say, 'I will forget my complaint, I will abandon my countenance and cheer up,'
I fear my sorrows, for I know you will not clear me.
I will be guilty – why then do I toil in vain?
If I should wash with snow and purify my hands with lye,
then you would plunge me in the pit and abominate my clothes.
For he is not a man like me, that we should come together for judgment (נבוא יחדו במשפט).
There is no arbitrator (מוכיח) between us, to place his hand on us both.
He should remove his rod from me, and not let dread terrify me.
I would speak and I would not fear him, for I am not thus in myself (9:27-35)

One cannot help but notice the overwhelming emphasis on *fear* in these chapters. The prospect of facing God in court is something Job knows is not

---

[89]As Sylvia Scholnick notes, "beginning in chapter 9 and continuing throughout the book, there is an interplay of the ideas of power and litigation." Sylvia Huberman Scholnick, *Lawsuit Drama in the Book of Job*, 135.

[90] Fullerton, 332.

possible, yet he both desires and fears this prospect. God is so overwhelmingly powerful that Job knows he would do nothing but cower in God's face, and
even his own mouth would testify against him.[91] Since even human courtrooms are places that provoke fear, how much the more so with regard to the
divine courtroom?[92]

Yet even so, Job still looks to the courtroom as the only place for him to
present his case, to redress his grievances. He calls out for a מוכיח (9:33) to
come and settle the dispute. Job knows that as it is, the situation can only resolve itself with a guilty verdict for Job (9:29), despite the fact that he is תם
(9:20-21).[93] If only there were a neutral third party who could judge the situation! But when the judge is an interested party, acting also as the prosecutor,
the inequity of the situation reveals itself.[94] The courtroom imagery only
serves to highlight this inequity. Because the courtroom should *ideally* be a
place where justice is served, it is in the courtroom that we can truly see
when, *in reality,* it is not served. The courtroom reveals injustice as much as
it reveals justice.[95] Because of the inherent inequity of the situation, Job can
only plead with God at least to let him know what the charges are: "Do not
condemn me; inform me why you contend with me" (10:2). In a just situation, the defendant would be informed of the charges and be able to present a
defense.

Job, indeed, clings to his innocence, even claiming that God knows that he
is innocent (10:7), and yet still oppresses him by hunting him (10:16). Job
expresses this hunt in both military and legal language (10:17). This impossible situation ultimately leads Job to wish he had never been born, accusing
God of bringing him into the world just to torture him (10:18-22). Though
this may at first look simply like a reiteration of what Job put forth in chapter
three, it here carries new weight precisely because of Job's exploration of
what is happening in the divine courtroom. As Edwin Good notes, "Here he
wants to be dead because the structure of things has fallen apart. He had
thought that divine power and divine justice were positively related, and that

---

[91] Cf. 15:6, when Eliphaz tells Job that his lips are already testifying against him. This may also be implied when Job places his hand over his mouth when God challenges him to respond
(40:4).

[92] As Fullerton states, "the thought which had earlier crossed his mind (9:3) of pleading his
cause before God does, indeed, return, but now only to drive him, after his brooding upon God's
irresponsible power, into an agony of fear. What if God should condescend to appear in court!"
Fullerton, "On Job," 331.

[93] Note also that the narrator confirmed this in 1:1.

[94] Later Rabbinic literature will sum up a related situation nicely in a refrain that reoccurs
throughout its varied texts, "Woe to the man whose advocate has turned into his accuser!" (Lev
Rab 30:2)

[95] Later Job will put the situation in even starker terms: "Indeed, I cry out 'violence' and I am
not answered; I swear an oath, and there is no justice (אין משפט)" (19:7).

divine power supported those weak ones who deserved divine justice. Sure
that he deserves justice, he is also sure now that, like those wicked people
who ought not to be supported, he is being attacked by the divine power. Distinction has dissolved into darkness, and Job would rather be dead.'"[96] The
friends's insistence on God's just administration of the world, as expressed
through the system of retributive justice, has forced Job to realize that his experience is utterly at odds with this system.

After emerging so strongly in chapters 9-10, the courtroom asserts itself
repeatedly throughout the friend dialogues, both on the lips of Job and on
those of his friends. Zophar, responding to Job's indictment of the divine
courtroom in Job 9-10, condemns Job for claiming to be innocent: "For you
say 'my teaching is clear (זך לקהי), and I am clean in God's eyes'" (Job 11:4).
Scholnick has demonstrated that the root זכך/זכה in Job has a forensic valence
and relates to the question of one's legal standing in a court of law.[97] The forensic possibilities of this particular word will be fully explicated many centuries later in the Rabbinic conception of "merits" (זכויות) and the specific
role they play in the divine courtroom. The seeds of this dramatic expansion
are already here, with this term found repeatedly throughout Job (15:14-16;
16:17; 25:4-6; 33:9) with this specifically forensic valence. Here, Zophar
uses the term to summarize what he feels is Job's main claim regarding his
own status.[98] Zophar sees Job as claiming that his legal slate is totally clean –
but Zophar believes that if God had the chance to speak, God would reveal
that Job is far guiltier than he thinks he is (11:5-6).[99]

Job refuses to be turned around by his friends's arguments and pleads for
him to admit his guilt and turn to God for aid and mercy. Everything they put
before him, he claims to have considered already:

Look, my eyes have seen all of this; my ears have heard and understood it.
What you know, I too know; I am not inferior to you.
Nevertheless, I will speak to God, and I desire to argue with God (והוכח אל-אל אחפץ).
And nevertheless, you are lie-smearers; worthless physicians, all of you.

---

[96] Edwin Good, *In Turns of Tempest: A Reading of Job* (Stanford: Stanford University Press,
1990), 229.

[97] Scholnick, *Lawsuit Drama*, 5-32. Scholnick especially points to the relationship of the verb
to the Akkadian *zakû* and the forensic use of the Hebrew cognate elsewhere in the Hebrew Bible,
such as in Proverbs 16:2 and especially Micah 6.

[98] Scholnick also suggests that the term "לקהי" in this particular construction could well be
translated "my testimony" rather than "my teaching," pointing to the juridical usage of this term in
Deuteronomy 32:3. Scholnick, *Lawsuit Drama,* 17.

[99] Interestingly, Zophar also points to the interplay between power and litigation, saying "If he
passes by and imprisons, and calls an assembly, who can turn him around?" (11:10). But for Zophar, this is not due to the inequity of the situation, but rather to the fact that God has far more
knowledge than humans, and can see all iniquity (11:11). The power dynamic, then, for Zophar, is
absolutely required given God's omniscience and the limitations of human knowledge.

Who will surely silence you, that it would be your wisdom!
Listen to my arguments (תוכחתי), and hear the contentions of my lips (שפטי רבות).
Will you speak injustice (עולה) for God, and speak deceit for him?
Will you show him partiality?[100] Will you contend for God (אם-לאל תריבון)? (Job 13:1-8)

Job raises the stakes in chapter 13. The courtroom metaphor is extended not only to imagine Job's relationship with God, and to point out the inequities of his situation, but also to condemn the friends for their own actions. Job here condemns the friends for taking inappropriate rôles in the proceedings. Job 13:8 is especially suggestive; in the first half of the verse Job condemns them for their perceived role as judges (asking if they will show God partiality), while in the second half of the verse he condemns them for behaving as God's attorneys, contending for God *in abstentia*. This is an ironic play on the problem of having God act as both prosecutor and judge – here Job accuses *the friends* of acting as both prosecutors and judges. While the friends should simply have been friends, consoling and comforting Job on his dung-heap, their adversarial positions towards him have forced him to consider what their true roles really are. From Job's perspective, the friends are trying to stand in for God, even when that forces them to speak injustice and deceit (13:7). His friends are trying to be his adversaries and his judges.

But the friends are not actually being allowed to judge Job. The entire time, the reader is the one who is silently judging, watching the drama unfold on the pages. This is illuminated by a trend in Jobian scholarship to compare the book to a dramatic composition. Something about Job lends itself to being imagined as taking place on stage. Indeed, one of the reasons Job is so jarring is because the framework seems to belong to the genre of comedy, whereas the dialogues are unmistakably tragic.[101] Some of the most penetrating comments on Job are those that make us imagine the book as if we were watching from the audience. A prime example of this is Luis Alonzo Schökel's article "Towards a Dramatic Reading of the Book of Job."[102] Schökel engages in a creative proposal for the dramatic staging of Job which imagines, among other things, two levels of stages: one main stage, in which Job and his friends engage in their dialogue, and a second, upper stage. Not only does Schökel suggest that this is the appropriate location to stage the prologue in heaven, but that the character of God should sit there for the entire unfolding of the drama until the final act.[103] What is important here about Schökel's insight is not that he reminds us of the presence of God throughout

---

[100] Literally "lift up his face," a forensic idiom relating to partiality in judgment.

[101] The Book of Job has in the modern world inspired several dramatic compositions, such as Archibald Macleish's *J.B.* (1958) and Robert Frost's lesser-known *A Masque of Reason* (1945).

[102] *Semeia* 7 (1977), 45-61.

[103] As Schökel states, "This gives an advantageous position to the audience but a powerless one to Job." Schökel, "Towards a Dramatic Reading," 47.

the whole book, but that he reminds us of the presence *of the audience* as being an active participant in the drama. A play is not staged without consideration of how the audience will respond and engage, and Schökel understands that this is true of Job as well:

> The sacred representation of Job is much too powerful to allow an indifferent reader or audience: he who does not enter into the action with his own responses or internal questions, he who does not participate, will not understand a play that through his own fault remains incomplete: if he enters and participates, he will find himself under the gaze of God and subjected to a test through the perennial drama of the man Job.[104]

Schökel suggests that "this also constitutes a magnificent irony: the character of God becomes a spectator and a judge of the audience viewed as characters."[105] But what Schökel does not realize and develop is that this also produces a situation in which the audience is judging the characters, including God.

The fact that the audience is an active character in the book of Job is often completely left out of scholarly discussions of the Jobian lawsuit. In her 1975 dissertation, Sylvia Huberman Scholnick carefully explicates many aspects of Job's *rîb*, including technical forensic vocabulary and overall thematic movement of the "lawsuit drama" she sees unfolding. However, despite characterizing what is taking place as a drama, Scholnick neglects to realize the essential role of the audience as the ultimate judge of the proceedings. This is especially clear in her discussion of chapter 13, which she believes represents the content of Job's *rîb*: "In chapter 13 Job begins his ריב, his lawsuit, against God. His friends then are challenged to hear the suit."[106] Scholnick argues that 13:6 is a direct appeal to the friends to act as judges in the case, and that "verses 7-12 serve to remind the friends of their proper role in the case and their responsibility as arbiters and witnesses to be impartial."[107] Scholnick has missed the biting irony in Job's words. Job does not want the friends to judge his *rîb* with God. He is using the language of *rîb* in order to accuse them of improper action, of taking *improper* roles in the proceedings, and to show his disappointment with them and their words to him. When Job says in 13:18 "Look, I've prepared a case (ערכתי-משפט), I know that I will be vindicated (אצדק)," he is not asking them to hear the case as a proto-rabbinic court,[108] but rather telling them to shut up as he contends alone. Job uses the language of the *rîb* to indict the friends, not to call upon them to hear his case impartially.

---

[104] Schökel, "Towards a Dramatic Reading," 48.
[105] Schökel, "Towards a Dramatic Reading," 48.
[106] Scholnick, *Lawsuit Drama*, 137.
[107] Scholnick, *Lawsuit Drama*, 139.
[108] As Scholnick suggests, *Lawsuit Drama*, 138.

Part of the reason why Scholnick and others have misread this is because they fail to take seriously the judicial rôle of the reader/audience. Scholnick neglects the fact that the reader is also a character in the proceedings; instead, she presents the *rîb* as having only six participants: Job, the three "friends," Elihu, and God. But there is a seventh active character. Job may not be explicitly appealing to the reader in a dramatic aside to hear the case, but there can be no doubt that he is doing so implicitly. I believe that what leads Scholnick to forget this is her overall project, which is to ask the question "whether the Book of Job is, in fact, a lawsuit drama with Job and God as litigants and their friends as witnesses and judges."[109] Scholnick's technical exposition is designed to provide an unmitigated "yes" to the question. However, Scholnick is in some ways taking the *rîb* far too literally. Instead of realizing that the *rîb* language and imagery is deployed for particular reasons and in a provocative manner, she instead suggests that the book of Job *is* a *rîb*, and therefore she must assign different rôles to each of the characters and to show how every aspect of Job fits into this schematic. This is spurious; the book of Job is not set in a courtroom – indeed, that is one of the points of the courtroom language within Job – and therefore it is inappropriate to treat it as if it were. Presenting Job as if it *is* a *rîb*, rather than a presentation of a character who *calls for a rîb*, does an injustice to the book as a whole and also fails to see the irony of the book and its profundity.

Indeed it also fails to take seriously the fact that Job is, in some way, getting a *rîb*, though not the one he intended, and its judges are the audience – not the friends. This is why the reader senses the biting irony and double meaning of Job 16:19, when he cries out "Even now my witness is in heaven, and my witness in the heights." On one level, this has dramatic irony, because Job does not realize that his witness is his adversary. On the cosmic level of the narrative, however, this is true – in the dispute between Job and his friends, his witness *is* in heaven. Not only will this be proven true when God rebukes the friends from the whirlwind, but it is also true as the reader judges this proceedings. And the reader also senses that there is a level on which the book is addressed entirely to them in 19:23-24: "Oh that my words were written down, put in a book and engraved, that with an iron stylus and lead they were engraved in a rock forever." This reaches entirely past the level of the narrative to the reader, in the ultimate position of judgment.[110] This is one of the functions of the courtroom imagery. As Stuart Lasine writes, "the trial

---

[109] Scholnick, *Lawsuit Drama,* 105.

[110] After her exhaustive presentation of the Book of Job as corresponding to the narratological features of the Neo-Babylonian trial, in which Yahweh finally judges and settles the dispute between himself and Job, in the very last paragraph of her conclusion Magdalene admits that ultimately the readers are the judges, writing that "The book's very mimicry of the trial form begs readers to adjudicate this dispute." (Magdalene, *On the Scales of Righteousness,* 265).

metaphor prompts readers to take on the role of juror in order to make ethical judgments about characters and events."[111]

While the courtroom language continues to appear throughout the friend-dialogues, the next place in which it asserts itself as the dominant aspect is in 23:1-9, in which it is intimately connected to the question of the presence of God:

Indeed today my complaint is rebellious, my hand is heavy on my groaning.
If only I knew where to find him, I would go to his dwelling place.
I would lay the case before him (אערכה לפניו משפט) and fill my mouth with arguments (תוחחות).
I would learn the words with which he would answer me, and perceive what he would say to me.
Would he contend with me with the greatness of his strength? No, he would pay attention to me.
There an upright person would argue with him, and I would be delivered forever from my judgment.
If I walk forward, he is not there; and backward, and I do not perceive him.
In his activity in the left, I do not grasp him; I turn right, and I cannot see.

Job here contends that if he could only find God, he would go to him and lay his case out so clearly that God would have no choice but to listen to him rationally and deliver him from his verdict. Part of the inequity that Job perceives in the divine courtroom is that God does not have to appear in court to answer for his actions. This is almost, for Job, the epitome of injustice, because God never has to face Job, and Job never gets to face God. If this was a true *rib*, Job asserts that he would win, as any upright person would. Pierre van Hecke has suggested that for Job, even more important that winning is the ability to *talk* to God, to have "an honest conversation" with God.[112] But Job cannot have that conversation if God does not answer him, and Job uses the legal metaphor to show just how unjust it is for God to hide himself from communication.

Job finishes his plaintive appeal to God to emerge from his hidden presence in a lengthy address that culminates in a challenge to God that some scholars see as the key to understanding the legal metaphor in Job.[113] Chapter 31 has been compared to the great "Negative Confession" or "Oath of Innocence" that the deceased undertakes before entering Osiris's hall of judgment (the "Hall of Two Truths") in the Egyptian Book of the Dead. The Negative Con-

---

[111] Stuart Lasine, "Job and his Friends in the Modern World," in Leo G. Purdue and W. Clark Gilpin, eds. *The Voice from the Whirlwind: Interpreting the Book of Job* (Nashville: Abingdon Press, 1992), 144.

[112] Pierre van Hecke, "'But I, I would converse with the Almighty' (Job 13:3): Job and his friends on God," in *Job's God*, 23.

[113] Cf., for example Michael Brennan Dick, "The Legal Metaphor in Job 31" *CBQ* 41 (1979), 37-50.

fession consists of a final confession in which the deceased asserts that he has
not committed a series of transgressions, such as we have in Job 31, particularly verses 5-34. Oaths were also a major part of trial procedure in the Neo-
Babylonian period, as Magdalene demonstrates.[114] At the beginning of this section, Job calls to God to "let him weigh me with accurate scales (מאזני-צדק) so
that God will know my integrity" (31:6). Not only does this heighten the comparison with the Egyptian materials, but we are reminded here of Job's initial
plea to be weighed in the balances in Job 6:2. Something has changed, though,
between chapter 6 and chapter 31. At first Job was confident that the scales
would demonstrate his righteousness and his unjust sentence of suffering. But
by the end of the dialogues, after Job has given full heed to his situation, he no
longer trusts even that small piece of the courtroom, calling instead for "accurate scales" – not just scales. Since Job distrusts the divine courtroom as a just
judicial system, there is the implicit charge that God could use dishonest
scales, or interfere with the scales in some way.[115] Job's use of the courtroom
imagery has led him to realize that the very system by which divine justice
seems to be administered is unjust at its fundamental core.

The close of chapter 31 brings together all of these aspects of the courtroom
imagery into one final cry: "If only I had someone to listen to me! Here is my
signature – let Shaddai answer me! And my adversary's writ ( ספר כתב איש
ריבי )– would I not carry it on my shoulder, bind it to myself like crowns? To
him I would narrate the number of my steps, I would approach him as a ruler"
(31:35-37). Michael Brennan Dick believes this verse is key to understanding
Job's use of the legal metaphor, writing that:

> An examination of biblical and extra-biblical legal documents establishes v 35 as a defen-
> dant's official appeal before a third party for a civil hearing at which the judge would com-
> pel the plaintiff to formalize his accusations and to present any supporting evidence. As we
> shall see, this request was ordinarily made only after all attempts at informal arbitration had
> been exhausted and was often accompanied by a sworn statement of innocence. In Job 31
> the oath of innocence has been expanded to embrace the entire chapter.[116]

Dick argues that an analysis of the Book of Job alongside what we know
about Ancient Near Eastern law can lead us to a better understanding of the
strategy that Job pursues throughout his dialogues, and that 31:35 specifically
is Job's "trial request before a judge," comparable to that which Dick finds in

---

[114] Magdalene, *On the Scales of Righteousness*, 188ff.
[115] This is a consistent motif in the use of the scale-imagery, as will be demonstrated throughout the manuscript.
[116] Dick, "The Legal Metaphor in Job 31," 38.

Ancient Near Eastern sources.[117] From Dick's vantage point, all of Job's speeches culminate in this one request for a public trial, formally enacted by Job's signature. He is not interested in pursuing any more conversation with the friends, and he will not be swayed from his resolve by their "windy words." He puts his signature to his name, and demands to face his adversary, his איש ריב.

But before that איש ריב answers Job's summons, a completely unfamiliar character appears on the scene, a character who has provoked fascinating interpretation, particularly in the last twenty years. After telling us that "the words of Job are completed" (31:40), the narrator breaks in for the first time since the end of the prologue:

So these three men ceased answering Job, for he was just in his eyes (צדיק בעיניו). And Elihu the son of Berachel the Buzite, from the family of Ram, became angry. He became angry that he justified himself more than God. And he was angry at the three friends, since they could not find an answer though they had condemned Job. And Elihu waited to speak to Job because they were older than he, but when Elihu saw that there was no answer in the mouths of the three, he became angry. (32:1-5)

Though we had not heard about Elihu, the narrator informs us that he has been there the whole time, silently waiting his turn, and finally could hold his tongue no longer because of the failure of the friends to answer Job (also 32:11-14), and at Job's insistent self-justification over that of God. Elihu insists that "I will speak, and I will have relief; I will open my lips and I will answer. I will not show partiality to anyone, and I will not flatter any man" (32:20-21). For the next four chapters (33-37), Elihu rebukes Job, particularly in his desire for a courtroom confrontation with God, and his self-righteousness, pointing instead to the majesty and sovereignty of God.

Forensic imagery and juridical vocabulary play a large role in Elihu's speeches, so much so that many scholars have understood his speeches in forensic categories. In particular, Norman Habel has presented a holistic interpretation of the Elihu speeches that suggests that they can all be read within a juridical context. For Habel, this begins with Elihu's initial rebuke of the friends in 32:12: "I considered you closely, and look, there is no arbiter for Job, no one of you to answer his claims." According to Habel, Elihu is sug-

---

[117] Dick, "The Legal Metaphor," 47. To Dick's great credit, despite being convinced that Job can be fruitfully illuminated by attention to this context, he still realizes that the author of Job has "shown characteristic artistic freedom in the use of this legal pattern," and thus avoids one of the pitfalls of modern scholarship, to attempt to fit all of Job's twists and turns into a specific box.

gesting that he will fill these technical juridical roles, arguing that "Job 32 is thus the apology of Elihu for assuming the role of arbiter."[118]

Elihu's appearance on the scene is jarring, and has led to two different schools of thought: either Elihu is a carefully plotted part of the author's narrative strategy, or he represents an intrusion onto the page by a later reader/author, unsatisfied (and angry) with the friends' failure to respond properly to Job's charges, and choosing literally to write himself into the argument of the book. Traditional arguments for this secondary nature of the Elihu material include: (1) Elihu is not mentioned in the prologue or in the epilogue; (2) The prose introduction of Elihu in chapter 32 differs from the introduction of the other characters, especially with regard to his extensive genealogy; (3) Elihu's refutation is different than the friends, particularly in that he calls Job by name nine times and quotes from the preceding dialogues; and (4) there may be a "distinctive linguistic profile" in the Elihu speeches.[119]

Newsom is among those scholars who are convinced by these arguments, believing that we can discern a different "culture of moral argumentation" in the Elihu speeches.[120] Newsom believes that Elihu is a reader who has literally written himself into the text, quoting from previous aspects of the debate. For example, in 33:8-11, Elihu explicitly quotes from Job's speeches in chapter 13: "Surely you have spoken in my hearing, and I heard the sound of your words: 'I am clean, without transgression; I am innocent, and there is no iniquity in me. Look, he finds oppositions to me, he reckons me as his enemy. He puts my feet in the stocks, he guards all my paths.'"[121] This summary quotes Job's own words at 13:24 and 13:27, as well as paraphrasing Job's claims to be clean (זך). Likewise Elihu explicitly quotes 27:2 at 34:5: "For Job said 'I am just, and God has taken away my judgment."[122] What is significant here with regard to the courtroom imagery, which figures heavily in the Elihu speeches, is that if Newsom and others are correct, Elihu represents an instance in which an ancient reader has adjudicated the dispute for himself,

---

[118] Habel, "The Role of Elihu," 83. Habel continues to provide a technical exposition of each of the chapters, suggesting that they all have juridical functions: in chapter 33, Elihu summons Job to a formal hearing and refutes Job's charge that God does not answer humans; chapter 34 represents Elihu's main trial speech, addressing Job's claim that God perverts justice; and 35-37 are Elihu's defense of "El's just governance." Habel, 95.

[119] Cf. Newsom, *The Book of Job*, 282 n.5.

[120] Newsom, *The Book of Job*, 201.

[121] Much has been made about the relationship between the Hebrew word 'enemy' (אויב) and the name of the protagonist (איוב). Even though the roots of the two words are not the same, they are similar enough that the ear might subconsciously connect the two, thinking that Job's name could mean 'the object of enmity.' Cf. Pope, *Job*, 6. Later Rabbinic Midrash exploits the connection.

[122] In addition, Newsom believes that Elihu also anticipates the whirlwind speeches, even though he cannot quote from them directly. Newsom, *The Book of Job*, 202.

emerged from his position of judgment, and decided to deliver his own verdict on the narrative. Elihu would thus be an example of the phenomena Lasine articulated when he suggested that "the book itself may prompt readers to 'rise from *their* chairs' to pass judgment on perceived injustice, as did Job, before and during his trial by God."[123] Elihu thus represents an instance of that very phenomenon already in the ancient world, evidence that at least one reader did think of himself as the judge of the dispute.[124]

On the other hand, arguments for the integrity of the Elihu speeches as original to the Book of Job are also compelling. Habel has presented a holistic interpretation of the Elihu speeches that sees them as being integral to the original design and plotting of the book.[125] The most recent attempt to present a full-length narrative interpretation of the Book of Job, that of F. Rachel Magdalene, also points to the integrity of the Elihu speeches within the text. By analyzing Job according to the narratological features of Neo-Babylonian legal procedure, Magdalene argues that we can account for many of the seemingly disjunctive literary features of Job, including the role of the Elihu speeches. According to Magdalene, Elihu can be identified as a "second accuser-prosecutor" such as those found in Neo-Babylonian legal documents, who do not rise to speak until the defense has finished making his case.[126] For entirely different reasons, Magdalene, like Habel, sees the Elihu speeches as integral to the Book of Job.

Both arguments are compelling and have merit. While they might seem incompatible, in both cases everyone agrees that Elihu has jumped into the conversation at an unexpected juncture that defers God's voice for six chapters. Even if one sees the Elihu speeches as integral to the book's design, it is still true that this represents an instance in which an audience member, a silent listener, has emerged to present his own "verdict" on the situation, suggesting that the author of Job himself realized and intended that readers would respond to the situation by attempting to adjudicate it for themselves. This was the intended reaction to Job. In Elihu, either we have proof that it *did* provoke this reaction, or we have an example of this intended reaction plotted by the author.

---

[123] Lasine, "Job and his Friends in the Modern World," 147.

[124] In Schökel's dramatic presentation of the book of Job, he describes Elihu's appearance thus: "all of a sudden there came a reader – a character of the audience – who, unable to contain himself any longer, jumped upon the stage and began to speak as if he were a member of the cast. His name is Elihu: he is an intruder in terms of the book's construction, an impulsive volunteer in terms of the cast; he is a witness to the provocative power of the book. This is why the book was composed: to transform the audience into the cast." Schökel, "Towards a Dramatic Reading," 48.

[125] Norman Habel, "The Role of Elihu in the Design of the Book of Job," in W. Boyd Barrick and John R. Spencer, eds. *In the Shelter of Elyon* (JSOT Supp 31; Sheffield: Sheffield Academic, 1984), 81-98.

[126] Magdalene, *On the Scales of Righteousness*, 225.

Job never responds to Elihu, because immediately following Elihu's defense, God emerges to speak to Job from a whirlwind. When God does speak, the courtroom imagery seems to have little or no place in his response. Unlike all of the other characters, God does not explicitly address Job's claims in a legal forum, or use the technical juridical vocabulary to set him straight. As Robert Alter has summarized, "God chooses for His response to Job the arena of creation, not the court of justice, the latter being the most insistent recurrent metaphor in Job's argument after Chapter 3. And it is, moreover, a creation that barely reflects the presence of man, a creation where human accounts of justice have no purpose."[127] In chapters 38-39, God questions Job repeatedly about his role in creation, taking Job on a cosmological and zoological tour, reminding him that he has a very limited perspective on the way God governs the world. According to God, Job does not have the vantage point to see everything and the purchase necessary to make accurate assessments and accusations.

However, as Scholnick has correctly noted, God's speeches are not entirely devoid of courtroom imagery; in fact, they continue to develop the metaphor. This is especially true in the way God frames his address. While Job has been requesting an "answerer" (עונה), instead God tells him that *He* will question *him*, and Job will be the one who is required to answer (38:3). This indicates that God is aware of Job's request to meet his accuser for a *rîb*, and is at least partially responding to it. This is explicit at the end of God's first speech, when God puts a direct challenge to Job: "Shall the one who contends with Shaddai (הרב עם-שדי) reprove? Let Eloah's accuser answer" (40:2).[128] The way God opens his second speech sharpens the image: "Gird up your loins like a man, I will question you, and you will declare to me. Will you invalidate my judgment? Will you condemn me to vindicate yourself?" (40:7-8). This explicitly juridical imagery turns the tables on Job, pointedly questioning Job's motivations and intentions in his *rîb*.[129]

The courtroom imagery in God's response points further to the fact that in forensic terms, God's response is somewhat unsatisfying. If it is God's answer in a *rîb*, God's participation in this lawsuit that Job has initiated, it is certainly

---

[127] Robert Alter, "The Voice from the Whirlwind," *Commentary* 77 (1984) 33-41.

[128] Scholnick argues that this is an "indication that God acknowledges his active participation in a *rîb*". Scholnick, "Poetry in the Courtroom: Job 38-41," 187.

[129] Scholnik presents an interpretation of the whirlwind speeches as God's "testimony" within Job's lawsuit, in which God answers the two charges brought by Job: (1) that "God is unjust in his role as judge"; and (2) that "God has committed *hamas*, 'offense,' which is a juridical term in the Hebrew Bible for the broad category of unlawful conduct." Scholnick offers a technical exposition of this section of Job to demonstrate and prove her claims, ultimately arguing that "God answers the complaint that he acted unjustly by defining for Job the true nature of divine justice as sovereignty," in other words, by picking up Job's courtroom imagery, God is showing Job that the courtroom imagery is inappropriate to understand God's just activity.

not what Job was anticipating – nor was it what the reader was anticipating. God never addresses Job's sufferings in his speeches; never informs Job of the heavenly wager, or what cosmic role Job's torment has served, the one *possible* justification for Job's seemingly unjust punishment. Instead, the speeches from the whirlwind seem, rather, like God is a bully. The reader knows that Job is, in fact, justified in most of his claims – he is being punished for a reason he cannot discern and cannot fit into his understanding of how divine justice is administered. However, the reader, being privy to the prologue, knows that there is a logic to Job's sufferings, even if it is a theologically troubling one. But God cannot inform Job about the true reason for his sufferings, because it *is* so theologically troubling – that God would allow Job's entire family to be murdered in order to prove his own point. Would this not just *strengthen* Job's case regarding God's justice? It is the reader who is expected to think about and process these questions. God's use of the courtroom imagery as the framework of his speeches reminds the reader just how evasive God is being, and how he is not providing "the truth, the whole truth, and nothing but the truth."

But Job has no answer, no choice but to recant – what else can he do? He has been predicting this all along. In his first response to God, when God challenges him to respond (40:1-2), Job has very little to say: "Look, I am of little account, what can I answer you? I place my hand over my mouth" (40:4). Job seems to be acquiescing to God's insistence that he get a new perspective on his own situation. However, this is tinged with irony. Job has been saying all along that God is far more powerful than man, and that they could never come together to court because God's power would far outweigh that of his own. Here Job is merely affirming what he has consistently asserted – the situation itself does not allow Job to respond; he has nothing to say. Job has no choice but to submit to God's will – but the reader watches all. So when Job says in his final response "I know that you can do all, and that no scheme can be thwarted from you" (42:2), he is not admitting that God is in the right – he is indicating that the situation leaves him no other choice.[130]

Norman Habel has shed further light on this response. Habel argues that a full consideration of the legal framework of Job reveals that "the final speech of Job (42:42-6) amounts not only to a summation of Job before he leaves the court, but to an indirect verdict on God by Job, the human litigant."[131] Habel correctly notes that "God's angry words to the friends include a backhanded

---

[130] Norman Habel suggests that Job's use of the מזמה מרת ("plot," "scheme,") is a deliberate response to God's insistence that Job does not understand his design (עצה) of the universe (38:2), and therefore when Job uses the term, he "is not praising God for his power but indirectly continuing his challenge to the way God runs the world." Norman Habel, "The Verdict on/of God at the End of Job," in *Job's God*, 29.

[131] Habel, "The Verdict on/of God at the End of Job," 27.

declaration of Job's innocence," and amount to an "out-of-court settlement."[132]
This, has implications for Job's final line of dialogue, where he seems to
completely submit to God: "Therefore, I despise (אמאס) and repent, on dust
and ashes" (42:6). Habel suggests that we should translate אמאס with forensic
valence as "retract,"[133] reading the verse as "Therefore I retract, and repent on
dust and ashes." For Habel, repenting on dust and ashes has a particular
nuance:

> For Job, being in 'dust and ashes' means being the public victim and more than a 'symbol of
> being mute and submissive before God.' He now repudiates the victim status. He chooses no
> longer to assume the role of victim, litigant, or adversary. He is leaving the court with his
> head held high, having 'seen' God. The implication of this dramatic exit is that Job believes
> he is vindicated.[134]

Habel's analysis suggests that Job does not simply capitulate to God, and the
author does not expect or desire the reader to do so either. In his reading,
Job's statement is more than it seems. In it, Job affirms God's power while
still maintaining his position. In effect, Job gives a verdict on God.

Ultimately this position of verdict-giver, however, is left to the reader. To
be sure, many readers do see God as, in the end, being in the right, seeing
Job's attempt to bring God to court as forcing human categories on the divine.
But many others leave the book questioning and even angry at the entire situation, at the "justice" of the end of the book, the return to the "moral imagination" of the prologue. This is the brilliance of the narrative presentation of the
divine courtroom, the reason that Job has withstood the test of time, the reason
that readers still find it so profound today. It has no easy answers. It does not
lend itself to being forced into complete narratological boxes. It is a *rîb*; it is
not a *rîb*. Job is innocent; Job is guilty of being innocent. God is guilty; God is
justified. Through all of this, the courtroom is a persistent presence, but it is a
confused one. One is never quite sure who is suing whom, who are the witnesses, who are the judges. The reader is forced to weigh the arguments and
judge for themselves. This confused courtroom scene sets the standard for
nearly all of the presentations of the divine courtroom that follow, which are
fraught with the Jobian background. Whenever we see images of God holding
trial, we are put in a position of judging God.

---

[132] Habel, "The Verdict," 35.

[133] Habel, "The Verdict," 33.

[134] Habel, "The Verdict," 33-34, quoting Samuel Balentine, "'What are Human Beings that
You Make so Much of Them?' Divine Disclosure form the Whirlwind: 'Look at Behemoth', in
Tod Linefelt and Timothy Beal, eds., *God in the Fray: A Tribute to Walter Brueggemann* (Min-
neapolis: Fortress, 1998), 277.

# F. Conclusion: God as Witness

In this chapter I have attempted to demonstrate the nature of the divine courtroom in the Hebrew Bible as a place where essential questions of God's justice emerge. Whether it is in the forensic appeals to God as judge, or in the prophetic law-court pattern of indictment and theodicy, or in the suggestive and provocative book of Job, the imagery of the courtroom emerges as an ideal way to place questions of God's justice squarely before the reader. The question is by no means resolved by any biblical author. There still remains the nagging question of God's justice and the possibility of inequity any time one must face God as a judge or prosecutor. These very real fears, heightened by the realities of human courtroom justice, are felt in the use of courtroom imagery and framework by biblical authors.

One final way in which the divine courtroom manifests itself in the Hebrew Bible is in the question of witnesses. Where there is a trial, there must be witnesses – at least two (Deut 19:15). The laws requiring two witnesses already remind us just how fraught human courtrooms were with the anxiety of injustice. This anxiety applies to the divine realm as well, and the issue of witnesses encapsulates many of the aspects of the divine courtroom discussed in this chapter.

A classic example of witnessing before God in the Hebrew Bible is found in the book of Deuteronomy. The book of Deuteronomy closes with the famous song of Moses (Deut 32-34), in which Moses appeals to heaven and earth to listen to his song (Deut 32:1). At first glance this appeal seems like a standard appeal to witnesses, either at a trial, or in the treaty form. But the situation is actually more complex, because the song *itself* is meant to serve as a witness against the people. God informs Moses that the Israelites are destined to forsake the covenant and whore themselves out to other gods (Deut 31:16-18). God is concerned, in particular, that when this happens, and he punishes them for it according to the established rules of the covenant, they will say "Isn't this because our god is not in our midst, that we have found these troubles?" (Deut 31:17). Wishing to anticipate the possible accusation that he has in some way abandoned them, God instructs Moses to "write down for yourselves this song, and teach it to the people of Israel; put it in their mouths, so that this song will be a witness for me against the people of Israel" (Deut 31:19). God (and the author of Deuteronomy) knows what will happen when Israel breaks the covenant, that Israel will have to be punished. He anticipates, however, a countercharge, in which *Israel* accuses *Him* of breach of covenant, attributing their sufferings to His unlawful absence. When this happens, "this song will be before them as a witness" (Deut 31:21).

But not only will the witness, therefore, testify against Israel, it also will testify *for God before Israel* – and before the reader, the ultimate judge of

God's actions in history. The Song will be God's proof that he has been acting justly all along by punishing them for breach of covenant. The Song is therefore God's witness in the imagined "trial" in which *he* is the defendant, needing to justify his actions before the community. In this case the community will not only be the historical Israel, but will be the imagined Israel of the future, those who are being told the history of God's relationship with Israel, those who are hearing the explanation of why Israel (and Judah) suffered such catastrophes throughout their history.

The song does not stand alone; there is also another witness called in the same chapter. Just as the song will be both God's testimony *before* Israel and God's testimony *against* Israel, so too will the book of the law (Deut 31:24-27). In this way God will have two witnesses prepared, both to convict Israel and to acquit himself. And as Moses calls both heaven and earth in Deuteronomy 32:1, the effect is that of witnesses within witnesses, attestation within attestation – all solidifying the case against Israel. But more importantly, they are all attempts to solidify the case for God's innocence and righteous behavior. Deuteronomy 31, and *any* time the biblical authors portray God calling witnesses and invoking the trial metaphor, is evidence of just how much question there was about the justice of God's actions in history, just how much anger and frustration there must have been at the time these texts were composed, probably after a long series of catastrophes in Israelite history. The more God protests his innocence, the more accusations there must have been.[135]

---

[135] After all, in what kind of equitable courtroom can the judge/prosecutor also act as a witness?

Chapter 3

# The Divine Courtroom After Life:
# Order and Chaos in Greek and Roman Literature

It is impossible to overstate the importance of Greek culture and literature for the depictions of the divine courtroom in Second Temple Judaism and early Christianity. Not only do we have comparable scenes of the god(s) administering justice from Homer to Lucian, but in addition we have an equally important literary tradition that posed the philosophical questions of justice, civic obligation, morality, violence, religion, ethics, etc. to an audience of judges – Greek tragedy. Greek drama put these questions, including questions of the justice of divine activity, on stage to be judged – literally – before a large audience, the same audience who regularly attended trials and lawsuits, the audience of the city. These two great literary traditions, that of the *Nekyia* and other such invocations or representations of the divine courtroom, and of the theatre and its interrogation of mythic figures and divine activity, form essential components of the context that surrounds and stands beneath depictions of the divine courtroom in Judaism and Christianity.

This chapter attempts to present a survey and analysis of the major works from Greek and Roman literature that discuss the divine courtroom, whether understood as taking place atemporally, in the past, or at the end of one's lifetime. This chapter will demonstrate that over time, the portrayal of the divine courtroom by Greek and Roman authors became more and more critical. While the earliest texts only allude to questions of the justice of Zeus and his ability faithfully and justly to administrate the cosmos, the later texts put this question front and center, using scenes of the divine courtroom not to present a post-mortem world that functions orderly and judiciously, but instead a post-mortem world that is incapable of ensuring justice and incompetent in judicial matters. Part of what makes the later texts so empowered in this regard is the dramatic tradition, which does not hesitate to put the gods on trial before the Athenian audience. Later writers who inherit both traditions, that of the *Nekyia* and post-mortem courtrooms, and the staged courtrooms of Greek tragedy (and sometimes Old Comedy), combine the two traditions in a way that exploits the courtroom setting to question the courtroom itself. This is best represented by Seneca in his *Apocolocyntosis*, and by Lucian of Samosata throughout his corpus. In this way the Greek and Roman literature, though having different characters and settings than those of the

Hebrew Bible, finds itself running a slightly parallel course in terms of the way this literary motif is employed in both cultures.

Before beginning to examine the presentation of the divine courtroom in the ancient Greek literature, it is useful to mention several aspects of Greek and Roman courtrooms, to remind us that our concept of the physical and social courtroom is far removed from that of antiquity.

## A. Courtrooms in Antiquity: Common Problems

Courtrooms in antiquity were not solemn places; they were loud, noisy, and boisterous, so much so that the authors of the rhetorical handbooks all insist that an absolute requirement for a forensic orator is a loud voice that can be heard above the crowd. This noise-filled atmosphere was a standard feature of the courtrooms from classical Athens to the Roman imperial era. Courtrooms were a standard feature of public life. Most trials were held in large public areas, and it was expected that people would come in and out, watching, listening, and cheering on their "side." Courtrooms in this way were very theatrical, arenas in which advocates performed for the judge, the jury (in Athens), the panel (in Rome), and the audience. In some ways, the audience was the ultimate arbiter in the case; while the judges or juries might pass down the legal verdict, it was the audience who ultimately tried the case in the vaunted "court of public opinion." Robert Bonner notes that "In many respects the trial was like a public debate with the audience acting as judges."[1] Just as today, while legally a person might be acquitted, public opinion on the matter – and on the system that provided that acquittal – may differ.

Courtrooms in antiquity were a standard and accepted part of society. While some may hold up the courts of classical Athens or Rome as the ultimate standard of judicial administration, just as today, all the problems with the legal system plagued those same courts. For example, jury corruption in fifth-century Athens was such a problem that a whole new complex system of assigning juries was invented to counteract it.[2] Fifth-century Athens also saw the rise of the sycophant, "the man who made a practice of prosecuting without justification, either because he hoped to get an innocent defendant convicted and so obtain a payment due to a successful prosecutor, or because he

---

[1] Robert Bonner, *Lawyers and Litigants in Ancient Athens* (Chicago: University of Chicago, 1927), 73.

[2] A summary of the new system, which involved the alphabet, wooden tickets, boxes, and other such technology, is described by Douglas McDowell, *The Law in Classical Athens* (Ithaca: Cornell University Press, 1978), 38ff.

hoped to blackmail the defendant into bribing him to drop the case."[3] The concern over false prosecution and unjustifiable charges was so strong that eventually laws were enacted to provide penalties against engaging in this type of action.[4]

Another issue that plagued the courts of Athens was misrepresentation of the law at trial. Unlike today, where laws are readily accessible by everyone, such was not always the case. In Athens, if a litigant wanted to argue that something was against the law, it was he (not a magistrate or other court official) who was responsible for producing that written law into evidence. This provided an opportunity for corruption if the litigant misrepresented the law or presented a false law, and therefore a new law was written punishing this action by death.[5]

All the normal and expected problems with witnesses continued: false witnessing, witnesses retracting their statements, fleeing the jurisdiction, succumbing to bribes, et al. Litigants in classical Athens were not allowed to testify for themselves, yet they could summon whomever they wished (provided they were not a disenfranchised citizen) and if the witness failed to testify, they could prosecute for *lipomartyrion* (failure to appear to give testimony). Monetary penalties were prescribed by law for witnesses who became hostile or refused either to confirm or deny testimony while on the side. If a witness was found to have given false testimony three times, that witness was "automatically disenfranchised."[6]

These very real problems that were associated with the judicial system made a significant impact on the public. Some of the best evidence that we have for this are in the literary portrayals of trials in antiquity, such as we find in the Greek novels and in New Comedy. The courtroom scene was a literary topos in the novel. Generic features of these scenes included "weep-

---

[3] McDowell, *The Law in Classical Athens*, 62-63. The classic treatment by Bonner still stands: "Further proof of the prevalence of sycophancy is found in the constant efforts of litigants to avoid being regarded as sycophants. When a man says, 'It is not by reason of fondness for litigation that I have brought this suit,' or 'I have tried by every possible method to come to terms with the defendant'; or 'I have never brought a public suit against a citizen nor have I harassed anyone when he was passing his accounts,' it is evident that he desires the jury to understand that he is not a professional accuser. And a litigant frequently brings a general charge of sycophancy against his opponent to ward off suspicion from himself. 'Not as a sycophant have I brought this suit, but because I myself was vexatiously prosecuted.' 'My opponent is an exceedingly clever speaker and is very familiar with the courts.' 'The case against me has been trumped up.'" (Bonner, 63)

[4] This did not eradicate the problem, as evidenced by the fact that these concerns and laws continue to appear and be enforced well into the Roman era.

[5] McDowell, *The Law in Classical Athens*, 242.

[6] McDowell, *The Law in Classical Athens*, 245. False witnessing did not just include giving testimony one knew not to be true, it also including bringing in evidence that was not allowed by law, such as hearsay evidence.

ing defendants, vengeful accusers, overblown speeches, and cheering mobs.... The fickleness of the jury, the clemency (or antagonism) of the judge, the last-minute introduction of crucial evidence, the injustice of false accusation, the pain of imprisonment and torture".[7] While much of this is literary hyperbole, intended to maximize dramatic effect, the novels must have a certain verisimilitude in order to "create a scenario plausible according to the assumptions shared by author and reader about what was real."[8] The same is true for the depictions of Roman trials in the satires of Horace, Juvenal and Martial.[9] In order for these texts which portray the judicial system – with all its flaws and opportunities for injustice – to have any resonance with the reader, they must contain recognizable elements that would strike chords of truthiness.

It is probably no surprise, then, that courtrooms were areas of heightened anxiety throughout the Greco-Roman world. This is evident in a wide variety of sources. For example, In his book on dream interpretation, Artemidorus of Daldis explains what it means if you dream about going to court:

Courts of law, judges, lawyers, and teachers of law prophesy disturbances, sorrows, untimely expenses, and the revelation of secrets for all men. They indicate days of crisis for the sick. If the sick are victorious in the dream, their health will change for the better. But if they lose in the dream, it means that they will die. But if anyone who is actually engaged in a lawsuit dreams that he is in the judge's seat, it signifies that he will not lose. For a judge passes sentence not upon himself but upon other men. Furthermore, for those who are involved in a lawsuit, doctors have the same meaning as lawyers. (*Oneirocritica* 2.29)[10]

Artemidorous easily identifies courtrooms as portents of sorrows, illness, and public revelations. Elsewhere in his treatise he makes an analogy between judges and rivers, because "they do what they wish with impunity and in accord with their own inclination" (*Oneir.* 2.27), and between a judge and the sea, because "it treats some people well and others badly" (*Oneir.* 3.16).[11]

---

[7] Saundra Charlene Schwartz, *Courtroom Scenes in the Ancient Greek Novels* (Phd. Diss.: Columbia, 1998), 1-2.

[8] Schwartz, *Courtroom Scenes*, 5.

[9] Leanne Bablitz has developed a methodology for using these texts within discussions of the realia of the Roman courtroom, involving "gradations of realism." In her gradation, the information most likely to be accurate in these texts is that which is "peripheral to the point of the satire," followed by "information central to the satire, but for which truthfulness is a necessity in order to set up the humorous point." Leanne Bablitz, *Actors and Audience in the Roman Courtroom* (London: Routledge, 2007), 6-7.

[10] Trans. Robert J. White, *Artemidorus Daldianus*, Park Ridge, NJ: Noyes Press, 1975.

[11] Artemidorus also makes an analogy between a law court and a weasel due to the numerical equivalent of the words (3.28). Lawsuits and courtrooms repeatedly show up in the *Oneirocritica*, indicating both the commonplace experience of being involved in a lawsuit and the propensity of lawsuits to show up in people's nightmares.

Like the courts of classical Athens, Roman courtrooms had their own share of problems, producing great anxiety for all participants. While Athenian litigants were required to represent themselves,[12] the emergence of a paid profession of legal advocacy brought with it its own set of problems. The disparity between the services available to the rich and those to the poor created a system that automatically and institutionally favored the wealthy. Compounding this issue was that the courtroom was very much an old boys club, with all the trappings of power, prestige, and status. Indeed, the Roman courtroom was a dominant arena for negotiating one's own status – a win in court could increase one's status, while a loss could decrease it. Advocates often decided which cases they would take based on the status of the litigant (and the opposing litigant), and how a win in court could affect their own status and climb up the social ladder.[13] Since judges in the Roman courtroom (like juries in Athens) were drawn from laymen, from all those listed in the *album iudicum*, the judges were vulnerable to the same concerns for honor, prestige, and status as the other participants. Favoritism was a common concern, as was the susceptibility of the judge to bribery and threats.

Another issue that plagued courtrooms in the Roman era was the length of time a case could occupy. Americans are intimately familiar with this issue from the way in which cases, with their seemingly infinite possibility for appeal, can drag on for years. In addition, while the Constitution may provide for a speedy trial, it is not uncommon for people to wait years simply to have their day in court. This is also the impression from sources around the Roman empire, despite the so called "one-day rule" that supposedly limited the time a civil trial could take.[14] In the papyri that survive from Roman Egypt, many records of individual trials exist (though some in very fragmentary form). One of the most common judicial verdicts recorded in the papyri, as J. A. Crook notes, was not a verdict at all, but rather a remittance of the matter to another court.[15] Crook calls these judgments "disappointing and disillusioning," summarizing that " One can well infer from these texts a very delay-ridden system of justice in Roman Egypt, whereby recalcitrance of parties and indecisiveness of judges can keep an issue on the docket, shuttling from court to court, for years; and sometimes the defendants have just simply not complied with judgment when given, and a year or so later petitioners are

---

[12] Although they could pay for the services of a logographer, who would write the speech they would deliver verbatim in court.

[13] A complete discussion is found in Bablitz, *Actors and Audience in the Roman Courtroom*, chapters six and seven.

[14] This rule, found in the *Twelve Tables*, provides that all civil trials must be presented over the course of one day. However, sources from across the empire provide evidence that this was not followed. See Ernst Metzger, *A New Outline of the Roman Civil Trial* (Oxford: Clarendon, 1997) 91ff.

[15] J. A. Crook, *Legal Advocacy in the Roman World* (Ithaca: Cornell, 1995), 68.

back starting the whole issue again and quoting earlier judgments in their fa-
vour."[16] It is hard not to imagine, if this was courtroom "justice" in Roman
Egypt, that this was not also the experience across the empire.[17] The information gleaned from the papyri is of particular importance because it is more
likely to reflect the realia of everyday courtrooms across the empire than the
information from Roman literary sources. Even the literary sources, however,
show a concern for these same problems and weaknesses.

It is fair to say that courtrooms in antiquity were not places where justice
always – or often – prevailed. Courtrooms were fearful in antiquity not only
if you were guilty, but also if you were innocent, just as they are today. Courtrooms were places of battle, in which audience members could be paid to
cheer or boo, where people squared off against each other in contests for
honor, prestige, and status.[18] It is no wonder that Paul reacts so strongly when
he hears that members of the bourgeoning Corinthian community are taking
each other to court (1 Cor 6). Perhaps nothing could tear the fabric of the
community apart more than having them choose sides in a Roman courtroom.

This, then, is the essential background to the literary portrayal of courtrooms in antiquity, including the divine courtrooms. Knowing that courtrooms in antiquity were plagued with issues and concerns over partiality,
injustice, manipulation, judicial misconduct, and inequity helps us to understand why this particular medium became a potent one for exploring issues of
divine justice.

## B. The Judgment of the Dead and the Justice of Zeus

One of the enduring legacies of the divine courtroom in Greek mythology is
the idea of the judging of the dead, either in the underworld itself, or on the
way to a sojourn in Hades or the Isle of the Blessed. Sometimes scholars
take it for granted that these scenes are plentiful throughout Greek literature
as they are in the Egyptian texts. However, a hunt for these scenes leaves one
nearly empty-handed, or, at least, with a handful of fragmentary information.
While it is clear that there was a tradition of the dead being judged, particularly by Minos and Rhadamanthys, we have only pieces of the puzzle surviving from the classical sources, and have to fill in the rest of the picture, or

---

[16] Crook, *Legal Advocacy*, 68.

[17] For a discussion of civil trials elsewhere, see Metzger, *A New Outline of the Roman Civil Trial*, in which he discusses the evidence from Roman Spain.

[18] Bablitz argues that the physical layout of the Roman courtroom reflects this agonistic atmosphere, in which the benches of the opposing sides faced each other, rather than facing the
judge as is common in contemporary courtrooms. The audience would literally be lined up behind their side, creating a literal battleground atmosphere in the Forum.

come as close as we can, by reference to later Roman literature such as Virgil's *Aenead* and even Ovid's *Metamorphoses*. Ironically, some of our best information about the judgment of the dead in Greek mythology comes from Plato (particularly in the *Gorgias* and the *Phaedo*), who repeatedly critiques the mythic discourse and uses myths in a remarkably variant and complicated way throughout his writings. Yet it is through Plato's use of these myths that some of this material survives, without which we would not have as complete of a picture as we do, nor would we be able to fully appreciate the parodies of this picture that we see in Aristophanes and Lucian, among others.

The earliest vision that we have of any sort of judgment among the dead is from the *nekyia* of the Odyssey. In book XI, Odysseus is granted a rare tour of the underworld, where he confronts the shades of those dear to him, including that of his mother (xi. 150-224). Towards the end of his journey through Death, he glimpses various scenes of life after death, including one of judgment:

Then I saw Minos, the radiant son of Zeus,
holding a golden scepter, judging the dead (θεμιστεύοντα νέκυσσιν),
and they were gathered sitting and standing round him in the wide-gated house of Hades requesting judgments (δίκας είροντο) upon them. (567-572)

Odysseus then glimpses scenes of punishment: that of Orion, Tityos, Tantalus, and Sisyphus (xi.681-717).

Scholars normally understand this depiction of Minos *not* as a full-scale judgment of the dead as he enacts in Plato's *Gorgias*, instead seeing Minos's activity as arbitrating disputes among the dead, a reflection of his mythological career on earth as an adjudicator.[19] This is most likely based on two factors: (a) the fact that this scene comes so near to the end of the tour of hell that it does not seem to predicate or ascribe people's sentences within the underworld but instead to reflect daily occurrences in the underworld; and (b) the use of the participle θεμιστεύοντα to describe Minos's activity. S. G. F. Brandon takes this to mean "legislating" rather than "judging," implying an administrative function.[20] In this reading, the term δίκαι is not understood to

---

[19] For example, Timothy Gantz explains that "the text seems clearly to indicate that the shades bring their *disputes* to Minos to be resolved. That beings as insubstantial as those the *Odyssey* describes could find anything about which to dispute, much less a way of paying back the offended party, strikes one as unlikely; probably we see here simply a reflection of Minos' role on earth, much as seems the case with Orion, the next figure viewed by Odysseus." Timothy Gantz, *Early Greek Myth: A Guide to Literary and Artistic Sources* (Baltimore: Johns Hopkins, 1993), 126. Such a view is also espoused by the most recent scholars to work on the *nekyia*, including Radcliffe Edmonds III, *Myths of the Underworld Journey* (Cambridge: Cambridge University Press, 2004), 56 n. 76.

[20] S.G.F. Brandon, *The Judgment of the Dead* (New York: Charles Scribner's Sons, 1967), 82.

mean "sentences" in its most extreme form, but rather "judgments," or minor arbitration decisions.[21] This understanding of Minos' role in the *Odyssey* has been the standard read since Merry's 1886 commentary on the *Odyssey*, who writes that Minos "only presents a shadowy counterpart of himself as he was when alive. Lawgiver, king, and judge in the flesh, he is also lawgiver, king, and judge in the shades."[22]

It is possible, however, that a larger judgment is alluded to here.[23] The two main pieces of evidence for this claim are (a) the later depictions of Minos, especially those of Plato and Virgil (as well as Lucian); and (b) internal evidence, both in the language used to describe Minos' activities and what immediately follows this brief mention of Minos' s judgment in *Odyssey* 11 itself.[24] In *Odyssey* 11.572-600, Odysseus witnesses the eternal torments of the mythic figures of Orion, Tityos, Tantalos, and Sisyphos. In all four cases, the punishments that these beings endure seem to follow a *lex taliones* principle: the punishment fits the crime. This sets the scene for what will become a standard trope in later versions of the *katabasis* from across the Mediterranean world: that one receives an eternal sentence that reflects the gravity and nature of the crime committed.[25] Christine Sourvinou-Inwood has analyzed this section of the Odyssey closely and elucidated how each one of these depictions illustrates a "punishment fits the crime" principle. For example, speaking about the punishment that Tityos receives for raping Leto, specifically mentioned here as Zeus' consort (11.579), she writes:

His excessive and transgressive sexual activity and aggression against a goddess' body is punished through immobility and painful erosion of his organ of sexual desire through the savage excruciating (continuous) invasion of his body by vultures – a lower form of life (which is what the vultures are in the Greek hierarchy of the cosmos) – as he himself was a lower form of life when compared to the goddess whom he attacked. Moreover, precisely because the liver is the organ of desire and passion, the vultures' attack on it may have con-

---

[21] Also contributing to this understanding of Minos' role is Lucian of Samosata's (much) later parody of Minos in *Dialogues of the Dead*, where Minos is depicted as having to judge such disputes as whether Hannibal or Alexander was more famous in his time.

[22] W. Walter Merry and James Riddell, *Homer's Odyssey* (Oxford: Clarendon Press, 1886), commentary on line 568.

[23] Debates as to the authorship of *Odyssey* 11 are beyond the scope of this study. For a classic argument as to why *Odyssey* 11 should not be considered Homeric, see Erwin Rohde, *Psyche* (New York: Harcourt, Brace & Co, 1925), 32-33.

[24] Admittedly it is impossible to make a convincing case based solely on the hands of later interpreters, who are fully capable of expanding these myths on their own based on their traditions, creativity, and agendas. But the second criterion, that of what constitutes and immediately follows this judgment scene, is not insignificant in thinking about the way this whole section functions.

[25] Such as in the later Christian *Apocalypse of Paul* and *Acts of Thomas*, as well as in Virgil's *Aeneid* and other Latin and Greek literature.

tained a metaphorical facet of sexual violence, sexual abuse to which he is submitting, unresisting – a reversal of his role as sexual aggressor.[26]

Sourvinou-Inwood also provides persuasive analysis as to the *Odyssey's* understanding of the crimes committed by Tantalos and Sisyphos, whose crimes are not spelled out by the text itself. In all three cases, Sourvinou-Inwood sees the principle of measure for measure at work, and additionally points out that what binds these three individuals together is that "all three sinners in *Odyssey* 11 are punished for crimes which constituted offences against the cosmic order which they had endangered, as well as personal offenses against the gods who are its guarantors, and also offenses against the social order which the cosmic order grounds."[27] These three tableaux, alongside the depiction of the punishment of Orion which Sourvinou-Inwood does not discuss, are given as paradigms of the types of punishment that exist in the *Odyssey's* underworld. While these may represent exceptional punishments for exceptional transgressions, they are not meant to be taken as the *only* instances of punishment in the underworld. It is not the goal of *Odyssey* 11 to give a comprehensive view of everything that happens in the underworld. On the contrary, the underworld is depicted quite hazily, as a world of shadows and shades, a world that humans can only see through a glass darkly, as it were.

This is a crucial point that should not be missed. The juxtaposition of these scenes of punishment next to the brief scene of Minos' judging suggests a more comprehensive judgment than is actually spelled out in *Odyssey* 11.[28] The mention of the judgment of Minos includes several key ideas that are often overlooked by those scholars who would dismiss this section of the *Odyssey* as an interpolation by later authors.[29] First, Minos is described specifically as the son of Zeus (11.568), linking the authority of this judgment to that of Zeus himself. In the juxtaposed punishment scenes, all the transgressions ultimately boil down to transgressions against Zeus. Leto, raped by Tityos, is specifically described as Zeus's honored (κυδρὴν) consort (11.580). The adjective κυδρὴν, which Sourvinou-Inwood explains is often reserved for goddesses, indicates Leto's intimate relationship with Zeus. She is not just his consort, she is his *honored* consort. This intensity not only magnifies the relationship between Zeus and Leto, but also magnifies the crime Tityos

---

[26] Christiane Sourvinou-Inwood, "Crime and Punishment: Tityos, Tantalos and Sisyphos in *Odyssey* 11" *BICS* 33 (1986) 37-58, 38.

[27] Sourvinou-Inwood, "Crime and Punishment," 54.

[28] This is *contra* Brandon, who sees absolutely no connection between the judgment scene and the punishment scenes. Cf. Brandon, *The Judgment of the Dead*, 84.

[29] For discussion, see Odysseus Tsagarakis, "*Odyssey* 11: The Question of the Sources" in Øivind Andersen and Matthew Dickie, eds. *Homer's World: Fiction, Tradition, Reality* (Bergen: Norwegian Institute at Athens, 1995), 123-132.

committed not only against Leto but against Zeus himself.[30] Minos's identifying characteristic as the radiant son of Zeus therefore links his authority to that of Zeus to pronounce judgment over the dead, perhaps even judgments that lead to this type of punishment.

Second, Minos is described as holding a golden scepter (χρύσεον σκῆπτρον). That this scepter comes to be associated with comprehensive judgment after death is clear from Plato, *Gorgias* 523a-527e, where all three of the afterworld judges have rods, but Minos holds the golden scepter, indicating that he has authority over the other two judges.[31] Likewise within *Odyssey* 11 itself, the other character who is indicated as holding a golden scepter is Teiresias (11.91), which may indicate Teiresias's authority to give Odysseus the prophecy he so seeks, and more importantly highlights his connection, like that of Minos, to Zeus.

While in Homer the golden object with which Zeus is most often depicted is a set of scales (cf. *Iliad* 21.248-254; *Il.* 8.78-87), in the *Iliad* it is Agamemnon's scepter that connects him to Zeus and gives him the authority to be "lord of many isles and of all Argos" (*Il.* 2.104). The scepter is specifically described as golden in *Iliad* 1.15, where Agamemnon, the very first character to appear in the epic, is described as holding in his hands "the ribbons of Apollo, who strikes from afar, on a golden scepter." Minos' golden scepter thus references (or at least allows the reader to reference) divinely mandated authority, here to carry out the judgments of Zeus.

Frederick Combellack's analysis of the (non-golden) scepter in Homer confirms this thesis. Combellack analyzes the thirty-six instances of scepters in Homer and concludes that while most scholars from the *scholia* onward have assumed that the scepter is a common mark of the speaker, and just serves to indicate that a speaker has the floor, in fact a close analysis of Homer reveals that "the scepter is not employed regularly by speakers, but only occasionally; and that its true function is to indicate clearly to the speaker's audience that he is about to make remarks of peculiar solemnity and importance."[32] Combellack persuasively argues that the scepter, therefore is a signal to the reader of the import of what is being said, and also notes that judges were also often depicted holding scepters.[33] If we carry this analysis forward into this brief description of Minos, his golden scepter would be appropriate for his forensic sentencing, especially if such *dikai* included the

---

[30] Likewise Sourvinou-Inwood illustrates how the crimes of Tantalos and Sisyphos, though not specifically mentioned, also are crimes against the gods.

[31] See below for a full discussion of this crucial passage.

[32] Frederick Combellack, "Speakers and Scepters in Homer" *JSTOR* 43 (209-217), 210.

[33] Combellack, "Speakers and Scepters in Homer," 214. Combellack directs the reader's attention here to *Il.* 1.223-244, where Achilles swears by the scepter. Combellack mentions Minos' golden scepter here (p. 215), but does not analyze it.

type of punishments undergone by the juxtaposed figures. This would serve to indicate a more serious and solemn type of judgment than previously interpreted by scholars.[34]

The final aspect of the description of Minos in *Odyssey* 11 that is relevant here is the location of the judgment scene, given as the "wide-gated house of Hades" (*Od.* 11.571). Gates are an essential part of afterlife imagery from Egypt to Dante, particularly because of their association with crossing a boundary from one world to another. In the *Iliad*, Homer uses this exact phrase again. The spirit of Patroclus appears to Achilles to ask him to bury him so that he can pass through the gates of Hades (*Il.* 23.70-71), and telling him that due to his lack of burial he is currently vainly wandering through the "wide-gated house of Hades" (*Il.* 23.74). For Homer, therefore, the gates have this afterlife resonance. More importantly, gates were often conceived of as places of judgment, both in depictions of the afterlife and in earthly reality.[35] City gates in antiquity were often the place of physical and earthly judgment, places of congregation and assembly. While some of the time it was bound to be the case that the disputes settled at gates were trivial and ultimately meaningless, the characteristics usually associated with the disputes Minos is settling, not all fell into this category. The depiction of Minos judging at the gate, therefore, can very well be read not as Minos judging trivial disputes, but as Minos passing down the sentences of Zeus, sentences like those being endured by the three paradigmatic examples of *Odyssey* 11. This brief mention of the judgment of Minos, a description that is only four lines long, is the starting point for a whole tradition in Greek literature of an afterlife judgment which is not confined simply to adjudicating minor disputes but, indeed, to determining one's eschatological destiny.

Following Homer, the next definite source in this line is the odes of Pindar (ca. 522-443 BCE), particularly the second Olympian ode, composed for the

---

[34] One more aspect of the scepter here is that in Pindar, the scepter of lawful judgment is said to be held by Zeus (*Olympian* 1.12), and the adjective used for lawful is θεμιστεῖον, the cognate adjective to the participle used to describe Minos' activity. This contradicts Brandon's too-rigid differentiation between "legislating" and "judging" to explain why Minos is not here depicted as a judge of the dead the way he is in later sources. Likewise also within the Homeric corpus itself θέμιστες are a characteristic aspect of the justice of kings, not just with respect to lawgiving but in all activity, and they come directly from Zeus (for example, at *Iliad* 9.98f).

[35] On judgment at the gates in Egyptian mythology, cf. H. Brunner, "Die Rolle von Tür und Tor im Alten Ägypten," *Symbolon* 6 (1982), 37-59.

76th Olympiad in 476 BCE.[36] One of the central themes in *Ol.* 2 is that of justice, particularly how it works through history, a note which is sounded right at the beginning of the ode. Pindar declares that Theron is "just with regard to guests" (*Ol.* 2.5-7), linking Theron with an attribute associated with that of Homer's Zeus.[37] Pindar's use of this epithet to characterize Theron immediately places the personal misfortunes and victories of Theron within the cosmic context sung in the successive strophes. This underscores one of the central themes of this *epinikion*, that of justice, and the way this justice works out in the good and bad fortunes befalling man.[38]

In the midst of this ode to Theron, Pindar includes an account of the afterlife, including brief mentions of the divine courtroom. This vision of the afterlife is unparalleled in his surviving odes.[39] The heart of the *epinikion* begins on a fatalistic note, with a prayer to Zeus to preserve the land "for once deeds are done, whether in justice or contrary to justice (ἐν δίκᾳ τε καὶ παρὰ δίκαν), not even Chronos, the father of all, could set aside the end of the deeds." (2.15-17). Pindar then goes on to hope for forgetfulness in the heights, yet still makes mention of the fates of Semele and Ino (2.25-30), and Oedipus (2.35-45), connecting that line to Theron, to whom his attention then turns. After detailing his accomplishment (2.48-52), Pindar declares:

> Truly, wealth embellished with virtues provides fit occasion for various achievements
> by supporting a profound and questing ambition;
> it is a conspicuous lodestar, the truest
> light for a man. If one has it and knows the future, that the helpless spirits of those who have died
> immediately pay the penalty – and upon sins committed here

---

[36] According to Race, the dating of most of the Olympian and Pythian odes is "relatively sound" due to the list of Olympic victors found on P. Oxy.222. Cf. William H. Race, *Pindar I* (LCL; Cambridge: Harvard University Press, 1997), 11. *Olympian* 2 celebrates Theron of Akragas' victory in the chariot race. However, the historical particularities of each of Pindar's poems should not be overly stressed, for, as John Finley Jr. stated, Pindar "sees his function as not merely or chiefly to give praise, but to uncover the hidden though inspired insight and to reveal truths which the future will confirm, though they are concealed by the uncertainties of any present as well as by common rancor." John H. Finley, Jr. *Pindar and Aeschylus* (Martin Classical Lectures 14; Cambridge: Harvard University Press, 1955), 50.

[37] As Lloyd-Jones writes, "Zeus in Homer possesses three of the functions later closely associated with that of protecting justice; he is protector of oaths (*Horkios*), protector of strangers and of the law of host and guest (*Xeinios*) and protector of suppliants (*Hikesios*); the last two functions are in their origins practically identical." Lloyd-Jones, *The Justice of Zeus*, 5.

[38] While I take seriously the appearance of this epithet in the prologue of this ode, I can hardly argue with William Fitzgerald, who notes also that presumably one of the guests to whom Theron showed justice was Pindar himself. Fitzgerald, "Pindar's Second Olympian," *Helios* 10 (1983) 49-70, 51.

[39] While the vision of the afterlife is unparalleled, the form in which it appears is not: it occupies the central section, where Pindar usually places a mythic narrative. Cf. Fitzgerald, "Pindar's Second Olympian," 49.

In Zeus' realm, someone judges beneath the earth [ἀλιτρὰ κατὰ γᾶς δικάζει τις ἐχθρᾷ]
pronouncing sentence with hateful necessity [λόγον φράσαις ἀνάγκα];
but forever having sunshine in equal nights
and in equal days, good men
receive a life of less toil, for they do not vex the earth
or the water of the sea with the strength of their hands
to earn a paltry living. No, in company with the honored
gods, those who joyfully kept their oaths spend a tearless
existence, whereas the others endure pain too terrible to behold (*Ol.*2.53-65)

This is followed by a depiction of the other option: the Isle of the Blessed, where people weave garlands and crowns "in accordance with the straight counsels of Rhadamanthys (βουλαῖς ἐν ὀρθαῖσι 'Ραδαμάνθυς)" who is seated at the side of Cronos (2.74-76).[40]

This doctrine of post-mortem retributive punishment has a direct antecedent in Homer.[41] Here, however, there can be no doubt that what is pictured here forensically is a post-mortem judgment based on man's actions. Pindar does not name this underworld (or post-world) judge; the focus is not on the identity of the judge itself but on his activity in passing down sentences. The judge here is ruled by necessity, a concept that will emerge in its fullest eschatological allomorph in Plato's *Republic*. This concept of necessity (ἀνάγκη) is of major import in Attic discussions of the nature of juridical justice.[42] Pindar sees this operational justice as being unavoidable and part and parcel of the justice of the universe. Sins committed here have their aftereffects in Zeus' realm, where the Zeus of the underworld *must* rule according to strict justice. The image sung by Pindar to express this understanding of the universe is a forensic one.[43]

However, Pindar is not important only for being the earliest definitive Greek literary reference to the post-mortem forensic judgment of the dead. The subtleties of Pindar bring out another facet of these images, which I argue is an essential component of these divine courtroom scenes, the question of divine justice. As Lloyd-Jones has well demonstrated, in the archaic period the qualities of divine justice are associated with Zeus as the supreme guarantor of the universe's *Dike*. One of the fascinating aspects of Pindar's second Olympian is that Zeus throughout the ode is often referred to by means of his

---

[40] Pindar then claims to have more arrows to shoot (i.e., things to say) on this subject, but that they need interpreters (ἐς δὲ τὸ πᾶν ἑρμανέων χατίζει; 2.85). Race takes this to mean that Pindar has more details about the afterlife to share, but that he forgoes their telling in order to praise Theron. Race, *Pindar I*, 72 n.2.

[41] Cf. also *Iliad* 3.279 and *Iliad* 19.259-60. Cf. Griffiths, *The Divine Verdict*, 294 n.62.

[42] Danielle Allen includes "necessity" as one of the elements of the "figurative grammar" used to talk about punishment in ancient Athens. Cf. Allen, *The World of Prometheus,* 74.

[43] Rhadamanthys, while he ultimately will find a home in the underworld alongside Minos and others, here instead is pictured not as a judge of the dead exactly, but more as a counselor. This also probably stems from the mention of Rhadamanthys at Elysian fields in *Odyssey* 4.561-569.

relationship to Kronos and Rhea. This is certainly the way Zeus is introduced in the ode (*Ol.* 2.12), and one could even argue that Kronos plays a more dominant role in the ode than Zeus himself. It is Chronos, Time, who is unable to undo the outcome of the deeds of either justice or injustice (2.16-17), and it is Kronos who sits on his throne next to Rhadamanthys on the Isle of the Blessed (2.75-76). William Fitzgerald argues that this is a deliberate move on the part of the poet:

> There are things that would be better forgotten in all family histories, and Zeus himself, the hierarchical absolute of the epinician world, has his own skeletons in the cuboard. To call him the 'Kronian son of Rhea' is to remind us that he *came* to power on Olympus, which was, for him as for Herakles, 'the firstfruits of war.' And it was a particularly impious war, in which the defeated enemy was his own father; it is probably no coincidence that Zeus is referred to as the son of Kronos a few lines before Chronos makes the implied reference to Zeus' crime, which Pindar hesitates to make explicit, all the more striking.[44]

What Fitzgerald is pointing to here is that, in the midst of a song that is ostensibly praise both of the athlete victor and of the head of Olympus, there is the shadow of Zeus's crime that appears around the edges. Not only this, but Zeus, the new guarantor of justice, directly associated with that judge in the underworld at 2.59-60 (and associated again with justice at 2.96), is a blemished divinity, not unimpeachable by any means in terms of his own actions.

I believe that the mention of this judgment, what happens in the realm of Zeus (*Ol.* 2.58) is not just a straightforward mention of the post-mortem judgment awaiting all those who have sinned upon earth. Instead, this is actually a *subversive indictment* of Zeus himself, perhaps for his known tendencies toward violence and injustice, such as the injustice carried out against Kronos that backgrounds this poem.[45] While I disagree with Fitzgerald's overall metempsychosis analysis of this ode, he is definitely correct in asserting that what Pindar is doing here is picturing Chronos as "the trace of Kronos in the dispensation of Zeus, unsettling the absolutes of the Olympian and Olympic context, which in turn threaten time with *latha.*"[46] While this ode supposedly celebrates Theron's victory in the Olympian *agon* of 476 BCE, what it references here is the true Olympian *agon* of Zeus and Kronos, casting a dark shadow over the current ruler of Mt. Olympus. What at first looks like a neat description of post-mortem justice in Pindar's second Olympian ode actually destabilizes the notion of the justice of Zeus, using the forensic scenario not to vindicate but to quietly indict. This move by Pindar is picked up again by Aeschylus, his contemporary, who will not be so quiet in his indictments.

---

[44] Fitzgerald, "Pindar's Second Olympian," 52.

[45] This charge is also leveled against Zeus in Aeschylus' *Eumenides*; see below.

[46] Fitzgerald, "Pindar's Second Olympian", 61.

The image of this forensic judgment brought forth in this ode carries with it the reminder that the judge of the underworld is still subject to Zeus' realm, an "other Zeus," and Zeus cannot be relied upon to embody perfect justice. This scene of the courtroom, therefore, carries with it an ominous warning that the means of justice by which the judge judges is not perfect justice, but "necessity," and necessity is not conceived of as being apart from the divine personality. Zeus' will will ultimately dominate, and Zeus' will is a frightening thing.

Pindar's allusions to Zeus's cosmic revolution cannot fully be understood without seeing the influence of Hesiod. While Homer assumes an understanding of how the Olympian regime came into existence,[47] it is Hesiod who provides us with a sustained account of the origins of the gods in the *Theogony*. Hesiod is the first Greek author whose work remains to us to give an account of Zeus's political activities in establishing his government. Jenny Strauss Clay describes the *Theogony* as "an attempt to understand the cosmos as the product of a genealogical evolution and a process of individuation that finally leads to the formulation of a stable cosmos and ultimately achieves its *telos* under the tutelage of Zeus."[48] The reign of Zeus is described as the result of a long and complicated succession of powers and forces that had to be harnessed and collected into a stabilizing cosmic order, not something that existed from eternity or was inevitable.

One of Hesiod's aims in the *Theogony* is to explain how the current Olympian pantheon came into existence. The question remains as to whether or not there is an apologetic concern, a concern to vindicate Zeus's actions, contained within the poem. Does Hesiod's account of the origin of Zeus' regime betray a concern to *justify* the origin of Zeus' regime? Daniel Blickman has argued in the affirmative, that the *Theogony* did provide a justification for Zeus's regime, in *Theogony* 383-403, the passage about how Styx collaborated with Zeus and "came first of all to Olympus with her children" (*Th.* 396-397).[49] In particular, Blickman calls attention to Hesiod's promise to Styx and her children, that "whoever of the gods would fight together with him against the Titans, him he would not strip of his privileges, but that every one would have the honor he had had before among the immortal gods; and that whoever had been without honor and without privilege because of Cronus, him he would raise to honor and privileges, as is established right (ἥ θέμις ἐστίν)" (*Th.* 392-396).[50] After Styx comes over to Zeus' side, Zeus

---

[47] Cf. Jenny Strauss Clay, *Hesiod's Cosmos* (Cambridge: Cambridge University Press, 2003), 12.

[48] Clay, *Hesiod's Cosmos*, 13.

[49] Daniel Blickman, "Styx and the Justice of Zeus in Hesiod's *Theogony*" *Phoenix* 41 (1987), 341-355.

[50] Trans. Glenn W. Most, *Hesiod I* (LCL; Cambridge: Harvard University Press, 2006).

lives up to his promise, and "he set her to be the great oath of the gods, and her sons to dwell with him for all their days. Just as he promised, so too he fulfilled for all, through and through; and he himself rules mightily and reigns" (*Th.* 400-404). Blickman argues that this passage is the place in the *Theogony* where Hesiod establishes the standard of justice by which Zeus operates, and thus provides a justification for Zeus's continued reign on Mt. Olympus, and his overthrowing of his father's government:

> *Zeus*, not these dumb creatures, is being justified, and quite explicitly. Zeus *earns* the alliance of Zelos, Nike, Kratos, and Bie by promising to guarantee proper honors (392-396) and by keeping this promise (399-403). The traditional phrase, ἥ θέμις ἐστίν (396 with West *ad loc.*), is not, I submit, being used casually. On the contrary, the upholding of θέμις by Zeus is being given a clear definition. His justice consists in his guaranteeing to the gods the enjoyment of their due τιμαί, including correction of abuses by Kronos (392-396). In maintaining such a fair and stable order, Zeus upholds θέμις. This passage expresses the *Theogony*'s definition of the justice of Zeus, and this justice is what establishes the legitimacy of his monopoly of force (=the attendance of the children of Styx), his right to be king.[51]

Therefore, for Blickman, "The protection of τιμαί is what differentiates his regime from that of Kronos."[52] According to Blickman, for Hesiod Zeus is not just another in a series of divine dictators, but is the legitimate cosmic ruler.

This says something about the view of Zeus in Hesiod's time. If Hesiod felt that he needed to give a justification for Zeus's rule within his account of the cosmogonic order, this indicates that there was a sense among others that Zeus's rule *needed* to be justified, that there was a question about whether or not the way Zeus took power was just at all. If it was not just, then how could Zeus be the upholder of justice in the cosmos? This would then call into question the scenes in the *Iliad* where Zeus sits on Mt. Olympus, holding court among the assembly of the gods, deciding the fate of Hector and Achilles, and of the battlefleets they represent: Is this divine justice, or the impetuous will of a tyrannical god who rose to power by unjust means? Hesiod's justification of Zeus indicates that this was a real concern.

The way Hesiod justifies Zeus's regime, through the protection of τιμαί and through the promise and fulfillment of that promise to Styx is significant. Not only does Zeus repay to Styx the honors she had before, and not only does he promise to do this for everyone, but Hesiod asserts that he established her as the "great oath of the gods" (*Th.* 400). In the world of Hesiod, Zeus therefore sets Styx as the principle of justice by which the world operates. This principle had direct relevance for humans, as oaths were a major

---

[51] Blickman, "Styx and the Justice of Zeus," 347.
[52] Blickman, "Styx and the Justice of Zeus," 348.

part of Greek legal procedure in Hesiod's time.[53] Before the advent of written law, and the consolidation of legal authority amidst archons and magistrates, arbitration procedures were based on evidentiary oaths. The oath, therefore, had a prominent place in adjudicating disputes. Here in Hesiod Zeus establishes Styx as the great oath, the ground of all other oaths. Hesiod must show that *that* oath, the great oath, is based on justice, in order for all oaths to be just, or to have claim to justice at all. By establishing Styx as the great oath, Hesiod places her at the center of the cosmos, establishing that not only was Zeus' rise to power just, but the way the cosmos itself functions corresponds to a notion of justice. This use of the forensic imagery of Styx vindicates Zeus, and allows him to play the role in the *Works and Days* of the foundation of cosmic justice. It is this passage on Styx, in many ways, that validates the cosmic nuptials of Zeus and Themis and father Eunomia, Dike, and Eirene (902). Zeus has proven through Styx that he truly *is* married to Themis and the father of Dike.

Yet even for Hesiod there is always the question of the unknowability of the will of Zeus, and the possibility that our understanding of how Zeus operates justly is limited and thus faulty. As Hesiod himself states, "There is no way to escape the intentions of Zeus" (*Works and Days*, 105).[54] The question of Zeus's justice, and whether he can order the universe through justice despite the bloody role he played in the overthrowing of Kronos and the Titans, creeps around the edges of these courtroom scenes, and continues to do so even in texts that use the courtroom framework in different ways. Ultimately, the use of the courtroom framework by these early authors, linking the judges of the dead back to Zeus, remind the reader that ultimately the standards and criteria of judgment are beyond their control, and in the hands of one much more powerful, ill-tempered, and violent. When Pindar refers to the judge of the underworld as the "other Zeus," and repeatedly refers to Zeus by means of his genealogy, he subtly alludes to the entire tradition of Zeus's battle for succession, inviting the reader to read it intertextually. He thus destabilizes the very justice that he is describing, quietly condemning Zeus while seeming simply to describe. The courtroom becomes a vehicle for exploring questions of justice and equity, particularly as it relates to the character of the expected judges. It was not a great leap from this use of the divine courtroom to anoth-

---

[53] On legal procedure in the time of Hesiod, see Robert Bonner, *Lawyers and Litigants in Ancient Athens: The Genesis of the Legal Profession* (Chicago: University of Chicago Press, 1927), 31f. That oaths play an important role in Hesiod's view of forensic procedure is clear from *Works and Days* 190-194, where the disgrace of the crooked oath is all the more clear.

[54] Glenn Most has shown that one aspect of the architectonic features of the *Works and Days* is to delineate the boundaries between gods, men, and animals. One of the boundaries between men and gods is that men must operate in the dark. Glenn Most, *Hesiod I*, xli.

er, in which the gods, particularly Zeus, actually had to stand trial for their actions.

## C. The Gods on Trial: Theatre as Courtroom

Recent scholarship has paid attention to the relationship between the courts of ancient Athens and the golden age of Greek tragedy, particularly the tragic competitions that took place there biannually. In her work *Dionysius Writes: The Invention of Theatre in Ancient Greece*, Jennifer Wise dedicates a chapter to "Courtroom Dramas," in which she argues that the relationship between the theatre and the courtroom in Athens was closely intertwined. Not only did all of the major playwrights each write relatively extensively on the legal system and devote at least one play to the topic, plays were performed before the same audience as would regularly come to witness the very public Athenian trials. Both the content of the plays and the context in which they were performed reflected Athens' burgeoning legal system.

For Wise, however, the relationship between the two systems goes even further. "Courtroom Dramas" refers not only to the prevalence of lawsuits and legal content on stage, but also to the fact that these dramas in many ways mimicked the courtroom setting: plays were performed to be *judged* by the audience, who would mark their votes on tablets similar to those used by jurymen at trials. As Wise writes, "In writing the winner's name, or voicing their approval or condemnation in the form of shouts, applause, or foot-stomping, theatrical audiences thus functioned essentially as jurors in a court of law. And as Jeffrey Henderson has demonstrated at length..., the identity between these two activities was obvious even to the participants at the time."[55] Audiences at these plays engaged with the plays as judges, and recognized their role as such. Wise, citing Aristotle, notes that both speeches in a law-court and staged dramas were both timed by the *klepsydra*, the water-clock.[56] This probably heightened the way all actors involved correlated both events in their minds, and by extension in the way they participated in each case. In addition, Wise also notes that there is a formal relationship between the ways that dramas were submitted to an archon for consideration and the ways that legal complaints were submitted for preliminary hearing before it was determined whether they had enough merit to stand trial. In this way, "the act of submitting a play for performance was identical in structure to the

---

[55] Jennifer Wise, *Dionysus Writes: The Invention of Theatre in Ancient Greece* (Ithaca: Cornell University Press, 1998), 133-134. Cf. Jeffrey Henderson, "The *Dēmos* and Comic Competition," in John J. Winkler and Froma I. Zeitlin, eds. *Nothing to do with Dionysus? Athenian Drama in its Social Context* (Princeton: Princeton University Press, 1990), 271-313, especially 276.

[56] Wise, 131, citing Aristotle, *Poetics* 1451a12.

act of submitting a legal complaint for trial: when Euripides handed in, say, the *Hippolytos* or the *Medea* for consideration for the theatre festival, he was in effect 'handing in an accusation' against these noble-blooded mythological figures, these great men and women."[57]

One of the most striking ways in which this theatre-as-courtroom relationship appears is in the similar terminology used by ancient authors to denote both participating in a lawsuit and competing on stage: each is called ἀγών ("struggle", "contest"), and the verb ἀγωνίζομαι refers to both activities. While the primary association of the *agon* is usually with the arena, the games, or other forms of athletic competition, the term is used frequently to refer also to theatrical competition and legal competition. This suggests an analogous relationship between what happens in all three of these competition stages. The term ἀγών referring to a trial or lawsuit and the cognate verb ἀγωνίζομαι to competing in that lawsuit, are found throughout the ancient forensic orators and logographers in both what we would now call civil and criminal proceedings. One such example is from Demosthenes:

> Let me begin, men of Athens, by beseeching all the powers of heaven that on this trial (εἰς τουτονὶ τὸν ἀγῶνα) I may find in Athenian hearts such benevolence towards me as I have ever cherished for the city and the people of Athens. May the gods so inspire you that the temper with which you listen to my words shall be guided, not by my adversary – that would be monstrous indeed! – but by the laws and by the judicial oath, by whose terms among other obligations you are sworn to give to both sides an impartial hearing. The purpose of that oath is, not only that you show equal favor, but also that you shall permit every litigant (τῶν ἀγωνιζομένων ἕκαστος) to dispose and arrange his topics of defense according to his own discretion and judgment. (18.1-2)[58]

On the theatrical side, one of the most important uses of the term ἀγών by an ancient dramatist is in the corpus of Euripides, who uses the term ἀγών to refer to a type of formal discourse within his plays. This, as Michael Lloyd has explicated, consisted of two parallel "set-speeches" of nearly equal length followed either by a sort of "judgment speech by a third party" or by dialogue in stichomythia.[59] Lloyd identifies thirteen of these Euripidean *agones*, as

---

[57] Wise, 132. Arthur Adkins explains that the question of justice was very much in the mind of Greek dramatists, particularly in terms of the seemingly unjust prosperity of some and how this relates to the image of the gods as responsible for upholding justice. The question was framed starkly by Euripides, in the mouth of Electra: "for if injustice is to get the better of justice, we must no longer believe that the gods exist." Euripides, *Electra* 583f, quoted by Adkins, *Merit and Responsibility: A Study in Greek Values* (Oxford: Clarendon, 1960), 139.

[58] Cf. also Dem. 21.7, 15; Lyc. 1.2, 5-7, 10; Ant. 5.4-7; 6.21; Isae. 1.1.

[59] Michael Lloyd, *The Agon in Euripides* (Oxford: Clarendon Press, 1992), 1-18, 1. Wise also notes the presence of stichomythia as being a distinguishing feature of law-court discourse and theatrical dialogue.

well as other scenes which he describes as "near-*agones*."[60] The use of this scene as a formal feature of Euripidean drama and its specific designation by Euripides as an ἀγῶν underscores the fact that both lawcourts and theatres were understood using the same language by ancient authors themselves, and not only by modern scholars who have the purchase to observe both institutions as Athenian social phenomena.[61]

The use of the term ἀγῶν to refer to both theatrical and legal competition highlights not only their analogous relationship, but also the conceptual relationship of each to athletic competition which pits one challenger against another. All three types of competition share certain characteristics, including the presence of an audience and the emergence of a victor to be rewarded. The reward, while sometimes material, also entailed honor and social status, as each type of *agon* was an arena for social enhancement. In the case of legal contests, the reward had its counterpart in punishment, as Danielle Allen notes: "Punishment, like reward, was the outcome of a contest for honor, but, a punishment was equivalent to a loss in a contest and a loss of honor. Andocides explicitly treats punishment as the inverse of reward when he describes a trial with the comment: 'This present contest [*agon*] is not for acquiring a crown [*stephanephoros*] but to determine whether it is necessary for one who has not wronged the city to go into exile [*phugein*] for ten years' (Andoc. 4.2)."[62] Courtrooms, like theaters and games, were areas in which complex negotiations for honor and dishonor were conducted.[63]

---

[60] Lloyd writes that "Euripides' agones clearly owe a great deal, both in form and in content, to a variety of situations in contemporary Athenian life which provided a formal context for the conflict of arguments. Prominent among these were the lawcourts, but political and diplomatic debates are also relevant."Lloyd, 2.

[61] Courtrooms continue to be equated with *agons* throughout the Hellenistic and Romans world. In his (second century CE) book on dream interpretation, Artemidorus of Daldis writes that "Fighting as a gladiator signifies that a man will be involved in a lawsuit or will fight in some other dispute or battle. In fact, a πυγμὴ is also called a 'fight' even though it is not fought with weapons, which signify the documents and legal claims of those fighting. The weapons of the man pursued always signify the defendant; the weapons of the pursuer signify the plaintiff." (Artemidorus, *Oneirocritica*, 2.32, trans. Robert J. White; Park Ridge, NJ: Noyes Press, 1975). Artermidorus also associates courtrooms and theaters: "If a man dreams that he is dancing in a theater, wearing make-up and possessing the other theatrical equipment, that he is held in high esteem and is praised, it signifies, for a poor man, riches that will not, however, last until his old age. For, on stage, the dancer plays the part of a king and is surrounded by many attendants. But, after the performance, he is left alone. For a wealthy man, on the other hand, the dream predicts turmoil and lawsuits because of the intricate complications that arise in the plot." (*Oneirocritica,* 1.76)

[62] Danielle Allen, *The World of Prometheus,* 60-61.

[63] This continued to be the case throughout the Hellenistic and even into the Roman Imperial era. For a complete discussion of this phenomenon in Imperial-era Rome, see Leanne Bablitz, *Actors and Audience in the Roman Courtroom* (New York: Routledge, 2007).

The agonistic nature of Athenian drama is relevant to the study of the divine courtroom because of its content. Throughout the plays of Aeschylus and Euripides, for example, we see characters from Greek legend and mythology on stage, with the audience judging their actions. These characters include gods and goddesses. The audience is put in the position of judging character's actions, intentions, and the very values of the city and of Greece. Gods therefore, in many ways, stand trial for their actions in Greek tragedy, to be judged by the Athenian audience. This, in turn, either reinforces or challenges the honor of those gods. Jean-Pierre Vernant notes that "tragedy establishes a distance between itself and the myths of the heroes that inspire it and that it transposes with great freedom. It scrutinizes them. It confronts heroic values and ancient religious representations with the new modes of thought that characterize the advent of law within the city-state."[64] Yet it does not just confront the "great men" of antique legend, it confronts the gods as well. Tragedy allows the audience to be the judge of those on stage, and all of the values and ideas that they represent. Indeed, "in drama, the great figures of mythology and public life were forced, like ordinary criminals, to stand public trial and justify themselves in speech."[65]

One of the most compelling instances of the divine on trial in Greek tragedy is in the *Prometheus Bound*, which has come down to us attributed to Aeschylus although some scholars doubt its authenticity. At first glance, there is no trial scene in *Prometheus Bound*. The trial has already happened: Prometheus has been sentenced by Zeus, and appears on stage as a tormented criminal, bound to a rock. Yet as the play unfolds, and Prometheus keeps asserting the injustice of his punishment to every character that emerges on stage, it becomes clear that what is unfolding is a trial of Zeus, in which Zeus is the defendant, Prometheus the accuser, and the audience the judge. Through the repeated interrogations of Prometheus, it emerges that these are really interrogations of Zeus, despite the fact that Zeus never appears on stage. His absence only highlights Prometheus's visceral presence. It is no accident that Prometheus is sometimes compared to Job: both protagonists cry out, accusing their respective deities of injustice, capriciousness and even malice, and both refuse to repent of their position in dust and ashes.

The very language of *Prometheus Bound* reflects the concern of the play with questioning the justice of Zeus and in putting the question before the audience to, as Demosthenes might put it, "be fought out and decided" (ἀγωνιεῖται δὲ καὶ κριθήσεται).[66] The tragedy begins with Kratos and Hephaestus, charged with shackling Prometheus, debating whether or not this is

---

[64] Jean-Pierre Vernant and Pierre Vidal-Naquet, *Myth and Tragedy in Ancient Greece* (New York: Zone, 1988), 26.

[65] Wise, 130.

[66] Demosthenes 21.7.

an appropriate punishment that Zeus has meted out. Hephaestus in particular shows immense sympathy for Prometheus, which sets the stage for the dialogue that follows. Near the start of the play, the chorus asks Prometheus to "unfold the whole story and declare to us upon what charge Zeus has taken you (ποίῳ λαβών σε Ζεὺς ἐπ' αἰτοάματι) that he thus visits you with ignominious and bitter outrage. Instruct us, unless, indeed, there be some harm in telling" (*Prometheus Bound* 188-189).[67] The harm in telling may be, in fact, that the audience has the liberty of hearing Prometheus' side of the story, and condemning Zeus for his prosecution and persecution of Prometheus. Indeed, Prometheus later in the play, after hearing of Io's plight also at the hands of Hera and Zeus, calls him "the tyrant of the gods" (ὁ τῶν θεῶν τύραννος) and asks "Doesn't it seem to you that the tyrant of the gods is violent in all his ways alike" (735-737)? This is the question put before the audience.

Throughout the play, the chorus, speaking for the audience, repeatedly uses legal vocabulary to condemn Zeus's actions, calling his use of the laws "arbitrary" (ἀθέτως; 150), and saying that Zeus is ruling by "his own laws" (ἰδίοις νόμοις κρατύνων; 404). Other characters also use legal vocabulary to accuse Zeus. Oceanus, for example, asserts that Zeus is "a harsh ruler who is accountable to no one" (326). The question is not whether Prometheus is guilty of the charges against him, for he confesses to them straightaway, in several long narrations throughout the tragedy. The question is whether his punishment is warranted, in other words, whether *Zeus* is guilty. In addition, Allen points out that "throughout the play, Prometheus's arguments that he does not deserve his punishment are intertwined with arguments that Zeus does not deserve to rule. The challenge to his punishment is a straightforward challenge to Zeus's political authority."[68] By challenging Zeus's decisions, Prometheus is challenging Zeus himself, and the challenge is put before the Athenian audience.

Prometheus has the last word at the end of the play. As he vanishes amid a thunder and lightening-filled storm, suggesting the wrath and power of Zeus, he turns to the heavens, crying, "Behold, this stormy turmoil advances against me visibly, sped of Zeus to work me terror. O holy mother mine, O firmament that revolves the common light of all, you see the injustices I suffer" (1089-1094). The *agon* could even perhaps be called a type of θεομάχια, but it is not necessarily Prometheus who has taken up legal arms, it is the *author*. Unfortunately, the realities of history leave us bereft of the sequels,

---

[67] Translations from H. W. Smyth, *Aeschylus I* (LCL; Cambridge: Harvard University Press, 1922).

[68] Allen, *World of Prometheus*, 26.

with only a few fragments remaining.[69] It is possible that Prometheus is acquitted in the *Prometheus Unbound,* but as the play is now lost it is impossible to know how this reversal took place, and what role Zeus played – on or off stage – in it. As it stands, though, the *Prometheus Bound* is a powerful example of how the art form of Greek tragedy can use the courtroom scenario as a means of indicting the divine.

Not only does *Prometheus Bound* take up the question of Zeus's justice in a forensic setting, but Aeschylus explicitly presents a divine courtroom scene in the *Eumenides,* the third and final act of the three-part *Oresteia.*[70] In the *Eumenides,* Orestes, fleeing the Erinyes, who demand strict justice and retribution,[71] comes to Athena as a supplicant at the urging of Apollo. Athena confronts the Erinyes by asserting that only half of the case had been heard (428), and the chorus of Erinyes relinquishes control over the proceedings to her, saying "question him and pronounce righteous judgment (κρῖνε δ' εὐθεῖαν δίκην)" (433). Athena at first agrees to hear the case, questioning Orestes and allowing him to present his defense. Orestes ends his *narratio* by stating "whether this was just or not, pronounce judgment: for however I fare at your ruling, I will rest content" (468-469). However, Athena refuses to give judgment on so grave an issue, and instead decides to take alternative action, to establish an everlasting court made up of mortal homicide judges, who will pass judgment on this and other such cases (480-486). She advises Orestes to prepare for trial by calling witnesses and preparing proofs (485-486), and she will return so that "they might decide this issue in accordance with the truth, having bound themselves by oath to pronounce no judgment contrary to justice (διαιρεῖν τοῦτο πρᾶγμη' ἐτητύμως, ὅρκον πορόντας μηδὲν ἔκδικον φράσειν)" (488-489). The famed Athenian homicide court of the Areopagus is thus directly linked to the divine courtroom, precisely because Athena could not dismiss the Erinyes's claim to justice.

The trial that takes place before this newly established court is really a trial between two different competing claims of justice. The Erinyes, on the one hand, claim that leaving Clytaemnestra's murder unpunished is unjust. Orestes, on the other, freely admits to having killed his mother, but asserts that he only did so on Zeus's order (spoken through Apollo), who bears wit-

---

[69] For a discussion of the fragmentary remains of *Prometheus Unbound,* see George Thomson, "Prometheia" in Erich Segal, ed. *Greek Tragedy: Modern Essays in Criticism* (New York: Harper & Row, 1983), 114-122. Thomson also discusses *Prometheus the Fire-bearer,* of which we know very little save the title.

[70] Theodore Ziolkowski, discussing the import of the *Oresteia,* argues that "the trilogy mirrors a critical moment in the history of Western civilization," the movement from a tribal culture which demanded strict retributive justice to a civilized society administered by state institutions. *The Mirror of Justice: Literary Reflections of Legal Crises* (Princeton: Princeton University Press, 1997), 20.

[71] Cf. Homer, *Iliad* 19.259-260.

ness to this fact (619-621). Orestes thus defers responsibility for his actions onto Zeus, and Apollo claims that it was just for Zeus to insist on the vengeance of his father's death while not caring about Orestes's mother (625-639). Orestes and Apollo thus claim that Zeus's will mitigates the necessity for strict justice and punishment. Yet before the judges come back with a decision, Athena interferes by casting her vote for Orestes, because she has no mother and therefore is on the father's side (her father, of course, being Zeus). This vote, the vote of the goddess in what was ostensibly the first human trial for bloodshed, proves to be the deciding vote when the judges return with a split decision. And yet the trial by no means ends the play. Indeed, the final third of the play is devoted to Athena's attempts to persuade the Erinyes that this decision (and her part in it) was valid and just.[72] The fact that so much time and space is devoted to this highlights the seemingly unjust nature of the court's decision, and highlights the fact that the true issue of the *Eumenides* is not the acquittal or condemnation of Orestes, it is the acquittal or condemnation of *Athena* and her vision of justice. This is emphasized by the fact that Athena seems to pacify the Erinyes only by bribing them into accepting the verdict.[73] One can only wonder what the audience judging this play might have thought of the way this drama envisioned the ending of the long saga of Orestes.

It is not insignificant that both of these plays belong to Aeschylus' corpus. While surviving lists of Aeschylus's writings attribute nearly ninety plays to the dramatist, only seven survive – and only six if *Prometheus Bound* is not included among them. Yet in all of the surviving plays Aeschylus shows enormous interest in exploring the issue of divine justice and in questioning – indeed interrogating – divine actions, particularly those of Zeus. Writing on the *Eumenides,* R. P. Winnington-Ingram comments that "for Aeschylus the will of Zeus is something to be anxiously explored."[74] No doubt one of the ways he explored it is through the genealogical relationship between Zeus and Dike; Lloyd-Jones points out that a fragment of one of the lost Aeschylean dramas has Dike explaining her relationship with Zeus in the first person.[75] It is not enough for Aeschylus that Apollo appeals to the will and commands of Zeus, it is not enough that Prometheus has been convicted.

---

[72] Ziolkowski argues that it is the argument over the Areopagus that "constitutes on the transcendental level the true dramatic conflict of the play." *The Mirror of Justice*, 37.

[73] Hugh Lloyd-Jones remarks that Athena appeases the Erinyes "by a dignified and tactful mixture of treats and bribery." *The Justice of Zeus* (Rev. Ed; Berkeley: University of California, 1983), 92. While the Erinyes appear to be pacified in the *Eumenides*, in Euripedes' *Iphigenia in Tauris* the Erinyes continue to bother Orestes after the verdict is given, setting the plot of the tragedy in motion.

[74] R. P. Winnington-Ingram, "Clytemnestra and the Vote of Athena" in Erich Segal, ed. *Greek Tragedy: Modern Essays in Criticism* (New York: Harper & Row, 1983), 84-103, 97.

[75] Fr. 530 Mette; Lloyd-Jones, *Justice of Zeus*, 35.

Aeschylus wants his audience to question the intentions, motivations, and justice of Zeus's decisions. As the chorus asserts in the *Suppliant Maidens,* referencing a future wished time "Zeus shall then be liable to the charge of injustice" (168-169). In his plays, Aeschylus insists that Zeus answer for his actions. Forensic language, the language of the legal system, is the way in which Aeschylus couches his *agones,* and by doing so he invites the audience to sit in trial on their gods and their cultural tradition.

## D. Plato: The Use of Myths for Philosophical Purposes

Not every ancient Greek author used the courtroom scenes as vehicles for indicting the gods. Instead, other authors used the divine courtroom scenes to indict humanity for failure to achieve justice. The best example of this is Plato, who, chronologically, is also the next source we have for the myths of the judgment of the dead. In many ways, this is an ironic twist of history, as Plato certainly seems to discount the value of mythological discourse in the *Republic* (particularly book II) and elsewhere in his dialogues, and yet he is a major source for mythological detail. Plato uses mythology (or speaks mythologically) in a different way from his predecessors, and in many ways subverts mythological discourse, certainly making it subservient to logical argumentation, as Luc Bresson has cogently argued.[76] In several important works, Plato ends his dialogues with the monologic retelling of a *mythos.* These *mythoi* close the discussion, and are the last impression of the discussion given to the reader. In three of the dialogues, the *Gorgias,* the *Phaedo,* and the *Republic*, these myths are explicitly about eschatological (in the sense of postmortem) destiny and judgment, giving depictions of the judgment that awaits humans after death. These myths are not just "tacked on" to the dialogues, rather they echo and illuminate themes in the dialogues, particularly the theme of justice. The most detailed of the three myths in terms of the process of judgment is that of the *Gorgias,* which is not surprising given the focus of the *Gorgias* on the question of whether it is better to suffer injustice than to perform it. In this section, I will focus my attention on the *Gorgias,* demonstrating that Plato uses this myth as part of his dialogical investigation of the nature of justice, equity, and man's ultimate role in the universe, questions

---

[76] Luc Bresson, *Plato the Myth Maker* (Chicago: University of Chicago Press, 1998).

that are part and parcel of the narratives of the divine courtroom, and I will make reference to the other myths when applicable.[77]

Though difficult to date, the *Gorgias* was probably written around 405 BCE, and is set in Athens.[78] Though the dialogue begins with Socrates questioning Gorgias on the nature of rhetoric, it leads from there into an extensive investigation on the nature of what is good, and on justice in particular.[79] What prompts this is Gorgias's claim that his art is the greatest good for men. When Socrates probes further, seeking clear articulation of this essential and superlative good, Gorgias replies:

> I say it is ability to persuade by speeches (λόγοις) judges in a lawcourt, Senators in the Council chamber, Assemblymen in the Assembly, or in political gatherings of any other kind whatever. Indeed by virtue of this power you will have the doctor as your slave, and the trainer too, and this businessman of yours will make his next appearance earning money not for himself but someone else – for you – because of your ability to speak and persuade the multitude. (452d-e)[80]

Socrates then further defines rhetoric as a "manufacturer of persuasion," particularly "persuasion in the soul of the hearers" (453a). Gorgias's mention here of the lawcourt with its judges signals the eventual question of the dialogue, which will be about the nature of justice and equity. However, the lawcourt is not here being envisioned as the place of just judgment. On the contrary, Gorgias is here stating that his art has power over the judges, maybe even to enslave them as it apparently can enslave the doctor and the trainer. The use of λόγοι here may have a deliberate double-meaning. While obviously a speech in a lawcourt is known as a λόγος, Bruce Lincoln has shown that in epic, the term λόγος has the connotation of beguiling speech, speech acts "through which structural inferiors outwitted those who held power over them."[81] This is clearly at play here for Plato. Plato is here not only question-

---

[77] For more complete discussions of the Myth of Er, see Claudia Baracchi, *Of Myth, Life, and War in Plato's Republic* (Bloomington: IUP, 2002); see also Lars Albinus, "The *Katabasis* of Er. Plato's Use of Myths, exemplified by the Myth of Er" in Erik Nis Ostenfeld, ed. *Essays on Plato's Republic* (Aarhus: Aarhus University Press, 1998), 91-105. A discussion of all three myths is found in S. P. Ward, *Penology and Eschatology in Plato's Myths* (Studies in the History of Philosophy 65; Lewiston: Edwin Mellen Press, 2002).

[78] Cf. R. E. Allen, *The Dialogues of Plato I* (New Haven: Yale University Press, 1984), 189.

[79] A complete discussion of the nuances of the argument of the *Gorgias* and how it reflects, utilizes, and critiques conceptions of retributive and restorative justice, including the relationship between this text and Aristotle's *Nicomachean Ethics* can be found in Allen, *Dialogues of Plato*, 189-230. See also the classic commentary by E. R. Dodds (Oxford: Clarendon Press, 1959).

[80] Trans. R. E. Allen, *The Dialogues of Plato*.

[81] Bruce Lincoln, *Theorizing Myth: Narrative, Ideology, and Scholarship* (Chicago: University of Chicago Press, 1999), x. Lincoln chronicles this usage of λόγος in chapter 1, "The Prehistory of *Mythos* and *Logos*."

ing the ethics of rhetoric, but also reminding the reader of the dubious nature of the modern lawcourt, where true justice is not to be sought.

That this is Plato's point of view is clear from later in the *Gorgias*. Socrates continues to press Gorgias on questions of definition, seeking to know the essence of rhetoric, first establishing the essence of persuasion. He leads Gorgias to admit that there are two different kinds of persuasion, "one providing belief without knowledge, the other providing knowledge" (454e), and that rhetoric produces the kind of persuasion from which arises belief. So Socrates clarifies Gorgias's earlier assertion: while Gorgias had said that rhetoric was about those things which are just and unjust (454b), this was not entirely correct, but rather "the rhetorician does not provide instruction to courts and other assemblies about things which are just and unjust. He only creates belief. For after all, it would be impossible to instruct so large a crowd in a short time about matters of such importance" (455a). Plato here establishes that rhetoric is art not aimed at reaching the truth but at reaching opinion, opinion based solely on the power of the persuasion (or persuader) and not on knowledge or truth. For Plato, Gorgias's courtroom seems to be a place of injustice, not justice. It only has the potential to be a place of justice if the rhetor uses his rhetoric justly, as Gorgias insists is required (457b). Even so this is only a potentiality and not the way Plato envisions actual courtrooms.

Not only is the courtroom, for Plato, not imagined as a place in which justice happens, it is also not seen as a vehicle for discerning the truth. Plato makes this abundantly clear when Socrates challenges Polus on the way he is attempting to refute him. When Socrates tells Polus he does not agree with anything he has said, Polus petulantly states "You don't want to agree, because what I say seems as true to you as it does to me" (471e). In response, Socrates states:

No, my dear friend. You keep trying to refute me rhetorically, as people in the lawcourts believe they refute. One party there actually thinks he refutes the other when he provides a multitude of well-esteemed witnesses for the things he says, while the opposing party produces only one or none. But that kind of refutation is worth nothing in regard to truth; sometimes a man may in fact be overwhelmed by the multitude of false but respectable witnesses against him. (471e)

Socrates here insists that the nature of the lawcourt is one that is contrary to discerning truth, here focusing on the question of false witnesses. He rejects Polus' methods of argumentation precisely because they are too much like lawcourt methods. Instead, he proposes a different way of investigation, more suited to reaching truth than trials: philosophical dialogues.

In a dialogue concerned with questions of justice, such as whether it is better to suffer justice than to do it, and whether it is more just to punish or not to punish, such a bleak picture of the mechanisms of human justice should not go unnoticed. It is impossible not to see in this dismal view of human trials a comment on what has happened to Socrates in the hands of human "justice." One can certainly not expect Plato to think optimistically about the potential of human lawcourts to reach the truth and be equitable given the historical circumstances of his hero. Indeed, Allen notes that "the *Gorgias* is a meditation on the meaning of Socrates' trial and death, and thereby on the moral foundations of law, politics, and human life."[82] When Socrates tells Polus that he was laughed at in the assembly for not knowing how to put a question to a vote (474a), the reader does not laugh, for he knows that this, ultimately, is the tragedy of Socrates, that he refused to engage in the games of the polis, and this was his downfall.[83] Polus cannot believe that Socrates would accept suffering injustice rather than do it (474b), and yet the reader remembers the ultimate fate of Socrates as described in the *Phaedo*, where Socrates prefers to drink the poison and die unjustly rather than escape against the law.

This foreshadowing of Socrates' death also closes the actual dialogue section of the dialogue, providing the entry-point into the "account" (λόγος) which Socrates narrates to Callicles at *Gorgias* 523a-527e. At 522b-c, Socrates paints a grim picture of what will happen to him if he is ever brought into court. Callicles cannot understand how, if this is what Socrates is expecting, such a man could consider himself well off, to which Socrates replies that if such a man has done no injustice, either to gods or men, he is well off, and this is man's greatest aid, adding: "But if I should reach my end for lack of flattering rhetoric, be assured that you would then see me bear death lightly. No man not utterly unreasonable and cowardly fears dying in itself; but he fears the doing of injustice. For the ultimate evil is for a soul to arrive at the place of the dead teeming with multiple injustices. But if you wish, I will offer an account of this too" (522e). According to Socrates, the injustices of a man penetrate his very soul, and this is the greatest of evils. Not to suffer injustice on earth, or to be convicted by an earthly court, but to arrive at Hades full of many injustices.

The way in which the story begins indicates that Socrates is about to retell a traditional story (albeit, obviously, with special Platonic nuance): "ἄχουε δὴ, φασί, μάλα καλοῦ λόγου, ὅν σὺ μὲν ἡγήσῃ μῦθον, ὡς ἐγὼ οἶμαι, ἐγὼ

---

[82] Allen, *The Dialogues of Plato*, 189.

[83] Cf. also *Gorgias* 522b-c: "I know that if I am brought into court, it will be the same with me. I will not be able to tell them of pleasures I've provided, the things they consider kindnesses and benefits; and I envy neither those who provide them nor those for whom they are provided. If someone accuses me of corrupting the youth by reducing them to perplexity, or of abusing their elders with sharp and pointed speech, in public or private, I won't be able to tell the truth, which is, 'I say all these things justly, Gentlemen and Judges, and do so for your benefit.' Nor will I be able to say anything else. The result, no doubt, will be that I'll take whatever comes."

δὲ λόγον (523a)." Dodds notes that ἄκουε δή, φασί is a traditional way "of calling the listener's attention to what follows."[84] This signals the reader to what kind of material he should compare or analogize to what follows. However, Plato immediately destabilizes this in the second clause. This is related as the truth: "ὡς ἀληθῆ γὰρ ὄντα σοι λέξω ἃ μέλλω λέγειν (523a)." On the question of Plato means here by the "truth," Dodds points us to what Socrates says in the *Phaedo* 114d about the myth (μῦθος) he narrates there:

> Now it would not be fitting for a man of sense to maintain that all this is just as I have described it, but that this or something like this is true concerning our souls and their abodes, since the soul is shown to be immortal, I think he may properly and worthily venture to believe; for the venture is well worth while.

Obviously the major formal difference between the two narratives are that that of the *Phaedo* is explicitly called a myth, while that of the *Gorgias* is deemed a logos, but it is appropriate to imagine that Plato had a similar understanding here when he deemed this account 'true': true in an absolute and universal sense, not historically accurate. True, therefore, in the ideal, and not in the particulars.[85]

The account begins here with a narrative illustration of the proportional theory of justice as it applies after life: he who passes his life justly goes to the Isles of the Blessed, but he who passes his life unjustly goes to "the prison of retribution and justice which they call Tartarus" (523b).[86] This corresponds to the theory of proportional justice discussed earlier in the dialogue: Socrates accuses Callicles of neglecting geometry (508a) and therefore recommending excess rather than balance. Likewise this is also evident in *Laws* VI 757c, where proportional justice, dispensing due measure according to what is in proportion to each, is presented as "the judgment of Zeus" (Διὸς γὰρ δὴ κρίσις ἐστι). Here the theory is being given narrative illumination. Those who are just will have their just deserts, and those who are not just will also have their just deserts, paying the penalties in Tartarus. Here in the Gorgias Socrates tells Callicles (and the reader) that it used to be the case in the time of Cronos and at the beginning of Zeus's reign that the judges were living men who judged the living on the day of their death (523b). However, there was a major problem with this system:

---

[84] Dodds, *Gorgias*, 376.

[85] This obviously does not do justice to the complicated relationship between Mythos and Logos in Plato; on this relationship see Luc Brisson, *Plato the Mythmaker* (Chicago: University of Chicago, 1998); Bruce Lincoln, *Theorizing Myth*; and most recently Radcliffe Edmonds III, *Myths of the Underworld Journey* (Cambridge: Cambridge University Press, 2004).

[86] It is significant that the prison is described as τίσις. Danielle Allen (following Foucault) has demonstrated that the Athenian penal system served to channel notions of ἀτιμία by inflicting τιμωρία. Cf. Allen, *The World of Prometheus*, 61ff.

Now, the judgments were badly rendered. So Pluto and the overseers of the Isles of the Blessed went to Zeus and told him that men were passing to each place contrary to desert. Now, Zeus said, 'I will put a stop to this. Judgments are now badly rendered because those judged are judged while still alive. Many people,' he said, 'have wicked souls dressed up in beautiful bodies, with ancestry and wealth, and when they come to judgment they bring many witnesses to appear in their behalf, testifying that they lived justly. The judges are confused by this, and at the same time, they are clothed themselves when they render judgment, and their souls veiled by eyes and ears and the whole of the body. All these things are impediments to them, both their own clothing and those of the people they judge. First of all then,' he said, 'it is necessary to put a stop to foreknowledge of death: for now people know in advance. And so Prometheus has already been told to put an end to this. Next, let all of them be judged naked, for they must be judged dead; and their judge too must be naked, and dead, contemplating the soul alone by itself at the very moment each person dies, bereft of all family and leaving behind on this earth all ornament and dress, in order that the judgment may be just. (523a-e)

Zeus recognizes the problem with the judgment: it is too easy to confuse human judges, who are swayed by aspects other than the nature of the soul itself, like money, prestige, and beauty, and that the unjust can easily persuade the judges by means of (false) witnesses. This reflects what Socrates has said about the nature of human judgment earlier in the dialogue. The human courtroom is not a place that is associated with revealing the truth, all the more so because everyone is "clothed," i.e., covered, veiled, and mediated.[87] This whole system has been set up in such a way that humans can prepare for the trial and come in with a coterie of supporters. This had to be completely restructured "in order that the judgment might be just" (524A).

The system that Zeus sets up, however, still retains some of the trappings of the human courtroom. Zeus explains that he has "appointed my own sons as judges: two from Asia, Minos and Rhadamanthys, and one from Europe, Aeacus. These then, when they die, shall render judgment in the meadow where three ways meet, whence lead two roads, one to the Isles of the Blessed, the other to Tartarus. Rhadamanthys shall judge those from Asia, Aeacus those from Europe, but I shall grant to Minos authority to judge on review, if either of the other two are perplexed, in order that judgment concerning the journey of men may be most just"(524A). This is still pictured using human conceptions of forensic justice: Rhadamanthys and Aeacus are each assigned a particular district, while Minos acts as the elder judge for the

---

[87] The mention of Prometheus here is really startling, especially since foreknowledge of one's death is not the main problem with the post-mortem judicial system as described here. Indeed, the mention of Prometheus, I believe, may be an intertextual flag to the reader, bringing with it a whole range of material involving the justice of Zeus.

other two to consult.[88] If Plato has such a negative view of the lawcourt, why is justice after death depicted as a law-court? Is the reader supposed to see this courtroom as functioning completely differently from the human courtroom, or does Plato assume that the reader will still be anxious about the possibility of justice even at the divine level? This is a central question regarding the way authors intend for their narratives of the divine courtroom to be understood. It is way too common for scholars to assume that authors intend for their readers to bring in only positive views on the ability of the divine courtroom to be a place of justice. However, when the human courtroom is not seen thus, can we really expect that readers will simply let go of all of their feelings about courtrooms in general when viewing the post-mortem courtroom?

I believe that Plato assumes that the reader will bring in anxieties and pessimism about the courtroom when confronting Minos, Rhadamanthys and Aeacus in this narrative. This is all the more so given that these three legendary figures were associated with exacting justice in their own lives, and that these three do not appear together in combination as judges of the dead before Plato, with the first time this combination appears together being at *Apology* 41a.[89] Indeed, there is no evidence for the tradition of Rhadamanthys as judging the dead before Plato at all. While Pindar places Rhadamanthys on the Isle of the Blessed at *Ol.* 2.74-76, his function there is more of a counselor, advisor to Cronos, not a judge per se. The choice of these three figures here seems to be a deliberate Platonic one, most likely because of the unique associations of these three figures. In *Laws* I.624b, Clinias of Crete affirms that Minos had a consultation with Zeus every nine years, and was divinely guided in laying down laws for the cities. In this same section Rhadamanthys is called δικαιότατος, and that he came by this title because of his "righteous administration of justice."[90] While Plato does not here mention Aeacus, according to Pindar he too had judicial assignments. In *Isthmian* 8.24 Aeacus's virtue is exemplified by the fact that "he settled disputes even among

---

[88] While some scholars have called Minos the appellate judge, this is really not an accurate statement of Minos's role, as the people *being judged* are not given the right to appeal to Minos, only the other two *judges* can turn to him if they are perplexed. Dodds is thus mistaken when he suggests that this role corresponds to what Plato sets out in *Laws* 767a regarding the mechanisms of human appeal.

[89] Along with Triptolemus: "For if a man when he reaches the other world, after leaving behind these who claim to be judges (τούτων τῶν φασκόντων δικαστῶν εἶναι), shall find those who are really judges (τοὺς ἀληθῶς δικαστάς) who are said to be judging there (οἵπερ καὶ λέγονται ἐκεῖ δικάζειν), Minos and Rhadamanthys, and Aeacus and Tritolemus, and all the others who were just men in their lives, would the change of habitation be undesirable?" (*Apol.* 41a)

[90] For more references, see Dodds, *Gorgias*, 374.

the daemons." Plato intends the reader to bring in this association when encountering these judges in the *Gorgias* account.

What truly separates these judges from those of normal human courts, and takes one out of what is familiar from a human courtroom, is their extraordinary vision that leads to an inability to be deceived. This is narrated by Socrates, who explains what happens at that unique courtroom. Just as the body bears the marks of illness and disease, so too does the soul when it is separated from the body at death:

> Now, when they come before their judge, as those from Asia before Rhadamanthys, Rhadamanthys stops them and inspects the soul of each, not knowing whose it is. Many a time he has laid hold of the Great King or some other king or potentate, and seen nothing healthy in their soul, whipped and scarred by perjury and injustice. Each act has left its stain on it, and it is all limping and crooked due to falsity and pretense, and nothing straight because it was brought up without truth. He saw that due to license and luxury, the insolence and intemperance of its deeds, it teemed with ugliness and lack of proportion, and seeing this, he sent it dishonored straight to the prison where, arriving, it suffers what befits it (524e-525a)

Such vision into the soul of the accused is obviously impossible in a human courtroom, and this is where the reader is able to leave the human courtroom and see above it the possibility of perfect justice, if that justice is conceived as proportional and restorative: the souls will then suffer punishment in order to "become better and profit by it" (525b) and to be "relieved of injustice" (525c). This, again, is a narrative illustration of something argued earlier in the dialogue, that "the person punished, therefore, is relieved of evil of soul" (477a), and therefore "corrective justice takes away intemperance and injustice" (478b). Here Plato provides a narrative illustration of this very principle: we see what happens if that corrective justice does not take place in one's lifetime. Only then can we truly understand one of the main themes of the *Gorgias*, that "to do injustice and not be punished is greatest of all and by nature first among evils" (479d). It is not evil in the abstract, or simply bad for society; it is bad for the soul, visibly marking it as diseased and infirm, unable to stand before Minos, Rhadamanthys, and Aeacus. This image of the administration of "the justice of Zeus" also is able to counteract the fear of false witnesses, presenting the soul itself as the ultimate evidence.

While some souls, continues Socrates, can be curatively relieved of injustice, others cannot, and their only benefit is to others: "they are no longer any good to themselves, because incurable, but others may profit from seeing them suffer the greatest and most painful and frightful sufferings for all time because of their sins. They therefore are gibbeted in the prison of the Dead simply as examples, spectacles and warnings to those who ever come there for injustice" (525c). This, too, is part of the celestial justice system according to Plato: if everyone could be cured, and there was not the threat of an eternal existence in Tartarus, what impetus would there be for keeping your soul unstained by the worst crimes? For Plato, strict and exacting punishment has its place in an ordered universe. Not everyone can be cured, though even the incurability of some has its place in the curing of others.

But there is also the possibility of being vindicated at the judgment and being sent to the Isles of the Blessed, especially if you are "a philosopher who has tended his own affairs and did not during his life officiously intermeddle with others" (526c). Socrates hopes that he will be among those souls, and strongly suggests that Callicles will not:

> Now, I am convinced by this account, Callicles, and I consider how I shall show my judge that my soul is as healthy as possible. So, bidding farewell to the honors of the majority of men, and practicing the truth, I shall really try to be and live in the truth, so that I may be as good as possible, and, when I die, to die in it. And I summon all other men, so far as I am able, and in answer to your summons, Callicles, I also summon you to this life and this contest (τὸν ἀγῶνα τοῦτον), which I claim is superior to all the other contests here. I reproach you because you will be unable to help yourself when you come to the trial and judgment I have just described. When you come before your judge, the son of Aegina, Aeacus, when he lays hold on you and drags you away, then your jaw will drop with dizziness, yours there no less than mine here, and it will be you, perhaps, who is ignobly punched on the chin and treated with foul insult. (526d-527a)

Socrates then closes the account with a lengthy paranetic section aimed far beyond Callicles at the reader, urging them to live their lives in virtue, to believe that "the doing of injustice is more to be guarded against than the suffering of injustice, that more than anything else a man must take care not to seem good but to be good, both in public and private; that if someone becomes bad in some respect he must be punished, and this is a second good after actually being just, namely, becoming just by paying the penalty and being punished" (527b). The account is to be used as a guide that signifies that this is the best manner of life, to "live and die in the practice of justice and the rest of virtue" (527e).

It is Plato's great hope that comes through this myth, that Socrates will have been proven such after life, since it is the human judicial system which so utterly failed him during his life. Plato's depiction of the divine courtroom carefully counteracts those failures he diagnoses in the human courtroom. The standard of justice so carefully articulated throughout the Gorgias is depicted and hoped for here. The courtroom of the three judges is proportional, equitable, and honest, free from *almost* every human trapping, save one's provenance. The *almost* is important – in this one allowance Plato is leaving the door open for the slightest bit of anxiety and perplexion. But overall, the courtroom that Plato depicts is far from the reality he knows. It is free from wrath, mocking, rhetoric. It is carefully drawn as different from a human courtroom. The very fact that it is depicted as a courtroom draws attention to how *different* it is from those Athenian courtrooms of Plato's lifetime. Through this, readers are invited to realize what is wrong with their judicial system, how it stymies justice rather than invites it, how fallible it is. We should not forget that before Minos, Rhadamanthys, and Aeacus, no one is allowed to speak. No witnesses, no rhetorical flourishes that distract and confuse the judges, that allow people like Callicles to prosper and succeed. Callicles, like everyone else, will be naked before the judges, stripped of his rhetorical whitewash. This depiction of the divine courtroom is a condemnation of the human courtroom, and a reminder to the reader just how far they are from achieving justice in their own judicial systems. Unlike other depictions of the divine courtroom, this one is used not primarily to vindicate or condemn the divine, but to vindicate Socrates and condemn the mechanisms of "justice" that allowed him to be poisoned.

However, despite the fact that it is not the purpose of this myth to try Zeus, we should not overlook the fact that once again we have a depiction of the justice of Zeus with reference to what is distinct about his rule from that of Cronos (523b). I believe Plato is not unaware of the way in which the depiction of Zeus' courtroom comes down with the taint of injustice, that Zeus took power unjustly and viciously, that he can thus not order the universe according to perfect justice. Instead, Plato very subtly here critiques that tradition, displaying that it was *Cronos* who was unable to order the universe justly, that under Cronos men were judged according to absolute incorrect standards which *perverted* the divine courtroom rather than allowed it to operate properly and proportionally, truly justly. Zeus's courtroom, on the other hand, stripped Cronos's system of these flaws, and provided a truly just way for souls to be judged. In this way, Plato is able to vindicate Zeus' courtroom from its detractors, and show how when he says that the world is ordered by "the justice of Zeus," this is actually justice, according to the most philosophically defensible standards. Even though this is not the main purpose of this courtroom scene, the fact that it still remains part of the myth shows that Plato is not unaware of this use of the divine courtroom by his predecessors and contemporaries.

## E. Seneca's *Apocolocyntosis* and the Critical Turn

While Plato's *Gorgias* presented a rather optimistic view of the power of the post-mortem world to correct the injustices of the mortal world, later Greek and Latin literature went in the complete opposite direction. Since the question of the justice of the gods, already is found in the margins of the earliest texts, it is not surprising that this sub-text later becomes explicit text, as later Greek and Latin authors present depictions of the divine courtroom that are explicitly critical of the systems and the actors therein.[91] One such text from the Roman period is Seneca's *Apocolocyntosis*, which was written soon after the death of the much-hated emperor Claudius, and depicts Claudius's failed apotheosis.[92] Though brief in length, the *Apocolocyntosis* packs a lot of plot and punch, taking the reader both to heaven and hell as Claudius attempts to find his place among the gods, and the gods try to figure out what to do with him. The *Apocolocyntosis* has both a depiction of the divine council on Olympus (though we are bereft of the beginning of this scene due to a lacuna in the text), and of Aeacus's tribunal at the gate of Dis. In both of these scenes, the divine courtrooms appear to be at a loss to function properly with regard to the figure before them. This is surprising, to say the least: Claudius is so unmistakably bad and guilty, particularly with respect to the charge of judicial misconduct, that the divine trial should be, in a Platonic view at least, very straightforward: trial, sentencing, punishment. This is the way the mythological judicial system is supposed to work according to the classical authors from Homer to Plato to Virgil. However, this is not the case: in fact the divine trial in heaven nearly fails to produce a just requirement, and the divine trial in hell is circumvented in a most unjust way.

At first glance the text might appear simply to be a lampooning of Claudius, but a closer look reveals that the object of amusement is not only Claudius, but also the system which is attempting to deal with Claudius, i.e., the divine system of cosmic administration. The *Apocolocyntosis* uses Claudius's divine trials to reveal the folly of the traditional portrayal of the gods, portraying the gods dubiously: not reliable, particularly in the arena of justice. Though hilarious, this comic piece is also a critique of the Olympian landscape and of the stability of classical mythology. Joel Relihan argues that "The *Apocolocyntosis* is not an attack on Claudius pure and simple, but an account of an occasionally sympathetic wanderer who is caught in a comic afterworld whose right to judge and condemn him is at least as questionable as his own right to become a god."[93] The fact of Claudius's obvious guilt highlights the failure of the divine judicial system. This is especially the case with regard to Claudius's "trial" by Aeacus, where we really see how Seneca puts the system on trial for the reader.

The first portrayal of the divine courtroom comes at *Apoc.* 8, after Claudius, upon arriving in heaven, manages to convince Hercules to stand up for him and vouch for him before the divine council. Claudius begins his argu-

---

[91] We will see a parallel development in the rabbinic literature, which takes the sub-text of the Hebrew Bible and turns it into supra-text.

[92] Though this text comes down in the manuscript tradition by different titles ("*Divi Claudii Apotheosis per saturam*", "*Ludus de morte Claudii*", et al), it has been identified with Seneca's *Apocolocyntosis* mentioned by Cassius Dio, *Hist. Rom.* 60.35.

[93] Relihan, *Ancient Menippean Satire*, 77.

ment to Hercules by reminding him that he, of all people, should vouch for him: "I hoped you would stand up for me among the others, and if anyone asked me for a person to vouch for me, I was going to name you, as you know me best. If you recall, I was the one who used to preside in court in front of your temple for whole days at a time in the months of July and August. You know what misery I went through there, listening to lawyers day and night. If you'd been dropped into that, mighty tough as you think you are, you'd have preferred to clean out the Augean sewers: I threw out a lot more bullshit." (*Apoc.* 7).[94] Unfortunately, the text breaks off here and we do not know what other arguments helped to convince Hercules to back Claudius before the council. Here, however, Claudius makes mention of his work in the judicial system. While he seems to think here that it is worthy of praise, what he does not realize is that this work will be his condemnation. The historical Claudius was well known for legal injustices; in particular for only hearing one side of a case, or for making summary judgments that led to executions without hearing any testimony at all.[95] This is not only mentioned several times in the *Apocolocyntosis*, but it becomes a crucial plot point at the very end.

When the text resumes, an unknown member of the divine council is speaking, questioning how Claudius could possibly be made into a god, and insisting that no one on Olympus was going to grant him this honor: "For Hercules' sake, if he'd asked this favor from Saturn, he wouldn't have got it, even though he celebrated his month all year round, a proper Saturnalian emperor. Still less would he get that favor from Jupiter, after he condemned him for incest, as far as he could: he killed his son-in-law Silanus. Why, I ask you? Because his sister, who was the most delightful girl in the world, he preferred to call Juno, when everyone called her Venus" (8). Claudius could hardly hope for Jupiter to grant him divinity if he had someone executed on the accusation of the very relationship Jupiter himself has with Juno. This mention is instructive: it is not really an attack on Claudius as much as it is a jab at Jupiter for engaging in activities that would get him executed if he were a regular human being and not the head of the Roman pantheon. While ostensibly it is the question of Claudius's proposed divinity that is being adjudicated here, the question provokes revelations about the nature of the gods themselves. It is not only Claudius's divine qualifications that are being challenged; it is the qualifications of the gods, the divine adjudicators.

This does not go unnoticed even by characters inside the text. After this address, Jupiter quickly realizes that things are getting out of hand, and this will have a negative impact on the gods's reputation: "Jupiter finally recol-

---

[94] Trans. John Patrick Sullivan (New York: Penguin, 1986).

[95] For these and other complaints about Claudius's injustice with regard to law, see Suetonius, *Claud.* 15; Dio, *Hist. Rom.* 61.33.

lected that with members of the public in the Senate-house it was out of order for senators to offer a motion or debate. 'Gentlemen of the senate,' he said, 'I permitted you to put some questions, but you're making the whole thing an absolute shambles. I request you to observe the rules of order in the House. What will this man think of us, whatever he is?" (9). Claudius's presence threatens to pull back the curtain on the way the gods operate and portray them in a negative light. While Jupiter says he is worried about the disorder of the divine council, what is also implied here is that he is worried that the gods are revealing themselves as having disorders, not being capable of running things properly. How will the gods keep order if they themselves are not orderly?

Various positions are entertained by the council as to whether or not Claudius should be deified, with Janus on one side and Diespiter, at some encouragement from Hercules, on the other (*Apoc.* 9). Jupiter's concerns about what Claudius will see in the gods are borne out here: Diespiter is described as someone who sells pieces of citizenships (9), and Claudius even appears to be winning after some valiant and dramatic Herculean advocacy, which in truth is nothing more than flat-out bribery (9).[96] But finally the Divine Augustus arises to present his opinion, expressing his indignation at the scene unfolding before him:

Was it for this that I brought peace to land and sea? Was this why I put an end to civil war? Was this why I laid a foundation of laws for Rome, beautified the city with public works – in order to... I can't think of what to say, gentlemen. No words can be equal to my indignation (10).

Augustus is disgusted with what he sees going on around him, that the gods are even considering Claudius's appointment. He reminds them of all the injustices Claudius perpetrated on earth, including those in his own family:

That man you see in front of you, after all those years of hiding under my name, thanked me by killing my two great-granddaughters, one Julia with cold steel, the other Julia by starving her to death, and by killing one of my great-great-grandsons, Lucius Silanus. You will decide, Jupiter, whether it was for an unjustified cause. Certainly it was one which reflects on you, if you are to be fair. Tell me, Divine Claudius, for what reason did you condemn any one of the men and women you killed, before specifying the charges, and before ascertaining the facts? Where is this usual? It doesn't happen in heaven.' (*Apoc.* 10)

Augustus specifically threatens Jupiter with what it will say about him if they are to deify Claudius, reminding him that his own reputation is on the line here. Augustus accuses Claudius of the worst possible impropriety in administering justice – condemning people without trial and sometimes even

---

[96] As Relihan states, "in fact, Claudius is thoroughly worthy of this heaven, as these Roman divinities are all sorry excuses for godhead themselves." Relihan, *Ancient Menippean Satire*, 85.

without cause.[97] Even Jupiter, he insists, did not kill – only "hung up" his wife and break Vulcan's leg (11; quoting *Iliad*). The irony here is not lost on the reader – Jupiter/Zeus's violent overthrowing of the previous regime of his father and his wrathful temper are well-trodden subjects in the mythological literature, so Augustus's insistence that Claudius has committed worse crimes even than Jupiter might ring slightly hollow. Even though it is Claudius's potential divinity which is at issue here, there are more than enough references to divine actions to signal to the reader that Seneca desires to illustrate something about the gods – or to at least put the question of the justice of the gods squarely before the reader.

Augustus is insistent that Claudius be required to pay for his actions, and motions that "he be severely punished, that he be denied any immunity from trial, and that he be deported as soon as possible, leaving heaven within thirty days and Olympus within three" (11). Claudius is thus kicked out of heaven, and out of Olympus forever, on his way to hell instead. So much for his apotheosis. Mercury is to be his guide, and on their way to hell they pass through the Via Sacra, where they witness Claudius's funeral, a gala event more like a party: "Everyone was happy and gay. The Roman people walked about like free men. Agatho and a few barristers were in tears, but they were clearly sincere. Legal authorities were emerging from the shadows, pale, thin, and scarcely breathing, like men who had just come back to life. One of them, seeing the barristers with their heads together, crying over their bad luck, went up and said: 'I told you it won't always be carnival time.'" (12) Claudius's death is the opportunity for justice to reign again.

The injustice of Claudius' reign is again mentioned during the dirges, which sarcastically proclaim despair over the death of Claudius's judicial activity:

"Weep, weep
For the man's good judgments.
Who could master
lawsuits faster,
hearing either
one or neither.
Who will warm
the bench and dock
through the year
and round the clock?
Minos, retire for him,
Let Claudius instead,
O Cretan lawgiver,
Be judge of the Dead." (12)

---

[97] His insistence that this doesn't happen in heaven will prove somewhat ironic later in the text.

Claudius, being the fool, fails to see the sarcasm in this dirge, and instead is "delighted" to hear these songs (13). He does not realize that speed is not to be desired in a lawsuit if it means sacrificing the actual trial. Seneca's ironic suggestion that Claudius should take over for Minos as judge of the dead is all the more appreciated since the reader is anticipating just such a confrontation with Minos in the near future, where Claudius will finally have to pay for his injustices on earth. Claudius's failure to appreciate the sarcasm here heightens the anticipation of the tribunal.

However, the trial before Aeacus, who Claudius meets instead of Minos, does not go as Claudius might have expected – nor as the reader expects. Aeacus, Seneca tells us, is sitting on cases "that fell on under the Cornelian legislation on murder" (14), a reference to Sulla's allocation of specific courts by crime in 81 BCE. That Hades is operating according to Roman law is amusing but also sort of terrifying – especially if it's the same kind of Roman "law" that Claudius was known for! The Roman courtroom was not a reliable place for justice, as the *Apocolocyntosis* has pointed out time and again. This small reference as to how Aeacus is conducting these trials is Seneca's signal to the reader that the divine judicial system is not all it is cracked up to be, maybe just as unreliable as the human judicial system.

What follows comes as a surprise to the inhabitants of Hades:

Pedo requests that Claudius be charged and he lays out the indictment: 'Executed 30 Senators, 221 Roman knights, and others 'to the number of the grains of sand and the specks of dust.' Claudius finds no counsel. Finally, an old crony of his, Publius Petronius, comes forward, a master of Claudian-style eloquence, and he requests an adjournment. It is not granted. Pedo Pompeius opens for the prosecution amid acclamation. The defence starts wanting to reply. The superbly impartial Aeacus denies the request, and with only one side of the case heard, finds Claudius guilty and quotes in Greek: 'What thou hast wrought shouldst thou suffer, Straight would justice be done.' There was a profound silence.

Obviously Claudius is here receiving the same treatment that he bestowed upon others, and while there is a certain Dantescan logic to this, this is dangerous precedent for post-mortem judicial procedure. As Relihan states, "this is poetic justice, but the fact remains that the most just judge of the underworld acts unjustly to secure justice."[98] There should have been no danger in Claudius being found not guilty, so why contravene procedure and cut off the trial? Indeed, the Hadeans are shocked at the "strange procedure," though it is familiar to Claudius. Seneca's use of the description "supremely impartial Aeacus" underscores just how partial Aeacus is being here. This was the perfect opportunity for the divine courtroom to operate smoothly, yet it fails miserably. Even though the result seems fair and poetically just, the procedure of attaining that justice falls short of its own standards. Throughout the *Apo-*

---

[98] Relihan, *Ancient Menippean Satire*, 86.

*colocyntosis* Claudius has been reviled for judicial misconduct, and so the appearance of judicial misconduct in Hades is unsettling.

And what kind of justice does this kangaroo court produce? Not even poetic justice. Sure, Claudius is condemned, but the underworld denizens cannot decide on a proper punishment for him. He is not turned into a pumpkin or gourd, as the title might suggest, but for a while he has to play everlasting dice (14). This is a parody of the classic punishment of Sisyphus to be sure,[99] but seemingly not so bad when you consider the magnitude of Claudius' own crimes. Then, just when it seems to be over, Caligula turns up claiming that Claudius is his slave, and Aeacus transfers custody of Claudius to Gaius, who in turn hands him over "to his freedman Menander to put him to work as legal secretary" (15). The very last line of the text, then, completely subverts the poetic justice of Aeacus's methods on a number of different levels. First, it's a pretty light sentence compared to what we normally see in these *nekyias*, and definitely in comparison to the classic Odyssean examples mentioned in *Apoc.* 14. Second, and more importantly, the ultimate result of this unjust trial is that Claudius himself becomes part of the legal bureaucracy of Hades, working as a law clerk! Seneca has thus revealed the divine courtroom to be completely incapable of standing up to what should have been the most straightforward of cases. Instead, Seneca shows it to be an utterly failed system, completely manipulable, and rotten at its very core. At the end of the text, Claudius is working for the very system that is supposed to ensure cosmic order, in a capacity in which he has already proven himself to be a complete failure.

This is a radical depiction of the divine courtroom, very pessimistic about the possibilities of post-mortem justice. It's a very funny text, but it's message is unsettling. The reader cannot help but realize that the gods are acting just as badly as Claudius. Okay, they might not be murdering. But they are failing to secure order on a cosmic level. Seneca's trials of Claudius are vehicles for him to display the incompetency and injustice of the divine courtroom system as it is portrayed in classical mythology. When Claudius is tried, it is truly the system which is on trial. If this has been sub-text in the earliest myths, Seneca has turned that sub-text into explicit text. This move by Seneca paves the way for later authors such as Lucian of Samosata, who takes advantage of all the possibilities inherent in the literary portrayal of the divine courtroom.

---

[99] And of the fact that the historical Claudius was a fan of gambling.

# F. The Parodist: Courtrooms and Chaos in Lucian of Samosata

There are a lot of courtrooms in Lucian's opera omnia. Lucian repeatedly takes advantage of the interplay between audience and judges/juries in his pieces, sometimes having entire pieces written as long addresses to the audience as jury (cf. *Tyrranicide, Disowned*, for example). This builds on the classic feature of Athenian audiences as judges of the cases presented on stage before them, and shows that this interplay between theatre and courtrooms was alive and well in the Second Sophistic. The litigious nature of society is also reflected in Lucian's works, as Lucian employs the mock courtroom over and over again in his writings even when such a scenario is not "required". An example of this is *The Hall*, in which Lucian enacts an entire trial scene on the totally banal and irrelevant question of whether the hall in question is the most beautiful and fabulous hall *ever*. This adoxography pokes fun both at the litigious nature of society and at the irrelevance of some philosophical and sophistic topics of debate. Even in Lucian's more narrative pieces, courtrooms often play a role in the action. In *Demonax*, for example, Lucian describes a courtroom similar to the one which indicted Socrates, attempting to condemn Demonax on the charges of anti-communal activity: not sacrificing to the goddess Athena, and being the only person in town who did not join the Eleusinian mysteries. Unlike Socrates, however, Lucian's protagonist escapes condemnation by means of clever words and well-placed humility, which turns the Athenian jury to his favor.[100]

Lucian also takes advantage of the common courtroom scenario as a way of justifying his own literary activity in two important dialogues, *The Dead Come to Life or the Fisherman*, and *The Double Indictment*. In both dialogues Lucian is responding to critiques leveled against him by his contemporaries, namely that he is disrespectful to, well, everything, but particularly classical philosophy, and the esteemed genres of rhetoric and dialogue. This is most likely a result of his *Philosophers for Sale*, in which Lucian roasts all the philosophical schools and their founders, except the Cynic Menippus, which does not go unnoticed by his critics.[101] *Philosophers for Sale* is twice alluded to in *The Fisherman* as having provoked particular ire (*Pisc.* 4, 27), though clearly the irritation with Lucian's particular ways of portraying figures from classical culture had probably been building for some time.

*The Fisherman* begins mise-en-scène with Socrates, of all people, proponent of suffering injustice rather than doing it, calling for the accursed man to be stoned with whatever is available, including ostraca (*Pisc.* 1). The very first words of the dialogue, "βάλλε βάλλε" set up the charged atmosphere that follows, in which the accused, Parrhesiades (Frankness, Boldness) is set

---

[100] Lucian, *Dem.* 11.

[101] This is clear from what "Diogenes" complains about in *Pisc.* 26.

upon by the eminence grises of Greek philosophy, Chrysippus, Epicurus, Plato, Aristotle, Pythagoras, Diogenes, "and all others whom you ripped apart in the texts" (*Pisc.* 4). Parrhesiades begs to be allowed to give an account of his intentions before they execute him. At first they refuse to do so; Plato accuses him of wanting to manipulate the courtroom by clever words and maneuverability, and insists that he cannot have a judge he could bribe (*Pisc.* 9). These set-up comments play to the audience's understanding of everyday courtrooms and keep the dialogue grounded in the pedestrian rather than sailing into the solely allegorical. This is the hallmark of Lucian's style, the playing with the tension between high and low culture, and genre games of audience expectation.

Finally the philosophers give in to allow Parrhesiades to have his waterclock, and contract Philosophy to serve as judge. When she finally arrives from her strolls, she agrees to take the case, and while traveling to the Areopagus to conduct the trial – where else would a trial be conducted? – Parrhesiades and Philosophy encounter Virtue, Temperance, Justice, Culture, and Truth, and they join the party (although Truth does not feel like going). When they finally reach their destination, and after a long quarrel among the philosophers as to who is best suited to conduct the prosecution, Diogenes lays out the case against Parrhesiades (*Pisc.* 25-28), and Parrhesiades gives a lengthy, frank, and bold response (*Pisc.* 29-38). He speaks so frankly, indeed, that Truth cannot help but agree that everything he said was true, and even the prosecution agrees that his case is airtight.[102] It is no surprise that Parrhesiades is acquitted – what is fun for the audience is watching the way he acquits himself, as it both glorifies their hero and jabs at those who would ruin their fun. The continued deferral of the trial in the first part of the dialogue allows Lucian to extend the fun and prolong the comic tension. The descent of the second half of the dialogue into the ridiculous provides a release of that tension and allows Lucian's actual response to his critics not to overwhelm his comedy. Choosing to present this seriocomic apology in an impossibly fictional courtroom allows Lucian an outlet to defend himself against his critics while retaining the light mood (and getting some good jabs in at the same time).

A similar technique is found in the *Double Indictment*, although this time Lucian expands his courtroom to include Zeus and the other Olympian deities. *The Double Indictment* begins with a long speech by Zeus in which he complains about all the gods must endure for the sake of men, ending with a long strophe about his personal responsibilities, including his requirement to

---

[102] The dialogue then moves in an entirely different direction, as contemporary philosophers become the object of the trial, and the two sides join together to "catch" those philosophers trying to escape prosecution (*Pisc.* 47ff).

be in so many places at the same time.[103] Zeus then rants about the criticism he and the other gods must endure from those on earth, and singles out one particular avenue of criticism:

Now here s a case in point: for lack of spare time we are keeping all these stale lawsuits (ἑώλους δίκας) filed away, already spoiled by mildew and spiders' webs, especially those brought against certain persons by the sciences and the arts – some of these are very ancient. People are making an outcry on all sides and losing patience and hurling reproaches at Justice and blaming me for my slowness, not knowing that the hearings have not been postponed, as it happens, on account of our negligence, but on account of the bliss in which they imagine we exist: for that is what they call our press of business. (Lucian, *Bis. Acc.* 3)[104]

Hermes acquiesces that he, too, has heard those complaints, and seems to agree with their validity (*Bis. Acc.* 4). This dialogue opening sets the scene for what follows, putting the courtroom scenes that follow squarely within the Olympian framework, even though Zeus himself will not sit as judge, a task which will befall his daughter Justice.

By opening the dialogue in this way, Lucian is able to connect several of his favorite comic themes: the pedestrian nature of life on Mount Olympus, philosophical critiques and comments on the divine, and the ludicrousness of his own critics. One of the critiques Lucian singles out is here is an Epicurean one: the perceived negligence of the gods with regard to matters of justice, and the failure of Zeus to hold trials long overdue. The call to the divine courtroom here is very openly a critique of Zeus; Zeus must call these courtrooms to session in order to sidestep the criticism. Indeed he does so, and gives Hermes the following instructions:

Fly down and proclaim that there will be a session of court (ἀγορὰ δικῶν) under the following regulations. All who have entered suit are to come to the Areopagus today; at that place Justice is to empanel juries for them out of the entire body of Athenians, the number of jurymen to depend upon the penalty involved; and if anyone thinks that his hearing has been unjust, he is to be allowed to appeal to me and have the case tried afresh, just as if had not been tried at all. (*Bis. Acc.* 4)

Lucian thus takes the traditional motif of the gods holding trial and reimagines it as it would look according to classical Athenian law. This is typical of Lucian's comedic style: he takes the extraordinary myths and discussions of the gods and brings them down to earth. Justice is not just going to hold a session of court, she will also conduct all the pre-trial procedures. If that does not work, there is an appellate option, as would be proper in a well-functioning judicial system.

In addition, the setting on the Areopagus and the identification of the human participants as Athenians creates comedic distance between the dramatic

---

[103] The complaining god is a familiar Leitmotif in Lucian's works; often it is Hermes who is seen complaining about the multitude of jobs that fall to him.

[104] Trans. A. M. Harmon, LCL.

personages and Lucian's own audience who are, of course, not members of
the classical Athenian community, but rather present in the second century
CE, far removed from the cultural ideal being enacted on stage. In this way
Lucian is very much at home in the Second Sophistic, "a time when much of
Greek literature and art reflected a cultural atavism marked by a deep and
pervasive fascination with the pre-Roman past stretching back over nine hundred years to Homer."[105] By removing the audience from their everyday lives
to the shared, familiar cultural memory of "classical Athens," Lucian allows
his audience to connect to the characters in a more universal, less realistic
way, similar to when modern comedy might take place in the "Middle Ages,"
which of course bears little to no resemblance to the actual Middle Ages.
This makes Lucian's incorporation of "realistic" details much funnier and
more ridiculous, creating a type of inside humor between him and the audience that provides ironic distance from the events on stage and reminds the
audience also of how not to take their own cultural memories so seriously.

Lucian does not let his audience imagine that this trial will go off without
a hitch, even though it is instigated at Zeus's command. First of all, Justice
does not want to go back to earth because she is afraid that she will be laughed at by Injustice (*Bis. Acc.* 5), and Zeus has to try to convince her that this
time will be different.[106] Ultimately Justice has no choice but to go hear the
cases, and after a lengthy discussion with Pan about what philosophers are
like "now," Hermes finally summons all the Athenians who have filed a lawsuit to the Areopagus for the hearings, where the jury pay will be three obols
per case. In addition, Hermes makes sure to announce that Aeacus, one of the
three post-mortem judges, will send back from the dead all those who have
filed lawsuits with Zeus but died before they came to trial (*Bis. Acc.* 12). The
Areopagus is immediately flooded with people, whom Justice compares to
buzzing wasps, an allusion to Aristophanes that Lucian's audience would
have appreciated. The cacophonous scene seems impossibly disorderly, but
right there in the middle Justice and Hermes begin calling the cases and assigning the appropriate number of jury-men for each one. There is a great
deal of verisimilitude here, given what we know not only about Athenian
courtrooms, but also to the Roman courtrooms of Lucian's own time. This
incongruity between the realities of human courtrooms and the supposed
ideal nature of the divine courtroom, presided over by Dike herself, is milked
for comic effect.

---

[105] R. Bracht Branham, *Unruly Eloquence: Lucian and the Comedy of Traditions* (Cambridge: HUP, 1989), 2.

[106] Unfortunately, Zeus takes a faulty tactic. He tells Justice that the philosophers have by now convinced the men to value her more highly than injustice, particularly "the son of Sophroniscus," i.e. Socrates (*Bis. Acc.* 5). Obviously this is not a great example of Justice prevailing over Injustice, which Justice is very quick to point out.

The roster of cases which Justice will hear includes ancient and long standing rivalries as The Stoa against Pleasure, Banking against Diogenes, and Painting v. Pyrrho. To these, Hermes asks Justice if she wants also to include the two cases filed recently against "the rhetor" (*Bis. Acc.* 14). Justice initially defers, but at Hermes's insistence that these two cases are really of the same type and ought to be included with the rest, she reluctantly agrees. Hermes calls the two cases, both against "the Syrian": the first instigated by Rhetoric, on the charge of neglect, and the second by Dialogue on the charge of maltreatment (*Bis. Acc.* 14). Justice asks "Who is this man? This name is not written down," but Hermes says it's okay if they record it anonymously.

By now the audience is totally in on the joke, and sees that Lucian is using the forensic setting to be able to answer his critics. Since the text is written by Lucian, the audience is well aware that the Syrian will emerge victorious from the trial. But Lucian does not allow them to view this immediately; instead the double indictments against the Syrian are postponed as Justice hears all the other cases on the docket ahead of these two (*Bis. Acc.* 15-25). Finally it is time for those cases against the Syrian, who wins on both counts, followed by the abrupt ending of the text as a whole.

The appropriation of the forensic setting allows Lucian to accomplish several goals at once: to defend himself in a somewhat serious way against those critics who find his writing odd and inappropriate, and to poke fun at the very use of the forensic setting as is common in philosophical dialogues and dramatic works that imagine these agonistic conversations quite seriously. But along the way, Lucian gets good jabs in at the traditional portrayal of the divine courtroom.[107]

While these two dialogues are set up in order for Lucian to defend himself against his critics, others of Lucian's pieces specifically poke fun at the classical portrayal of the divine courtroom such as we have in Homer, Plato, Virgil, and the lost *Nekyia* of Menippus. Lucian has three main ways in which the divine courtroom figures in his writings. The first corresponds to what we have seen in the *Double Indictment*, in which the courtroom takes place in some sort of timeless "classical" world and include a mixture of historical figures, ideas personified, and divine figures. We have such a setting, albeit with less formal judicial proceedings, in *Zeus Refuted* and *Prometheus*. The second two ways in which the divine courtroom appears, however, both revolve around the courtrooms of the underworld and at Elysian Fields, the courtroom that awaits everyone in the afterlife. In this way Lucian finds himself the literary descendant both of the Aeschylean tradition and the *Nekyian* tradition. Post-mortem courtrooms appear in two distinct ways in the Lucianic corpus: 1) when a character narrates such a scene (*True Story, Menippus,*

---

[107] And at the inconsistencies that plague classical culture's portrayal of the Olympian deities.

*Icaromenippus, On Funerals*), and 2) when the scene is presented entirely through a dramatic dialogue (*The Downward Journey, Dialogues of the Dead*).[108]

Of the post-mortem courtrooms that Lucian narrates, only the *True Story* narrates an Elysian scene in which Rhadamanthys holds court at the entrance to the Isle of the Blest.[109] In Book II of the *True Story*, the narrator and his traveling companions arrive at a many-harbored island that smells like Arabian perfume and in which the mellifluous notes of Pandean pipes sound constantly. He is told that they have arrived at the Isle of the Blest, and that the Cretan Rhadamanthys is its ruler. Lucian then narrates the scene at Rhadamanthus's court, in which Rhadamanthys is portrayed as arbitrating minor disputes among such classical heroes as Ajax, Menalaeus, and Alexander (4-10). This is a great example of a Lucianic take on a traditional scene. Plato had placed Rhadamanthys along with Minos and the other post-mortem judges at the crossroads of the afterlife, sending people either to the Isles of the Blest *or* to an alternative, nasty destination. However, traditional Greek myth places Rhadamanthys squarely in Elysium.[110] Lucian therefore correlates the two traditions by placing Rhadamanthys as a judge on the Isle of the Blest – but the question then remains: why is a judge is needed on the Isle of the Blest if everyone there has already been found just? In his portrayal of the Rhadamanthene courtroom, Lucian has diagnosed both the inconsistency and the comic potentiality found therein. He thus decides to portray Rhadamanthys as judging minor disputes among the blest inhabitants, much in the same way as he will, on occasion, portray Minos as judging minor disputes among the dead.

This is funny on several accounts: first, that these eminent inhabitants of the Elysian paradise still find things that need to be adjudicated, even in the beauty of paradise, says something recognizable and laughable about the human condition; and second, the cases themselves brought before Rhadamanthys poke fun at inconsistencies and classical elements in Greek culture. One case includes the age old question: If someone had two husbands while on earth, whose wife will she be afterwards?[111] That Lucian poses this question with regard to one of history's greatest and most well-known beauties, Helen of Troy, adds to the fun because of the way Lucian combines, for comic ef-

---

[108] While *Menippus* is technically a dialogue, it is included among the narratives because the dialogue is only a loose framework for Menippus to narrate his journey; whereas in the *Downward Journey* and the *Dialogues of the Dead*, the dialogue is actually the scene of the divine courtroom.

[109] For a recent discussion of the *True Story* as a whole, see Peter von Möllendorff, *Auf der Suche nach der verlogenen Wahrheit: Lukians Wahre Geschichten* (Tübingen: Narr, 2000).

[110] Homer, *Od.* 4. 561-9; Pindar, *Ol.* 2.75.

[111] Note the Judeo-Christian variation on this question with regard to the resurrection in Matthew 22:23-30.

fect, the entire Greek canon of traditions, be they mythological, philosophical, or historical. This is all presented in straight-face narration: true story!

Lucian's narrator must queue up before Rhadamanthys, and their appearance seems to cause consternation.

> We were brought up fourth, and he asked us how it was that we trod on holy ground while still alive, and we told him the whole story. Then he had us removed, pondered for a long time, and consulted with his associates about us. Among many other associates he had Aristides the Just, of Athens. When he had come to a conclusion, sentence was given that for being inquisitive and not staying at home we should be tried after death, but that for the present we might stop a definite time in the island and share the life of the heroes, and then we must be off. They set the length of our stay at not more than seven months. (10)

When they tell him the whole story, Rhadamanthys has to withdraw to think about it, even needing to consult with his advisors. It is good news for the narrator that Aristides the Just is one of them, a man so celebrated in Antiquity for his absolute fairness and justice in all legal activity. His inclusion in this picture is significant: it displays the quality of Rhadamanthys' judgments and suggests the equity of the trials. Lucian's mention of Aristides here counters anticipated objections such as those of the *Apocolocyntosis*, that post-mortem courtrooms are as skewed and imbalanced as human courtrooms. On the contrary – if Aristides is there advising Rhadamanthys, his readers can be sure that everyone will get a fair hearing.[112] The fact that Lucian puts him here is more evidence that there is some concern about the equity of these trials.[113]

Like in *A True Story*, Lucian includes narrated scenes of post-mortem courtrooms in both *Menippus or A Consultation with the Dead* and *Icaromenippus or Over the Clouds*. Since the protagonist in both works is the Cynic Menippus (third century CE), the two works are often viewed together as a literary pair.[114] Both of the two works are dialogues in which a friendly inter-

---

[112] Georgiadou and Larmour point out that this arrangement also parallels the Sophoclean presentation of Zeus with Dike sitting nearby at Soph, *Oed. Col.* 1382. Cf. Aristoula Georgiadou and David H. J. Larmour, *Lucian's Science Fiction Novel True Histories* (Mnemosyne 179; Leiden: Brill, 1998), 188. That presentation was definitely designed to show Zeus's proper administration of the cosmos, which was very much a concern or topic of classical Greek theatre. Cf. Lloyd-Jones, *The Justice of Zeus*.

[113] In addition, by placing Aristides at the very height of Elysian honor, Lucian manages to vindicate Aristides, since on earth he was eventually ostracized and exiled from Athens, and also manages to vindicate the Athenians' decision to welcome and honor him upon return from exile. Lucian accomplishes all of this, at the same time, in one sentence, and that is the reason that his genius has been so admired through the ages. Lucian never underestimates his audience.

[114] *Menippus* probably owe its literary inspiration to the lost *Nekyia* of the actual Menippus, though we are unable to gauge the exact relationship between the two texts. Helm famously argued that Lucian had plagiarized most of Menippus's *Nekyia*, but contemporary Lucian scholars have rejected Helm's claims on various grounds. *Icaromenippus*, on the other hand, has no known precedence among the Menippean corpus.

locutor ("Friend") questions Menippus about the voyage from which he recently returned, and Menippus proceeds to narrate – with some interspersed questioning – his adventures. The two works are very similarly structured, as Relihan's side-by-side analysis has demonstrated.[115] Additionally, the stated "goals" of both of the voyages are similarly themed. In *Menippus*, Menippus explains that he headed to Hades in order to find out what kind of life was best (*Menippus* 6); while in *Icaromenippus,* Menippus heads to the skies to find out which philosophical truth was unassailable and irrefutable with regard to the universe (*Icaromenippus* 10). Just as the goals are similar, so too are the "lessons" that emerge from these voyages. After the lengthy trip to Hades, Menippus finally finds Teiresias, Odysseus's great guide, who tells him that the best kind of life is the simple one which does not seek out great investigations. Quoting Simonides, Teresias tells him to "above all, pursue only how to put the present in its proper place and run on, laughing at most things and worried about nothing" (*Menippus* 22). Likewise Menippus learns a similar lesson in Heaven, that all the philosophers are ultimately screwed and headed for destruction (*Icaromenippus* 33).

In the *Icaromenippus,* after a long journey involving a birds-eye view (*katascopia*) of the idiocy and ant-like behavior of man, Menippus arrives in heaven and witnesses exactly how Zeus responds to the prayers and petitions he receives from humanity below (*Icar.* 25-26). The actions Zeus takes are executive and judicial, using vocabulary that indicates that the reader should understand this as Zeus's sitting in judgment on human affairs much in the way he is depicted in the *Iliad*: "Pursuing such things, we arrived at the region where it seemed good to him to sit to hear the prayers. There were openings like mouths of wells, with covers on them, and beside each stood a golden throne. Sitting down by the first one, Zeus took off the cover and gave his attention to the people who were praying" (*Icar.* 25). The reference to the golden thrones here recalls Zeus's golden scepter (and golden scales) in the Homeric corpus, while the throne clearly indicates Zeus's sovereignty and capacity as universal ruler.

The prayers themselves are comically varied, as one man wishes to become king, another for his onions and garlic to grow, and another to emerge victorious in his lawsuit (25). In addition, several of the prayers are at complete odds with each other: "Among seafaring men, one was praying for the north wind to blow, another for the south wind; and the farmers were praying for rain while the washerman were praying for sunshine" (25). Lucian thus indicates just how contradictory and conflicting are the goals of man, which recalls Menippus's reason for heading to heaven in the first place, to try to

---

[115] See Relihan, *Ancient Menippean Satire*, pgs. 104-114.

resolve the conflicting theories proposed by the philosophers. Lucian then describes just how Zeus deals with this seeming dilemma:

Zeus listened to each prayer, weighing precisely but not promising everything, *but on the one hand father granted one, but denied another.* You see, he let the just prayers come up through the orifice and then took them and filed them away at his right; but he sent the impious ones back ungranted, blowing them downward so that they might not even come near Heaven. In the case of one petition I observed that he was really in a dilemma: when two men made contrary prayers and promised equal sacrifices, he didn't know which one of them to give assent to; so that he was in the same plight as the Academicians and could not make any affirmation at all, but suspended judgment for a while and thought it over, like Pyrrho (*Icar.* 25, quoting *Iliad* 16.250)

This portrayal is subversive: while it starts off well, with Zeus carefully weighing each petition in the manner of the Homeric Zeus, it does not end well, as Zeus proves himself just as incapable of solving dilemmas and dealing with conflicting claims as the philosophers. Menippus's journey to heaven is not going to bring him the answers he so desires, and moreover, the audience is treated to a view of Zeus as incapable of judicial activity. It is not a portrayal of an *unjust* Zeus, but a portrayal in which Zeus is revealed to be incompetent – or, at least, no more competent than the philosophers. Though this portrayal of Zeus's judicial activity is comic, particularly in terms of Lucian's imagining of the various openings to heaven in which the petitions arise, it is horribly pessimistic. The possibility of attaining divine justice in heaven seems quite slim, if even Zeus is incapable of making decisions and instead just delays action.

Worse, later in the text, when Menippus finally gets around to revealing what the gods have to say about the philosophers, Zeus and the other gods reveal themselves to be wrathful and unjust, sentencing the philosophers to death for their activities.[116] While there may be comic comeuppance for Menippus, who gets to go tell the philosophers what is in store for them (*Icar.* 34), sentencing the philosophers to annihilation is massive overkill, and reveals that the vaunted "divine council" can be just as hot-tempered and vengeance-seeking as any human council. The two portrayals of divine judicial activity in the *Icaromenippus* point not towards the possibility of a just administration of the universe, but to the exact opposite, revealing that perhaps the best attitude towards philosophical contemplation, which includes speculating about the gods and about the way they decide matters with regard to the fate of man, is not doing it at all, and throwing up one's hands at the whole thing.

This is certainly the lesson intended by the *Menippus*, which seems to be its companion-piece. The courtroom scene of the *Menippus* is longer and more explicitly juridical than the *Icaromenippus*, but the same dubious atti-

---

[116] Though a delayed death, as the action is postponed for the festival season (*Icar.* 33).

tude toward the possibility of post-mortem justice and proper divine administration of the cosmos is evidenced. At the beginning of the text, Menippus, in
the course of a casual conversation, tells his friend ("Friend") that the rich
have no idea what is waiting for them in the underworld (*Men.* 2). His friend
expresses interest in hearing about this new legislation, but Menippus expresses some concern about publishing the details, for "someone might bring
a suit against us for impiety before Rhadamanthys" (2). This foreshadows the
trial scene that the audience will hear about later.

Without much encouragement, Menippus agrees to narrate what he witnesses in Hades. Though at first he goes right to the heart of the matter, his
friend interrupts him and asks him to tell the whole tale. Menippus thus starts
at the beginning, with the reasons for his journey. He explains that he was
perplexed about the contradiction between the myths of the gods and the ethical instructions of the philosophers, which seem to propose a different sort
of life than one actually practiced by the gods in the myths of Homer and Hesiod (*Men.* 3-4). He also finds himself dissatisfied with the fact that the philosophers contradict each other, and that the philosophers themselves act
contrary to their own instructions (5). He thus decides to head to Babylon,
where he can address one of the Magi of Zoroaster, who knows how to open
the gates to Hades and bring people down and back safely, so that he can go
down and ask Teiresias for himself (6).

After elaborate description of the complex machinations by which Menippus actually managed to get down to Hades, Menippus is ferried across the
river by Charon and arrives at the court of Minos:

Going ahead little by little we arrived at the tribunal of Minos. And it happened that he was
seated on a certain high throne, and the Tormentors, the Erynies, and the Avengers stood
beside him. From one side a great number of men were being led up in line, bound together
with a long chain; they were said to be adulterers, procurers, tax collectors, toadies, sycophants, and all that crowd of people who create confusion in life. And separately the wealthy
and the money-lenders came up, pale, pot-bellied, and gouty, each of them with a neck-iron
and a hundred point crow upon them. Standing by, we watched the goings-on, and listened
to the defenses. For they were condemned by new and surprising rhetors. (*Men.* 11)

When Menippus's friend asks him who these surprising prosecutors were,
Menippus explains that they are our shadows, and "when we die, they bring
charges and testify against us, exposing whatever we have done in life, and
they are considered extremely reliable because they are always with us and
never leave our bodies" (*Men.* 11). This is a great example of how sometimes
Lucian not only envisions the divine courtroom as operating successfully, but
at times Lucian even makes the divine courtroom operate *more* smoothly than
Homer, Plato, and the other myth-makers that come before him. While Plato
explains in the *Gorgias* that one's own body will witness against them before
the judicial trio, bearing physical scars for the errors and transgressions of

their earthly life, Lucian actually comes up with an even better witness. Here, Menippus tells his friendly interlocutor that he won't believe one of the major players in the court of Hades – one's own shadow, who, since he was there with you through your whole life, can testify to every single thing you did, good and bad (at least during the daytime). It's a funny notion, but it works, and since it speaks, it's better at bearing witness than just physical scars.[117]

Menippus describes Minos's judicial activity here by saying that Minos examined each carefully and sent each one to be punished in accordance with his crimes. The most harsh punishments are reserved for those puffed up with arrogance, self-importance, and hybris (*Men.* 12). Menippus, of course, delights in this state of affairs, and does not hesitate to rub it in by reminding the tormented of their previous position in life (12). So far, Lucian's *Menippus* seems to reveal a post-mortem world governed judiciously, in which those most deserving of punishment are punished accordingly. Minos's court *works*, and the inclusion of the funny detail about the shadow only makes it work better. At this point this seems like a conservative view of the post-mortem courtroom, upholding and expanding what the philosophers (particularly Plato) have said. This is an optimistic view; Lucian's portrayal of the divine courtroom reveals an orderly and functioning cosmos.

However, this is Lucian. Such optimism about the fate of the rich and, by extension, the state of the post-mortem world to eventually work things out and right society's wrongs is tempered by what happens next:

> But to return to Minos, one certain instance was judged by favor. For many terrible and impious things had been charged against the Sicilian Dionysius by Dion and testified to by his shadow, but Aristippus of Cyrene appeared – for they hold him in honor, and he is able to do great things among those in the underworld – and when he [Dionysius] was just about to be bound to the chimera, he released him from his punishment, saying that he was found to be obliging with regard to money by many of the educated men. (*Men.* 13)

This explicit favoritism by Minos with regard to the case of Dionysius, to free him from punishment despite the overwhelming evidence against him, casts a shadow of doubt over the whole courtroom scene. The fact that Minos is able to be so swayed by Aristippus's testimony that he is willing to overlook all the many dreadful and impious crimes shows that all is not impartial in the underworld, and that the courtrooms of the underworld are just as susceptible to rhetorical manipulation as those of earth. It is not as pessimistic a portrayal as we have in the *Apocolocyntosis*, in which the courtroom is completely discarded in favor of summary judgment, but it is still a dose of cynicism as to the possibilities for justice even in the divine judicial system, and

---

[117] This little detail is a nice addition to Greek lore of the post-mortem courtroom, and is not dissimilar from the Pauline notion that one's own inner thoughts testifies against them before God.

thus for cosmic order. If even Minos will judge some cases by favor, what hope is there for people who do not have Aristippus of Cyrene to show up for them? The optimism evinced by the original scene of Minos's court is tempered by this example of judicial impropriety – or, if that is too strong, of favoritism and partiality even in Hades.[118]

Lucian's *Menippus* is an example of one consistent literary use of the divine courtroom: as a potent medium to explore the issues of cosmic order and the possibilities either for justice or for entropy. While at first everything seems to be operating smoothly, moving according to the system described by Homer and philosophically envisioned by Plato, Dionysius' reprieve suggests that the system has within it the potential for failure, the potential for injustice. Even in the post-mortem world, in which the gods and their representatives have dominion, there is still manipulation, favoritism, and the possibility of injustice. Despite the light-heartedness and good cheer of the *Menippus*, this is a potent indictment of the divine courtroom, showing that "the machinery of Hades is inadequate to prove the triumph of justice and the rightful exaltation of the poor over the rich".[119] The divine bureaucracy, while maybe not totally impotent, is just as flawed as the human bureaucracy. Just as Lucian's earthly courtrooms (as he portrays them in his texts) often show the frustration of justice rather than the administration of justice, so too do his divine courtrooms. Rhetoric is here also indicted: it is not only used in service of unjust ends on earth (a la *Gorgias*), but also in the next world. The tools of manipulation, negotiation and distraction in life are also seen to be at play in Hades. This is all very depressing: If one cannot even count on the gods to maintain order and stability, what is one left to do? Ultimately, Tieresias provides the answer: the best life is an unexamined one, and one should go forth in life "laughing a lot and taking nothing seriously" (*Men.* 21). Lucian does not attempt to "fix" the system, or to provide philosophical solutions to the problems with the way classical Greek culture envisions the divine courtroom, even if he does smooth out some of its wrinkles by providing some ingenious and clever suggestions. But he does point out the problems, milks them for comic effect, and leaves the audience to do with his insights what they will.

The third way in which the divine courtroom appears in Lucian's writings is in those text which enact the courtroom scene in dialogue form. The best example of this is Lucian's *The Downward Journey, or the Tyrant*, an entire dialogue devoted to Charon's underworld ferry and the trial before Rhada-

---

[118] Relihan states this more dramatically, saying that the point here "is not the mutability of fortune, but of the influence that philosophers have in the other world for evil. The moral order of Hades, to which Menippus turns for guidance, is a shambles." Relihan, *Ancient Menippean Satire*, 109.

[119] Relihan, *Ancient Menippean Satire*, 114.

manthys that awaits its passengers. The dialogue is filled with illusions to classical myths of the underworld courtroom, particularly the *Gorgias*. And unlike the courtrooms of the *Menippus* and the *Icaromenippus*, here, like in the *True Story,* Rhadamanthys's courtroom seems to be functioning just fine. Lucian's "target" in this dialogue is not the administrative bureaucracy of Hades (though of course he finds some opportunities to get some jabs in here as well), but rather the comic reversal of fortune that awaits the wealthy in the next life. Though this theme echoes that of the *Menippus*, and the two texts both involve courtroom scenes, the way in which Rhadamanthys's courtroom operates in the *Downward Journey* is far better than Minos's courtroom of the former text. It is possible that Lucian has more confidence in the Rhadamanthene judgments than in the Minean ones, given the historical Rhadamanthys's reputation for severity in judgment.

The dialogue starts mise-en-scene, with Charon impatiently waiting for Hermes, complaining that he hasn't earned any obols yet and about all the jobs that Hermes has to do. Hermes shows up panting, with a man in fetters, and identifies him as a runaway, "a king or a tyrant, to judge from his lamentations and the wailing that he makes, in which he makes out that he has had great happiness taken away from him" (*Cat.* 3). He describes the tyrant's attempted escape, and after said tyrant Megapenthes rants and raves about the injustice of his untimely death, Clotho tells him to "stop threatening and get aboard; it is already time for you to make your appearance before the tribunal" (*Cat.* 13). When Megapenthes asks "and which man is worthy to pass judgment on a tyrant," Clotho replies "On a tyrant, no one, but on a corpse, Rhadamanthys. You shall soon see him impose on every one of you the sentence that is just and fits the case" (*Cat.* 13). Not only will Megapenthes see this judicial activity, but the audience will as well. After an extensive ferry-journey, in which the audience is introduced to other passengers such as Micyllus and Cyniscus, the boat finally alights on the shore (*Cat.* 21). When they do, they meet Tisiphone, one of the Erinyes, who brings them to Rhadamanthys for trial. The entire rest of the dialogue (23-29) is a dramatic presentation of the courtroom.

Cyniscus is up first, by his own request, explaining to Rhadamanthys that "I wish to prosecute a certain tyrant for those terrible deeds that I know him to have done in life, and I am not worthy of belief when I speak unless I first make it clear what sort of man I am and according to what manner I led my life" (*Cat.* 23). When Rhadamanthys instructs Hermes to call the accusers (τοὺς κατηγόρους), no one comes, but the trial is not over: Rhadamanthys tells Cyniscus to "strip yourself, so that I can judge you from the marks on your back" (24). Rhadamanthys explains that each wicked deed leaves a mark on his soul, a clear allusion to *Gorgias* 524d-525a. These deeds, represented by their marks will serve as witnesses against Cyniscus. However, in his case, the marks tell a different story. Rhadamanthys exclaims that "the man is altogether free from marks, except for these three or four, very faint and uncertain. But what is this? There are many traces and indications of brandings, but somehow or other they have been erased, or rather, effaced" (24). Cyniscus explains that his turn towards philosophy gradually washed away his scars. This is a dramatic presentation of the belief in the curative nature of philosophy. Here, Cyniscus's turn towards philosophy literally has wiped away his scars. They bear witness not against him, but rather for him, for his transformation and rehabilitation. Rhadamanthys calls the cure good and most efficacious, and tells him to "go your way to the Isles of the Blest to live with the good, but first prosecute the tyrant you spoke of" (24).

Cyniscus does just that: what follows is an extended prosecution of Megapenthes. Cyniscus begins with an opening statement in which he lays out exactly the crimes with which Megapenthes finds himself charged: putting to death ten thousand people without a hearing, "ravishing maids, corrupting boys, and running amuck in every way among his subjects" (*Kat.* 26). To these horrors Cyniscus adds the less tangible ones of pride, haughtiness, and arrogance, insisting that these are so great it would never be possible to exact a penalty for them (λαβεῖν τὴν δίκην). To witness to these horrors – since anything is potentially possible in the underworld – Cyniscus brings in Megapenthes's murder victims (*Cat.* 26). Megapenthes cops to the murders, but refuses to admit to the other crimes, at which point Cyniscus brings in witnesses to these acts as well – Megapenthes's bed and lamp (*Cat.* 27). The way these previously inanimate objects bear witness is surprising – they bear witness by claiming to be so outraged and upset by Megapenthes's actions that they refuse to talk about them, just agreeing that Cyniscus's charges are accurate (*Cat.* 27). Rhadamanthys, responding to Bed, asserts that "therefore you have testified most clearly by being reluctant to speak of these things." The lack of explicit testimony is taken by Rhadamanthys to be most damning evidence against the tyrant.

Rhadamanthys thus proceeds to the physical examination. Ordering Megapenthes to be stripped, Rhadamanthys exclaims "the fellow is all livid and crisscrossed; indeed, he is black and blue with marks. How can he be punished? Shall he be thrown into the River of Burning Fire or turned over to Cerberus" (*Cat.* 28)? But Cyniscus has a better idea, a "new and fitting punishment," suggesting that Megapenthes be the only one who is not to drink from the water of Lethe, so that "he will pay a bitter penalty in that way, by remembering what he was and how much power he had in the upper world, and reviewing his life of luxury" (*Cat.* 29). Rhadamanthys is pleased with this sentence, and ends the dialogue by asserting "let him be so condemned (καταδεδικάσθω), and let this man be led off and bound near Tantalus, remembering those things he practiced in life." (*Cat.* 29).

The Rhadamanthene courtroom that Lucian presents in *The Downward Journey*, like that of the *True Story*, is far more conservative than that which he put forth in the *Icaromenippus* and the *Menippus*, despite his comic elaborations and presentations of the trial, and the presence of non-human witnesses therein. In the *Downward Journey*, Lucian upholds the judicial functioning and operational reliability of Rhadamanthys's courtroom, just as he upheld the reliability and justice of Justice's courtroom in the *Double Indictment*. In these texts, he does not use the courtroom scenes in order to critique the courtroom itself. Instead, despite all of his variations, anecdotes, jabs, and basic needling, he does not do any damage to the basic image of the courtroom as a place in which correct sentences are meted out correctly. It is when the courtroom is sidelined in favor of immediate punishment, the threat against Parrhesiades in *The Fisherman* or indeed, against Prometheus, that Lucian sees the most injustice and the failure of the system. In these texts, Lucian's divine courtroom works. For someone who is so radical in terms of genre-bending, seeing the humor in tradition, and willing to take shots at the most esteemed and serious figures of his day, and is capable of being so radical in presentations of the divine courtroom, *The Downward Journey* is surprisingly conservative and indeed optimistic about the possibilities for actual post-mortem justice. Cyniscus and Micyllus are sent off to the Island of the Blessed, and the tyrant Megapenthes, who so tried to escape Hermes at the beginning of the dialogue, is sentenced accordingly. There is still, however, the question of Cyniscus's influence before Rhadamanthys, conducting a full prosecution and suggesting an appropriate sentence, but ultimately it is the physical evidence of Megapenthes's own body which seals his fate.

Lucian is thus capable of employing the imagery and actors of the divine courtroom in a variety of ways throughout his writings. We should not be surprised to see the courtroom presented optimistically in one text (*Downward Journey, True Story*) and pessimistically in another (*Menippus, Icaromenippus*), for it is the nature of Lucian comically to point out contradictions, and this is no exception. While some scholars have seen the influence of the historical Menippus and his lost *Nekyia* in Lucian's *Menippus*, and attempted to understand Lucian's critique in the *Menippus* as reflecting Menippus's own writings, we do not need to jump to this conclusion to understand that Lucian is capable of presenting contradictory portraits of the same scenario to make different points and to serve various purposes. In fact, Lucian seems to embrace the contradictions of classical culture as a source of humor and constitutive of the tensions of life. Lucian fully appreciates the traditions he has inherited, including all of the contradictions therein.

# G. Conclusion

It seems clear from its consistent presence in varying literary genres that scenes of the divine courtroom remain a potent aspect of Greek and Roman mythology from classical culture through the Second Sophistic. Indeed, the fact that these scenes are set in a physical environment familiar from everyday life, the courtroom, makes them particularly viable media for exploring questions of justice, of divine characterization, and of fate and destiny, as the image of the courtroom already carries with it a variety of cultural attitudes. These attitudes include but are not limited to fear, skepticism, anxiety, and a concern for personal honor and vengeance. Why should Lucian's Cyniscus be so quick to jump into a prosecutorial role if not for a) the honor this may bring him; and b) the personal satisfaction he can feel from conducting a successful prosecution against a tyrant? Audiences of the Second Sophistic were capable of recognizing these prosecutorial goals without Lucian needing to spell them out for the reader. These courtrooms, then, are not benign settings for revealing the process of administrating cosmic order.

Second, these scenes, unlike those of monotheistic culture, do not share the same concern for role differentiation in the courtroom as a focus of the inequity. The presence of multiple deities in the Greek (and later Roman) pantheon allows for judicial scenes to have several actors acting independently of each other, without one having to act both in a prosecutorial and a judicial role, in the way that YHWH is in the Hebrew Bible. However, the lack of focus on role differentiation allows the focus instead to be on the one sitting in judicial capacity, and whether or not that judge administers justice with equity. This most often becomes a question of the justice of Zeus, as Minos, Rhadamanthys, and Aeacus act as his representatives. Zeus is haunted by the tradition of his violent overthrow of his father and the Titans, and often this memory clouds the courtroom scene. Zeus's propensity to tyranny and violence leads authors to cast shadows over his ability to act as impartial judge.

The courtroom scenes thus, for many authors, become media not only for issues of Justice, but more specifically for exploring issues of Zeus's justice.

Chapter 4

# Books, Angels, and Scales, Oh My:
# The Divine Courtroom in Second Temple Judaism

## A. Introduction

Scenes of the divine courtroom continue to emerge throughout the years of
formative Judaism under Greek and Roman rule. These scenes carry new
cultural currency as they are reformed and reimagined through the lenses
of Greek, Egyptian, and Roman mythology. In particular, the location of
the court moves from an atemporal, eternal address as we have in the Hebrew Bible, to a more permanent residence. This residence is either in the
immediate afterlife, as God, with the help of biblical figures such as Abraham, Enoch, and Moses, sits in judgment on the fate of individual souls, or
at the end of days, as God acts as ultimate judge of Israel and the nations.
Additional influence from non-Israelite culture can be found in the cast of
characters who play roles in the forensic systems. While the polytheistic
cultures of the Greco-Roman world find various gods serving judicial
rôles, Second Temple Jewish literature sees these same functions being
performed by a host of ministering angels and/or biblical characters. Notable is the fact that Jewish authors recognized the need for separate actors
to fill these functions, a development of the courtroom scenario found in
the Hebrew Bible, and a possible response to the criticism put forth by Job
and Jeremiah.

   Scenes of the divine courtroom are found in a variety of literary genres,
including the "Rewritten Bibles," and in apocalyptic literature, particularly
with regard to otherworldly journeys undertaken by biblical patriarchs,
most prominent of these being the possibly parodic and definitely entertaining *Testament of Abraham*. Often these scenes are used to provoke a
number of attitudes on the part of the reader, such as humor, consolation,
fear, or a reaffirmation of personal piety and commitment to God. However, these scenes are also part of an ongoing conversation that began in the
Hebrew Bible: the question of God's ultimate justice in the universe and
the issue of theodicy. These scenes become opportunities for authors to
work out their visions of ultimate justice, often attempting to vindicate
God of charges of injustice, impropriety, or abandonment. In particular,
Second Temple literature deals with the complicated relationship between

justice and mercy. How much mercy tips the balance in favor of *injustice* rather than justice? When is it appropriate for God to display mercy, and when does justice require strict punishment? Alongside these questions are those that circulate regarding intercession and advocacy: what room is there for intercession before God? If intercession is favorable, what type of arguments are successful? Are there some cases when intercession subverts justice?

This chapter will demonstrate that throughout the Second Temple period there is a consistent concern by authors to prove to their readers that God is justified in his actions. Forensic scenarios become the carriers of these conversations. The courtroom scenes serve as vehicles in these authors's attempts literally to vindicate God, affording them the opportunity to show God's judicial activity firsthand. What is exceptional is that this does not go unnoticed even by contemporary (or slightly later) authors. I will argue that in the most elaborate of these courtroom scenes, the longer recension of the *Testament of Abraham*, the author actually parodies these very attempts to vindicate God, forcing the reader to take a step back and look at what they are doing in these courtroom scenes. This not only is an example of when trying Man is trying God, but indeed where trying Man forces the reader to realize that they have been trying God.

## B. The Divine Courtroom in the Rewritten Bibles: *Jubilees*

James Kugel has plainly demonstrated that the genre of the "rewritten Bible" was a popular one in Second Temple Judaism.[1] The rewritten Bibles that exist from this time period, such as the book of Jubilees, Flavius Josephus's *Jewish Antiquities,* and the *Biblical Antiquities* of Pseudo-Philo, bear witness to lively and creative imaginations capable of filling in the narrative gaps of biblical literature, or of reframing biblical stories for new purposes. In the pages of these rewritten Bibles there is evidence of sustained interest in the operations, procedures, and choreography of the divine courtroom. Courtroom scenes are included in the narratives even when such scenes are not indicated in the biblical text. In this way the authors of the rewritten Bibles seem to have located the court in the margins of biblical narrative, writing their understanding of the divine courtroom into texts that originally had no such imagery, finding sub-text that emerged from sustained intertextual readings of the canon as a whole.

Likely the most popular of the rewritten Bibles, the book of *Jubilees,* probably written in Hebrew, was composed in the mid-second century

---

[1] James Kugel, *The Bible as it Was* (Cambridge: Harvard, 1997).

BCE in Judah during the Maccabean period. Fragments of the text were found amidst the caves of Qumran, the oldest of which dates to ca. 100 BCE.[2] *Jubilees*, fifty chapters in length, purports to be an account of the revelation received by Moses on Mt. Sinai (Jub 1:1-4). A central concern for *Jubilees* is God's justice, particularly in his dealings with Israel. This is evident from the very beginning of the book. According to Jubilees 1, while Moses was on Sinai, God instructed him to:

> Pay attention to all the words which I tell you on this mountain. Write (them) in a book so that their offspring may see that I have not abandoned them because of all the evil they have done in straying from the covenant between me and you which I am making today on Mt. Sinai for their offspring. So it will be that when all of these things befall them they will recognize that I have been more faithful than they in all their judgments and in all their actions. They will recognize that I have indeed been with them. Now you write this entire message which I am telling you today, because I know their defiance and their stubbornness (even) before I bring them into the land which I promised by oath to Abraham, Isaac, and Jacob: 'To your posterity I will give the land which flows with milk and honey.' When they eat and are full, they will turn to foreign gods – to ones which will not save them from any of their afflictions. Then this testimony will serve as evidence. For they will forget all my commandments – everything that I command them – and will follow the nations, their impurities, and their shame. (Jub 1:5-9)[3]

This introduction places the question of God's justice in the forefront. This book is intended to serve as testimony in the future for accusations that God anticipates: specifically, that he is not just, abandoned the people in some way, and whatever has happened to them was due to this abandonment. In Deuteronomy 31, before Moses' death, God instructs Moses to write such a book for the same purpose. Here, the author places the instruction to write not before Moses' death, but indeed all the way back on Mt. Sinai, suggesting that the future apostasy of the people was not something God expected only after their desert foibles, but indeed was anticipated by God even at the moment he created the covenant with Israel.[4]

The fact that this book (identified by the title as *Jubilees* itself) is meant to serve as testimony in this anticipated lawsuit-like accusation places the book of *Jubilees*, and its readers, as participants in a cosmic courtroom drama. This is the implied narrative frame in the whole work. On the level of the narrative, the book is written to convince the readers of the justice of

---

[2] The complete text only survives in Ethiopic, first edited by R. H. Charles, *The Ethiopic Version of the Hebrew Book of Jubilees* (Oxford: Clarendon Press, 1895), and recently by James VanderKam, *The Book of Jubilees: A Critical Text* (Corpus Scriptorum Christianorum Orientalium 510; Louvain: Peeters, 1989).

[3] Translation from James VanderKam, *The Book of Jubilees* (Corpus Scriptorum Christianorum Orientalium 511; Louvain: Peeters, 1989).

[4] However, included in this anticipation is also the knowledge that this apostatic situation will not last forever; God tells Moses that they eventually will return "in a fully upright manner and with all (their) minds and all (their) souls" (Jub 1:23).

God's actions in history, serving as God's own evidence. This places the implied reader in a judicial stance, evaluating the evidence presented by God alongside the evidence presented by his or her own experience and history.[5]

While the book as testimony plays an important role in the narrative framework of Jubilees, books inside the narrative also serve functions in the divine courtroom. Especially relevant here is the description of the activity of Enoch found in *Jubilees* 4:16-26. Enoch is described as "the first to write a testimony" (Jub 4:18). We are told that Enoch "saw everything and understood. He wrote a testimony for himself and placed it upon the earth against all mankind and for their history" (Jub 4:19). The testimony that Enoch wrote is described not only as testimony for one side, but actually as "judgment and condemnation of the world" (Jub 4:23). Enoch's book is understood as serving a forensic role, either as evidence against a particular group, as a record of the sentence against such group, or as a combination of both roles. Both these books, therefore, are explicitly said to serve judicial functions in a courtroom setting.

Cosmic books are mentioned again in *Jubilees*, along with the related concept of the heavenly tablets. The two are mentioned close together in *Jubilees* 30, during the narration and justification of Levi and Simeon's attack on Shechem to avenge Dinah's defilement (Jub 30:1-23). The text, which clearly wants to vindicate Levi in particular of any wrongdoing,[6] insists that the retaliation was carred out because "the punishment had been decreed against them in heaven" (Jub 30:5). This is followed by the description of a law prohibiting intermarriage (Jub 30:7) and the prescription of death for any man who "defiles": "For this is the way it has been ordained and written on the heavenly tablets regarding any descendant of Israel who defiles (it): 'He is to die; he is to be stoned'" (Jub 30:9). The "heavenly tablets" here seem to refer to records of legal proscriptions, not unlike the tablets said to be written by the finger of God on Mt. Sinai (Ex 31:18; 34:1). This concept of the heavenly tablets appears throughout *Jubilees* (3:9-11; 4:5; 33:10-12).

Following further elaboration of this and related laws (Jub 30:10-17), *Jubilees* explains the result of Levi's actions:

Levi and his sons will be blessed forever because he was eager to carry out justice, punishment, and revenge on all who rise against Israel. So blessing and justice before the

---

[5] This is clearly intended by the Deuteronomistic Historian in Deuteronomy 31, but here this is used as the overarching narrative for the rewritten Pentateuch it presents.

[6] This, in conjunction with other emphasis on matters reflated to the priests, probably reflects a priestly *Vorlage*. On this see James VanderKam, "The Origin and Purposes of the *Book of Jubilees*," in in Matthias Albani, Jörg Frey and Armin Lange, eds. *Studies in the Book of Jubilees* (Tübingen: Mohr Siebeck, 1997), 3-24.

God of all are entered for him as a testimony on the heavenly tablets. We ourselves re-member the justice which the man performed during his lifetime at all times of the year. As far as 1000 generations will they enter (it). It will come to him and his family after him. He has been recorded on the heavenly tablets as a friend and a just man. I have writ-ten this entire message for you and have ordered you to tell the Israelites not to sin or transgress the statutes or violate the covenant which was established for them so that they should perform it and be recorded as friends. But if they transgress and behave in any impure ways, they will be recorded on the heavenly tablets as enemies. They will be erased from the book of the living and will be recorded in the book of those who will be destroyed and with those who will be uprooted from the earth. (Jub 30:18-22).

This understanding of the heavenly tablets has a different nuance. Here, rather than understanding the tablets as containing divinely-sanctioned le-gal prescriptions and codes, the heavenly tablets are understood to contain records of people's behavior and actions. The tablets are also here men-tioned in association with two books: the book of life and the book of those who will be destroyed. Not only will someone who breaks the cove-nant be written down in the tablets as enemies, they will also be blotted out of the book of life (recalling Moses' request in Ex 32:32), and written down in what is basically the book of death.[7] The concept of a heavenly book which contains a record of one's deeds probably originates in Sumer[8] and becomes popular in Second Temple Jewish Literature as foundation for ethical paraenesis and reflection.[9]

Here in *Jubilees*, however, given the narrative framework of the book, the tablets/books with this valence have additional forensic import. The existence of these tablets implies that at some point those tablets will be consulted as evidence. Just like the book of *Jubilees* itself, and the testi-mony of Enoch mentioned in *Jubilees* 4, these tablets and books are un-derstood to serve as evidence of people's actions before the ultimate judge at the appointed time of judgment. In other words, people's actions and their category as either "friend" or "enemy" is understood to have judicial power. Someday, it seems to be suggesting, those books are going to be opened. Someone is going to *read* them. Someone is going to take action

---

[7] Florentino García Martínez discusses these tablets under the heading of the "Heavenly Register of Good and Evil," which he also sees in Jub 19:9, and relating to the concept of the tablets as the "Book of Destiny," which he locates in a number of passages. Cf. García Martínez, "The Heavenly Tablets in the Book of Jubilees," *Studies in the Book of Jubilees,* 243-260. García Martínez offers a taxonomy of the heavenly tablets in Jubilees that divides the scattered references into five major categories: 1) The Tablets of the Law; 2) Heavenly Register of Good and Evil; 3) The Book of Destiny; 4) The Calendar and Feasts; 5) New Ha-lakhot.

[8] Shalom M. Paul, "Heavenly Tablets and the Book of Life," *JANES* 5 (1973) 345-352.

[9] For a complete discussion of the function of books in *Jubilees*, see Leslie Baynes, "'My Life is Written Before You': The function of the motif 'heavenly book' in Judeo-Christian apocalypses, 200 BCE-200 CE" PhD Diss; University of Notre Dame, 2005.

based on the contents of those books/tablets. In *Jubilees*, the existence of these heavenly record-books is given within the context of *Jubilees* itself constituting evidence for God and against the people in a meta-trial conducted by the implied reader. For the author, this witnesses that the people have been warned about these books, and therefore cannot appeal to ignorance of their existence later on. *Jubilees* thus has books within books, piling up the courtroom scenarios. There is an implied courtroom scenario of Man before God, in which the tablets serve as evidence, and this itself is evidence in the implied courtroom scenario of Man vs. God before the reader, the framework of *Jubilees* itself.

In this overarching courtroom scenario, one of the pieces of "evidence" the reader hears is that of God's overwhelming justice with regard to his decision-making and judicial role. In his retelling of the story of the Watchers (Jub 5:1-19), which is connected to the account of the flood (Jub 5:20-6:16), the author of *Jubilees* includes an assurance to his readers about God's righteousness and justice. This begins with the description of the punishment of the angels, followed by the insistence that "the judgment of them all has been ordained and written on the heavenly tablets; there is no injustice" (Jub 5:13), and continues with the assertion that judgment has been written down for every creature:

All their judgments have been ordained, written, and inscribed. He will exercise judgment regarding each person – the great one in accord with his greatness and the small one in accord with his smallness – each one in accord with his way. He is not one who shows favoritism nor one who takes a bribe, if he says he will execute judgment against each person. If a person gave everything on earth he would not show favoritism nor would he accept (it) from him because he is the righteous judge. Regarding the Israelites it has been written and ordained: 'If they turn to him in the right way, he will forgive all their wickedness and will pardon all their sins'. It has been written and ordained that he will have mercy on all who turn from all their errors once each year. To all who corrupted their ways and their plan(s) before the flood no favor was shown except to Noah alone because favor was shown to him for the sake of his children whom he saved from the flood waters for his sake because his mind was righteous in all his ways, as it had been commanded concerning him. He did not transgress from anything that had been ordained for him. (Jub 5:13-19)

Here *Jubilees* goes out of its way to convince the reader that God's action in punishing the angels is completely justified. Such a description of the justice of God's actions, here speaking not only with regard to the particular situation but also generally about the character of God in his role as judge, is not found in the earlier Watchers material, nor in its brief origin in Genesis 6. However, Genesis 9 may bear witness to a tradition that questioned God's justice with regard to destroying the world. When God establishes the covenant with Noah following the flood (Gen 9:1-17), God promises that he will never cut off all of humanity by flood again (Gen

9:11), promising that "I will remember my covenant that is between me and you and every living creature of all flesh; and the waters shall never again become a flood to destroy all flesh" (Gen 9:13-15). This promise to "remember" is repeated again in the next verse (9:16). This repetition is good indication that there was some fear about God forgetting or abandoning his covenant.

While this passage from Genesis 9 is not explicitly about God's justice, it is not difficult to see this as evidence that the Genesis redactor understood that people were troubled by the tradition of the flood.[10] The flood tradition implied a certain willingness on the part of God to punish his creation with devastating violence, an unsettling accusation. This may be the initial source of the exposition in *Jubilees,* which stands right in the middle of the description of God's punishment of the angels and his punishment of the whole world. When the two traditions were connected more explicitly than in Genesis,[11] the author seems to have felt compelled to provide a more explicit justification of God's decision. Here the justification is not only about God's decision in this instance, but about his very capacity to make those decisions at all. In *Jubilees* 5, God's character as a judge is explained: he will judge everyone according to their own essence (5:15), he will not "lift up faces," i.e., show partiality (5:16), and he will not take bribes (5:16). This description of God's judgments as having "no injustice" (5:13), and the description of God's judicial activity serves within the overarching framework of *Jubilees* as an *argument* for God. Here, this argument is placed in the narrative at one of the most tendentious moments of God's "career": the decision to destroy the world by means of the great flood. By placing this right before the description of the flood, the *Jubilees* redactor attempts to anticipate one of the great objections to the case for God's justice in his dealings with Israel.

This same strategy can also be observed in the *Jubilees* expansion of Genesis 22, the binding of Isaac (Jub 17:15-18:19). While Genesis 22 merely informs the reader that "God tested Abraham" (Gen 22:1), *Jubilees* provides detail as to the reasons for and the circumstances of that test (*Jub* 17:15-18). Here the reason for God's command to offer Isaac up in sacrifice is given: due to Abraham's great piety, Prince Mastema instigates God to initiate the ultimate test, whether Abraham's love of God surpasses that of his love for Isaac. This expansion of the text obviously reflects the abiding influence of the book of Job, as Mastema's instigation mirrors that of

---

[10] Which existed in other cultures as well, as the Atrahasis Epic witnesses.

[11] Michael Segal believes this connection occurred as a result of 1 Enoch. For complete discussion see Segal, *The Book of Jubilees: Rewritten Bible, Redaction, Ideology and Theodicy* (Leiden: Brill, 2007), 139.

the Accuser in Job 1-2.[12] Jon Levenson notes that "the effect of this trans-
ference of the motif of the prologue to Job to the aqedah is to provide a
ready answer to a question that also bothered the rabbis of the midrash:
what provoked this gruesome test, what could have been 'these things' on
which the aqedah logically followed (Gen 22:1; see *Gen Rab.* 55:4)?"[13]
The prologue to Job provided the author of *Jubilees* with an example of a
seemingly unimpeachable man being subject to unimaginable suffering due
to that very unimpeachability. By interweaving these two stories together,
the author finds a reason for the *aqedah*, and uses this in his overall justification of God's actions for the reader. Abraham's willingness to submit to
this command has the effect, according to *Jubilees*, of shaming Prince
Mastema (Jub 18:12), and thus serves a cosmic purpose. It is not merely an
arbitrary decision on the part of God. This becomes part of *Jubilees*'s defense of God's actions that serves as the framing for the entire narrative.[14]

In sum, the book of *Jubilees* bears witness to the continuing interest and
use of divine courtroom imagery in Second Temple Judaism. Its major
contribution to the development of this imagery is in the narrative frame,
which places the reader in a courtroom scenario that shapes the way these
stories must be read and understood. It thus expands on the concept of the
heavenly books that appear sporadically in the earlier material, and stands
as evidence of the questions regarding God's justice that continue to nag
ancient readers, as well as the strategies that ancient authors took to address those very questions. Here the strategy was to retell the stories of
Genesis and Exodus as part of a forensic defense of God's actions, so that
the reader is persuaded to acquit God of wrongdoing and injustice. Though
God is repeatedly referred to as judge, and his unique judicial qualities are
extolled throughout the book, it is the reader whom the author is trying to
persuade, who stands as the immediate judge of God's actions in history.

---

[12] For a discussion of this and other exegetical choices of the author of Jubilees with re-
gard to this story, see Jon Levenson, *The Death and Resurrection of the Beloved Son: The
Transformation of Child Sacrifice in Judaism and Christianity* (New Haven: Yale University
Press, 1993), 177ff.

[13] Levenson, *Death and Resurrection,* 178.

[14] This also bears witness to a major development in the expansions of the Abraham story,
the linking of the character of Abraham with that of Job.

# C. The Divine Courtroom in the Apocalyptic Literature

Scenes of the divine courtroom are often found in the apocalyptic literature, where biblical patriarchs are taken on cosmic tours and shown the mysteries of heaven. The apocalypses of this time period show sustained interest in the choreography and procedural details of the heavenly judicial system. These texts introduce and develop a number of motifs that later become standard in descriptions of the divine courtroom, such as the props involved (scales, books), the setting (throne/court rooms), and the figures present (Enoch, Abel, and a host of ministering angels). In particular the apocalyptic literature is concerned with the questions of intercession, and what arguments can be brought forth in favor of man before God. The apocalypses show a concern to anticipate and rebut possible objections brought as to proper procedure and judicial propriety in the divine courtroom. This is evidence that these questions and concerns existed both for author and reader.

## I. The Trendsetter: 1 Enoch and the Emergence of Topoi

It has long been recognized that the book of Enoch occupied an authoritative place within Second Temple Judaism and, later, within earliest Christianity. The number of copies or fragments of the Enochic corpus found at Qumran testify to the book's popularity among that particular form of Judaism, and the number and variants of the manuscript tradition indicates that this popularity continued well into the Christian era. The date of the composition is certainly a matter of debate, but it is nearly universally agreed that parts of 1 Enoch predate the biblical book of Daniel, making it our earliest known piece of apocalyptic literature.[15] 1 Enoch in many ways sets the trends for the literature that follows it. This is true with regard to overall form and content, individual topoi, and broad thematic issues that continue to be central in Jewish and later Christian apocalyptic literature.

One such issue that emerges in 1 Enoch is the question of the relationship between justice and mercy and the efficacy and propriety of intercession at the final judgment that awaits all humanity. As noted in chapter two, the biblical attributes of God include both those of justice and punishment, and those of grace and mercy (Ex 34:6-7). The biblical author understood God's justice and mercy as working in tandem with each other, and that part of God's mercy includes the *delay* of punishment, but not the *abandonment* of punishment. God's mercy is so great that he will bear the sins and wait patiently, but the biblical author does not imagine that God

---

[15] Though there is considerable debate about the dating of the Similitudes; see below for discussion.

will leave the sin unpunished forever. This remains the case in apocalyptic literature, which includes an understanding of an eventual "final judgment," in which the fate of all mankind will be sealed forever. This apocalyptic scenario envisions the final judgment as the moment when God's patience runs out and God finally acts to punish and condemn those trespassers.

This is the scenario envisioned in *1 Enoch* 1-5. The opening verse sets the upcoming judgment as the focus of the collection of materials: "The words of the blessing with which Enoch blessed the righteous chosen who will be present on the day of tribulation, to remove all the enemies; and the righteous will be saved" (1 En 1:1).[16] The "day of tribulation" is subsequently described as a judgment day (1 En 1:8), and this judgment day is the focus of every section of *1 Enoch*, despite the divergent nature of sections of the text.[17] It can be argued that the sustained focus on the upcoming future judgment, from the vision of the Book of the Watchers to the tribunal of the Animal Apocalypse, is what links the corpus together thematically.[18]

A recurring theme in these visions of the upcoming judgment is the efficacy of angelic intercession. The first vision of the judgment that Enoch receives occurs in Book I, the "Book of the Watchers." Enoch's vision includes an etiology for the degenerate nature of mankind: the fall of the angels and their interaction with human women, a longer narration of the capsule story found in Genesis 6:1-6 (1 En 6-8). Upon observing the oppression of the earth from heaven, Michael, Sariel, and Gabriel explain that "The earth, devoid (of inhabitants), raises the voices of their cries to the gates of heaven. And now to <us>, the holy ones of heaven, the souls of men make suit, saying, 'Bring in our judgment to the Most High, and our destruction before the glory of the majesty, before the Lord of all lords in majesty.'" (1 En 9:2-4). The angels then intercede before God on behalf of the people being oppressed by the wicked angels (1 En 9:4-11). The language they use to present the case is explicitly juridical, as they state that the souls are "making suit" before God (1 En 9:10), asking the angels

---

[16] Translation by George Nickelsburg and James VanderKam, *1 Enoch: A New Translation Based on the Hermeneia Commentary* (Minneapolis: Fortress Press, 2004).

[17] As George Nickelsburg writes, "The oracle that introduces the collection sets the tone for what follows, announcing God's coming judgment and its consequences: blessings for the righteous and curses for the sinners (chps. 1-5). All the major sections of 1 Enoch and many of their component parts either provide background for this theme or elaborate on it and give it prominence." Nickelsburg, *1 Enoch 1* (Hermeneia; Minneapolis, MN: Fortress Press, 2001), 37.

[18] *1 Enoch* is traditionally divided into five sections, the Book of the Watchers (1-36), the Book of the Similitudes (37-71), the Book of the Heavenly Luminaries (72-82), the Book of Dreams (83-90), and the Epistle of Enoch (90-108).

to "bring in our judgment to the Most High" (1 En 9:3). In this way the angels act as advocates before God on behalf of the people.[19] Their advocacy is effective, as the Most High acts in response, giving the angels tasks to bind the wicked angels and hold them over for punishment, warning of all the calamities that will befall the angels "until the everlasting judgment is consummated" (1 En 10:12). Asael in particular is singled out by name to be bound and cast into darkness (10:4-5), a punishment that recalls that of the Titans at the hands of Zeus.

However, the efficacy of the angelic intercession is not the end of the story. Following God's announcement of the sentence upon the wicked Watchers, Enoch receives the unfortunate commission of messenger, charged with bearing the bad news to Asael and the others (1 En 12:4-6). Enoch proceeds to tell them that "You will have no relief or petition, because of the unrighteous deeds that you revealed, and because of all the godless deeds and the unrighteousness and the sin that you revealed to humans" (1 En 13:2). Noteworthy in this grave announcement is the insistence that the judgment includes an inability of the fallen angels to supplicate on their own behalf. As a result, the wicked angels beg Enoch to make supplication and intercede *for them* (1 En 13:4). In this way one instance of intercession brings another: the angelic intercession on behalf of the people leads to Enoch needing to intercede on behalf of the fallen angels. Enoch does what they ask, writing down their prayers and petitions (1 En 13:6) and going to recite them by the waters of Dan, falling asleep in the process.[20]

When Enoch awakes, he has bad news, having received another vision, this time of a series of great and terrifying houses in heaven (1 En 14:1ff). Recounting his vision, Enoch describes what he saw inside the second house:

Its floor was of fire, and its upper part was flashes of lightning and shooting stars, and its ceiling was a flaming fire. And I was looking and I saw a lofty throne; and its appearance was like ice, and its wheels were like the shining sun, and the voice of the cherubim, and from beneath the throne issued rivers of flaming fire. And I was unable to see. The Great Glory sat upon it; his apparel was like the appearance of the sun and whiter than much snow. (1 En 14:17-20)

---

[19] Sisson has described this intercession as having "a three-part structure typical of intercessory prayer. It begins with a lengthy doxology (9:4-5), addressing the deity as lord, god, and king and extolling him as the creator and all-powerful authority from whose sight nothing is hidden. A statement of motive (9:6-10) follows, citing the transgressions of the fallen angels and the sufferings of humankind, to which a plea for help (9:11) on behalf of the latter in the form of a lament has been added." Jonathan Paige Sisson, "Intercession and the Denial of Peace in 1 Enoch 12-16" *HAR* 11 (1987), 371-387, 377.

[20] An appropriate place for this activity, given the etymology of the tribal name.

Scholars have long noted that this scene bears a very strong resemblance to the throne room scene of Daniel 7, as well as to a fragmentary text found at Qumran called the Book of the Giants (4Q530). Of particular similarity is the throne with wheels (cf. Dan 7:9) and the streams of flaming fire (cf. Dan 7:10), as well as the description of the garments as "whiter than snow."[21] There is considerable debate over the direction of the relationship both in this case and in the case of *1 Enoch* 46 and 47, which also look remarkably like the Danielic tradition with regard to the "Son of Man." Helge Kvanvig has convincingly argued that the Watchers's vision predates and influenced Daniel 7, rather than the other way around.[22]

In both of these scenes (as well as in the Qumran text), the throne-rooms are locations for judgment. In Daniel 7, the judgment is issued against the eleven-horned arrogant-speaking beast, and in *1 Enoch* 14, the throneroom scene has juridical implications, as Enoch receives a message of particular import there. Enoch is told that he shouldn't be interceding on behalf of the watchers, but indeed the Watchers should be interceding on behalf of Men, given what kind of corruption and pollution they had sown in Mankind as a result of their actions (1 En 15:1-2). God gives Enoch an account of exactly why the Watchers are to be punished and what will happen to their descendants (1 En 15:3-16:3). The form of the account includes an accusatory question (1 En 15:3), an explanation of how they have gone wrong and the consequences of their actions (1 En 15:4-16:2), and a sentence of judgment, which Enoch is to pass on: their petitions are denied (1 En 16:3).

Jonathan Paige Sisson has argued that the form of this speech "resembles that of a *rîb*-patterned denouncement speech which Enoch is called upon to witness," and reads the entire scene as having a full juridical context: "It is clear that the watchers are the defendants in the present context, while the deity takes on the role of the plaintiff. Enoch's part in the lawsuit derives from both his advocatory role on behalf of the watchers and his duties as a scribe. He not only pleads the case of the accused before the divine council, but also records the testimony and delivers the word of judgment."[23] Sisson is right on the essentials, but needs one slight corrective. While Enoch certainly plays the role of advocate, God is not really presented as the plaintiff (though his judicial sentence does include an accusatory question). It is the *people of the earth* that have been presented as

---

[21] Cf. Dan 7:9, "white as snow."

[22] Helge S. Kvanvig, "Throne Visions and Monsters: The Encounter between Danielic and Enochic Traditions" *ZAW* 117 (2005), 249-272. However, in the case of the passages from the Similitudes, John Collins has argued for the opposite relationship. John Collins, *A Commentary on Daniel* (Hermeneia; Minneapolis: Fortress Press, 1993), 80.

[23] Sisson, "Intercession," 383, using the criteria put forth by H. Huffmon (see above, chapter 2).

the plaintiffs in *1 Enoch* 9:2, represented well by the intercessory activity of Michael, Sariel, and Gabriel. There the language is explicitly juridical.[24]

This is an important distinction because the classic employment of the *rîb*-pattern in the Hebrew Bible ascribes both the accusatory and the judicial roles to God, while here the book of Enoch is careful to assign the different judicial rôles to a number of participants. A significant difference is present between this divine courtroom and those of the biblical prophets. Not only do the oppressed people receive efficient advocacy (Michael, Sariel, Gabriel), but *1 Enoch* has even provided the *accused* with vigorous advocacy (in the figure of Enoch himself). God therefore just acts as judge, not as both judge and prosecutor, effectively "solving" the biblical *rîb* - pattern issue pointed out forcefully by Job. No longer does God play all the courtroom roles. The development of the angelic intercessory force assures that an entire and orderly process of judgment proceeds apace in heaven.

However, that does mean that not every intercessory advocate will be successful at pleading their cause. Not all intercession is effective; not everyone will be saved from punishment. Some defenses will not stand, because in this cosmic judicial system, actions deserve punishment, and no plea for mercy will sway the divine sentence. To punctuate this theological point, Enoch is taken on one of several tours of heaven and earth, in which he bears witness to the ordering of astronomical and natural phenomena, including the cornerstone of the earth, the pillars of heaven, and the "prison for the stars and the hosts of heaven" (1 En 18:14; cf. 21:1-10), where the wicked Watchers will be held forever. In contrast, however, Enoch also sees a place far less terrible:

From there I traveled to another place. And he showed me to the west a great and high mountain of hard rock. And there were four hollow places in it, deep and very smooth. Three of them were dark and one, illuminated; and a fountain of water was in the middle of it. And I said, 'How smooth are these hollows and altogether deep and dark to view.' Then Raphael answered me, one of the holy angels who was with me, and said to me, 'These hollow places (are intended) that the spirits of the souls of the dead might be gathered into them. For this very (purpose) they were created, (that) here the souls of all human beings should be gathered. And look, these are the pits for the place of their confinement. Thus they were made until the day (on) which they will be judged, and until the time of the day of the end of the great judgment that will be exacted from them.' (1 En 22:1-4)

This is the first mention in a Jewish text of a sort of "intermediate" holding pen for souls, where souls are kept between the time of death until the final judgment, where they will be sentenced eternally. This is an important step

---

[24] And bears resemblance to the language used to describe the crying of Abel's spirit in 1 En 22:5-7 (see below).

in the development of Jewish eschatology, because it reflects an attempt to synthesize a cultural concern with the immediate post-mortem afterlife (as we find in Greek literature) with the Jewish (and ultimately Christian) concept of a final reckoning for all of humanity, including the resurrection of the dead. *1 Enoch* posits that the future judgment will include everyone, even those that have died already.[25] In addition, Enoch is informed that the souls being held there have already been separated one from the other based upon their conduct in life (1 En 22:8-14). That these souls have already been separated even within the holding pen suggests a type of preliminary judgment, although no description is given of the process of that initial judgment. This, will emerge later as its own topic of illustration in future texts. Here, however, the immediate post-mortem selection and separation is not narrated, although the suggestion is that something has already taken place that provides an order even within the holding pit. In effect, the pit described is not dissimilar to the modern jail, where people are held awaiting and during trial, as opposed to prison, where people go when they are sentenced. This penology suggests an ordered universe that operates according to its own processes, and this is the overwhelming characteristic of the cosmos that Enoch witnesses in this, his first heavenly tour.

The process may be indicated by its preceding verses. When Enoch is shown this jail-like pit, he reports that:

There I saw the spirit of a dead man making suit, and his lamentation went up to heaven and cried and made suit. Then I asked Raphael, the watcher and holy one who was with me, and said to him, 'This spirit that makes suit – whose is it – that thus his lamentation goes up and makes suit unto heaven?' And he answered me and said, 'This is the spirit that went forth from Abel, whom Cain his brother murdered. And Abel makes accusation against him until his posterity perishes from the face of the earth, and his posterity is obliterated from the posterity of men. (1 En 22:5-7)[26]

Enoch asks no further questions about this accusing spirit or about the lawsuit that the spirit seems to be participating in continually. This is a crucial piece, however, for the development of the tradition which ultimately has Abel presiding over the judgment scene in the *Testament of Abraham*. The biblical verse that seems to inspire this forensic location of Abel is Genesis 4:10, when God informs Cain that the voice of his brother's bloods are crying out to him from the ground. *1 Enoch* 22:5-7 understands these cries very literally: as forensic petitions, making lawsuits, crying out for vengeance. It suggests that this crying did not cease in Genesis 4, but contin-

---

[25] According to 1 En 27:1-5, the future judgment will take place in the "accursed valley," the forerunner of the later Gehinnom/Gehenna.

[26] For the textual variants, cf. Nickelsburg, 301.

ues until all of Cain's descendants are wiped out.[27] The inclusion of this reference to Abel's continuing lawsuits suggest a divine courtroom process for individual souls such as that witnessed for the Watchers. This suggested process results in the separation of the souls into their appropriate jails, held over for ultimate judgment. Though this is not spelled out, it is a key building block for the eventual depiction of that very process, with Abel at the center, in the *Testament of Abraham*.

Thus the Book of the Watchers, though not really including a full courtroom scene such as we see in the later literature, does include the narration of an extended juridical process that culminates in the judicial sentence handed down in God's throneroom. This is also featured in other sections of *1 Enoch*. The Book of the Similitudes (1 En 37-71), which probably *postdates* the canonical book of Daniel, also contains glimpses of this type of process, including an extended prediction of the coming judgment (1 En 38), and a vision of what will happen to the sinners on "that day," when "my Chosen One will sit on the throne of glory, and he will test their works" (1 En 45:3). The Chosen One is further referred to as the "son of man" (1 En 46:3), chosen by the Lord of Spirits, and is revealed to have an extensive role in the coming judgment. Enoch tells us that "he will judge the things that are secret" (1 En 49:3), "the unrepentant will perish in his presence" (1 En 50:4), and he shall sit on the throne to make the selection (1 En 51:2-3).

This throne is referred to repeatedly throughout the Similitudes (1 En 47:3; 51:3; 55:4; 60:1-6) as the judgment-seat, whether it be in the future or the primordial past. The throne is specifically contrasted with the thrones of earthly kings (1 En 56:5), and is alternately occupied by the Chosen One and the Lord of the Spirits.[28] The most extensive vision of the process of judgment that occurs on the throne is given in 1 En 61:8-9, where it is part of the overall cosmic order put forth by the Lord of the Spirits:

And the Lord of the Spirits seated the Chosen One upon the throne of glory and he will judge all the works of the holy ones in the heights of heaven, and in the balance he will weigh their deeds. And when he will lift up his face to judge their secret ways according to the word of the name of the Lord of Spirits, and their paths according to the way of the righteous judgment of the Lord of Spirits, they will all speak with one voice, and bless and glorify and exalt and santify the name of the Lord of Spirits.

---

[27] Nickelsburg, following T. F. Glasson, suggests a similarity to "the restless spirit of the murdered Clytemnestra (Aeschylus, *Eumenides* 98), who cries out for revenge on the murderer." Nickelsburg, *1 Enoch 1*, 305; cf. T. F. Glasson, *Greek Influence in Jewish Eschatology* (London: SPCK, 1961), 16.

[28] Compare, for example, *1 Enoch* 61:8-13 with *1 Enoch* 62:2ff.

Here, the Chosen one and the Lord of the Spirits work in tandem: the Chosen one is judging, but he judges "according to the word of the name of the Lord of Spirits," and "by the way of the righteous judgment of the Lord of Spirits." Though we are not told exactly what that method is, we see the imagery of scales and the assurance that the judgment is righteous, i.e., just.[29] Despite the fact that it is not God himself seated on the throne, but rather a chosen representative, the reader is assured that the method of judgment is still God's and therefore unimpeachable.

The emphasis on the equity of God's judgment practices is found again in 63:7-9, where the kings and other earthly rulers bemoan their fate, pleading for respite from their punishment: "Our hope was on the scepter of our kingdom and <throne of> our glory. But on the day of our affliction and tribulation it does not save us, nor do we find respite to make confession, that our Lord is faithful in all his deeds and his judgment and his justice, and his judgments have no respect of persons. And we vanish from his presence because of our deeds; and all our sins are reckoned in righteousness." The emphasis on the equity of God's judgment indicates that the author has recognized classic complaints and concerns about the divine courtroom and has taken steps to try to alleviate these concerns for the reader. However, unlike the Book of the Watchers, there is no indication here that these earthly rulers have any one, angelic or heroic, to advocate for them. They are forced to plead for themselves, but their pleas go unheard. In the view of the author, the method of the righteous judgment does not, apparently, include the kind of vigorous advocacy granted in the Book of the Watchers.

One thing briefly mentioned in the Similitudes but not fully developed until the Book of the Heavenly Luminaries are the heavenly books. In *1 Enoch* 39:2-3, one of the predictions of what will come to pass "in those days," Enoch receives the "books of jealous wrath and rage and books of trepidation and consternation." Though no elaboration is given, these do not sound like the kind of books in which people want to be recorded, such as the "books of the living" opened before the throne of glory in 1 En 47:3. Instead, these sound like the books Enoch is shown in the Book of the Heavenly Luminaries, where Enoch is given access to sapiential information regarding the order of the cosmos and the movement of the heavenly bodies (1 En 73-80). To conclude this section, Enoch is shown one more heavenly object:

He said to me: 'Enoch, look at the heavenly tablets, read what is written on them, and understand each and every item.' I looked at all the heavenly tablets, read everything that

---

[29] The use of the instrumental dative here to refer to how the elect one is judging may be the antecedent of *T. Abr.* 13 (Recension A), where Dokiel weighs the deeds of the soul "by means of the righteousness of God."

was written, and understood everything. I read the book of all the actions of people and of all humans who will be on the earth for the generations of the world. From that time forward I blessed the great Lord, the king of glory forever, as he had made every work of the world. I praised the Lord because of his patience; I blessed (him) on account of humanity. Afterwards I said: 'Blessed is the one who does righteous and good; regarding him no book of wickedness has been written and no day of judgment will be found.' (1 En 81:1-4)

This heavenly tablet seems to contain records of human history, including the minutia of existence – the type of books, perhaps, appropriate to be judicially examined in a throne-tribunal. These books become recurrent objects in this type of divine courtroom scene, such as the multi-cubit sized book that sits on the gilded table before Abel in *T. Abr.* A. Here Enoch does not see the books in a throneroom context, but given the content of the tablets and Enoch's reaction to them there can be no doubt that these books are understood to play a crucial role on that day and in that room.

This is reinforced by the appearance of book in two other sections of *1 Enoch*, the "Animal Apocalypse" and the "Epistle of Enoch." In the Animal Apocalypse (1 En 85-90), Enoch witnesses the entire scope of human history played out before him with animal protagonists.[30] The extensive vision, which includes detailed zoological tableaux of highlighted moments from Israelite history such as the Flood, the Exodus, and the Division of the Kingdom, culminates with an extensive judgment scene. The judgment scene beings with a mention of the by-now familiar throne- and book- imagery: "And I saw until a throne was constructed in the pleasant land and the Lord of the sheep sat upon it, and he took all the sealed books and opened those books before the Lord of the sheep" (1 En 90:20). The books refer to the many books of testimony that had begun to be written by the shepherds following the destruction of Jerusalem and shown to the Lord of the sheep (1 En 89:68-71; 89:73-77; 90:17). Books again play a prominent role in the Epistle of Enoch (1 En 91-108), where Enoch cries "Woe to you, sinners, for your riches make you appear to be righteous, but your heart convicts you of being sinners; and this word will be a testimony against you, a reminder of (your) evil deeds" (96:4). Given Enoch's vision of the heavenly tablets, we should not understand this as an analogical statement (this matter shall be *like* a witness), but rather concretely – these matters are physical records. Indeed, Enoch specifically admonishes his readers: "Do not suppose to yourself nor say in your heart, that they do not know and your unrighteous deeds are not seen in heaven, nor are they written down before the Most High. Henceforth know that all your unrighteous

---

[30] For full discussion see Patrick A. Tiller, *A Commentary on the Animal Apocalypse of 1 Enoch* (Atlanta: Scholars, 1993).

deeds are written down day by day until the day of your judgment" (1 En 98:7-8).[31]

The Epistle of Enoch explicitly links the coming judgment described throughout the book to a message of consolation for the righteous, promising that their names are also being inscribed (1 En 104:1), and they will see justice:

Take courage and do not abandon your hope, for you will have great joy like the angels of heaven. And what will you have to do? You will not have to hide on the day of the great judgment, and you will not be found as the sinners, and the great judgment will be (far) from you for all the generations of eternity. Fear not, O righteous, when you see the sinners grow ng strong and prospering, and do not be their companions; but stay far from all their iniquities, for you will be companions of the host of heaven. Do not say, O sinners, 'None of our sins will be searched out and written down.' All your sins are being written down day by day. And now I show you that light and darkness, day and night, observe all your sins. Do not err in your hearts or lie, or alter the words of truth, or falsify the words of the Holy One, or give praise to your errors. For it is not to righteousness that you're your lies and all your error lead, but to great sin. (104:4-9)

This exhortation encourages those righteous to continue to have hope and trust that God will remember them and that all of their just actions as well as the sinful actions of their oppressors are being meticulously recorded in heaven. They are encouraged to cry out for judgment, much like the peoples of the earth cried out as a result of the actions of the Watchers, and much like the spirit of Abel continually cries out for judgment against the sons of Cain. But this exhortation does not only console, it also warns, using the divine courtroom as a motive for ethical paraenesis: don't think you can hide, your sins are being recorded every day. The readers are exhorted to recognize that it is they who ultimately decide their own fate by their actions. This, too, is an implicit appeal to the reader to judge for themselves whether the process is just. By reaffirming that ultimately, one holds one's fate in their own hands, 1 Enoch is arguing that the final judgment will be one of the utmost justice and equity. The Epistle recalls aspects of the courtroom scenes not only to remind the reader of what awaits them, but to reassure the reader that what awaits them is just, and thus to persuade the reader to judge the situation accordingly.

The Book of Enoch thus plays an important role in the development of literary topoi that become part of standard divine courtroom imagery in Hellenistic Jewish literature. In Enoch we see the development of the angelic bureaucracy, particularly as it relates to intercession and advocacy;

---

[31] Cf. also .03:2-3: "For I have read the tablets of heaven, and I have seen the writing of what must be, and I know the things that are written in them and inscribed concerning you – that good things and joy and honor have been prepared and written down for the souls of the pious who have died; and much good will be given to you in the place of your labors, and your lot will exceed the lot of the living."

the emergence of the throneroom as almost synonymous with a forensic and judicial setting; an extensive spacial description of the heavenly penal system, and the expansion of the already biblical notion of the heavenly record-books, here specifically associated with coming judgment and legal action. These scenes continue to function as vehicles of conversations regarding God's justice, as the reader is once again asked to evaluate and ultimately vindicate God and the cosmic plan.

## II. The Book of Daniel

Following *1 Enoch*, the next major moment in apocalyptic literature that features the divine courtroom is the canonical book of Daniel, particularly the visions in chapters 7-12. While there is still some debate about the dating of the court tales of chapters 1-6, it is universally acknowledged that the visions contain clear allusions to the Maccabean period, suggesting a date for this latter half of Daniel in the mid-second century BCE.[32] All twelve chapters of Daniel were found at Qumran, some in multiple copies, leading John Collins to conclude that "The book of Daniel was widely accepted as a reliable and authoritative document by the end of the second century BCE."[33] The visions of Daniel contain a vision of the divine courtroom that, due to its canonical status, was widely influential on future depictions of this heavenly moment, such as those in the New Testament and the early Church fathers.

In the prominent apocalyptic scene of Daniel 7, Daniel receives a vision of four great beasts, each more terrifying than the last, culminating in the beast with ten horns, of which three are uprooted by a little one (Dan 7:1-8). Following this vision, later given the interpretation of a series of kingdoms that must presage the everlasting kingdom of God (Dan 7:15-22), Daniel has a vision of the divine throneroom, over which the Ancient of Days presides:

As I watched, thrones were set in place, and an Ancient of Days too his throne, his clothing was white as snow and the hair of his head like pure wool; his throne was fiery flames, and its wheels were burning fire. A stream of fire issued and flowed out from his presence. A thousand thousands served him, and ten thousand times ten thousand stood attending him. The court sat in judgment, and the books were opened ( דינא יתב וספרין פתיחו). (Dan 7:9-10)

---

[32] John Collins notes that this was recognized as early as Porphyry, whom Jerome quotes as saying that "Daniel did not so much say what was yet to happen as he narrated past events" and "whatever he spoke of up till the time of Antiochus contained authentic history, whereas anything he may have conjectured beyond that point was false." John Collins, *Daniel* (Hermeneia; Minneapolis: Fortress, 1993), 25, quoting Jerome, *Preface to Daniel*.

[33] Collins, *Daniel*, 72.

Daniel then watches the condemnation of the horn and the removal of the dominion of the beasts (Dan 7:11-13), followed by a now iconic vision of the arrival of the "one like a son of man" (Dan 7:13-14). This scene in Daniel becomes the prototype for almost all later scenes of final judgment and the ushering in of the messianic era. It itself is a type of interpretation or reimaging of those biblical poems which talk about God's future judgment over the nations, bringing condemnation to some and victory to Israel (e.g., Isa 2 2-22).

As in *1 Enoch*, Daniel 7 includes what are becoming popular features of the courtroom scene, thrones and books. The throne in particular here, as in *1 Enoch* 14:8-15, seems also to reference the chariot-vision of Ezekiel 1, given its wheels and its fiery emissions. This brings together two theophanic varieties, that of the throneroom and the chariot. Added to this is the now forensic role of the throneroom, so that multiple layers of divine encounter become fused in one semantic field of throne-chariot-courtroom.[34] This is reinforced by what seems to be the merging of two divine images from the Ancient Near East, that of El, the prototypical judge/Ancient of Days figure, with Baal, the "cloud-rider" and warrior God.[35] The fusion does not just reduce all the imagery into one; on the contrary, the fusion of these theophanic types enhances the vision dramatically. The combination of motifs provides an "overwhelming" quality to the vision that increases its solemnity, importance, and awesomeness. In this way the vision has the effect of simultaneously and intertextually (both on the literary and cosmological levels) linking all of the visual manifestations of the divine together into this one world-changing scene in a form of eschatological figuration. This has implications also for the books: when the books are opened before the court (Dan 7:10), the scene implies that the entire range of books mentioned in the the Bible and Jewish literature are being recalled, so that the Ancient of Days has access to all of human history at his fingertips.

What makes this scene different from *1 Enoch* is its compact nature. Daniel 7 manages to bring all these links and motifs together with excep-

---

[34] Kvanvig has suggested that the Qumranic Book of the Giants (4Q530) is the link between the Enochic and Danielic traditions in terms of the combination of motifs, writing that "The vision in Enoch is not a vision of a court, but a vision of the heavenly temple, introducing a 'prophetic' commissioning. Nevertheless the court motif is essential in the context, both in the beginning of the vision, 'the book of righteousness and reproof', and at the end, Enoch sent to pronounce judgment. In Giants this motif is lifted into the throne scene itself, it is a scene of judgment. This feature is taken over by Daniel." Kvanvig, "Throne Visions and Monsters," 257-258.

[35] The Mesopotamian references were first noted in 1895 by Herman Gunkel. Complete discussion of the relationship between Yahweh, El, and Baal can be found in Cross, *Canaanite Myth and Hebrew Epic*, with discussion of this passage at p.17.

tional brevity. If the Book of the Watchers is the source for much of this material, then what the author of Daniel has done is a remarkable amount of innovation and shaping that actually produced a stronger text. By not saying too much, the author of Daniel has, in effect, said *more*, requiring and allowing the reader to do the intertextual work for themselves, to experience this vision in a theologically meaningful way. This, in turn, subtly requires the reader to think about the divine courtroom here presented in a more elusive way, which in turn reminds them of the power and overwhelming transcendence of God. Not for nothing does the author present the response of Daniel to this vision and its interpretation as one of profound fear (Dan 7:28). By not filling in the gaps, the author of Daniel presents a vision of the divine courtroom that becomes definitive precisely because it leaves the details of the definition unexpressed. This has the effect of requiring the reader always to keep in mind the limitations of visionary experience, and indeed human experience, a fearful notion indeed.

This in turn is a subtle apology for God, one that includes a recognition of the nature of humanity to be mere participants in an entire cosmological drama. Written in the midst of a crisis, the author of Daniel seeks to convince the reader that God has a plan for history with a beginning, middle, and end that includes the seemingly endless dominion of that little horn. Here he presents an argument for God's just administration of the universe that has the courtroom at its boiling point. The readers are asked to trust in this courtroom while, at the same time not being given the details of its procedure, just the outline, and being reminded throughout of God's overwhelming power and nature.

What we have here in Daniel 7 that is a departure from the Book of the Watchers, something that is subsequently also found in the Similitudes of *1 Enoch* is the presence of a figure other than God on the judicial throne. This continues throughout Second Temple literature. One parallel to the imagery of both Daniel 7 and the Similitudes is the figure of Melchizedek in 11Q13, an exceedingly fragmentary text from Qumran. The text, consisting of thirteen fragments from cave 11, is an eschatological description of what is to come on the final jubilee, when the prophecy of Isaiah 61:2, the promise of release to the captives, will be fulfilled. The best-preserved section of the text concerns the figure of Melchizedek and his role in the divine courtroom. Speaking of the end of the tenth jubilee, the text reads:

For this is the moment of the Year of Grace for Melchizedek. [And h]e will, by his strength, judge the holy ones of God, executing judgment as it is written concerning him in the Songs of David, who said, ELOHIM *has taken his place in the divine council, in the midst of the gods he holds judgment* (Ps 82:1). And it was concerning him that he said, (Let the assembly of the peoples) *return to the height above them;* EL *will judge the peoples* (Ps 7:7-8). As for that which he s[aid, *How long will you] judge unjustly and show partiality to the wicked? Selah* (Ps 82:2), its interpretation concerns Belial and the

spirits of his lot [who] rebelled by turning away from the precepts of God to... And Melchizedek wil. avenge the vengeance of the judgments of God...and he will drag [them from the hand of] Belial and from the hand of all the sp[irits of] his [lot]. And all the 'gods [of Justice'] will come to his aid [to] attend to the de[struction] of Belial..."
(11Q13.9-14)[36]

Here, Melchizedek is clearly portrayed as having a distinct role in the divine courtroom. His activity is described as "executing judgment," and we are told that he will "avenge the vengeance of the judgments of God" ( יקום נקמת משפטי אל). Further, the two quotes from Psalms 7 and 82, which in the Hebrew Bible clearly refer to God's role in the divine courtroom,[37] are here applied to Melchizedek, as the text tells us that these verses are "concerning him."[38] Melchizedek's legal rôle seems to be both that of judge and of avenger. This is similar to that ascribed to God by Hebrew Bible authors, particularly those who invoke the rîb pattern, but it is still distinct because no prosecutorial role is here definitely attributed or even intimated to the Melchizedek character. The rôle of judge is not incompatible with that of avenger/executor assuming that the two aspects follow sequentially.

The identity of the figure of Melchizedek here is an issue of much scholarly dispute. 11QMelchizedek was first edited and published by A.S. van der Woude, who believed that Melchizedek was the same figure as Michael, an angelic intermediary acting as the eschatological judge and savior.[39] This view has been challenged by Paul Rainbow, who argued that this text portrays Melchizedek not as an angel but as a Messiah figure,[40] and Franco Manzi, who argued that we should understand "Melchizedek" as a divine title for YHWH.[41] Recently, Rick van de Water has persuasively argued that Manzi's thesis can in fact be reconciled with the understanding of Melchizedek as an intermediary.[42] Van de Water believes that this text, much like the understanding of "one like a son of man" in Daniel 7, portrays a figure who both acts in a God-like role and stands as distinct from God.

11Q Melchizedek, like 1 Enoch, demonstrates the desire to introduce other actors into the divine courtroom, creating a whole slew of judicial

---

[36] Reconstruction and Translation from Geza Vermes, *The Complete Dead Sea Scrolls in English*.

[37] See above, chapter two.

[38] The alternate possibility that this should be read as "concerning it," i.e. the day of judgment, is not at all convincing, as the focus of the verses is clearly on the figure of God.

[39] A.S. van der Woude, "Melchizedek als himmlische Erlösergestalt in den neugefundenen eschatologischen Midraschim aus Qumran Höhle XI," *OTS* 14 (1965), 354-373.

[40] Paul Rainbow, "Melchizedek as a Messiah at Qumran," *BBR* 7 (1997), 179-194.

[41] Franco Manzi, *Melchisedek e l'angelologia nell'Epistola agli Ebrei e a Qumran* (Rome: Pontifical Biblical Institute, 1997).

[42] Rick van de Water, "Michael or Yhwh? Toward Identifying Melchizedek in 11Q13," *JSOP* 16 (2006), 75-86.

operators where the Hebrew Bible, for the most part, saw just one. The existence of this type of heavenly bureaucracy has parallels in both Egyptian and Greek mythology, where different gods perform different judicial functions. By introducing angels and eschatological features as prominent participants in the divine courtroom, apocalyptic literature attempts to provide a solution to the problem of monotheism with regard to rôle differentiation and judicial fairness as conceived by the Hebrew Bible. This can be taken as evidence that Second Temple Jewish readers did in fact respond to the scenes of the divine courtroom in a critical and judicial manner, recognizing that the claims of Job have validity and do, in fact, suggest that God's courtroom is not a just one. Early Christian authors will obviously see a different actor as the solution to the problem, as Christ/ the Son takes on major judicial roles in their understanding of the same procedure. Notable here is that Melchizedek seems to perform many of the same roles ascribed to Christ. This is evidence that both Jewish and Christian authors recognized the same potential issue and posed similar solutions to it, despite the fact that the figures taking those roles vary significantly. This introduction of a figure who is both part of the divine judicial system and yet distinct from God is an example of the way authors attempted to answer these criticisms and thus *vindicate God* from charges of injustice. As the strategy for this vindication, these authors chose the divine courtroom, expecting their readers to approach courtroom scenes from this discursive viewpoint of the reader-judge.

*III. The Apocalypse of Zephaniah*

One of the more frustrating texts of import to the study of the divine courtroom is the *Apocalypse of Zephaniah*. The text, which Wintermute dates between the first century BCE and the second century CE, is preserved in part in a fifth-century Akhmimic manuscript which also contains the *Apocalypse of Elijah*.[43] What makes the text so frustrating is not its content, but rather the fact that the text has a serious lacuna right in the middle of the courtroom scene, almost to the point of parody.

The text itself shares classic features of apocalyptic literature. When we enter the Akhmimic text, the seer is being taken on a tour of his city by "the angel of the Lord" (*Apoc. Zeph* 2:1). The tour seems a classic *katascopia* in which the seer has a birds-eye view of human activity. Immediately after this vision, in which Zephaniah sees "the whole inhabited world hanging like a drop of water which is suspended from a bucket when it

---

[43] Two pages are also preserved in a Sahidic manuscript also containing the Elijah Apocalypse, and a short quotation from Clement of Alexandria, *Strom.* 5.11.77. For discussion see O.S. Wintermute, *OTP* I:497-515.

comes up from a well" (*Apoc. Zeph* 2:5), Zephaniah sees the souls of men in punishment, and pleads with the Lord to have compassion on them (2:8-9). Perhaps in response, the angel then takes him to Mount Seir, where he sees angels who have a particular function:

> Then I saw two other angels weeping over the three sons of Joathan the priest. I said, 'O angel, who are these?' He said, 'These are the angels of the Lord Almighty. They write down all the good deeds of the righteous upon their manuscript as they watch at the gate of heaven. And I take them from their hands and bring them up before the Lord Almighty; he writes their name in the Book of the Living. Also the angels of the accuser who is over the earth, they also write down all of the sins of men upon their manuscript. They also sit at the gate of heaven. They tell the accuser and he writes them upon his manuscript so that he might accuse them when they come out of the world and down there. (*Apoc. Zeph.* 3:5-9)

The angel thus identifies two different sets of recording angels, each with their own function. One set works directly for God, bringing their manuscripts to him so that he can then record their names in the ultimate book, but the other works for "the Accuser," bringing him their manuscripts so that he can accuse those people after their death.[44] Here we see a differentiation also being made between two different types of written material: the manuscripts, and the Book of the Living. This suggests that there is a two-step process in which any errors can be found and corrected, similar to an editing or even an appellate process. It is not the case that *only* the angels are responsible for engraving a soul's fate; God then reviews their work and then puts the seal on it. This procedure leaves less of a margin of error than a one-step process.

The manuscripts appear again later in the text. After a vision of terrifying angels who escort the souls of the ungodly (*Apoc. Zeph* 4:1-7), and a glimpse at the gates of the heavenly city (5:1-6), Zephaniah has a dramatic encounter at the edge of Hades, described as a fiery sea (6:1-3). First Zephaniah sees a terrifying creature (6:8-9), and prays to the Lord Almighty to assist him (6:10).[45] He then is visited by Eremiel, "who is over the abyss and Hades, the one in which all of the souls are imprisoned from the end of the Flood, which came upon the earth, until this day" (6:15). Eremiel informs him that the creature he encountered was "the one who accuses men

---

[44] The text does not here specify whether the Accuser also works for God or whether he works on his own, but this seems to be implied by a later scene, in which the protagonist triumphs over the Accuser and thus is allowed to cross over to the righteous (*Apoc. Zeph* 9:1-5).

[45] Zephanah's petition here is important for a dating of the text: "You will save me from this distress. You are the one who saved Israel from the hand of Pharaoh, the king of Egypt. You saved Susanna from the hand of the elders of injustice. You saved the three holy men, Shadrach, Meshach, Abednego, from the furnace of burning fire. I beg you to save me from this distress" (6:10). The references to the book of Daniel, including to the story of Susanna, require a date later than the second (and possibly even the first) century BCE.

in the presence of the Lord" (6:17). The creature has a manuscript in his hand, which Zephaniah realizes contains a written record of all of his sins:

If I did not go to visit a sick man or a widow, I found it written down as a shortcoming upon my manuscript. A day on which I did not fast (or) pray in the time of prayer I found written down as a failing upon my manuscript. And a day when I did not turn to the sons of Israel – since it is a shortcoming – I found written down upon my manuscript so that I threw myself upon my face and prayed before the Lord Almighty, 'may your mercy reach me and may you wipe out my manuscript because your mercy has [co]me to be in every place and has filled every [p]lace.' Then I arose and stood, and saw a great angel before me saying to me, 'Triumph, prevail because you have prevailed and triumphed over the accuser, and you have come up from Hades and the abyss. You will now cross over the crossing place.' Again he brought another manuscript which was written by hand. He began to unroll it, and I read it, and found it written in my (own) language... (7:1-11)

Unfortunately, this is the moment at which the text breaks off for a lacuna of what is believed to be approximately two pages. When the manuscript resumes, Zephaniah is being placed on a boat for the trip out of Hades (*Apoc. Zeph* 8:1). The statement of 8:5 that sums up the previous scene informs us that "Now, moreover, my sons, this is the trial because it is necessary that the good and the evil be weighed in a balance." This may suggest an appearance of some form of scales or weighing protocol, such as in the Egyptian scenes of post-mortem judgment and in *Testament of Abraham* A. What it certainly indicates is that we are to understand the previous scene including its two-page lacuna as a trial scene. In the preserved section of the text, Zephaniah is confronted by his past, and throws himself before the Lord, pleading for mercy. Though we do not hear God's response, Zephaniah is informed that he has triumphed over the accuser. He is then brought another manuscript, which presumably contains the record of his good deeds that counteract those on the other text (which include, importantly, sins of omission). Zephaniah is told (9:2) that his name has been written down in the Book of the Living.

From the little that we have, it appears that, as in other literature from this period, the questions of mercy and intercession played a major role in this text. In addition to the aforementioned instances of pleading for mercy Zephaniah sees multitudes in heaven praying to God to have mercy for those in torment, and learns that they do so daily (11:1-6). The text as we have it now ends with Eremiel beginning to describe the great wrath that awaits the earth and the heavens (12:1-8). The four page lacuna that follows probably contained another plea for mercy by Zephaniah. Unlike other literature, the emphasis in the *Apocalypse of Zephaniah* does not appear to be on the question of the propriety of intercession, but rather on its proper role within the overall heavenly protocols. The fact that the multitude in heavens pray for mercy daily suggests that intercession is part of the structure of heaven. This most likely was meant to console readers who may be thinking about what is on *their* manuscripts. However, it is not insignificant that God does not speak in the *Apocalypse of Zephaniah* (at least not in the preserved text). Nowhere does God respond directly to any petitions. In fact, though the angels refer to God, God does not appear anywhere in the text. This seems to be a deliberate move by the author to keep God in the background and focus instead on the procedures of heaven and Hades.[46]

In one of the central procedures, Zephaniah's "trial," God is not present. While of course it is possible that he could have appeared during the lacuna, we have no reason to suspect that this is so, since this would not be in keeping with the content of the Apocalypse. The trial is conducted entirely by God's agents, Eremiel and the Accuser. Like the differentiation between the manuscripts and the Book of the Living, this procedural separation seems to be part of the administration of the post-mortem world. This may also be a temporary situation; in chapter 10, when Zephaniah sees the punishment of the non-perfected catechumens (10:9), he asks how long they are to be so punished, and is told "Until the day when the Lord will judge" (10:11). This may mean that the *Apocalypse of Zephaniah* understands that post-mortem trials are conducted by the angelic host, while the eschatological event will be presided over by God. If this is so, we would then have a parallel here to the longer recension of the *Testament of Abraham*. By setting up the divine judicial system this way, the author thus leaves room for error by developing a two-stage process. There is room for appeal, nothing is final – yet.[47]

The existence of the possibility of an appellate process that serves as a check on each divine courtroom is a crucial innovation, because it recognizes that readers may be scrutinizing these scenes and judging for themselves whether or not God is administering the universe justly and, by extension, whether God is just and fair. By adding additional steps in the judicial process, the author is attempting to anticipate and mitigate this concern. This is already implied in the *Apocalypse of Zephaniah*, but it will be explicit in the *Testament of Abraham*. The fact that authors chose

---

[46] It is possible that the author is building to something here. Perhaps later in the text, during the lacuna that appears in the description of the eschaton, these intercessions are referenced and the reader is informed about their efficacy. As it stands, though it looks like chapter 12 would include a description of the eschatological woes and likely a mention of the eschatological trial, there is no way of knowing whether the intercession theme returns.

[47] Richard Bauckham notes that "This idea of the possibility of repentance and deliverance from hell is rare in the apocalypses, but the motif of prayer for mercy for the damned, either by the righteous in paradise or by the apocalyptic seer who sees the sufferings of the wicked in hell, is common in many of the apocalyptic descriptions of visits to hell." Bauckham, *The Fate of the Dead: Studies in the Jewish and Christian Apocalypses* (Supplements to Novum Testamentum 93; Leiden: Brill, 1998), 91.

to include checks on God's procedures implies real concern about those very procedures, and an attempt to ensure the reader, the true judge of all these proceedings, that God has recognized all of the potential moments of corruption and judicial misconduct, and has taken steps to correct that very problem.

## D. Is Justice Just? The Use of the Courtroom Scenes for Philosophical Investigation

As the above discussion has demonstrated, scenes of the divine courtroom become potent media for discussion of God's justice. Two texts in particular use the divine courtroom as a locus for these issues that is more explicit than in other pieces of apocalyptic literature. These texts explicitly acknowledge the critical stance of the reader. When Uriel admonishes Ezra that "You are not a better judge than God, or wiser than the Most High" (4 Ez 7:19), one cannot fail to see the admonishment directed at the implied reader as well.[48] In the *Testament of Abraham*, the reader is taken on the most detailed tour of heaven yet, and the overwhelming number of details force the reader into a critical stance, not only at what is being presented but also at themselves and what they expect from this type of scene.

### I. 4 Ezra

One of the most prominent examples of the use of the imagery of the divine courtroom and in an explicit context of theodicy and discussion of God's justice is the pseudepigraphical work 4 Ezra. Though the work is difficult to date precisely, the most recent scholarly assessment is that the work was originally written as a result of the destruction of the Second Temple.[49] The extensive manuscript tradition is well-documented, indicating the relative popularity of this text, and revealing its multiplicity of translations, most likely from a Hebrew original. It seems that this text sparked off a wave of interest in Ezra, as evidenced by the number of literary variations of the Ezra-apocalypse tradition thought to have been inspired by this book.[50] While these texts are believed to have circulated in

---

[48] This will also be the case in the later *Apocalypse of Peter*, discussed in chapter 5.

[49] This date is reached based on historical, literary, and linguistic evidence. As Michael Stone points out, Clement of Alexandria quotes this text in the second century CE, which establishes the latest possible dating. A complete discussion of the relevant issues involved in the dating of 4 Ezra can be found in M. E. Stone, *Fourth Ezra* (Hermeneia; Minneapolis: Fortress Press, 1990).

[50] Good discussions of the varied texts and traditions surrounding Ezra in Jewish and Christian circles can be found in Robert Kraft, "'Ezra' Materials in Judaism and Christiani-

predominantly Christian communities, 4 Ezra itself stems from a Jewish milieu and is written at least in part to encourage the community after the destruction of the second temple. In particular, Philip Esler argues that the destruction of the Second Temple created a situation of intense cognitive dissonance "between the hopes which had been focused on Jerusalem and the reality of its destruction".[51] Discussing the *Sitz im Leben* of the text, Esler argues that "At its most fundamental level, the social function of 4 Ezra is to provide a mode of reducing the almost unbearable dissonance which beset the Jewish people after 70 CE to an acceptable level."[52]

Given this probable situation lying behind the book's composition, it is not surprising that one of the dominant responses themes in the book is the question of God's justice. Such a response to catastrophe is also found in Lamentations, written following the destruction of the first temple. Lamentations 2 and 4 attempt to explain why God's actions were just, placing the blame for the destruction of Jerusalem on the people and their leaders, vindicating God of any misgivings. The poems place the blame for the desolation squarely with the community, not with God.[53] This theodicy is expressed over and over again in Lamentations precisely because the natural reaction to such a catastrophe might have been to *indict* God for unjustly punishing the people. Such is the case in 4 Ezra. Though written in response to the destruction of the Second Temple, the narrative setting of the book is the wake of the destruction of the First Temple. From the very beginning of the text, the issue of God's justice is at the fore. The language of God's justice and administration of justice in a forensic context is particularly explicit. The use of the divine courtroom imagery in this context is revealing, both because of how the author employs the imagery, and how he *refrains* from employing the imagery. One of the dominant themes of 4 Ezra is the question of God's justice given the partiality of revelation and the limitations of human sight. Thus, the limited nature of Ezra's visions, including that of the divine courtroom, reveals an additional way in which imagery of the divine courtroom can be employed in narrative philosophical inquiry.

4 Ezra, a first-person narrative, begins with a grieving Ezra lying on his bed thirty years after the destruction of Jerusalem. The narrator introduces himself as "Salathiel," the Greek translation of the Hebrew Shealtiel, a fitting name for this protagonist, as it means "I asked God" or "I inquired of

---

ty," *ANRW* II.19.1, 119-136. See also the explication of Ezra's trajectory in M.E. Stone, "The Metamorphosis of Ezra: Jewish Apocalypse and Medieval Vision," *JTS* 33 (1982), 1-18.

[51]Philip Esler, "The Social Function of 4 Ezra" *JSNT* 53 (1990), 108.

[52]Esler, ' The Social Function of 4 Ezra," 114.

[53]For interpretation of each lament, see Robert Gordis, *The Song of Songs and Lamentations* (New York: Ktav, 1974).

God." This name clues the reader that this narrative is going to be all about questions. Indeed, the opening questions come fast and furious, culminating in 3:28-36:

> Then I said in my heart, Are the deeds of those who inhabit Babylon any better? Is that why she has gained dominion over Zion? For when I came here I saw ungodly deeds without number, and my soul has seen many sinners during these thirty years. And my heart failed me, for I have seen how you endure those who sin, and have spared those who act wickedly, and have destroyed your people, and have preserved your enemies, and have not shown to anyone how your way may be comprehended. Are the deeds of Babylon better than those of Zion? Or has another nation known you besides Israel? Or what tribes have so believed your covenants as these tribes of Jacob? Yet their reward has not appeared and their labor has borne no fruit. For I have traveled widely among the nations and have seen that they abound in wealth, though they are unmindful of your commandments. Now therefore weigh in a balance our iniquities and those of the inhabitants of the world; and so it will be found which way the turn of the scale will incline. When have the inhabitants of the earth not sinned in your sight? Or what nation has kept your commandments so well? You may indeed find individual men who have kept your commandments, but nations you will not find."[54]

Ezra here indicts God for what he perceives as injustices on his part, unfairly punishing Zion when Babylon is just as guilty. Very much at issue here is God's "way" (3:31). Ezra is throwing down a challenge to God: *show me* how this is just.

The language of the weighing of the soul here is explicitly forensic in nature. Ezra indicts God here for acting against the mechanisms of justice. He is convinced that if God would weigh their sins against those of the rest of the world, they would come out on top, because they have kept the commandments better than anyone. This is very similar to the use of the scales motif in the book of Job. Twice Job calls upon God to place him onto the scales, to prove his righteousness, to acquit him of wrongdoing. Job is confident that those scales would show that the anguish and torment he has experienced so outweighs any transgression that he would be acquitted and his punishment overturned. So too here Ezra believes that if God would only follow his own judicial technologies, his people would be vindicated. Michael Stone notes the forensic nature of the whole of 4 Ez 3:4-36, writing "this passage clearly formulates and sets forth in quasi-legal forms charges laid against God. A case is argued using the same techniques and forms that elsewhere are part of the indictment of Israel before the divine court. This passage is therefore better called an address

---

[54]Translation from the Latin by Bruce Metzger, *OTP* I.525-569.

or a speech or a plaint than a prayer."[55]  Karina Martin Hogan goes further, arguing that "The first lament (3:4-36) may be read as a parody of the covenant *rîb* form, since Ezra uses a selective recital of *Heilsgeschichte* (from the creation of Adam to the fall of Jerusalem to Babylon) to indict God, not Israel."[56] This would place 4 Ezra in the same trajectory as Jeremiah, who realizes that the *rîb* can be used to indict God for injustices against Israel. This sets the tone for the whole book: Ezra is indicting God on the charge of injustice, noting especially the question of God's "way," how God administers the universe justly.[57]

What follows this challenge is the appearance of the angel Uriel and a series of back-and-forths in which Uriel attempts to convince Ezra that as a human, he cannot possibly understand God's justice and way.  Hogan argues that we should take seriously the back-and-forth nature of the conversation as a debate, believing that it represents an actual debate between two schools of theology over how to interpret the catastrophic events that befell them.[58] During the initial meeting, Uriel tells Ezra that the end is approaching and that there will be "signs" of this event. Uriel describes the signs and promises Ezra more revelation as time progresses (4 Ez 5:13). After seven days Ezra begins with the questioning again, explicitly telling the angel "I strive to understand the way of the Most High and to search out part of his judgment" (4 Ez 5:34).  The angel is insistent that Ezra is not able to discern this:

He said to me, 'You cannot.' And I said, 'Why not, my Lord? Why then was I born? Or why did not my mother's womb become my grave, that I might not see the travail of Jacob and the exhaustion of the people of Israel?' He said to me, 'Count up for me those who have not yet come, and gather for me the scattered raindrops, and make the withered flowers bloom again for me; open for me the closed chambers, and bring forth for me the winds shut up in them, or show me the picture of a voice; and then I will explain to you the travail that you ask to understand.' 'O sovereign Lord,' I said, 'who is able to know these things except he whose dwelling is not with men? As for me, I am without wisdom, and how can I speak concerning the things which you have asked me?' He said to me, 'Just as you cannot do one of the things that were mentioned, so you cannot discover my judgment, or the goal of the love that I have promised my people.' (4 Ez 5:34-40)

---

[55] Stone, *Fourth Ezra*, 62. See also Egon Brandenburger, *Die Verborgenheit Gottes im Weltgeschehen: das literarische und theologische Problem des 4. Esrabuches* (Abhandlungen zur Theologie des Alten und Neuen Testaments 68; Zürich: Theologischer Verlag, 1981), 29.

[56] Karina Martin Hogan, *Theologies in Conflict in 4 Ezra: Wisdom Debate and Apocalyptic Solution* (Leiden: Brill, 2008), 103.

[57] On the "way" see M. E. Stone, "The Way of the Most High and the Injustice of God in 4 Ezra" in R. van den Broek, T. Baarda, and J. Mansfield, eds. *Knowledge of God in the Graeco-Roman World* (Leiden: Brill, 1988), 132-142.

[58] Hogan, *Theologies in Conflict*, 35-40. Hogan argues that the debate is between "covenantalized" and "eschatological" schools of Jewish wisdom.

The explicit allusion to Job 3:11 at 5:35 invites the reader to draw on the entire book of Job, with its intense and furious questioning of God and its refusal to accept personal circumstances as being justified, as an intertext intended by the author.[59] References to Job are found throughout the book.[60] Two particularly vital aspects of Job are of import. One is the imagery of the divine courtroom that dominates the book of Job, both with its narrative frame set in the divine courtroom, and in the forensic resonances throughout the poetry. Like Job, Ezra is indicting God and using known forensic elements to do so. The second is related and centers on the question of the knowability of God's ways and the partiality of revelation. In Job, this is most viscerally represented in the voice from the whirlwind (Job 40-41), in which God himself speaks – answering the charges posed against him – to put an end to the questioning. The main thrust of this address is that Job cannot possibly contend with God because he is God, and Job is not.[61] Ultimately this leaves Job no choice but to recant. Job does not receive a full revelation in this book. God never tells Job what his plans were or are, nor does he let Job know about the cosmic wager between him and the accuser that frames the poetry and is given as the reason for Job's horrible suffering. God just reminds Job that as a human he has no legal standing by which to contend against God.[62]

This is precisely what is going on in 4 Ezra. Ezra will receive revelations and visions, but the revelations are partial and only serve to emphasize the limitations of what Ezra as a human can see and understand. Only through divine intervention is Ezra able to experience any revelation at all. In the second half of the book, Ezra experiences intense revelations of di-

---

[59]There are basically two theoretical approaches to intertextuality, one focused on the *reader* (represented by theorists such as the French structuralists Julia Kristeva, Jacques Derrida, and Roland Barthes), and one focused on the *author* (such as Michael Riffattere, who is interested in particular and demonstrative relationships between texts), although Ellen van Wolde has attempted to create a third paradigm of intertextuality based on Charles Pierce's concept of iconicity, in which attention is given to both the author (as intertextual director) and reader (as intertextual selector). Here the author is clearly directing the reader to look at Job and see it as a dialogue partner.

[60]Note, for example, the clear allusions to Job in 6:49-52.

[61]God gives specific examples of his creation and power to make this case, which is clearly stated in his opening words to Job (Job 40:1-9). Likewise in the conclusion not only to this section but to all of the poetry, Job highlights the limitations of his knowledge in comparison to God's purchase (Job 42:1-6).

[62]Many scholars have found this ending to the poetry infuriating. Edwin Good sees a lot of sarcasm in the way God addresses Job, writing that "Yahweh is not merely exhibiting objectively what is there in the cosmos or showing Job the majesty and glory of the god in contrast to human frailty. The sarcasm proposes that Job is not only limited and out of his depth in trying to joust with the deity but also off limits, out of order." Edwin Good, *In Turns of Tempest* (Stanford: Stanford University Press, 1990), 345.

vine mysteries, what Hogan describes as Ezra's "religious conversion."[63] Only through these revelations is Ezra able to relinquish his attempts fully to understand God's way; the dialogue between Uriel and Ezra is not successful in bringing Ezra to this conclusion.

Uriel attempts to shows Ezra by means of questioning that he does not know anything, and simply cannot know anything. But Uriel is not successful in convincing Ezra on this point. Despite the angel's repeated remonstrations that Ezra does not have the knowledge necessary to make these kinds of contentions against God, Ezra continues to question Uriel. It is impossible not to hear Uriel's frustration with Ezra when he admonishes him: "You are not a better judge than God, or wiser than the Most High!" (4 Ez 7:19). Uriel attempts to prove this to Ezra by explaining that "God strictly commanded those who came into the world, when they came, what they should do to live, and what they should observe to avoid punishment.... They scorned his Law and denied his covenants; they have been unfaithful to his statutes and have not performed his works" (4 Ez 7:21, 24). This is followed by a description – not a vision – of the arrival of the Messiah and the day of judgment, in which "the Most High shall be revealed upon the seat of judgment, and compassion shall pass away, and patience shall be withdrawn; but judgment alone shall remain, truth shall stand, and faithfulness shall grow strong" (4 Ez 7:26). The pit of torment and place of rest will be opened, and the Most High will have words for the nations that have been raised from the dead (4 Ez 7:26-38). Uriel describes this for Ezra because he believes that Ezra needs to focus on the future judgment, when God will decide the fate of every soul.[64]

However, this is as close as Ezra gets to a vision of final judgment. An essential thing to realize is that, when Ezra receives divine revelations that enable him to move past his "crisis of faith" to a trust in God, he does *not* receive a vision of final judgment. Though Uriel is insistent that there will be a final judgment that will decide the fate of each individual, this is not communicated to Ezra in the revelations of the second half of the book. This undercuts the power of the imagery of the divine courtroom, and is significant because it invites the reader to question whether or not Uriel's vision of the divine courtroom is a satisfactory view of the justice of God. As Hogan correctly notes, part of the power of the debate between Uriel and Ezra lies in the fact that neither presents a satisfactory argument to the

---

[63] Karina Martin Hogan, *Theologies in Conflict*, 161.

[64] Hogan argues that "In his view, asking 'why?' is a misuse of the mind, which should be kept focused on the goal of one's own salvation in the final judgment.... In Uriel's view, human life is a 'contest' (4 Ez 7:127) that will be decided at the final judgment, and human understanding is useful only insofar as it enables people to make the correct moral choices that lead to victory in the contest." Hogan, *Theologies in Conflict*, 126.

other. Uriel's answers to Ezra do not succeed in convincing either him or the reader. This forces the reader to look at the traditional divine courtroom imagery in a particular light, questioning whether the vision of God's justice put forth by the divine courtroom does justice to the plans of God, and whether represents an acceptable view of God's justice, or does more damage to the image of God. In this way the reader is forced not to try God, necessarily, but to try the image of God represented by these texts. By not including an image of the divine courtroom in the revelations received by Ezra, the author is making a statement about the accuracy and the viability of such a scene.

This is all the more striking given that this is classic apocalyptic imagery both biblical and extrabiblical. If Hogan is correct, and the solutions of the author represent a form of "apocalyptic theology,"[65] it is one that is critical of traditional apocalyptic imagery. The author knows these scenes of the divine courtroom, employs their imagery and language, but does so in a specific, truncated, and mediated way that points just as much to what is *not* satisfactory, what is *not* being revealed, as to what is. This is crucial: we must pay attention to this use of the divine courtroom. It is being brought in explicitly to provide a theodicy – that ultimately God's justice will become evident and eschatologically final – but it is a theodicy that is being questioned, being "tried," not one that the audience is being asked to trust implicitly.

This is the key to understanding 4 Ezra. Scholars have long noted the lack of consistency within the text, as the arguments within the book push and pull the reader in opposite directions. It was for a long time de rigeur to attribute this to a patchwork of sources clumsily stitched together by a redactor. It was not until a penetrating article by Earl Breech in 1973 that scholars began to examine the form of the book as being inherently tied up with its content. Breech suggested that "the structure and meaning of 4 Ezra are mutually determinative" and that the entire book should be understood as following the "pattern of consolation," writing that "the form of the work is constituted by the narrative of Ezra's (*not* the author's) movement from distress to consolation, from distress occasioned by the destruction of Jerusalem to consolation by the Most High himself who reveals to the prophet, in dream visions, his end-time plans."[66] Breech took seriously the fragmentary nature of 4 Ezra as being deliberate, and proposed a holistic reading of the narrative for the first time.

In her study of 4 Ezra, Hogan made significant contributions to this discussion by arguing that the form of the text is deliberately structured to

---

[65] Hogan, *Theologies in Conflict*, 39.

[66] Earl Breech, "These Fragments I have Shored Against My Ruins: The Form and Function of 4 Ezra" *JBL* 92 (1973), 269.

make theological arguments about the limits not only of human understanding but of the sapiential approaches to the problem of theodicy. Hogan argues that the debate between Ezra and Uriel is designed to show that
neither the arguments offered by Uriel nor the charges and statements
made by Ezra are totally satisfactory. Hogan believes that the positions of
the two protagonists are meant to represent actual schools of thought regarding how to understand the destruction of the Jerusalem temple in 70
CE, and that the author wants to show that these positions are inherently
flawed and cannot put forth adequate solutions to the problem of theodicy
raised by the destruction of the Second Temple. [67] She sees the solution of
the author in the "apocalyptic theology" of the visions of the second half
of the book. According to Hogan, "the outcome of the dialogues as seen in
Ezra's lament at the beginning of the fourth lament at the beginning of the
fourth episode is purely negative, an ironic illustration of the incompatibili-
ty of the two forms of wisdom, analogous to a Socratic *aporia*. The three
apocalyptic visions fill this void with imagery that appeals to the imagination, and they succeed in consoling Ezra where Uriel's arguments failed."[68]

I agree with Hogan that 4 Ezra is structured deliberately and that it is reflecting the limits of human understanding, but I would further argue that 4
Ezra also emphasizes the weaknesses of the apocalyptic theology
represented by the visions. Rather than seeing, as Hogan does, the visions
as the "solution" put forth by the author, I would suggest that 4 Ezra demonstrates that even the solution has its own weaknesses and requires it
own leap of faith. In this way I would argue that 4 Ezra also emphasizes
the limitations of revelation itself to aid in human comprehension.
Throughout the narrative while Ezra is privy to some esoteric truths about
the universe, he is not privy to all of them. Ezra does not receive full revelations, only partial revelations. Since the back-and-forth debate of the first
half of the text is designed to force the reader really to examine the arguments being put forth, the reader carries this attitude of suspicion and critical engagement through to the visions as well. There is no doubt that the
visions are designed to show the reader the limits of the human capacity
logically to understand the universe. But the revelations that Ezra receives
are also fragmentary and partial. This, I believe, is also designed to call
into question the reliability of visionary experience as an adequate solution
to the problem. While it is presented as leading to Ezra's own "conver-

---

[67] On the one hand, Ezra represents a form of "covenantalized wisdom," which believed
strongly in God's election of Israel and the primacy of God's mercy in his dealings with his
people. On the other, Uriel represents a form of "eschatological wisdom" which argues for a
focus on individual salvation at the final judgment, the moment in which God's "way" will
become clear in the fulness of time.

[68] Hogan, *Theologies in Conflict*, 38.

sion" experience, it is not capable of bringing this experience to the dislocated reader. The reader can only feel at least partially frustrated, then, by the willingness of Ezra to give up all of his previous charges and commitments, because they cannot experience what Ezra experiences. The detailed argumentation of the first half of the book brings the reader into a critical stance that does not disappear in part two.

This itself is part of the design of the author. Throughout the narrative Ezra asserts his desire to comprehend the justice of God, and thus implicitly asserts his *ability* to comprehend that justice. The partial and sometimes contradictory natures of the visions he does receive emphasize Ezra's *inability* to comprehend fully, even with the revelations, and, more importantly, that his inability to comprehend fully *is proper and appropriate*. Thus Ezra sometimes receives visions that seem fragmentary and unsatisfactory. This is so, the author asserts, because he literally cannot see the whole picture. If we were to have a full tour of heaven and hell, a full throne room scene, a full otherworldly experience, this would thwart this authorial purpose. The author is playing on the expectations of his readers, even in the revelation section. The revelations Ezra does receive, and the juxtaposition of these revelations next to the debate, creates a sort of hermeneutical circle in which the reader is consistently frustrated. In this way Ezra finds itself like Job, seeming to assert the primacy of revelation while at the same time calling that primacy into question.

This read of 4 Ezra has the additional benefit of refuting the scholarly lament that the solutions posed by the text are not as interesting as the questions. I would argue that this text is actually quite subversive in that it seems to suggest that the standard solutions to the problem of theodicy are only partially acceptable. In other words, on one level this text upholds apocalyptic theolgoy as a proper understanding of God's "way," and determinative of the ultimate justice of God, but on another level this text rejects that answer as sufficient. The author of 4 Ezra thus highlights the connection between the partiality of revelation and Man's desire and need to justify God. No human solutions are found to be adequate, not even the human solution of putting faith in revelatory experiences.

One example of this phenomenon in 4 Ezra regards the nature of intercession. Ezra asks about the nature of intercession on the day of judgment (4 Ez 7:102), which Uriel insists will not be proper:

He answered me and said, 'Since you have found favor in my sight, I will show you this also. The day of judgment is decisive and displays to all the seal of truth. Just as now a father does not send his son, or a son his father, or a master his servant, or a friend his dearest friend, to be ill or sleep or eat or be healed in his stead, so no one shall ever pray for another on that day, neither shall anyone lay a burden on another; for then everyone shall bear his own righteousness or unrighteousness....Therefore no one will then be able to have mercy on him who has been condemned in the judgment, or to harm him who is victorious. (4 Ez 7:104-105, 115)

The angel insists on the impropriety of intercession, focusing instead on the personal responsibility of each for their own actions. Intercession is considered unacceptable because it allows individuals to be carried by another. While that was okay in the past (4 Ez 7:112), it will not be acceptable in the final reckoning. Ezra is not happy with this response and continually pleads with God to have mercy by allowing mercy on the day of judgment (4 Ez 7:132-140; 8:4). Ezra reminds the angel that the Most High is called merciful, gracious, and patient, bountiful, abundant in compassion, and giver (4 Ez 7:132-139, referencing the divine attributes of Ex 34:6). He concludes by reminding the angel that the Most High is also called judge, "because if he did not pardon those who were created by his word and blot out the multitude of their sins, there would probably be left only very few of the innumerable multitude" (4 Ez 7:140). This is a nice turn of argument here: Ezra is focusing the attention on the judge's ability *to pardon*, not the judge's ability *to sentence*. Ezra is insisting that the very nature of God's identity of judge includes the ability to pardon at will, and to set aside the criterion of judgment normally associated with judges's identities.

After the first prayer seems to go nowhere, Ezra employs a different strategy of appeal (8:4-36). While Ezra seems to understand the logic behind using observance to the law as the strict criterion for judgment, he implores God to remember how small and pitiful is humanity. For Ezra, this anthropological consideration justifies extra mercy on God's part:

For if you have desired to have pity on us, who have no works of righteousness, then you will be called merciful. For the righteous, who have many works laid up with you, shall receive their reward in consequence of their own deeds. But what is man, that you are angry with him; or what is a mortal race, that you are so bitter against it? For in truth there is no one among those who have been born who has not acted wickedly, and among those who have existed there is no one who has not transgressed. For in this, O Lord, your righteousness and goodness will be declared, when you are merciful to those who have no store of good works. (4 Ez 8:32-36)

Mercy, for Ezra, is determined by positive judgment for those who have no works of righteousness, not positive judgment for those who have stored up good deeds. The allusion to Psalm 8:4 at 4 Ezra 8:34 heightens the contrast Ezra intends between God and man.

As we have seen, many texts in this time period are especially concerned with the question of the propriety of intercession at the divine courtroom, and of negotiating the boundaries between God's justice and God's mercy. 4 Ezra clearly participates in this conversation. Ezra insists over and over again in this text that intercession should be proper, that God should allow mercy to overtake the criterion of strict justice, and that it is the very nature of Man versus God that requires this. Just as with the other topics of the debate between Uriel and Ezra, Ezra's position is not necessarily the position of the author, as Ezra's arguments are continually shut down. Ezra is told again and again that God will not be merciful on the day of judgment, and that intercession will not be allowed. Ezra does not win this argument with God. The revelations that constitute the second half of the book remind Ezra of the gulf between his perspective and that of God's, and to convince him that his views, including those on divine mercy and justice, are limited. However, the reader cannot help but remember. Ezra's argument: that this distance between Man and God *required* God to exercise extensive mercy. The insistence of the visions on the gulf only highlights Ezra's points, even if on the level of the narrative he seems to be refuted and convinced.

4 Ezra represents a particularly nuanced use of the imagery of the divine courtroom. By including a description of the divine courtroom in the debate between Uriel and Ezra, the author invites the reader to think seriously about this image, and what it is saying about God. The text is not totally dismissing the view of the divine courtroom, but rather calling the question. In the end, the text both partially accepts that this is the a valid theodicy, and subtly denies that this is so. The divine courtroom, like in the *Testament of Abraham*, becomes a vehicle for questioning God, for questioning traditional interpretations of God, for discussion of theodicy, history, and justice. Recognition of its intertexts and subtle nuances leads us more fully to appreciate 4 Ezra, with its insistence that while writers seem to package questions of theodicy nicely, that package is always threatening to irrupt.

## II. The Testament of Abraham

The most extensive divine courtroom scene in the literature from Greek Judaism is that of the *Testament of Abraham*. The text exists in two variant manuscript traditions and shows definite signs of Christian interpolation and redaction. Each of the manuscript traditions, which are discussed in detail in the recent commentary by Dale Allison,[69] has a detailed courtroom scene, though the two scenes differ greatly in terms of their content. Both recensions show a serious concern and engagement with the question God's justice, particularly in terms of the relationship between justice and mercy, and how much mercy tips the balance in favor of *injustice* rather than justice. This is coupled with an extensive engagement with the question of intercession: what room is there for intercession before God, what

---

[69] Dale Allison, *Testament of Abraham* (New York: de Gruyter, 2003).

kind of intercession is efficacious, and what is the precise effect of that intercession? However, like Lucian of Samosata, though the concerns are serious and sustained, the text is comic and possibly parodic, and reveals an author with the reflexive ability to poke fun at oneself and one's traditions while still asking and probing serious questions.

### 1. T. Abr. A: The Long Recension

In chapter nine of the longer recension, Abraham successfully bargains with God: If he is allowed to see the entire world which God has created, he will acquiesce to Death, something he has refused to do up to this point in the narrative (*T.Abr.* A 9:7-8). God agrees, and so the archangel Michael takes Abraham on a tour of the world, showing him the people of the world engaged in various acts (T. Abr. A 10:2-3). Abraham is so enraged by the bad acts, however, that he begs God to destroy the perpetrators. First he encounters robbers, and petitions God to set wild beasts upon them (A 10:6); then asks God to swallow up some fornicators (A 10:9), followed by a request to have fire come down from heaven to consume several thieves (A 10:12). At this point a voice from heaven suggests to Michael that he better stop the tour, because if Abraham was allowed to see the entire world, Abraham would not be able to refrain from calling destruction upon all of creation:

And immediately a voice came down from heaven to the Commander-in-chief, speaking thus, 'O Michael, Commander-in-chief, command the chariot to stop and turn Abraham away, lest he should see the entire inhabited world. For if he were to see all those who pass their lives in sin, he would destroy everything that exists. For behold, Abraham has not sinned and he has no mercy on sinners But I made the world, and I do not want to destroy any one of them; but I delay the death of the sinner until he should convert and live. Now conduct Abraham to the first gate of heaven, so that there he may see the judgments and the recompenses (κρίσεις καὶ ἀνταποδόσεις) and repent over the souls of the sinners which he destroyed. (*T. Abr.* A 10:12-15)

The way this is phrased is of import. Abraham's desire to punish sinners is here contrasted with God's mercy in not punishing the sinners and instead allowing them the opportunity to repent. God's ultimate authority in this manner, what distinguishes him from Abraham, is his activity in creation and thus the stake that he has in preserving life for as long as possible. Abraham's intercession is here shown to be *very* effective: every time Abraham asks God to destroy someone, God acquiesces. But the *value* of this intercession is here being called into question. Though this is a narrative fable, there is a serious comment being made here: one should not necessarily wish or call for the destruction of sinners, for that destruction leads to a complete abandonment of the possibility of salvation.

Instead, God commands Michael to bring Abraham up to the gates of heaven, so he can have better purchase on the situation. Abraham's trip to heaven is thus God's proof that Abraham's decision to have those sinners murdered was a bad one, and God's decision to let them go on sinning ultimately is more just. George Nickelsburg is correct when he notes that "the judgment scene is not intended to convey eschatological information for its own sake. It plays a crucial role within a pericope (chs. 9-14) that has an ethical, didactic function."[70] While Nickelsburg sees the didactic function as being that of correcting Abraham's "self-righteous indignation that leads him to condemn a multitude of sinners,"[71] I would argue that this goes further than mere pedagogical instruction: the function of this section of the text is to prove to Abraham, and the reader along with him, that God knows what he is doing and is just in his administration of the cosmos. This is obviously related to the ultimate framework of the story which is Abraham's refusal to set his house in order and die. His refusal is a refusal to submit to the will of God, and is thus implicit criticism of God's decisions. Abraham's cosmic tour is designed to prove to Abraham that he is incorrect on many levels.

It is in heaven where Abraham witnesses the great judgment of souls, beginning with the division of souls into two gates and the appearance of the "first-formed" (πρωτόπλαστος) Adam, weeping at the destruction of so many (*T. Abr.* A 11:1-12). This scene is a narrative illustration of the classic "two-ways" theology of Wisdom Literature and Second Temple Judaism. As G. H. McCurdy notes, this scene bears a strong resemblance to Plato's Myth of Er (*Republic* 614a-615c), in which the souls of departed are divided into two openings in the earth, with the judges sitting between them.[72] Though these are not gates per se, they are clearly portals or passageways, and therefore serve the same function as gates. The parallel only goes so far, however: an important distinction is that though Adam is sitting on a throne, associated with judicial functions in other texts, he does not seem to be performing any judicial activity here. Instead, he watches and reacts to the separation, with which he seems to have nothing to do. No information is given as to the mechanisms of separation or the criteria by which people are so separated. We are only told that one group is "righteous" and conducted through the narrow gate to Paradise (A 11:10), and

---

[70] George Nickelsburg, "Eschatology in the Testament of Abraham: A Study of the Judgment Scenes in the Two Recensions," in ibid., *Studies on the Testament of Abraham* (Septuagint and Cognate Studies 6; Missoula, MT: Scholars Press, 1976), 26.

[71] Nickelsburg, "Eschatology," 27.

[72] There are also two openings across, in which souls emerge; some from the earth, "travel-stained and dusty," and others from heaven "clean and pure" (*Rep.* 614a).

the other group is "sinners" and the broad gate "leads to destruction and eternal punishment" (A 11:11).

Following this is an extensive scene (chs. 12-14), which Michael calls the "judgment and the recompense" (A 12:15). Abraham sees two angels "of fiery appearance and pitiless mind" driving souls through a wide gate into destruction (A 12:1-2). When they follow them, they witness the following scene:

> Between the gates there stood a fearsome throne which looked like awesome crystal, flashing lightening like fire. And upon it was seated a wondrous man, looking like the sun, like a sun of God. Before him there stood a crystalline table, all of gold and byssus. Upon the table lay a book six cubits thick and ten cubits broad. On its right and its left stood two angels holding parchment and ink and pen. Before the table sat a luminous angel, holding a scale in his hand. <on> his left hand there sat a fiery angel altogether merciless and severe (ὅλος ἀνιλέως καὶ ἀπότομος), holding a trumpet in his hand, holding within t all-consuming fire for the testing of the sinners (δοκιμαστήριον τῶν ἁμαρτωλῶν). And the wondrous man who sat up the throne was himself judging and sentencing the souls. The two angels of the right and of the left were recording. The one on the right was recording the righteous deeds, the one on the left the sins, and the one who was before the table who was holding the scale was weighing the souls, and the fiery angel who was holding the fire was testing the souls. (A 12:4-14)

Michael informs Abraham that this is "judgment and recompense," and the two watch what happens to one particular soul:

> And behold, the angel who was holding the soul in his hand brought it before the judge. And the judge said to one of the angels who were attending him, 'Open this book for me and find me the sins of this soul.' And opening the book he found its sins and righteous deeds were equally balanced, and he handed it over neither to the tormentors nor to those being saved, but set it in the middle. (12:16-18)

This scene takes place entirely within the broad gate (A 12:3). In other words, this is a judgment scene of those people already adjudicated to be sinners. No one here is purely righteous; those people have been taken through the narrow gate already. What we have here is a judgment scene of one individual soul who has already received a preliminary judgment of sorts.   Several actors appear in this scene: the "wondrous man" who "judged and sentenced the souls" (A 12:11), two recording angels, a "light-bearing angel" who holds the balance, and the fiery angel who is "merci-less and relentless" (A 12:10) and examines (δοκιμάζειν) the souls with fire. This judgment scene seems to consist of several parts: the weighing, the fire-testing, and the reading of the book.   However, it is slightly ambiguous because we are not actually told that the individual soul being followed was tested by fire or weighed, rather we only see the book being read to the judge.

The scene continues with Abraham questioning Michael as to the identity of the judge and the two angels who hold the scales and fire. Abraham's questions lead to Michael's revelation of the nature of divine judgment, and this crucial passage is rich for discussion of the divine courtroom. Michael tells him that the "fearsome man" who sits on the throne is Abel, who has been given the judgment until the parousia, when there will be "perfect judgment and recompense, eternal and immutable, which no one can overrule" (A 13:4).[73] At that point, there will be further trials:

> And in the second coming they will be judged by the twelve tribes of Israel, both every breath and every creation. And third, they will be judged by God the despot of all, and then the end of that judgment is near, and the sentence is fearsome (καὶ φοβερὰ ἡ ἀπόφασις), and there is none who releases. And finally through three tribunals shall be the judgment of the cosmos and the recompense. And therefore in the end a matter shall not be secured (ἀσφαλίζεται) upon one or two witnesses, but every matter shall stand upon three witnesses. The two angels, the one on the right and the one on the left, these are those who record the sins and the righteous deeds. The one on the right records the righteous deeds and the one on the left the sins. The heliomorphic angel who holds the scale in his hand is the archangel Dokiel, the just scale-bearer (ὁ δίκαιος ζυγοστάτης), and he weighs the righteous deeds and the sins by means of the righteousness of God (ἐν δικαιοσύνῃ θεοῦ). The fiery and pitiless angel who holds fire in his hand is the archangel Puruel who has power over fire, and tests the deeds of men through fire. If the fire consumes the deeds of a certain man, immediately the angel of judgment takes him and leads him away to the place of the wicked, a most bitter correction house. But if the fire tests the act of a certain one and does not touch it, this man is justified (δικαιοῦται) and the angel of righteousness takes him and leads him up to be saved in the lot of the righteous. Therefore, most just Abraham, all in all are tested by fire and scales. (A 13:6-14)

Though this scene is far more detailed than previous depictions of the divine courtroom, antecedents of all of its components can be found elsewhere.[74] One of the most visible elements of this judgment scene is the weighing of the soul, worthy of a short excursus before returning to examination of the details of this pericope and the important role of the quote from Deuteronomy within it.

### 2. Excursus: The Weighing of the Soul

Though unique in its particular formulation and combination of motifs, this scene is part of a continuum of visual and textual imagery from the Mediterranean and Mesopotamian worlds picturing the *psychostasia*. The most obvious antecedent is that of the famous judgment of souls in the Egyptian

---

[73] Further discussion of Abel's role as judge can be found below in the analysis of Recension B.

[74] Philip Munoa has argued that the source of the imagery of the judgment scene is Daniel 7, writing that "T. Abr. 11.1-13.6 can be identified as a haggadic midrash in which the biblical text being adapted, Dan. 7.9-27, is taken as authoritative and used as the springboard for a 'new revelation' about the judgement of the dead." Philip B. Munoa III, *Four Powers in Heaven: The Interpretation of Daniel 7 in the Testament of Abraham* (JSoP Supplement Series 28; London: Sheffield, 1998), 81.

Book of the Dead, particularly the glorious illuminations of the papyrus of Ani. There, Anubis weighs each heart against the feather that symbolizes Maat, while Thoth records the balance.[75] We perhaps see an adherence to this belief of what awaits the soul after life in the discovery of small golden scales in the chamber tombs of Mycenae, adorned with butterflies, which may represent the soul.[76] The motif is not exclusive to Egypt and Greece; references to God's scales are scattered throughout the Hebrew Bible as well, particularly in the wisdom literature.[77]

To date, the most thorough investigation of this motif has been that of S. G. F. Brandon, who traced the development and analyzed the symbolic resonance of this motif from Egypt to Christendom in his 1969 article "The Weighing of the Soul," published in the Festschrift for Mircea Eliade. In this article, Brandon puts forth an analysis of this motif, particularly in classical Egypt, as representing an immediate, impartial assessment of one's individual worth and measure. Brandon writes that:

> The important factor involved in this conception would seem to be that the individual's eternal destiny would be decided by his own past actions and not by the prosecuting counsel or the judges. In other words, the verdict on a man's life would be automatically determined and, therefore, impartial and objective. By invoking such a notion, it is possible that the author of the document, mindful of the perversion of justice in this world, sought to show that the judgment after death would be immune from external interference.[78]

As Brandon traces the historical development of the weighing of the soul, he sees a change in the way the motif took shape in medieval Christian art, where the scales no longer represent an impartial assessment but are rather subject to interference and tampering. This is dramatically evidenced in the tenth century Muiredach cross, upon which there is carved a figure weighing souls while another figure, probably the devil, pulls down on one of the scale pans.[79] For Brandon, this represents a completely different under-

---

[75] Papyrus of Ani sheet 31. See the still-classic discussion by E. Wallis Budge, *The Book of the Dead: The Chapters of Coming Forth by Day* (London: Kegan Paul, Trench, Trübner & Co, LTD, 1898), xciff. See also E. Wallis Budge, *The Egyptian Heaven and Hell* (La Salle, IL: Open Court, 1974 [1925]); J. Spiegel, *Die Idee vom Totengericht in der ägyptischen Religion* (LAS 2; Glückstadt, 1935); and, more recently, J. Gwyn Griffiths, *The Divine Verdict: A Study of Divine Judgment in the Ancient Religions* (Leiden: Brill, 1991), 201ff.

[76] A. J. B. Wace, *Chamber Tombs at Mycenae* (Oxford: J. Johnson, 1932). Griffiths (*Divine Verdict*, 287) discusses these scales as part of a crucial link between Egypt and Greece.

[77] E.g., Prov 16:2, 21:2; Isa 40:15. The Nachleben of this motif can be seen in the medieval Christian "dooms" reliefs and the illustrious midrashim of the *Pesikta Rabbati*, which portray the scales of judgment on Rosh HaShanah.

[78] S. G. F. Brandon, "The Weighing of the Soul" in Joseph M. Kitagawa and Charles H. Long, eds. *Myths and Symbols: Studies in Honor of Mircea Eliade* (Chicago: University of Chicago Press, 1969), 96.

[79] Brandon, "The Weighing of the Soul," 101.

standing of the weighing of the soul, distinct from its earlier, original, meaning.

I believe that there is actually more consistency in the symbolic resonances of the weighing of the soul than Brandon has posited. In particular, I believe that Brandon has overstated the idea of the scales as automatic, impartial, and not subject to interference. While there is no doubt that in their ideal form, scales represent a means of impartial assessment, this was not the experience that people had with actual scales all the time. In fact, consistently in the art and literature there is reflected cultural anxiety over the exactness and veracity of scales and measures, an anxiety that may also be at play in the symbolic range of meaning associated with depictions of the weighing of the soul. Much like other motifs with regard to the divine courtroom, the weighing of the soul functions powerfully as a symbol or pictorial representation of this anxiety over the afterlife and its judicial system, as it perfectly captures both the ideal and the reality: the ideal, that one's life will be fairly and impartially weighed, and the reality: that in truth, we just do not know how impartial that assessment is going to be.

Already in the Egyptian texts there is a range of ways in which the representation of the weighing of the soul appears. The pictorial representations of the weighing differ one from the other, even on the level of what is being weighed against what. Most famously in the Papyrus of Ani the heart is weighed against a feather, the symbol of Maat. Other pictorial representations in the Book of the Dead contain variations of this theme. An eighteenth dynasty vignette at the beginning of chapter 30B represents the heart being weighed in one scale pan against the deceased himself, who sits in the pan opposite. The scale itself varies from image to image. In the famous image from the Papyrus of Ani, the scale consists of a central balance, above which lies a beam that holds the two scale pans, suspended from gold chains. However, in another representation of this scene from the Book of Gates, the scale differs in one very important and suggestive manner: the balance is not an inanimate piece of metal or wood, but is instead the god Thoth himself.[80] This representation is suggestive: just how impartial can a scale be, if a god is the balance? Gods in the ancient world are not usually known for their impartiality. Even more suggestive is an example from the Coffin Texts, eventually incorporated into the Book of the Dead, in which the scales are hypostasized as a monstrous deity.[81]

The existence of this type of representation of the weighing, in which a god balances the scales, or the scales *are* in some way deified, invites us to reexamine the vignette of the Papyrus of Ani. In this pictorial representa-

---

[80] Book of Gates, Division VI; discussed by Budge, *Egyptian Heaven and Hell*, 162-163.

[81] S.G. F. Brandon, "The Proleptic Aspect of the Iconography of the Egyptian 'Judgment of the Dead' *Ex Orbe Religionum* 21 (1972), 16-25, 21.

tion, Anubis, the mortuary god, kneels next to the balance of the scales, with both hands touching the scales. His left hand holds one scale pan by its chain, and the second holds a small object that is suspended from a chain on one side of the beam. The words used to describe this scene betray its interpretation. Anubis has been described as "calibrating the balance" of the scales, to ensure a fair weighing. Budge writes that Anubis is "testing the tongue of the balance."[82] Brandon describes this thus: "The plummet of the scales is carefully attended by the jackal-headed mortuary god Anubis."[83] All of these descriptions portray the actions of Anubis here in a positive light. Anubis is doing nothing more than making sure that this weighing goes off fairly and accurately. However, we should not overlook the fact that what we have here is Anubis touching the scales. And not only this, but the side he touches, the Maat side, is the side which is lower than the other, signifying a good verdict for the heart on the other side of the scale. This at least leaves open the possibility that what Anubis is doing is actually tipping the balance of the scales in favor of Ani, therefore interfering with the impartial and automatic assessment. In fact, if you look closely at those scales, you will see that the beam itself is longer on one side than the other, and not insignificantly so. Is this balance really balanced?

Whether or not scales were properly calibrated was a common concern and anxiety throughout the Mediterranean, and is also attested in the Egyptian literature. In the Book of the Dead, before and during one's journey into the Hall of Two Truths, the great Judgment Hall of Osiris, the deceased is required to recite the so-called "Negative Confession" or the "Declaration of Innocence," a form of final confession in which the deceased asserts that he has not committed a series of transgressions. In the first declaration, the confessions of the deceased include the following:

I have not caused pain to anyone.
I have not diminished the food offerings in the temples.
I have not spoiled the bread of the gods.
I have not stolen the loaves of the glorified.
I have not had sexual relations with a boy.
I have not committed a sexual act in the sanctuary of the god of my town.
I have not added to, nor diminished the corn-measure.
I have not altered the *aroura* [land-measure].
I have not falsified a half-aroura.
I have not added to the weights of the balance.
I have not warped the index of the scales.[84]

---

[82] Budge, *Book of the Dead*, XCIB.

[83] Brandon, "The Weighing of the Soul," 93.

[84] Text and Translation from S. G. F. Brandon, *The Judgment of the Dead: The Idea of Life After Death in the Major Religions* (New York: Charles Scribner's Sons, 1967), 33.

The declarations continue, and include other transgressions. It is significant that included in this list are several which involve being appropriate in transactions, specifically mentioning both ways one could interfere with proper weighing, either by using false measures themselves, or by miscalibrating the beam. These were common fears held by people in the marketplace, fears that are directly associated with the image and meaning of scales, including those scales pictured in the afterlife. Ideally, scales should be impartial and objective, but in reality, that was not always how things turned out. We must keep this in mind when looking at depictions of the weighing of the soul.

This anxiety is also felt in the Hebrew Bible. Throughout the prophetic and wisdom literature, we see evidence that the ancient Israelites and Judahites had experience with false scales and balances. This is already evident in the book of Amos. In his scathing indictment of the northern kingdom, particularly those wealthy members of the cultus, he specifically mentions one of their transgressions as their immoral business practices: "Hear this, you that trample on the needy, and bring to ruin the poor of the land, saying 'when will the new moon be over so that we may sell grain; and the sabbath, so that we may offer wheat for sale? We will make the ephah small and the shekel great and practice deceit with false balances, buying the poor for silver and the needy for a pair of sandals, and selling the sweepings of the wheat'" (Amos 8:4-6). Likewise Hosea, speaking of the sins of the northern kingdom half a century later, writes " a merchant, in whose hands are false balances, he loves to oppress" (Hosea 12:7). In addition to these prophetic critiques, several biblical authors specifically tell us that God cannot stand false weights. Proverbs 20:23 asserts that "The Lord detests differing weights, and deceitful scales are not good." Micah, in a divine oracle, asks the rhetorical question "Can I tolerate dishonest scales, with a bag of false weights" (Mic 6:11)? Deceit in business practices is seen as particularly dishonorable by the prophetic and wisdom literature; a practical and physical example of ethical and social dishonesty and immorality. The fact that this practice is repeatedly singled out does not only attest to its widespread provenance, but also to the fact that this continued to provoke great anxiety among the people, who had very little course to defend themselves against such interference.

The command to use accurate weights and measures is also given positively throughout the Hebrew Bible. Leviticus 19:35-36 combines both the negative and the positive formulation of the commandment, as part of the so-called Holiness code: "You shall not cheat in measuring length, weight, or quantity. You shall have honest balances, honest weights, an honest ephah, and an honest hin: I am YHWH your God, who brought you out of the hand of Egypt." It is significant that this commandment appears at the very end of Leviticus 19, which begins with the command to be holy, for God is holy. It is not only cultic rituals that make one holy, it is also social ethics and appropriate business practices. In the sweep of biblical literature this command appears at crucial points in Israel's history. Ezekiel, looking forward to the return to the holy land, exhorts his exiled countrymen to "use accurate scales, an accurate ephah, and an accurate bath" (Ezek 45:10). But he does not stop there; Ezekiel continues to give precise weights for the different units of measurement: the ephah, the bath, the homer, and the shekel." This attempted to rectify what was a problem throughout the Mediterranean world; the lack of standardization of currency. In Greece, for example, the weight of the drachma varied from 2.9 grams in Corinth to 6.28 grams in Aigina. It was not until the time of Solon that Athens adopted the Euboic standard for the drachma, setting a weight of about 4.25 grams of pure silver.[85] This Athenian coinage was highly sought out because it was made entirely of silver, scrupulously checked for stability, and never devalued, not even in wartime. Athens was the exception and not the norm. The lack of consistency in measurements contributed to the deep-seeded anxiety and unease about being taken advantage of in business dealings, an unease that is, perhaps, most acutely attested in the Hebrew Bible, but was no means unique to ancient Israel.

The anxiety about the scales extends not only to the fear of miscalibration or interference by humans, but there is also a sense in much of the Greek literature that it is possible also for *gods* or divine beings to interfere with scales. Often in the dramatic literature, when a character's fate is seen as unjust, it is metaphorically envisioned as divine interference in balances. One such example is from Aeschylus. In several of Aeschylus's plays characters make reference to the weighing of the scales with regard to the fates of humans and human events. In *The Persians*, his earliest surviving play, the following exchange takes place between Atossa, the Queen Mother, and the messenger who has brought her news of the battle of Salamis:

ATOSSA

Alas! The words I hear put the very crown upon our woes – a disgrace to the Persians and cause for shrill lament. But retrace thy tale and tell me clearly this: how great was the number of the ships of Hellas that gave them assurance with their armed prows to join battle with the Persian armament?

MESSENGER

Were numbers all, be well assured the barbarians would have gained the victory with their fleet. For the whole number of the ships of Hellas amounted to ten times thirty, and, apart from these, there was a chosen squadron of ten. But Xerxes, this I know, had under

---

[85] Jean Philippe Lévy, *The Economic Life of the Ancient World* (trans. John G. Biram; Chicago: University of Chicago, 1967), 25,

his command a thousand, while those excelling in speed were twice a hundred, and seven more. Such is the reckoning. Think'st thou we were outnumbered in this contest? No, it was some power divine that swayed down the scale of fortune with unequal weight and thus destroyed our host. The gods preserve the city of the goddess Pallas. (*Persians* 331-347)

Though this is clearly poetic, it does serve as evidence that it was possible to imagine that divine forces interfered with the scale of fortune. If this is so, then the scales cannot possibly be, in every circumstance, a symbol of the impartial assessment of anything, much less one's soul or heart. Likewise in Aeschylus's *The Suppliant Maidens*, the Chorus cries out to Zeus for aid:

Shriek aloud, with a cry that reaches unto heaven, strains of supplication unto the gods; and do thou, O Father, give heed that they in some wise be accomplished to my safety and tranquility. Behold deeds of violence with no kindly glance in thy just eyes! Have respect unto thy suppliants, O Zeus, omnipotent upholder of the land! For the males of the race of Egypt, intolerable in their wantonness, chase after me, a fugitive, with clamorous lewdness and seek to lay hold of me with violence. But Thine altogether is the beam of the balance, and without Thee what is there that comes to its accomplishment for mortal man? (808-824)

Zeus is here being evoked to go against what seems to be the fated course of events, and he has the power to do so because he is the beam of the balance. This recalls the Egyptian visual of Thoth as the ballast at the judgement of the dead, and reminds us that the image of the scales leaves room for the possibility of partiality. This is true even in the most basic representation of Zeus with his golden scales in the Iliad. Often times scholars who wish to assert the scales as impartial and objective will point to Homer's famous representation of Zeus balancing the fates of Hector and Achilles at *Iliad* 21.248-254, or that of the Argives and Achaia at *Iliad* 8.78-87.[86] However, what many people fail to acknowledge is that Zeus has already made his decision as to who will be victorious in the end. Indeed, at every time in the *Iliad* where Zeus raises those scales, it is at a point where he has already made up his mind as to what the future holds. The scales are not objective even on the level of the narrative, and not even to the characters *in* the narrative. Even the fighters of the *Iliad* recognize that the tip of those scales is at Zeus's will, evident by Odysseus' attempt to calm Achilles at 19.262-267: "So let your heart be swayed by what I say. Now fighting men will sicken of battle quickly: the more dead husks the bronze strews on the ground the sparser the harvest then, when

---

[86] This became visually featured on Attic vase painting. See Emily Vermule, *Aspects of Death in Greek Art and Poetry* (Sather Classical Lectures 46; Berkeley: University of California, 1979).

Zeus almighty tips his scales and the tide of battle turns – the great steward on high who rules our mortal wars."

Anxiety over scales continues to be felt through the Hellenistic and Roman worlds. We know that a special class of administrators, the *metronomoi*, were active in the Athenian agora, whose sole job it was to inspect and test scales, weights, and measures, and to provide an immediate avenue for complaint or appeal in the case of suspected malfeasance. From the evidence available it seems that the function of the *metronomoi* was passed over to the Roman *aediles* in the Roman agora.[87]

To be sure, these passages are not about the weighing of the soul, the weighing of the heart, or the weighing of one's individual deeds or merits. But by including them in the conversation, we are able more fully to appreciate the strong cultural resonances that scales provoke. Scales are a particularly provocative object in antiquity, producing both anxiety over their accuracy as well as a sense of the possibility of perfect equity and justice. What makes the scale so perfect a motif for discussions of the final judgment is that the scale both stands as a metaphor for ideal and impartial justice, and leaves room for the possibility of doubt and fear. Ultimately, everyone is holding their breath about the afterlife. The more conversation

---

[87] Strong textual evidence for the continued fear and condemnation of falsifying weights and balances is found in the rabbinic material, such as in a strong example from the midrash *Pesikta d'Rav Kahana,* commenting on the Biblical command to "remember Amalek": "R. Banai, citing R. Huna, began his discourse with the verse *A false balance is an abomination to the Lord* (Prov 11:1). And R. Banai, citing R. Huna, proceeded: When you see a generation whose measures and balances are false, you may be certain that a wicked kingdom will come to wage war against such a generation. And the proof? The verse *A false balance is an abomination to the Lord*, which is immediately followed by a verse that says, *The insolent will come and bring humiliation* (Prov 11:2). Citing R. Abba bar Kahana, R. Berechiah said: It is written, *shall I be pure (zkh) with wicked balances [and with a bag of deceitful weights]?* (Micah 6:11). How can a man ask such a question as 'shall I be pure with false balances?' and the verse itself answers: *If gemstones got through deceit are in a man's purse, he will find himself deceived.* According to R. Levi, Moses intimated to Israel that the specific consequences of not keeping honest measures and balances are to be inferred from the following four verses in Torah, beginning with these two: *You shall not have in your pouch diverse weights, a great and a small. You shall not have in your house diverse measures, a great and a small* (Deut 25:13-14). If you do have diverse weights and measures, know that a wicked kingdom will come and wage war against your generation. And the proof? The third verse: *All that do such things...are an abomination unto the Lord your God* (Deut 25:16). What warning against the abomination of using false measures and balances follows in the fourth verse? *Remember what Amalek did unto you* (Deut 25:17)." Here, using classic Rabbinic hermeneutical techniques, they find biblical support for the connection of the injunction to remember Amalek, the nation of their destruction, with the specific command to be honest with weights and measures, even going so far as to argue that when a generation uses false measures and balances, it is a sign that that generation will be destroyed. Examples of this kind of strong condemnation of this particular transgression are found throughout the rabbinic literature, continuing the strong preoccupation or cultural interest in this topic.

emerges about how just that final judgment will be, the more we realize how much doubt and fear there is about final judgment, even for those who believe they have led a fair and balanced life. The use of the scales in literary and visual representations of final judgment, therefore, both assure their audience of the faithfulness and trustworthiness of God while still leaving room for the human reality of doubt and unconfidence which goes along with trusting in a divine plan and in an all-powerful God; a God who *could* interfere with those scales should he so desire, whether it be by lifting one's bad deeds out of the scale-pans, or using impartial scales to begin with.

Returning to the *Testament of Abraham,* close examination reveals that the author is well aware of the anxiety over the scales. Dokiel is specifically called the "just scale-bearer," ὁ δίκαιος ζυγοστάτης (A 13:10). The addition of the predicative adjective δίκαιος attempts to ensure the reader that this scale is quite literally in good hands. Second, Michael tells Abraham that Dokiel weighs the deeds "by means of the righteousness of God," (13:10). This additionally reaffirms that Dokiel's weighing technique is proper, as its means is that of God himself. This double affirmation of Dokiel's proper weighing technique is evidence that the author expected at least some of his readers to have skeptical if not dubious reactions to the presence of scales in this judgment scene. This piling on of assurances regarding the scales' reliability is coupled with the fact that the scales are not the only means of adjudication in this scene. Indeed, the scales are combined with the fire-testing trumpet and the reading of the book. The author has gone out of his way to insist that even if by some means the scales are compromised, there are two additional steps to this trial which will act as checks against any mistakes, whether intended or unintended.[88]

But this is not the only way in which the author makes this claim. In addition to describing this three-fold trial procedure, the author insists that this is not the *only trial.* Instead, the author makes it clear that this is only one of *three* trials that will determine the soul's ultimate fate. First is this trial, presided over by Abel, and then a trial presided by the twelve tribes of Israel, and then finally the ultimate trial run by God himself. Michael tells Abraham that "finally through three tribunals (βημάτων) shall be the

---

[88] The name Dokiel may itself be an additional nudge in this direction, since there is no evidence for an angelic figure with this name outside of the Testament of Abraham. While G. H. Box suggests that the name derives from the Hebrew דוק, meaning "to examine," Francis Schmidt argues that Δοκιήλ should be understood as שרקאל, equated with צדק אל, God's justice. Schmidt points to an Egyptian engraving of the name SATQVIEL next to an image of Anubis as evidence for this read as well as for the association with Anubis, the soul-weigher in Egyptian tradition. If either of these explanations is correct, an additional "proof" of the justice of this activity is packed in to the name Dokiel itself. For other possibilities, see Allison, *Testament,* 289.

judgment of the cosmos and the recompense. And therefore in the end a matter shall not be sealed (ἀσφαλίζεται) upon one or two witnesses, but 'every matter shall stand upon three witnesses'" (A 13:8). The end of this sentence is a near quotation of LXX Deuteronomy 19:15, and adds a crucial new dimension to the presentation of the divine trial, in which each trial itself witnesses not only to the sins or righteousness of each individual, but to *the validity of the decision reached by each tribunal.* The trials themselves thus become evidence for God's proper sealing of everyone's fate, and indeed for God's justice itself.

On the level of the narrative, Michael, at God's behest, is trying to convince Abraham that the divine judicial system operates well, and his idea of "justice," calling down immediate punishment on sinners on earth without trial or sentencing, is indeed unjust, or at least not appropriate for God's cosmic plan. The viewing of the "judgment and the recompense" is designed to prove that God is just in his dealings with the world – including in God's decision that it is time for Abraham to die. But beyond the pure narrative level, this insistence that the heavily described tribunal, with its three-part procedure, is only one of three trials that secure the fate of an individual, is designed to convince the reader that the system designed by God is proper, just, and foolproof, with built in checks to secure against a false verdict or misconduct of any sort. In this way, the entire text is set up to persuade the reader that God's courtroom is a proper one, and thus that God himself, the "despot of all," is a just God, beyond reproach.

The piling on of checkpoints, the insistence of even more trials beyond this one conducted by Abel, almost falls into the category of "me doth protest too much." The author is going out of his way to insist on God's justice. This amplification of checkpoints to the point of superfluity may be additional evidence that the Testament of Abraham should be read as parodic.[89] It is certainly comic – the sheer length of the description of this tribunal, with each step in the trial followed by another and another, has comic potential, possibly parodying both the extensive post-mortem procedures described in the Egyptian material and in the numerous motifs found in the Jewish (and then Christian) texts.[90] Not just scales, but scales and a trumpet. And not just scales and a trumpet, but also a book. And not just scales, trumpet, and a book, but the whole process is repeated twice more. The emphasis on the redundancy of the motifs as found in the tradi-

---

[89] Many Egyptian texts have a combination of the motifs of the confession in the hall of truths with the *psychostasia.* Allison calls this a "redundancy" (Allison, *Testament of Abraham,* 256). For discussion, see S. G. F. Brandon, *The Judgment of the Dead,* 31-42.

[90] Allison gives extensive references for parallels to each judgment motif. See Allison, *Testament of Abraham,* 256-293.

tional material adds to the comedy – perhaps one's entire afterlife is spent in the judicial system!

It has long been noted that the *Testament of Abraham* is funny. Nickelsburg believes that the *Testament of Abraham* is a parody of the character of Abraham as he appears in the patriarchal narratives of Genesis. Nickelsburg writes that "the author has composed a startling portrait of Abraham. Although he ascribes to the patriarch some of the virtues traditionally attributed to him (righteousness, hospitality), the author has glaringly omitted the most celebrated of these, viz., Abraham's obedient faith. Instead, he has created a veritable parody on the biblical and traditional Abraham. He fears God's summons to 'go forth' (cf. *T. Abr.* 1 and Gen 12:1), and his haggling with God takes on the character of disobedience."[91] Additionally, Nickelsburg points to Abraham's propensity in the *Testament of Abraham* to call down punishment on individuals without mercy or second thought, a portrayal opposite to the Abraham who argues with God over the fate of Sodom and Gomorrah.[92] Recently, Jared Ludlow has challenged the classification of the *Testament of Abraham* as a parody of the biblical character of Abraham. Ludlow argues that "classifying the *Testament of Abraham* as a parody of Abraham may not be the best genre classification since it does not technically parody the traditional biblical account of Abraham."[93] Instead, Ludlow argues that the *Testament of Abraham* is a parody of testamentary literature, particularly Recension A, in which Michael repeatedly tells Abraham to set his house in order (i.e., prepare a testament), and yet the testament never comes. Ludlow sees this at work in Recension B as well, though not to the same extent. Ludlow explains that "both recensions excluded any testament by Abraham, yet both included direct commands by a messenger from God for Abraham to make one. Recension A obviously plays with the reader's expectation of a testament much more by setting up several perfect testamentary situations only to have Abraham refuse; yet even Recension B, which lacks many of Recension A's humorous touches and stubborn characterization of Abraham, leaves the reader's expectation of a testament unsatisfied."[94]

I concur with Ludlow that the *Testament of Abraham* plays on the expectation of the reader with regard to the conventions of a testament, and that this adds to the humor of the text. Whether or not we should understand the entire text as a parody of the testamentary genre is another story,

---

[91] George Nickelsburg, "Structure and Message in the Testament of Abraham," in ibid., ed. *Studies on the Testament of Abraham* (Septuagint and Cognate Studies 6; Missoula, MT: Scholars Press, 1976), 87.

[92] This aspect is also highlighted by Allison, *Testament of Abraham*, 51.

[93] Jared Ludlow, *Abraham Meets Death: Narrative Humor in the Testament of Abraham* (JsoP Supplement Series 41; London: Sheffield Academic, 2002), 13.

[94] Ludlow, *Abraham Meets Death*, 27.

particularly since the formal elements of a testament, including first-person narration and ethical exhortation, are not present in the *Testament of Abraham*. What we probably have instead is an entertaining text that pokes fun at many different literary conventions, as well as shining a different light on a much beloved and serious traditional character. In this way the humor of the *Testament of Abraham* is similar to that of Lucian, who also plays on the traditionality of classical characters and conventions in innovative ways.

However, with regard to the judgment scene of Recension A, I find Ludlow's read lacking. Ludlow seems to believe that we should not take any part of the scene at face value. In particular, Ludlow takes issue with Munoa's read of the judgment scene of Recension A:

> Phil Munoa's reading of Adam's role in the *Testament of Abraham*'s judgment setting focused on Adam's 'terrifying' appearance, as Munoa conveniently elided Adam's exaggerated weeping and laughing at the fate of the souls. Thus Munoa has taken Adam's description as a didactic piece with parallels to other terrifying appearances of Adam in the book of Daniel. But this episode seems to be very comical with Adam repeatedly falling off his throne and tearing the hair of his head and beard. If it is comical, can we accept its description of the heavenly setting at face value as indicative of their religious thought, or would that lead us astray since its intention may not have been to give a true rendering of the setting, but simply to have fun with the figure of Adam? It would seem that the presence of comic elements in a text should raise a warning about taking too literally the presentation before the reader.[95]

This is problematic. Ludlow believes that because the Testament of Abraham has exaggerated the portrait of Adam, we should not understand anything resembling "true rendering" in the intentions of the author. First, Ludlow is exaggerating the comedy of this moment. Contrary to the impression given by Ludlow, the author does not highlight Adam's "repeated" falling and getting up. Instead, in two verses we are told that "when the wondrous one who was seated on the throne of gold saw few entering through the strait gate, but many entering through the broad gate, immediately that wondrous man tore the hair of his head and the beard of his cheeks, and he threw himself on the ground from his throne crying and wailing. And when he saw many souls entering through the strait gate, then he arose from the earth and sat on his throne, very cheerfully rejoicing and exulting" (*T. Abr.* A 11:6-7). If the author wanted to hit a comic note in this passage, he could have had Adam fall down, get up, fall down, and get up again. Then Ludlow's read would have more validity. Instead, what we have here seems just to be a description of Adam taking on a traditional

---

[95] Ludlow, *Abraham Meets Death*, 45.

role of weeping and rejoicing over the fate of souls,[96] much as indicated by Munoa.

Second, the presence of comic elements in a scene does not necessarily mean that there is nothing serious intended by the author. There is a message behind the judgment scene of the *Testament of Abraham*, which is twofold. First, it is trying to convince the reader that God's justice is perfect and operational, and second, it is trying to make the audience realize that *they require convincing on this point*, i.e. that traditional understandings of the divine courtroom contain within them inherent contradictions and complexities about which people need to be self-reflexive. The piling on of different courtroom images into one very extended and seemingly never-ending trial process reminds people that their attempts to portray afterlife judicial procedures are only attempts, built on very human ideas about justice, and that these attempts themselves ask serious questions about God's justice that need to be answered. This is a serious message, even if it is comic in its execution. Yet the author is not challenging the *validity* or the potential truth of any one of these symbols or images. There is nothing inherently comic in the book, the trumpet, or the scales. It is the combining of the motifs together that gently pokes fun at traditional renderings of the divine courtroom.[97]

Ludlow seems to approach this when he discusses the judgment scene as being structured according to "problems" and "solutions." For every problem encountered, a solution is presented.[98] But what he does not seem to articulate is that it is fact that the solutions are so perfect that makes the comedy – as if the whole world was a logical puzzle that the author is sorting out. The perfection of the solutions creates, I believe, a mutual understanding between author and reader that the problems themselves stem from a hyperliteral and very human understanding of the divine. The solutions thus invite the reader to take another look at the *problems*. And one of those problems that the author is pointing to, is that every depiction of

---

[96] See, for example, *Apoc. Zeph* 3:1-9, where angels alternatively weep and rejoice over the fate of the souls. Allison also points to the actions of Mary in *Prot. Jas.* 17:2 and Ps.-Mt. 13. cf. Allison, *Testament of Abraham*, 248.

[97] Nickelsburg takes an entirely different approach to the issue of the superfluity of motifs, seeing the multiplicity as being a result of a Jewish core having been "fleshed out with detail from a comparable Egyptian piece." (Nickelsburg, "Eschatology in the Testament of Abraham: A Study of the Judgment Scenes in the Two Recensions", *Studies on the Testament of Abraham*, 39). He posits five stages of textual development that produced recension A (46). Nickelsburg's historical approach, while illuminating certain aspects of the tradition, especially the choice to follow one soul through the judgment process, does not attempt to take a step back and examine the potential purpose of the combination of motifs as the text has been handed down. Instead, the historical approach posits the text almost as a repository of tradition rather than a product with literary goals and purposes.

[98] Ludlow, 134ff.

the divine courtroom contains within it inherent issues when applied to God. By adding the detail about the expected three tribunals, and quoting Deuteronomy 19 as evidence for God, the author is attempting to make the reader realize that traditional portrayals of the divine courtroom are attempts to justify *God*. By showing them his perfect justification, his solution, he is reminding them of the problem. In this way the comedy of the *Testament of Abraham* is effective because it makes the reader take another look at themselves even though they are not center stage in the dramatic action. Perhaps the *Testament of Abraham*, like the writings of Lucian, should be described as σπευδογελἀιος, seriocomic.[99]

The comedy of Recension A takes somewhat of a backseat in the next scene (14:1-15). After Michael explains the judicial process with all of its intricate steps, Abraham asks Michael what will happen to the soul whose initial trial he had witnessed (14:1). When he learns that all that is required to be saved is one more righteous deed, Abraham implores Michael to pray with him on behalf of the soul. When his prayer is granted, Abraham proceeds to glorify God, and to beg God to show the same mercy to the sinners for whom he was previously responsible for condemning:

> Abraham said to the Commander-in-chief, "I beg you, archangel, listen to my plea, and let us again call upon the Lord, and let us prostrate ourselves for his pity. And let us entreat his mercy for the souls of the sinners whom I, once despising, destroyed, those whom, because of my words, the earth formerly swallowed, and the wild beasts rent in two, and the fire formerly consumed. Now I know that I sinned before God. Come, Michael, Commander-in-chief of the upper powers, come let us beg God with earnestness and many tears, that he might forgive me my sin and grant them absolution." And immediately the Commander-in-chief hearkened to him and they prayed before the Lord God. After they called upon the Lord for a long while, a voice from heaven cam saying: "Abraham, Abraham, the Lord has heard your prayer and your sins are forgiven. And those you earlier thought I had destroyed, I have recalled them and brought them unto eternal life on account of my utter goodness. But for a time I repaid them with judgment, but those I requite while they live on the earth, I will not requite in death." (14:10-15)

There is really nothing funny about this scene. Instead, this scene concentrates on the efficacy of intercession: Abraham's prayer is enough to tip the balance in favor of righteousness and literally save a soul from punishment. Unlike in the marketplace, when scales are used to balance one object against another, these scales must be tipped in favor of righteous deeds in order for the soul to receive a positive verdict. This balance cannot be balanced if the soul is to be saved. But due to Abraham's prayer, the soul merits salvation and immediately disappears to paradise. There is no mention, as in 4 Ezra, of any moment in which intercession will not be permitted. This text points instead to the necessity of human intercession

---

[99]For discussion, see R. Bracht Branham, *Unruly Eloquence: Lucian and the Comedy of Traditions* (Cambridge: HUP, 1989).

to ensure good outcomes for those on the fence. Not for those whose balance is already far tipped, but for those who are really on the brink of salvation.[100] Likewise this passage shows the efficacy of all prayer, reminding us of how efficacious was Abraham's original prayer that called down fire and brimstone on the earthly sinners. This scene thus ties up Abraham's journey to heaven by having Abraham realize his mistake and repent for it. From now on Abraham will submit to God's will and set his house in order to prepare for death – or so we believe at this point.[101]

The last line of this chapter has received some attention because it seems to suggest that those who die violently escape the described judgment, because they paid for their sins in life. Allison suggests that this idea "harmonizes with the rabbinic notion that suffering and death may atone and allow entrance into the world to come."[102] Anitra Bingham Kolenkow has argued that the *Testament of Abraham* has presented Abraham's calling down punishment as a "new sin," the sin of "wanting to destroy sinners."[103] Kolenkow reads God's statement here as suggesting that those who would call down punishment to destroy sinners are actually *saving* them, since their sin would thus have been requited on earth. As Kolenkow writes, "the reader would be shocked and yet agree – recognizing that the common desire to catch a sinner in his sins (so that the sinner would immediately go to judgment) might mean that one would save sinners from dire punishment in the judgment. God has arranged his salvation so that those who destroy sinners are really saving them."[104] This, Kolenkow believes, undercuts the boasts of Death in chapters 17 and 19.[105] It should be noted, though, that if this is what God is saying to Abraham, then the *Testament of Abraham*'s theology paints an awful picture of God, a God who would desire to punish people after death rather than punishing people in life. This would also completely contradict God's earlier words to Abraham in 10:14, when God says that he does not want to destroy anyone, and would rather wait until the sinner "turns and lives." Rather, we should be more cautious in our reading of 14:15, understanding instead that God is

---

[100] Later rabbinic parallels suggest that when the righteous and evil deeds of a person are balanced, God himself inclines the scale towards righteousness, eiher by removing a bad deed or by God's grace. cf. *b. Rosh HaShanah* 17a, *y. Qiddushin* 1:10, *y. Sanhedrin* 10:1.

[101] The comedy continues as Abraham still refuses to follow Michael in chapter 15, despite his heavenly journey.

[102] Allison, *Testament of Abraham*, 306. Allison points to *Mekh.* on Ex 20:20, *Sifre Deut* 32, *b. Berakhot* 5a, and 2 Bar 78:6 in support of this position.

[103] Anitra Bingham Kolenkow, "The Genre Testament and the Testament of Abraham," *Studies on the Testament of Abraham*, 143.

[104] Kolenkow, "The Genre Testament," 144.

[105] Allison basically concurs with Kolenkow, saying that "if those who die violently are not condemned at the judgment, then the horror of chaps. 17 and 19 is shown to be without substance." Allison, *Testament of Abraham*, 306.

promising Abraham ultimate equity, and reassuring Abraham that his hasty words have not led to eternal punishment. Instead, when God – not Abraham – decides to requite someone on earth, that decision is well thought out, and means that God has already planned not to requite them again later. Unlike Abraham, who gave no thought to the consequences of his actions, God makes decisions in a just manner following a well-thought out – if not redundant – cosmic plan.

*3. Recension B*

The judgment scene of the shorter recension (Recension B) differs significantly from that of Recension A, not just in terms of length. The situation which prompts the heavenly journey in Recension A, Abraham's calling down punishment on the sinners he witnesses in his katascopy, exists in Recension B, but not until *after* Abraham's cosmic tour. It does not, therefore, represent the cause for Abraham's cosmic tour, as it does in Recension A. Instead, in Recension B the only reason given for Abraham's cosmic tour is a request by Abraham. When Michael tells Abraham to make a testament (B 7:18), Abraham replies to Michael, "I beg you, Lord, if I am to go out of the body, I would like to be lifted up so that, before I am carried away, I might see all the creation which the Lord created in heaven and on earth" (B 7:19). Michael then relays the request to God, who honors Abraham's request. This significantly changes the effect of the judgment scene which follows, as it no longer has a major didactic and ethical purpose to prove to Abraham that he is in the wrong (and, consequently, that God is in the right). The stated purpose of the tour, then, is just "seeing," not "seeing and learning," and indeed the reader will see that Abraham learns very little on his cosmic tour.

Just as in Recension A, Abraham first witnesses Adam sitting on a throne between the two gates, and asks after the identity of the man (B 8:3-16). However, Recension B milks the moment for comedy, as Abraham frets over his inability to fit through the narrow gate: "And Abraham said to Michael, 'is it the case then that the one unable to enter through the narrow gate is unable to enter into life?' Michael said to him, 'Yes.' Abraham cried out saying, 'Woe to me! What will I do? For I am a man of broad girth, and I will be unable to enter into the narrow gate, because only a child of about ten would be unable to enter through it'" (B 9:1-3). Michael has to reassure Abraham that all holy people will be able to fit through the gate. This pokes fun at Abraham because of his inability to get the symbolism of the gates, and it takes a shot at the hyperliteral interpretation of the tradition: these are not necessarily real gates, they are metaphorical gates. It's a pretty funny take on the two-ways tradition, taking the narrow/broad dichotomy to an extreme hyperliteral degree.

Abraham then sees an angel driving thousands of sinners away, and asks Michael if they are all going to destruction. Michael says yes, but suggests that they look to see if maybe they could find one righteous among them. Though they cannot, they find one whose sins and deeds are equally balanced (B 9:8). Unlike Recension A, which has a full description of the weighing process, Recension B only alludes here to this motif by saying the angel had found the soul's sins and good deads balanced. The fate of this soul is thus the motif which carries through to the trial scene, as Abraham wants to see what will happen to this soul next (B 9:11).

The trial scene that follows is far more detailed in its description of the verbal aspects of the courtroom than that of Recension A. While Recension A seemed to be more interested in the scales, trumpet, and books, Recension B is interested in the trial procedure, and the roles of all of the actors therein:

When he arrived at the place where the judge was, an angel came and handed over to the judge that soul which the angel held in his hand. And he heard the soul crying out, "Have mercy on me, Lord." The judge said to him, "How can I show mercy to you when you did not show mercy to your daughter? But you rose up against the fruit of your womb and you murdered her." And the soul answered and said, " I did not commit murder, but she spoke falsely against me." The judge commanded the one who writes down the record to come. And behold, there were Cherubim bearing two books, and with them was a man, exceedingly great, who had three crowns on his head. And one was higher than the other crowns. These are called witnesses. And the man had in his hand a golden reed. And the judge said to him, "Exhibit the sin of this soul." And the man opened up one of the two books with the Cherubim and looked up the sin of the soul. And the man answered and said, "O wretched soul, how can you say thàt you have not committed murder? Did you not, upon the death of your husband, go forth and commit adultery with the husband of your daughter, and then kill your daughter?" And he spoke to her in that hour of the other sins that she had committed. Hearing these things, the soul opened her mouth and cried and said, "Alas, because all the sins that I committed while I was in the world, I had forgotten. But here they are not forgotten." Then the servants of wrath took her and tortured her." (B 10:2-16).

Again, the comedy is emphasized here. This is the soul whose sins were *equal* to her good deeds, which seems ridiculous given that her evil deeds include *murder*. What did she do that was so good that it balanced this out enough for her to warrant this tribunal? Also, the extremity of the sin makes the fact that she "forgot" about it all the more funny. The description of this scene amplifies the straightforwardness of this case, and of the tribunal. This is not nuanced or requiring sophisticated judicial ability; this case is open and shut. The defendant pleads not guilty, the crime is found in the book, the defendant claims to have forgotten committing the crime, and she is sentenced to punishment.[106] Every one has a clearly delineated role – the judge is separate from the witnesses, and not just one but three witnesses are there to present testimony. There does not seem to be a prosecuting or a defending angel, as in the *Apocalypse of Zephaniah* and as there will be in later rabbinic literature; if anyone is bringing the case against this soul, it is the pre-trial procedure in which the deeds were perfectly balanced against the sins.

Just as in Recension A, Abraham here desires Michael to explain to him exactly what is going on and who the actors are in the trial. Michael identifies three figures, Abel (the judge), Enoch (the exhibitor of evidence), and the Lord (the sentencer). Abel's role in essentially the same as that in Recension A, as judge over this sentencing process. Most commentators agree that Abel's role developed out of an interpretation of Genesis 4:10. In *1 Enoch* 22:5-7, discussed above, this is understood in a forensic context, as Abel becomes the one who brings suit not only against Cain but also against his descendents. Here in recension B no real reason is given for the choice of Abel; Michael simply calls him the "first martyr" and tells Abraham he was brought here to judge. In some way the author of this recension thought that Abel's status as the first martyr was enough to justify this selection. Allison suggests that this is a parallel to Egyptian tradition, in which Osiris, the judge of the underworld, was the first martyr, who also died at the hands of his brother.[107] Recension A has more explanation, though it is enigmatic. The *archistrategos* explains that Abel "sits here to judge all the creation, and he carefully examines the righteous and sinners, for God said, 'I do not judge you, but every person will be judged by a person'....Every person has arisen from the first-formed, and because of this, each will first be judged by his son" (A 13:3-5). Munoa suggests that the cause for Abel's selection is an understood equation of "son of Adam" with the "one like a son of man" in Daniel 7:13, who has a forensic role in the divine courtroom.[108] However, it should be noted that it is not the "one like a son of man" who has a *judicial* role in Daniel's courtroom, so this is not totally satisfactory; we would have to understand a figure more like the son of man in *1 Enoch* 46 and 49, or a merging of the two.

The source of the quote that the *archistrategos* offers here is unknown. Recently, Jan Dochhorn has suggested that "This information can only be considered an explanation of Abel's role if it points to a subtext, which in

---

[106] This is what *should* have happened in the *Apocolocyntosis* – if the system had been functioning properly!

[107] Allison, *Testament*, 281. Cf. Danielle Ellul, "Le Testament d'Abraham: Mémoire et source d'imaginaire, la pesée des âmes," *FoiVie* 89 (1990), 73-82.

[108] Munoa, *Four Powers*, 34ff.

turn explains why Abel, and no one else, judges the dead."[109] Dochhorn believes that this subtext can be identified "with a high degree of certainty" as Genesis 9:6:

> Whoever sheds the blood of a human, for this human shall the person's blood be shed.« In this text God himself speaks – as he does in *T. Ab.* A 13:3b, and the text can be read as an etiology of the human legal system. It thus corresponds well with *T. Ab.* A 13:3, which is also concerned with the origins of judgment passed by a human. And this text can indeed explain why Abel is the judge in *T. Ab.* A 13:6. It mentions the shedding of blood, and the blood theme is central to the story of Abel, especially in Gen 4:10 where God says that Abel's blood cries to him from the earth. As was common in the narrative-exegesis typical of early Judaism, the author of *T. Ab.* 13:2-3 interpreted this link between Gen 9:6a and Gen 4:10 as evidence that Abel also plays a role of Gen 9:6a.[110]

This seems far from certain, and highly speculative. An alternative explanation is put forth by Allison, who points out that a contributing factor may be that early Christian authors who redacted the *Testament of Abraham* saw Abel as a Christ figure, and therefore may have seen Abel filling a Christ-like judicial role here as prescribed by the New Testament (see following chapter). Obviously given the pseudepigraphic setting of the *Testament of Abraham*, Jesus would be an unlikely figure for Abraham to encounter in heaven, so it may be that the author wanted the audience to understand Abel as a stand in for Christ.[111] In any case, we must recognize, in the words of Allison, that "which one of these explanations, or which combination of them, is right, or whether the truth lies elsewhere, remains beyond recovery."[112] It seems clear that the presence of Abel in *1 Enoch* plays a significant role in the appearance of Abel in apocalyptic texts, but the exact reasons the author chose to put Abel in this role remain unknown.

Enoch is the second figure identified in Recension B, as the exhibitor of evidence (B 11:3). Michael identifies Enoch as the "teacher of heaven and the scribe of righteousness" (B 11:3). The title "scribe of righteousness" is also attested in *1 Enoch* 12:4, when Enoch is given his charge to go to the Watchers. Birger Pearson argues that this Enochic epithet was especially prominent in Egypt.[113] Abraham challenges Enoch's qualifications to play

---

[109] Jan Dochhorn, "Abel and the Three Stages of Postmortal Judgement: A Text-Critical and Redaction-Critical Study of the Christian Elements in *Testament of Abraham* A 13:2-8" in Ian H. Henderson and Gerbern S. Oegema, eds. *The Changing Face of Judaism, Christianity, and Other Greco-Roman Religions in Antiquity* (Munich: Gütersloher Verlagshaus, 2006), 398-415, 413.

[110] Dochhorn, "Abel," 413.

[111] For discussion, see Allison, *Testament of Abraham*, 282.

[112] Allison, *Testament of Abraham*, 282.

[113] Birger Pearson, "Enoch in Egypt," in Randall A. Argall, Beverly A. Bow, and Rodney Werline, eds. *For a Later Generation: The Transformation of Tradition in Israel, Early Judiasm, and Early Christianity* (Harrisburg, PA: Trinity Press, 2000), 216-231.

such an important role in the trial, given that Enoch never died.[114] Michael
here goes out of his way to insist that Enoch's role is just, explaining to
Abraham that he would be correct in his objection if Enoch were the one
who passes sentence, but Enoch is only the recorder of the sentence – God
is the one who passes the sentence (B 11:6-7). In addition, Michael tells
Abraham that this is by design, because Enoch prayed to God not to be the
one who passes sentence (B 11:8), and God acquiesced and agreed to give
Enoch the high sign to record the sins (B 11:9-11). This removes the onus
from Enoch, and downplays his role in the trial, ensuring Abraham and the
reader that this is just despite Enoch's lack of having gone through the
process himself.

But why? What has prompted such a passage? That this is given so
much attention seems to suggest that there was concern that Enoch was not
an appropriate actor in the trial, and that the author is trying to convince
the reader that these concerns are moot. In an earlier article, Pearson points
to the similarities between Recension B and the fragments of a Coptic
Enoch Apocryphon.[115] In this text, concern is expressed that Enoch may
be "too harsh in his score-keeping."[116] In particular, Enoch is admonished
not to be too quick to write down sins (fol 7v).[117] This may reflect a tradition in which Enoch, perhaps like Abraham in Recension A, is quick to
jump to judgment and needs to be reminded to temper strict justice and the
urge for punishment with mercy. Especially if Enoch himself never had to
experience the judgment, and does not know what it is like to go through
the process of weighing and trying, he may not understand the role that
mercy and compassion must play when determining the fate of human
souls. Both of these texts may reflect an important tradition here related to
the figure of Enoch and his role in the divine courtroom.

But the concern over Enoch is not only a concern about Enoch, it is really a concern over whether or not the entire process is corrupt, or at least
has serious weaknesses. Recension B, which lacks the "over-the-top" qual-

---

[114] The way in which the question is framed is suggestive. Abraham asks how Enoch "is
able to weigh the lot of every soul (βαστάσαι τὸ βάρος τῶν ψυξῶν)," a seeming allusion to
the *psychostasia*, although no description of such weighing is found in this recension. Earlier,
there also seemed to be a similar allusion, when the soul's sins were found to be "of equal
weight (ἰσοζυγούσας)" to her works (9:8). Those scholars who take Recension B as prior to
Recension A believe these metaphors are the source of the elaborate description of Recension
B. See especially Schmidt, *Testament* II, 132. The opposite view is taken by Nickelsburg,
"Eschatology," 56ff.

[115] Birger Pearson, "The Pierpont Morgan Fragments of a Coptic Enoch Apocryphon,"
*Studies on the Testament of Abraham*, 227-284.

[116] Pearson, "Pierpont Morgan Fragments," 236.

[117] Another important parallel that Pearson notes is that this text has an elaborate depiction
of the *psychostasia*, in which, if the scale pans are equal, Michael puts his rod down to tip the
balance in favor of the soul (fol 7v).

ity of Recension A, attempts to address this concern seriously. The author here is attempting to convince the reader not only that Enoch is qualified in his (limited) role in the courtroom, but that *God* has established a fair process that can be trusted to bring the appropriate results. In this way Recensions A and B are in agreement in terms of one of their ultimate goals, though they accomplish them in different ways.

It is only here at this point in Recension B that Abraham is taken on a tour of the cosmos, where he witnesses humans committing sins and calls down punishment against them (B 12:1-13). That this activity comes *after* the heavenly tour and not before, as in Recension A, highlights that Abraham learned nothing from his heavenly tour. While in Recension A the tour is prompted by Abraham's lack of mercy or trust in God's ultimate plan to deal with sinners, here in Recension B Abraham sees just how hard afterlife judgment is, and yet he still sends people to their deaths immediately. This certainly paints a more ruthless picture of Abraham than in Recension A.

The judgment scene of Recension B paints a picture different in its details than Recension A, but both texts use the divine courtroom scene as a way to make arguments to the reader about the possibility of divine justice and the need to temper justice with mercy. In Recension A, Abraham is taught a lesson, as God proves to him that his way of dealing with sinners is more just than Abraham's hasty condemnation. Yet Abraham still refuses faithfully to obey God's command that he set his house in order and prepare to die. In Recension B, no lesson is explicit, but the reader cannot help but notice that Abraham seems to have gained nothing from his heavenly adventures. Abraham, who promised in B 7 that if he was granted heavenly access he would submit to God's will, still does not do so even when returned to his house to find the death of his wife. Both texts use humor in their presentations, though Recension A finds humor in the amplification of motifs and procedural steps, while Recension B finds humor in Abraham's willingness to take a metaphor literally and in the outlandishness of the individual soul's claims to have "forgotten" committing murder. Both recensions take pains to convince the reader that God's system is well-thought out and just, reflecting real tensions regarding the divine courtroom and in the fate of souls in the afterlife, and once again demonstrating an understanding that it is truly the reader who is in the judicial position.

# E. Conclusion

This chapter has examined the divine courtroom in Second Temple Judaism, focusing in particular on the way these scenes are used within a broader conversation about the way God ultimately administers justice. Jewish authors introduce a host of figures into these courtroom scenes, who act in various judicial roles. In particular, certain figures like Enoch and Abraham become particularly associated with the divine courtroom, and will continue to be so in rabbinic literature. The appearance of angels fulfilling judicial functions also has a long afterlife, culminating in the extensive angelology of medieval Judaism and Christianity. Each text analyzed above has its own agenda and concerns that it wants to address in the text, from the desire of *Jubilees* to vindicate God from accusations of abandonment, to the desire of 4 Ezra to challenge those very types of vindications.

It is not sufficient, as some scholars do, to dismiss these scenes as "apocalyptic motifs." One cannot simply substitute one scene for another, for it is in the details of each scene that reveal the ways in which authors accomplish their goals and thus reveal the concerns that lie behind them. Those concerns vary – they can be regarding God's power, the way in which God balances justice and mercy, a lack of role differentiation in the courtroom, or anxiety about the very technology involved in administering justice. In all of these texts the authors attempt, by their descriptions of the process, to convince the reader that the judicial system they are describing is just and well-administered. Nowhere do we have an *Apocalocyntosis*, nowhere is the system described as being corrupt. On the contrary, all of these texts show a desire to portray a totally uncorrupt system. Just how hard they try to convince their readers of this is evidence of just how hard they needed to be convinced – especially as things became worse on the ground. This sets the stage for the messianic hopes and expectations that become the background for the rise of Christianity.

Chapter 5

# Courtrooms Without Law: The Tensions of Paul

## A. Introduction

For the development of the imagery and theology of the divine courtroom, just as for any other theological development in early Christianity, Paul of Tarsus is both crucial witness and frustrating antagonist. At times, reading Paul, it is clear that he employs and deploys the imagery of the divine courtroom alternatively to console, threaten, or conciliate his readers. Such is certainly the case in 1 Corinthians 3, where he assures the readers that everyone's work will be tested individually by fire in the day of the Lord, although they stand together in the building of God. It is present in Romans 2, where he unexpectedly affirms that God will recompense to each according to their deeds, and Romans 14:10: πάντες γὰρ παρα-στησόμεθα τῷ βήματι τοῦ θεοῦ, we will all stand at the judgment-seat of God. Even a cursory glance at the Pauline letters reveals the forensic and juridical metaphor of justification to be at the center of Pauline theology, christology, cosmology, soteriology, and eschatology. Ultimately, Paul finds himself within the long-standing tradition of using the language of the divine courtroom as an opportunity to acquit God of perceived injustic-es. Here, as in the book of Job and the intertestamental literature, trying man is trying God, and God is found not guilty.

Yet even though this is the case, Paul's use of the imagery of the divine courtroom stands in tension with one of his central tenets: that justification is by faith alone, and not by works of the law. In other words, Paul *rejects* the legal metaphor as an appropriate way to imagine the relationship be-tween God and the new Israel, the *ekklesia*. If the period of the law is over, as Paul argues in Galatians 3-4, then so too are the protections that the law offers for humanity. People no longer have recourse to the law as a means for argumentation and complaint against God, nor can they use the con-tractual arrangements of the covenant as arguments in their own defense. Paul's understanding of the anthropological nature of man *vis-à-vis* that of God strongly hampers the ability of mankind successfully to stand trial be-fore God. What Paul has done is take the law out of the courtroom.

It would seem that the divine courtroom no longer would carry the same currency for Paul as a medium for picturing man's destiny, and yet Paul continues to use the forensic metaphor to picture what will come at the end of days, as well as use the scene of the courtroom to shame the Corinthians, who think that they – not God – should be Paul's judge and jury (2 Cor 10-12). The forensic metaphor continues to be a part of Pauline discourse, but it now stands in a tension previously not present. Throughout Paul's letters, in particular Galatians, 1 and 2 Corinthians, and especially Romans, we see Paul navigating this tension and attempting to articulate the criteria of judgment in a courtroom without law – at least not the way previously envisioned. This chapter will explore the ways in which Paul employs the imagery of the divine courtroom in the seven undisputed letters that make up his correspondence.

## B. Pauline Anthropology: How Can Man Stand Before God?

In Romans 14, in exhortation to the new community of Rome, Paul makes the following plea:

The one who eats should not despise the one who does not eat, and the one who does not eat should not judge (μὴ κρινέτω) the one who eats, for God has received him. For who are you to judge another's servant? He will stand or fall before his own lord. And he will stand, for the Lord is able to make him stand. For some, on the one hand, judge a day ahead of another day, but some judge every day. Let each be fully convinced in his own mind. The one who reckons the day reckons it to the Lord, and the one who eats eats to the Lord, for he gives thanks to God. And the one who does not eat, does not eat for the Lord and gives thanks to God. For none of us live for himself and none of us dies for himself. But f we live, we live for the Lord, and if we die, we die for the Lord. If we therefore live or die, we are the Lord's. For this reason Christ died and lived, in order that he might be Lord of the dead and the living. But you, why do you judge your brother? Or you, why do you despise your brother? For this reason we will all stand before the judgment-seat of God. For it is written, 'As I live, says the Lord, every knee will bend and every tongue will confess (ἐξομολογήσεται) to God. Therefore each of us will give a reckoning to God concerning himself (περὶ ἑαυτοῦ λόγον δώσει τῷ θεῷ) (Rom 14:3-12).

Here Paul argues that the Romans should not pass judgment on each other for any reason, particularly on the issues of dietary preferences and on which day they choose to celebrate as the Lord's. His ultimate reason for why the Romans should not condemn each other and act as each other's moral and ritual judges is because that function belongs to God and to God alone. This statement is perfectly in line with Pauline understanding of God as the ultimate judge found throughout his correspondence. Here the crux of the argument is found in 14:10, "we will all stand before the judgment-seat of God." The Greek term for judgment seat, βῆμα, is of course a well-documented technical term, referring to the raised place or tribune in the law-courts, and sometimes referring to the tribunal as a whole.[1] Here the reference to the judgment seat of God is a clear way in which Paul employs the language of the divine courtroom as an assumption that he shares with his audience. It is the acknowledged existence of such a βῆμα that is what Paul thinks will convince the Romans to cease and desist from judging each other, knowing that each will be judged by God in the end. If this assumption were not a shared one, this argument would not work. This use of the language and imagery of the divine courtroom in Romans 14:10 is a representative example of the way Paul employs this motif throughout his writings. He never describes the divine courtroom in narrative form (just as he hardly ever describes *anything* in narrative form), yet he assumes his existence and calls it to mind when it can serve a purpose in his argument.

1 Corinthians 4 uses the imagery of the divine courtroom in much the same manner, although in a different context:

Thus let a man reckon us as servants of Christ and stewards of the mysteries of God. And moreover, it is sought out among the servants whether one is found to be faithful (πιστός), but for me this is the smallest thing, that I might be judged by you (ὑφ' ὑμῶν ἀνακριθῶ) or by a human court. I do not even judge myself. For I am not aware of anything against myself, but I am not acquitted by this (οὐκ ἐν τούτῳ δεδικαίωμαι), for the one who judges me is the Lord. Therefore do not judge anything before the time when the Lord comes, who will both illuminate the hidden things of darkness and disclose the intentions of the heart. Then there will be praise for each from God. (1 Cor 4:1-5)

Here Paul employs the divine courtroom imagery in much the same way as in Romans 14, as part of his exhortation to the Corinthians to stop judging one another, for the role of judge properly belongs to the Lord (1 Cor 4:4). There is also an element of warning here – even though the Corinthians might not be aware of any evidence against them, this does not mean that they are acquitted (or "justified"). It is clear from 1 Cor 1-3 that Paul has diagnosed the Corinthian community as having a bit of a hybris problem, and this passage uses the legal imagery to remind them of their proper place in the cosmological order. Both ἀνακρίνω and δικαιόω have clear forensic resonances, and this passage as a whole participates in Paul's overall use of forensic imagery in the Corinthian correspondence as a whole, which I will discuss below.

Both of these passages, though, along with corresponding pericopes throughout the Pauline epistles, pose a crucial question that is truly at the heart of Pauline theology: How can man stand before God? What happens

---

[1] See also 2 Cor 5:10, where Paul insists that we must all appear before the judgment-seat of Christ (ἔμπροσθεν τοῦ βήματος τοῦ Χριστοῦ).

when one presents himself at the βῆμα? This is not just a question of court-room choreography, although that in itself is worthy of discussion. This question revolves around the essential nature of Pauline anthropology, and how Paul conceives of the relationship between Man and God. This question is also christological: how did the death and resurrection of Jesus affect this relationship? This question is one of *standing*, not just physical standing, but *legal* standing. What stand does Man have before God?

It is nearly universally acknowledged that Paul has what is called a "low" anthropology, an idea of man that sees him as separated from God by a vast gulf. Paul is overwhelmingly negative about the possibility of humans participating in their own salvation. The essential text here, though by no means the only place where Paul touches on this issue, is the Epistle to the Romans, particularly Romans 1:18-3:21 and its consequences for the remainder of the letter.

In modern scholarship, the import of Paul's anthropological pessimism was felt most strongly by Rudolf Bultmann in his seminal *Theology of the New Testament*. Bultmann not only explicated the degree of Paul's articulation of the human condition, but argued that it was truly at the center of Paul's thought:

> Pauline theology is not a speculative system. It deals with God not as He is in Himself but only with God as He is significant for man, for man's responsibility and man's salvation. Correspondingly, it does not deal with the world and man as they are in themselves, but constantly sees the world and man in their relation to God. Every assertion about God is simultaneously an assertion about man and vice versa. For this reason and in this sense Paul's theology is, at the same time, anthropology.[2]

Bultmann continues to explain how interconnected Paul's soteriology and christology are, arguing that "Paul's theology can best be treated as his doctrine of man: first, of man prior to the revelation of faith, and second, of man under faith, for in this way the anthropological and soteriological orientation of Paul's theology is brought out. Such a presentation presupposes, since theological understanding has its origin in faith, that man prior to the revelation of faith is so depicted by Paul as he is retrospectively seen from the standpoint of faith."[3] Bultmann therefore argues that Paul's anthropological considerations are at the very center of Paul's thought, and indeed in many ways are the starting point for Paul's thought – or at least for an investigation of Paul's thought. Though many of Bultmann's conclusions about Paul in general came under fire with the publication of E. P. Sanders's *Paul and Palestinian Judaism* and the windstorm that followed

---

[2] Rudolf Bultmann, *Theology of the New Testament* (trans. Kendrick Grobel; New York: Charles Scribner's Sons, 1955), 190-191.

[3] Bultmann, Theology of the New Testament, 191.

it,[4] one of the main critiques of Sanders continues to be that he did not contend with Bultmann's assertions regarding Paul's anthropological outlook and the effect that might have had on his claims regarding Paul.[5] This study stands with Bultmann in believing that the investigation of Paul's use of the language of the divine courtroom must begin with the exposition of Paul's anthropological precepts, his understanding of the world in which he stood and how he stood in it. Only then can we fully understand how he expects his readers to stand before God's judgment seat.

The overwhelming theme of Romans 1:18-3:21 is the fact that all of mankind, both Jew and Gentile, stand in a state of condemnation before God, the overturning of which is only possible with Christ's death and resurrection, which form the necessary conditions of the potentiality of man's salvation. Paul presents this argument after introducing himself and his gospel (Rom 1:1-6), indicating his desire finally to visit the church at Rome (1:8-15), and stating the crux of the letter's message in 1:16-17:[6] "For I am not ashamed of the gospel, for it is the power of God towards salvation for everyone who believes, to the Jew first and to the Greek. For the justice of God (δικαιοσύνη θεοῦ) in it is revealed from faith to faith, just as it is written, 'the one who is just (ὁ δικαιός) will live by faith.'"[7]

---

[4] The so-called "New Perspective" on Paul. Sanders argued, among other things, that Judaism at the time of Paul was characterized by "covenantal nomism," an understanding that Jews did not believe that one "earned" salvation through works, but rather was granted the opportunity for salvation through the grace of God in the election of Israel, and obedience to the commandments was a secondary response. Sanders argued that Paul's understanding of grace and works finds itself within this context and not opposed to it. So Sanders, *Paul and Palestinian Judaism* (Minneapolis: Fortress Press, 1976), 543. For a review of the impact of the New Perspective and contemporary reflections see Steven Westholm, "The 'New Perspective' at Twenty-Five," in D. A. Carson, Peter T. O'Brien, and Mark A. Seifrid, eds. *Justification and Variegated Nomism II: The Paradoxes of Paul* (Tübingen: Mohr Siebeck, 2001).

[5] See, for example, Timo Laato, "Paul's Anthropological Considerations: Two Problems," in Carson, *Justification and Variegated Nomism*, 345. Laato goes so far as to claim that Sanders "ignored" Bultmann's claims.

[6] Despite the variety of perspectives on the meaning, purpose, and composition of Romans, most scholars are in agreement that Romans 1:16-17 represent the thesis of the letter. See, for example, James Dunn, *Romans 1-8* (Word Biblical Commentary 38a; Dallas: Word, 1998); Joseph A. Fitzmyer, *Romans* (AB 33; New York: Doubleday, 1993), 253-255; Douglas Moo, *The Epistle to the Romans* (NICNT; Grand Rapids, MI: Eerdmans, 1996), 63-70; A. Katherine Grieb, *The Story of Romans: A Narrative Defense of God's Righteousness* (Louisville: Westminster John Knox, 2002), 12-20.

[7] I find myself at odds with the standard translation of δικαιοσύνη θεοῦ and ὁ δικαιός as "the righteousness of God" and "the righteous one" respectfully. Since I believe the overwhelming theme of Romans is God's justice and the place of the gospel within the mechanisms of that justice, I believe it is much more appropriate to translate these terms using the terminology of justice (which, of course, is equated with righteousness; the two are not opposed terms). This choice also seems to me better to fit the original context of Habakkuk,

Having asserted the salvific power and function of the gospel, Paul recognizes that the next logical step in his argument is to explain exactly *why* one needs salvation, and so the next two chapters begin by illustrating the conditions of man before the advent of Christ.

First in this argument is a section which has alternatively been taken to refer to humankind as a whole, or to the pagans in particular:

For the wrath of God is revealed from heaven against every impiety and injustice of those men who suppress the truth by injustice. For what can be known of God is plain to them, for God revealed it to them. Ever since the creation of the world his eternal power and diving nature, invisible though they are, have been understood and seen through the things he has made. So they are without defense (ἀναπολογήτους[8]): although knowing God they did not reckon or give thanks to him as God, but they speculated futilely in their reasoning and their senseless heart was darkened. Asserting themselves to be wise, they were foolish, and they exchanged the glory of the incorruptible God for the likeness of the image of a corruptible person and of birds and four-footed animals and reptiles. Therefore God handed them over to the desires of their hearts, to impurity, to the dishonoring of their bodies among them, who exchanged the truth of God for deception and worshiped and served the creature instead of the creator, who is praised forever, Amen. (Rom 1:18-25)

Paul continues by listing the results of such a disgraceful exchange: the advent of homosexual inclinations (1:26-27), and a whole catalogue of vices (1:29-31), into all of which God allowed them to fall because of their actions (1:28). Such a debased and disgraced state is that of man that they should not fool themselves into thinking that they can make adequate judgments about anything, much less the actions of other people (2:1-2). Ultimately, whether one thinks that this passage condemns Gentiles in particular or humanity as a whole, the conclusions Paul draws in Romans 3 make it clear that Paul considers all of humanity indicted by sin. Anticipating the questions that follow his argument, Paul asserts that "we have already accused everyone, both Jews and Greeks, to be under sin, just as it is

---

both in the MT and the LXX. This assertion is *contra* VanLandingham, who forcefully asserts that neither ἐικαιοσύνη nor related terms "refer to right relationship, acquittal, or any kind of judicial accounting or declaration." This assertion is completely baffling, considering the very nature of Δίκη as the goddess of justice, and the almost universal semantic resonance of δικαι-terminology as being forensic in nature in the Greek literature. VanLandingham has come to this conclusion based *only* on an examination of the LXX and post-biblical Jewish texts, and therefore misses the larger picture here, all the more relevant for Paul given the overwhelmingly Gentile makeup of his readership. See Chris VanLandingham, *Judgment & Justification in Early Judaism and the Apostle Paul* (Peabody, MA: Hendrickson, 2006), pp. 242-271.

[8] Traditional renderings of this as "excuse" miss the clear forensic nature of the verb and so fail to identify or point to the clear Wortmotif that sets up the use of the imagery of the divine courtroom in Romans 2.

written, 'there is no just (δίκαιος) one, not even one, there is no one who understands, there is no one who seeks God'" (Rom 3:9-11).

It is what lies between these two passages that is particularly relevant for this study. Romans 2 is a passage of utmost importance not just for an understanding of Pauline anthropology but for the *effects* of that anthropological situation in man's ability to stand before God at judgment. It is perhaps an understatement to say that Romans 2 is a widely debated passage. Romans 2, particularly Romans 2:6-8, is at the center of the long-standing debate over whether or not Paul believed in judgment by deeds – or even justification by works (though not by works of "The Law."[9] Of the many scholars who have entered into this debate, the most important here is Klyne Snodgrass, who seems to have appreciated *what* this passage is accomplishing overall, and not removed it from its context. Snodgrass argues that one of the overall themes of Romans is the vindication of God, and that Romans 2 finds its place within that thematic.[10] Snodgrass is correct, though he has not fully appreciated just how appropriate the language of Romans 2 is to Paul's goals. Since it is the argument of this study that scenes of the divine courtroom are almost always attempts to acquit (or to condemn!) God of perceived injustices, Paul's use of the leitmotif of the courtroom in Romans 2 (and in Romans overall) perfectly fits this overall thematic. An understanding of what Paul is doing in Romans 2 thus may help to smooth out (or at least articulate) the tensions that some feel in Romans 2:6-8 without falling into the trap that so many have done in holding that these two verses (and a few others from elsewhere, including 1 Corinthians 3) contradict Paul's overwhelming belief in justification by faith and the necessity of faith for securing good judgment before God.

---

[9] The secondary literature here is substantial and growing, as the "New Perspective" continues to attempt to de-Lutherize Paul, particularly on the question of one's deeds during life, provoking extensive conversation. Some of the most important studies here include: Floyd V. Filson, *St. Paul's Conception of Recompense* (Leipzig: J. C. Hinrichs'sche Buchhandlung, 1931); Calvin Roetzel, *Judgement in the Community* (Leiden: E. J. Brill, 1972); Karl Paul Donfried, "Justification and Last Judgment in Paul," *Interpretation* 30 (1976), 140-152; Nigel Watson, "Justified by Faith; Judged by Works? Another Look at Romans 2," *BBR* 3 (1993), 131-158; Kent Yinger, *Paul, Judaism, and Judgment According to Deeds* (Cambridge: Cambridge University Press, 1999); VanLandingham, *Judgment & Justification*.

[10] Klyne Snodgrass, "Justification by Grace – To the Doers: An Analysis of the Place of Romans 2 in the Theology of Paul," *NTS* 32 (1986), 72-93. Recently J. Daniel Kirk has argued that all of Romans should be understood as a theodicy (Kirk, *Unlocking Romans: Resurrection and the Justification of God* [Grand Rapids, MI: Eerdmans, 2008]), though he focuses on the role that resurrection plays within Romans. Despite his compelling argument that Romans is a theodicy, he spends almost no time discussing Romans 2.

Having set up in Romans 1:18-32 the essential state of condemnation in which man finds himself, Paul asserts that one should not be under any illusions as to what this means for individual people and for the community as a whole. Just as Paul asserted that those who suppressed the truth are without defense, so now he applies this universal truth to his readers in particular:

Therefore *you* are without defense (ἀναπολόγητος), O man, each who judges. For by whatever you judge (κρίνεις) another, you condemn (κατακρίνεις) yourselves, for the one judging is acting the same. For we know that the judgment of God (τὸ κρίμα τοῦ θεοῦ) is in accordance with the truth against those doing the very same things. Do you reckon this, O man who judges those doing such things and doing them yourself, that *you* will escape the judgment of God? Or do you despise the riches of his goodness and his forbearance and patience? Are you ignorant that the goodness of God leads you to repentance? But according to your hard and unrepentant heart you treasure up for yourselves wrath in the day of wrath and revelation of the just judgment of God (δικαιοκρισίας τοῦ θεοῦ), who will repay to each according to his works: on the one hand, eternal life to those who seek glory and honor and immortality according to the steadfastness of good work; on the other hand, wrath and fury to those who out of selfish ambition despise the truth and are persuaded by injustice. There will be affliction and distress upon every soul of man who does evil, to the Jew first and the Greek, but glory and honor and peace for everyone who does good, to the Jew first and the Greek, for there is no partiality before God. For as many as who sin apart from the law will also perish apart from the law, and as many as who sin in the law, will be judged through the law. For it is not the hearers of the law who are just (δίκαιοι) before God, but those who do the law will be justified (δικαιωθήσονται). When the Gentiles who do not have the law naturally do what is of the law, these, though not having law, are a law to themselves. They display that the work of the law is written in their hearts, to which their own conscience co-testifies (συμμαρτυρούσης αὐτῶν τῆς συνειδήσεως) and their conflicting thoughts will condemn or even defend them (κατηγορούντων ἢ καὶ ἀπολογουμένων) on the day (ἐν ἡμέρᾳ)[11] when God will judge the secret things of men according to my gospel, through Jesus Christ. (Rom 2:1-16)

It is hardly necessary to assert the import of this passage both for a study of Paul's anthropology and for a study of the divine courtroom. Even a cursory overlook can spot the forensic language being employed here, and being employed deliberately. To begin with, we have the use of the verbs κρίνω, its intensified version κατακρίνω, and the cognate noun τὸ κρίμα (2:1-3). Likewise the verb ἀπολογέομαι at 2:15 recalls ἀναπολόγητος at 2:1 (and at 1:20) and refers specifically to legal defense, and συμμαρτυρέω (2:15) brings in the language of calling witnesses in a fo-

---

[11] We should not miss the potential legal connotations of ἡμέρα which Paul has employed elsewhere (cf. 1 Cor 4:3).

rensic context. It should be obvious in this context that δίκαιοι and δικαιωθήσονται (2:13) have their technical semantic resonance here.[12]

The scene, therefore, in Romans 2 is that of the divine courtroom. Paul is affirming to the Romans that they will one day find themselves on that day (or in that courtroom) where God, through Jesus Christ, will pass judgment (2:16). They should not be under the illusion that they will be able to withstand that day. Paul clearly does not want them to think that they are going to be among those who receive those rewards listed in verse 7. His intention in this passage is to warn them not to behave in a hypocritical fashion and to recognize the inevitable consequences of such behavior. In order to do this, he situates their behavior, and the condition of man in general, in its cosmological place: they are not just Romans, subject to legal authorities and perhaps even participating in those legal authorities, but they are all going to be accountable to the ultimate Judge, God. In essence, Paul is asserting that they need to get some perspective (his perspective). They need to see the larger picture. For Paul, the divine courtroom *is* that larger picture.

Taken on its own, Romans 2 does not in itself pose a pessimistic outlook on the conditions of man as a whole, in fact, just the opposite: 2:6-8 is hope for some optimism, as it asserts man's actions as God's criteria for judgment. This certainly sounds like man has some recourse to defense in front of God: if he has behaved according to the steadfastness of good works, he will be rewarded. However, Romans 2 does not stand on its own and should not be taken that way. The perceived optimism of 2:6-8 is completely outweighed by the overwhelming pessimism of Romans 1-3, which sets up the real cause for optimism: the death and resurrection of Christ and the advent of the gospel. In addition, in 3:12, Paul insists that "there is no one doing good, not even one." The criterion set forth by 2:6-8 cannot be met by humanity. Indeed, the discussion of man's situation in Romans 2 continues with yet another Pauline indictment, this time of the Jews in particular, for their hypocrisy and their completely misguided (in his opinion) reliance on the law for their salvation (2:17-29). Romans 2:1-16, therefore, must be taken within its context as part of the discussion of the condemnation of man, reframing the issue in terms of its full juridical consequences: man will be in real trouble before God on that dreaded day.[13] As N.T.

---

[12] As Mark Seifrid has clearly explication. Cf. Mark A. Seifrid, "Paul's use of Righteousness Language Against its Hellenistic Background," *Justification and Variegated Nomism*, 39-74. Additionally, on the resonances of προσωπολημψία (2:11), including legal resonances, see the excellent dissertation by Jouette Bassler, *Divine Impartiality: Paul and a Theological Axiom* (SBL Dissertation Series 59; Atlanta: Scholars Press, 1982).

[13] For another scholar's perspective on the importance of Romans 2 for an understanding of Pauline anthropology, see Oda Wischmeyer, "Römer 2.1-24 als Teil der Gerichtsrede des Paulus gegen die Menschheit," *NTS* 52 (2006), 356-376.

Wright has said, "all humankind is thus in the dock in God's metaphorical law-court."[14] One further aspect of this passage is especially relevant here: Paul's use of the phrase δικαιοκρισίας at 2:5. The use of the prefix δικαιο- here magnifies one of Paul's intentions. God's judgment is no longer just referred to as τὸ κρίμα (2:1-3), but δικαιοκρισία – *just* judgment. God s judgment, for Paul, will be perfectly just – it cannot be any other way. Paul here is emphasizing this for the benefit of his readers. The just judgment of God is contrasted with the non-just judgments of the Romans in 2:_-3. Snodgrass is absolutely correct when he claims this passage highlights one of Paul's themes in Romans – the vindication of God.[15] I wish to highlight the way Paul here attempts to vindicate God – through the use of forensic imagery. This is a theodicy in its truest sense of the word – an *acquittal* of God. Even though this passage is ostensibly about the trial of man, it is truly about the trial of God. This finds Paul very much in line with both biblical and extra-biblical authors (both Jew and Greek). Paul uses the forensic backdrop of this passage both to condemn the Romans and to acquit God of any misguided ideas held by the Romans as to whether or not this judgment will be one of justice.

## C. A Law-less Courtroom?

Paul's view of the low status of Man before God leads to one of the dominant themes of the surviving letters of Paul: the Jewish law cannot lead to one's justification (Gal 2:16, 3:11, et al.). While we can see some development in Paul's articulation of this tenet from Galatians to Romans,[16] its essence remains the same: justification comes through faith, and not through works of the law (Rom 3:28).[17] This understanding, for Paul, is completely based on and informed by his conception of the cosmological

---

[14] N.T. Wright, *What St. Paul Really Said* (Grand Rapids, MI: Eerdmans, 1997), 106.

[15] Snodgrass, "Justification by Faith," 76.

[16] On this development see J. Louis Martyn, "Romans as one of the Earliest Interpretations of Galatians," in *Theological Issues in the Letters of Paul* (Nashville: Abingdon Press, 1997). See also U. Wilkens, "Statements on the development of Paul's view of the Law," in M.D. Hooker and S.G. Wilson, eds., *Paul and Paulinism: Essays in Honor of C.K. Barrett* (London: SPCK, 1982), 17-26.

[17] W. D. Davies is completely correct in asserting that Paul's view of the law is not "monolithic." (W. D. Davies, "Paul and the Law: Reflections on Pitfalls in Interpretation," *Paul and Paulinism*, 10). There are subtle nuances in his discussions in Galatians, the Corinthian correspondence, and Romans. We should not expect otherwise, as all of Paul's letters are occasional in nature and their epistolary situations guide their *heuresis*. Nevertheless, Paul makes certain claims that remain consistent, including that of the inadequacy of the Law for justification.

effects of Christ's death and resurrection. Whether or not Paul thought theoretically about the law prior to his calling is unknowable. While some scholars have postulated about Paul's life as a Pharisee and the theological presuppositions of that association,[18] our access to Paul's thought is limited to his surviving writings which obviously all date post-crucifixion. It is essential to remember Paul's vantage point, and that his thought is grounded in post-crucifixion reflection on a stage of history that he believes has passed.[19] Paul's understanding of what was accomplished through Christ's death and resurrection leads him to the development of a theology of history that sees all of history as divided into two basic periods: the period of the law, and the period of the Spirit. According to Paul, the law had its purpose for a period of time (Gal 3:23-24), but now is no longer valid (Gal 3:25-26).[20] In Paul's address to the Galatians, he insists that it is toxic for them to follow even one precept of the law:

For I Paul say to you: if you circumcise yourself Christ will benefit you not at all. And I again testify to every man who circumcises himself: he is obligated to do the whole law. You were nullified (κατηργήθητε) from Christ, whoever "is justified" by the law (οἵτινες ἐν νόμῳ δικαιοῦσθε), you fell away from grace. For we, by the spirit, from faith await the hope of justice (δικαιοσύνη). For in Christ Jesus neither circumcision counts for anything, nor uncircumcision, rather faith working through love. (Gal 5:1-6)

In the notoriously difficult allegorical reading of Sarah and Hagar in Galatians 4 Paul attempts to convince the reader to want to line themselves up with the free, law-less woman, *not* Hagar, the slave, the present Jerusalem, Mount Sinai, the covenant of the law (Gal 4:21-31). Though the details of the allegory can be interpreted variously, the effect is to place the two covenants into two corresponding columns: one bad (the law), one good (the Spirit).

---

[18] cf. Floyd Filson, *St. Paul's Conception of Recompense*; Martin Hengel, *The Pre-Christian Paul* (London: SCM, 1991).

[19] On this point Sanders is certainly correct; cf. Sanders, *Paul and Palestinian Judaism*, 474.

[20] Wilkens nicely summarizes Paul's position on the Law in Galatians: "Paul answers the expected question, 'Why then the Law?' (3.19), with a rough rejection. *First*, the Law has a secondary and not a primary significance in salvation history. God only *added* it in reaction to sin, namely 'because of transgressions', i.e. to condemn them as such (not to cause them!). *Second*, the time of the Law is limited – until the coming of Christ. *Third*, the Law is not even given directly by God but is mediated by angels (3.19f), which shows its inferiority to the promise God has given directly to Abraham. *Fourth*, therefore, Law and promises cannot even be regarded as directly opposed to each other, for the Law is not able to create life like the promises (3.21). On that account, finally and *fifthly*, the function of the Law is to be compared with that of an 'attendant slave' whose time has come to an end: faith in Christ has taken over the position of the *Torah* (3.23-4.6)." U. Wilkens, "Statements on the development of Paul's view of the Law," 22.

Whatever nuances one claims about Paul's attitude to the Mosaic law, it seems fairly clear that he considers it to be an un-ideal and no longer valid way of conceiving of God's relationship with humanity. For Paul the law is an inadequate means of attaining justification.[21] This is the essential nature of the gospel – that it brings justification *apart* from the Law:

> But now, apart from the law, the justice of God (δικαιοσύνη θεοῦ) has been revealed, having been testified to by the law and the prophets, and the justice of God is through faith in Jesus Christ for all those who believe. For there is no distinction, since all sinned and fell short of the glory of God, all are justified as a gift by his grace through the redemption in Christ Jesus, whom God put forth as an atoning-place through the faith in his blood, as evidence of his righteousness (ἔνδειξιν τῆς δικαιοσύνης αὐτοῦ ) through the pardoning (πάρεσις) of those sins previously committed. In the forbearance of God, as evidence of his righteousness in the present time, in order that he be just and the one who justifies (εἰς τὸ εἶναι αὐτὸν δίκαιον καὶ δικαιοῦντα) the one who has faith in Jesus. (Romans 3:21-26)

It is the gospel that is the evidence of *God's* justice, and Paul goes so far in this passage as to suggest that God put forth Christ Jesus *as his own theodicy*, to demonstrate and provide evidence of his own justice/righteousness. This is perhaps to demonstrate that he is not partial, that he wants to assist all in their own justification. This seems shocking at first but I find no other way to understand verses 25-26. Paul is here saying that God's reason for Christ's redemptive blood-sacrifice was to prove that God himself is a just God. The technical term ἔνδειξις should not be dismissed too lightly here. This is law-court terminology found repeatedly Demosthenes and Aeschines to refer to the laying out of evidence. Other terms in this passages (besides δικαιόω and cognates) with forensic contexts include μαρτυρέω (3:21) and πάρεσις (3:25).[22] This may also relate back to the quotation of Hab 2:4 at Rom 1:17. In Habakkuk, the prophet engages God on questions of justice in this world, asking why God allows violence to reign on the world and why "justice never prevails" (Hab 1:1-4). Hab 2:4 is part of God's response to the prophet. Habakkuk is told to "write down the vision and engrave it on the tablet" (Hab 2:2). The vision

---

[21] It is this "traditional" view of Paul that has come under attack from the adherents of the "New Perspective." W. D. Davies has asserted that this traditional view owes more to the Protestant Reformation than to Paul himself (cf. W. D. Davies, "Paul and the Law", 4, 6.) I, however, believe that Martin Luther was *entirely correct* in asserting this as the key to understanding Paul. We should not forget that Luther's read of Paul is almost entirely in accordance with that of Augustine of Hippo, who did not require the Protestant Reformation to read Paul in this way. It seems to me that to read Paul otherwise requires one actually to read *past* Paul.

[22] The legal resonances of πάρεσις have been recently well articulated. See Romano Penna, "The Meaning of πάρεσις in Romans 3:25c and the Pauline Thought on the Divine Acquittal," in Michael Bachmann, ed., *Lutherische und Neue Paulusperspektive* (Tübingen: Mohr Siebeck, 2005), 251-274.

that follows, concerning "the end" (Hab 2:3), includes the promise of violence for the wicked, and insistence that "the just one will live by his faith" (Hab 2:4). This vision in Habakkuk is presented as God's direct reply to the charges that Habakkuk levels against him. In other words, this passage in Habakkuk is part and parcel of God's proof that everything will be "made right" in the end. Paul's quotation of Hab 2:4 at Rom 1:17 already introduces the issue of theodicy into Romans, foreshadowing that this will be a major concern in the letter. Here we have the payoff – Paul is arguing that Jesus was God's evidence, his proof, of his own δικαιοσύνη.

The divine courtroom thus functions in this passage for Paul as a means to acquit God, even though ostensibly the conversation under discussion is the acquittal of man, and the inadequacy of the law as a vehicle for man's acquittal.[23] Yet here we have a central issue in Paul's use of forensic terminology and imagery as a way of imagining the relationship between Man and God. The rejection of the Law as the criteria for achieving justification leads Paul into a terminological and conceptual quandary. Since he continues to use the forensic backdrop as a way of exhortation; he finds himself trying to assert both a courtroom setting and the lack of law within the courtroom. It is this quagmire that leads Paul seemingly to double-talk, speaking about the "law of God" (Rom 7:22; 8:7), the "law of the Spirit of life in Christ Jesus" (ὁ γὰρ νόμος τοῦ πνεύματος τῆς ζωῆς ἐν Χριστῷ Ἰησοῦ; Rom 8:2), the "law of faith" (Rom 3:27), and other such assertions that continually prove vexatious for students and scholars alike. Paul is searching for a law that makes sense both in the conceptual framework of the courtroom and within his cosmological understanding of the effect of Christ's death and resurrection for man's relationship with God.

Likewise, this quagmire leads Paul at times to assert that the criteria for judgment will be one's actions, as in Romans 2:6-7, for example. These isolated statements within the Pauline correspondence have led to an extraordinary number of books trying to reconcile these verses with Paul's conception of justification by faith. I submit that it is the use of the divine courtroom imagery that leads Paul to make these kinds of claims, because a courtroom implies a standard of judgment, and when you remove obedience to the law as that standard of judgment, there remains a gaping hole which needs to be filled. Paul is trying to find the language for what

---

[23] On this passage Andrew Lincoln explicates that "the apostle stays with his picture of the lawcourt from 3:19 not only through his mention of righteousness with its forensic connotations but also through his assertion that, although righteousness cannot come through the law, both the law and the prophets act as *witnesses* to the righteousness of God which comes through faith in Jesus Christ." Andrew Lincoln, "From Wrath to Justification: Tradition, Gospel, and Audience in the Theology of Romans 1:18-4:25" in David M. Hay and E. Elizabeth Johnson, eds., *Pauline Theology III: Romans* (Atlanta: Society of Biblical Literature, 2002), 147.

he knows *implicitly* to be true – that there is going to be a judgment-seat, there *is* criteria for judgment, and although it is not "The Law" (i.e., the Jewish Law), it is some form of *law*, either the Law of Christ, or the Law of Spirit, or "faith working through love" (Gal 5:6). It is Paul's search for this articulation that causes the tension. Paul feels the tension and knows his readers feel the tension, and yet he knows it to be true. This tension will have a profound effect on early Christian understandings of the Divine Courtroom and the last judgment.

What we have, then, in Paul, is simultaneously a rejection of the idea of man's relationship with God as being able to be conceived as a legal relationship, and a continued use of the forensic metaphor and forensic language to talk about God and humanity. It is this tension that causes scholars such headache when trying to articulate how Paul feels about the Law. An understanding of the basis of the tension, the law-less courtroom, can ease the tension somewhat by drawing attention to one of its root causes. It is simply much easier to talk about God using the language of the courtroom (justice, defense, condemnation, intercession, accounting, witnessing, judgment-seat) when there is a clear sense of what the Law in operation in the courtroom *is*.

In addition, Paul's removing of the Law leaves man at a serious disadvantage. As discussed in chapter two, ancient Israelite writers, including some of the Psalmists and Prophets, invoked the legal relationship between God and Israel through the *rîv*-pattern style of writing. At times they described God as presenting a lawsuit against Israel, but often it was just the opposite: authors indicted God for failing to live up to his end of the treaty. This is the benefit of a legal relationship: it protects *both* parties, especially the weaker party. There are *benefits* to having a legal system (otherwise we wouldn't have one in society!). The Law protects the weaker party in an arrangement, and gives people a standard by which to appeal potential injustices. This is part of the brilliance and logic of ancient Israelite conceptions of reality. When one conceives of the Law as a contractual relationship, and its articulation in the Pentateuch (particularly Deuteronomy) as most likely based upon a Suzerain-Vassal Treaty, then one can understand the benefits of such an arrangement. This aspect of legalism is, sadly, often overlooked by scholars, who are hesitant to talk about "legalism" because they perceive it in such negative terms. Without the law, humans have no means of redress, and nothing to hold on to in the courtroom. This is the situation Paul envisions and needs his readers to recognize, and it is for precisely this reason that Paul attacks so virulently the attitude of those Jewish colleagues who feel that the legal criteria are still valid in their upcoming courtroom drama (Rom 2:17-24).

# D. Paul's use of the Forensic Metaphor: 2 Corinthians 10-13

Not every instance of divine courtroom imagery in Paul has to do with final judgment. In fact, sometimes the most effective use of this motif is when he is not referring to final judgment at all. One of the most impressive and sustained uses of the forensic metaphor in Paul is in 2 Corinthians 10-13, the so-called "fool's speech," where Paul uses the scene of the courtroom to shame the Corinthians, who think that they − not God − should be Paul's judge and jury. An extended look at this section of 2 Corinthians − which most likely should be identified with the "letter of tears" described in 2 Cor 2:3-11[24] − reveals Paul's brilliance at employing the imagery of the divine courtroom in a variety of contexts.

2 Cor 10:1-18 lays out Paul's reason for composing the epistle: to counter charges that have been brought against him (10:9-10). We can deduce that the charges brought against Paul were: that he was boasting (10:8), that he was trying to frighten the Corinthians (10:9), and that he was inconsistent, being strong by letter but weak in person (10:10). We know from earlier correspondence with the Corinthians that Paul was also accused of not having letters of recommendation (2 Cor 3:1), and therefore his authority was doubted and he was accused of not being ἱκανός, qualified, for his position (2 Cor 2:16). Implicit in all of these accusations is the charge that Paul, who brought the faith to the Corinthians and established the church there, is not a credible apostle, and is not δόκιμος ("testworthy," or "able to pass the test successfully").[25]

Paul's first and consistent strategy to counter these charges is to remind the Corinthians of the larger picture, and the cosmic implications of their particular situation. Charges that are brought against him are therefore identified as obstacles "against the knowledge of God" (10:5). In order to make this comparison, Paul sets up a dualistic view of the word, comparing those who work by human standards to those who work in the standards of God (10:1-5).[26] He continues to employ this strategy with the dis-

---

[24] Following the "five-letter hypothesis" for reading 2 Corinthians, laid out by Gunther Bornkamm in a 1968 presentation to the Akademie der Wissenchaften in Heidelberg. For a good discussion of the different theories regarding the literary composition of 2 Corinthians, see Hans Dieter Betz. *2 Corinthians 8 and 9* (Hermeneia; Philadelphia: Fortress Press, 1985), 1-36.

[25] See 2 Cor 13:6 and following.

[26] In good rhetorical form, Paul insists that he is not, in fact, comparing himself to these people (10:12), because of the insufficiency, indeed impiety, of human standards to mediate such a comparison. By engaging in this type of *synkrisis*, Paul will give too much value to the other side, and give validity to their position. Therefore Paul must make his comparison in a much more subtle way, so as to consistently undermine the position of the opponents while not doing an overt point by point comparison, which would undermine his entire case.

cussion of the limits of boasting: the opponents are those who commend themselves (10:18), i.e. those who believe that authority is to be obtained from other humans, but the true workers are those who are commended by God (10:17-18). This strategy is also in place on a much less explicit level. 2 Cor 10-13, and specifically 11:1-12:13, is Paul's attempt to show that he is engaged in an apocalyptic battle at work on the ground, in which Paul and the Truth fight against Satan and Deception. Paul's presentation of the world in this light points to the cosmic implications of the historical actions of the Corinthians.

The main issue at hand, what an ancient author might call the *iudicationem*, the "point to be decided,"[27] is Paul's δοκιμή, which is shorthand for whether or not Paul has met the criteria for apostleship – specifically, whether he has met *the Corinthians's* criteria for apostleship. Major arguments against Paul have presented themselves. Paul is physically weak (2 Cor 10:10), which is normally taken both as a sign of divine disapproval and displeasure, and also as an indication of his lesser moral worth. He has continually suffered afflictions (11:23b-29), normally understood as divine punishment. The task of the Apostle is to prove that he is indeed approved by the Lord, that he has stood the test successfully. He must therefore present all these seeming weaknesses as strengths, and explain how it is these apparent weaknesses prove his δοκιμή rather than argue against it. The theme of δοκιμή appears time and again in 2 Corinthians 11-13, beginning in 10:18, the verse which concludes the epistolary prologue and makes the transition to the fool's speech.[28] Paul states that "it is not the one who recommends himself, rather whom the Lord recommends, this one is δόκιμος.' Likewise 13:3 makes this clear: "you are seeking a δοκιμή that Christ is speaking in me." Both the beginning and end of this section of 2 Corinthians, therefore, revolve around the question of δοκιμή, culminating in the exhortation of chapter 13: "examine yourselves [to see] if you are in the faith, test yourselves (ἑαυτοὺς δοκιμάζετε). Or do you not realize that Jesus Christ is in you? Unless you are test-failers (ἀδόκιμοι). But I hope that you know that we are not test-failers."

2 Cor 11:1-12:13 presents a carefully designed argument brought by Paul, in the guise of the fool, to counter the charges brought against him by illustrating his δοκιμή and his credibility as an apostle. He does this both by presenting positive arguments (as to his character and person), and negative arguments (by casting his opponents as ministers of Satan, and opponents of the work of Paul, which is identified with work in the service of Christ).[29] 2 Cor 12:1-10 is a crucial part of this argument, tying together

---

[27] *Rhet. Her.* I.xvi.26.

[28] I.e., a verse where we should expect to see the main themes of the letter appear.

[29] This double strategy is consistent ith that laid out in *Rhet. Her.* I.vi.7.

and focusing interlocking strands of a thesis that revolves around the central claim that Paul's weaknesses prove his δοχιμή: a claim which comes directly from the Lord (12:8-9). What is especially relevant here is that the question of δοχιμή is one that found its home in the Greek law courts. A prevalent type of legal examination was the δοχιμασία, an examination (or scrutiny) of a candidate for office at Athens. According to M. H. Hansen, the *dokimasia* was "not an examination of the candidate's competence, but only of its formal qualifications, conduct, and political convictions."[30] The court was required to reject a candidate if he was guilty of any crime normally punished with *atimia*, and a candidate could be turned down for office even if he possessed all the formal qualifications of office, if he was found to be "unworthy to hold office."[31] Though we have no evidence that the *dokimasia* was still in place in the first century CE, or that Paul has modeled his apology on one for a *dokimasia*, the fact that the *dokimasia* existed proves that there was was a tradition of proving one's δοχιμή in a legal context. Even the term δοχιμή might have provoked legal images in the mind of the Corinthians.

I contend, among others before me, that 2 Corinthians 10-13 is modeled after a forensic apology, and constitutes Paul's defense to the charge that he is ἀδόχιμος. Within this context, 11:1-12:13 stands as a discrete unit beginning and ending with reference to "foolishness" (11:1; 12:11), and is understood as the central speech within the apology. In this manner, it can be read as following the traditional form of Greek forensic oratory. 11:1-4, the introduction of the fool, is thus to be understood as the *prooimiom;* 11:5-6, the *prothesis;* 11:7-12:10, the *pistis,* or "proof"; and 12:11-13 the *epilogos,* the conclusion. The entire section is to be read as the proof-section of the greater epistle 10-13.[32] The Corinthians would certainly have been familiar with this format. We know from Paul's condemnation in 1 Corinthians 6:1-11 that the Corinthians were taking each other to court "before the unrighteous," which presumably means a secular law court. They would have thus most likely been able to recognize the standard format of a legal defense.

---

[30] M. H. Hansen, *The Athenian Democracy in the Age of Demosthenes* (Oxford: Blackwell, 1991), 218.

[31] Hansen, Athenian Democracy, 219.

[32] This outline is based on a schema outlined by Margaret M. Mitchell at the University of Chicago, 7 November 2000. For additional discussion, see Hans Dieter Betz, *Der Apostel Paulus und die sokratische Tradition: eine exegetische Untersuchung zu seiner Apologie 2 Korinther 10-13* (Beiträge zur historischen Theologie 45; Tübingen: J. C. B. Mohr, 1972).

In a formal apology, one of the most effective forms of proof is the production of witnesses.[33] Paul knew that the Corinthians expected him to produce witnesses for his case (13:1). Paul's best witness – since the Corinthians, who should have been his witnesses, have failed him – is God. We know that Paul is comfortable calling upon God as a witness from 2 Cor 1:23,[34] and his repeated use of the refrain "God knows" (11:11; 12:2; 12:4) may have the effect of a witness's testimony. This is true despite the fact that Paul never explicitly calls upon God as a witness as he does in 2 Cor 1:23. This too is part of Paul's strategy: if he were to call explicitly upon God as a witness, he would run the risk of pointing to the fact that he was defending himself. This would give too much credibility to his opponents, as well as too much credibility to the Corinthians as an appropriate judge of his δοχιμή. In 2 Cor 1:23, there are no Pauline opponents to speak of, so he can call upon God as a witness without this risk.[35] Paul himself knows that the Corinthians would be able to recognize his strategy as that of a forensic defense. In 2 Cor 12:19, Paul states (perhaps with a sigh): "You have again thought that we are defending (ὑμῖν ἀπολογούμεθα) ourselves to you." Though Paul is using the model of a forensic apology, he cannot admit to doing so, and so he must bring in his witnesses "under the table," in order to make his case on his terms without succumbing to those of his opponents.

In this courtroom scene, Paul stands alone, accused, with his opponents, the "lying apostles," as his accusers, and the Corinthians as judge and jury. Paul will then introduce God, the Lord, and even Satan as witnesses for his defense. This is a complete inversion of the forensic scene described above, which sees *God* as the judge. In the trial here envisioned by Paul, the scene has shifted, and Paul finds himself facing judgment not by God but rather by the Corinthians, and though his opponents are seemingly those who accuse him,[36] his real opponents are indeed *the Corinthians*. The only person whose role has not shifted is Paul, who remains at the center of the imagined courtroom. The Corinthians have failed Paul: they

---

[33] The *Rhet. Her.* disagrees, writing that "signs and presumptive proof deserve more credence than witnesses, for these first are presented precisely as they occurred in reality, whereas witnesses can be corrupted by bribery, or partiality, or intimidation, or animosity." *Rhet. Her.* II.vii.11 (trans. Harry Caplan, Loeb Classical Library).

[34] Though this is the most explicit instance, other examples of Paul's use of God as witness (though this is often inside an oath formula) include 1 Thess 2:10 and Phil 1:8.

[35] In 2 Cor 1:23, Paul's task is to prove that the reason he did not follow through with his intended travel plans was because of his goodwill towards the Corinthians. As part of the reconciliation process, Paul must answer any charges brought against him by the Corinthians. Calling upon God as a witness in this case thus affirms the validity of the Corinthians's charges, which in turn will pave the way for reconciliation.

[36] Here identified as "ministers of Satan" (11:14-15).

should have been there to testify for him, to bear him witness (12:11). Instead they are presenting themselves as the arbiter of Paul's δοχιμή.[37] Because of this inversion, Paul needs to employ a strategy of defense that makes it clear that it is precisely this type of tribulation that proves his δοχιμή. To do this he employs the character of the fool to outline the case, in which he is able to lead the Corinthians back to the cosmic picture by showing how his being singled out for testing is proof of his δοχιμή itself.

Paul's central claim in this section is that the fact that he has consistently been singled out for negative attention is proof of his δοχιμή. In line with Jewish law, quoted by Paul in 13:1 ("every charge stands from the mouth of two or three witnesses"), Paul needs to bring proofs of this claim. Paul thus details major instances in which he has received negative attention, which, by his logic, thus prove his δοχιμή. These same events could normally be understood as "weakness" and thus, from the point of view of his opponents, discount his credibility as an apostle.

The first section in which Paul engages in this strategy is 11:21b-29, in which Paul describes how he has been singled out for consistent torture and dangers he has received at the hands of the Jews (11:23-25), nature (11:25-27), his own people and Gentiles (11:26). This taxonomy of trauma ends with Paul reminding the Corinthians that he is constantly anxious about the cares of the churches, and affirming that he is indeed weak (11:28-29). This leads right into the second section, in which Paul describes his near-escape from the Ethnarch of Aretes in Damascus. According to Paul, the entire city is guarded in a thwarted attempt to seize and capture him (11:30-33). Paul's strategy here is to show that the fact that the Ethnarch singled him out as a threat is proof of his apostolic credibility and δοχιμή. The third section of Paul's proof is an ascent narrative that is perhaps expected by the Corinthians (2 Cor 12:1-10). Here Paul is again the subject of extended personal attention. After being chosen as the recipient of exceptional revelations in heaven, Paul is singled out as "a thorn was given to me in the flesh, a messenger of Satan, to strike me" (12:7). The giver of the thorn is intentionally left ambiguous – is it God or Satan? – but the message is clear: Paul is enough of a threat to warrant Satanic harassment.

Sine in light of Paul's revelation from the Lord these instances of harassment prove that he is δόχιμος,[38] the instigators of these circumstances have the rhetorical effect of being brought in as witnesses in Paul's defense. This completely undercuts the argument of Paul's opponents. If their central argument is that Paul is weak, rendering him ἀδόχιμος, then they could call upon the above events as proof *for them*. By inverting and

---

[37] Whereas, according to Paul, the judge of one's δοχιμή is God (1 Thess 2:4).

[38] Cf. 2 Cor 12:9, "My power is perfected in weakness."

diverting the conversation, Paul argues that these witnesses are in fact not witnesses for the prosecution, but witnesses for Paul himself. Paul thus does what he sets out to do in 11:12 – denies every opportunity of these "lying apostles" (who are really ministers of Satan, cf. 11:14-15, and are thus be identified as Paul's "thorn") to prove him ἀδόκιμος. Paul's inversion of the courtroom scene is reminiscent of that in the book of Job, discussed in a previous chapter. As in Job, the question of who is the judge and who is the adversary is confused. Both authors have recognized and brought to light the fundamental tension in the image of the heavenly court: the confusion of the roles of tester, witness, and judge. In Job, this tension provokes anger, lament, and frustration; Paul celebrates this tension as proof that it is his faith and actions that provoke his testing, and thus prove his δοκιμή. In the forensic context of 2 Corinthians, Paul takes advantage of the confused courtroom scene, and is able to bring in Satan as a witness on his behalf. Since he is afflicted by Satan, and has passed the test, he is, therefore, δόκιμος. Paul thereby uses the courtroom scene for purposes of his own argumentation. But, again, just as in Romans 14:10, if there was no shared assumption of the operation of the divine courtroom, this argument would have limited resonance. It is precisely Paul's intent to shame the Corinthians and make them realize their own illusions of self-governance and authority that lies behind this extensive metaphor. The metaphor has no currency if the Corinthians do not share Paul's assumptions about the cosmological tribunal.

One other place where Paul takes advantage of the confused courtroom scene is Romans 8:31-34, where Paul asks, "If God is on our behalf, who is against us? God who indeed did not spare his only son, rather handed him over on behalf of all of this, will he not indeed also grace us with all things in him? Who will bring charges against the elect of God? Is it not God who justifies? Who is the condemner? Christ who died, but rather was raised, who also is at the right hand of God, who pleads (ἐντυγχάνει) with God for us." This is the very paradox of the confused courtroom. God is both the justifier and the advocate, the one on our behalf (8:31). Yet if this is so, how can you have a courtroom? Who is bringing charges? Who is condemning? Though this is highly disputed, it is possible that Paul is here arguing that *Christ* is the condemner (ὁ κατακρινῶν), the one bringing the charges – indeed the only one *able* to bring the charges. It is a brilliant use of the verb ἐντυγχάνω – a word that can mean both "to plead, to entreat" and also "to lay charges against." In Paul's eyes Christ by his very nature both pleads and condemns – similar to the way the Gospel of John imagines the crisis that has come into the community, as I will argue in the following chapter.

Paul did not have to make this argument; he is perfectly capable of imagining Satan as the great condemner, the ultimate threat to humanity's
justification. He certainly sees himself as being the object of Satanic harassment in the Corinthian correspondence, and famously tells the Thessa-
lonians that he had intended to visit them, but Satan blocked his way (1
Thess 2:18). But Satan is absent from Romans, and thus absent from the
cosmological schema envisioned therein. Courtrooms need condemners;
they are not (*contra* Seifrid) simply two parties contending with each other.[39] By the time of Paul, courtrooms had significantly more parties involved, including public prosecutors (sometimes the individuals bringing
the case, other times people acting officially) and advocates.[40] Paul could
not have expected his readers to imagine a courtoom without a prosecutor.

What hope does humanity have if their defender is also their accuser! In
following chapters I will demonstrate that this is a central question and lament in rabbinic midrash. Though at least half a millennium – if not closer
to three quarters of a millennium – passes between the composition of the
Pauline epistles and the collation of rabbinic traditions, the same issue
persists. How can man stand before God, and how can this seemingly unfair courtroom be fair and just at all?

## E. Courtrooms with Love: the *non*-tensions of Paul

One of the most dominant aspects of the intertestamental literature, an aspect that will reach its full tensive potential in the Rabbinic material, is the
tension between conceptions of God's attributes. As I have argued in previous chapters, scenes of God holding trial are part of an ongoing conversation that began in the Hebrew Bible with the book of Job: the question of
God's ultimate justice in the universe and the complicated relationship between justice and mercy. In particular, the testamentary and apocalyptic
literature seems concerned with the question of how much mercy tips the
balance in favor of *injustice* rather than justice. Specifically, this question
is focused on the nature of intercession: What room is there for intercession before God? What is remarkable about Paul is that despite the fact
that his employment of divine courtroom imagery creates new tensions,

---

[39] Seifrid is thus mistaken in his critique of Wright that closes his otherwise erudite work
"Paul's use of Righteousness Language," cf. especially p.66.

[40] While it has often been taken as axiomatic that Greek law did not have a professional
class of advocates that one could hire, the most recent scholarship has taken an axe to this
axiom, noting both the use of professional speech-writers and supporting speakers
(συνήγοροι) that one could hire in one's own defense. See, for example, Lene Rubinstein,
*Litigation and Cooperation: Supporting Speakers in the Courts of Classical Athens* (Stuttgart:
Franz Steiner Verlag, 2000).

tensions that will have an effect on early Christian understanding of the administration of God's justice and the use of the motif of the divine courtroom, this central tension between justice and mercy is almost completely *lacking* in Paul. It is Paul's particular understanding of the grace of God through its concrete realization in the death and resurrection of Christ that allows this tension to be diffused.

Paul does not use just one metaphor to talk about what was made possible by the Christ-event: he variously uses terms such as salvation, redemption, sanctification, reconciliation, and justification. It is therefore misguided to argue, as some scholars have done, for *either* a forensic model of salvation *or* a participatory model. Both are present and have their place in Paul. He uses the whole range of terminology, metaphor, and analogy available to him to articulate the import of the events at Golgotha. It is precisely the magnitude of the event that makes it *impossible* for Paul to limit himself to just one avenue or image, or one set of words. An additional impact of the controversial statement in 1 Cor 9:19-23 is that Paul has basically announced to his readers that he will use *all identities and categories* that he can to "win some" for the new faith, for the sake of the gospel. This chapter, therefore, does not argue that the divine courtroom is somehow the *most important* aspect of Paul's thought, only that Paul makes use of it often, and that this use is not without its own problems and tensions.

One tension that it resolves, at least somewhat, however, is that between the justice and mercy of God. For Paul, the death and resurrection of Christ is the ultimate event for illustrating *both* God's justice and mercy. It is the Christ-event that creates the conditions of the possibility for justification, for the divine courtroom to operate at all. For Paul, there was no way of moving humanity out of that dock before Christ came. We were all, in Paul's mind, hopelessly stuck in a state of condemnation. It is only through Christ that humanity *can* successfully stand before God in the first place. Agreed, Paul sometimes uses the term justification, δικαιοσύνη in a seemingly contradictory manner. On the one hand, he often uses the present tense to speak about being justified, yet on the other he speaks of justification as something people are striving *for*, something that hasn't happened yet. So, for example, both are present in Galatians 2:15-16, when Paul castigates Peter for his hypocrisy:

We are Jews by nature and not sinners from the Gentiles, knowing that no man is justified (δικαιοῦται) from works of the law except through faith in Jesus Christ, and we believed in Christ Jesus, in order that we might be justified (δικαιωθῶμεν) from the faith of Christ and not from works of the law, for no flesh will be justified (δικαιωθήσεται) from the works of the law.

Three uses of the verb, three tenses of the verb. This one example is enough to highlight the "yet, not yet," feel of much of Paul's writings on this issue. He understands justification as something that has taken place with the death and resurrection of Christ, that wiped the slate clean for humanity, something that is taking place right now, and one that will take place in the future, probably the eschatological future. The second and the third aspects – what is happening right now and what will happen in the future – are conditional on πίστις 'Ιησοῦ – whatever that means.[41] Πίστις 'Ιησοῦ is, for Paul, the criteria for justification, and perhaps the new operative law in the courtroom, the "law of faith," as Paul seems to suggest in Romans 3:27-31:

> Through what sort of law? That of works? No, but through the law of faith (νόμου πίστεως). For we reckon that a man is justified by faith apart from works of the law. Or is God the God of the Jews alone? Isn't he also of the God of the Gentiles? Indeed, also of the Gentiles, since God is one, who will justify the circumcision from faith and the uncircumcision through faith. Do we then nullify (καταργοῦμεν) the law through faith? Μὴ γένοιτο, rather we confirm (ἱστάνωμεν) the law.

Though it seems clear from this passage (and is perhaps the only thing that *does* seem clear from this passage) that Paul believes faith is the *only* operative criteria in the courtroom, again we have the problem of reconciling those passages that seem to suggest other criteria (see above). It is perhaps not surprising that ultimately Paul resorts to the language of wisdom literature to close the kerygmatic section of Romans:[42]

> Oh the depth of riches and wisdom and knowledge of God:
> How unfathomable are his judgments (τὰ κρίματα) and incomprehensible his paths.
> For who can know the mind of the Lord?
> Or who was his counselor?
> Or who has offered previously to him, and has been repaid by him?
> For all things are from him and through him and for him:
>     To him be the glory forever, Amen. (Rom 11:33-36)

One can only hope that the declaimer of this letter (perhaps Phoebe?) was able to nuance the reading of this letter through her voice and movement!

Nevertheless, for Paul it is the death and resurrection of Christ that provides the conditions of the possibility for justification, and the death and resurrection of Christ are examples both of God's justice and mercy – inexorably intertwined attributes of God. Though Paul certainly has not de-

---

[41] This study cannot take up the question of what exactly Paul means by πίστις 'Ιησοῦ, whether he means the personal faith of Jesus or man's faith in the person of Jesus.

[42] So Fitzmyer: "this hymn also forms the conclusion to the whole of the doctrinal section of Romans (1:16-11:36). For not only God's dealings with Israel are unsearchable and manifest his uprightness to his chosen people, but all God's dealings with humanity are so. No one holds God in his debt." Fitzmyer, *Romans*, 633.

veloped th s understanding of what was accomplished on the cross to the extent that Anselm of Canterbury will, Anselm finds the building blocks of his theory of salvation as satisfaction *in Paul*: it is because of God's great justice – that he cannot leave sin unpunished – and mercy – that he desires to redeem humanity from their fallen state – that out of love for humanity he sends Christ to die on the cross. Paul expresses this fundament in Romans 5:8, writing that "God demonstrates his love for us, for while we were yet sinners Christ died on our behalf." In other words, the death and resurrection of Christ is proof both of God's love for humanity, and is God's proof of his ultimate justice and righteousness (Rom 3:26, see above). Paul thus *resolves* the essential tension between justice and mercy that is often at the center of the divine courtroom by seeing the resolution in the figure and accomplishments of Christ himself. While the courtroom is still very much alive in Paul's thoughts, this aspect of it is no longer in tension. Christ conditions the courtroom, and this is what gives the people of faith the ability to move out of the dock.

God's justice and mercy are the central issue in the entire section of Romans 9-11, where Paul deals with salvation history and the identity of God's elect Israel. After the hymn to love at the end of Romans 8, Paul turns to the question of Israel, arguing that the word of God to Abraham has not failed – Israel are still Abraham's descendants – but rather the identity of the people Israel has been reestablished. Not all Israelites are truly a part of Israel (9:6); it is the children of the promise, not the children of the flesh, who are to be counted as descendants (9:8). God has placed a stumbling block in Zion (9:32-33) that has led historical Israel astray, and so the Gentiles have become God's elect, attaining righteousness (9:30). In the future, however, both Jew and Greek will be saved (10:12-13; 11:26), for the gifts and the calling of God are irrevocable (11:29). These three chapters provide a sustained historical proof for Paul of both the inherent justice and mercy of God realized in the figure of Christ, and these two attributes *are* δικαιοσύνη θεου. As N. T. Wright has argued, *contra* Ernst Käsemann:

This divine righteousness always was, and remained throughout the relevant Jewish literature, the *covenant faithfulness* of god. The fact that, as Käsemann observed, this 'righteousness' includes the idea of the justice of the creator being put into effect vis-à-vis the whole cosmos does not mean that the covenantal idea has been left behind. It should remind us that the covenantal idea itself *always included in principle* the belief that when the creator/covenant god acted on behalf of Israel, this would have a direct relation to the fate of the whole world, to the rooting out of evil and injustice from the whole creation. Paul's Christian theological reflection begins, I suggest, from within exactly this matrix of thought, with the realization that *what the creator/covenant god was supposed to do for Israel at the end of history, this god had done for Jesus in the middle of history.* Jesus as an individual, instead of Israel as a whole, had been vindicated, raised from the dead, after suffering at the hands of the pagans; and this had happened in the middle of ongoing 'exilic' history, not at its end.[43]

For Paul, therefore, Christ is the physical embodiment and proof of the resolution of God's justice and mercy. This tension between the two attributes of God, which will have such a dominant role in rabbinic literature, is resolved in Paul.

# F. Conclusion: Echoes of Job in Paul

It is no accident that throughout Romans 9-11 Paul reinterprets and adapts traditional Wisdom texts for his readers, texts which seek to answer and ask questions about the nature of divine reasoning and the place of man in the universe. In particular, one hears repeated echoes of the book of Job throughout these three chapters.[44] Perhaps nowhere else in the Hebrew Bible do we find this question of man's role in a divinely ordained universe so rawly exposed. When confronted with absolute debasement and despair, Job refuses to compromise his position as he is faced with arguments from his friends who extol God's consistency and insist that Job would not be punished in this way unless he had transgressed the law. The readers, being privy to Job 1-2, know that it is precisely because Job is unimpeachable with regards to the law that he is being faced with this ultimate test. The readers know that there has been an intrusion into the divine plan, a divinely warranted intrusion, but an intrusion nonetheless. This intrusion has completely overturned the divine courtroom. Job does not know this, but he realizes that by the criteria of the law he has not done anything to warrant such punishment. He cannot accept his friends's rational explications for his punishment. Allusions to Job in this section of Paul thus represent a concrete scriptural example of the inadequacies of having confidence in the law as a vehicle for justification. For Paul, the only confidence one can

---

[43] N.T. Wright, "Romans and the Theology of Paul," in David M. Hay and E. Elizabeth Johnson, eds., *Pauline Theology III: Romans* (Atlanta: Society of Biblical Literature, 2002), 33-34.

[44] So, for example, the allusions to Job 5:8-9, 9:10-12, 15:18, and 41:3 found at Romans 11:33-35; Job 34:29 at Rom 8:34; 12:7-9 at Rom 1:20. See also the likely allusion to the Targum of Job 41:3 at 11:35, as argued by A. T. Hanson, *The New Interpretation of Scripture* (London: SPCK, 1980), 85.

have is in God and Christ, and Paul uses the imagery of the divine courtroom throughout Romans both in order to attack traditional understandings of the role of the law in that court, and to acquit God of any wrongdoing.

Likewise the portrayal of Satan as a Pauline witness in 2 Corinthians 10-13 recalls the role of the Accuser in the divine courtroom envisioned in Job 1-2. As explicated in a previous chapter, present within the book of Job, not just in the prologue but in the poetry as well, is the repeated image of a trial, a judge, and a courtroom. As in Job, the question of who is the judge and who is the adversary in 2 Corinthians is confused. Both authors have recognized and brought to light the fundamental tension in the image of the heavenly court: the confusion of the roles of tester, witness, and judge. In Job, this tension provokes anger, lament, and frustration; Paul celebrates this tension as proof that it is his faith and actions that provoke his testing, and thus prove his δοκιμή. In the forensic context of 2 Corinthians, Paul takes advantage of the confused courtroom scene, and is able to bring in Satan as a witness on his behalf. Since he is afflicted by Satan, and has passed the test, he is, therefore, δόκιμος.

The book of Job provides Paul with a cultural model on which to build and to envision the world, both in terms of his own position and that of his readers. Throughout his writings Paul alludes both to specific verses of Job but also to the overall mise-en-scene imagined by Job. In the book of Job, his friends repeatedly try to persuade Job that he simply *must* have done something wrong, had broken the law, to be punished in this way. Job refuses to concede this crucial point; instead, he insists that he is being punished *unjustly* and repeatedly uses forensic imagery to argue this point. As Norman Habel has argued, "the book of Job is as much about God as it is about the specifics of Job's crisis."[45] Job indicts God for unfairly indicting him. This is the backdrop to Paul. Using the language of the divine courtroom, he shares with Job a rejection of the conception of the courtroom with its traditional criteria for judgment. Like Job, he too uses the forensic language to talk about God. However, unlike Job, Paul *acquits* God of any wrongdoing. While Job may ultimately come to that conclusion after the Voice from the Whirlwind that closes the majority of the book, it is the opposite of the dominant force of his fire and fury in the poetry. Indeed, the appearance of the whirlwind is necessary for *God to acquit himself* – because Job refuses to do so. Perhaps this, too, is the force of Paul. God had to send Jesus as a ἱλαστήριον (Rom 3:25) in order to acquit him-

---

[45] Norman Habel, "In Defense of God the Sage," in Leo G. Perdue and W. Clark Gilpin, eds. *The Voice from the Whirlwind: Interpreting the Book of Job* (Nashville: Abingdon Press, 1992), 21.

self, and it is up to Paul and others to explain just how Christ changed all the courtroom rules, changed the laws of the courtroom entirely.

Chapter 6

# "Judge with Just Judgment:"
# The Divine Courtroom in the Gospels and Revelation

## A. Introduction

Despite the fact that the future manifestation of the divine courtroom plays an important role in the Pauline epistles and in later Christian theology, the divine courtroom is not a central feature of the Synoptic Gospels. While glimpses of the courtroom appear periodically, it is not of primary concern to the first three evangelists. The Gospel of John, on the other hand, develops the cosmic courtroom and the concept of a heavenly lawsuit as an overarching motif. This is an innovation of the Fourth Gospel that represents a unique way of presenting the Jesus narrative. Of the synoptics, Matthew seems the most interested in invoking the divine courtroom on the lips of Jesus, usually as a warning in order to provoke fear and a change of behavior in the audience. In other words, Matthew uses the rhetoric of the coming courtroom as an ethical spur to action, which may be why the divine courtroom plays a role in the Sermon on the Mount as well.

Trials play a role in all four canonical gospels. In each gospel the readers are brought in to the story of Jesus' trial/interrogation/hearing before the Jewish authorities and then before the Roman tribunal of Pilate. Though these represent human courtrooms, these trials become crucial paradigms for later Christians in thinking about what it means to have the Son of God undergo a very human process of justice. The divine courtroom becomes connected to the human courtroom especially in the Gospel of John, where it has long been noted that when Jesus appears before Pilate, he appears to be judging Pilate rather than the other way around. In John, this is the culmination of his development of the "lawsuit motif" of his entire gospel, a moment of irony in which the one who seems to be being judged is revealed to be the ultimate judge.

In the book of Revelation we have several presentations of the divine courtroom at the end of days, the canonical fulfillment of the predictions outlined in Matthew. Not only does the author paint a picture of the final judgment of mankind, but he also opens a door into the heavenly courtroom, inviting the reader into the process of divine decision making. I will demonstrate these two courtrooms are very much connected, and central issues are at stake in his presentations, including the most important of all: whether God's judicial decisions are just, and the wrath of Revelation deserved.

In what follows, I will examine the way the divine courtroom appears in the gospels of Matthew and John, and the book of Revelation. First, I will discuss the way Matthew uses the divine courtroom, showing where in the Markan outline he has inserted these invocations and demonstrating that his use of the divine courtroom is designed to provoke fear and repentance. Following that discussion, I will examine the unique innovations of the Gospel of John and its "lawsuit motif," engaging especially with the important work of Andrew Lincoln on this matter. Finally, I will turn to the presentation of the divine courtroom at the end of days that appears in Revelation. In all three of these cases, I will demonstrate that far from simple dioramas of the courtroom, the authors paint a picture of the divine courtroom that expects the reader to take an active role in the proceedings, and use this knowledge as part of their compositional strategies. Though this is most evident in John and Revelation, it is also part of the way Matthew has structured and presented his Gospel, as will become evident from the following discussion.

## B. The Divine Courtroom in Matthew

It has long been recognized that future judgment is a central motif in the Gospel of Matthew.[1] Beginning with the proclamation of John the Baptist (Matt 3:1-12), Matthew repeatedly invokes the coming judgment as a motivation for repentance and the turn towards ethical action throughout the Gospel. This culminates in the famous depiction of the future separation of the sheep and the goats in 25:31-46, understood early on to be a description of what the grand assize of the nations will resemble. Writing on the centrality of the judgment-motif in the Gospel, Ulrich Luz remarks that "God's judgment is at the center of Jesus' proclamation of the kingdom of God and keeps it from becoming a message of harmless love."[2] Daniel

---

[1] This has been the case since Gunter Bornkamm's 1956 article, "Endwartung und Kirche im Matthäusevangelium," available in G. Bornkamm, G. Barth, and H. J. Held, eds., *Tradition and Interpretation in Matthew* (London: SCM, 1963) 15-51. See also the important works by D. Marguerat, *Le Jugement dans l'évangile de Matthieu* (Geneva: Labor et Fides, 1981), and David C. Sim, *Apocalyptic Eschatology in the Gospel of Matthew* (Cambridge: Cambridge University Press, 1996).

[2] Ulrich Luz, *Matthew 8-20* (Hermeneia; Minneapolis: Fortress Press, 2001), 154.

Marguerat notes that out of 148 pericopes in Matthew, the theme of judgment is present in 60 of them.[3]

Jesus speaks about the coming judgment and the need for humans to change their actions in his first public address in Matthew, the Sermon on the Mount (Matt 5:1-7:27). Immediately following the Beatitudes (5:3-12), Jesus reminds the people of their role and responsibilities in the universe, including observing the commandments, which he has come "not to abolish, but to fulfill" (5:17), and which if they do not follow, they "will never enter the kingdom of heaven" (5:20). After laying out these "hermeneutical principles,"[4] Jesus then applies them by proclaiming a more intensified interpretation of the law, using language that repeatedly reminds the audience of the judgment that awaits them if they fail to live up to the requirements of the law (5:21-48). This section, referred to as the "Antitheses," consists of six examples, the first of which specifically calls upon the language of judgment to make its ethical claims (5:21-26). Formally, this unit has three distinct subsections: (a) the protasis: Jesus' reference of the biblical commandment not to commit murder and its correllative punishment, being liable to judgment (5:21); (b) the antidosis: Jesus' reinterpretation of that commandment as being not only regarding murder but regarding anger, the root cause of murder, which in *itself* makes one liable to judgment (5:22). Jesus insists that even insulting one's brother makes one liable – not only to judgment but to the high council and indeed to fiery Gehenna. This takes the reader out of a purely human realm of justice and into an eschatological one; (c) The practical examples on how to put this teaching into action (5:23-25): the first regarding the proper state required for cultic participation (5:23-24), and the second regarding the need to seek reconciliation for legal trespass outside of the courtroom, which can have dire consequences, setting off a chain of events beyond one's control (5:25).

The concept of judgment in this pericope is both human and divine. Obviously Jesus cannot be suggesting that everyone who is angry is liable to human courtrooms in the same way as those who commit murder. Instead, already by this first intensification, Jesus has moved the reader into understanding judgment not only as an earthly court of law, whether Jewish or Roman, but as having a heavenly counterpart, and impresses upon the reader that the heavenly judgment is interested in more than just whether or not the person has committed a justifiable offense. It is indeed possible that Matthew's use of συνέδριον in 5:22 represents the first use of this

---

[3] Marguerat, *Le Jugement*, 13. Marguerat notes that in Mark, the count is only 10/92, and in Luke 28/146.

[4] Following the description and definition of Hans Dieter Betz, *The Sermon on the Mount* (Hermeneia; Fortress Press, 1995), 167-200.

term to refer to the divine high council rather than the historical Sanhedrin of Jesus' time.[5] The parallelism with this liability to that to fiery Gehenna in the second half of this verse certainly suggests this meaning, as is it difficult to think that saying "Raka" vs. "Fool" would result in two different jurisidictional claims.

What Matthew is here doing is what will remain a consistent part of his Gospel, which is the use of the rhetoric of the divine courtroom to provoke fear and a change of behavior in his readers. It is certainly not the case that the imagery of heavenly judgment is here supposed to be a comfort or a source of hope for the Matthean community, even though other Christian texts employ the rhetoric in this way. Indeed, the example that closes this section reinforces the intended implication by reminding the readers just how dangerous *any* courtroom is, much less one that is controlled by an all-powerful judge with the power to sentence individuals to fiery Gehenna. Jesus here encourages the disciples to settle issues with their adversaries out of court because of the chain of events that could occur at trial: "lest the adversary hand you over to the judge and the judge to the guard, and you be thrown in prison. Truly I tell you, you will not get out of there until you have paid back the last quadran" (5:24). Scholars have suggested that on the historical level the intended reference is to a debtor's prison, and the legal issue suggested here is that of debt collection.[6] But what is more important is the role this example is playing in the pericope. This example serves as a reminder to the reader of just how dangerous the legal system is, given the way one circumstance can lead to another and spiral out of one's control. The syntax of Matt 5:24 especially bears this out, with the sequence of events being described with the verb παραδίδωμι at the beginning, and a simple καὶ separating each recipient, as "you" are handed down from one judicial actor to another ("μήποτέ σε παραδῷ ὁ ἀντίδικος τῷ κριτῇ καὶ ὁ κριτὴς τῷ ὑπηρέτῃ καὶ εἰς φυλακὴν βληθήσῃ"). The impression of this verse is that these events can take place in rapid-fire succession, and thus reminds the reader of the power of the imperial judicial apparatus. I believe there is an implied *a fortiori* argument here: if this can happen so quickly and easily, with such dreadful results, on the human level, *how much the more so* with someone who has the power to sentence you to fiery Gehenna. Especially since that someone

---

[5] Later Rabbinic literature will develop the concept of the "Bet Din Gadol" as the heavenly counterpart to the earthly Bet Din (see below, chapter 7); Matthew may intend a similar semantic resonance here.

[6] Cf. Bernard Jackson, *Theft in Early Jewish Law* (Oxford: Clarendon, 1972), 144; Betz, *Sermon on the* Mount, 226; Ulrich Luz, *Matthew 1-7* (Hermeneia; Minneapolis: Fortress Press, 2007), 241.

can sentence you for crimes not justiciable by human courts – like calling your sibling a moron.

This example, then, is an instance of Matthew using the rhetoric of the divine courtroom to provoke fear and a change of behavior in his readers. What is crucial to remember is that the imperial judicial apparatus, represented by the procedure involved in a case of owing money here, was a frightful thing not only for people who were guilty of the crime, but for people who were *innocent* of it as well. As argued in chapter three, Roman courtrooms and courtrooms of antiquity in general were not places known for the administration of perfect justice, but rather places in which *injustice* was perpetrated just as often. Courtrooms were places to be avoided at all costs – which is why Jesus encourages the audience to settle out of court (5:24). While he does not specifically say that even people who are innocent of the crime should settle, the implication is that *everyone* facing an adversary (ἀντιδίκος) should do so. As Betz notes, "Only fools rush into lawsuits! The dreadful risks implied in a lawsuit can be avoided if the opponents settle the dispute out of court."[7] Even if one was innocent, one should avoid the courtroom, for it is a place to be feared. Everyone should attempt to be reconciled with their adversary, if they meet them "on the road". This has additional meaning when understood on the eschatological level. Ulrich Luz notes that "The 'way' – in the original commonsense advice merely the way to where the court is located – becomes the time granted people before God's final judgment. Thus beneath the surface of the commonsense advice the perspective of the last judgment becomes visible."[8] This example, therefore, is meant to provoke fear in the audience and to urge the hearers to change their behavior. For if the worst thing that could happen is that they are thrown into a debtor's prison, how much the more so should they fear the divine courtroom if the punishment there is fiery Gehenna. One should fear the divine courtroom even if that person believes they are innocent and righteous.[9] The use of a specific example from the human legal system buttresses this eschatological message because it invites them to make the analogy with their own time and draw the appropriate conclusions. "Final Judgment" is not an empty threat – it is given a concrete analogy and reference point to non-final, regular judgment, and how tumultuous and unpredictable it can be.

---

[7] Betz, *Sermon on the Mount*, 228.

[8] Luz, *Matthew 1-7*, 241. This is buttressed for Luz by the "ἀμὴν λέγω σοι" in 5:25, which he argues always introduces an eschatological warning.

[9] This, in turn, links back to one of the central messages of the Sermon on the Mount, that of pointing to the immense gulf between human *self*-righteousness and actual *righteousness*. Throughout the Sermon, Jesus consistently reminds the disciples of just how much hypocrisy and self-satisfaction stands between them and living up to the ethical demands of the law.

Later in the Sermon on the Mount, Matthew again invokes the rhetoric of final judgment as a warning against hypocrisy and inappropriate judgment of others (Matt 7:1-5). In particular, Jesus warns the disciples "Do not judge, that you may not be judged (μή κρίνετε, ἵνα μὴ κριθῆτε). For by what judgment you judge you will be judged (κριθήσεσθε), and by what measure you measure, it will be measured to you (μετρηθήσεται ὑμῖν)" (Matt 7:1-2). Betz correctly notes that this maxim is not intended to suggest that humans should abolish the entire judicial system, but rather this refers specifically to "fraternal correction," writing that:

> The imperative in vs 1a implies the observation that in ordinary life people are relentlessly preoccupied with what is prohibited: passing judgment on one another. This habit involves everything from mere gossip to community regulations to court actions. The habit of passing judgment on others also involves a mechanism of tit for tat. The kind of judgment one passes on others comes back to the person who started it. Gossipers become targets of gossip; critics must face being criticized, and so forth. The prudent person, so goes the advice, will break the vicious cycle by withholding such judgment because the same mechanism will work in the reverse direction as well. Restraint will motivate others to exercise equal restraint.[10]

The instruction not to engage in this type of conduct includes a warning to those who choose not to heed this advice: they "will be judged" and "it will be measured" to them.[11] These are eschatological warnings, and we should understand these future passives as divine passives, indicating what action God will take against those who engage in this type of activity.[12] Thus the criterion at the final judgment will be the very standards employed by humans. This corresponds to a reciprocal notion of justice, the eschatological *"ius talionis"*.[13] But this implies something important about the divine courtroom: God plays by human rules. God will judge according to human standards of justice, and he will execute punishment according to human standards of punishment. Even though the activity warned against here may be ethical in nature and broader than simply judicial conduct, there is certainly a warning against inappropriate judicial conduct included here. This has larger resonance within the Gospel of Matthew, as the readers will be called upon to evaluate what happens to Jesus in the human judicial system, and effectively to pass judgment on the conduct of the participants in that trial. The theological assertion that God plays by human rules, that he operates according to human standards, is not a comforting one.

---

[10] Betz, *Sermon on the Mount*, 490.

[11] Luke sharpens this warning, and includes a positive imperative along with the negative; "Do not judge, and you will not be judged; Do not condemn, and you will not be condemned (καταδικάζετε); Forgive, and you will be forgiven" (Luke 6:37).

[12] cf. Betz, *Sermon on the Mount*, 491; Luz, *Matthew 1-7*, 351.

[13] Betz, *Sermon on the Mount*, 491.

This is reinforced by the second half of the verse, when Jesus informs the disciples that it will be measured to them according to the standards by which they measure (7:2). As I argued in the previous chapter, anxiety over weights and measures was common in Antiquity across cultures, and needs to be taken into consideration when analyzing scenes of weighing in the divine courtroom. Here we have an explicit warning about those measures that might be found there – they might be the very same measures that human use when judging others. Here these measures are metaphorical, and no doubt refer to the criteria people use when making judgments on one another. However, the metaphor works because of the associations people have with measures in antiquity, and the commonality of bad business practices across the Ancient Mediterranean World.[14] People's lived experience in the economic and the judicial realm stand behind these warnings. Matthew is here warning his readers about how God will judge them, using the rhetoric of the divine courtroom with an eye to changing human behavior, but by doing so he is reminding them that the divine courtroom is not a place at which they should look forward to being. It is a courtroom at once both unlike any other but also just like the ones they know – operating according to standards they may not like. Standards for which, according to Matthew, they themselves are responsible – he is certainly suggesting a *quid pro quo* arrangement here – but standards they won't like, and standards of which they should be very, very afraid.

This is consistent with the way Matthew employs the rhetoric of the divine courtroom throughout his Gospel. In Matthew, Jesus often includes tense references to the impending day of judgement to reinforce instructions to his disciples. Referring to certain cities, Jesus insists that it will be worse for them on the day of judgment than it was for Sodom and Gomorrah (10:15; 11:20-24). Jesus asserts that at "the judgment of this generation" the people of Nineveh will rise up and witness against the Pharisees and the scribes,[15] and so will the Queen of the South, who came from the ends of the earth to see Solomon (12:38-42). The implication here is that if the people of Nineveh, non-Israelites, could understand the severity of their situation and repent, then the Pharisees, who *are* of the people of God, should be able to do so. If the Queen of the South, aka the Queen of Sheba, could come from the ends of the earth to see Solomon, then the Pharisees, who are right there in Judea, should recognize what is right in front of them, even greater than Solomon.

---

[14] See Bernard Couroyer, "De la measure dont vous measurez il vous sera measuré" *Revue Biblique* 77 (1970), 366-370. Couroyer argued that this is an economic metaphor and a warning against bad business practices.

[15] This is part of the discourse of the "Sign of Jonah," mentioned again at 16:4.

This assertion regarding the people of Nineveh and the Queen of the South comes at the end of a lengthy discourse in Matthew 12 that again makes clear the connection between human ethical behaviour and the appearance before the heavenly tribunal. This pericope is characterized by the intensifying conflict between Jesus and the Pharisees. First, Jesus argues with the Pharisees after they castigate him for picking grain on the Sabbath (12:1-8), an argument that climaxes with Jesus' assertion that "the Son of Man is Lord of the Sabbath" (12:8). The rising conflict continues as the Pharisees again question Jesus' religious practice by (not so innocently) asking him whether or not it is lawful to heal people on the Sabbath (12:9-10). Jesus rises to the bait, admonishing the Pharisees and healing the man with the shriveled hand (12:11-13). The narrator then tells us that "exiting, the Pharisees took counsel against him in order to destroy him (ἀπολέσωσιν)" (12:14). The tone of the pericope continues to darken as the Pharisees accuse Jesus of performing exorcisms by the power of Beelzebul (12:24), leading Jesus to a strong warning:

> Either make the tree good and its fruit good, or make the tree rotten and its fruit rotten: for the tree is made known by the fruit. Brood of vipers, how are you able to speak good things, being evil? For the mouth speaks from the abundance of the heart. The good man casts out good things from the good treasure, and the evil man casts out evil things from the evil treasure. But I say to you that for every idle word they speak, humans will have to give an account of it (ἀποδώσουσιν περὶ αὐτοῦ λόγον) on the day of judgment. For by your words you will be justified (δικαιωθήσῃ), and by your words you will be condemned (καταδικασθήσῃ). (12:33-37)

This is then followed by the Pharisees's request for a sign and Jesus' statements about who will testify against them at the judgment (12:38-42). These warnings about judgment punctuate this pericope, providing an exclamation point to the entire conflict-section between Jesus and the Pharisees. Though Jesus is speaking to the Pharisees when he warns them about how their words will come back to haunt them on the day of judgment, Matthew is clearly speaking past the level of the narrative to his readers, warning *them* about their words and about what will happen to them if they fail to repent or change their behavior. It is significant that Jesus here does not tell the Pharisees "*you* will be required to give an account of your words," but rather that "*humans*" will have to give that account (12:36).[16] This extends the object of the warning past the Pharisees to everyone, and

---

[16] The NRSV translation completely loses this distinction, translating Jesus' words as "on the day of judgment *you* will have to give an account for every careless word you utter," missing Matthew's larger audience here.

makes the second person singulars of the following verse (δικαιωθήσῃ, καταδικασθήσῃ) applicable to every reader individually, every human.[17]

The theology being expressed here is that of recompense; specifically, Jesus is here saying that not only will humans pay back for their actions, which he has already asserted in the Sermon on the Mount, and will assert again even more strongly in 16:27 ("For the Son of Man is about to come in the glory of his father with his angels, and then he will repay to each according to his work" [ἀποδώσει ἑκάστῳ κατὰ τὴν πρᾶξιν αὐτοῦ]), but that humans will have to account even for their *words*. Πρᾶξις in 16:27 should thus be understood to include the entire range of human activity, understanding speech as a type of action. On this passage, Blaine Cherette writes that "words reveal the basic orientation of the heart, and for that reason they are important. One will be held accountable at the judgment for even the most useless words, which are consequential because they too are able to divulge the true character of the person. The day of judgment will be a time when such words are weighed and their true significance is established."[18] The revelatory character of one's words – even idle ones – makes them appropriate evidence against man on the day of judgement. According to Mathew, one's own worst nemesis, in its full legal connotations, is not necessarily the people of Nineveh and the Queen of the South, but is one's own self. This is not dissimilar from the contemporary claim of Lucian of Samosata that everyone's shadow testifies against them in Minos's courtroom – who better to report one's secrets than that which follows you around all the time? Here it is the very words one speaks that he will need to confront.

This all paints a very terrifying picture, especially since it is not only the case that one needs to confront those words, but that the words themselves will become the instruments of judgment, the criteria of adjudication. Once again, just like in the Sermon on the Mount, Matthew is asserting that humans are setting the conditions of judgment, that the divine courtroom will play by human rules. Just as one would have to get up and defend against one's own assertions in a human courtroom, so will be the case in the divine courtroom – except the scope of those assertions is so much broader, encompassing everything ever said, not just what others have overheard or to which one has officially attested. As Marguerat notes, Matthew puts humans in a state of *radical responsibility*, not only for what

---

[17] This reading has the added benefit of explaining why these are not second person *plurals* if Jesus is speaking to the multiple Pharisees, his immediate audience in the narrative.

[18] Blaine Cherette, *The Theme of Recompense in Matthew's Gospel* (JSNT Supp Series 79; Sheffield: Sheffield Academic, 1992), 130.

they do, but also for what they say, even without thinking or in a moment of weakness.[19]

The terror is compounded by the assertion throughout the Gospel of Matthew that the judge humans will face in the eschatological courtroom will be the Son of Man/Jesus, i.e., the very person who is giving them the warnings now. As Marguerat argues, "Quand bien même le rédacteur accueille des traditions rattachant la rétribution finale à Dieu, il ne fait pas de doute qu'à ses yeux, *le Dieu qui juge arborera les traits de Jésus*."[20] This identification of the eschatological judge represents a departure from one strand of Second Temple Judaism that, building off the assertions of the Hebrew Prophets and the vision of Daniel 7, understands this role as belonging and proper to God alone. Instead, the Gospel of Matthew informs the reader that this role will be filled by the Son of Man.[21] This also represents a departure from the way the Son of Man's eschatological role is understood in Mark. In particular, Mark 8:38 states that with regard to those who are ashamed of Jesus, the Son of Man will be ashamed of them when he comes in the Father's glory. David Sim has correctly noted that Mark does not predicate judging activity on the Son of Man, but rather simply notes that he will be ashamed. Sim also believes that the Son of Man as eschatological judge is a tradition not found in Q. Pointing to the shared tradition of Matt 10:32-3//Luke 12:8-9, Sim notes that "the Son of Man clearly acts as an advocate at the court of judgment in which the holy angels play a leading part."[22] However, Matthew differentiates from Mark, Q, and Luke by clearly depicting the Son of Man as the eschatological *judge*, not merely an advocate or a witness.

One such way that Matthew expresses this theology is in his portrayal of the Son of Man as sitting on the throne, which by this time has come to be associated as the location of divine judgment. In Matt 19:28 Jesus tells his disciples that "truly I tell you, you who have followed me, at the renewal, when the Son of Man is seated on the throne of his glory, you also will sit on twelve thrones, judging the twelve tribes of Israel." Sim notes that the throne here is specifically that of the Son of Man, and not that the Son of Man is seated on *God*'s throne.[23] This distinguishes this text from others, including 1 Enoch, which includes both sections on the Son of Man

---

[19] Marguerat, *Le jugement*, 41.

[20] Marguerat, *Le jugement*, 82.

[21] Marguerat notes that this is not dissimilar from the Pauline epistles, which "manifests un transfert similaire de la compétence judiciaire de Dieu à la personne du Christ." Marguerat, *Le jugement*, 83.

[22] Sim, *Apocalyptic Eschatology*, 98.

[23] Sim, *Apocalyptic Eschatology*, 119.

and elaborate throneroom depictions (see previous chapter), but does not have the Son of Man specifically seated on his own throne.

However, this Matthean concept does share a resemblance to the throne-rooms of the *Testament of Abraham*. In Recension A, Abraham encounters two thronerooms. First, he sees "the protoplast" Adam, sitting on a throne between the two gates of post-mortem destination (T. Abr. A 11:1-12). He then sees a second throneroom/courtroom with a fearful man seated on the throne (T. Abr. A 12:1-18), and is informed that the fearful man is "the son of Adam the protoplast, who is called Abel, whom Cain the wicked killed" (T. Abr. A 13). Likewise Abel is also identified as the judge in recension B, though the scene there is more specifically a courtroom with less throne imagery (T. Abr. B 11). As explained in the previous chapter, it is possible that the choice of Abel as judge might be related to his role as "son of Adam," referring back to the forensic role of "one like a son of man" in Daniel 7:13. This, merged with the judicial role of the Son of Man in 1 Enoch 46 and 49, may lead to the presentation of Abel as post-mortem judge. If so, this might provide a trajectory or parallel presentation of a "son of man" acting as an ultimate judge, not entirely dissimilar to the role of the Son of Man as the *eschatological* judge of Matthew 19:28.

A second parallel between the two texts may provide more evidence of this connection. Matthew 19:28 ascribes a judicial function in the eschatological courtroom to the disciples as well, asserting that they will sit on twelve thrones, judging the twelve tribes of Israel. Suggestively, in the complicated eschatological judicial procedures envisioned by the *Testament of Abraham*, Michael tells Abraham that at the parousia, each soul, after first being judged by the son of Adam, will then be judged "by the twelve tribes of Israel," and then, finally, by God himself (T. Abr. A. 13). While obviously Matthew has the twelve disciples *doing* the judging, and the twelve tribes of Israel *being judged*, rather than the twelve tribes doing the judging as asserted by *T. Abr.* A, this seems very similar, especially since no parallel tradition can be found for the tradition preserved in *T. Abr.* A, nor is the relationship between the judicial function of the Son of Man and that of the disciples clear in Matthew. Does one take place before the other? Do the disciples judge the tribes and the Son of Man judge the rest of the nations, as has been proposed by some scholars? If, however, we understand these traditions as being related in some way, Matthew 19:28 becomes more clear. It would be another example of Matthew as creative redactor of tradition, this time of the tradition that asserts a special forensic role to the twelve tribes of Israel at the eschatological judgment.[24]

---

[24] Obviously as we have it now, the longer recension of the Testament of Abraham is much later than the Gospel of Matthew. However, it is certainly possible if not probable that parts of the recension were composed earlier, and certainly that the traditions that they con-

Here the forensic role is shared by the disciples, perhaps portrayed as the spiritual heirs of the thrones previously occupied by the twelve tribes. The irony would then by that the twelve tribes who perhaps expected to be sitting on those thrones, would instead find themselves before the thrones, having lost their inheritance.[25]

The throne of the Son of Man is again the location of the most elaborate depiction of eschatological judgment in Matthew, that of Matt 25:31-46, the separation of the lambs from the kids. It hardly needs to be said that this is not your typical courtroom scene, though it contains elements thereof, particularly the throneroom setting and the interrogation and adjudication. The pericope is presented using the language of similitude. It is not a parable, though it contains features of a parable, and it is not a full vision, though it seems to be descriptive.[26] The "just as" (ὥσπερ) in 25:32 throws the rest of the pericope into slight ambiguity: is the whole pericope meant to be *analogous* to final judgment, or is it a description of final judgment?

The activity of separation is not one that is usually associated with courtrooms, and yet it is the first activity here specifically predicated on the Son of Man: he will separate (ἀφορίσει) the nations before him just as a shepherd separates the lambs from the kids. This is not without parallel, as it is reminiscent of the "pre-trial" division of humanity into two gates before the throne of the protoplast in *Testament of Abraham* A 11:1-12. The likely antecedent of this activity as part of judgement is the oracle of Ezekiel 34, a lengthy section of condemnation of both the shepherds (the rulers of Israel) and the sheep (the people). The oracle includes 34:17: "As for you, my flock, thus says the Lord YHWH, behold I will judge between sheep and sheep, between rams and goats ( הנני שפט בין-שה לשה לשה לאילים ולעתודים)."[27] However, in Ezekiel the activity is not described as separating, but as judging (שפט; LXX διακρίνω), and the activity is predicated on YHWH, not on an intermediate figure or proxy. This is emphasized by Ezekiel 34:20, when Ezekiel reports YHWH as asserting that "I myself

---

tain are far earlier than the final product. For discussion, see Allison, *Testament of Abraham*, 29ff.

[25] This read of 19:28 would buttress Charette's assertions regarding the role of the reward of inheritance in the Gospel of Matthew's theology of recompense, and the way Matthew uses the theme of inheritence in both its positive and negative formulations in the Gospel. 19:28 would then be an example of how the author employs *both* of these aspects of the inheritance formulation in one verse.

[26] So Luz: "Only vv. 32b-33 are a brief parable. The main part of the text is composed to the two major 'judgment dialogues' (vv. 34-40, 41-45). A way out of the dilemma might be to call Matt 25:31-46 a 'depiction of judgment.'" Luz, *Matthew 21-28*, 264.

[27] LXX: "καὶ ὑμεῖς πρόβατα τάδε λέγει κύριος ἰδοὺ ἐγὼ διακρίνω ἀνὰ μέσον προβάτου καὶ προβάτου κριῶν καὶ τράγων."

will judge between the fat sheep and the lean sheep." If this is the Hebrew Bible antecedent of the Matthean scene, Matthew has adapted the prophecy to transfer YHWH's judicial activity to the Son of Man, much as in previous pericopes.

The importance of this pericope is emphasized by its strategic placement in the Gospel. As Bornkamm first noted, all of the Matthean discourses end with anouncements or warnings of the coming judgment.[28] This, the culmination of the Olivet Discourse, not only stands as another announcement, but as the climax of *all* the announcements.[29] Right after the close of this pericope, Jesus warns the disciples about the upcoming Passover festival and handing over of the Son of Man (Matt 26:1-2), introducing the chain of events that will form the rest of the Gospel. This depiction of the future judgment, which has no Synoptic parallel, is, as Luz writes, "simply the culmination of something that has always been cantus firmus, leitmotif, and goal of the Matthean Jesus proclamation."[30]

One of the central issues in the scholarly literature on this pericope is the identity of those who are being judged, likened in the description to lambs and kids. In particular, some question whether or not the new Christian community is understood to be among those gathered for judgement. The passage calls those who appear before the throne "πάντα τὰ ἔθνη" (Matt 25:32), which would seem to include *all* the nations of the world, inluding Israel and the new Christian community. However, some scholars believe that Matthew does not intend his readers to see themselves among the flock, but rather among the "least of my brothers" in 25:40.[31] In this read, this passage would not be a description of universal judgment, but rather of the judgment on the rest of the nations. I do not believe that this a viable interpretation. Rather, I concur with Luz that we must understand this judgment scene to include the Christian community as well, as this is the only interpretation that makes relevant the entire Olivet Discourse. Luz

---

[28] Bornkamm, "End-Expectation," 15-24.

[29] The importance of the Olivet Discourse is well-noted in the scholarly literature. See, for example, Klaus Wengst, who argues that "This sermon has a prominent position both in its narration and also within the Gospel itself. Jesus delivers it upon the Mount of Olives at the end of his earthly mission, looking towards Jerusalem and particularly at the Temple. Directly thereafter comes his passion. Therefore, what we have here is a view both towards the future and also of his legacy." Wengst, "Aspects of the Last Judgment in the Gospel According to Matthew," in Henning Graf Reventlow, ed. *Eschatology in the Bible and in Jewish and Christian Tradition* (JSOT Supp 243; Sheffield: Sheffield Academic Press, 1997), 233-245, 233.

[30] Luz, *Matthew 21-28*, 285.

[31] See, for example, Eugene Pond, "Who are the Sheep and Goats in Matthew 25:31-46?" *Bibliotheca Sacra* 159 (2002), 288-301. An exhaustive survey of the literature on this passage is found in S. Gray, *The Least of My Brothers: Matthew 25:31-40: A History of Interpretation* (SBL Diss. Series 114; Atlanta: Scholars Press, 1989).

notes that "Since 24:3 Jesus has been speaking to the disciples alone. Since 24:32 he has been warning them in ever new images of the judgment that awaits them also. However, Matthew has not yet portrayed the judgment on the church. The entire parenesis of 24:32-25:30 would be in vain if it did not end in a portrayal of judgment that includes the church."[32]

The depiction of judgment that follows the description of separation is very specific. The judgment on each group is proclaimed first (Matt 25:34-36; 41-43), and then explained as each group questions their fate (25:37-40; 44-46). It does not correspond to the other Matthean warnings of final judgment: no one has to give account of their words (12:37), no one is judged by the same standards of judgment or measured by the same measures (7:1-2), and the disciples do not sit on twelve thrones judging the twelve tribes of Israel (19:28). This is not actually bares very little resemblance to a trial, even if it might bear resemblance to a sentencing hearing. Luz deals with this discrepancy by arguing that Matthew "feels little need to describe apocalyptic images or go into detail about his worldview. Instead of describing the actual act of judgment he represents it with a comparison but then expands it with a judgment dialogue."[33]

However, this is still a courtroom if you understand the participants differently. This is an example of a depiction of judgment being used to explain why final judgment will be *just*; why the judgments proclaimed here by the Son of Man are fair and equitable. In this passage, Matthew is explaining to his readers the justice and wisdom of the future judgment of the king. He is using this dialogue to show, painstakingly, that their behavior in the present towards "these my brothers," stands in for their behavior towards the king himself. This is why he explains this in both its positive and negative formulations. He does not just explain to those adjudicated to be righteous how they ministered to him, but also to those going to Gehenna how they did not do so. In this way, Matthew is anticipating the objections of the readers as to the justice of this threatened judgment. The readers are given this depiction of final judgment, complete with very detailed

---

[32] Luz, *Matthew 21-28*, 275. In an attempt to negotiate a middle ground on this issue, John Paul Heil has argued that Matthew's readers are supposed to identify with *both* the flock gathered for judgment and the least of the brothers in 25:40. Heil believes this passage "performs a double pragmatic effect upon its audience: (1) On the one hand, it urges them to behave as the righteous sheep and take care of the neediest, the 'least ones' in the world as a way of serving Jesus himself until his final coming. By doing so they will be blessed at the last judgment by inheriting the eternal life of the kingdom God has prepared for them. (2) On the other hand, and in a different way, it encourages them to further adopt the humility required of disciples (cf. 10.42; 18.1-5), by becoming needy least ones in their mission of bringing the kingdom to the world." Heil, "The Double Meaning of the Narrative of Universal Judgment in Matthew 25.31-46" *JSNT* 69 (1998) 3-14, 13.

[33] Luz, *Matthew 21-28*, 287.

explication of the criteria of judgment, for their own edification. There is an interrogation here, but it is not an interrogation of those gathered for judgment, it is an interrogation of the *judge* himself. It is not an accident that the king is the one who answers the questions, not the one doing the questioning. This is an example of Matthew anticipating that the readers are going to judge for themselves whether or not this is equitable and just, and thus whether or not *the judge* is equitable and just. Matthew anticipates that it will be the readers asking the questions of his Gospel, interrogating what is handed down to them.

This is also why this passage bears so little resemblance to the other warnings that are found throughout the Gospel of Matthew. This passage is a warning on a base level, but it is not meant to threaten and incite fear. On the contrary, the reason it is so lengthy in comparison to the other logia is because it is an appeal to reason. Matthew wants his readers to be aware of their behavior and actions, and he also wants his readers to be thinking about the equity of the future judgment. This passage thus constitutes a *defense* of future judgment, in which the readers are judging and evaluating the scene depicted before them.[34] This climax of the Matthean discourses, therefore, builds on the warnings that have been sounding notes throughout Matthew's gospel by ending with a reasoned appeal and argument to the readers. At first this looks like simply another warning of what is to come, but its power lies in the fact that it is explained so clearly and logically – what more powerful warning could there be?

# C. Trying God in John

The Gospel of John does not adhere to the standard depiction and use of the divine courtroom. The Gospel of John develops the cosmic courtroom and the concept of a heavenly lawsuit as an overarching structural motif for the entire Gospel. Throughout the Gospel of John, the author invites the reader to realize that the divine trial is not something that will occur at a future time, but that the divine courtroom is already in session. In John the reader is asked to view the world's rejection of Jesus, represented on the narrative level by the hostile reception of Jesus by the Jews, as an on-

---

[34] Luz correctly identifies the "ignorance motif" as a "literary device" (*Matthew 21–28*, 279). However, he does not explore the implications of using this device in a forensic setting. It is not simply a technique to provoke surprise in the hearers, it is an apologetic argument in defense of the justice of judgment.

going trial in which people bring about their own condemnation.[35] In this trial, the world testifies against itself by its own actions, just as Jesus says his works testify *for* him (John 5:36).

What scholars have not fully investigated in this divine courtroom scenario and how it functions in the Gospel of John is the role of John's readers in the courtroom. Viewing this trial from the purchase of temporal, geographical, and narrative distance, the reader is led to evaluate the choices of the characters and the decisions made by actors in the text. The reader is the only character in the Gospel who has the true insight to be able correctly to evaluate the choices of the characters and the decisions made by actors in the text. The reader is, therefore, not just a spectator in this trial, not just someone paid to sit behind a prosecutorial or defense bench, or someone passing through a forum or tribunal. The reader instead is invited into the action as a judge: judging the trial of the world, judging the correct course of action, and judging whether or not to bring judgments on themselves by refusing to believe in the message. "Blessed are those who have not seen and yet have believed," Jesus proclaims after Thomas's climactic confession (John 20:29). This statement, like so many others in the Johannine corpus, is tinged with irony. The reader, who has not "seen" Jesus in the plain sense of the term, has been able to *see* more clearly than the characters in the Gospel, and this sight makes them qualified – δόκιμοι – to sit as judges on the action.

The reader is explicitly addressed in this judicial capacity in John 7:24. Jesus, being questioned by the Jews as to the authority of his teaching, admonishes them "Do not judge by appearances (κατ᾽ ὄψιν), but judge the just judgment (τὴν δικαίαν κρίσιν κρίνετε)." John is not here only speaking to Jesus' Jewish interrogators, he is speaking past the characters in the Gospel directly to the reader in their judicial capacity. On the plain level of historical-event-interpretation, the trial appears to be over: Jesus was condemned, handed over, and crucified. But that is just "appearances." John asks the reader to look past appearances to judge the just judgment – the trial continues, and they have the responsibility to make the correct judgments on what *really* occurred, and what is still in process. The reader is thus an active character in John, whose distinct rôle is revealed by the forensic simile – The life of Jesus as heavenly courtroom – which represents the deep structure of the Gospel. In what follows, I will explore this motif with regard to three elements of the Gospel: the statements of Jesus in John 5, the figure of the Paraclete and its forensic function, and the trial of Jesus before Pilate in its unique Johannine composition.

---

[35] Cf. Nils Alstrup Dahl, "The Johannine Church and History" in William Klassen and Graydon F. Snyder, eds. *Current Issues in New Testament Interpretation* (New York: Harper and Brothers, 1962), 124-142, esp. 139-140.

## *I. John 5*

In his magnum opus *Truth on Trial: The Lawsuit Motif in the Fourth Gospel*, Andrew Lincoln argues convincingly that the Fourth Gospel presents the narrative of Jesus' life and death using the overarching metaphor of a trial scene or courtroom scenario, in which God convicts the world of injustice. Lincoln, like others before him, points to John's use of juridical vocabulary throughout the Gospel over and against the synoptics.[36] Lincoln argues that the choice of vocabulary reveals the overarching theme of the Gospel, that of the lawsuit or trial. After dividing the Gospel into four main sections, the prologue (1:1-18), Jesus' public ministry (1:19-12:50), the departure of Jesus (13:1-20:31), and the epilogue (21:1-25),[37] Lincoln argues that each of the four main sections of the Gospel contains the lawsuit motif in a significant way, and thus "both the pervasiveness and the positioning of the motif encourage readers to view the narrative, as a whole, from the perspective of a trial."[38] Lincoln argues that the actors in the trial are not just Jesus and the Jews. Given the cosmic backdrop provided by the prologue, the trial is between God, for whom Jesus acts as the ultimate representative, and the world, whom the Jews represent in microcosm.[39]

Obviously central to Lincoln's argument is the Johannine understanding of the κρίσις that has come into the community with the arrival of Jesus. At several key points in the narrative, Jesus makes definitive statements about what his arrival means for the world. The first is John 3:17-21:

For God did not send the son in order to condemn the world (ἵνα κρίνη τὸν κόσμον), but rather in order that the world might be saved through him. The one who believes in him will not be condemned (κρίνεται), but the one who does not believe has been con-

---

[36] Rudolf Schnackenburg noted that the verb μαρτυρεῖν appears thirty-three times in John, six times in 1 John, and 4 times in 3 John, compared with only thirty-two instances of the verb in the rest of the New Testament as a whole. Μαρτυρία by his count appears fourteen times in John, six times in 1 John and once in 3 John, while only sixteen times in the rest of the NT. Schnackenburg, *The Gospel According to St. John* (vol 1; New York: Herder and Herder, 1968), 251 n. 106. Lincoln adds to this by pointing out that μαρτυρεῖν only appears in the synoptics twice, with μαρτυρία only appearing four times in the synoptics. Additionally, Lincoln's word count on the verb κρίνειν reveals that the verb appears nineteen times in John compared to six times in Matthew and four in Luke. Lincoln, *Truth on Trial* (Peabody, MA: Hendrickson, 2000), 12.

[37] Though Lincoln does not like Raymond Brown's classification of the two major sections of the Gospel into the "Book of Signs" and the "Book of Glory," he does not alter Brown's classic division of the majority of the Gospel into these two separate stages. Lincoln, *Truth on Trial*, 14-15; cf. R. E. Brown, *The Gospel According to John i-xii* (AB; New York: Doubleday, 1966), cxxxviii-cxxxix.

[38] Lincoln, *Truth on Trial*, 21-22.

[39] Lincoln, *Truth on Trial*, 23.

demned already (ἤδη κέκριται), for he has not believed in the name of the only-born son of God. For this is the judgment (κρίσις), that the light has come into the world and men have loved darkness rather than light. For their works were wicked. For every one who does evil hates the light and does not come toward the light, in order that his works might not be proven guilty (ἐλεγχῇ). But every one who does good comes toward the light, in order that it might be revealed that his works were worked in God.

Schnackenburg sees this as an example of the Johannine "realized eschatology," that the judgment which other authors might ascribe to the end of time, has already occurred in John.[40] Jesus' coming has literally shed light on the true nature of man, revealing who might be saved and who has already been condemned because of their lack of belief.[41] The force of the perfect tense κέκριται in 3:18 is to indicate that the verdict is already in; the trial is underway, or has happened already. While the *sentencing* may still need to occur, the outcome has been already determined. The criteria, apparently, for the verdict, is the same as the criteria imagined by Paul: whether or not one believes in Jesus, the monogenes son of God. In this way the courtroom scenario imagined by the Gospel of John is radically different from previous understandings of the divine courtroom. Rather than envisioning a future, fixed courtroom, in which the divine trial will have a linear beginning, middle, and end, the Gospel of John imagines the courtroom as taking place in the arena of history, in which people are constantly testifying, offering evidence, and being judged.

This is confirmed by the second crucial passage regarding the κρίσις, John 5:19-30. After healing a paralytic on the sabbath (5:1-13), Jesus is rebuked by the Jews, who seek to kill him not only for his activity, but because he "said that God was his own father, making himself equal to God" (5:18). Jesus insists that none of his actions are his alone, but that of both the Son and the Father (5:19), and that "the Father does not judge anyone, but he has given all judgment to the Son" (5:22), for he is the Son of Man (5:27). Jesus insists that "I am not able to do anything by myself. I judge just as I hear, and by judgment is just (καὶ ἡ κρίσις ἡ ἐμὴ δικαία ἐστίν), for I do not seek my own will but the will of the one who sent me" (John 5:30).

This passage elaborates on the reality of the crisis that has come to the community, a crisis which was already asserted in 3:17-19. Jesus' arrival has brought the two poles of either life or judgment into the world. In this passage, Jesus not only claims the authority to perform miracles on the sabbath, but claims ultimate judicial authority. The Son has been given the authority to judge the community from the Father, and the judgment is in

---

[40] Schnackenburg, *The Gospel According to John 1*, 401-402.

[41] So Brown: "Jesus is a penetrating light that provokes judgment by making it apparent what a man is.' Brown, *The Gospel According to John i-xii*, 148-149.

process, though its final ratification is not yet apparent (5:24-29). The Father has given the son authority to execute judgment because he is the Son of Man (5:27). This concept most likely has its background in the judicial rôle of the Son of Man in both Daniel 7:14 and the Enochic traditions (Enoch 37-41, 49:4).[42] Jesus insists that his judgment is just because it is not his alone, but that of the one who sent him (5:30).

Though Jesus should really be on the defensive here, being accused by the Jews, his words to them show that he is taking an entirely different rôle. It is not merely a switch from defense to offense, from defendant to prosecutor, but it is a claim to truly be the authorized judge of the proceedings, a judge who far exceeds human judges. This is the force of the word δικαία in 5:30.[43] The judgment that he is able to pronounce – and pronounces by his very being, according to the Johannine theology, is of the utmost ontological significance. As Lincoln explains "Jesus claims that the divine prerogative of delivering the final verdict in the cosmic lawsuit has been entrsted to him. This should indeed be a cause for astonishment (v. 20b), for those who have brought their charge against Jesus are being told that the accused is in fact the judge."[44]

Jesus, however, does not only claim to be his accusers's judge. In this same interaction, Jesus seems to concede that, at least on one level, he is the defendant, and needs to call upon witnesses to affirm his identity and authority:

> If I testify concerning myself, my testimony is not true. But there is another who testifies concerning me, and I know that the testimony which he testified concerning me is true. You have sent to John, and he has testified to the truth. But I do not receive testimony from a human, but I say these things in order that you might be saved. For that one was the lamp which burns and shines, and you desired to rejoice for a while in his light. But I have a testimony greater than John's. The works which the father gave in order that I might complete them, the very works which I am doing, testify concerning me that the father sent me. And the father who sent me himself has testified concerning me. You have never heard his voice or seen his form, and you do not have his word abiding in you, because you do not believe him whom he sent. (5:31-38)

Here Jesus calls three witnesses to testify on his behalf, picking up the language of μαρτυρία that has been so much a part of the Gospel since the

---

[42] Though the one like a Son of Man is not given authority to judge in MT Dan 7:14, in the LXX the Ancient of Days gives the judgment to the saints of the Most High. For discussion see Schnackenburg, *The Gospel According to St. John* (vol 2; New York: Seabury Press, 1980), p.107.

[43] As Schnackenburg explains, "'just' does not here mean merely that quality which all judgment ought to have (cf. 7:24); when Jesus pronounces judgment, it means something more. It is a true and effective judgment in accordance with the authority of God, who stands behind it (cf. 8:26)."Schnackenburg, *The Gospel According to St. John* 2, 468 n. 103.

[44] Lincoln, *Truth on Trial*, 75.

prologue.[45] This passage shows cognizance of traditional Deuteronomic laws concerning witness testimony (Deut 19:15), that no testimony is valid unless confirmed by two or three witnesses, and that one's own testimony does not constitute appropriate evidence.[46] Here Jesus calls upon the testimony of John the Baptist, the works that he performs (i.e., his own actions, particularly the "signs" that he accomplishes), and the testimony of the Father, which they can find in the Scriptures (5:39).

After claiming the role of judge, and yet still providing witnesses in his own defense, Jesus uses the language of one more forensic actor to effectively uproot the situation once more. Castigating the Jews for refusing to believe in him, and instead turning their hopes to the scriptures (5:39-44), Jesus insists that the scriptures will indeed be their downfall, because of their failure to understand them correctly. Jesus warns his Jewish accusers: "Do not think that I will accuse you (κατηγορήσω) before the Father. The one who accuses you (ὁ κατηγορῶν ὑμῶν) is Moses, in whom you have hoped. For if you believed in Moses, you would believe in me, for he wrote about me. But if you do not believe in his writings, how will you believe in my words" (5:45-47)? Jesus insists that He's not the one who will act as their accuser; their accuser is Moses, the one in whom they have placed their hopes. Indeed, just as the Johannine κρίσις is something occurring in the present, the accusation is also occuring in the present. The contrast between the future tense of κατηγορήσω in verse 45 and the present active participle κατηγορῶν in the next verse points to the sense that the accusation is not something that will occur in the future time but is something that is going on right now due to their own unbelief.

This is laced with irony. The background of this statement is the Jewish understanding of Moses not as a heavenly accuser but as a heavenly *intercessor*. This tradition is found in writings as diverse as the *Testament of Moses*, the *Assumption of Moses*, and Philo of Alexandria's *De Praemiis et poemis*.[47] Discussing these traditions and their relevance to this passage, Wayne Meeks points especially to the *Assumption of Moses* 12:6. Moses, preparing to leave Joshua in charge of the Israelites, tells Joshua not to worry, because God "has on their behalf appointed me to pray for their sins and make intercession for them." This is a task made possible by the tradition found in the *Assumption of Moses* and other Second Temple Jew-

---

[45] The entire Gospel is framed using the language of testimony, from the Prologue and discussion of John the Baptist (1:6-8; 1:15-23) to the conclusion of the appendix (21:24).

[46] Although Jesus will later contradict this claim; see below.

[47] This tradition reached its full elaboration in the multitude of references to Moses as a heavenly intercessor in rabbinic literature, for example b. Sanhedrin 11a-b; see below, chapter 7.

ish texts that Moses did not die, but was translated to heaven.[48] This heavenly vocation is seen as the natural continuation of Moses' biblical role as the great intercessor who saved Israel from certain destruction time and again in her desert sojourn.

This understanding of Moses' continual intercession is a reversal of what the Bible says will happen after Moses' death. In Deuteronomy 31, God predicts the future apostasy of the people of Israel, and instructs Moses to write both the Song (Deut 31:19-21) and the book of the Law (Deut 31:26) as witnesses against the people, so that they will not be able to say "Isn't this because our god is not in our midst, that we have found these troubles?" (Deut 31:17).[49] The outlook of Deuteronomy 31 sees Israel, after Moses' death, as being 'on their own,' without their great intercessor, and with the Song testifying against them. Those later texts which argue that Israel is not truly without Moses, who continues to plead on their behalf and present their defense before God, are reading against the literal meaning of Deuteronomy. What Jesus says here in John 5:45, that Moses is the one who is *condemning* them, is actually much closer to the situation envisioned by the Pentateuch.[50] Jesus' words here inform the Jews that they cannot appeal to the Bible for assistance, because it is their own biblical literature which witnesses against them.

On first glance, Jesus' comments here would seem to claim that he is turning the tables on his accusers, by accusing them. The culminating force of this entire section of John, then, would be that Jesus claims *all* the rôles in the unfolding cosmic trial: Judge, defendant, and accuser. But actually, what he is doing here is telling them that they cannot think of him as their accuser, their prosecutor, because that rôle is already being filled by another – Moses, their great hope. It is true, here, that the accusers become the accused, but Jesus refuses to take a prosecutorial role in these proceedings. He will not allow the Jews to claim that he is out to get them in a forensic way. Once again, though Jesus is informing the Jews of this, it is the reader who is really being asked to understand and see clearly. Jesus claims on the one hand not to need to provide testimony, but he is provid-

---

[48] For discussion, see Wayne Meeks, *The Prophet-King: Moses Traditions and the Johannine Christology* (Leiden: Brill, 1967), 124-160. Meeks demonstrates that this tradition is found not only in the apocryphal literature, but also in the writings of Philo and Josephus. See also the discussion in Louis H. Feldman, "The Death of Moses, According to Philo," *Estudios Bíblicos* 60 (2002), 225-254.

[49] See above, chapter 2.

[50] This is correctly noted by Lincoln, who states that "the depiction of Moses' writings as a positive witness to Jesus not only removes them as a court of appeal for 'the Jews' but also makes their writings a negative witness against them. The latter function of their witness is precisely a role that, according to Deuteronomy, Moses himself had envisaged for the law." Lincoln, *Truth on Trial*, 81.

ing testimony – for the reader. They are the true judges envisioned in this account. It is the forensic scenario that draws them into this role, the juridical vocabulary that invites them into the proceedings. The juridical vocabulary that surfaces at key junctions in the Gospel reminds the reader of their true role in the proceedings, that they are not passive spectators but active judges, and that, as Rudolf Pesch once titled his monograph, "the trial of Jesus continues."[51]

## II. The Paraclete

To make it clear that the trial is not a static event but a dynamic process, John introduces a figure that will play an active role in the life of the community after Jesus' death, the figure of the Paraclete (ὁ παράκλητος). The word Paraclete in Greek can be translated as Counselor or Comforter, but more importantly the word has the technical translation of Advocate. The figure of the Paraclete is introduced in John 14:15-17, when Jesus informs the disciples that "I will ask the Father, and he will give you another advocate in order that he might be with you forever, the spirit of truth, which the world is not able to receive, for it does not see or know it. But you know it, for it abides in you and will be in you." The phrase "another Paraclete" suggests that Jesus has been functioning as their paraclete already. While in 1 John 2:1, Jesus functions as a heavenly paraclete, interceding on behalf of the believers with the Father, this represents a departure from the understanding of Jesus as paraclete presupposed here, which sees Jesus as providing *paraklesis* to the disciples on earth.[52] Sayings about the Paraclete occur five times in John, all clustered in these few chapters signalling the end of Jesus' earthly ministry and the preparation for his departure. The role of the Paraclete, we learn, is that of a teacher and reminder after Jesus' departure (14:25-26).[53]

---

[51] Rudolf Pesch, *The Trial of Jesus Continues* (trans. Doris Glen Wagner; Allison Park, PA: Pickwick, 1996).

[52] Cf. Schnackenburg, *The Gospel According to John* (vol 3; New York: Crossroad, 1982), 74.

[53] The passages concerning the Paraclete have been the subjects of much scholarly attention, with various figures and paradigms being offered as possible reference for the Johannine use of this term. Both Sigmund Mowinckel and Nils Johannson believed that the most relevant referent was that of the angelic intercessor found in the Jewish apocalyptic tradition. Mowinckel believed that the tradition of the Paraclete could be traced back to the Hebrew מלאך מליץ referenced by Job in Job 33:23. (S. Mowinckel, "Die Vorstellung des Spätjudentums vom heiligen Geist also Fürsprecher und der johanneische Paraklet," *ZNTW* 32 [1933], 97-130.) Johannson, on the other hand, believed that special attention should be paid to the angelic intercessor and forensic advocate envisioned by the Enochic literature, particularly with regard to the Son of Man figure. (Nils Johannson, *Parakletoi: Vorstellungen von Fürsprechern für die Menschen vor Gott in der alttestamentlichen Religion, im Spätjudentum*

The Paraclete is more than a mere counselor or "representative."[54] In the farewell discourses of John 15-16, Jesus elaborates on the role of the Paraclete, which has explicitly forensic connotations. In John 15:26-27, Jesus says that he will send the Paraclete to them from the father, and "he will testify concerning me, and you will testify, that you were with me from the beginning." Jesus further elaborates this forensic rôle of the Paraclete in 16:7-11:

> And when he comes he will refute the world concerning sin and concerning justice and concerning judgment (ἐλέγχει τὸν κόσμον περὶ ἁμαρτίας καὶ περὶ δικαιοσύνης καὶ περὶ κρίσεως). Concerning sin, that they do not believe in me; concerning justice, that I am going to the father and you will no longer see me; and concerning judgment, that the ruler of this world has been judged.

The explicitly juridical terminology in these passages suggests that the Paraclete has a forensic role in an expected trial in which the entire world is rebuked, that of an *advocate*. As Schnackenburg eplains, "the activity of the Paraclete with regard to the world is presented in this verse as a legal battle or cosmic trial. This is clear not only from the term ἐλέγχειν, which summarizes the Paraclete's function, but also from the concepts 'sin, righteousness and justice' that are elucidated in the verses that follow and in the context of ideas created by them."[55]

---

*und Urchristentum* [Lund: Gleerup, 1940]. In a similar though not identical trajectory, Otto Betz argued that the Paraclete has its antecedant in the dualistic imagination of the Qumran community and their belief in a heavenly spokesman petitioning before God. (Otto Betz, *Der Paraklet: Fürsprecher im häretischen Spätjudentum, im Johannes-Evangelium und in neu gefundenen gnostischen Schriften* [Leiden: E. J. Brill, 1963], esp. 56-72.) Though each of these three proposals has its difficulties, as has been well pointed out by scholars (cf. Johnston, *The Spirit-Paraclete)* the overall impression of the genesis of the Johannine Paraclete within the Jewish literature is entirely convincing. As the previous chapter noted, the necessity and propriety of intercession at the divine tribunal was a major concern of Jewish apocalyptic literature in the Second Temple period. Angelic, patriarchal, and other intercessory figures figured largely in this literature, and John has already referenced this motif in 5:39-47. Given the heavy use of forensic language throughout the Gospel, it makes sense for John to portray this new figure in the same conceptual framework, building on the literature that came before him while suggesting that the game has changed with the arrival of the incarnate Logos. A major trend in Paraclete scholarship has focused on its pneumatic identification. For this type of read see Brown, "The Paraclete in the Fourth Gospel"; Stephen S. Smalley, "The Paraclete: Pneumatology in the Johannine Gospel and Apocalypse" in R. A. Culpepper and C. Clifton Black, eds. *Exploring the Gospel of John: In Honor of D. Moody Smith* (Louisville, KY: Westminster John Knox, 1996), 289-300.

[54] To use the English translation preferred by George Johnston, *The Spirit-Paraclete in the Gospel of John* (Cambridge: Cambridge University Press 1970), 87.

[55] Schnackenburg, *The Gospel According to. St. John* 3, 128. For discussion of the grammatical issues, see D. A. Carson, "The Function of the Paraclete in John 16:7-11" *JBL* 98 (1979), 547-566, and Lincoln's response to Carson in *Truth on Trial*, 117-123.

As has long been noted, in classical Greek the term παράκλητος developed the meaning not just of generic "advocate" or "lawyer," in modern parlance, but of "defense counsel," comparable to the Latin *advocatus*.[56] Eventually the term became a loan word in Hebrew and Aramaic (פרקליט), appearing in the Mishnah as the counterpart to קטיגור.[57] Not only does the Paraclete, then, find a home within the repeated announcement of κρίσις in John, but he seems to be the counterpart to the Mosaic accuser of John 5. However, the forensic rôle of the Johannine Paraclete goes beyond that of defense counsel or advocate. The rôle as envisioned in 16:7-11 is one of a prosecuting attorney, more of a κατήγορος than a συνήγορος. His job is to *convict* the world, to prove that it is guilty in the matters of sin, justice, and judgment.

On the other hand, the previous passages envision the Paraclete as the one who provides comfort, consolation, one who teaches, and represents the disciples in their ongoing trials. The Johannine Paraclete, therefore, seems to fill both of these forensic rôles. This is possible because of the way the Gospel functions on multiple levels. The Paraclete will function as a defense counsel for the disciples, assisting them in their continuing struggles against a hostile world after Jesus' departure. But this very assistance in the disciples's defense is an offensive role against the world in the cosmic lawsuit.[58] The Paraclete's ability to assume multiple rôles is part and parcel of the way the courtroom scenario is rotated in John. And if we rotate it again, recognizing that all of this is being "tried" in the court of the reader, the Paraclete truly becomes yet another witness, testifying to Jesus, God, and the Christian community in front of the reader-judge. In this way the Paraclete fills the function envisioned in 15:26-27. The different rôles assigned to the Paraclete by the author invites the reader to realize the multi-faceted nature of this courtroom, and to see themselves as active participants within it, not just spectators on the sidelines.[59]

---

[56] Still helpful is the article by J. Behm, "παράκλητος," *ThWb* 5 (1954), 798-812. See also R. E. Brown, "The Paraclete in the Fourth Gospel," *NTS* 13 (1966), 113-132; Schnackenburg, "Excursus 16: The Paraclete and the Sayings about the Paraclete" *Gospel According to St. John* 3, 138-154.

[57] Cf. m. Avot 4:11: "R. Eliezer b. Jacob says: He that performs one precept gets for himself one advocate [פרקליט]; but he that commits one transgression gets for himself one accuser [קטיגור]."

[58] As Lincoln notes, he is both "the defending counsel for the disciples but the prosecutor or accuser in regard to the world."Lincoln, *Truth on Trial,* 117. Lincoln quotes Bultmann, *Gospel of John* 561-562: "The image that comes before the eyes is that of a lawsuit of cosmic dimensions, taking place before the court of God. The world is accused, and the Paraclete is the prosecutor."

[59] Schnackenburg summarizes the situation well: "just as the accused is really the accuser in Jesus' trial, the one who is condemned is the one who is justified and the one who is defeated is in fact victorious, so too is this the case in God's 'trial' with the unbelieving world,

## III. The Trial of Jesus

Perhaps nowhere in John is the multi-faceted courtroom so apparent than in the literary masterpiece that is the Johannine passion narrative of chapters 18 and 19. Through deliberate use of irony, ambiguity, and careful architectonics, the evangelist leads the reader to realize that the trial of Jesus is really a trial of Pilate and the Jews, representing the hostile world, in which Jesus pronounces the ultimate verdict. This culminates quite beautifully in the ambiguous use of the verb ἐκάθισεν in John 19:13, where it is unclear whether it is Pilate or Jesus who winds up seated on the βῆμα in front of the Jewish leaders at Lithostratos/Gabbatha.[60] However, it is not only Jesus who serves as the ultimate judge in these scenes. The elaborate and cinematic drama that unfolds in these chapters invites the reader into the action, not just as spectator but as true judge of the proceedings. It is the reader who is asked to realize what is truly occurring on the cosmic stage, what has taken place before them. Just like the courtroom dramas of antiquity, the reader is being asked to figuratively cast their ballot on the action.

But here, where Jesus is linked so closely with God, the cumulative effect is that the reader is truly judging God – judging his decision to send his Son, judging his plans for the world, judging his plans *for them*. Lincoln forcefully argues that the Johannine trial narrative reveals that "in the Fourth Gospel, through identification with the incarnate Logos in the outworkings of human history, this God takes the final consequences of a willingness to be tried and judged. This is not simply a sovereign judge who remains aloof but a judge who is judged and undergoes the sentence of death. This narrative's discourse justifies speaking of a God so involved as to become 'the crucified God.'"[61] Lincoln, however, believes that the judging that is taking place is the judging of God by Pilate and the Jewish authorities. I believe that this is only one aspect of the judging. The true judging that is occurring is that which is taking place in the discursive space between the evangelist and the reader, as the reader listens, contemplates, evaluates. The reader is judging God, on a fundamental level. The reader is judging what has taken place, making evaluative decisions on all

---

which the trial of Jesus before Pilate represents in a hidden way and which also takes place in the encounter between Jesus' community and unbelieving and hostile men.... Helped by the Spirit as the counsel for their defence, Jesus' disciples are no longer accused, but become accusers, and this means that the Paraclete's function also changes. He has been defending the disciples; now he is God's advocate against the world, with the task of proving that world guilty." Schnackenburg, *The Gospel According to St. John* 3, 143.

[60] Complete discussion in Ignace de la Potterie, "Jésus roi et juge d'après Jean 19:13," *Biblica* 41 (1960), 217–247.

[61] Lincoln, *Truth on Trial*, 192.

the characters in the narrative, including, if not primarily, the activities of God himself. It is the forensic scenario which has brought this to the fore, really set it in front of the reader and invited them to participate in the action in this way.

In many ways, it is the architectonic of the Johannine trial narratives that allows the reader to participate in the process on a deeper level, perhaps, than the synoptic versions. Brown and Schnackenburg have convincingly demonstrated that the trial narratives unfold in a series of seven scenes, which are marked by Pilate's physical movements from his private conversations with Jesus to his public encounters with the Jewish leaders. Schnackenburg's outline is helpful here:

| | |
|---|---|
| Exposition: | Jesus led into the praetorium, the Jews outside (18:28). |
| 1st scene: | Outside: Pilate and the Jews (18:29-31[32]) |
| 2nd scene: | Inside: Pilate and Jesus (18:33-38a) |
| 3rd scene: | Outside: Pilate and the Jews (Release of Barabbas) (18:38b-40) |
| 4th scene: | Inside: Scourging and crowning with thorns (19:1-3) |
| 5th scene: | Outside: Pilate's presentation of Jesus (19:4-7) |
| 6th scene: | Inside: Pilate and Jesus (second discussion) (19:8-12) |
| 7th scene: | Outside: Condemnation of Jesus by Pilate to the accompaniment of the Jews' shouts (19:13-16a).[62] |

This breakdown of the seven scenes cannot be accidental. Rather, it reveals a carefully designed narrative that is dramatic in nature. One can easily imagine how to stage this action; it is not an accident that it is the Passion according to John which became the basis for so many medieval passion plays. The architectonic invites the reader to imagine the action unfolding in front of them, watching the movements of Pilate as he goes from stage to stage.

It hardly needs to be said that this is a literary device employed by the author and not a historically accurate representation of the actual mechanics of the trial of Jesus. As Ernst Haenchen sums up, "It is clear from the outset that historical exactitude does not matter to the narrator. It would never enter the mind of any Roman governor to run back and forth between the Jews outside and Jesus inside as Pilate is represented as doing here."[63] The use of this literary device, however, creates contrasts for the reader, as it creates two different physical environments that are strikingly different in tone and content. While inside, Pilate and Jesus have conversations that are calm, serious, and theologically and christologically fraught, on the outside Pilate confronts what is basically an angry mob, unwilling to engage in conversation at all, filled with vitriol. The contrast is truly be-

---

[62] Schnackenburg, *The Gospel According to St. John* 3, 242.

[63] Ernst Haenchen, "History and Interpretation in the Johannine Passion Narrative," *Interpretation* 24 (1970) 198-219, 206.

tween the human and the savage. When Pilate finally brings out Jesus – *ecce homo* – the Jews are not willing to confront him as an anthropos, much less in his true Johannine identity as the incarnate logos. The movement of Pilate from inside to outside illuminates the dramatic contrast, creating "two distinct theatres."[64]

The movement from inside to outside is not only spatial, but, like everything else in the Gospel of John, provides a contrast between those who are truly insiders – able to see past appearances – to those who only exist on the outside, not able to make just judgments (cf. 7:24). This reflects the insider/outsider dichotomy which is present throughout the Gospel. By means of their reactions to Jesus, characters within the Gospel of John present themselves in varying degrees to be insiders or outsiders, being among those who fundamentally "get it" and those who do not.[65] But perhaps no one in the Gospel of John is a true insider – except the reader, who is privy to the Johannine prologue (1:1-16), and thus is able to "see" more than any of those inside narrative. The true insider, in the Gospel of John, is the reader. Characters are able to see in part; never in full. Only the reader is privy to everything in the Gospel; this enables him to judge with just judgment.[66] The inside/outside movement in the trial scenes calls attention to the insider/outsider mentality present throughout the Gospel, which provides the reader with a privileged position and thus a special responsibility and rôle in the trial.

This privileged position allows the evangelist to make use of the literary strategies of ambiguity and irony in the unfolding trial drama. From the very first conversation between Pilate and the Jews, John uses the techniques of irony and ambiguity to invite the reader to look beyond the plain sense of the action to see on a different level. For example, when Pilate asks the Jews what charge (τίνα κατηγορίαν) they bring against Jesus (18:29), the Jews do not specify a charge, but using the classic logic of obfuscation, they reply that were he not a criminal, they would not have handed him over (οὐκ ἄν σοι παρεδώκαμεν αὐτόν; 18:30). The reader is required to supply the missing information, and understand why the Jews have brought Jesus to Pilate, knowing that they are deliberately avoiding

---

[64] Haenchen, "History and Interpretation," 206.

[65] A classic contrast in the Gospel of John is that between the Beloved Disciple and Peter. The Beloved Disciple fundamentally gets it, Peter does not. This climaxes in Jesus' obviously annoyed exchange with Peter in the appendix to John, particularly at 21:20-22, but is present throughout the Gospel. In every point where we encounter the Beloved Disciple within John, the BD is always contrasted with Peter in a situation where he is portrayed in a positive light which always manages to cast an equally negative shadow on Peter.

[66] This is similar to the way the reader participates in the action in the Gospel of Mark. For discussion, see the excellent analysis by Mary-Ann Tolbert, *Sowing the Gospel: Mark's World in Literary-Historical Perspective* (Minneapolis: Fortress Press, 1989).

the question, as they cannot find anything with which to formally charge Jesus according to Roman law. But John has chosen his words carefully to allow the reader to realize what is truly occuring here. The verb παραδίδωμι, which the Jews use to describe their action, is certainly a juridical vert and is used forensically in cases of jurisdictional transfer or, as in 19:16, the formal turning over of a prisoner for punishment.[67] But for John's readers, and early Christians in general, παραδίδωμι had another set of referents, as it was the word that signified Jesus' betrayal and rejection by those that should have accepted him (cf. 6:64; 6:71; 12:4; 13:2; 13:11; 13:21). The word appears 15 times in John alone, including five times within the trial narratives (18:30; 18:35; 18:36; 19:11; 19:16). It is a signal word that points to the great cosmic tragedy of John, that the Logos "came to his own, and his own did not receive him" (John 1:11). This obfuscating response by the Jews invites the reader to recognize that all that the Gospel had predicted was being fulfilled, and that people were tragically playing their roles in a great cosmic drama unfolding before them.

Likewise, the insider conversations between Pilate and Jesus are fraught with irony and ambiguity. In the first conversation (18:22-38), Pilate tries to ascertain Jesus' identity, and figure out why the Jews have handed him over. Jesus answers using typically Johannine logic. When Pilate asks Jesus what he has done (18:35), Jesus responds "My kingdom is not from this world. If my kingdom was from this world, my servants would be fighting (ἠγωνίζοντο), that I not be handed over to the Jews. But now my kingdom is not from here" (18:36).[68] The verb ἀγωνίζομαι, as demonstrated in chapter 3, has decisively forensic resonances, as courtrooms were envisioned as great *agons* in which complex negotiations for honor and dishonor were conducted, and legal competitions were envisioned as sides contending against each other in a manner similar to athletic competition. The use of this verb here reminds the reader of two separate aspects of what is transpiring. First, on the narrative level, Jesus is alone in his trial; no one is there to contend for him. His disciples have abandoned him; this is represented quite viscerally in the way John, unlike the other evangelists, juxtaposes the scenes of Jesus' interrogation by Annas and Peter's denials (18:1-27). No one is willing to agonize for Jesus at his trial. Second, a great agon – much greater than the one before Pilate – is unfolding on the cosmic level. Jesus is literally from another world. No one has been able to see who he is and his unique relationship with the Father stigmatizes him to the world. His presence has indeed provoked a great

---

[67] Cf. Schnackenburg, *Gospel According to St. John* 3, 266.

[68] This is similar in logic to the statement Jesus makes to the Jews in 8:31-38, when he informs them that they have demonic ancestry, for if they were children of Abraham, they would recognize him for who he is.

*agon*, but it is not an agon in which people must agonize *for Jesus* – it is an agon in which Jesus must agonize *for God*, so that people do not condemn themselves by their own judgment. Jesus has been testifying in this agon since he arrived; it is up to the people to judge the situation and take correct action.

When Pilate, responding to Jesus' statement, then asks him if he is a king (18:37), obviously this has additional meaning for the reader as the reader knows that Jesus *is* a king, just not the kind that Pilate expects. But more important for us is what Jesus says next: "you say that I am a king. I have been born and I have come into the world for this reason: that I might testify to the truth (μαρτυρήσω τῇ ἀληθείᾳ). Everyone who is of truth listens to my voice." Jesus is not in the world to announce his reign as king, or even to *be* a king. Jesus is here to bear testimony.[69] He is not really or only bearing testimony in a divine courtroom in which God is holding the trial of man, as 1 John 2 later imagines. Jesus is bearing testimony *in front of man* as to the truth about the world and of God. He is avering before the reader. So when Pilate infamously asks, "what is truth" (18:38), the reader is able to put the pieces together, realizing that it is Jesus who is "the way, the truth, and the life" (John 14:6). Jesus' identity shines light on the identity of men. Here Pilate reveals himself not to be of the truth, but there is still hope for the reader.[70]

Pilate's question, "what is truth?" has deservedly received much attention from Johannine scholars. Raymond Brown suggests that "John is interested in Pilate as an archetype, i.e., the man who does not have the courage to decide for the truth and hear Jesus' voice (18:37) even though he knows Jesus is innocent."[71] In a penetrating article, Andreas Köstenberger examines this scene for its relevance to ancient and contemporary readers. Köstenberger believes, along with many other scholars before him, that the tables are turned on Pilate during these trial scenes. While supposedly it is Jesus who is the one who is being judged, the trials reveal that truly it is Pilate who is being judged by Jesus.[72] In this framework, Köstenberger

---

[69] So Brown: "He will not refuse the title of 'The King of the Jews' if Pilate wants to put it that way; but the real reason he came into this world was *not* to be a king...it was to bear witness to the truth (18:37)." Brown, "The Passion According to John," 129.

[70] Though he does not frame the issue as I do, Andreas Köstenberger recognizes that this question has meaning for the reader, writing that "In the context of the entire Johannine narrative, similar to the ending of Luke-Acts, Pilate's question, 'What is truth?' remains open-ended, and still rings through the ages, calling for an answer from every reader of the Gospel." Köstenberger, " 'What is Truth?' Pilate's Question in its Johannine and larger Biblical Context" *JETS* 48 (2005) 33-62, 45.

[71] Raymond E. Brown, *The Death of the Messiah* (New York: Doubleday, 1996), I.90.

[72] So Brown, *Death of the Messiah*, 34; Schnackenburg, *Gospel According to St. John* 3, 260; Lincoln, *Truth on Trial*, 33;

argues that "Pilate serves as a representative character of all those who fail to recognize that they are called to render a verdict regarding Jesus and who deem *themselves* to be in the judgment seat regarding Jesus while in fact it is *they* who will be judged on the basis of their decision concerning Jesus."[73] Köstenberger is correct to insist that this question provokes the reader to reexamine their own presuppositions about who is doing the judging and who is being judged. What Köstenberger recogizes that the reader is the one who is in the judgment seat. He believes that this statement from the evangelist is meant to provoke the reader to think twice before passing judgment. This is not entirely correct. This statement is meant to provoke the reader to make the *correct* judgment, the *just* judgment, the judgment that is in accordance with truth. There can be no escaping the reality that readers are going to make judgments. What John can do is attempt to *persuade* the reader towards the correct decision. The question "What is truth?" is part of this persuasive technique, to ring bells for the reader, to signal them to look beyond the tragic figure of Pilate to realize that they cannot be, as Köstenberger frames the issue, "apathetic about the issue of truth itself."[74]

One of Köstenberger's great contributions to this discussion is his considered discussion of the role of truth as it relates to the courtroom. Köstenberger quotes Miroslav Volf:

> Trials are supposed to be about finding out what happened and meting out justice. In Jesus' trial, neither the accusers nor the judge cared for the truth.... The judge scorns the very notion of truth: 'What is truth?' he asks, and uninterested in any answer he leaves the scene of dialogue...For both the accusers and the judge, the truth is irrelevant because it works at cross-purposes to their hold on power. The only truth they will recognize is 'the truth of power.' It was the accused who raised the issue of truth by subtly reminding the judge of his highest obligation – find out the truth.[75]

Volf believes that this exchange between Pilate and Jesus points to the illegitimacy of the Roman trial, because it reveals itself to be incapable of executing justice, and uninterested in attempting to do so. I cannot argue with this conclusion. But the reason why this comment from Volf is so illuminating is because *Volf is here doing exactly what the forensic scenario calls for* – he is making a judgment about the forensic situation, judging the system, evaluating whether or not it can distribute justice, or whether it fails to do so. The courtroom setting explicitly provokes this type of reac-

---

[73] Köstenberger, "What is Truth?," 52.

[74] Köstenberger, "What is Truth?," 51. Köstenberger elaborates: "a *neutral* stance toward Jesus is a decision *against* Jesus." Köstenberger, 52.

[75] Miroslav Volf, *Exclusion and Embrace: A Theological Exploration of Identity, Otherness, and Reconciliation* (Nashville: Abingdon, 1996), 266, quoted by Köstenberger, "What is Truth?," 58.

tion, and this is understood and anticipated by the evangelist. The reader is called upon to judge the situation and to judge the characters, Pilate, the Jews, and Jesus himself.

The levels of discourse and irony builds through the second and third conversations between Jesus and Pilate. After Pilate dresses Jesus up as a mock-king, perhaps trying to demonstrate to the Jews how ridiculous their charges are, and twice declaring that he can find no legal cause (αἰτία) against Jesus (19:4, 19:6), the Jews finally declare to Pilate that the true charge against Jesus is blasphemy (19:7). When the Jews reveal this to Pilate, he becomes more afraid (19:8), and returns to the Praetorium to question Jesus again, this time regarding his provenance (19:9),[76] pestering Jesus to answer him, for he has the power to release, and the power to crucify (19:10). Once again Jesus' response hits on the theologically laden παραδίδωμι: "you would have no authority over me unless it had been given to you from above (δεδομένον); therefore the one who handed me over to you (ὁ παράδους μέ σοι) has the greater sin" (19:11). The contrast between δίδωμι and παραδίδωμι is explicit. God has given Pilate the authority; but those who should have given Jesus authority – his own people – have instead given him over to Pilate to be killed. Schnackenberg suggests that "with these words, Pilate, who subjects Jesus to his supposed power, becomes the one subjected, and Jesus, the seemingly powerless one, shows himself to be the one who is free and possesses power."[77] Jesus' words ask the reader, the only witness to this interchange, to judge not by appearances, but to look past the image of Jesus subjected to Pilate to realize that it is Pilate who is truly subject to Jesus.

All of this multi-layered conversation leads up to a great moment of Johannine ambiguity, which Ignace de la Potterie has studied in detail.[78] After the Jews threaten Pilate by suggesting that he will incur the wrath of the emperor if he releases Jesus (19:12), the seventh and culminating scene opens with Pilate bringing Jesus out before the Jews (19:13), where inside and outside meet at Lithostratos/Gabbatha. According to the Greek text, Pilate "ἤγαγεν ἔξω τὸν Ἰησοῦν καὶ ἐκάθισεν ἐπὶ βήματος εἰς τόπον λεγόμενον Λιθόστρωτον, Ἑβραιστι᾽ δὲ Γαββαθα." Pilate is the subject of the verbs ἄγω and καθίζω, and Jesus is the direct object of ἄγω. But the verb καθίζω can be either intransitive or transitive. Either Pilate simply sits down on the βῆμα, as would be proper for a Roman governor pronouncing judgment, or, as de la Potterie suggests, we should take Jesus as

---

[76] Haenchen believes that Pilate's question "Where are you from?" is transparently the question of "are you in fact a god?" and that every reader understands this. Cf. Haenchen, "History and Interpretation," 213.

[77] Schnackenburg, *Gospel According to St. John* 3, 261.

[78] Ignace de la Potterie, "Jésus roi et juge d'après Jean 19:13."

the direct object of *both verbs*, and read the verse to describe Pilate seating Jesus on the βῆμα.

Obviously these are two very different images! Grammatically both options can be supported, but de la Potterie, summarizing his research, suggests that the stronger argument is for a transitive reading:

> It is enough to say that there are various literary and philological arguments in favour of the transitive meaning of *ekathisen*. One of the principal arguments is that the sentence contains two verbs indicating Pilate's movements: *egagen*, he brought him out, and *ekathisen* followed by the words *eis topon legomenon Lithostroton*, towards a place called Lithostrotos. One cannot sit *towards* a place; that is nonsense. But everything is normal if we regard the phrase as indicating the place to which the *two* movements lead: Pilate brings Jesus out towards a place called Lithostrotos and there makes him sit on the *bema*, the platform. This presumes that the same person, Pilate, is the subject of two active verbs with a transitive meaning.[79]

De la Potterie believes that John has brought the action together in a highly symbolic way, with Jesus sitting in his true rôle as judge, and that John has marked this action for the reader with two spatial markers (Lithostratos and Gabbatha) and two temporal markers (the sixth hour; the day of preparation for the Passover, 19:14).[80] Not everyone is convinced by this argument. Schnackenburg, for example, believes that it is historically unlikely, if not impossible, that Pilate would have ever seated Jesus on the judgment seat, and therefore cannot opt for this reading of John 19:13.[81] Both Schnackenburg and de la Potterie are correct. John certainly knows that Pilate did not seat Jesus on the βῆμα. However, a close read of the Johannine trial narratives reveals that John understands Jesus to be the one who *properly belongs* on that judgment seat. I believe John chose his words carefully and was deliberately ambiguous so to allow both reads, to signal for the reader that things are not always as they seem, that it is truly Jesus who was seated on the judgment seat, even if Pilate historically was seated there. The choice of this word, I believe, was not accidental – its ambiguity allows for John to retain a certain amount of verisimilitude while opening up a higher level of reading for his audience. The reader does not have to choose; the reader has to recognize that, in some very real way for John, *both* reads are happening simultaneously.[82]

---

[79] Ignace de la Potterie, *The Hour of Jesus: The Passion and the Resurrection of Jesus according to John* (Slough: St. Paul Publications, 1989), 109-110.

[80] "The mention of this combination of symbolic details – Jesus seated on the *tribunal*, the place with two *names* (a Greek name and a Hebrew name), and the *hour of the Preparation* – all this indicates that for John it is an event of momentous significance. This makes no sense unless Jesus himself is actually 'seated.'" de la Potterie, *The Hour of Jesus*, 110-111.

[81] Schnackenburg, *The Gospel of John* 3, 264.

[82] de la Potterie's read of John also helps us to understand why *two* later texts portray Jesus as being seated on the judgment seat. *Gospel of Peter* 3:7 tells us that the Jews "threw

Though the Johannine trial narratives obviously end with Jesus sentenced to death and remanded to "their" custody,[83] the reader cannot help but feel that it is the world who was truly condemned in this forensic scenario. John has been preparing the reader for this from the beginning of the Gospel. But it is up to them to judge this for themselves, truly to sit on the βῆμα and watch the Logos, who is God (1:1), undergo trial and execution. They judge the equity of this trial, they judge truth itself, and by doing so they are doing exactly what John wants them to do – judging the divine wisdom and the divine plan, judging whether or not the Johannine kerygma of 3:16-21 has proven to be the truth. They have been given judicial instructions throughout the Gospel. In 7:24 they are warned not to judge by appearances, but to judge with just judgment. In 8:12-18, the reader is urged to take Jesus' testimony as legally valid. When the Pharisees tell Jesus that self-testimony is invalid (8:13), Jesus informs them that his unique identity and provenance provides the criteria for reliable testimony:

Even if I am testifying about myself, my testimony is true, for I know from where I came and where I am going, but you do not know from where I came of where I am going. You judge according to the flesh, I judge no one. But even if I judge, my judgment is dependable, for it is not I alone, but I and the father who sent me. And it is written in your law that the testimony of two men is true. I testify concerning myself, and the father who sent me testifies concerning me. (8:14-18)

Though on the narrative level Jesus is speaking to the Pharisees, on another level altogether John is speaking to the reader, who is the one judging the testimony. The readers are not to fall into the trap of the Pharisees by judging according to the flesh, they must look beyond Jesus' carnal body to understand his incarnate logos. They are the recipients of the testimony, and, as the original ending of the Gospel indicates, they are the true addressees of the Gospel, which is written "so that you may come to believe

---

around him a purple robe and set him on the judgment seat and said, 'Judge rightly, King of Israel!" Admittedly the Gospel of Peter is not the best representative of Christian orthodoxy, but no less a figure than Justin Maryr also references such a scene: "Then they jeered him, as the prophet says, and placed him on the judgment seat and said, Judge us!" (Justin Martyr, *Apology* i.35.6). Haenchen does not believe that these two texts necessarily had John; he believes instead that John "proffers a correction of the tradition. The Jews did not place Jesus on the judgment seat for that was impossible for them, but Pilate, the judge, did it." Haenchen, "History and Interpretation," 216.

[83] Another highlight of Johannine ambiguity is his repeated use of the third person plural "they" or "their" to describe Jesus' captors and executioners in John 19:16-18. The most obvious antecedent on the literary level is the Jews, though clearly it is the Roman Soldiers who crucify Jesus and divide his clothes in 19:23-25. But by choosing the ambiguous "they," John is able to highlight who he believes to be Jesus' real executioners – the Jews, even though he knows, as 19:23-25 clearly demonstrate, that it is the Roman soldiers to whom Pilate remands Jesus for crucifixion.

that Jesus is the Christ, the Son of God, and that by believing you may have life in his name" (20:31). The reader is the one who must be convinced, so that they judge correctly and justly, and the unique nature of John makes it clear that everything is at stake in their decision.

This analysis of the Gospel of John reveals that the evangelist has taken seriously the distinct judicial rôle for the reader in the imagined and narrated courtroom. Throughout the Gospel the evangelist has taken the traditional imagery of the divine courtroom and used it as a framing and structuring device which requires the reader to take a significant role in the proceedings. Only by recognizing the role of the reader in the presentations of and allusions to the divine courtroom can we fully appreciate the discursive dynamic of texts like the Gospel of John, which expect the reader to judge everything that is put before them, including the plan of God itself.

## D. Justice at the End of Days:
## The Divine Courtroom in Revelation

Just as in the Gospel of John, the author of Revelation takes advantage of the fact that his readers will serve as judge of his composition, using this knowledge as part of his literary strategy for presenting the events of the last times, including the manifestation of the divine courtroom. At several key points in Revelation, characters reiterate the justice of God's actions. After the description of the cosmic war, the dominion of the beast, and the cosmic reaping (Rev 12-14), those who had conquered the beast (15:2) sing a song which is described as "the song of Moses the slave of God and the song of the Lamb" (15:3):

Great and wonderous are your works, Lord God the Almighty!
Just and true (δίκαιαι καὶ ἀληθιναὶ) are your ways, O King of the nations.
Who will not be afraid, Lord, and glorify your name?
For you alone are holy, that all nations will come and will make obesience before you,
For your judgments (δικαιώματα) have been revealed. (Rev 15:4)

Likewise, after the plague of the third bowl (Rev 16:4), John hears another voice, this time of the "angel of the waters":

You are just (δίκαιος), O one who is and who was, O Holy one,
for you judged these things.
Because they poured out the blood of the saints and prophets,
indeed you have given blood to them to drink; they deserve it (ἄξιοί εἰσιν).
And I heard the altar saying: Yes, Lord God the Almighty,
true and just (ἀληθιναὶ καὶ δίκαιαι) are your judgments. (Rev 16:5-7)

These two heavenly refrains serve as an answer to the challenging question posed earlier by the martyrs at the close of the opening vision of the heavenly throneroom, "Until when, O holy and true ruler, will you not judge and avenge (οὐ κρίνεις καὶ ἐκδικεῖς) our blood on those dwelling on the earth" (Rev 6:10)? The subsequent actions seem to answer this question satisfactorily; this is the force of "the altar" confessing and confirming God's just and true judgments (Rev 16:7). Richard Bauckham, discussing the concept of judgment in Revelation, believes that first and foremost Revelation asserts the justice of God: "The desire for justice in an unjust world or – better – the desire for a just world is a central concern of the book of Revelation. It is axiomatic for Revelation that God, the universal Judge, is perfectly righteous and judges with absolute justice. He is the judge whose justice must prevail in the end. The hope for a just world would be futile were there not this universal Judge who is willing and able to implement justice universally."[84] Bauckham believes that the numerous mentions of God's just and true judgments are designed to praise God, and to display that "God's judgment brings to light the evil intrinsic in the act itself. God's judgment is not an external authority imposing its will on people, but the light of truth exposing evil for all to see."[85] Bauckham is certainly correct to note that Revelation insists on the justice of God's actions, and repeatedly asserts this tenet throughout the text. However, Bauckham is not entirely correct when he notes that God's perfect justice is "axiomatic" for Revelation. While the *author* of Revelation may believe this to be so, this claim is not axiomatic *for the reader*. In fact, I believe that the numerous mentions of God's perfect and totally just judgments are designed *to persuade the reader* that God is just and perfect in judgment, in other words, *to justify God*. This is necessary precisely because this claim is not axiomatic.[86]

Within Revelation there is significant evidence to buttress this claim, not the least of which is the question posed to God from inside the heavenly court (6:9-11). The question posed by the martyrs specifically brings up the issue of God's justice, subtly suggesting that the delay in action is

---

[84] Richard Bauckham, "Judgment in the Book of Revelation" *Ex Auditu* 20 (2004) 1-24, 1.

[85] Bauckham, "Judgment," 3.

[86] That Revelation contains within it an argument for God has been recently articulated by Sigve K. Tonstad in his intriguing analysis *Saving God's Reputation: The Theological Function of* Pistis Iesou *in the Cosmic Narratives of Revelation*. Tonstad believes that Revelation is best understood as a theodicy, and that the question of God's justice is at the heart of Revelation: "In the most gripping moments in the story there is profound apprehension, an unresolved dispute centring on the character and the actions of the One who sits on the heavenly throne. Witnessess in heaven and earth stand puzzled and aghast at the apparent discrepancy between conditions on earth and the expectd divine action." Tonstad, *Saving God's Reputation* (Library of New Testament Studies 33; London: T & T Clark, 2006), xv.

causing individuals to question God's decision making.[87] The way the question is framed is also instructive. Most English translations, in an effort to create a smoother English translation, translate 6:10 with positive valence. For example, NRSV Rev 6:10: "Sovereign Lord, holy and true, how long will it be before you judge and avenge our blood on the inhabitants of earth?"[88] This translation puts the emphasis on the fact that God has *not yet* executed justice. But this fails to bring out the *negative* force of the Greek: ἕως πότε, ὁ δεσπότης ὁ ἅγιος καὶ ἀληθινός, οὐ κρίνεις καὶ ἐκδικεῖς τὸ αἷμα ἡμῶν ἐκ τῶν κατοικούντων ἐπὶ τῆς γῆς – up to what point, O holy and true Master, will you *not judge and avenge* our blood? The way the question is framed actually points to the actions that God is *not taking* in the present, actions that they believed are required and necessary. The English frames the question more nicely, as if the martyrs were simply asking when the delay will be over. But the Greek is more accusatory: it suggests that God is not taking the necessary action, and asks when they can expect that to change. The predication of "holy and true" on God (the "despot") is a challenge to God to live up to his responsibilities and attributes. The question is not at all innocent, and not simply just a call for vengeance and a petition for God to hasten the judgments. It is an accusation leveled against God that goes to the nature of God's judicial administration, to the justice of God itself.[89]

The fact that Revelation includes this question as well as the instance in which the martyrs seem to be satisfied that God has answered them satisfactorily (Rev 16:7) shows just how seriously Revelation takes potential accusations against God, and how thoroughly it wants to answer them. By including the objection and accusation, Revelation gives itself the opportunity to respond to it. In many ways the entire sequence of events that follows is designed to show the reader just how seriously God takes his responsibilities as Judge.

However, this is not the only accusation regarding the nature of God's justice that Revelation addresses. The points at which these "praises" of

---

[87] John Paul Heil has argued that these verses are central to the book of Revelation, because "in a book imbued with references to worship, the opening of the fifth seal in Rev 6,9-11 contains the only example of a prayer of supplication and its answer." John Paul Heil, "The Fifth Seal (Rev 6, 9-11) as a Key to the Book of Revelation" *Biblica* 74 (1993) 220-243, 220.

[88] So too NIV: "How long, Sovereign Lord, holy and true, until you judge the inhabitants of the earth and avenge our blood?"

[89] Tonstad explains this well: "In the martyr's question, too, there is concern about God's apparent failure to maintain justice, a sense of distress in the face of justice delayed, even a hint of delinquency on the part of God in upholding the moral order." Tonstad, *Saving God's Reputation*, 134.

God's justice appear are deliberate; they appear at moments in which God seems to be executing *too much punishment*, or at points at which the punishments/judgments administered by God's agents seem very severe, if not downright cruel. Rev 16:5-7, for example, comes after the entire earth suffers for the sins of mankind, after the second bowl takes out every living thing in the sea, and after the third bowl turns all water into blood. The insertion of the praise of God's just judgment here is deliberate; the author believes that this praise is necessary here to convince and reassure the reader that what is unfolding before them is "true and just."

By inserting this type of comment, in the form of heavenly hymns and praises, the author of Revelation shows keen awareness that his audience may require affirmation or interpretation of the action unfolding before them. Following the work of scholars who point to dramatic features of Revelation, Elisabeth Schüssler Fiorenza argues that these hymns (such as Rev 16:5-7) have the same function as the chorus in a Greek drama, "preparing and commenting upon the dramatic movements of the plot:"[90]

The forward movement of the narrative is also interrupted through the interludes. They are visions or hymns of eschatological protection and salvation (e.g., 7:1-17; 11:15-19; 12:10; 14:1-5; 15:2-4; 19:1-9; 20:4-6). Insofar as the author interrupts the patterns of continuous narrative and cyclic repetition through the insertion of these anticipatory visions and auditions, he expresses in his composition the relationship between present reality and eschatological future. The hymns and acclamations serve as a commentary on the apocalyptic action of Rev. Their contribution to its structure is interpretation and comment. Thus they function in a manner similar to the chorus in the Greek tragedy which commented and explained the actions of the principals in the drama.[91]

These hymns, then, are not just "praises," as Bauckham suggests, they are comments meant to instruct the reader and direct them in their evaluation of the action. In other words, they are *arguments*. The author of Revelation is keenly aware that the actions he describes could be seen as cruel and unusual, particularly the mass devastation of the earth such as had not been seen since Genesis 6-9. While it is axiomatic in the Bible that man's actions have terrible consequences for the earth, the attribution of these consequences to God's own bowls goes far beyond the normal cause-and-effect understanding present in biblical ecology, and comes much closer to the visions of the end of time present throughout the prophetic literature.[92] But just because these actions have been predicted and the people have been warned about what will happen to the earth if they continue in their

---

[90] Elisabeth Schüssler Fiorenza, *The Book of Revelation: Justice and Judgment* (2nd ed; Minneapolis: Fortress Press, 1998), 166.

[91] Schüssler Fiorenza, *The Book of Revelation*, 172.

[92] For discussion, see Tikva Frymer-Kensky, "The End of the World and the Limits of Biblical Ecology" in Adela Yarbro Collins and Margaret Mitchell, eds., *Antiquity and Humanity: Essays on Ancient Religion and Philosophy* (Tübingen: Mohr Siebeck, 2001), 15-26.

course,[93] this does not mean that the depictions of the actions itself are expected to be anything less than shocking and saddening.

Revelation anticipates objections here, and even though it firmly believes that the literal pouring out of God's wrath is warranted, necessitated, and even called for by participants in the action, it still needs to convince the reader that this is true. So it reminds the reader that it is just that the third angel "poured out his bowl" (ἐξέχεεν τὴν φιάλην αὐτοῦ; Rev 16:4), causing the waters to become blood: "because they poured out (ἐξέχεαν) the blood of the saints and prophets, indeed you have given them blood to drink" (Rev 16:6). This is conceived of as following the law of *lex talionis*, proportional, measure-for-measure justice, and Revelation adds a strong voice of hymnic ascent: "ἄξιοί εἰσιν," "they deserve it", or "they are worthy [to receive this punishment]" (Rev 16:6).[94] Bauckham points to Obadiah 15 as a good summary statement of the principle, and explains that "the basic idea is that the punishment should fit the crime. This can take many forms, some of which seem highly artificial to us. In this case, blood is the factor that corresponds in both crime and punishment: they have shed blood and so they must drink blood."[95] This sounds good until one realizes that it is not just the *people*, the *perpetrators*, that are being punished for their murderous activities, but it is indeed the *earth itself* which is subject to the punishment. Perhaps anticipating this objection, Bauckham concludes that "in this surreal visionary context we should not be too concerned that the correspondence of crime and punishment does not really insure that the severity of the punishment is appropriate to the seriousness of the crime. The point is rather a graphic way of claiming that strict justice is being done, a point emphasized in the added insistence that those judged deserve what they get."[96] Bauckham is too quick to smooth over the discrepancy between action and consequence present in Revelation. He seems to argue that we should not take it too seriously because it is a surreal vision. This explicitly, I believe, reads *against* the text. Bauckham is correct to argue that the author of Revelation presents this punishment as being totally justified. However, what he fails to realize is that this is an *argument* being made by the text, and the author knows full well that this action needs to be justified before the reader, or at least the reader needs to

---

[93] So, for example, the warnings in Joel 3, Zechariah 14, and Malachi 3-4.

[94] Just as the Lamb is worthy or deserving (ἄξιος) of opening the scroll in Rev 5 because of his actions, and God is worthy (ἄξιος) of receiving glory, honor, and power because of his activity in creation (Rev 4:11), those who shed the blood of the prophets are worthy of receiving their due. The word ἄξιος in Revelation becomes shorthand for the sense that the described action is perfectly appropriate, fitting, and just.

[95] Bauckham, "Judgment," 2.

[96] Bauckham, "Judgment," 2.

be reassured that this punishment does, in fact, fit the crime – because on the surface this may not appear to be so.

One of the main moments in Revelation in which the author is clearly taking pains to justify God's action or convince the reader that God's judgments are just is the dramatic depiction of the fall and punishment of Babylon and the heavenly response in Rev 17-19:8. God's justice is illustrated dramatically in the description of the double measure for measure judgment on the Whore of Babylon:

Render to her as she herself rendered (ἀπόδοτε αὐτῇ ὡς καὶ αὐτὴ ἀπέδωκεν) and pay her double for her deeds (διπλώσατε τὰ διπλᾶ κατα τὰ ἔργα αὐτῆς). In the cup which she poured pour her double (διπλοῦν); as much as she glorified herself and lived luxuriously, give her torment and sorrow. For in her heart she said "I sit as a queen and a widow I am not; I will never see sorrow." For this reason her plagues will come in a single day, death and sorrow and famine, and she will be burned up with fire, for mighty is the Lord God who judges her. (Rev 18:6-8)

Many scholars have recognized that paying Babylon double for her actions (Rev 18:6) seems to circumvent the logic of *lex talionis*. If *lex talionis* is designed to ensure that punishment does not exceed what is warranted by the crime, and thus provide a measure of protection for the accused, the punishment of Babylon here is presented as illegal in the sense that it specifically goes again the theoretical penal code. Bauckham attempts to "solve" the issue by arguing that the standard translation of 18:6 is incorrect, and offers an alternative: "Render to her as she herself has rendered [cf. Ps 137:8], give her the exact equivalent (*diplōsate ta dipla*) of her deeds [cf. Isa 40:2]; and in the cup she mixed mix for her the exact equivalent (*diploun*)."[97] Bauckham is following the work of M.G. Kline, who argues that διπλόω should be translated as "duplicate" rather than "double". However, David Aune convincingly demonstrates that this type of argument does not take into account what are almost certain references to Jeremiah 20:29b (LXX 27:27b), "Requite to her according to her deeds; do to her according to all that she has done (ἀνταπόδοτε αὐτῇ κατὰ τὰ ἔργα αὐτῆς, κατὰ πάντα ὅσα ἐποίησεν, ποιήσατε αὐτῇ)," and further that "The notion of a *double* recompense, which cannot be regarded as just retaliation (Exod 21:24-25; Lev 24:19-20; Deut 19:21), is probably based on Jer 16:18, καὶ ἀνταποδώσω διπλᾶς τὰς ἀδικίας αὐτῶν, 'I will recompense their iniquities twofold' (cf. Isa 40:2)."[98] Aune further notes that this type of double-restitution is frequently mentioned in Greek literature,

---

[97] Bauckham, "Judgment," 2.

[98] David Aune, *Revelation 17 -22* (Word Biblical Commentary 52c; Nashville: Thomas Nelson, 1998), 992.

"though it is never claimed that this is just," and quotes Kenneth Dover, who calls this type of punishment "a head for an eye."[99]

It seems that Bauckham is determined to justify this presentation of the punishment of Babylon. He admits that the "usual English translation...suggests a grossly unjust punishment by the standard of the *lex talionis*".[100] However, his alternative translation fails to do justice to the deep intertextual relationship that exists between this verse and the prophetic literature. Overall, what Bauckham fails to realize is that the author is aware of this seeming discrepancy between crime and punishment, and that is the reason the author inserts the extensive statement of Babylon's crimes (Rev 18:1-24) and the following auditory "comment" by the "loud voice of a great multitude":

> Hallelujah! The salvation and glory and the power of our God – for true and just are his judgments! For he judged the great whore who corrupted the earth by her fornication, and he avenged (ἐξεδίκησεν) the blood of his servants by her hand. (Rev 19:1-2)

This is followed by yet more accolades and worship (19:3-10) before the arrival of the Faithful and True rider on the white horse (19:11ff). Not only are these verses deliberately placed to convince the reader of the justice of Babylon's punishment, the vocabulary of these two verses deliberately recalls the question of the martyrs in Rev 6:9-11. This suggests that God, in his destruction of Babylon, is specifically responding to the accusation and challenge posed by the martyrs.[101] The destruction of Babylon, therefore, is the author's *proof* that God's judgments are true and just, and does not let the blood of his servants go unvindicated.

Schüssler Fiorenza partially realizes the forensic connotations of this scene in her analysis of Revelation 15:5-19:10, arguing that:

> The central images and theological motifs of Rev. 15:5-19:10 are the splendor, wealth, and power of Babylon/Rome, and the justice of God's judgments. The whole scene is conceived of in terms of a universal courtroom, in which a 'class-action suit' takes place. The plaintiffs are the saints who represent the class of all those killed on earth (18:24), the defendant is Babylon/Rome, the charge is exploitation and murder in the interest of power and idolatry, the judge is God. As was previously announced in 14:8, Babylon/Rome has lost its lawsuit and therefore its associates break out in lamenting and mourning, while the heavenly court and the Christians rejoice. The judge has acknowledged their legal complaints and claims to justice (18:20) and has pronounced the sen-

---

[99] Aune, *Revelation 17-22*, 992, quoting Kenneth J. Dover, *Greek Popular Morality in the Time of Plato and Aristotle* (Berkeley: University of California, 1974), 184.

[100] Bauckham, "Judgment," 2.

[101] Heil notes in particular that the verb ἐκδικέω only appears here in Rev 19:2 and in the prayer of the martyrs in 6:10, and therefore "this exclamation serves as a climactic answer to the souls' prayer for God to 'vindicate (ἐκδικεῖς, 6,10) their blood." Heil, "The Fifth Seal," 138.

tence against Babylon/Rome which will be executed by the beast and the ten horns as divine henchmen.[102]

Schüssler Fiorenza is right to assert that there is a concern to demonstrate that God's actions are just and his judgments proceed in like manner. She is also correct to recognize that there is a long accusation against Babylon contained in this section of the text, that the martyrs have made an official complaint, and that God is called "Judge" repeatedly throughout this section. However, she has not fully comprehended all of the actors in this courtroom scenario. It is true that God is here portrayed in his judicial function, exercising judgment against Babylon and vindicating the blood of the martyrs. But, like all other views of the heavenly courtroom and divine judicial procedures, the true purpose of this presentation is *to convince the reader of God's just judgments*. God is not really the judge in this scene. Though he may be the judge "on the page," or "on stage," if one thinks about Revelation in dramatic terms, he is not the true judge, being convinced or not convinced of Babylon's guilt. The readers are the true judges, judging the question of whether or not this double-punishment meted out by God is just and deserved, not whether Babylon is ἄξια, but whether God is δίκαιος in his determination of Babylon's liability and his corresponding actions.

But even further than that, the readers are also ultimately being asked to judge whether God is ἄξιος to act as judge. Sigve Tonstad, who believes that theodicy is a central issue of Revelation, believes that the story of Revelation is connected to the events of Genesis 3, particularly the charge leveled against God by the serpent, that God is arbitrary and thus capricious.[103] Tonstad envisions the actions of the serpent, and the war in heaven that followed, to have created a crisis in the heavenly council, arguing that this crisis is at the center of Revelation.[104] The crisis, argues Tonstad, is one of challenge to God's sovereignty and authority, a challenge to God's ability properly to govern.

The challenge, therefore is *whether or not God is ἄξιος to sit on the throne*. As we have seen, the question of worthiness appears over and over again in Revelation. Tonstad demonstrates that Revelation 12 is at the center of the plot of Revelation, and stands as the deep background for the entire narrative, including the scenes that take place in the heavenly throneroom. In a real insight into the function of the image of the throne in Revelation, Tonstad reminds us that "according to the war-in-heaven theme the throne of God is contested territory not only in the sense that the reader of Revelation must contend with claimants of earthly sovereignty in the

---

[102] Schüssler Fiorenza, *The Book of Revelation*, 7-8.
[103] Tonstad, *Saving God's Reputation*, 105.
[104] Tonstad, *Saving God's Reputation*, 118.

form of Roman emperors who make demands on his life and loyalty. John's vision of the throne and of the One who sits on the throne recalls the initiation of the conflict and the ambition expressed in the neglected passage in Isaiah, 'You said in your heart, I will ascend to heaven; I will raise *my throne* above the stars of God; I *will sit enthroned* on the mount of assembly, on the utmost height of the sacred mountain. I will ascend above the tops of the clouds; I will make myself like the Most High.' (Isa 14.13-14)."[105] According to Tonstad, therefore, the image of the throne in Revelation is a visible icon that captures the entire essence of the cosmic battle for sovereignty and the challenge to God's authority that is present throughout the central section of Revelation.

Tonstad's understanding of the way that the throne functions in Revelation is buttressed by the work of Cameron Afzal, who argues that we should understand the throne as a "communal icon", a "cognitive-social appropriation of an image by a community."[106] Afzal believes that the throne in Revelation is an example of a communal icon, one that is shared between reader and audience, and that the reader will understand the throne as participating in a conversation with a specific set of resonances. Afzal understands the throne is an example of the communal icon *merkabah*, which draws its generative force from a particular set of texts.[107] Afzal further believes that the use of the *merkabah* imagery in Revelation, particularly in chapter 4, directs the reader toward a particular conversational framework, arguing that "the presence of the *merkabah* in the text is a pointer that John has invoked traditions typically concerned with mysteries involving the nature of the created order and the mystery of the role of evil in God's redemptive plan."[108] Afzal pursues this trajectory, leading him towards an interpretation of the throne-chariot as representing the

---

[105] Tonstad, *Saving God's Reputation*, 119.

[106] Cameron Afzal, "Wheels of Time in the Apocalypse of Jesus Christ," in April DeConick, ed. *Paradise Now: Essays on Early Jewish and Christian Mysticism* (Atlanta: SBL Publications, 2006), 195-210, 196-197. See also C. Afzal, "The Communal Icon: Complex Cultural Schemas, Elements of the Social Imagination" in V. Wiles, Alexandra Brown and G. F. Snyder, eds. *Putting Body and Soul Together* (Valley Forge: Trinity Press Intl, 1997), 58-80.

[107] "Among these there is a general consensus regarding the use of imagery from Isaiah (1:6, 66:1) Ezekiel (1-2:7); Dan 7; *1 En.* 18; 39; *2 En.* 20-22, as well as elements taken from the iconography of Iranian and Greco-Roman royal courts." Afzal, "Wheels of Time," 198. The literature on the *merkabah* is extensive; among the most important works see Ithamar Gruenwald, *Apocalyptic and Merkabah Mysticism* (Leiden: Brill, 1980), and David Halperin, *The Faces of the Chariot: Early Jewish Responses to Ezekiel's Vision* (Tübingen: Mohr Siebeck, 1988).

[108] Afzal, "Wheels of Time," 202.

cosmos itself, uncovering markers in the text that point to the movement of the seasons, zodiacal imagery, and a vision of the night sky.[109]

Afzal's discussion is useful because it suggests that by its very nature, the image of the throne may be connected to a specific set of discussions, and this understanding is shared between reader and author. Using Afzal's definition of a "communal icon," I might further suggest that the throne is not only an instance of the communal icon *merkabah*, but also an instance of the communal icon *judgment seat*, or βῆμα, as thrones are a consistent part of judgment seat imagery from the Hebrew Bible through Second Temple Jewish and Early Christian literature. In fact, as I argued in the previous chapter, the image of the throne in texts such as Daniel 7 and 1 Enoch 14:8-15 bring together two theophanic varieties, that of the throne-room and the chariot, and add to this the now forensic role of the throne-room, so that multiple layers of divine encounter become fused in one semantic field of throne-chariot-courtroom. This is the imagery that is encapsulated in the communal icon of the throne in Revelation 4.

Since thrones carry with them this entire field of sovereignty-related issues, including that of the majesty of God in his full judicial capacity, when the door opens in heaven (Rev 4:1) and the author narrates the vision of the throne surrounded by twenty-four thrones (4:2-4), the reader is already prepared to engage with these issues and attuned to the heightened importance of all that is transpiring before him. Even within Revelation itself the author has prepared the reader for this encounter. The first mention of thrones in Revelation occurs in 3:21, in the close of the letter to the church in Laodicea: "the one who conquers – I will give to him to sit with me on my throne, just as I also conquered and sat with my father on his throne."[110] The mention of the throne(s) here anticipates what the reader is

---

[109] Afzal, "Wheels of Time," 202-209. Summarizing, Afzal writes that "in Rev 4 the Lord of creation is enthroned upon his handiwork; before him are the seven spirits, the sevenfold holy spirit, aflame with the life of the world, and the abyss into which all things fall that do not return to God. The throne is creation itself, the four living beings, representing the motion of the stars symbolize the movement of the four seasons. The throne of God, creation, 'moves' through time."

[110] "Conquering" is a significant term in Revelation. At the end of each of the letters of Rev 1:9-32, John makes a promise to each person who 'conquers.' Ultimately, Revelation develops a theology of conquering that means rising above the limitations of this life, i.e., to reject all associations with the political and material world of the first century in favor of a life with Christ. This theme is developed slowly within the promises. First John promises the conqueror that he will be given permission to eat from the tree of life that is in the paradise of God (2:7), a real place that exists in a world outside of the first century. All those who conquer will not be harmed by the second death (2:11) and will receive a life immortal in the Lamb, a theme which is fully developed in the heavenly throneroom of chapters 4-5. Christians are being called to conquer and move into a life beyond their own in Asia, a life in the heavenly city, "the new Jerusalem that comes down from my God out of heaven" (3:12). The

about to witness in chapters 4-5, part of the internal structure of anticipation present throughout the book of Revelation.[111] Here the throne seems to be something that has the ability to be *shared*, not only between Jesus and the Father, but also with anyone who conquers. Thrones are also a central and recurring image throughout Revelation. As J. Massyngberde Ford notes, "the word 'throne' appears in every chapter of Revelation except 9, 10, 15, 17. 18. Twice it is used with reference to 'Satan's' throne: Rev 2:13, 16:10 (the beast's throne)." [112] For Ford, this emphasis on the throne points to sovereignty and dominion as a central concern of the Apocalypse, and "suggests that the main theme of the work is theocracy versus dominion of Satan."[113]

In this context, I believe Tonstad is correct to refuse to understand the praises sung by the occupants of the heavenly throneroom (e.g., 4:8; 4:11; 5:9-14) as being the product of "spending another routine day at the office, mindlessly repeating their prescribed hallelujahs."[114] Rather, Tonstad argues that the participants "are expressing their admiration for God in a context where God's worthiness is contested. Worship and adoration take place in intense awareness of the searing memory that one of their own created order aspired to occupy God's throne, and in full recognition of the fact that advocacy for the aspiration of 'the Shining One' won a staggering measure of support (12.4)."[115]

Throughout all of this, the reader is set up as a participant in the action by seeing what is transpiring in heaven through John's eyes. They are given the purchase to understand why and how things are to unfold on the earth, to prove once and for all that God has a plan to rectify the stituation caused by the war in heaven and that his means of doing so are just and deserved, δίκαιοι, ἀληθινοι, ἄξιοι. The author invites the reader to participate in the action; he anticipates that the reader will judge the situation and so attempts to persuade the reader of the justice of God's actions. That the reader will be so persuaded is not a foregone conclusion. The means in which God will rectify the situation are harsh and difficult to endure and

---

heavenly city is a very real prospect for John, and a place which Christians can attain if they are able to conquer. Here in 3:21, Christians are being called to conquer just as Jesus himself conquered: to be prepared to shed one's own blood and to walk the path of martyrdom to bear true witness to God.

[111] In 3:20, John writes "Behold! I have stood at the door and I am knocking. If anyone hears my voice and opens the door, I will come in to him and eat with him, and he with me." This anticipates the opening words of Rev 4:1: "After this I looked and behold! A door was open in the heavens."

[112] J. Massyngberde Ford, *Revelation* (AB; New York: Doubleday, 1975), 76.

[113] Ford, *Revelation*, 76.

[114] Tonstad, *Saving God's Reputation*, 122.

[115] Tonstad, *Saving God's Reputation*, 122-123.

swallow. Bauckham notes that "Many readers of Revelation recoil with horror from its lurid depictions of judgment, which seem to them the actions not of the just God but of a wantonly cruel deity," and that "the first step in dealing with this reaction must be to recognize that Revelation itself insists emphatically on the justice of God and his dealings with the world." [116] But we must also recognize that the author of Revelation knows that he has a hard sell, and that is why there are repeated insistences on the justice of God's actions, and the deserving nature of those that receive the judgments, throughout the text.

Revelation leaves the reader with final images of sentencing, of a "grand assize" of the dead before God's throne. At the end of all the woe-filled septets described in Revelation 4-19, John describes a series of events that include a depiction of the judgment of the dead (Rev 20:11-15). This judgment scene comes with a sense of relief – *finally* – because it signals the final word, the final pronouncement that seals the fate of the unworthy and heralds the emergence of the New Jerusalem (Rev 21:1-27). After the milennium, when Satan is once again allowed out to deceive the world (Rev 20:7-8), and is finally thrown into the lake of fire (20:10), John describes the following:

> And I saw a great white throne and one sitting upon it, from whose presence the earth and the heavens fled, and a place was not found for them. And I saw the dead, the great and the small, standing before the throne. And books were opened, and another book was opened, which is [the book] of life, and the dead were judged from that which had been written in the books according to their works. And the sea gave its dead which were in it, and Death and Hades gave the dead in them, and they were judged, each according to their works. And Death and Hades were cast into the lake of fire. This is the second death, the lake of fire. And whoever was not found written in the book of life was cast into the lake of fire. (20:11-15)

This image is peaceful compared to the horrors that have unfolded throughout the book, despite the haunting presence of the lake of fire and the warning of the possibility of a second death. It is peaceful because the reader recognizes that all other claims to occupy that throne have been vanquished, and that the process of final, step-by-step courtroom procedure, can take place. This scene comes as somewhat of a relief because it is so familiar; it is a typical courtroom scene in the tradition of 1 Enoch and other Second Temple Jewish literature. There are books, there is a throne, there is judgment according to works. Everything *makes sense*, proceeds logically. But because this scene comes at the end of a book which has been anything but typical and logical, this scene is "fraught with background" – the background of what has been taking place in the heavenly throneroom up to this point. It is the very typical and standard nature

---

[116] Bauckham, "Judgment," 4.

of this scene that is so jarring in its context. There are no adversaries, there is no pleading, there are not even praises or insistences of God's justice. There is no talking at all. In comparison to the heat which has blazed throughout Revelation, this scene is cold. There is no *personality* in this courtroom. The occupant of the throne is not even named. While it seems clear that it is God, the silence of the text on this issue leaves the reader with an image almost of facing a faceless, implacable monolith. Is there no room for compassion, for mercy, for intercession in this courtroom? Is there no room for *identity?*

This standard apocalyptic scene, therefore, is anything but standard. The author has effectively played on the standard imagery, the "communal icon," by infusing it with tension, ambiguity, and questions of theodicy. While the divine personality and character is at issue in the book of Revelation, this issue is noticeably absent in this final scene. The reader, I believe, is left questioning whether even this cold, hard, procedural justice, is just at all. The system is effectively presented as something to fear. Is this scene meant to reassure, to comfort, or to terrify? Not for nothing does Revelation end with a series of warnings of how quickly these events will move from visionary to actuality. The author is attempting in Revelation to acquit God of charges of injustice, of caprice, of arbitrariness, but he may not be entirely successful in his endeavor. In a courtroom without mercy, what is there?

## E. Conclusion

Not surprisingly, the way in which these authors, along with Paul, include the imagery of the divine courtroom in their writings had enormous impact on the way later Christian authors thought about the divine courtroom. As the following chapter will demonstrate, the New Testament authors effectively set the stage for the various tendencies of early Christianity and the way in which the imagery of the divine courtroom played a crucial role in the arguments of the second and third centuries. By expecting and inviting the reader into the courtroom, the authors opened the doors for the readers to do exactly what the courtroom scenarios invited them to do – interrogate the issues presented in these texts and make judicial decisions about the characters and arguments presented therein – including God.

Chapter 7

# "Righteous is the Judgment of God":
# The Divine Courtroom in Early Christian Literature

## A. Introduction: In the Shadow of the Roman Courtroom

In a penetrating article, Brent Shaw examines the effects of the experience of going to Roman court on early Christians, analyzing the descriptions of courtroom dreams that appear in late antique Christian literature. To begin with, Shaw argues that the Roman trial left an indelible impression on the subjects of the Roman Empire:

> For the subjects of the Roman Empire, the experience of witnessing and participating in a trial was arguably *the* quintessential civic experience of the state. It was the most intense and widespread public and ceremonial imperial presence found in a myriad local venues in the provinces of the empire. In the management of the concerns that struck most directly at the state and its subjects, urgent problems were resolved in the forum of the civil trial that was staged in a public and dramatic fashion by elite officials of the state. The formal rituals and frightening apparatus of the court and public punishment had a powerful effect on persons caught up in the direct confrontation with the authority of the state.[1]

In Shaw's analysis, the public trial was the most common way in which people across the empire encountered the state in all its power and magnitude. That this experience was frightening is an understatement. Moreover, Shaw believes that this experience was *designed* to be frightening:

> The Roman state consciously intended its punishments to be public and strikingly visual precisely in order to achieve the terror-effect that was to provide the desired deterrent. The public trials staged by Roman governors were calculated to be preventative spectacles, visual sights that were meant to startle: an ekphrasis of administrative power and of undisguised coercion so riveting that it was further developed in internal pictures of the mind. Hence the significance of judicial dreams and punitive nightmares. They are symptoms of a collective picturing and memory of a specific kind of power.[2]

According to Shaw, the Roman empire had a real stake in making these experiences frightening, so as to perform the power of the state and to demand subjectivity and submission from its populace. Shaw believes that

---

[1] Brent Shaw, "Judicial Nightmares and Christian Memory," *JECS* 11 (2003) 533-563, 535.

[2] Shaw, "Judicial Nightmares," 535.

we have access to some of the effects of this phenomenon from the judicial nightmares that survive from antiquity, including those left behind by Christian authors such as Jerome, and in Christian texts such as the *Passion of Perpetua and Felicitas*. These texts, he believes, show that "the possibility of being involved in a public spectacle, either a trial or a public display of physical torture and punishment, was one of the imminent hazards of life that was deeply embedded in the conscience of the ordinary people of the time – enough to evoke the nightly apparitions that were regularly commented on in the dream-interpretation manuals of the time."[3]

Shaw's analysis focuses on the visual effect of the Roman trial, and on the effect of seeing and recalling these images, arguing that "memories of trial and punishment became a kind of recollection that was an ekphrasis of the experience."[4] Pointing to depictions of Roman courtroom procedures from authors as diverse as Seneca and Cyprian of Carthage, Shaw argues that the images provoked by the Roman courtroom were replayed in the minds of ordinary people to the point where merely the recollection of them provoked terror and submission.

In the course of his analysis of this ekphrasis, Shaw discusses some early Christian dream-experiences that focus not just on the human courtroom, but on the *divine* courtroom, including the vision of Marian from the *Passion of Marian and James* (*Passio Mariani et Iacobi*), a text from North African Christianity that is set during the Valerian persecution of 259 CE.[5]   After being arrested, interrogated, tortured, and awaiting yet another tribunal, Marian had a vision in his sleep:

Indeed, Marian after this bodily torture fell into an unusually deep sleep, and what the divine favor revealed to him to confirm his hope of salvation he thus narrated to us when he awoke. 'My brothers,' he said, 'I was shown the towering front of a shining, high tribunal, in which, instead of the prefect, sat a judge of very handsome countenance. There was a scaffold there, whose lofty platform was reached not merely by one but by many steps and was a great height to climb. Up to it were brought ranks of confessors, group by group, whom the judge ordered to be executed by the sword. It came to my turn. And then I heard a loud, clear voice saying, 'Bring up Marian!' So I started to climb the scaffold, when all of a sudden Cyprian appeared at the judge's right hand. He stretched out his hand and lifted me up to a higher spot on the scaffold; then he smiled at me and said, 'Come and sit with me.' So it happened that I too formed the audience while the other groups were being tried. Then the judge rose and we escorted him to his palace. Our road lay through a country with lovely meadows, clad with the joyous foliage of bourgeoning woods, shaded by tall cypress and pine trees that beat against the heavens, so that you would think that the entire spot all round was crowned with fertile groves. In the center

---

[3] Such as that of Artemidorous, see above, chapter 3. Shaw, "Judicial Nightmares," 538.

[4] Shaw, "Judicial Nightmares," 533.

[5] Published by P. Franchi de' Cavalieri, "La Passio ss. Mariani et Iacobi" *ST* 3 (1900), 47-61; reprinted with English translation in Herbert Musarillo, *Acts of the Christian Martyrs* (Oxford: Clarendon Press, 1972), 195-213.

was a hollow that abounded in pure water and in the fertilizing watercourses of a crystal spring. And lo! All of a sudden the judge vanished from our sight. At the edge of the spring lay a drinking-cup; Cyprian picked it up, and when he had filled it thirstily from the spring he drank. Then filling it again he handed it to me, and I drank gladly. I say 'Thank God,' and (he said) aroused by the sound of my own voice, I awoke. (*Passio ss. Mariani et Iacobi* 6.5-15)

The vision that Marian recounts here is of a tribunal that far exceeds the one he expects to face. The tribunal is high and shining (*excelsi et candidi*), and the judge is handsome. As Marian ascends the steps of the scaffold, he is greeted by Cyprian, who was martyred in 258 CE.[6] Cyprian lifts Marian to the heights of the scaffold, where the two watch the ongoing trials and executions that follow. The implication is that, like Cyprian, Marian's impending execution by the Roman prefect will allow him to avoid the trials and executions of this handsome judge. Marian's martyrdom will give him a position of privilege in this courtroom and with this judge.

Marian's vision, as Jan Bremmer correctly notes, "conflates an earthly court scene with a heavenly one."[7] The imagery of the Roman tribunal is present, but amplified. Like a Roman tribunal, there is a scaffold, but it is higher than normal, and shiny. There is a judge, but instead of a prefect it is a handsome man. But obviously this is no ordinary tribunal, as all of a sudden the location changes from the scaffold platform to the woods, which are not like ordinary woods but have also an open water source at the center. The contrast between the tribunal, which in Roman North Africa was a major feature of the urban landscape, and the pastoral imagery of the route through the forest – not familiar Carthaginian topography – is stark. This tribunal, unlike Roman tribunals, is presented peacefully and quietly, a noticeable change from the violence and noise of the earthly judicial system. Marian dreams of a tribunal which is and is not like that he expects to face.[8]

This peaceful vision was not the only way in which the divine courtroom appeared in the dream-world of early Christian literature. Another text discussed by Shaw is Jerome's letter to Eustochium (*Ep.* 22). The letter, written at Rome in 384 CE, is the letter in which Jerome lays out his position on virginity and arguments for how Eustochium and other Chris-

---

[6] For ancient depictions of the martyrdom of Cyprian of Carthage, see the *Vita Caecilii Cypriani*, supposedly written by his deacon Pontius, and the *Acta proconsularia Cypriani*.

[7] Jan Bremmer, "Contextualizing Heaven in Third-Century North Africa" in Ra'anan S. Boustan and Annette Yoshiko Reed, *Heavenly Realms and Earthly Realities in Late Antique Religions* (Cambridge: Cambridge University Press, 2004), 163.

[8] Shaw does not go into extended analysis of this text, but uses it as evidence that "from actual dreams and literary evocations of them, therefore, we know that the judicial process impressed itself upon the individual consciousness of defendants of the time." Shaw, "Judicial Nightmares," 544.

tian women and men should lead their lives. Full of Scriptural quotations, Jerome argues that it is necessary for Christians to avoid all the temptations of Roman society, whether they be sexual, dietary, or other. Speaking about his own experiences, Jerome recounts a vision that he had that led him to give up his greatest temptation – his library of pagan books:

> Suddenly I was caught up in the spirit and dragged before the judgment seat of the Judge; and here the light was so bright, and those who stood around were so radiant, that I cast myself on the ground and did not dare to look up. Asked who and what I was I replied: I am a Christian. But He who presided said: Thou liest, you are a follower of Cicero and not of Christ. For *where your treasure is, there will your heart be also* [Matt 6:21]. Instantly I became dumb, and amid the strokes of the lash – for He had ordered me to be scourged – I was tortured more severely still by the fire of conscience, considering with myself that verse, *in the grave who will give you thanks?* Yet for all that I began to cry and to bewail myself, saying: Have mercy upon me, O Lord: have mercy upon me. Amid the sound of the scourges this cry still made itself heard. At last the bystanders, falling down before the knees of Him who presided, prayed that He would have pity on my youth, and that He would give me the space to repent of my error. He might still, they urged, inflict torture on me, should I ever again read the works of the Gentiles. Under the stress of that awful moment I called upon His name, saying: Lord, if ever again I possess wordly books, or if ever again I read such, I have denied You. Dismissed, then, on taking this oath, I returned to the upper world, and, to the surprise of all, I opened upon them eyes so drenched with tears that my distress served to convince even the incredulous. And that this was no sleep nor idle dream, such as those by which we are often mocked, I call to witness the tribunal before which I lay, and the terrible judgment which I feared. May it never, hereafter, be my lot to fall under such an inquisition! (Jerome, *Ep.* 22.30)

This is a far cry from Marian's peaceful vision of the divine courtroom! This courtroom, despite being shiny, is terrifying and violent, including interrogation and physical torture. This courtroom is one where even a practicing Christian like Jerome has much to fear, a courtroom which can do far more physical and psychological damage than even than humans face in Rome. Shaw notes that "here the whole courtroom experience is replayed in the mind: the ritualistic obeisance before the raised dais of the tribunal on which the presiding magistrate, the governor, sat as judge, and the use of bodily torture to elicit the truth."[9] While Marian's dream combined elements of the Roman courtroom with imagery unfamiliar to this context, Jerome's dream is "a quintessentially Roman experience."[10] The courtroom he sees, though divine in nature, harnesses the terrible everyday imagery to depict what awaits all Christians – even good Christians, who have successfully competed with most of their temptations.

It is a wonder, then, that after discussing these and other examples of how writers like Tertullian and Augustine use this terrifying imagery in their exhortations and apologetics, that Shaw asserts the following:

---

[9] Shaw, "Judicial Nightmares," 548.
[10] Shaw, "Judicial Nightmares," 548.

It is in the martyr acts from the mid-second century, and in the defenses, explications and debates connected with these texts by early church Fathers like Tertullian, that the interplay between the actual court days faced by Christian defendants and the development of the concept of a divine tribunal becomes more and more explicit. The relationship between the Christian and his or her God came to be configured as a judicial one. Fairness and justice, vengeance and retribution became the principal qualities of God the Judge.[11]

What Shaw does not take into account here is the effect on the reader of using the terrifying imagery associated with *injustice*, coercion, and persecution to depict the final judgment. Are people supposed to put aside all the associations they have with everyday courtrooms when they ekphratically view the depictions of the divine courtroom? On the contrary, the use of the Roman courtroom imagery necessarily invites the reader to make the comparison between the courtrooms they face now and the courtroom they must face ultimately. If the comparison were not intended, if the analogy were not expected and anticipated, these scenes would not have the power that they do. But the comparison cannot be reduced to simple shades of black and white, with the Roman courtroom standing in for all that is terrible, and the divine courtroom representing everything just and honorable. It is more significant than that. People do not leave their associations at the steps of the divine tribunal. They are invited to carry them with them, to fear the divine courtroom *more* than they do the Roman courtroom, because they are told that the power contained within it exceeds even that of the Imperial state.

And just as authors like Job and Paul, Jerome and other later Christian authors who harness the imagery of the Roman courtroom to paint their terrifying pictures, to persuade their readers that the Roman courtroom is *nothing* compared to the divine courtroom, rely on the fears of the courtroom to substantiate their rhetorical goals. They rely on the fact that people are scared of the courtroom, not only guilty people, but innocent people as well, people who have committed no crimes, because of the ability of innocent people to be unjustly acquitted, caught up in the "heaving tide of impious judgments," as Tertullian reminds his readers so vividly. The divine courtroom is an image designed to terrify even the innocent, designed to make people realize the awesomeness of the Judge they will face, and their complete powerlessness before him. These images work because people have negative associations with courtrooms, and they carry these fears and anxieties with them in their collective imagining of the divine tribunal, both textual, visual, and those that are replayed in the mind.

The judicial nightmares recalled and recounted in these texts and analyzed by Shaw demonstrate that the terrifying imagery of the courtroom seeped into the subconscious of those subject to Roman imperial power.

---

[11] Shaw, "Judicial Nightmares," 556.

Shaw is correct that early Christian authors depict God as Just. But their depictions of God as at least in some ways analogous to a Roman judge, only with significantly more skills and power, has the effect of encouraging readers to fear the divine courtroom even if they believe they have nothing to fear, just as subjects of the Roman empire feared the Roman tribunal even if they were not guilty of committing a crime. This fear of the courtroom is part and parcel of depicting God in this manner, and it is why so many early Christian readers judged and questioned the justice depicted in these texts. Early Christian authors did not *have* to use the imagery of the courtroom to describe the activity of God at the end of days. They could have harnessed different rhetorical images, such as the image of the testing fire in 1 Corinthians 3, or the river of fire in the *Apocalyse of Peter*. Their choice of the judicial environs was deliberate, and took advantage of the very real fears and associations people had with courtrooms, fears and associations that Shaw himself does an excellent job of enumerating. Shaw notes that early Christian epigraphy often refers to the "fearful day of Court" (*per tremendam diem iudicci*), or talk about Christ as a "venerable and terrible judge" (*iudex venerabilis atque terribilis*).[12] People feared the courtroom because of all the things they knew could go wrong in courtrooms. No wonder, then, that the question of intercession, and whether or not people could intercede on behalf of the defendants, was so pressing and appears in so much literature.

In this chapter, I will examine the extensive courtroom scenes found in the *Apocalypse of Peter* and the *Visio Pauli*, demonstrating that the authors used these courtroom scenes to answer criticisms regarding God's justice, fully intending the reader to play the true judicial rôle in the proceedings. These texts are full of signposts to the reader, guiding them to what the author believes is the correct verdict on God and God's justice. But the verdicts they want their readers to hand down are not necessarily commensurate with what modern commentators believe is just. This, in turn, provokes some modern scholars to do exactly what the courtroom scenario presupposes – judge the proceedings – but come up with an alternative verdict regarding the justice of God as presented in the text. Following this examination, I will then demonstrate that this exact same process occurred in antiquity, at least one very vocal early Christian reader – Marcion of Sinope – did exactly what the courtroom scenario expected him to do, act as judge on the proceedings. Marcion, however, came to the conclusion as some modern readers: that the god of these scenes was entirely unjust and not truly God. God was truly on trial for Marcion, and Marcion pronounced him guilty. In the latter half of this chapter I will examine Marcion's critique and the response of Tertullian, who attempts to demon-

---

[12] Shaw, "Judicial Nightmares," 560.

strate, using the exact forensic criteria that Marcion interrogated, that the judicial attributes are entirely appropriate to God's justice and, indeed, appropriate to God. Tertullian makes an impassioned defense of these attributes, and indeed an impassioned defense of God. Again a verdict is demanded, this time from the readers Tertullian hopes to reach.

# B. The Divine Courtroom in the Christian Apocalypses

In the *Apocalypse of Peter*, possibly dating to the Bar Kochba revolt but set during the transfiguration atop the Mount of Olives, Jesus reveals to Peter (along with James and John) on the palm of his hand the image of all that will happen on the last day (*Apoc. Pet.* 3).[13] The image includes "how the righteous and the sinners shall be separated and how those will do who are upright in heart, and how the evil-doers will be rooted out for all eternity" (*Apoc. Pet.* 3). The image of judgment as separation comes from Matthew, both the image of the separation of sheep from goats in Matthew 25, and from the parable of the wheat and the tares. Here the final separation leads to great sorrow on behalf of the heavenly community, both sinners, righteous, angels, and even Jesus (*Apoc. Pet.* 3). Peter is greatly provoked by this sight:

And I asked him and said, 'Lord, allow me to speak your word concerning these sinners: 'It were better for them that they had not been created.' And the Saviour answered and said 'O Peter, why do you speak thus, 'that not to have been created were better than them?' You are resisting God! You would not have more compassion than he for his image, for he has created them and has brought them forth when they were not. And since you have seen the lamentation which sinners shall encounter in the last days, therefore your heart is saddened, but I will show you their works in which they have sinned against the Most High. (*Apoc. Pet.* 3)

Peter here, reflecting on what he has seen, quotes the words of Jesus (Mark 14:21) to Jesus. But Jesus responds to him quite harshly, probably more than what the character might have expected. Peter comments as a spectator, a passive witness to the action who has formed an opinion on it. But Jesus informs him that his comment does something else: it resists God.

---

[13] For careful discussion of the issues involved in dating the *Apocalypse of Peter*, see Richard Bauckham, "The Apocalypse of Peter: A Jewish Christian Apocalypse from the Time of Bar Kokhba," *Apocrypha* 5 (1990), 7-111, reprinted in Bauckham, *The Fate of the Dead: Studies in the Jewish and Christian Apocalypses* (Supplements to Novum Testamentum 93; Leiden: Brill, 1998); cf. also E. Tigchelaar, "Is the Liar Bar Kokhba? Considering the Date and Provenance of the Greek (Ethiopic) Apocalypse of Peter" in Jan Bremmer and István Czachesz, eds. *The Apocalypse of Peter* (Leuven: Peeters, 2003), 63-77; Martha Himmelfarb, *Tours of Hell: An Apocalyptic Form in Jewish and Christian Literature* (Philadelphia: University of Pennsylvantia Press, 1983), 222.

The reason Jesus' rebuke is so harsh is that Jesus is informing Peter that his comment is more than a passive remark, it is in fact an active condemnation of what he has seen. Peter is more than a passive spectator, he has acted as an active judge. Perhaps without realizing it, Peter has, by his comment, *pronounced judgment on God and God's wisdom in these matters.* Peter has not acting as a spectator, he is acting as a judge – one who thinks that he is more just than the Most High (to paraphrase 4 Ezra).

This conversation between Jesus and Peter sets the stage for the otherworldly tour that makes up the bulk of the *Apocalypse of Peter.* The focus of the tour will be Jesus' proof to Peter that it is just for the wicked to suffer, and it is not just for Peter to have compassion for them.[14] In other words: that *God's* decisions are just, and, by extension, that God is just, and has a plan for the universe that is commensurate with justice. This is necessary, because Peter's comment here is representative of the type of comments that early Christian readers were making when they reflected on the visions of final judgment present in their literature. Peter is here an example of the judicial stance of the early Christian reader, sitting in judgment on what plays out before them. Perhaps it was an unintended consequence, and perhaps it was intended by the author, but the scenes of the divine courtroom caused readers to make judgments about the justice of the courtroom procedures. The *Apocalypse of Peter* provides us with good evidence that courtroom scenarios in antiquity provoked the same type of impulses that courtroom scenarios provoke in the modern era: an impulse to judge the proceedings and the system, so that the system and the proceedings become the defendant in the rotated courtroom.

Peter, as a character, stands in for early early Christian readers who "watch" the visions of final judgment that authors place before them. He has pronounced a judgment, and perhaps he does not even realize the severity of the judgment. The *Apocalypse of Peter* was written at least in part to combat this type of judgment and sentence being pronounced by early Christian readers. Jesus' harsh rebuke of Peter and the extended proof-section that follows is designed (1) to make ancient readers realize that this is the rôle they have been playing, and moreover (2) to defend God from the charges that have been leveled against him by these readers, particularly the charge that his judicial decrees are too severe and that God lacks compassion for sinners.

---

[14] As Roig Lanzillotta explains, ""The measure of punishment, according to Jesus, strictly correlates with the measure of their transgressions. His urging Peter to pay attention not only to the sufferings but also to the nature of the sins that provoked them relies on the notion of distributive justice." Lautaro Roig Lanzillotta, "Does Punishment Reward the Righteous? The Justice Pattern Underlying the *Apocalypse of Peter*" in Bremmer, *Apocalypse of Peter*, 127-157, 139.

Jesus begins this proof by describing the events that lead up to the pronouncement of judgment (*Apoc. Pet.* 4-6), which culminate with the arrival of Jesus on a shining cloud, à la the depiction of the Son of Man in Daniel 7. Jesus is throned and crowned, and the nations weep at his presence. Following this, God "shall command them to go into the river of fire, while the deeds of each individual one of them stand before them. <Recompense shall be given> to each according to his work" (*Apoc. Pet.* 6). This vision combines two kinds of judgment imagery, that of the judicial ordeal, particularly the river ordeal, and that of courtroom testimony, in which witnesses give evidence against the accused. Here the witnesses go far beyond what could be found in a human courtroom: the witnesses are the personifications of the deeds of the accused, who stand as undeniable accusers before the defendants.[15] This is very similar to the way the near-contemporary humorist Lucian of Samosata imagines post-mortem witnesses: the accused is forced to deal with the testimony of his shadow, who has been with him his whole life (*Men.* 11).[16] The presentation of the deeds as witnesses here in the *Apocalypse of Peter* is designed to demonstrate that one (i.e., Peter, standing in for the early Christian reader) cannot argue that the sinners were unjustly condemned. This is the first step to proving that the punishments are just as well, and that God's judicial activity is appropriate, proper, and righteous.

After describing the events that lead up to the pronouncement of judgment (*Apoc. Pet.* 4-6), Jesus begins the lengthy description of the punishments of sinners that forms the majority of the text.[17] An unusual and important feature of the *Apocalypse of Peter* is that periodically characters in the narrative comment upon the punishments being witnessed. Sometimes

---

[15] So Bauckham: "The significance of the image is clearly that the evil deeds are personified as witnesses against the sinner, accusing him. We should remember that in Jewish judicial practice the witnesses were the accusers. It was they who accused the person on trial of the crimes which they had witnessed. So the idea in these apocalyptic passages is that whereas human justice is imperfect – because people can be convicted only of crimes which have been witnessed and because witnesses may not always be reliable – in the eschatological judgment of God sinners will not be able to escape condemnation for every sin, because the sins themselves will be the witnesses accusing them. Even sins witnessed by no other human being, sins done in secret, will come to light and will be undeniable. If the evidence presented against the sinner is his sins themselves appearing to accuse him, then the evidence against him will be irrefutable." Bauckham, "The Apocalypse of Peter," 52.

[16] See also Lucian's *Downward Journey*, in which Cyniscus brings in Megapenthes' bed and lamp to testify against him in the post-mortem courtroom (*Kat.* 27). Other examples from Jewish and Christian literature include Wis 4:20 and *6 Ezra* 16:65.

[17] The Ethiopic and Akhmim texts differ in an important way in this regard. While the Ethiopic text is in third person narration, with Jesus describing the different places of punishment, the Akhmim text is continues in first person, with Peter describing what he saw.

it is the sinners themselves who comment,[18] while at other points it is witnesses, angels, or even victims who make comment. One such example is in *Apoc. Pet.* 7, with regard to the punishment of the murderers. Jesus informs Peter that Ezrael will bring the souls of murder victims to witness the murderers's torment: "and they shall see the torment <of those who> killed <them> and shall say to one another, 'Righteous and just is the judgment of God. For we have indeed heard, but did not believe that we would come to this place of eternal judgment.'" The souls here quote Psalm 19:9, which was paraphrased in Revelation 16:7 and 19:2 by the heavenly chorus of martyrs who challenged God to execute justice. Their comment on the action directs Peter, standing in for the reader, to interpret the torments properly, as being part of the retributive justice of God. The presence of the victims is meant to remind Peter that the suffering now occurring is part of the justice of desert, and is sufficient for the victims to believe that they have been vindicated. This is a fairly sophisticated way of answering anticipated objections. It reminds Peter, and all readers, that there are victims who require justice, who have the most potential objections and the most potent charges to level against God. By bringing in these characters here to pronounce that they are satisfied, and proclaim God's justice wholeheartedly, the author is attempting to convince the reader that they have no legal standing by which to level charges against God or by which to pronounce judgment on God's judicial verdicts.[19]

The pronouncement that God is righteous and just, and his verdicts are righteous, just, and good, is repeated several times in the *Apocalypse of Peter*, but perhaps none more poignant than when the sinners themselves make this pronouncement in *Apoc. Pet.* 13:

Then the angels brought my elect and righteous, who are perfect in all righteousness, bearing them on their hands, clothed with the garments of eternal life. They shall see (their desire) on those who hated them, when he punishes them. Torment for everyone is

---

[18] So *Apoc. Pet.* 7, where the fornicators remark that "we did not know that we would come into everlasting torture."

[19] Michael Gilmour takes a slightly different but complimentary position on what these scenes are doing, arguing that they are designed to convince the early Christian reader that it is perfectly appropriate for them to feel satisfaction at the visions of the punishment of sinners at final judgment. Building off of John Portmann's philosophical investigation of the concept of *Schadenfreude*, Gilmour suggests that the *Apocalypse of Peter* is designed "to relieve a dissonance he and some of his readers experienced, created by the combination of three things: (a) certain teachings of Jesus (for example, 'forgive your enemies, pray for those who persecute you' [Matt 5:44]); (b) their own painful experience as victims of violence...; and (c) the (guilty?) pleasure they (or at least the author of this text derived from imagining the eschatological carnage to come. If this is correct, the text functions as an apologetic, one giving readers permission to fantasize about the fate of the damned." Gilmour, "Delighting in the Sufferings of Others: Early Christian *Schadenfreude* and the Function of the *Apocalypse of Peter*," *BBR* 16 (2006) 129–139, 131.

forever according to his deeds. And all those who are in torment will say with one voice, 'Have mercy upon us, for now we know the judgment of God, which he declared to us beforehand, and we did not believe.' And the angel Tatirokos will come and chasten them with even greater torment and will say unto them, 'Now do you repent when there is no more time for repentance, and nothing of life remains.' And all shall say, 'Just is the judgment of God: for we have heard and perceived that his judgment is good, since we are punished according to our deeds.

If the sinners themselves believe that their punishment is just, and affirm God's justice in tormenting them, who is Peter – and who are early Christian readers – to argue? Here the sinners affirm in no uncertain terms that they had been warned about the judgment, they did not believe it, and they are punished according to their deeds, in other words, proportionally and appropriately.

The *Apocalypse of Peter* ends the way it began; with a return to the scene of the transfiguration and the heavenly voice declaring Jesus as Son of God (*Apoc. Pet.* 16-17). In this Apocalypse, Jesus has attempted to prove to Peter that God's justice is perfectly just, and that he has no standing on which to accuse God otherwise. However, the second part of Jesus' rebuke – that Peter has no standing on which to judge God's *compassion* for his creatures – goes unanswered.

This has not gone unnoticed by readers, both ancient and modern. Monika Pesthy has argued that the *Apocalypse of Peter* is not complete on its own. Pesthy argues that Peter's rebuke only *appears* to go unanswered because scholars have not fully considered the relationship of the *Apocalypse of Peter* to the Pseudo-Clementine work in which it is embedded in one of only two manuscripts of the text,[20] and that we should not understand the *Apocalypse of Peter* as a work on its own, but as part one of a three-part work that incorporates this pseudo-Clementine text.[21]

Pesthy notes that the second part of this text is initiated by Peter asking the same question that plagued him at the beginning of the *Apocalypse of Peter,* whether or not it would have been better for the sinners if they had not been created at all. Jesus' answer to Peter is described by Pesthy as "enigmatic": "Because the mercy of my father is like this: as the sun rises and the rain falls in the same way, so shall we have mercy and compassion for all our creatures" (140 r b). This mention of mercy pulls the conversa-

---

[20] The text, entitled *"The Second Coming of Christ and the Resurrection of the Dead"* compiled from manuscript d'Abbadie 51, was published by Sylvain Grébaut, "L'ittérature Éthiopienne Pseudo-Clementine", *ROC* 15 (1911) 198-214; 307-23; 425-439.

[21] Monika Pesthy, "Thy Mercy, O Lord, is in the heavens; and thy righteousness reacheth unto the clouds" in Bremmer, *Apocalypse of Peter*, 40-51, 42. Pesthy argues that the second section of the text goes from d'Abaddie 51 137rb-141 vb (p. 309, 1.5 to p. 316 in the Grébaut edition), beginning at the Mount of Olives during the transfiguration scene, where the *Apocalypse of Peter* left off, and the third section picks up from there to the end.

tion back to the beginning of the *Apocalypse of Peter*, where Jesus rebuked Peter for believing that God did not have mercy and compassion on the sinners. Jesus further explains to Peter that God's mercy shines on everybody like the sun, but that when Christ comes, he will separate the righteous from the sinners and the sinners will be tortured by merciless angels (140 v b - 141 v b). Summarizing this section, Pesthy notes the seeming contradiction between the mercy promised and the merciless torment that results for the sinners.[22] This contradiction is directly related to the charges leveled against God in the *Apocalypse of Peter*, this seeming contradiction between punishment and mercy that has led some to believe that God is unjust.

In Pesthy's outline, the third section includes a secret revelation just for Peter (142 r a), in which "Jesus reveals that at the Last Judgment the sinners who believe in Christ will be pardoned, because Christ assumed their body and they ate his body and drank his blood."[23] Peter is admonished not to tell anyone, because it is assumed that if the sinners knew about the forthcoming mercy, they would never behave ethically (142 v b). In other words, the "answer" posed by this Pseudo-Clementine text to the tension felt between God's mercy and the punishment of sinners at the second death is that, secretly, all of these expositions and descriptions of the punishment of sinners – the *entire content of the Apocalypse of Peter* – is a noble lie told to instigate sinners to repentance. According to the theology posed by this three-part treatise, God's mercy is such that he will forgive everyone who believes, presumably regardless of what punishment is appropriate to their deeds in a retributive justice system.

This is a highly subversive theology, and has the effect of totally undercutting the *Apocalypse of Peter*. On a literary level, it does pose an answer to the charges leveled by Peter and those early Christian readers whom he represents, who are struggling with the tension they feel between the need for ultimate justice and the need for God to have mercy. But the answer it poses brings with it the possibility of different charges against God. Is it just to leave sins unpunished? Does this promise of sweeping mercy to all believers go against the principle of retributive justice? What about all those murder victims in the *Apocalypse of Peter* – how will they feel if God pardons all the sinners, and commutes all their sentences? Will they feel betrayed by God, if they had affirmed that his torments were just? Does this grand lie that Jesus suggests everyone is telling in effect *weaken* the justice that he and God will be able to execute?[24]

---

[22] Pesthy, 45

[23] Pesthy, 45

[24] As I will demonstrate in the next section, at least one important early Christian thinker – Tertullian of Carthage – argued so.

Rather than believing that the *Apocalypse of Peter* was always meant to be read as part one of a three part work, we should instead understand the Pseudo-Clementine manuscript as an example of the way ancient authors themselves were reading, reacting to, and annotating the apocalypse. This work demonstrates that that some ancient readers found the idea of eternal punishment of sinners repugnant and incompatible with God's mercy. The author of this pseudepigraphon was dissatisfied with the presentation of the issues in the *Apocalypse of Peter*. While the *Apocalypse of Peter* went out of its way to insist that the torments of sinners is just, this pseudo-Clementine work, which takes the *Apocalypse of Peter* as its starting point, argues that this is not really the case, and eventually God's mercy will simply not allow him to punish believers, even if they had sinned heinously in their lifetimes. This seems to be related, in some way, to the tension between a judgment according to deeds and a justification according to faith that exists within the Pauline literature. This postulated three-part work argues that ultimately, no matter what one has done, one is justified by faith alone, and this justification is a result of God's great mercy and the shedding of Christ's blood – just as Paul argues in Romans. This pseudo-Clementine work thus suggests a two-stage process: there will be punishment of sinners after death, but the second death leaves open the possibility of total mercy-based amnesty.[25] Such a distinction by design undercuts the force of the *Apocalypse of Peter*, and specifically rejects its claim that the punishments it describes are eternal (*Apoc. Pet.* 6, 13).[26] This Pseudo-Clementine work is an example of exactly the literary dynamic present in courtroom scenes – the author of this text judged the vision presented by the *Apocalypse of Peter* to be inadequate and unjust, and therefore amended the text according to his own standards and concepts of what God's justice entails.

Pesthy is not the only scholar who believes that the *Apocalypse of Peter* is not totally complete on its own. Richard Bauckham has repeatedly argued that the text is not complete without a paragraph known as the Rainier fragment. Though the Ethiopic text is for the most part coherent and well-preserved, one paragraph, numbered 14 in the Schneemelcher edition,

---

[25] As Pesthy explains, "our treatise gives a perfectly clear definition of the respective places of justice and mercy in divine economy: in this world and as well as in the first judgment, justice reigns, but at the end of the world mercy will prevail." Pesthy, 50.

[26] Bauckham notes that "in the Ethiopic version of the account of the various punishments it is explicitly stated eleven times that they are eternal, and this point is also vary emphatically made in each of the chapters which frame the account of the punishments (chapters 6 and 13)." Bauckham, "Apocalypse of Peter," 59.

is corrupt and "largely unintelligible."[27] Part of the Rainer collection in Vienna, a fragment from the third or fourth century seems to be a Greek version of the corrupt text. Coming after *Apoc. Pet.* 13, in which the sinners confirm that God's judgment is just even though the angel Tatirokos has told them the time for repentance is over, the fragment (R) follows:

> Then I will give unto my called and my chosen whomsoever they shall ask me for (ὅν ἐὰν αἰτήσωνταί με), out of torment, and will give them a fair (χαλὸν) baptism in (or unto) salvation from the Acherusian lake which men so call in the Elysian field, even a portion of righteousness with my holy ones. And I will depart, I and my chosen, rejoicing, with the patriarchs, unto mine eternal kingdom, and I will perform for them the promises which I promised them, I and my Father which is in heaven.[28]

This fragment describes a further step in the judicial process: the intercession of the elect on behalf of whomever they wish to save, and the subsequent salvation by baptism of the former tormented.[29] This, coming after *Apoc. Pet.* 13, would suggest that there will still be one more opportunity to save those who find themselves in eternal torment. The choice, however, of whom to save would not belong to God or Christ, but to those already saved. The attitude towards intercession here in this fragment is optimistic to say the least: it gives an enormous amount of power and choice to the elect, and seems to make the salvific will of God and Christ entirely dependent on the desires of the elect and chosen.

James is not convinced that this is a faithful translation of the Ethiopic text. He argues that "the Ethiopic exhibits relics of the Greek text throughout, but in two places is gravely corrupted, and in one place is guilty of an important omission."[30] James notes that there is no evidence in the Ethiopic text to suggest that the elect have the power to save whomever they desire. The Ethiopic text at this point is not corrupted, and instead reads "Then will I give to my elect and righteous the baptism and the salvation for which they have besought me, in the field Akrosja which is called Aneslesleja" (*Apoc. Pet.* 14). The corruption of the Ethiopic text begins with the *following* sentence. James instead believes that the editor of the Ethiopic version "has designedly omitted or slurred over some clauses in

---

[27] M. R. James, "The Rainer Fragment of the Apocalypse of Peter," *JTS* 32 (1931), 270-279, 270.

[28] Text and translation from James, "The Rainer Fragment," 271. The fragment continues for another three lines: "Lo, I have manifested unto thee, Peter, and have expounded all this. And go thou into a city that ruleth over the west, and drink the cup which I promised thee, at the hands of the son of him that is in Hades, that his destruction may have a beginning; and thou acceptable of the promise..."

[29] Alan Bernstein believes that Christian Sybillines 2.330-38 also represents such a reaction to the *Apocalypse of Peter*. Cf. Bernstein, *The Formation of Hell* (Ithaca: Cornell, 1993), 290-291.

[30] James, 272.

the passage beginning, 'Then will I give unto mine elect," because "the doctrine – which is indeed a very curious one – was thought dangerous."[31] In other words, James believes that the Ethiopic translator deliberately omitted these verses. The Rainer fragment, in his view, is an ancient editorial amendment to the *Apocalypse of Peter*, preserving a reaction to the theology contained in these verses. Their "danger" lies in the fact that they seem to give away the power of salvation from God and Christ to other, non-divine beings. Other problems emerge from thinking through this doctrine. Why are the righteous allowed to ask for some to be saved and not others? Why aren't those who are in torment allowed to ask for their own salvation? Does this give the righteous power over God?

In contrast to James, Bauckham believes the Rainer fragment is crucial to an understanding of the *Apocalypse of Peter*.[32] Bauckham believes that the Rainer fragment is integral to the structure and meaning of the text, because it is what brings the conversation back to the theme of mercy introduced in *Ap. Pt.* 3, and thus frames the account of God's justice by two passages on God's mercy. To the question of why, if the text is eventually going to forgive sinners and dismiss the judgment, Jesus rebukes Peter so harshly in chapter 3, Bauckham argues that:

> Peter's compassion is rejected at this stage because it is cheap. It takes no account of the demands of justice. The chapters which follow (4-13), with their account of the judgment itself and the punishment of each sinner specifically for his or her particular sin, are designed to demonstrate to Peter that hell is required by God's justice. Only when this has been made abundantly clear, by means of a whole series of traditional themes, can mercy be allowed a voice which does not detract from justice.[33]

Furthermore, Bauckham believes that only the righteous elect can ask for people to be saved because they are the ones *owed* justice by God, since they were the victims, and therefore "no one else has the right to forgive oppressors."[34] According to Bauckham's understanding of the way justice operates in the *Apocalypse of Peter*, God and Christ owe the righteous justice because of their suffering, and therefore the righteous have the power to insist that they have been properly compensated. Only then can there be mercy.

Bauckham's claims are problematic. To begin with, he has not adequately answered James's objections regarding the exact passages in the Ethiopic text which are corrupted. But moreover, he has failed to recognize that this still does not adequately deal with the question of *God's* compas-

---

[31] James, 273. The doctrine does, as James notes, appear in *other* Christian texts, including Sybilline Oracles 2:330-338, and *Epistula Apostolorum* 40.

[32] Bauckham, "Apocalypse," 83.

[33] Bauckham, "Apocalypse," 84.

[34] Bauckahm, "Apocalypse, 85.

sion, the substance of Jesus' rebuke of Peter in *Apoc. Pet.* 3. This fragment
suggests that there is room for compassion, but it is not the compassion of
God but rather that of the elect. Moreover, the addition of the Rainer fragment to the *Apocalypse of Peter* seems to undercut the entire effect of the
tour of hell, which is to vindicate God's judicial decisions, by announcing
that ultimately everything is up to the whim of the righteous elect. James is
probably correct when he argues that the Ethiopic edition of the text did
not contain this material, especially not this particular section. The Rainer
fragment does not resolve the tensions felt in the *Apocalypse of Peter*; it
creates new tensions, tensions which Bauckham is trying to resolve.

What Bauckham is doing, however, is enacting the critical response that
this type of imagery provokes in readers ancient and modern: judging the
situation, pronouncing a verdict. Though the *Apocalypse of Peter*, I believe, was written as a response to early Christian "judicial pronounce-
ments" on images of the divine courtroom and God's judicial operations, it
in turn, by using this genre and writing these new scenes, provoked the
same kind of response in others. Both the Pseudo-Clementine text discussed by Pesthy and the Rainier fragment are evidence that this critical
and judicial attitude and role was taken by ancient readers. Bauckham is
but a modern example of this very ancient type of reader response. And, in
turn, Bauckham's attempt to vindicate this conception of justice has itself
been challenged in the scholarly literature, as other scholars have taken
issue with this envisioned justice. Roig Lanzillotta, for example, takes issue with Bauckham's claims, arguing that "as far as the conception of a
justice owed to the victims is concerned, such an interpretation of the
theodicy dangerously slides, in my view, from a general to a particular notion of justice. From this perspective, God's justice is no longer the mate-
rialisation of righteousness, but simply a compensation owed to particulars. And, naturally, this implies that punishment and reward are no longer
effects of the restitution of justice, but rather its cause."[35] Lanzillotta himself attempts to vindicate the justice pattern in the Apocalypse by trying to
distinguish between the principle of *lex talionis*, which he considers too
close to a concept of justice that is based on revenge, and "mirror punishments", which punish not the *act* of sin, but the *guilt* that sinners have accumulated. Lanzillotta believes it is mirror punishments which are present
in the text, not an application of a divine *lex talionis* principle as most
scholars have asserted.[36] What we have here is another modern attempt to
vindicate the image of God's judicial system, and with it the image of ultimate justice presented by the *Apocalypse of Peter*.

---

[35] Lanzillotta, 144.
[36] Lanzillotta, 145.

All of these modern scholars are reacting to the text as judges and arbitrators of the issue of God's justice precisely because this is the type of reaction provoked by the use of courtroom imagery. The second-century *Apocalypse of Peter* responds to exactly this type of ancient reaction by having Peter stand in for the ancient reader who is pronouncing judgment on God and God's wisdom in the operation of justice. As demonstrated, the *Apocalypse of Peter* was written at least in part to combat this type of judgment and sentence being pronounced by early Christian readers, by suggesting to them that this type of activity is a form of "resisting God." The *Apocalypse of Peter* attempts to prove to Peter, standing in for the reader, that God's justice is entirely just. But its own use of the courtroom scene to prove this point and to answer these objections in turn provoked new questions, as the Pseudo-Clementine text and Ranier fragments demonstrate. This reaction continues through the twenty-first century in the interpretive impulses of modern authors such as Pesthy, Bauckham, and Lanzillotta. Though it attempts to direct the reader to a particular judicial verdict, the *Apocalypse of Peter* was clearly not successful in its pursuits, as not every reader came to this decision, and not every ancient judge acquitted God of the charges leveled against him.

### I. The Visio Pauli

The Christian *Apocalypse of Paul* (the *Visio Pauli*) is best known for its graphic and disturbing tour of hell, in which Paul views the detailed punishments of sinners for a variety of crimes after death (*Vis. Paul* 31-43), including ecclesiastical crimes such as improper behavior in church (*Vis. Paul* 31) and not executing the episcopate properly (*Vis. Paul* 35). Probably dating from the late fourth century,[37] the text enjoyed a lively career in the middle ages, being translated into multiple languages and having over ten Latin redactions.[38] Recently, Jane Baun has drawn attention to the particular surge of popularity of the *Visio Pauli* in the ninth and tenth centuries, arguing that the medieval *Apocalypse of the Theotokos* and *Apocalypse of Anastasia* both find their literary predecessor in the *Visio Pauli*.[39] Many scholars have argued that the *Apocalypse of Paul* is the literary antecedent to Dante's *Inferno*, drawing attention to the way in which the pu-

---

[37] The text was known by both Augustine and Prudentius (ca. 348-410 CE). For discussion, see Bernstein, *The Formation of Hell*, 292ff.

[38] For discussion see A. Hilhorst, "The Apocalypse of Paul: Previous History and Afterlife," in Jan Bremmer and István Czachesz, eds. *The Visio Pauli and the Gnostic Apocalypse of Paul* (Leuven: Peeters, 2007); for a critical edition of three Latin versions see Theodore Silverstein and Anthony Hilhorst, *Apocalypse of Paul: A New Critical Edition of Three Long Latin Versions* (Geneva: Patrick Cramer, 1997).

[39] Jane Baun, *Tales from Another Byzantium: Celestial Journey and Local Community in the Medieval Greek Apocrypha* (Cambridge: Cambridge University Press, 2007).

nishments in Paul's hell correspond to the sins as a precursor to Dante's highly developed poetics of *contrapasso*.

But the tour of hell is only one section of the *Visio Pauli*, and is preceded by one of the longest and most fleshed-out examples of the heavenly courtroom process in late Antique Christian literature. Several different cases are brought to trial, witnesses give testimony, and verdicts are pronounced. These scenes set the stage for the way the reader is to understand what Paul witnesses on his tour; they serve as directions from the narrator. The courtroom scenes are filled with affirmations of God's justice as a judge and his righteousness in executing judgments. Many of these affirmations are then repeated throughout the tours themselves, either by Paul or by the victims themselves. In this was the *Visio Pauli* stands in the same tradition as the *Apocalypse of Peter*, using the courtroom scenes as an attempt to vindicate God from charges of injustice and cruelty. In the courtroom scenes the author anticipates the reactions and concerns of his readers to the graphic and disturbing images that will follow. By devoting so much space to the presentation of God's justice, the author is trying to convince the reader that the decisions to send souls to these horrible fates were not the arbitrary and cruel whims of a tyrannical deity, but rather the verdicts of a carefully adjudicated process than ensures that everyone receives their just deserts. The author expects the readers to pronounce a verdict on the entire process, and on God in his capacity as judge.

At the beginning of the *Visio Pauli*, one of several narratives based on 2 Corinthians 12:1-12, a document is found which contains a record of Paul's ascent to the third heaven (*Vis. Paul* 1). The document does not begin with a description of Paul's ascent, but rather with a litany of complaints that have been lodged against the people with God. God tells Paul to inform the people that protestations have been filed against them by the sun, the moon and stars, the sea, the waters, and the earth (*Vis. Paul* 4-6). These natural bodies protest against the ungodliness and unrighteousness of men, and ask God to allow them to punish the people "so that they may know that you are God." In each case God tells them that he knows, "but my patience bears with them until they are converted and repent. But if they do not return to me, I will judge them."[40] This culminates with the cries of the earth, who insists that she has suffered more than any one else, for she has to put up with "the fornications, adulteries, murders, robberies, false oaths, sorceries and evil enchantments of men, and every evil which they commit" (*Vis. Paul* 6). But God informs her not that his patience bears with them, but that "my holiness endures them until they are converted and repent."

---

[40] This exchange is also later repeated between the angels and God (*Vis. Paul* 10).

Though the complaints are lodged against the people, it is obvious that the complaints really being lodged here are against God, for he has not punished the people for their sins. The undertone to these opening passages in the *Visio Pauli* is that the heavenly and earthly bodies believe that God has waited too long to punish the people, and that they are deserving of immediate punishment. They call on God to take action, for they cannot take watching the people any more. In each case God repeats the same refrain: he is waiting for them to repent, but if not, he will Judge them. But the final complaint by the earth provokes a different response: his holiness, one of his attributes, necessitates this endurance – but it has limits, for if they do not return, he will judge them.

The document continues in Paul's voice, with Paul telling them that humans need to bless the Lord God every hour, but especially at sunset:

> For at that hour all the angels go to the Lord to worship him and bring before him all the deeds of men, whether good or evil, which each of them does from morning until evening. And one angel goes forth rejoicing from the man he indwells but another goes with sad face. When then the sun has set at the first hour of the night, in the same hour (come) the angel of each people and the angel of each man and woman, (the angels) which protect and preserve them, because man is the image of God; and similarly at the hour of morning which is the twelfth hour of the night all the angels of men and women meet God to worship him and to bring before him every deed which each man has done, whether good or evil. Every day and (every) night the angels present to God an account of all the actions of mankind. Therefore I tell you, children of men, bless the Lord continually every day of your life. (*Vis. Paul* 7)

By informing the people that God is watching everything they do, and telling them that every day brings its own record-keeping and accounting, Paul is asking the people to imagine what their angel might be bringing to God every day. He asks the audience to realize that they are constantly being surveilled and their activities are constantly being recorded. Harry Meier discusses this aspect of apocalyptic literature with particular attention to what this means for apocalyptic representations of punishment and reward, which will occur later in the *Visio Pauli*, but his comments are relevant here as well. Meier notes that "plots of coming judgment, or visions of judgment figuring in larger narratives, present audiences to themselves in order to persuade them of the necessity of new performances of self."[41] Though Meier is talking about texts with depictions of a future judgment, this is all the more relevant for this conception of the divine courtroom (or divine accounting office), which sees evidence as being presented continually and immediately, not in some far-away future. Audiences are being asked to see themselves as God sees them, every day, and to use that exceptional vision to transform themselves in the present.

---

[41] Meier, "Staging the Gaze," 145.

Paul is shown the angels who guide both the souls of sinners and the souls of the righteous to their respective post-mortem abodes (*Vis. Paul* 11-12), but is troubled by something in the process, asking "must the righteous and the sinners meet the witnesses when they are dead?" (*Vis. Paul* 12). His angelic tour guide tells him that everyone must pass over to God in the same way, "but the righteous, because they have a holy helper with them, are not troubled when they go to appear before God." This exchange anticipates and attempts to answer an objection to the justice of the heavenly process: whether it is fair for those who are righteous to have to face the same fearful process as the sinners. "Meeting the witnesses" seems to be shorthand for facing up to one's life in an immediate way, especially since the witnesses, as evident from what follows, are nothing less than the personification or hypostatization of one's deeds and desires (*Vis. Paul* 14). Here the angel asserts that everyone must face the same process – regardless of what that process entails – but that the presence of helpers makes it much easier for the righteous. This attempts to play down the fears associated with courtrooms and especially the divine courtrooms by asserting that there is a procedure in place to assist those who "deserve" to have it easier.

Paul asks to see the process by which the souls and the righteous leave their respective bodies (*Vis. Paul* 14), which sets the scene for the next major section of the apocalypse (*Vis. Paul* 14-19. Paul is allowed to witness what happens to the soul of both a righteous man (*Vis. Paul* 14) and that of a sinner (*Vis. Paul* 15) as they leave the body and pass over to their post-mortem "lives." When Paul witnesses the soul of the righteous man, he sees firsthand what kind of "help" is given by the angels who watch over the righteous. They give the soul a sort of heavenly pep-talk, assuaging its fears and exhorting it to be confident. The soul's individually assigned angel assures the soul that he has taken care to report to God all of its good deeds, and the angels together ward off the evil angels who attempt to block the soul's path to heaven.

After passing through these obstacles, the angels again attempt to build up the soul's confidence for the real challenge – the presence of God. The angels lead the soul to worship God, but before God can speak, "an angel ran on ahead of it and declared, saying: Lord remember its works; for this is the soul on whose deeds I reported to thee daily, acting according to thy judgment." This testimony is buttressed by that of the spirit, who testifies to the quality of the soul: "I am the spirit of quickening, breathing on it and dwelling in it. For I was refreshed in it during the time I dwelt in it. It behaved according to thy judgment." (*Vis. Paul* 14). The soul never speaks at all, but instead these two testimonies are immediately followed by God's declaration that Michael should lead the soul to Paradise until the resurrection. This divine verdict is immediately affirmed by the heavenly chorus: "And after that I heard the voices of a thousand times a thousand angels and archangels and the cherubim and the twenty-four elders who sang hymns and glorified God and cried: Righteous art thou, O Lord, and righteous are thy judgments; there is no respect of persons with thee and thou dost requite every man according to thy judgment." This affirmation of God's righteousness contains explicit allusions to the affirmations of the heavenly chorus in Revelation, where the function of the heavenly affirmations is to assert God's justice and to direct the reader to assert it as well.

Following this exultant scene, Paul is allowed also to view its counterpart, what happens to the soul of an unrighteous person when it leaves the body (*Vis. Paul* 15). The soul is described as having "provoked the Lord day and night by saying: I know nothing other than this world; I eat and drink and enjoy what is in the world. For who has gone down into the underworld and coming up has told us that there is a judgment there?" But just like the soul of the righteous man, at the hour of death this soul is confronted by all of his deeds, standing before him to confront him with his own activities and thus with the essence of his earthly life. And just as the soul of the righteous had to confront the wicked angels, so too does this soul, but this time it is the holy angels which find no place within it, and the wicked angels are the ones who lead the soul out of the body.

Like that of the righteous, this soul also has a meeting with its "familiar angel," but the substance is quite different. The angel says to him:

O unfortunate soul, I am the angel who clung to you and reported daily to the Lord the evil deeds which you did night and day. And if it had been in my power I would not have served you one single day, but I was not able to do that. For God is merciful and a righteous judge and he has ordered us not to cease to serve a soul until you repent. But you have wasted the time for repentance. And today I am become a stranger to you, and you to me. Let us then go to the righteous judge; I will not discharge you before I know that from the present day I am become a stranger to you. (*Vis. Paul* 16)

Twice here the angel informs the soul of God's justice. First the angel informs him that it is *only* due to God's justice, which includes mercy, that the angel was forced to serve as this soul's personal daemon. God's justice in judgment is mentioned again as he is called the "righteous judge." The emphasis is clear: God has set up a just process, despite how unjust the recipient. Everything bad that is about to happen to the soul, therefore, is entirely due to the soul's nature and activity, and has nothing to do with God, because God gave the soul ample opportunity to repent, and the soul did nothing about it.

And just as the soul of the righteous man was greeted upon his arrival at the gates of heaven, so too the soul of the wicked has a heavenly host prepared to conduct him to meet his maker, "so that it may know there is a

God whom it has despised" (*Vis. Paul* 16). But this time the cries of the
"thousands of thousands" of angels have a decidedly different tone, weeping over its inevitable fate, and over its foul smell that has permeated the
angelic community. And the angel who runs before the soul to present it to
God has an entirely different motivation, asking God to "deal with it according to thy judgment" (*Vis. Paul* 16). Its spirit also speaks similarly,
testifying that "I am the spirit which dwelt in it from the time when it was
made in the world, and it did not follow my will. Judge it, Lord, according
to thy judgment" (*Vis. Paul*. 16).

But whereas in the case of the righteous soul these testimonials were
followed immediately by the declaration of the verdict, here in the case of
the wicked soul, God offers the soul an opportunity to speak, asking (albeit
rhetorical) questions: "And the voice of God came forth to it and said:
Where is your fruit which you have brought forth corresponding to the
good things you received? Did I set even the difference of one day between you and the righteous? Did I not make the sun to rise over you just
as over the righteous? It however kept silent because it had nothing to say"
(*Vis. Paul*. 16). This deviation from the sequence of events in the case of
the righteous soul is significant. The reader is here being asked to realize
that despite the fact that the soul did not do anything to deserve this opportunity to defend itself before God, God is such a just God that he allows
him to do so. This is marked by the text given what happens next:

> And again a voice came saying: God's judgment is righteous and there is no respect of
> persons with him. For whoever has shown mercy, to him will mercy be shown, and
> whoever has not been merciful, God will not have mercy on him. Let him therefore be
> handed over to the angel Tartaruchus, who is appointed over punishments, and let him
> send him into outer darkness where there is wailing and gnashing of teeth, and let him
> remain there until the great day of judgment. After that I heard the voice of the angels
> and archangels who said: Righteous art thou, O Lord, and righteous is thy judgment. (*Vis.
> Paul* 16)

There is a bit of deliberate ambiguity here which is significant, in that the
speaker of "a voice" is not identified. Presumably the voice is the voice of
God, in that it pronounces the verdict, that the soul is to be handed over to
Tartaruchus for punishment. This voice would then be identical to "the
voice of God" in the previous passage. However, because what is pronounced before the verdict is an affirmation of the justice of God and the
righteousness of his judgments,[42] this has the effect of feeling like an independent voice, pronouncing judgment on the verdict that God is to deliver.
This feeling is confirmed by the "verdict" pronounced by the heavenly

---

[42] Here in particular, the voice asserts that "there is no respect of persons with him" – in
other words, God does not show partiality in judgment, that even to the souls of the wicked
God gives the opportunity to speak and defend oneself.

chorus that closes this section, affirming the righteousness and justice of God's decisions. Thus, in addition to having two witnesses (the angel and the spirit) that here testify to the guilt of the soul, we also have two witnesses that testify to the justice of God and God's judgment, the "voice" and the heavenly chorus. These two witnesses act as signposts to the reader, directing him to register his own verdict, that God was perfectly just in consigning this wicked soul to Tartaruchus, and has thus proven to be a just and righteous Judge. The heavenly chorus functions here in the same way it does in the book of Revelation, pointing towards the "correct" position the author would like the reader to take.

But if the preceding two cases have "proven" that God is righteous and just, they have not necessarily proven that God is merciful. In the verdict on the wicked soul, the "mercy for the merciful" standard (Matt 5:7) was asserted. But no illustration of this principle, or exploration of the way God functions as a merciful judge – which the angels have asserted throughout the text – has yet appeared. This is the function of the next scene, which is devoting to proving this claim about God:

> I looked again and behold two angels were leading a soul which was weeping and saying: Have mercy on me, O God, righteous judge. For it is seven days today since I came out of my body and was handed over to these two angels and they have led me to places which I had never seen. And God the righteous judge said to it: What have you done? You never showed mercy, and for that reason you have been handed over to such angels as have no mercy; and because you did not do what was right they have not treated you compassionately in the hour of your need. Confess therefore the sins which you committed while you were set in the world. (*Vis. Paul* 17)

Here the question of God's mercy is explicit. The soul asks for mercy, and God asks it what it thinks it has done that deserves mercy, explaining that it has been given over to the merciless angels precisely because it failed to show mercy. This explanation presumes a measure-for-measure standard of judgment that is akin to poetic justice: souls will experience in the afterlife a response which is proportional to their own actions on earth. By asserting this standard of justice, the author argues that God is not to blame for harsh verdicts; rather, that people are themselves to blame for their eventual fates. It is debatable, as I have argued when discussing the Sermon on the Mount, and Seneca's *Apocalocyntosis*, whether this type of envisioned punishment is just at all, and whether certain authors do not carry with this type of assertion some form of interrogation of it. But here in the *Visio Pauli*, this is accepted without question as a totally just operating procedure, in fact the most just operating procedure imaginable.

Yet even so, the reader is here being asked to realize that despite the fact that it would be just for God to end the conversation here, God is so merciful that in fact he gives the soul the opportunity to confess its sins. Perhaps if the soul were to confess them, God would show mercy on that soul and pardon it, or at least relent from the harshness of its punishment. The author expects and directs the reader to come to this conclusion, to imagine that God is here so merciful that he is giving the soul an opportunity to change its fate, to alter its post-mortem trajectory, even though the soul has done nothing to deserve this chance. But the soul, rather than seizing the opportunity to confess and ask for forgiveness, lies to God, saying "Lord, I have not sinned. And the Lord God, the righteous judge, burned with anger when it said, 'I have not sinned,' because it was lying; and God said: Do you think that you are still living in the world, where each of you sins and conceals it and hides it from his neighbour? Here, however, nothing is hidden. For if souls have come to worship in the presence of the throne then the good works of each and his sins are revealed. And when the soul heard this, it kept quiet, for it had no answer" (*Vis. Paul* 17).

The theme of God's mercy recurs through this section, as God revisits this soul's case by asking the soul's angel to come forward. The angel brings forth a document which contains all the sins of the soul's whole life, and offers to "recount its deeds from when it was fifteen years old" (*Vis. Paul* 17). But God does not take the angel up on his offer. Instead, the narrator tells us that "the Lord God, the righteous judge, said: I tell you, angel, that I do not expect from you an account from the time when it was fifteen years old, but set forth its sins for the five years before it died and came here. And again, God, the righteous judge, said: I swear by myself and by my holy angels and my power, that if it had repented five years before it died, because of a conversion one year old the evils which it had formerly done would now be forgotten and it would have remission and pardon of sins; now however let it perish" (*Vis. Paul.* 17) Twice the narrator here calls God "the righteous judge," asking the reader to recognize that what God is doing is exceedingly just, offering only to take the sins of the last five years into account, rather than the sins of the soul's entire adult career. The reader is asked to realize that this is not only exceedingly just and righteous, but deeply merciful. This scene is used to prove this to the reader, that God cannot be faulted with regard to any of his judicial decisions. By the criteria for mercy laid out in Matthew 5 and repeated above, that God will show mercy to whomever showed mercy in their own life, the soul should not have had an opportunity to confess his sins. But God gave him that opportunity anyway, and he bold out lied to God. Again, by all standards of judgment, God has every right to ask – and it would be considered just – to be presented with the evidence of this man's entire adult life. But instead God stops the angel from doing so, only wanting to hear the sins of the last five years. Though the narrator does not say to the reader "this is an example of God's mercy," it is clear that this is what the narrator hopes the reader to recognize and to adjudicate.

When the souls who suffered at the hands of the wicked soul come forth to give testimony against him (*Vis. Paul* 18), the wicked soul has no choice but to admit his sins. This is followed by yet another reference to God as the "righteous judge," an explanation of what the souls who suffered are doing there, and the final verdict:

> And the Lord God, the righteous judge said: Or did you not know that whoever has done violence to another, if the person who has suffered violence should die first, he is kept in this place until the one who has committed the offence dies and then both stand before the judge, and now each has received according to what he did? And I heard the voice of one who said: Let that soul be handed over into the hands of Tartarus, and it must be led down to the underworld. Let it be led into the prison of the underworld and be cast into torments and be left there until the great day of judgment. And again I heard thousands and thousands of angels who were singing a hymn to the Lord and crying: Righteous art thou, Lord, and righteous are thy judgments.

This detail, which is unique to the *Visio Pauli*, regarding the delay of judgment for the victims so that they can bear testimony against the accused and force that soul to confront its crimes, has the effect of adding an exclamation point to the case the author wants to make regarding God's justice. Not only is God's mercy illustrated in this section by his willingness to overlook years of sins and the opportunity he gives the accused soul to make a statement before the judgment-seat, but his justice is illustrated here not only by having the wicked soul finally admit to his crimes, but also by giving those souls who have suffered the opportunity to hear the verdict against their persecutor. The impression is that, if given a choice, they too might join the heavenly chorus affirming God's justice and righteousness.[43]

These extensive descriptions of the courtroom process direct the reader towards the proper way to interpret and view the torments which the reader views with Paul in the latter half of the apocalypse. The author of the narrative clearly expects the reader to make a judgment on God and on whether or not the heavenly judicial system is a just one. The courtroom scenes are presented so as to convince the reader to acquit God of potential charges.

Despite this, however, the author clearly knows that the reader might be in need of further convincing during the Tartarus trip. At several points during the tour of hell, the author directs the reader toward the "proper" attitude to have toward the punishments he is witnessing. For example, at

---

[43] This is important because one of the theories of justice in antiquity was that justice should be compensatory: that it should perform restitution for the victims, and that justice was *owed* to the victims. Lanzillotta's objections to this concept of justice when applied to the divine courtroom have already been noted with regard to the *Apocalypse of Peter*. Yet the *Visio Pauli*, though post-dating the *Apocalypse of Peter*, clearly also reflects some aspects of compensatory justice, at least enough to answer potential objections. For discussion of the concept of "receiving justice," see Danielle Allen, *The World of Prometheus*.

the very start of the tour, Paul views the measureless abyss of souls, weeping and crying out for God's mercy (*Vis. Paul* 32), and reacts to the sight and its explanation: "Now when I had heard that, I wept and sighed for the race of men. The angel answered and said to me: Why do you weep? Are you more compassionate than God? For since God is good and knows that there are punishments, he bears patiently the race of men, permitting each one to do his own will for the time that he lives on earth" (*Vis. Paul.* 33). Paul's reaction here is what the author anticipates the readers might feel: sorrow and upset, and compassion for the souls crying out for mercy. But just like in the *Apocalypse of Peter*, the character is informed that his reactions are inappropriate, and even by having those reactions he is actually challenging the authority and attributes of God. In essence, the author believes that to have those reactions is actually to pronounce a verdict on God, and to believe that one is more righteous, more compassionate, more right than God. Though it is Paul who is being literally put in his place here, it is the reader whom the angel is truly addressing.  How seriously the author takes these potential and anticipated objections and reactions is evident by the fact that Paul experiences this same reaction again just a couple of torments later, and receives nearly the same response (*Vis. Paul* 40). This duplication is not accidental; it is perceived as *necessary* to counter these anticipated objections. It is part of the author's strategy to persuade the reader to pronounce the correct verdict on God's justice.[44]

Not only does the author desire the reader to come to the conclusion that God's judgments are just, and that God is a righteous judge, within the narrative this verdict is requested even from those being tormented. Twice figures appear to tormented souls to "explain" the justice of what has befallen them. In *Vis. Paul* 40, for example, Paul witnesses the following scene: "And I looked and saw other men and women on a fiery pyramid and wild animals were tearing them to pieces, and they were not allowed to say: Lord have mercy on us. And I saw the angel of punishments laying punishments most vigorously on them and saying: Acknowledge the judgment of the Son of God! For you were forewarned; when the divine Scriptures were read to you, you did not pay attention; therefore God's judgment is just; for your evil deeds laid hold on you and have led you into these punishments" (*Vis. Paul* 40). Here, by insisting that the punished had been forewarned, the angel makes a case that God is just.[45] This is yet

---

[44] The *Apocalypse of Peter* and the *Visio Pauli* by no means succeed in convincing everyone that their compassion is misguided. Augustine is still dealing with this very issue at *De. Civ. Dei* 21.18. For discussion, see Richard Bauckham, "Augustine, the 'Compassionate' Christians, and the Apocalypse of Peter," in *The Fate of the Dead*, 149-159.

[45] Though it may seem odd to force the guilty to acknowledge the justice of their sentence, this was also a major part of the *Apocalypse of Peter*, as previously discussed. In the *Apoca-*

another example of how the author attempts to negate or at least mollify the reactions he anticipates from the reader, by repeatedly having characters assert the justice and righteousness of God's decisions to punish. The author seems here, like in the *Apocalypse of Peter*, to be giving his audience permission *not* to feel upset at viewing these scenes.

The tour of hell, containing within it this continued exploration of the issues of God's justice and mercy, culminates with a scene in which the figure of the Son of God appears for the first time. Witnessing the freezing punishment of those who denied the resurrection of Christ (*Vis. Paul* 42), Paul weeps for the fate of mankind in much the same way as Peter does in his apocalypse, claiming that "it would be better for us if we who are all sinners had not been born." This time, however, he is not scolded as Peter is in the *Apocalypse of Peter*. Instead, the tormented resurrection-denying souls cry to God for mercy, and Michael and the host of angels appear to them (43). Seeing him they cry to Michael for mercy, and Michael responding, tells them that he prays for the human race continually before God, despite the sinful activities and lack of repentance on the part of humans. He adds:

Where are your prayers? Where is your repentance? You have squandered time contemptibly. But now weep, and I will weep with you, and the angels who are with me together with the dearly beloved Paul, if perchance the merciful God will show mercy and give you ease. And when they heard these words they cried out and wept much and said all together: Have mercy on us, Son of God. And I, Paul, sighed and said: Lord God, have mercy on what thou hast fashioned, have mercy on the children of men, have mercy on thine own image. (*Vis. Paul* 43)

There seems to be a real tension here. Since the beginning of the tour Paul has been chided for his compassion, for desiring to have mercy on the tormented souls. He has in essence been told that having these feelings constitute challenging the authority and wisdom of God and believing oneself to be more righteous, more just than God. Yet here Michael informs the souls to go ahead and ask for mercy, for perhaps God will show them mercy. This seems to go against the trajectory of the text thus far.

But it is important to note to whom the souls pray for mercy here. They do not turn to God; instead, they pray to the Son of God. This represents a departure from the object of their address in the opening verse of this paragraph. In the opening verse the souls cried out "O Lord God, have mercy on us," but here they direct their prayers slightly differently. It is not an accident that Christ appears for the first time here (*Vis. Paul* 44). The *Visio Pauli* understands Christ as the only way for those tormented to receive respite, their only access to mercy, after God has delivered his divine ver-

---

*lypse of Peter*, this acknowledgment was made by the tormented, but here there is no such statement.

dict. Christ is not quick an appellate judge here, as he does not – or cannot – reverse the verdict or grant a stay, but what he can do is provide a weekly respite from their torments. Here in the *Visio Pauli* he gives them the Lord's day off from their punishment.[46] It almost seems like the author has deliberately held this character back from appearing in any other scenes in order that he can show up here, not quite as a *deus ex machina*, but to make his appearance all the more powerful and meaningful. It might also be surprising – if the reader has not realized that Christ has not appeared thus far, his appearance may cause the reader to reflect on why Christ has of yet played no role in the text, and thus make them think differently about the courtroom process. If God has deliberately allowed for this extra avenue of mercy, this adds another layer to the tribunal proceedings, and reminds the reader that though they have been making judgments on God, they have not the purchase to understand God's entire plan and procedure.

With regard to the respite, the author is very clear that this act of mercy is granted not because of anything the souls themselves have done, but rather on the merits of others. After berating them for not deserving mercy at all, and having done nothing to merit it on their own sakes, Christ proclaims that:

> Now, however, for the sake of Michael, the archangel of my covenant, and the angels who are with him, and for the sake of Paul, my dearly beloved, whom I would not sadden, and for the sake of your brethren who are in the world and present offerings, and for the sake of your children, because my commandments are in them, and even more for my own goodness – on the very day in which I rose from the dead I grant to you all who are being punished a day and a night of ease forever. (*Vis. Paul* 44)

This is very similar to the rabbinic doctrine of imputed merits which will be discussed fully in the next chapter. For the sake of others, Christ will show mercy to these wicked souls. The reader is directed to understand this as an example of Christ's great mercy – and God's great mercy – that the divine process allows for even the wicked to be shown yet another mercy after their torments have already begun. By the time Christ appears, the reader has been directed over and over again to understand the punishments as totally deserved, and directed not to feel compassion for them, but rather to acknowledge the justice of God at work in these post-mortem destinations.

The reader is given one more instruction, one more direction here. As perhaps to be expected, the souls do not fully appreciate this great mercy. After thanking Christ for giving them a day's ease, the souls insist that "if we had clearly known that this was appointed for those who sin we would

---

[46] This is very similar to the Medieval Hebrew Apocalypse *Gedulath Moshe*, in which souls in Gehenna have a Sabbath respite from their torments. Full text in Moshe Gaster, "Hebrew Visions of Hell and Paradise," *JRAS* 25 (1893) 571-611.

have done no other work at all, have practiced nothing, and have committed no evil. What need was there for us to be born into the world" (*Vis. Paul* 44)? These words are familiar, as they are similar to those uttered by Paul at the beginning of this vignette (*Vis. Paul* 42), and those which caused Peter so much trouble in the *Apocalypse of Peter*. But the mention of the earthly lives of these souls invites the reader to recall what caused these souls to be tormented in the first place – the denial of the resurrection, both the resurrection of Christ and the future resurrection of the body (*Vis. Paul* 42). This is an ecclesiastical sin, and comes after Paul views the punishments of those who committed another series of ecclesiastical sins, including that of those who professed docetism and those who refuse to admit the doctrine of transubstantiation (*Vis. Paul* 41). This clearly places those who are currently being tormented and crying out to Christ here within an ecclesiastical context. These are not people who never heard of Christ and never had the gospel proclaimed to them; these are those who heard and rejected the orthodox teachings of the Church. In other words, the claim of the souls that they did not know that this place was prepared for sinners rings very, very false. They may not have believed it, but they certainly were forewarned – these are the conclusions the author expects the reader to draw.[47] And this is reinforced by the angry response of the angels in charge of the punishments:

When they said this, the wicked angels and those in charge of the punishments were angry with them and said: How long have you wept and sighed? For you have shown no mercy. This indeed is the judgment of God on him who has shown no mercy. However you have received this great grace – ease for the day and night of the Lord's day for the sake of Paul, the dearly beloved of God, who has come down to you. (*Vis. Paul* 44)

The *Visio Pauli* ends on a positive note, with Paul witnessing what awaits the righteous, meeting such luminaries as Lot, Elijah, and Noah at the close of his journey. This concluding vision of the fate of the righteous provides a hopeful contrast for the reader, and allows the reader to leave the text with fear being balanced by optimism. The author of the *Visio Pauli*, like the author of the *Apocalypse of Peter*, has gone out of his way to persuade the reader that the judgments awaiting sinners after death are totally compatible both with God's justice and with God's mercy. The extended courtroom scenes at the start of the text ask the reader to make a careful judgment on God, viewing his judicial process at work in a number

---

[47] There may be an intertextual echo here directed to the story of the Rich Man and Lazarus (Luke 16:19-31), in which the Rich Man, punished in Hades, asks Abraham to send Lazarus back to his house to warn his family what will happen if they do not act justly and righteously in the world. Abraham replies that they have been forewarned – they have Moses and the Prophets (Luke 16:29). The reader may be asked here to recall this story, and to come to the conclusion that whatever punishments these people are enduring are completely deserved, since they had been forewarned explicitly.

of cases, not just one. Early Christian authors knew that their readers would sit in judgment on what was presented before them. In the next section, I will demonstrate that this judicial rôle was undertaken with serious consequences by a notorious early Christian reader, Marcion of Sinope.

## C. Trying Man, Trying God: The Verdict of Marcion of Sinope

Marcion of Sinope is an example of an early Christian reader who judged God. Marcion judged God on the basis of the portrayal of God in the Old Testament, particularly the portrayal of God *as a judge*, laying down laws and punishing transgressions. Marcion believed that the qualities associated with judging were not appropriate to God, and stood in contradistinction to the God of loving kind-ness revealed by Jesus Christ. He thus argued that the God of the Old Testament was nothing more than a demiurge, a lesser god, and that the Old Testament God therefore had no relevance to Christ's good news. Marcion did exactly what these courtroom scenes and depictions of God's judicial activity ask a reader to do – he passed judgment on the events transpiring before him, thought critically and judiciously about the question of divine justice, and ultimately pronounced his own verdict: the God of these passages was guilty of injustice, in a way that was entirely inappropriate to his concept of God. Tertullian painstakingly refuted Marcion precisely by *defending God's judicial attributes*, arguing that it is entirely appropriate and necessary for God to act as a judge, and that God's judicial activity in both Testaments reveals his ultimate divine justice. Tertullian's *Adversus Marcionem* is thus evidence for my overall argument: that the divine courtroom imagery provoked readers to think critically about God's judging powers and rôles. Moreover, Tertullian's defense of God once more requires the reader to sit in judgment on the divine – and Tertullian implores the reader to make the correct judgment in these crucial matters.

Though our evidence for the life and thought of Marcion is certainly wanting, it is clear from what remains that the questions and answers posed by Marcion set the agenda for most of the theological debates of the second century. Marcion was the first early Christian author to determine a canon of authoritative Christian writings, which for him included ten epistles of Paul (all the current canonical epistles excluding Hebrews and the Pastorals) and a heavily edited and abbreviated – Tertullian would say "mutilated" – version of the Gospel of Luke. Marcion forced early Christian thinkers like Justin, Irenaeus, and Tertullian to consider the questions he found relevant, including what writings should be considered authoritative, the relationship between the God of the Hebrew Scriptures and the

God preached by Jesus, the nature of humanity and the way humans should live in the world, and the relationship between Christians and Jews. It seems that Marcion's teachings were immensely popular, and Marcionite Christianity spread quickly around the Roman Empire. Stephen Wilson notes that "beyond personal charisma and organizational advantage, Marcionism exhibited a rigor and clarity of thought that were uncommon in their day. It is no accident that the title of Marcion's major work (no longer extant) was *Antitheses*. He favored clear-cut, decisive solutions to otherwise baffling and murky issues, and this may help to account for his appeal."[48] Wilson points out that Celsus, Origen's great foil, knew only two branches of Christianity, and one was Marcionite, and that the sheer number of early Christian writings dedicated to opposing Marcion are evidence of how seriously second century thinkers took his thought and influence.[49]

Our sources for Marcion are limited. Though we have many references to the *Antitheses*, his most extensive treatise, the text itself is not extant, and the "Marcionite prologues," brief introductions to the Pauline epistles written in Latin, were written later by Marcion's followers and are therefore not totally reliable witnesses to the thinking and writing of Marcion himself. Moreover, as Joseph Tyson notes, most of our information about Marcion and quotations from his writings come from his opponents – early Christian heresiologists like Ireneaus and Tertullian – whose writings are undoubtedly polemical, designed to cast his thinking in the worst possible light and to defend against it.[50] However, we should not on that basis assume that nothing of what the heresiologists say is correct or reliable. Many of Ireneaus's descriptions of the beliefs of gnostic sects were confirmed with the discovery of the Nag Hammadi gospels. Moreover, it was not in Ireneaus or Tertullian's best interests to misrepresent the views of Marcion in their defenses against his thought. In order for them to be able to convince people of the dangers and theological inconsistencies in Marcion's thought system, they needed to present it in a way that was impossible – or at least difficult – to deny, so that readers sympathetic to the Marcionite doctrines would not automatically discard their considerations of his system. We can therefore view the writings of Irenaeus and especially Tertullian, whose tractate is the longest extant from antiquity – not to mention the longest extant writing Tertullian himself left behind – as for the

---

[48] Stephen G. Wilson, *Related Strangers: Jews and Christians 70-170 CE* (Minneapolis: Fortress, 1995), 211.

[49] Wilson, *Related Strangers*, 208.

[50] Joseph B. Tyson, *Marcion and Luke-Acts: A Defining Struggle* (Columbia, SC: University of South Carolina Press, 2006), see especially chapter 2, "The Challenge of Marcion and Marcionite Christianity."

most part reliable witnesses to the basic tenets of the *Antitheses* and Marcionite doctrine.

According to Ireneaus (*Adversus haereses* I.27), Marcion believed that the God of the Old Testament was a warmonger and the author of evil. He believed that the God who was revealed through Jesus Christ was the true God of the universe, a God of loving kindness, who was above the lesser-god portrayed in the Old Testament. Marcion believed and taught that Paul was correct in maintaining an absolute distinction between law and gospel and, as Tyson explains, "he found that the characteristics attributed to the divine in the Hebrew Scriptures were at fundamental odds with those associated with the divine in the letters of Paul. For him there was an irresolvable contrast between a God who enacted laws and judged humans in accordance with their obedience or disobedience of them and a God who justified sinners."[51] The heresiologists, particularly Tertullian, focused on countering this objection, demonstrating that the God of Ancient Israel and the God of Jesus Christ were identical, and that the two activities – judging and justifying – were not at all opposed to each other, but in fact were complimentary and mutually necessary and appropriate to God. Analyzing the ancient witnesses, Gerhard May has concluded that Tertullian is our best source for information about Marcion.[52] Tertullian characterizes Marcion's doctrine as being about separating the divine attributes: "we know full well that Marcion makes his gods unequal: one judicial, harsh, mighty in war; the other mild, placid, and simply good and excellent" (*Adv. Mar.* I.6). Tertullian diagnoses the heresy of Marcion as refusing to acknowledge that justice and punishment are attributes proper to God. As Tertullian explains with regard to how Marcion describes his god, Marcion "has removed from him all the severity and energy of the judicial character" (*Adv. Mar.* I.25). For Tertullian, it is of the utmost imperative to prove that it is Marcion's 'god,' not the God of the Old Testament, who is unjust, and demonstrate that "the judicial character" is good, just, and utterly befitting the deity. This strategy for defeating Marcion leads Tertullian to spend a lot of time reflecting and discussing God's role as judge and the operations of the divine courtroom.

The final five-book form of Tertullian's *Adversus Marcionem* is Tertullian's third edition of the work, composed between 207-208 CE, during the fifteenth year of Severus (*Adv. Marc.* I. 15). Speaking of the necessity for yet another version of the text, Tertullian tells us that "my original tract, as too hurriedly composed, I had subsequently superseded by a fuller treatise. This latter I lost, before it was completely published, by the fraud of a per-

---

[51] Tyson, *Marcion and Luke-Acts*, 31.

[52] Gerhard May, "Marcion in Contemporary Views: Results and Open Questions" *Second Century* 6 (1987) 129-152.

son who was then a brother, but became afterwards an apostate. He, as it happened, had transcribed a portion full of mistakes, and then published it. The necessity thus arose for an amended work; and the occasion of the new edition induced me to make a considerable addition to the treatise" (*Adv. Marc.* I.1). Ernst Evans has proposed a date as early as 198 CE for the first edition, due to the way Tertullian refers to the Judaean campaign at III. 24.[53] Tertullian continues the preface by noting that "This present text, therefore, of my work – which is the third as superseding the second, but henceforward to be considered the first instead of the third – renders a preface necessary to this issue of the tract itself that no reader may be perplexed, if he should by chance fall in with the various forms of it which are scattered about" (*Adv. Marc.* I.1). Obviously Tertullian could not issue a recall of the other forms of the text, so he needed to explain to his readers why they might run into divergent editions of the work. As Harry Gamble explains, "Tertullian assumed that the third edition would have to compete with the other two, and that a reader might encounter all three and be confused. This obviously implies that the previous versions of the work were widely available and thus that dissemination had been rapid."[54] There is good reason, then, to think that the *Adversus Marcionem* was read by a good number of people. In addition, the fact that Tertullian took this opportunity to add even more to the treatise suggests that the Marcionite threat was a continuing one that he took seriously, that he believed adding to the treatise would strengthen it, and that he had time to look over and perfect his arguments to his satisfaction. Our present form of the text, therefore, was carefully compiled, edited, and revised by Tertullian himself over a decade.

The final version of the work is five books long, but the majority of the argument itself is found in books I and II, on which I will concentrate. Book III presents Tertullian's scriptural evidence for the agreement between the Hebrew Scriptures and the figure of Christ, while books IV and V go through Marcion's "scriptures" and attempt to demonstrate that they cannot support the claims Marcion has put upon them. The work is apologetic – Evans describes it as "envisioned as a case in court against Marcion as defendant".[55] Tertullian implores the reader to judge the dispute in his favor, and sometimes speaks directly to the reader in their judicial position, as I will demonstrate below. Eric Osborn has called the *Adversus*

---

[53] Ernst Evans, *Tertullian Adversus Marcionem* (Oxford: Clarendon Press, 1972), xviii.

[54] Harry Gamble, *Books and Readers in the Early Church: A History of Early Christian Texts* (New Haven: Yale University Press, 1995, 119-120.

[55] Evans, *Tertullian*, xvi.

*Marcionem* "the first extended work of Christian argument."[56] It is by all accounts a highly successful piece of argumentation, though it did not completely silence the Marcionite threat. What it did do, however, was present an impassioned defense of the judicial qualities of God as being appropriate and necessary to God, to the point where we realize how seriously people were questioning these very attributes. Tertullian's strident defense is evidence that early Christian readers were thinking critically about the divine courtroom: whether it was a place of justice or injustice, and whether it was not theologically and philosophically appropriate to conceive of God in this manner *at all*.

In book one of the *Adversus Marcionem*, Tertullian argues that one cannot, as Marcion has done, attempt to remove the judicial attributes from God, because to do so weakens God, for it denies him the authority of following through on his commands: "For how is it possible that he should issue commands, if he does not mean to execute them; or forbid sins, if he intends not to punish them, but rather to decline the functions of the judge, as being a stranger to all notions of severity of judicial chastisement?" (*Adv. Marc* I. 26). Tertullian believes that the power of God is manifest in God's ability both to command and to institute penalties for those who do not follow those commands. This, he believes, are essential components of the judicial rôle of God, and removing God's ability to act in this manner limits God's ability to do anything: "If it is unbecoming for God to discharge a judicial function, or at least only so far as becoming that He may merely declare His unwillingness, and pronounce His prohibition, then He may not even punish for an offence when it is committed." (*Adv. Mar.* I. 26). This, for Tertullian, is truly unjust, and goes against the power and the authority of God:

> Now, nothing is so unworthy of the Divine Being as not to execute retribution on what He has disliked and forbidden. First, he owes the infliction of chastisement to whatever sentence or law He promulges, for the vindication of His authority and the maintenance of submission to it; secondly, because hostile opposition is inevitable to what He has disliked to be done, and by that dislike forbidden. Moreover, it would be a more unworthy cause for God to spare the evil-doer than to punish him, especially in the most good and holy God, who is not otherwise fully good than as the enemy of evil, and that to such a degree as to display His love of good by the hatred of evil, and to fulfill His defense of the former by the extirpation of the latter. (*Adv. Mar.* I. 26)

For Tertullian, nothing could be more dangerous or improper to a God that is good as to deny that God the ability act judicially, both in its positive and negative forms.

---

[56] Eric Osborn, *Tertullian, First Theologian of the West* (Cambridge: Cambridge University Press, 1997), 90.

While the *Adversus Marcionem* is written to combat the teachings of Marcion, Tertullian's strategy is apologetic: He must *defend God* from Marcion's charges that the way God acts as revealed in the Old Testament is unjust, unreasonable, and not befitting the true God. To do so, he must prove to the reader that it is fitting that God *should* be a judge, and should act in his judicial capacity as he does in the Old Testament. Tertullian thus attempts to *vindicate God* from the charges leveled at him by Marcion. As befits apologetic literature, even though God's role as judge is being discussed, that is the point to be adjudicated before the court of the reader. This effectively rotates the courtroom, and puts the portrayal of God exercising judgment "on trial" before the reader. As Tertullian explains, at the start of Book two, "we must first vindicate those attributes in the Creator which are called into question" (*Adv. Marc.* II.5).

Tertullian confronts especially the Marcionites' claim that God, following the fall of man, "became a judge both severe and, as the Marcionites will have it, cruel" (*Adv. Mar.* II.11). Tertullian attempts to prove that the judicial determinations set forth by God following the events of Eden are part and parcel of the nature of God as good. Tertullian demonstrates that in order to argue that the judicial attributes of God are incompatible with the Good, "you will undoubtedly have to accuse justice herself, which provides the judge, or else to reckon her among the species of evil, that is, to add injustice to the titles of goodness. But then justice is an evil, if injustice is a good" (*Adv. Mar.* II.11). For Tertullian, this is logically and philosophically untenable, since "you are forced to declare injustice to be one of the worst of things, and by the same rule are constrained to class justice among the most excellent" (*Adv. Mar.* II.11). If justice is classified amongst the good, and injustice among the bad, Marcion's refusal to allow God to punish those who transgress his commands (i.e., to execute or perform justice) turns God into a God of *injustice* rather than justice, and therefore it is *Marcion's* god who is not good, not vice versa.

Tertullian, appropriate to his training as a jurist, then turns to Marcion's claim that the punishments of God are evil and thus not appropriate to God, since God cannot be the author of evil (II.14). Tertullian confronts this opposition by distinguishing between two classes of evils, the sinful evils (*mala culpae*) from the penal evils (*mala penae*). Tertullian argues that the devil creates the sinful evils, but that God is the author of the penal evils, which are not in fact morally bad, but are instead to "be classed as the operations of justice passing penal sentences against the evils of sin" (*Adv. Mar.* II. 14). Tertullian does not see them as evil at all, but rather as *good*, since though they are "evil to those by whom they are endured," they are still "on their own account good, as being just and defensive of good and hostile to sin" (II.14). In other words, Tertullian believes that punishing those who commit sins is part of the good and just operations of God.

Having dispensed with the issue of whether penal evils are in substance good or evil, and proving that Marcion is incapable of denying that the function of Judge is appropriate to God, Tertullian then proceeds to demonstrate that even what Marcion perceives as the severity of God is itself compatible with reason and justice (II. 15). Tertullian poses a challenge to Marcion:

> Consider well, then, before all things the justice of the Judge; and if its purpose be clear, then the severity thereof, and the operations of the severity in its course, will appear compatible with reason and justice. Now, that we may not linger too long on the point, (I would challenge you to) assert the others reasons also, that you may condemn *the Judge's* sentences; extenuate the delinquencies of the sinner, that you may blame his judicial conviction. Never mind censuring the Judge; rather prove Him to be an unjust one. Well then, even though He required the sins of the fathers at the hands of the children, the hardness of the people made such remedial measures necessary for them, in order that, having their posterity in view, they might obey the divine law.

This passage demonstrates that one of the main charges against God's penal system was that God the judge was *unjust* in the execution of justice. In particular, we can see from the way Tertullian confronts the issue that one of the main pieces of evidence brought against God in this case was the concept of imputed guilt and deferred punishment, that God punishes children for the iniquities of their parents, part of the divine attributes of Exodus 34:6. Tertullian attempts to demonstrate that this decision was just and compatible with reason, for "if the blessing of the fathers was destined likewise for their offspring, previous to any merit on the part of these, why might not the guilt of the fathers also redound to their children? As was the grace, so was the offense" (II.15) Tertullian acknowledges that this theological understanding of the way God's justice operates through history was ultimately rejected by biblical authors (quoting Jer 31:29; cf. also Ezekiel 18), but then turns back around and suggests that Matthew 27:25 proves that God still operates by this system of requital.

Tertullian spends a lot of time trying to prove that the God of the Old Testament was, in fact, a just God, despite being severe. This is not surprising since this was at the heart of Marcion's rejection of the God of the Old Testament. At times one can sense Tertullian's frustration, as when he declares that "your conduct is equally unreasonable, when you allow indeed that God is a judge, but at the same time destroy those operations and dispositions by which he discharges his judicial functions" (II. 16). Despite his characterization of this position as "unreasonable," Tertullian takes great pains to defend God against these charges, which signal just how seriously he took them, and how much he realized that God *needed* to be defended against them.

While his attention is prima facie directed at Marcion, he implores the reader directly: "do not therefore look at God simply as Judge, but turn your attention also to examples of His conduct as the Most Good. Noting Him, as you do, when He takes vengeance, consider Him likewise when He shows mercy. In the scale, against His severity place His gentleness" (II. 17). It is not Marcion nor Marcionites to whom this directive is addressed; it is the reader, and Tertullian instructs the reader to weigh the arguments carefully. Scales obviously were associated with judicial functions, and here Tertullian acknowledges what is really going on in this defense. He is making an impassioned plea to the reader to acquit God of the charges of improperly executing his judicial functions. The remainder of Book II goes into detailed defenses of particular elements of God's justice, such as individual prescriptions of the law and the actions of God in Israelite history (II. 18-28), including the decision of God to reject Saul after anointing him King over Israel (II.23), and God's decision to refrain from destroying the Ninevites (II. 24). This section of book II constitutes the evidence that the reader is to weigh. Book II concludes with Tertullian arguing that he has made a sufficient case, despite not focusing all of his attention on Marcion's *Antitheses:*

But I would have attacked Marcion's own *Antitheses* in closer and fuller combat, if a more elaborate demolition of them were required in maintaining for the Creator the character of a good God and a Judge, after the examples of both points, which we have shown to be so worthy of God. Since, however, these two attributes of goodness and justice do together make up the proper fullness of the Divine Being as omnipotent, I am able to content myself with having now compendiously refuted his *Antitheses*, which aim at drawing distinctions out of the qualities of the (Creator's) artifices, or of His laws, or of His great works; and thus sundering Christ from the Creator, as the most Good from the Judge, as One who is merciful from Him who is ruthless, and One who brings salvation from Him who causes ruin. The truth is, they rather unite the two Beings whom they arrange in those diversities (of attribute), which yet are compatible in God. (*Adv. Mar.* II. 29)

This is Tertullian's closing argument of Book II. That which Marcion believes is antithetical is proved to be compatible, and thus Tertullian attempts to persuade the reader to acquit the God of the Old Testament from the charges of severity, cruelty, and injustice, charges that have nagged not only readers of the Old Testament but even characters *in* the Old Testament.

Many modern readers do not like Tertullian's argument. Osborn writes that "above all, Tertullian seems to fail in his account of divine justice and love. In his rejection of Marcion, he claims that only retributive justice can discourage sin."[57] Osborn thinks that many of Tertullian's arguments are

---

[57] Osborn, *Tertullian,* 4.

totally unconvincing, especially since "he accepts without qualification the avenging God of the Deuteronomist."[58] Authors like Osborn are not really arguing with Tertullian's *logic*, however – what they are arguing with is Tertullian's portrait of God. These readers find themselves sympathetic – at least in part – to Marcion's criticisms of God's judicial activity, particularly as it is presented in the Hebrew Bible. In critiquing Tertullian in this way, these modern readers arerevisiting the same questions and concerns as those of Marcion and those of the *Apocalypse of Peter*. They are still judging God for themselves, because by talking about the divine courtroom the authors have *asked them* to consider this very question.

## D. Conclusion

In many ways, the variant strains of early Christian literature, and the way the divine courtroom is variously presented and interrogated, is a direct result of the tension within the New Testament itself. One can easily see the nachleben of Revelation in the *Apocalypse of Peter* and the *Visio Pauli*, not only because of the generic similarities but also in the way the authors use the heavenly chorus as a signpost to the reader as they contemplate their verdict. Texts like Matthew and John find their natural descendants in the martyrological literature while the legacy of trials in Luke-Acts is continued by the *Acts of Andrew*, although not discussed in this chapter. Marcion, of course, takes his cues from Paul. The tensions found in Paul, discussed in detail in the previous chapter, are acutely felt by Marcion, who finds them impossible to reconcile. Marcion correctly recognizes that Paul's understanding of the anthropological nature of man *vis-à-vis* that of God strongly hampers the ability of mankind successfully to stand trial before God, and thus, in favor of a theology of grace alone, rejects the judicial proceedings still found in the Pauline literature as unjust and not befitting the true God of Christ. Ultimately Marcion is so successful at bringing out the tensions in Paul that Paul to a certain degree falls out of favor with subsequent Christian authors, and it takes an Augustine to bring him back into the mainstream of Western Christianity. While early Christian literature wrestled with the challenges posed by the Pauline anthropology, Rabbinic literature had no such tension to overcome, and to this corpus of literature we turn in the next chapter.

---

[58] Osborn, *Tertullian*, 101.

# Chapter 8

# The Divine Courtroom in Rabbinic Literature

## A. Introduction

In tractate *Beshallah* of the *Mekhilta de-Rabbi Ishmael*, three interchanges are preserved between R. Akiba and R. Pappias (פפייס), a second century Tanna who seems to have been closely affiliated with R. Akiba.[1] Expounding on the verse "And the children of Israel walked on dry land in the midst of the sea" (Ex 14:29), Pappias gives an interpretation that points to Song of Songs 1:9, "I liken you, my beloved [דמיתיך רעיתי] , to a mare in Pharaoh's chariet [לססתי ברכבי פרעה]." Connecting this verse further to Hab 3:15, Pappias suggests that when Pharaoh rode on a mare, God too, "כביכול" appeared to him on a mare. Pappias seems to be reading "דמיתיך" not as "I liken you," but as "I appeared to you," suggesting that the speaker of this verse from Song of Songs is God. At this point, R. Akiba breaks in to cut Pappias off with the interjection "That's enough for you, Pappias, "דייך פפיס". R. Akiba seems to be reacting to Pappias's suggestion that God is polymorphous or appears in multiple guises, but he stops Pappias from continuing before we can see the trajectory of Pappias' thought. R. Akiba proposes a different interpretation of Song of Songs 1:9, and the exposition ends here.

However, we get a glimpse of why R. Akiba is so insistent that Pappias quiet himself by the next interchange:

R. Pappias also expounded *But he is at one with himself* [והוא באחד], *and who can turn him, etc.* (Job 23:13). He judges all that come into the world by himself and there is no one to argue against his words. R. Akiba said to him, 'that is enough for you, Pappias.' He said to him: 'How do you interpret *But he is at one with himself, and who can turn him*? He said to him: There is no possible argument against the words of Him who spoke and the world came into being, for every word is in accordance with truth and every decision in accordance with justice. [הכל באמת והכל בדין] (*Mekh. Beshallah* 7)[2]

Here Pappias turns his attention to the plaintive cry of Job in Job 23:13, who points to the reality of what happens if one finds himself against God.

---

[1] See also b. Berakhot 61b.

[2] Text from J. Z. Lauterbach, *Mekilta de Rabbi Ishmael: A Critical Edition on the Basis of the Mss and Early Eiditions with an English Translation, Introduction and Notes* (3 vols; Philadelphia: Jewish Publication Society, 1933-1935).

As detailed earlier, Job frames his situation and explores his predicament in terms of courtroom imagery, pointing to the impossibility of facing down God in a courtroom given the enormous power imbalance between the two parties. Job 23 itself contains explicit courtroom imagery in verses 1-9, where Job contends that if he could only find God, he would go to him and lay his case out so clearly that God would have no choice but to listen to him rationally and deliver him from his verdict. However, this is followed by Job's realization that "He is one, and who can turn him? He does whatever he desires. Indeed he will carry out his decree against me and there are many like it with him. For this reason I am terrified of him; I understand and I am afraid of him" (Job 23:13-15). This chapter vacillates between Job's optimistic belief that if he could lay out his case, God would have no choice but to see it his way, and his realization that no one can turn God from his decisions, since God is One.

Picking up on the explicit courtroom imagery in Job, Pappias restates what he sees as Job's ultimate complaint: that God's power is unchecked; there is no appeal or anyone who can turn him from his verdicts. He judges everyone that comes into the world by himself. R. Akiba cuts him off here because he quite correctly sees that Pappias is stating that this is unfair, and an unjust situation.[3] Pappias, not unlike Marcion of Sinope, has performed the forensic rôle of the ancient reader, viewing the divine courtroom, and judged the situation to be radically unjust. R. Akiba wants nothing to do with Pappias's critique. When Pappias challenges him to come up with an alternate interpretation, R. Akiba agrees that there is no argument against God, but declares the question moot because everything God does is in accordance with truth and justice. In other words, there is no need for anyone to be able to turn God, because God's decrees are totally just to begin with.

Pappias is certainly not the only sage to wonder out loud about the equity of God's justice. The Tanna R. Eleazar b. Azariah recognizes that humans will be at a serious disadvantage, if not in a totally impossible situation, on the day of judgment. Commenting on Genesis 45:4, R. Eleazar notes that "Joseph was but mere flesh and blood, yet when he rebuked his brothers they could not withstand his rebuke. How much less then will man of flesh and blood be able to withstand the rebuke of the Holy One,

---

[3] Alan Segal argues that R. Akiba was deeply engaged in countering the heretical doctrines contained under the category "two powers in heaven." Though Segal does not discuss these exchanges between Akiba and Pappias, they seem to reflect this concern, which Segal locates in the second century. Here in particular there might be a reflection in Pappias's challenge of Marcion's understanding of the "justice" of the OT God. On the heresy, see Segal, *Two Powers in Heaven: Early Rabbinic Reports about Christianity and Gnosticism* (Leiden: Brill, 1977)

blessed be He, who is Judge and Prosecutor, and who sits on the throne of judgment and judges every single person!" (Gen. Rab. 93:11). Nor is this concern confined to the Tannaitic era; the Amora R. Judah b. Simon, within the context of a discussion about Job and Abraham's challenges to God to act justly, points to the difference between the courtrooms of earth and the courtrooms above:

R. Judah b. R. Simon said: 'Even in the case of a human judge, an appeal can be made from the commander to the prefect and from the prefect to the governor, but you, because no appeal can be made from your judgment, will you not do justly?' R. Judah said further: When you desired to judge your world, you did entrust it to two, Romulus and Remus, so that if one wished to do something the other could veto him; while you, because there is none to veto you, will you not do justly? (Gen. Rab. 49:9)[4]

R. Judah here seems to be using the contrast between God's ways and the ways of human judges to pose a challenge to God: since you have set up a situation in which you are באחד, you have all the more responsibility to act justly. R. Judah also seems to suggest here that Romulus and Remus, the legendary Roman protogenitors, were actually authorized by God as part of a specific divine plan, and uses this assertion to buttress his claims regarding God's own responsibility to act justly. R. Akiba may have succeeded in quieting Pappias, but he could not silence this concern among the rabbis, a concern which is deeply rooted in biblical literature. The use of the courtroom imagery for figuring God and the process of divine decision making carried with it a challenge to the reader to think critically and judicially about God.

In many ways, a study of the divine courtroom in Rabbinic literature is nothing less of an undertaking than a study of rabbinic literature itself, since the courtroom imagery is so pervasive and touches upon issues of fundamental importance to the entire rabbinic corpus. The divine courtroom is a vehicle for rabbinic discussions of the nature of man, the nature of God, including his attributes and modalities, the doctrine of merits and the way God operates in history, the ongoing issue of the relationship between God's justice and God's mercy, the role of Torah, the election of Israel, and so forth. To a certain degree the divine courtroom is a perfect microcosm of the phenomenon of "organic thinking" as discussed by Max Kadushin:

Rabbinic thought is concerned with numerous rabbinic concepts, terms peculiar to itself. These concepts are certainly not united in logical fashion and their relationship with each other defies diagrammatic representation. Instead, every concept is related to every other concept because every concept is a constituent part of *the complex as a whole*. Conversely, the complex of concepts as a whole enters into the constitution of every concept; and

---

[4] Text from J. Theodor, *Berischit Raba: mit kritischem Apparat und Kommentar* (Jerusalem: Wahrmann, 1965).

thus every concept is in constant, dynamic relationship with every other concept. Rabbinic thought, hence, is organismic, for only in an organism are the whole and its parts mutually constitutive.[5]

The imagery of the divine courtroom can be marshaled by various rabbis in different ways, but discussing the imagery in isolation is nearly impossible because it is part of the nexus of rabbinic thought as a whole. This chapter, therefore, can attempt no more than a good series of snapshots, piecing together an album that illuminates some of the rabbinic pursuits and priorities while giving a sense of the range of potential albums still to be collated.

One aspect of the divine courtroom in rabbinic literature that really stands out in contradistinction to the way the divine courtroom appears in early Christian literature is that in rabbinic literature, the courtroom is used most often as a way to narrate and explain how God acted in the past. In early Christian literature, attention is most often focused either on the divine courtroom after-life or on the expected "Grand Assize" such as predicted in Matthew 24 and in Revelation. Certainly there are depictions of the grand assize in rabbinic literature, such as the great trial of Israel presented in b. Avoda Zara 2a-3b. In general, however, it is far more common to find the divine courtroom in the rabbinic literature used as a vehicle for narration and explanation of how God acted in the past, in other words, to fill in perceived gaps in Scripture. The rabbis's primary interests, therefore, could be described as *exegetical*: their attention is focused on the biblical text, and they locate the divine courtroom in the margins of that text. Obviously, however, they have purposes that go beyond simple exegesis, and may always have at least one eye on the future horizon, but their comments are grounded in Scripture. Scripture is thus the entry point of Midrash.

But Scripture is not only the entry point of midrash, it is truly the language by which Midrash speaks. As Michael Fishbane argues, following the closing of the canon and the cessation of prophecy, the rabbis became Scriptural mediators, opening up the now-closed Scriptural canon to find new meaning within its boundaries.[6] Since the closing of the canon meant that nothing could be added or subtracted from Scripture, the rabbis developed new methods of interpretation that had as their first epistemological principle the fact that everything could be found within the lines of the Hebrew Bible. The rabbis were thus able to reinvigorate and renew Scripture through Midrash. Through this process of renewal by means of

---

[5] Max Kadushin, *Organic Thinking: A Study in Rabbinic Thought* (New York: Jewish Theological Seminary of America, 1938), vi.

[6] Michael Fishbane, *The Exegetical Imagination: On Jewish Thought and Theology* (Cambridge: Harvard University Press, 1998).

midrashic techniques such as the recombination of words, the innovative combinations and juxtapositions of Biblical verses, and the written form of anthology and enchainment in which these techniques are animated and made manifest, Scripture is revealed "as a rabbinic work."[7]

The divine courtroom in the rabbinic literature, therefore, is something that the rabbis locate within Scripture itself, explicating verses that do not seem to suggest a courtroom scenario in precisely that manner. This has the effect of creating an entire Scriptural background, almost as if the rabbis are lifting up the curtain of Scripture to reveal what is happening backstage, while at the same time locating this doctrine not in extra-biblical traditions but within Scripture itself, so that Scripture becomes the proof for the existence and operations of this courtroom. The rabbis present the divine courtroom almost as a postulate, something everyone agrees upon, and use that to read Scripture. The divine courtroom can thus be called upon or invoked to explain elusive verses, to justify divine action, or to explain why a figure like Moses is sometimes able to sway God's decision and sometimes not. In this chapter I will explore some of the aspects of the way the divine courtroom appears in the rabbinic literature, trying to parcel out this imagery which is very pervasive, and demonstrating that the rabbis assumed the existence of the divine courtroom almost as a presupposition of the way God operates.

## B. The Doctrine of Merits

In the previous chapter, I demonstrated that in the *Visio Pauli* Christ finally grants respite to tormented souls not for their own sakes, but for the sakes of others, including Paul, who prayed for their ease. This concept has a rabbinic counterpart in the doctrine of merits, which forms a crucial role in the imagined operations of the divine courtroom. Throughout rabbinic literature, from its earliest strata to its latest, we see elements of this doctrine at work, as people seek to accumulate merits in heaven, rely on the merits of others to plead their arguments before God, and think about the way God's justice operates "on the ground" in heaven.

The classic work on the doctrine of merits is still that of Arthur Marmorstein. In his monograph *The Doctrine of Merits in Old Rabbinic Literature*, Marmorstein traces the history and development of the doctrine of merits in Rabbinic literature from the Tanaaitic through the Amoraic periods, covering a span of time that encompasses roughly the first five cen-

---

[7] Fishbane, *The Exegetical Imagination*, 20.

turies of the common era.[8] Part of Marmorstein's program, which focuses almost exclusively on the Aggadic material, is unapologetically apologetic, seeking to address what he sees as misconceptions regarding the relationship between merits and faith that arose from critical readings of the church fathers and their distinctly anti-works and anti-ritual attitudes. However, the apologetic tenor of the work, which emerges most prominently in the introductory and concluding sections, frames an otherwise invaluable discussion of a crucial doctrine that informs the entire lexica of Rabbinic traditions. The impact of this doctrine emerges and is felt throughout not only the Midrashic literature, but what will become later Talmudic tradition.

Marmorstein summarizes the doctrine by explaining that the sages taught that man had the ability to acquire merits (זכויות) before God, merits that could then be used almost as barter or accumulated credits to ensure a place in the world to come, both for oneself and also for one's descendants. Alongside the doctrine of merits Marmorstein also examines its obverse, the doctrine of imputed sin, which holds that just as a merit could be passed down from generation to generation, so too can a demerit. This important pair of doctrines has at its center the profound proposition that man is not alone in the world, and his actions have meaning beyond himself. One person's action, either meritorious or notorious, will have an effect for generations.[9]

Marmorstein divides the positions of the sages into two main categories: those who believed in events being merited by the works of the fathers, and those who believed in the merits of the righteous. According to Marmorstein, the school which held to the value of imputed merits enjoyed greater popularity. However, relying *solely* on the merits of the fathers posed a theological danger, in that it lessened man's responsibility for his own actions, and thus a compromise was formed "as early as the time of Hillel," with the result that "in the later Aggadah again the traces of these differences were lost and the views assimilated with each other."[10]

At the heart of the rabbinic discussion of merits, according to Marmorstein, is the desire to know God and understand the reasons behind God's activity in the world, even so far as to why God created the world in the first place. In other words, the rabbis, by anxiously investigating the concept of merits, were trying better to capture the reasons behind divine ac-

---

[8] Arthur Marmorstein, *The Doctrine of Merits in Old Rabbinic Literature* (London: Oxford University Press, 1920).

[9] As Marmorstein explains, "One man, or one set of society, or even one people cannot do good or harm without influencing beneficially or adversely the fate of their nearest kith and kin as well as their whole environment, yea, even the whole world." *Doctrine of Merits*, 4.

[10] Marmorstein, *Doctrine of Merits*, 25.

tion, particularly as it related to the fate of man. The implications of this for imagining the divine courtroom are evident. By believing that man, by his actions in the world, could store up credits in heaven, the rabbis were suggesting that they could directly impact the divine judge and secure a positive verdict. By asserting that others were able to earn those credits, the rabbis built up a hopeful theology that suggested that even if one had personally not stored up as much credits as possible, one could call upon the credits earned by others, again with the goal of securing a positive outcome. For this reason the doctrine of merits plays an important role in the overall way the rabbis picture the operations of the divine courtroom, and the way God arrives at his judicial verdicts.

Following Marmorstein, the next scholar seriously to engage the issue of merits in Rabbinic literature was Ephraim Urbach, who discusses the rabbinic doctrine of merits in his magnum opus *The Sages, their Concepts and Beliefs*.[11] Like Marmorstein, Urbach's discussion focuses on the relationship of the action of one individual to the consequences for the future. Urbach's discussion falls side by side with an examination of the rabbinic belief in a causal nexus between sin and punishment, the "doctrine of requital."[12] Urbach's discussion of merits, alongside his discussion of the Sages's attempt to deal with the problem of suffering, falls within his chapter on "Man's Accounting and the World's Accounting," thus echoing Marmorstein's view of bartering and weighing as being the central paradigm in the Sages's theological exploration. In this chapter, Urbach attempts to provide a description and analysis of rabbinic ideas about reward and punishment, sin and death, the reasons for suffering, and the attributes of justice and mercy, among other such sub-units. Urbach thus sees the doctrine of merits as being one component of an entire rabbinic matrix of ideas related to the operation of God's justice.

Urbach believes that the rabbinic doctrine of merits emerged out of a concern by the sages to understand why sufferings fell upon the righteous. In particular, Urbach believes that much of this conversation can be traced back to the profound effect of Hadrian's religious persecution on rabbinic thinking regarding suffering. Because observing the commandments (thought to be the method of acquiring merits) was the cause of death and suffering, which had formerly been thought to be the result of *not* acquiring merits, the persecution required the rabbis to rethink the relationship between reward and punishment and the way in which observing the com-

---

[11] trans. Israel Abrahams (Jerusalem: Magnes Press, 1975; fifth ed. Cambridge: Harvard University Press, 2001).

[12] Urbach, *The Sages*, 420. The *locus classicus* of this rabbinic dictum can be found in m. Sotah 1.7-10, "with what measure a man measures, it will be meted out to him," with Scriptural proofs adduced.

mandments still stored up merits for the future. As a result of the persecution, which saw the death of R. Akiba, a new understanding of suffering arose, and it became the tradition that suffering received its rewards in the world to come.[13] In addition, the sages believed that righteous accumulated merits through their suffering.[14]

Despite the theological debates over the suffering of the righteous, and the need to formulate new solutions to the questions this raised for theodicy, Urbach notes that "numerous dicta, aphorisms, stories, and parables were added by the Sages to those already found in the Bible in order to prove that the principle of 'measure for measure' was not abolished."[15] The rabbis believed in a direct correlation between reward and punishment in the administration of divine justice. For this reason, great attention is given in the Rabbinic literature to the "weighing and measuring of details, down to the minutest particulars, of actions and their consequences."[16] That so much attention is paid to this pursuit is not just an indiction that this was "an unfailing source of expository-poetic enjoyment," as Urbach suggests,[17] but indeed that there were concerns that this needed to be demonstrated; in other words, these dicta are evidence that the doctrine of measure-for-measure was hotly debated, and not simply a presupposition of rabbinic theology.

Like Marmorstein, Urbach points to the popularity of the doctrine of זכות אבות, the merits of the patriarchs. Both Marmorstein and Urbach believe that there was a fundamental מחלוקת amongst the Tannaim as regarding what kind of merits were efficacious in securing divine action and a positive divine verdict, and that this dispute can be traced to the time of Shemaih and Abtalion, the earliest generation of rabbis. Abtalion and the Tannaim who succeeded him were afraid of the reliance on the merits of the patriarchs to achieve results, for this implied a "consequent weakening of the sense of duty and the need to fulfill the commandments."[18] Urbach tries to explain how the Amoraim attempted to reconcile the different opinions on merits, noting that the objections raised to the doctrine of זכות אבות did not succeeded in countering its popularity. He concludes his discussion by showing how the rabbis believed the generations were tied together: sons could atone for the sins of their fathers, and in like manner, the merit of future generations could affect present events. This understanding of the doctrine of merits points to an implicit theology of history

---

[13] Urbach, *The Sages*, 445, quoting Tannatitic traditions preserved in b. Sotah 4b and b. Berakhot 61a.

[14] cf. b. Yoma 67a.

[15] Urbach *The Sages*, 439.

[16] Urbach *The Sages*, 439.

[17] Urbach *The Sages*, 439.

[18] Urbach *The Sages*, 497.

in which all moments are connected through the divine. Urbach's discussion is particularly effective in explaining the interrelationship of Rabbinic thought on issues of merit, punishment, and theodicy, themes that are connected due to their focus on "spiritual stocktaking of the world and of the individual Jew."[19]

The doctrine of merits is an integral part of the rabbinic imagery of the divine courtroom, which neither Marmorstein nor Urbach thoroughly engage in their discussions of the doctrine. We see, for example, passages in which merits are figuratively cashed in in the courtroom to balance or tip the scale pans. In Tosefta Qiddushin, for example, we have the following illustration:

> R. Simeon b. Eleazar said in the name of R. Meir: because the individual is judged by his majority [of deeds], the world is judged by its majority. If one sees himself half meritorious and half liable, and the world is half meritorious and half liable, if he does one commandment, fortunate is he, for he has inclined the balance for himself and for the world to the side of merit. If he commits one transgression, woe is he, for he has inclined the balance for himself and for the world to the side of liability. And with respect to him it is said *One sinner destroys much good* – by the single sin which this one committed, he cost himself and for the world many good things. (t. Qidd. 1.11)

Here the deeds of the individual can have drastic consequences for the merit of the world. Just like in the apocryphal literature, scales are part of the figuration of divine justice, and one deed is enough to drag the scale pan down in the wrong direction.[20]

A good example of the way merits are brought in to the divine courtroom imagery can be found in the *Pesiqta d'Rab Kahana*:

> *Who directs you in the way you should go* (Isa 48:17). R. Levi in the name of R. Hama b. Hanina: [the matter is similar] to a prince who was on trial before his father. His father said to him, if you want to succeed [לזכות] before me at trial, hire for yourself so-and-so as a lawsuit-pleader [וניקולוגוס], and you will succeed in the trial. Likewise the Holy One, blessed be He said to Israel: My children, if you want to succeed before me at trial, make mention before me of the merits of your fathers, and you will succeed before me at trial. (*Pesiq. Rab Kah.* 23:7)[21]

---

[19] Urbach, *The Sages,* 511.

[20] Cf. the expansion of this tradition in b. Qiddushin 40b, which includes comment from R. Simeon b. Yohai, who exclaims "let it be regarded as half transgressions and half merits," hoping, perhaps, that God would then tip the scale in the right direction, as suggested in Midrash Psalms 86:2: "*For you, Lord, are good, and forgiving* (Ps 86:5). R. Phinehas the Priest taught: When the scales are evenly balanced with sins and merits, what does the Holy One, blessed be He, do? He takes a debt out of the sins and inclines the balance towards the merits side, as is said: *Who is a God like you, that bears* [נושא] *iniquity* (Micah 7:18)?"

[21] Text from B. Mandelbaum, *Pesiqta de Rab Kahana: According to an Oxford Manuscript with Variants* (2 vols; New York: JTSA, 1962).

Here R. Levi, speaking in the name of R. Hama, comments on Isaiah
48:17, which states that God will give Israel directions that they should
follow. The context of this passage in Isaiah is that of an oracle in which
God announces that he is about to bring Judah back from Babylon (Isa
48:1-20). The immediate context of this quotation is the assertion "I am
YHWH your God, who teaches you for your benefit, who leads you in the
way you should go. If only you had listened to my commands, your peace
would have been like a river, your righteousness like the waves of the sea.
Your descendants would have been like the sand, your offspring like its
numberless grains; their name would never be cut off nor destroyed from
before me" (Isa 48:17-19). In Isaiah, these passages are designed to persuade Israel that if they had followed God's directions the first time, they
would have been successful in their endeavors; that God had a plan for
them that would have guaranteed them success.

Here R. Levi expounds on the phrase "who directs you in the way you
should go," by providing a parable to a royal courtroom, in which a king
helps his son the prince ensure a positive victory at trial. R. Levi then applies this to the relationship between God and Israel, and how God will
help Israel secure a positive verdict in the divine trial. Writing on the way
parables operate, David Stern notes that "In parables a set of parallels is
suggested between an ideal event and the immediate one confronting the
parable's author and his audience."[22] In this parable, God is like the king,
and Israel is like the prince. The merits of the patriarchs also have an analogous role. They are described here as being analogous to an advocate in
the human courtroom. By calling upon the merits of the patriarchs, Israel is
guaranteed a positive verdict in the divine courtroom. This imagines the
courtroom function of זכות אבות almost as if the patriarchs were there physically defending the accused. They are here likened to the way an advocate
operates inside a royal courtroom. But not just any advocate – a surefire
winner, as citing the merits of the patriarchs guarantees a positive verdict.[23]

This may seem to suggest that somehow the patriarchs have power over
God, and encroach on the concept of divine sovereignty. Such was a concern, as discussed in the previous chapter, with the overwhelming power
given to the righteous in the *Apocalypse of Peter*. However, a closer look
at this passage reveals an attempt by the tradent to alleviate or at least
ameliorate these concerns. The set up of the *mashal* indicates that this entire situation rests on the pre-existing relationship between the accused and

---

[22] David Stern, "Rhetoric and Midrash: The Case of the Mashal," *Prooftexts* 1 (1981) 261-
291, 262.

[23] R. Levi is obviously playing off the relationship between the verb to succeed [לזכות] and
the rabbinic word for merits, [זכיות].

the judge, here described as the relationship between a son (the prince) and his father (the king).[24] It seems to be suggested here that the king's advice to the prince rests on this pre-existing relationship, in other words, the king wanted the prince to win his case, so he advised him on how to do so. In the *nimshal*, when this is likened to the relationship between God and Israel, this same assertion applies: God wants Israel to emerge victorious at the divine trial, so he informs them how they can do so. The relationship between God and Israel, likened to that of a father and his son, is what causes God to give Israel this winning strategy. This does not encroach upon but rather reinforces the concept of divine sovereignty. According to this logic, God did not have to advise Israel in this manner should he not have wanted to. Israel's success at the trial is entirely within his power and their citation of the merits of the patriarchs is presented as within God's sovereignty, not external to it. However, while providing a solution to the issue of divine sovereignty, the mashal still leaves open the issue of fairness and equity in the courtroom. Was it fair for the judge to give the defendant "inside information" on how to win the case? This issue will appear again in rabbinic literature, as I will demonstrate below.

This midrash interprets "who leads you in the way you should go" with reference to the divine courtroom. There is certainly a didactic intent behind this midrash. If one follows God's direction, one will secure a positive verdict. It is not difficult to see the source of the didactic element of the verse, as right before "who directs you in the way you should go" is the assertion that God "teaches you for your benefit" (Isa 48:17). The midrashic tradent asserts that God wants Israel to succeed and is giving Israel the tools to do so. This is not so dissimilar from the purpose of the Isaianic oracle, although in Isaiah 48, this is part of a reminder of what *would* have happened if the Israelites had listened to God all along (Isa 48:17-19), while the midrash uses this to point towards the future – what *will* happen or *could* happen if people follow God's directions (as explained by the rabbis). The question still remains as to what engendered the interpretation of this midrash with regard to the specific instruction of calling upon זכות אבות as a defense strategy in the divine courtroom. Was there something in Isaiah that called forth this interpretation, or was this simply a midrash in search of a verse?[25]

---

[24] For a complete discussion of the "king-mashal" in rabbinic literature, and the theological impact of likening God to a king, see David Stern, *Parables in Midrash: Narrative and Exegesis in Rabbinic Literature* (Cambridge, MA: Harvard University Press, 1991).

[25] This remains a debated issue with regard to the conditions of the production of midrash. With regard to interpretation of *meshalim* specifically, there are two schools of thought on the issue, one represented by Stern and one by Daniel Boyarin. Stern argues that midrashic texts are written to serve rhetorical purposes, and thus behind each text there is a rhetorical intent that guides the composition and structure of the text. Boyarin would not disagree, but he iden-

Two aspects of the Isaiah passage, in my opinion, seem to be a factor in the association of this midrash with this verse. First of all, there is enough in the chapter to bring this verse into a discussion of merits, and why God takes action in general. There is a mention of a patriarch within Isaiah 48. Right after this section of the chapter, God tells the Israelites to "Go out from Babylon, free from Chaldea, declare this with a shout of joy, proclaim it, send it forth to the end of the earth; say 'YHWH has redeemed his servant Jacob'" (Isa 48:20). Obviously "Jacob" here is a metonym for the nation, as the whole people are called the "house of Jacob" in 48:1. However, the use of the metonym "Jacob" here instead of "Israel" or "Judah" could have led certain rabbis to question the reasons behind the choice of this name. As it is axiomatic in rabbinic literature that nothing in the Bible is superfluous or accidental, certain tradents could have believed that the use of "Jacob" suggested that God was bringing the people back from Babylon on Jacob's merits, i.e., בזכות אב. It is certainly not for anything the people merited on their own. In fact, the question of why God is taking the step to return Israel is explicitly mentioned earlier in the chapter. God explains that he is deferring his anger and restraining himself "for my own sake, for my own sake (למעני למעני), I do it; for why should it be profaned – my glory I will not give to another" (Isa 48:11). Marmorstein briefly discusses למען as part of the vocabulary of merits,[26] but does not give it full attention. There can be no doubt, however, that למען signals an explanatory clause as to the reasons for divine action. Both of these sections of Isaiah 48 have possibly signaled the rabbis to examine the question of why God chooses to end the exile and allow the people to return, thus providing certain rabbis the opportunity to connect this passage to a discussion of merits.[27]

---

tifies the rhetorical text as being simply a matter of the exegesis of Scripture. For Boyarin, midrash is guided by exegetical questions, while Stern asserts that exegetical questions are not always the driving force of midrash. For Boyarin's understanding of the nature and function of midrash, see *Intertextuality and the Reading of Midrash* (Eugene, OR: Wipf and Stock, 1990). A series of back and forth articles between Boyarin and Stern that focused this debate on the *mashal* appeared in *Prooftexts* over the course of a decade. This began with Stern's 1981 article "Rhetoric and Midrash," followed by the debate between Stern and Boyarin entitled "An Exchange on the Mashal; Rhetoric and Interpretation: the Case of the Nimshal," *Prooftexts* 5 (1985) 269-280. The debate had its most acrimonious moments in Boyarin's review essay of Stern's *Parables in Midrash*, (*Prooftexts* 11 [1991] 123-138), in which Boyarin accuses Stern of misrepresenting his (Boyarin's) argument and characterizes Stern's argument as accusing the rabbis of lying (see, especially p. 132). To the best of my knowledge Stern has not yet in print responded to Boyarin's allegations, effectively ending the urgency of the dispute, and this indeed seems to be for the best.

[26] Marmorstein, *Doctrine of Merits*, 11-12.

[27] The question of why "for my own sake" is repeated twice is discussed at Midrash Tehillim 107:1.

Still the question of how this then became associated with a divine courtroom scenario remains. This too, however, need not be solely attributed to the rabbis's exegetical imagination, although this always remains a possibility. As discussed earlier in chapter two, these chapters of Second Isaiah make use of the genre of the *rîb*-pattern. Köhler identified two sections of Isaiah 48 as belonging to the category of "Streitgespräch" (Disputation).[28] In this extended use of the *rîb*-pattern, God defends his actions before the people who sit as his judges on the entire question of the justice of the destruction of Jerusalem and the Babylonian exile.[29] This already places this passage within a courtroom scenario. Obviously this is not the same one imagined by the rabbinic tradent. However, the forensic resonances attached to this passage may have been a contributing factor to the interpretation of this passage as regarding the importance of זכות in the divine courtroom.

It is not just זכות אבות that can be called upon as a winning strategy in the courtroom, but זכות בנים, as in this remarkable passage from the midrash on Ecclesiastes. Commenting on Ecclesiastes 4:1, "Again I looked and saw all the oppression that was taking place under the sun," R. Judah asserts:

These are the children who were cut off in their lives on account of the transgressions of their fathers. In the future to come they will stand on the side of the fellowship of the righteous, and their fathers on the side of the wicked, and they will say before him: 'Master of the Universe, didn't we die for no other reason than on account of the transgressions of our fathers? Let our fathers come over on our merits [בזכיותינו].' And he will say to them: 'your fathers sinned after you [died], and their sins accuse them [מלמדין קטיגור].' R. Judah b. R. Hai said in the name of R. Joshua b. Levi: 'In that very hour Elijah (may he be remembered for good) will sit and present a defense [יושב ומלמד סניגוריא], and say to hem: 'Say before him: Master of the Universe, which attribute is greater, the Attribute of Good or the Attribute of Punishment?' Say: the Attribute of Good is greater and the Attribute of Punishment is lesser, and we died on account of the transgressions of our fathers. If the Attribute of Good is greater, isn't it the case [לא כל שכן] that our fathers should come over to us!' He said to them: 'Well have you presented a defense: let them come over to you, as it is written: *And they will live with their children, and they will return* (Zech 10:9).' They will return from descending to Gehenna and they will be saved on the merits of their children. Therefore every one is required to teach his son Torah, for he will save him from Gehenna.

This passage portrays a successful petition, this time by children on behalf of their parents. As in the passage from the *Pesiqta*, calling upon merits is a winning strategy in court. The tradent R. Judah describes this petition as a סניגוריא, a technical legal defense. God here praises the children for mak-

---

[28] Ludwig Köhler, *Deuterojesaja (Jesaja 40-55) stilkritisch undersucht* (BZAW 37; Giessen: A. Töpelmann, 1923).

[29] For discussion of this section of Second Isaiah, see above, chapter 2.

ing use of that defense well, and he grants them their request as a result of
their successful defense. In addition, God here praises the children for
making use of that defense well, and he grants them their request as a result of their successful defense. The image is that of a heavenly courtroom,
in which God is the judge. The prosecutor seems to be the sins themselves,
similar to the way deeds are personified in the apocryphal literature. The
technical term is used here: the sins "מלמדין קטיגור". Here Elijah comes in
as an advocate for the defense, teaching the children the technical skills
they will need to succeed in arguing their case before God.[30]

## C. Snegoria and Kategoria

The above midrash uses specific terms for defense and prosecution,
סניגוריא and קטיגוריא, cognates of the Greek συνηγορία, advocacy, and
κατηγορία, accusation, which derive from the verbs συνηγορέω and
κατηγορέω, respectively. Both Greek terms are well documented and appear in classical Greek texts such as those by Plato, Aristotle, and Demosthenes as part of the forensic terminology of the classical world.[31] The
terms continued to be used in Late Antiquity; for example, Plutarch uses
the term συνήγορος to refer to the great advocate Cicero (Plut. *Cic.* 26, 8),
and uses the term συνηγορία throughout his *Lives* to refer to law-court
speeches.[32] As noted in a previous chapter, the verb κατηγορέω was used
in the New Testament to describe the activity of Moses in the divine courtroom (John 5:45-47).

These two terms, seen as opposite to each other, are found throughout
the corpus of rabbinic literature, in both early and late compilations.[33] At
one point it seems that the term פרקליט, from the Greek παράκλητος, was
favored over סניגור: in m. Avot 4:11, for example, the tradent R. Eliezer b.
Jacob says that "he that performs one precept gets for himself one advocate (פרקליט); but he that commits one transgression gets for himself one

---

[30] For discussion of this midrash within the context of salvation through children, see Dov
Weiss, "Between Values and Theology: The Case of Salvation through Children in Rabbinic
Thought – Part 1" *Milin Havivin* 3 (2007) 1-15.

[31] For discussion, see Douglas McDowell, *The Law in Classical Athens* (Ithaca: Cornell
University Press, 1978, 61ff.

[32] Noted by J. A. Crook, *Legal Advocacy in the Roman World* (Ithaca: Cornell University
Press, 1995), 35 n.24.

[33] Though, surprisingly, they are not discussed in the excellent article by Saul Lieberman,
"Roman Legal Institutions in Early Rabbinics and in the Acta Martyrum," first published in
*JQR* 35 (1944) reprinted in *Texts and Studies* (New York: Ktav, 1974).

accuser (קטיגור)."[34]   The terms are found in contexts that refer to earthly courtrooms, but they are most often found within the context of the divine courtroom. In the *'Abot de Rabbi Nathan*, for example, the ministering angels are described as mounting a prosecution (קושרין קטיגור) against Moses (*'Abot R. Nat.* 1.2). The most common way the terms are found together is in the talmudic dictum that "an accuser cannot become a defender" ( אין קטיגור נעשה סניגור).[35]

Here in Ecclesiastes Rabbah, Elijah appears to teach the children how to mount a successful defense before God, and thus how to save their fathers from Gehenna. This is, to my knowledge, the only time in rabbinic literature that Elijah serves such a forensic rôle. Though Elijah appears in various guises and forms throughout the Aggadah,[36] he is not usually found in a courtroom context. Several figures, however, do appear in this context frequently, advocating on behalf of defendants before God. The figure most often associated with this task is Moses. Given Moses' inordinate and unparalleled success at arguing before God in the Hebrew Bible, especially during the Golden Calf incident (Exodus 32) and again at Numbers 14:11-20, it is not surprising that various rabbis wish to hire Moses for this rôle. This has precedents in Second Temple Judaism, as discussed above.

Sometimes the discussion of Moses as an advocate is directly called upon by the verse under consideration. So, for example, discussing the verse "and he said he would destroy them" (Ps 106:23), directly referring to God's decision to destroy Israel at Mt. Sinai, R. Berechiah, in the name of R. Judah bar Simon explains: "[it is comparable] to a prosecutor [קטיגור] who was prosecuting the son of the king. What did the defender [סניגור] do? He pushed the prosecutor aside and stood in his place. Likewise, *had not Moses his chosen stood before him in the breach to turn back his wrath* (Ps 106:23)" (Midr. Ps. 106:6).[37] Moses' petition before God at Mt. Sinai was here understood as being similar to that of a סניגור at a trial.[38]

---

[34] As discussed previously with regard to the figure of the paraclete in the Gospel of John, παράκλητος developed the meaning of "defending counsel" in Greek, similar to the Latin *advocatus*. See above, chapter 4.

[35] So, for example: b. Rosh HaShanah 26a; b. Berakhot 58b-59a; Lev Rab 21:10. This dictum is also phrased as a question; so b. Hagigah 13b; b. Hagigah 5a. In y. Sukkah 3:1 this appears as a warning: אי לא לזה שנעשה סניגורו קטיגורו; see also Lev Rab 30:6.

[36] Including that, surprisingly, of a Roman official; cf. b. Ta'anit 21a.

[37] This comment from R. Berechia occurs right after another presentation of the interchange, found at Mekhilta *Beshallah* 7, between Pappias and R. Akiba on Psalm 106:20, "And they destroyed their glory in the building of an ox which ate grass." The exchange is presented and then the midras moves directly to the discussion of Ps 106:23.

[38] It is noteworthy that here, again, Israel is compared to a prince. Despite the fact that this mashal does not specifically liken God to a king, it is explicitly implied. The same set of relationships are assumed here as discussed in the mashal from *Pesiqta de Rab Kahana*.

This same exegetical situation is the background to one of the most descriptive and important collection of midrashic traditions on the divine courtroom, preserved at Exodus Rabbah 43:1. The midrash preserves a series of rabbinic comments on Exodus 32:11, "And Moses besought (יחל) YHWH his God." This verse begins Moses' petition not to destroy the people of Israel (Ex 32:11-13). As in Midrash Psalms, several of the comments liken Moses' activity to that of a defense attorney. The commentary begins thus:

*And Moses besought* (Ex 32:11). R. Tanhuma b. Abba opened: *He said he would destroy them, had not Moses his chosen one stood in the breach before him* (Ps 106:23). R. Hama b. Hanina said: the good advocate (סניגור) shows a bright face at trial. Moses was one of two advocates who arose to mount a defense on behalf of Israel and set their faces, as it were [כביכול] against the Holy One, blessed be He. These were Moses and Daniel. From where do we know this? As it says, *had not Moses his chosen one, etc.* And with regard to Daniel? As it says, *And I set my face towards the Lord God to ask, etc* (Dan 9:3). These were two men who set their faces against the Attribute of Justice to ask for mercy for Israel.

Here R. Hama b. Hanina praises Moses' ability successfully to mount a defense, and then categorizes Moses, along with Daniel, as one of the two successful biblical advocates who were able, "כביכול," to set themselves before God. The term כביכול is a signal term that marks that the tradent realizes that he is saying something that could perhaps border on a theologically problematic or uncomfortable statement. Here, the idea that Moses and Daniel set themselves *against* God, i.e., against God's will and God's plans – and are able to emerge victorious when doing so – may not have sat well with some sages, as it suggests a) that God is not always correct in his decision making; and b) that Moses and Daniel have power over God, and can face God down.

Michael Fishbane discusses the term כביכול in the context of an analysis of *Mekhilta de-Rabbi Ishmael, Bo'* 14.[39] Fishbane notes that כביכול often appears in midrash within the context of rabbinic statements about God that have a mythic context or tendency, in particular in contexts of divine anthropomorphism or divine anthropopathism.[40] Fishbane thus argues that an examination of כביכול suggests that the term originally "functioned to qualify the *exegetical basis* of the mythic fabulations asserted about God. That is to say, the teachers exhibit a self-conscious awareness about the tenuous scriptural nature of their bold teachings."[41] Here the tradent uses the term to qualify his interpretive comment that Moses and Daniel set themselves against God, in other words, faced God down – and won, by

---

[39] Michael Fishbane, *Biblical Myth and Rabbinic Mythmaking* (New York: Oxford, 2003).

[40] "God's own *imitatio hominis*," cf. Fishbane, *Biblical Myth*, 110.

[41] Fishbane, *Biblical Myth*, 138.

suggesting that this comment is scripturally based, and that he is aware that we can only say this "as it were." As Fishbane suggests, "the term *ki-vyakhol* is used to indicate that these myths about God are in fact grounded in Scripture – but only midrashically so, as it were."[42]

R. Hama bar. Hanina here says that Moses and Daniel faced down the Attribute of Justice (מדת הדין), in order to plead for mercy. I will return to the question of the divine attributes in detail, but it is sufficient to note that here the Attribute of Justice is understood to be that aspect of God or the modality of God which desired to destroy Israel because of their immediate disregard for the first and second commandments prescribing exclusive worship of God and prohibiting the production of idols. According to this tradent, by the criteria of strict justice, God should have destroyed Israel. The decision not to destroy Israel is here attributed to Moses' great advocacy power and skill, that he succeeded in making God, כביכול, not abide by the rules of justice and show mercy instead.

The midrash continues with a mashal, attributed to Rabbenu:

R. Berechiah said two things, one in the name of Rabbenu and the other in the name of R. Samuel b. Nahman. Rabbenu said: to what can the matter be compared? To a king who was judging his son and the accuser (קטיגור) was standing and accusing (מקטנרג). What did the son's instructor do? When he saw him being found liable, he pushed the accuser outside the courtroom and stood in his place, mounting a defense on behalf of the son. Thus in the hour that Israel made the calf the Accuser (השטן) was standing within, accusing, and Moses was standing outside. What did Moses do? He pushed the Accuser outside and stood in his place, as it is said *He stood in the breach before Him*, he stood in the place of the breacher.

If the previous midrashic comment contained within it some theologically problematic assertions, this mashal ups the ante. The previous comment suggested that Israel's prosecuting attorney, whom Moses needed to face down, was God, acting as both judge and prosecutor. The Attribute of Justice was specifically named as that which threatened to destroy Israel. Here, however, the courtroom is portrayed differently. Moses is no longer facing down God, but facing down the Accuser, i.e., Satan. The king, standing in for God, is remarkably passive in this mashal. The king sits in judgment over the defendant with two separate attorneys petitioning before him. This contains within it a radical assertion about God's decision in the biblical text to destroy Israel, suggesting that had God gone through with his decision, it would have been because he listened to the Accuser, not because of his own commitment to justice. In other words, if R. Hama bar Hanina was willing to acknowledge that according to the laws of strict justice, God was perfectly justified in his decision to destroy Israel, this mashal attributed to Rabbenu asserts the opposite: God would *not have been*

---

[42] Fishbane, *Biblical Myth*, 139.

*justified* in destroying Israel, and if he had done so, it would have been because the Accuser mounted a good prosecution. Only due to Moses' heroic advocacy, and his physical dispossession of the Accuser, was this not to be. Moses here is portrayed in the same vein as Elijah in the passage from Qohelet Rabbah, as the instructor, who mounts a defense for his charge. Here, Moses is not facing down God, but facing down the Accuser, and literally throws him out of the divine courtroom to plead his case. This midrash glorifies Moses, pointing to the profound impact of his petition, but it paints God, perhaps, in a lesser light, as it suggests that the Accuser had enormous sway over God.[43]

Not surprisingly, perhaps, the midrashic compilation does not end here. This image of the courtroom is counteracted immediately by an alternate picture painted by R. Samuel b. Nahman:

R. Samuel b. Nahman said: *He stood before him in the breach* is difficult. A parable: it can be compared to a king who was angry with his son, sat on the judgment-seat (בימה), tried him, and found him liable. As he took the reed to sign the decree – what did his associate (סונכתדרו) do? He took the reed from the hand of the king in order to appease his wrath. Likewise in the hour when Israel did that deed, the Holy One, Blessed be He sat in judgment against them to find them liable, as it says, *Leave me alone so that I can destroy them* (Deut 9:14), but he did not do it. Rather, he came to sign their decree, as it says, *Whoever sacrifices to the gods will be destroyed* (Ex 22:19). What did Moses do? He took the tablets from the hand of the Holy One, blessed be He in order to appease his wrath. To what is the matter comparable? To a king who sent a marriage broker to betroth a woman. While he was going, the woman corrupted herself with another. What did the marriage broker, who was innocent, do? He took the ketubah which the king had give him and tore it, saying: it is better that she be judged as single than as married. Thus did Moses. When Israel did that deed he took the tablets and broke them, as if to say that had they seen their punishments they would not have sinned. Moreover, Moses said: it is better that they be judged as unintentional sinners and not as deliberate transgressors. Why? Because on the tablets was written *I am the Lord your God* (Ex 20:2), and the punishment *whoever sacrifices to the gods will be destroyed*.

R. Samuel b. Nahman offers another mashal to a king sitting on trial, but imagines the courtroom differently. Sticking, I would argue, more closely to the sequence of events presupposed by Exodus 32, Samuel b. Nahman suggests that Moses is not really analogous to an advocate here, but rather to an "associate," literally a co-chair, who will not let the king *sign* the decree. In other words, R. Samuel b. Nahman realizes that the decree has already been handed down by the time Moses appears on the scene, but not sealed yet. This midrash actually contains two meshalim. The first, to that of a trial, seems to have been presented in order to counteract or present a counter-image to that of Rabbenu's. It is the second mashal that R. Samuel b. Nahman brings in to demonstrate *how*, exactly, Moses was able to over-

---

[43] Similar to the sway held by the Accuser over God in Job 1-2.

turn the decree, by demonstrating to God that Israel didn't have a sense of what would happen to them if they broke the commandment, and thus to appease God's wrath and beseech God to give Israel another chance.

These two meshalim actually contain two divergent images of Moses, one that amplifies his relationship to God and one that downplays it. The first likens Moses to a "co-chair," a provocative title that suggests that Moses perhaps has as much power as God and is almost co-seated with him on the judgment seat. The second, however, sees Moses as nothing more than a servant entrusted with a special task. The juxtaposition of these two meshalim downplays the quite substantial theological opposition that might have occurred to seeing Moses as God's co-chair. The initial statement by R. Samuel b. Nahman here, that it is "difficult" to agree with the statement of Psalm 106:6 is of extreme import. It seems that R. Samuel b. Nahman does not like the כביכול statement of the first interpretation, that Moses was able to face God down successfully, nor the image presented in the second interpretation, that God could have been swayed by Satan. R. Samuel b. Nahman is probably not the only sage who would have difficulty with these two statements. The placement of this comment *after* the first two in this anthology of rabbinic opinion might reflect a desire by the anthologist to "tone down" the theological complications or perceived dangers of those of R. Hama b. Hanina and Rabbeinu.

It is not difficult to understand why the imagery of the divine courtroom was attractive to certain rabbis as a way of figuring God and imagining the way God makes decisions, even decisions that occurred in the past, such as the decision not to destroy Israel at Mt. Sinai. As I argued when discussing the prophetic *rîb*-pattern, courtroom imagery attempts to mediate the powerful violence of God's punishment through a series of actions that channel that wrath through the legal administration of justice, presenting any penal decision as one upon which there has been proper deliberation and analysis. By figuring God as a judge, operating within a divine courtroom, authors are not only emphasizing that no decision by God is arbitrary and capricious, but they are also suggesting that God has engaged in a particular process that seeks to channel his understandable anger appropriately. However, it is just as easy to understand why some sages may have taken issue with such a figuration. The divine courtroom is freighted with issues of inequality and power, as God, by his very divine nature, seems to need to operate in some capacity as both judge and prosecutor, and as prosecutor, he must win. A central concern from Job onward is that God's power procludes anyone from successfully mounting a defense against him. So the sage notes in b. Arakhin 17a: "If the Holy One, blessed be He, were to bring Abraham, Isaac, and Jacob to judgment, they could not stand before the indictment."

Indeed, though the Aggadah contains many examples of successful petitions before God, and paints Moses as a great סניגור, perhaps unparalleled in his distinct abilities, elsewhere in Midrashic literature there exist examples of this type of petition that are not successful, notably Moses' petition for his life in Deut. Rabbah 11:10. The passage is of import because Moses uses all sorts of rabbinic techniques to reverse the decree against him, techniques that are portrayed as efficacious elsewhere in midrash, yet none of them hold sway. The passage begins with a comment by R. Johanan that "Ten death penalties are ascribed upon Moses…this teaches that up to ten times it was decreed against him that he would not enter the land of Israel and the harsh decree was still not inscribed until the High Court revealed itself to him. It said to him: 'This is my decree – you shall not pass over,' as it is said. *indeed you will not cross the Jordan* (Deut 3:27)." The specific language of the High Court immediately sets the stage for the nature of Moses' petition here, and places it squarely within the tradition of arguing with God in the divine courtroom.

The midrash immediately tells us that Moses does not take the decree seriously; Moses cites numerous examples of when God has decreed the destruction of Israel and has spared them after Moses had prayed for them successfully. In other words, Moses here relies on his own ability to mount a successful סניגוריא. Moses then turns this into his own *a fortiori* argument, deducing that "Seeing then that I have not sinned from my youth, won't it be the case that when I pray on my own behalf God should answer my prayer?" The Midrash tells us that Moses' inability to take this decree seriously itself provokes God: "Immediately he jumped upon him and swore by his great Name that he will not enter the land of Israel." This exposition of Moses' immediate activity after receiving his decree leaves the reader with the impression that had Moses taken the decree seriously to begin with, he would have indeed been able to enter the land of Israel. His petitionary prowess has been proved time and time again, and the Midrash does not shy away from citing particular examples of this. However, there is a difference, for the Rabbis, between having the capacity to reach God in prayer and actually doing the action. Moses' hubris here lies in the fact that he believed that since he would be able to annul the decree he didn't actually have to engage in that very activity. The Rabbis are quick to condemn Moses for this fact. For the Rabbis, there is a time and place for petitionary prayer, and when that time is opportune, one must seize it immediately and not tarry.

This lesson from the Rabbis is all the more striking considering what happens next in the Midrash. Deuteronomy Rabbah tells us that when Moses saw that his decree had been sealed, he then engaged in precisely the sort of activity that the Rabbis prescribe for annulling a decree of God:

he drew a small circle around him,[44] began to fast, donned sackcloth, and engaged in weighty prayer and supplication to such an extant that the Midrash tells us "the heavens and the order of nature were shaken." The impression is that, had Moses engaged in this activity to begin with, he would have been spared. In other words, this passage seeks to affirm Moses's ability as the great סניגור while explaining why Moses' self-defense failed. The Rabbis do not doubt the ability of Moses to petition on behalf of himself and others, rather, they point to that very ability as something not to be taken for granted. Moses' ability to pray is so powerful that God has to instruct the heavens not to receive Moses' prayer:

What did God do? At that hour he had it proclaimed in every gate of each of the heavens, and in every Court, that they should not receive Moses' prayer, nor bring it before him, because the degree against him had been sealed. Now at that hour God hastily summoned the Angel in charge of Proclamations, Achzeriel by name, and he commanded the ministering angels: 'descend quickly, bolt all the gates of every heaven, because the voice of the prayer threatens to force its way to heaven.' And the angels sought to ascend to heaven because of the sound of Moses' prayer, for his prayer was like a sword which tears and cuts its way through everything, and spares nothing, seeking that his prayer was the nature of the Ineffable Name which he had learnt from Zagzagel the Master Scribe of the children of Heaven.[45]

This passage suggests that Moses is such a successful advocate that God took pains to make sure that no divine courtroom was even in session to hear Moses' petition.

The use of the term סניגוריא to describe the activity of defense in which Moses and others are engaged is notable not just because it reflects the Greco-Roman legal culture in which these texts emerged, but also because of the cultural resonances this term carried with it. Just as today, the ability to mount a successful συνηγορία was highly prized, but it was not prized because of any sort of associations with truth or with achieving perfect justice. On the contrary, as J. A. Crook explains:

Legal argument is not in the sphere of truth-and-falsehood but in that of right-and-wrong; it is a search for a way of deciding who is entitled to win within the rules of a game, a contest, an *agon*. The ancient jurisprudents were using argument to establish and refine upon the rules: the advocates were helping the parties to achieve maximum success with-

---

[44] Judah Goldin has written extensively upon the use of circles in rabbinic literature, particularly the case of Honi the circle drawer. cf. J. Goldin, "On Honi the Circle Drawer: A Demanding Prayer," *Studies in Midrash and Related Literature*, ed. Barry Eichler and Jeffrey Tigay (Philadelphia: Jewish Publication Society, 1988), 331-335.

[45] Text from Saul Lieberman, *Midrash Devarim Rabah* (Jerusalem: Wahrmann, 1974). A counterpart to this story is the prayer of Menasseh at *Pesiqta de Rab Kahana* 24:11 and b. Sanhedrin 103a. In the *Pesiqta*, the ministering angels begin to lock up the windows of heaven in order that God could not hear Menasseh's prayer. God in response carves out an opening right under his throne in order to hear the supplication.

in the rules, and, what is more, it was in their field, that of individual circumstances, that truth and falsehood came into the matter.[46]

Just as in a modern courtroom, lawyers in Antiquity were not necessarily truth-tellers, though they certainly could tell the truth. Instead, they were gamers, masters of spin; arguers, rhetors. Decisions were "won," earned because of argumentary skill.[47] This aspect of Roman lawcourts is absolutely present in the application of these terms to the divine courtroom in the rabbinic literature. This is evident in the passage above from Ecclesiastes Rabbah. When Elijah shows up, he does not instruct the children to pray, to appeal to God's compassion, or to concede anything. He teaches them to *win*, to mount an argument. The use of the technical term סניגוריא heightens the aspect of legal strategy that is at play here. This seems to have been a highly prized ability amongst the rabbis, hence the didactic comment that closes the text. The rabbis believed that a well mounted legal argument, a συνηγορία, was prized by God and could be successful in the divine courtroom. One need not look further than the famous rabbinic story of the oven of Akhnai (b. Baba Metzi'a 59b) to see that the rabbis believed God prized this ability.[48]

Since the ability to win and prove an excellent legal strategist seems to have been a crucial aspect of the divine courtroom imagery, it is not surprising that throughout rabbinic literature there are many examples of how one can successfully defeat God in argument. The rabbis believed that one of the best strategies for mounting a successful סניגוריא was a well-placed *a fortiori* argument.[49] Joseph Heinemann, in his study *Prayer in the Talmud*, notes that the *a fortiori* argument is sometimes found within rabbinic presentations of petitionary prayer. So for example, R. Tanhuma's petition for rain (appearing in both Genesis Rabbah 33:3 and Leviticus Rabbah 34:14):

At that moment, R. Tanhuma turned his face heavenward and said: Lord of all worlds! If this man, upon whom the woman has no claim for sustenance, beheld her in distress and was filled with compassion for her, then how much the more so must Thou, about whom

---

[46] Crook, *Legal Advocacy*, 4-5.

[47] Crook further notes that "Of both Roman advocates and Athenian logographers and *synegoroi* it has endlessly been complained that they engaged in unscrupulous distortions for the purpose of winning their clients' cases: thus, even Isaeus' speeches, written in the most purely civil and technical field of inheritance law, are notable – notorious – for brilliantly unscrupulous rhetoric. In fact, it is often taken for granted by Roman lawyers that that wicked, perverted activity was an import from Greece without which the Romans would have been content with a more sober and jurisprudential kind of advocacy." Crook, *Legal Advocacy*, 34.

[48] Note that here, too, it is Elijah who brings this lesson to the rabbis.

[49] See, for example, the highly developed midrashic presentation of the prayer of Hezekiah at Ecc. Rab. 5:6.

it is written, *The Lord is gracious and compassionate* (Ps 103:8), be filled with compassion for us, thy children, thy beloved ones, the descendants of Abraham, Isaac, and Jacob! Immediately the rain fell.[50]

Here R. Tanhuma, pleading for rain, does not humble himself or rely on God's mercy to produce rain. Instead, he mounts a legal argument, and his argument causes an immediate divine response.

Heinemann believes that this prayer of R. Tanhuma falls into a category called the "law-court pattern in prayer." In this type of petition, the petitioner addresses his appeal to God as if he was addressing a judge in a forensic setting. Heinemann identifies three formal elements of this pattern: an opening address, a plea and statement of the facts, and a concluding petition.[51] More important than the formal elements, however, is the overall *mise-en-scène* that is projected from this type of prayer, which is that of the divine courtroom. Prayer is conceived of as a type of argument, and in order to win, you need good strategy. Inherent to these petitions and prayers is a high degree of rhetorical and argumentative prowess; in a law court it is not the facts that will acquit or stay a sentence; it is the ability to argue those facts and present them in a manner that will assure a logical victory. In the example of the children, the Rabbis end the pericope with an overarching conclusion that all men should teach their children torah in order that they will be able to argue for them in the next work. The Rabbis thus view the ability to argue as essential to survival.

A beautiful example of the success of proper legal argument before God is that of Rachel in the twenty-fourth proem to Lamentations Rabbah. This proem presents a lengthy tradition in which Biblical figures approach God after the destruction of the Temple, weeping over the predicament of Jerusalem and the people of Israel. Abraham comes to God weeping, and God tells Abraham: "Your children sinned and transgressed the entire Torah and the twenty-two letters by which it arises, as is written *all of Israel transgressed your torah* (Dan 9:11)." Abraham attempts to argue with God by asking who testifies against the people of Israel [מִי מֵעִיד בִּישְׂרָאֵל]. The language of witnessing makes the courtroom scene explicit. Not only has Israel transgressed, but the passage paints the picture of a courtroom at which accusations against Israel have taken place. In response to Abraham, God calls forth the Torah to come and give testimony against Israel, but Abraham silences the Torah and shames it from testifying.[52] Next God

---

[50] trans. J. Heinemann, *Prayer in the Talmud* (Studia Judaica IX; Berlin and New York: Walter de Gruyter, 1997), 211.

[51] Heinemann, *Prayer in the Talmud*, 194.

[52] Abraham says to the Torah: "My daughter, are you coming to testify against Israel, that they transgressed your commandments, and you have no embarrassment before me? Remember the day that the Holy One, Blessed be He, returned you to every nation and tongue and they did not wish to receive you, until the day my children came to Mt. Sinai, received you

calls upon the letters of the alphabet to give testimony, and Abraham uses the same technique to force aside the aleph, bet, and gimmel, until all the remaining letters are shamed and do not testify. However, while Abraham's arguments prevent the testimony, they do not succeed in convincing God. Abraham, Isaac, Jacob, and Moses – all the great defenders – attempt to convince God that he should spare the people on account of their merits, but God does not pay heed to their words. Finally Rachel the matriarch pleads with God to spare Israel:

Master of the Universe! It is revealed before you that Jacob your servant loved me with an extraordinary love and served my father for seven years on my account. And when the time of my marriage to my husband arrived, my father planned to exchange me from marrying my husband on account of my sister. The matter was very hard for me because the plan was known to me, and I informed my husband and I transmitted him a sign by which he could differentiate between me and my sister, in order that my father would not be able to make the exchange. And after this I relented within myself, and I bore up my desire and had compassion on my sister that she should not go out in shame. In the evening they switched my sister for me for my husband and I passed on to my sister all the signs that I passed to my husband, in order that he would think that she was Rachel. And moreover, I entered under the bed in which he was lying with my sister, and when he spoke with her she was silent, and I responded to everything in order that he would not recognize my sister's voice. And I was kind to her, I was not jealous, and I did not expel her to shame. And what am I? I am flesh and blood, dust and ashes, I was not jealous of my opponent, and I did not expose her to embarrassment and shame, and you are the king who lives forever, compassionate, why are you jealous of the service of stars, in which there is nothing, and exile my children so that they are being killed by the sword, and their enemies are doing what they will with them?[53]

Rachel's cry, exegetically drawn, perhaps, from Jeremiah 31:15 ("A voice is heard in Ramah; Rachel crying for her children"), succeeds where the Patriarchs did not. While her petition does not contain within it the technical "how much the more so," it does use the same logic. Using the lesser example of herself, Rachel argues that since she, a creature of flesh and blood, was able to be compassionate for her sister, avoid the pitfalls of jealousy, and not treat her wrongly, how much the more so should God, the eternal king, be able to overlook the nothingness of idolatry and have compassion upon Israel. Rachel's petition poses a challenge to God to "man up," as it were. If flesh and blood can still be compassionate towards rival forces, surely God too should be able to do so.[54]

---

and honored you, and now you come to give testimony against them in the day of their trouble?"

[53] Text from M. Margulies, *Midrash Wayyikra Rabbah: A Critical Edition based on Manuscripts and Genizah Fragments with Variants and Notes* (5 vols; Jerusalem: Wahrmann, 1953-60).

[54] Cf. also the prayer of Hannah in b. Berakhot 31b.

One of the most striking aspects of the law-court pattern of prayer is that the petitioner often seems to be making demands of God and to be suggesting that God is in some way already acting unjustly. In other words, by engaging in סניגוריא as a petitionary strategy, the petitioner seems to be asserting that they justified in doing so. It hardly needs to be said that this would not go over well in the *Apocalypse of Peter* or the *Visio Pauli*, in which even a declaration of compassion for the tormented is taken as a challenge to divine justice. Heinemann, looking at Rabbinic comments on the nature of the law-court patter of prayer, points out that often times the Rabbis seem to be critiquing its use, citing examples from both Talmudic and Midrashic literature.[55] Heinemann makes special note of the fact that the petitioner who attempts to justify his own actions is "soundly denounced by the Sages as one who 'approaches with insidious-ness' according to Rashi's commentary: 'for they did not approach God to petition in prayer, but rather to defeat him in argumentation'), or as one who 'approaches in disputation.'"[56] The Rabbis were not unaware that these petitions had an air of the impertinent. Indeed, the fact that some rabbis notice this shows that they are acting in their judicial capacity by judging the courtroom scenarios posed by the midrashim of other rabbis. They are critiquing the entire system, including the way God is portrayed in that system. They recognize that these petitions are more like accusa-tions, and are uncomfortable with the idea that God has found himself guilty to the point that he chooses to "obey" the demands of the petitioner.

So far our discussion has focused on the figure of the סניגור, and the techniques used to mount a successful סניגוריא. There are many midrashim and traditions on this aspect of the divine courtroom, since the rabbis have additional didactic interests here, e.g. to model successful rabbinic tech-niques of argumentation for their successors. But behind every סניגור there is a קטיגור, mounting an accusation that needs to be defended. Sometimes this accuser is, as in the *Apocalypse of Peter*, the sins them-selves, as in the passage from Ecclesiastes Rabbah, in which the sins of the fathers מלמדין קטיגור. No other קטיגור is needed to counteract the defense taught by Elijah; the deeds of the fathers speak for themselves. The same understanding of sin is already present in m. Avot 1:11: "R. Eliezer b. Ja-cob says: He that performs one precept gets for himself one advocate, but he that commits one transgression gets for himself one accuser [קטיגור]." The accusers can also be heavenly beings; in a tradition preserved in Levi-ticus Rabbah, the letters of the Torah mount a קטיגוריא against Solomon (Lev Rab 19:2), similar to the קטיגוריא the ministering angels mount against Moses at *Abot de Rabbi Nathan* 1.12.

---

[55] Heinemann, *Prayer in the Talmud*, 200.
[56] cf. b. Sanhedrin 101b. Heinemann, *Prayer in the Talmud*, 198.

In a passage imagining what the future manifestation of the divine courtroom will be like, the role of קטיגור is assigned to Samael:

Just as the Holy One, Blessed be He, did in this world through the hand of Michael and Gabriel, so will in the future to come will he do by their hands, as it says: *And saviors shall come up on Mt. Zion to judge the Mount of Esau* (Obad 1:21) – this refers to Michael and Gabriel. Our holy teacher says this is Michael only, as it says: *And at that time Michael will stand up, the great prince who stands for the children of your people* (Dan 12:1), for he presents Israel's requirements and pleads for them, as it says: *Then the angel of the Lord answered and said: O Lord of hosts, until when will you not have compassion on Jerusalem* (Zech 1:12), and also: *And there is none that holds with me against these, except Michael your prince* (Dan 10:21). R. Jose said: To what may Michael and Samael be compared? To an advocate and an accuser before a tribunal [ דומין סניגור וקטיגור עומדין בדין]. One speaks and then the other speaks, and when each finishes his words the advocate sees that he won, and he begins to praise the judge that he may issue his verdict [איפופסין].[57] When the accuser asks to add something, the intercessor says to him: 'be quiet and let us hear the judge.' Likewise Michael and Samael stand before the Divine Presence; the Accuser brings charges [השטן מקטרג], while Michael asserts the merits of Israel, and when the Accuser comes to speak again, Michael silences him, because, as it says: *I will hear what God YHWH will speak; for He will speak peace unto his people* (Ps 85:9). (Ex Rab 18:5)

In this passage, part of a series of midrashic interpretations preserved with relation to the verse "it happened at midnight" (Ex 12:29), the Tanna R. Nehemiah offers a lengthy comment on God's love for Israel with relation to setting Michael and Gabriel as guardians (שומרין) over Israel, discussing how Michael and Gabriel saved Israel at various times through its biblical history. This discussion, which draws from Obadiah 1:21, forms the background and precedent to R. Nehemiah's view of what God will do for Israel in the future. R. Judah ("our holy Teacher"), however, believed only Michael would arise in the future, drawing on Daniel 12:1 for Scriptural support. The reference to Daniel 12:1 is the bridge to thinking about Michael's role in a judicial context. Though the biblical verse does not explicitly mention a courtroom as the context for Michael's "standing up for Israel," George Nickelsburg has argued that we should understand עמד with its forensic valence, seeing Michael's role in Daniel 12 as that of judicial advocate before God. The "deliverance" then would be forensic vindication by God.[58] Nickelsburg's argument is based on Hebrew passages which use עמד in a legal context, such as Deuteronomy 19:17, Isa 3:13, and especially Zechariah 3:1, in which both the angel of YHWH and the Accuser stand as forensic disputants. Though Nickelsburg may not be correct in reading an initially intended forensic valence to Daniel 12:1, he is

---

[57] From the Greek ἀπόφασις, "verdict" or "sentence."

[58] George W. E. Nickelsburg, *Resurrection, Immortality, and Eternal Life in Intertestamental Judaism and Early Christianity* (Expanded ed.; HTS 56; Cambridge: Harvard University Press, 2006), 24.

undoubtedly correct that this was a way in which Daniel 12:1 was read and interpreted, as this passage from Exodus Rabbah demonstrates.

Nickelsburg is also correct to bring in Zechariah 3:1 as a potential intertext here, as it seems to stand behind R. Jose's interpretation of this passage from Daniel and what it can tell us about the future manifestation of the divine courtroom. By means of a mashal, R. Jose compares the future activity of Michael and Sammael to that of two litigants pleading before a judge at a tribunal. Sammael is then explicitly called "the accuser" (השטן) in the nimshal, which seems directly to link this judicial scene to that of Zechariah 3:1. Again in this passage more attention is paid to Michael's activity as סניגור than Sammael's activity as קטיגור. We note, however, that one of the anticipated arguments seems to be that God is too compassionate, as that is the force of the quotation from Zechariah 1:12. Though we do not know of the content of Sammael's accusations, the inclusion of this verse brings this particular accusation into the foreground. The presentation of the trial, in many ways, seems to be attempting to answer this charge. The tradent has presented this trial at least in part to demonstrate that God's compassion is entirely in line with justice, as well as the orderliness and proper procedure of the future trial. This is nothing less than a defense of God's justice – even though he is accused of having too much compassion, the trial demonstrates that Sammael is given the opportunity to speak his accusations, and that the decision even to *be* compassionate is undertaken judicially. God's compassion, it is demonstrated, is entirely in line with his justice.

## D. The Attributes of Justice and Mercy

Despite common wisdom, this understanding of Sammael as the great קטיגור, and connecting him to the figure of the Accuser (even if it is not yet the fully-formed mythological Satan), is not a common one in rabbinic literature. We do, periodically, see Satan assuming a forensic function, particularly in rabbinic explanations of what happens on Rosh HaShanah and Yom Kippur.[59] Much more often, however, do we find another "figure" mounting accusations, that of the Attribute of Justice (מדת הדין). Several midrashic traditions suggest that the figure mounting a prosecution before God, whether against an individual or against Israel collectively, is one of God's own attributes, hypostasized into an active courtroom agent. So, for example, in Lamentations Rabbah 1:41 we find the tradition: "*O God, who*

---

[59] See, for example, b. Yoma 19b-20a.

*is like unto thee* (Ps 71:19): since you subdue the Attribute of Justice.[60] At the time [when the enemy conquered Jerusalem] Accusation sprang up [קפצה קטיגוריא] before the Throne of Glory and exclaimed, 'Master of the universe, shall this wicked person boast, saying 'I ruined the house of God, I burnt his temple!' If so let fire descend from above and let him burn. What is immediately written? *From on high he sent fire into my bones* (Lam 1:13)." Here an example of the power of the Attribute of Justice is given through the personification of an accusation which sprung up before God's throne to accuse a specific individual, resulting in direct divine action. The courtroom imagery illustrates the power of God's attribute, and the implication is that this could happen any time, to anyone. God is thus to be praised for subduing that very attribute.[61]

The power of the Attribute of Justice, seen here as always ready to mount an offense against Israel, in the rabbinic imagination is only matched by the power of the Attribute of Mercy.[62] This understanding of God having two fundamental modalities that work in tandem – though sometimes at odds – with one another is found throughout rabbinic literature. Prior to the terms "attribute of justice" and "attribute of mercy" becoming the standard ways for the rabbis to refer to these two modalities of God, we find the phrases "attribute of punishment" [מדת הפרענות] and "attribute of good" [מדת הטוב].[63] So, for example, we read in t. Berakhot 6.1: 'For every judgment with which he judges you is by the attribute of good or by the attribute of punishment." Marmorstein notes that these terms appear in discussions between R. Gamaliel II and Akiba, and so are likely to be early.[64] Alan Segal believes that these names for the divine attributes can be found even in the works of Philo of Alexandria, who uses

---

[60] On the issue of "subduing" the Attribute of Justice, see Fishbane, *Biblical Myth and Rabbinic Mythmaking*, 125ff. See also David Stern, "*Imitatio Hominis*: Anthropomorphism and the Character(s) of God in Rabbinic Literature," *Prooftexts* 12 (1992): 151-174.

[61] Likewise in Esther Rabbah 7:14, R. Isaac Nappaha comments that Mordechai issued a proclamation to the Jews of Shushan, saying "do not go to eat at the feast of Ahasuerus, sine he has invited you only in order to mount a prosecution [קטיגוריא] against you, so that there would be an opportunity for the Attribute of Justice to accuse you before the Holy one, blessed be He.' cf. also the successful argument of the Attribute of Justice in b. Shabbat 55a.

[62] So, for example, Sifre Deut 49: "These are the ways of the Omnipresent (מקום): *YHWH, God, merciful and gracious* (Ex 34:6). And it says, *And it will be that whoever is called by the name of YHWH will be delivered* (Joel 3:5). And is it possible for a person to be called by the name of the Omnipresent? Rather since the Omnipresent is merciful, you too be merciful. The Holy One, blessed be He, is called gracious, so you too be gracious. As it says, *YHWH, God merciful and gracious*."

[63] As in Ecc Rab 4:1.

[64] cf. Midrash Psalms 119f; b. Sanhedrin 81a. See the discussion in Segal, *Two Powers in Heaven*, 44-45.

the terminology of δύναμις ἀγαθότητος and δύναμις κολαστήριος.[65] At some point, however, these terms fell out in favor of the justice/mercy terminology. Marmorstein argued that R. Meir and R. Simeon bar Yohai were the first to use these terms in the middle of the second century, and Segal argues that this would be "entirely appropriate to the gnostic menace of the early and middle second century."[66] Segal believes that the debate over the relationship between God's justice and mercy was spurred by gnostic authors and concerns. This is certainly plausible, as the discussion of the critique of Marcion reveals. However, one does not need the specter of Gnosticism to understand why this became such a hot-button topic in the second century, particularly following the Hadrianic persecution and the unsuccessful Bar Kochkba revolt. The second century was a time in which both Jews and Christians were dealing with essential questions of identity and definition, and part of the question of identity involved questions of one's relationship to God, which in turn invited examination of the identity and character of God himself.

The understanding of God as having two separate and fundamental modalities, whether they are called good/punishment or justice/mercy is biblically supported by the attributes revealed to Moses at Exodus 34:6-7, and referenced throughout the Hebrew Bible.[67] There are thirteen named attributes, but they can be easily broken up into two groups, one focusing on God's mercy and *hesed,* while the other focusing on God's justice in exacting punishment. It is not difficult to understand, then, how the rabbis developed an understanding of God's attributes that focused on the two attributes of justice and mercy. One seemingly influential and early rabbinic tradition linked these two attributes to the two most common names for God in the Hebrew Bible, YHWH and Elohim. According to *Sifre Deuteronomy* 27, "Wherever 'YHWH occurs, this is the attribute of mercy, as is said 'YHWH, YHWH, God gracious and compassionate' (Exod. 34:6); wherever 'Elohim' occurs this is the attribute of judgment, as is said 'The case of both parties shall come before the Elohim' (Ex 23:8), and 'Do not curse Elohim' (Ex 22:27)."[68] The rabbis, believing that nothing in Scripture was accidental, developed this theological and hermeneutical principle that suggested that the choice of referring to God either as YHWH or as Elohim was deliberate.[69]

---

[65] Segal, *Two Powers*, 46.

[66] Segal, *Two Powers*, 46.

[67] For example, by Moses at Numbers 11:14-20; in arguments before God in the Psalms (e.g., Psalm 86), and notably, one half of the attributes are quoted by Jonah (Jonah 4:2).

[68] Text from Louis Finkelstein, *Siphre ad Deuteronomium* (New York: JTSA, 1969).

[69] For discussion of the nature of midrashic interpretation and fundamentals of rabbinic understanding of the Bible, see Fishbane, *The Exegetical Imagination,* esp. chapter 1.

This tradition, which is here passed down anonymously, occurs during a discussion of Moses' petition on behalf of Israel at the Golden Calf incident.[70] This location is not accidental. According to this anonymous tradent, Moses' language of supplication was deliberate. Moses, narrating his petition, explains that he prayed to YHWH (Deut 9:25-26). For this tradent, this means that Moses prayed to God to listen to or to heed his attribute of mercy, beseeching YHWH, i.e., God's merciful side. This suggests that Moses had an understanding of the divine attributes and used them strategically, even though they are not revealed until Exodus 34, two chapters later. Moses does use the divine attributes in his petition to God in Numbers 11:14-20. This appeal by Moses to the divine attributes as a means of petitioning is the background to the rabbinic imaging of the rôle of the divine attributes in the divine courtroom. Already in the Hebrew Bible authors utilize the divine attributes in their own appeals (or presentation of appeals) to the divine. Rabbinic literature takes this further, imagining the attributes themselves as courtroom actors. The attributes prove paramount in their understanding both of the way God functions as a whole, and in particular in the way God's courtroom operates, in the way God functions judicially.

For this reason, we find in rabbinic literature that these attributes appear in association with the divine courtroom quite often. This is not surprising, given that the rabbis use the courtroom as a vehicle for depicting, exploring, and even interrogating the process of divine decision making. The attributes are in some way seen as fundamental to the way God operates, as clues to the identity and being of God.[71]

---

[70] As Fishbane notes, this tradition went through slight modification fairly early. In Genesis Rabbah 33:3, R. Samuel bar Nahman explains that sometimes, however, the names can refer to the other modalities, and this is due to the actions of the individual: "*And Elohim remembered Noah.* R. Samuel b. Nahman said: Woe to the wicked who turn the Attribute of Mercy into the Attribute of Judgment. Whenever it says YHWH, it is the Attribute of Mercy, as it is written, YHWH, YHWH *God, merciful and gracious* (Ex 34:6), yet it is written, *And YHWH saw that the wickedness of man was great* (Gen 6:5), *And YHWH repented that he had made man* (Gen 6:6), *And YHWH said, I will blot out man* (Gen 6:7). Fortunate are the righteous who turn the Attribute of Judgment into the Attribute of Mercy. Wherever it says *Elohim* it is the Attribute of Judgment: Thus: *You shall not revile Elohim* (Ex 22:27); *the cause of both parties shall come before Elohim* (Ex 22:8); yet it is written, *And Elohim heard their groaning, and Elohim remembered his covenant* (Ex 2:24); *And Elohim remembered Rachel* (Gen 30:22); *And Elohim remembered Noah*" (Gen Rab 33:3). As Fishbane explains, "Hence on this understanding, when Scripture records an apparent contradiction of the principle of divine powers, we are to understand that the Name given represents God's providential mode *ante quem*, prior to the human actions that change it." Fishbane, *Biblical Myth,* 183.

[71] Urbach believed that the Tannaim understood the attribute of good to be far greater than the attribute of retribution, pointing to passages like t. Sotah 4:1 and Mekhilta *Nezikin* 18, where this assumption forms part of a קל וחמר argument. In Urbach's view, "the use of the

Both the Tannaim and the Amoraim use the imagery of the divine attributes to explore the nature of divine action and the judicial operation of God. This is nothing less than an exploration of the divine "personality" itself. By personifying or hypostasizing aspects of God, the rabbis seek to understand the way in which God functions and operates. At first in the Tannaitic literature there is an understanding that the attribute of Good far exceeds that of punishment, in other words, that it is in God's nature to forgive rather than apply the criteria of strict justice.[72] Numerous Tannaitic dicta may shed some light on why they believed this, attesting to a belief that no one – not even the patriarchs – could withstand a close scrutiny according to the criteria of strict justice.[73] Since Scripture provides ample evidence of God forgiving and giving second changes, the rabbis may have seen this as the proof they needed that God, as Urbach puts it "is wont to enlarge the measure of good due to a person."[74] However, in some respects sages are aware that this statement contains within it a significant amount of wishful thinking. There is real concern even among the tannaim that God may not choose this path. This is implied in the beautiful depiction of the death of R. Johanan ben Zakkai at *Abot de-Rabbi Nathan* 25:

In the hour of the death of R. Johanan ben Zakkai he raised up his voice and wept. His disciples said to him: Teacher, tall pillar, light of the world, mighty hammer, why are you crying? He said to them: Am I going to be received before a king of flesh and blood, whose anger, if he should be angry with me, is of this world; and whose chastising, if he should chastise me, is of this world; and whose killing, if he should kill me, is of this world? Whom, moreover, I can appease with words or bribe with money? Indeed I am

---

correlatives 'attribute of retribution – attribute of good' points to the extrusion of 'compassion' [or 'mercy'] from the sphere of justice, although we found it still included therein in Scriptural passages and even in ancient translations and Rabbinic sources. The attribute of justice – including the elements of beneficience and punishment inherent in it – was completely separated from that of compassion in heavenly as in human judgements" (*The Sages,* 450-451). Urbach's claims here cannot be supported by the texts. There are numerous texts in which both the attribute of justice and mercy, once these epithets replace the older terminology, are both seen to play rôles in the divine courtroom. Urbach would like to see this, however, as an Amoraic tradition rather than a Tannaitic one. The claim, perhaps, is that the Amoraim have bastardized the initial Tannaitic tendence. See, for example, Urbach's comments on p. 457. Speaking about the views of R. Hanina and R. Aha with relation to the attribute of mercy, Urbach writes that "These Amoraim were not only opposed to making the attribute of compassion the one, absolute attribute of the Lord..., but they maintained the view that the attribute of justice was of primary importance, and that the function of the attribute of compassion was to delay and slow down the collection of the debt." This is in contrast to Urbach's presentation of the Tannaim, whom he believed were very careful "to preserve both attributes." Urbach, *The Sages,* 453.

[72] cf. t. Sotah 4:1; Mekh. *Nezikin* 18. Indeed, this assertion forms the basis of the סניגוריא at Ecc Rab 4:1.

[73] cf. b. Arakhin 17a.

[74] Urbach, *The Sages,* 450.

going to be received by the King of kings of kings, the Holy One, blessed be He, whose anger, if He should be angry with me, is of this world and the world to come; whom I cannot appease with words or bribe with money. Moreover I have before me two roads, one to the Garden of Eden and one to Gehenna, and I do not know whether he will sentence me to Gehenna or admit me into the Garden of Eden. Of this the verse says, *Before him shall be sentenced all those that go down to the dust* (Ps. 22:30).

R. Johanan ben Zakkai here does not rely on the Attribute of Mercy to outweigh that of the Attribute of Justice; on the contrary, he recognizes that there is a real possibility of God's anger awaiting him, and nothing he could do, not even those methods of last resort available to those awaiting earthly judgments, could sway God's decision.

It is far rarer to see the Attribute of mercy assuming an independent role in the divine courtroom than it is to see the Attribute of justice doing so. Many midrashic and talmudic comments, seeking to explain why something has or has not happened, will attribute it to the active engagement of the Attribute of justice. So for example, R. Simeon bar. Nahmani insists that the reason the messianic age has yet to occur is because the Attribute of Justice has delayed it (b. Sanhedrin 97b), and likewise R. Tanhum explains that the Attribute of Justice was responsible for Hezekiah not being appointed as the messiah (b. Sanhedrin 94a). Urbach suggests that at some point instead of "being a contest between two attributes it becomes a struggle between the Attribute of Justice and the Almighty, who becomes identified with the Attribute of Compassion."[75] For Urbach this represents a shift, as the Attribute of Justice becomes increasingly seen as a hostile force that sways God away from his more compassionate and benevolent nature.

In some ways this understanding gives the rabbis an "out." By understanding the Attribute of Justice almost as a full-fledged independent being, they are able to separate God from some of his activities, especially those that are more difficult, in their minds, to justify. They thus seem to be able to separate God from God's wrath, holding on to an image of God that is inherently merciful, only acquiescing to punish and execute justice when persuaded to do so. God's initial impulse, then, would be to have mercy and compassion, and only through a courtroom session would justice be executed. This would represent a change from the way the biblical authors – and, in Urbach's view, the tannaim – understood the process. In, for example, the story of the Golden Calf, God is represented as initially full of wrath, and it is Moses through petitionary argument who is able to turn him from that wrath (Exodus 32). If, however, the Attribute of Justice is understood as separate from God – or separable from God – in some way, then the situation would be reversed. God's initial impulse would be

---

[75] Urbach, *The Sages*, 460.

to forgive, but be persuaded to act in accordance with Justice. This is exactly the situation presented in Midrash Psalms 106:6, with the *mashal* that suggests that Moses was like a defender who thrust the prosecutor aside. God's wrath and decision to destroy Israel is presented as something that came from outside, rather than something inherent to God. Likewise, in Midrash Psalms 8:2, when Moses goes up a second time to receive the tablets, the following exchange takes place between God and the ministering angels:

> the ministering angels asked: Master of the Universe! Wasn't it just yesterday that they [Israel] sinned against her [the Torah] in which you wrote *You shall have no other gods before me* (Ex 20:3)? The Holy One, blessed be He, said to them: Every day you have been accusers [קטיגורן] between me and Israel. And yet wasn't it the case that when you went down to Abraham, you ate milk and meat together, as it is said *and he took curd, and milk, and the calf, etc* (Gen 18:7-8)? Even one of their children, when he comes home from his teacher's house, and his mother sets out bread, meat, and cheese for him to eat, will say to her: 'This day my teacher taught me: *Thou shalt not cook a kid in his mother's milk* (Ex 34:26).' They found no answer for him. In that very hour the Holy One, blessed be He, said to Moses: *Write these words* (Ex 34:27).

Here, God himself insists that his decision to destroy Israel, which Moses had succeeded in overturning, was due to outside forces – the prosecution by the ministering angels. The implication is that had they not tried to accuse Israel, God would never have attempted to destroy Israel. What Exodus 32 attributes to God's wrath, this midrash attributes instead to a nearly-successful קטיגוריא from an outside source.

## E. Imaging God Judicially

What makes the rabbinic discussion of the divine attributes so fascinating is that they are depictions of God as constituted by fundamental modalities and needing to navigate between them. By figuring God in this way, the rabbis are depicting a God who is dynamic and reflective, having what resembles a personality. David Stern describes this aspect of the rabbinic figuration of God as one who has "felt interiority,"[76] while Michael Fishbane says these texts bear witness to an "inner divine dynamic."[77] Texts in which God has to hide things from or subdue the Attribute of Justice open a window on the way the Rabbis chose to portray God, as being not unlike a human being. As Stern explains, "The irony, even the paradox, behind rabbinic anthropomorphism is that the only model of sufficient complexity that the Rabbis possessed to portray God's character – and to communicate

---

[76] Stern, "Imitatio Hominis," 168.
[77] Fishbane, *Biblical Myth*, 125.

the complexity of their own feelings *about* God – was that of human character."[78] Depicting God in this way, anthropomorphically and anthropo-
pathically, has implications not only on the metaphysical or the theological
level, but also on the literary level. What was the literary effect of presenting God in this way? Was the tradent trying to elicit a certain reaction from
the rabbinic audience, and if so, what was it?

I believe that the reason these texts are so powerful is that depicting
God in a human-like manner, has the effect of inviting the reader to *identify* with God in some way, and to relate to God. By suggesting that God
sometimes has to hide what he is doing from his own self, as in the Genesis Rabbah passage discussed by Stern, or to contend with his conflicting
priorities and desires, represented quick viscerally in the hypostasization
of the Attributes of Justice and Mercy, the tradent is asking or inviting the
readers to view God as being not unlike them, caught between responsibilities and desires, perhaps even as being stuck between the proverbial rock
and a hard place, and simply doing the best he can. In many ways this
represents an apologetic strategy, as the tradents seek to explain God's actions to the reader in a way that is close to a justification of those actions.
This is heightened by the courtroom imagery. When God is presented as a
judge, or even as being *like* a judge, the reader is invited to evaluate the
way God comes to these decisions. In the judicial scenario posed by the
courtroom imagery, this has the effect of asking the reader to judge God's
courtroom, and judge God. When this judicial modality of God is tied to
the activities of his Attributes, the readers are being asked to understand
how and why God came to certain decisions, and to relate to the process of
divine decision-making. This can be a deliberate strategy by a tradent to
justify God, to vindicate God from anticipated or expected charges.

One such example of this occurs at *Pesiqta de-Rab Kahana* 7, in which
tradents give a list of examples to show that God is reluctant to kill even in
the exercise of justice, discussing how the instances of Job, Mahlon and
Chilion demonstrate this. The midrash continues:

Thus also with regard to the plagues which come upon man. First he [God] starts with his
house. If he repents, only the plagued stones must be taken out, as it says, *and they took
out the stones* (Lev 14:40). If he does not repent, the stones must be destroyed, as it says,
*and he will destroy the house, the stones of it* (Lev 14:45). After this he begins with his
clothes. If he repents, the plagued parts must be torn out, as it says, *and he shall tear it
out of the garment* (Lev 13:56). If he does not repent, the plagued parts must be burned,
as it says, *and he shall burn the garment* (Lev 13:52). After this he begins with his body.
If he repents, he will redeem him, and if not *he shall sit alone outside the camp* (Lev
13:46). Likewise it was in Egypt. At the beginning the Attribute of Justice plagued their
property, as it says, *and he smote their vines and their fig trees* (Ps 105:33). After that *he*

---

[78] Stern "Imitatio Hominis," 157.

*gave over their cattle to hail* (Ps 78:48). And after that *he killed every first-born* (Ps 78:51). (*Pesiq. Rab Kah.* 7:10)[79]

Here the tradent attempts to vindicate God from potential charges regarding his decision to kill all of the Egyptian first-born sons. His tactic for vindication is to demonstrate that God's procedure for executing justice is logical and specific, not emotional and arbitrary, and that God takes every possible precaution to avoid taking human life. At the close of this passage, however, the tradent goes one step further and attributes the final execution to the Attribute of Justice, almost viewing the attribute as a separate being to whom God acquiesces.

Another example of using courtroom imagery to vindicate God and to acquit God of any charges occurs at *Pesiqta de-Rab Kahana* 9:1:

*Your righteousness is like the great mountains, your ordinances are like the great deep* (Ps 36:7). R. Ishmael and R. Akiba: R. Ishmael said for the righteous who obey the Torah that was handed down from the great mountains, the Holy One, Blessed be He, performs righteousness like the great mountains. But for the wicked who do not obey the Torah that was handed down from the great mountains, the Holy One, blessed be He, will deal strictly with them [מדקדק] to the great deep. R. Akiba said: the Holy One, blessed be He, deals strictly with both. He deals strictly with the righteous and holds them accountable for the few wicked deeds they commit in this world so he can give them a good reward in the world to come. Likewise he overflows goodness and ease for the wicked in this world, rewarding them for the few good deeds they do in this world, in order that he can destroy them in the world to come.

Here the anticipated charge seems to be that of partiality. The reason that R. Akiba proposes a different interpretation than that of R. Ishmael is that R. Ishmael suggests that God follows a different judicial procedure with regard to the righteous and the wicked. Though this seems to suggest a type of poetic justice, of the type Matthew warns of in the Sermon on the Mount, R. Akiba insists that this is not the case, and that God is just as strict with the righteous and the wicked so that in the next world the righteous can be amply rewarded. The implication is that God has to be just as strict so that no one can accuse God of showing partiality in judgment. God must be beyond judicial reproach. R. Akiba seems to be particularly involved in the debates of how God executes judgment. This is most likely due to his second-century provenance, a time when this issue was very much on the table cross-culturally, as people like Marcion – and, perhaps, like Pappias – were arguing that the god of the Old Testament was cruel in justice in a way inappropriate to the deity. R. Akiba here recognizes that R. Ishmael's interpretation can lead people down a path that will lead them to pronounce such a sentence on God – that he is guilty of partiality in

---

[79] Text from B. Mandelbaum, *Pesiqta de Rab Kahana: According to an Oxford Manuscript with Variants* (2 vols; New York: JTSA, 1962).

judgment and in exercising one standard of judgment with regard to one type of person and another elsewhere. R. Akiba thus interprets the verse differently to persuade the reader not to come to this verdict, but to find God innocent of these charges.

By arguing that God's activity follows a specific procedure that is judicial and judicious, tradents like R. Akiba and the anonymous tradent of Piska 7 are presenting an apology for God, attempting to justify God's judicial procedures, even in the case of what could have been a difficult passage theologically for many readers, the slaying of the Egyptian first-born. In so doing, the authors uses courtroom imagery to liken God to a judge and to vindicate God from charges of wrath, caprice, arbitrariness, and rash action. But asking readers to view God judicially has additional implications, in that it invites readers to think about human judges and their experiences with them. This is amplified by the fact that so many of the images of the divine courtroom and explanations of God's judicial activity are found through the use of meshalim, rabbinic parables, in which God is likened to a judge. By likening God to a judge, readers are invited to think about those judges with whom they have had experience in their own time. Needless to say, not all of those judicial encounters were positive ones. Indeed throughout the rabbinic literature there are found negative portrayals of human judges and the human judicial system in general, such as in the depiction of the trial of R. Eleiezer b. Hyrcanus for *minut*. By depicting God as a judge, the reader is invited to bring with them all of the associations they already have with human judges.

This is not unlike what Stern talks about with regard to the common analogical depiction of God as a king in the rabbinic meshalim. Stern believes that a close look at the rabbinic mashal is imperative for any discussion of the way the rabbis viewed God, for "the mashal represents the greatest effort to imagine God in all Rabbinic literature."[80] Stern notes that the only character in the meshalim who is not a stock character is the king, since "he is the only character consistently to possess a personality – or personalities, since he can change utterly from one mashal to another – and this distinction among characters may stand, from a theological perspective, as an emblem of God's profound difference from all else in the universe."[81] However, by likening God to a king, Stern notes that the rabbis are actually not saying that God is so different; on the contrary, they are pointing to the *similarities* between God and a human king, especially to the Roman emperor. As Stern explains, the king in the meshalim is "not only modeled upon the historical figure of the Roman emperor (or of the imperial representative in Palestine), he bears a plethora of human details

---

[80] Stern, *Parables in Midrash*, 93.
[81] Stern, *Parables in Midrash*, 93.

and markings that are without parallel in earlier Israelite literature; and because of the nature of the analogy underlining the mashal, all those details
and markings are inevitably transferred to God."[82] In other words, asking
the reader to imagine God as in some way like a king, the tradent is asking
the reader to consider every aspect of kingness that they know in thinking
about God. God is in some real way *like* (דומה) a king; kings contain clues
to ה' דמות , the image of God.

Stern considers this a powerful statement about the complexity the rabbis ascribed to God, which he calls the "anthropomorphic paradox":

> Indeed, this is the sum meaning of the anthropomorphic paradox: the Rabbis were able to
> portray God's full complexity only by imagining Him in the human image. Why? Be-
> cause only human behavior presented the Rabbis with a model sufficiently complex to do
> justice to God.

This is relevant when we consider that many of these meshalim liken God
to a king *in his judicial capacity*, or specifically to a judge. This reflects a
widely-held rabbinic belief that God undertakes decisions through a deli-
berative process, similar to the way the prophets imagined God operating
when they employed the *rîb*-pattern. By likening the activity of God to that
of a judge, the rabbis are suggesting that God operates in a way similar to
that familiar from courtrooms. In Exodus Rabbah 38:8, for example, we
find the following mashal given as part of the discussion of why there were
so many stones on Aaron's breastplate:

> Why were all these stones placed there? So that God should look at them and at the gar-
> ments of the priest as he entered on the Day of Atonement and remember the merits of
> the tribes. R. Joshua of Siknin said in the name of R. Levi: it can be compared to a prince
> whose tutor went in before him [the king] to mount a defense on behalf of his son [ ללמד
> סניגוריא על בנו], but was afraid of the bystanders, that one of them should attack him.
> What did the king do? He clothed him in his royal purple garment, so that all who saw
> him might fear him. Likewise, Aaron would enter the Holy of Holies every hour, and
> were it not for the many merits which entered with him and helped him, he would not
> have been able to go in. Why? Because of the ministering angels that were there. What
> did the Holy One, blessed be He do for him? He gave him the pattern of the holy gar-
> ments, as it says, *And for Aaron's sons you shall make tunics*, etc (Ex 28:40); just as it is
> written, *And he put on righteousness as a coat of mail, and a helmet of salvation upon
> His head, and he put on garments of vengeance for clothing, and was clad with zeal as a
> cloak* (Isa 59:17).

A whole courtroom scenario is imagined here. God is likened to a king sitting as a judge, and Aaron is likened to an advocate, coming in to mount a
defense on behalf of the prince (the people of Israel). What is fascinating
occurs next: in order to make sure that the advocate will not be harmed, the
king dresses the advocate in royal robes. Who are these assailants that

---

[82] Stern, *Parables in Midrash*, 93.

threaten the advocate? This is stated without explanation, but the nimshal likens them to angels, who apparently threaten to harm either Aaron, the people, are both. The robes, like the stones, are visual reminders to the king/God to sway the judicial decision and keep the assailants/angels from doing harm to the advocate/Aaron. This mashal may reflect some of the "ministering angels mount a prosecution" suggested in other rabbinic passages. But more so, by likening the activity of God and Aaron on Yom Kippur to that of a Judge and advocate, the tradent is asserting or opening the possibility that in the divine courtroom as well as the human courtroom there lurks the danger of the prosecution, and even the danger of physical harm. On the human level, this must reflect a certain amount of realia. Though it seems dubious that a king should have to protect people from harm in his own courtroom, this part of the mashal is given as an assumed shared reality, as it is essential to the building of the mashal. This must have been a common enough occurrence that people would recognize this situation and accept it as a common scenario appropriate to a mashal. Then these figures are likened to angels, suggesting that apparently even God has the same issues in the divine courtroom, and has taken precautions to ensure order and safety in his courtroom actors, specifically Aaron. Once again the wisdom and forethought of God is praised here, to protect Aaron from danger by giving him the breastplate.[83] The mashal, by likening God's courtroom to a human courtroom, suggests that the divine courtroom may be fraught with the same issues as that of the human courtroom, issues that may *impede* justice, not be conducive to it.

Sometimes a well-placed mashal can specifically call attention to the inherent inequity of the divine courtroom. Commenting on the verse "Lord, I cry out to you, quicken to me, hear my cries" (Ps 141:1), Midrash Psalms preserves the following tradition:

What is meant by *quicken to me?* I quickened to do your words, so quicken to me. To what was this comparable? To a man who had a lawsuit before a ruler. He saw that everyone had advocates [סניגורין] to speak for them. He called to the ruler and said: 'I ask of you: everyone needs their advocates. I, I have no advocate, I have no one to speak on my behalf. You are the judge and the advocate [אתה הדיין ואתה הוא הסניגור]. Likewise David said: One has confidence in the officious and upright deeds he has. Another has confidence in the deeds of his fathers. But I have confidence in you. Even though I have no righteous acts, answer me because I have called to you. Hence it says: *I cry out to you, quicken to me* (Midrash Psalms 141:1)[84]

---

[83] We should note also that this mashal from R. Joshua of Siknin has the effect of undercutting the previous suggestion, that the stones of the breastplate serve as a visual aid to God to remind him of the merits of the tribes and thus sway God's judicial decision. The mashal suggests this is not the case – the stones are not there to remind God to hand down the correct verdict, but they are there for protection.

[84] Text from S. Buber, *Midrash Tehillim* (Vilna: Ram, 1891).

Here it is suggested that the deeds and righteous acts should act as David's advocate before God, but David, having no righteous acts, must ask God to be both his judge and advocate. But there may also be a hint of something more here. What is the divine courtroom but a place in which God by nature is both judge and advocate – and perhaps prosecutor as well? This was already noted in the Hebrew Bible by Jeremiah and Job. The reader is asked to realize how much a petitioner like David is "at the mercy of the court," not just because he has committed iniquity rather than acts of righteousness, but also just by nature of being human.

Some traditions, in fact, are more explicit, and ask the readers to realize how *different* God's ways are from man's, using judicial imagery to drive this point home. In Exodus Rabbah 15:29, for example, an anonymous tradition notes: "The way [מדת] of the Holy One, blessed be He, is not like the way of man. In the way of man, two stand before the king, one mounting his prosecution [קטיגוריא] and one mounting his defense [סניגוריא]. He who mounts a prosecution does not mount a defense, while he that mounts a defense does not mount a prosecution. But not with regard to the Holy One, blessed be He, he both mounts a defense and mounts a prosecution." Scriptural verses are then produced which show God in both his defending and accusing capacities. On first glance this tradition seems to be in the same vein as those that talk about God acting according to his Attribute of Justice and his Attribute of Mercy, acting both as prosecutor and as advocate depending on his circumstance. But actually this tradition is even more subversive. Though the tradition asks humans to realize just how different God's courtroom is from a human courtroom, by likening God to both a prosecutor and a defense attorney, the tradent has implicitly invited the reader to realize that God fills one other function in the courtroom, that of Judge. In this scenario painted by the anonymous tradent, God fills all of the rôles in the divine courtroom. The comparison to the human courtroom points to God's all-encompassing presence in his own courtroom. By omitting any mention of God's judicial rôle, the tradent is drawing even more attention to it.

The divine courtroom, therefore, functions in a number of different ways in Rabbinic literature. Sometimes it is used as a vehicle for exploring the nature of God, for discussion of the relationship between God's justice and God's mercy. Often, however, it is used as a way of interrogating the issue of God's justice, whether by displaying through these courtroom scenes that God goes out of his way to execute justice, or to beg the question of whether God is just at all, by bringing up the parallels to the human courtroom, not notable for their abilities faithfully and consistently to execute justice. In the following section, I will demonstrate that the rabbis engage in the same literary strategy as their forerunners and contempora-

ries, using an extended presentation of the divine courtroom to argue before the reader that God is just and fair in the execution of final judgment,
expecting the readers to act as judges in this courtroom scenario.

## F. Trying the Nations, Trying God: b. Avodah Zarah 2a-3b

Perhaps the fullest presentation of the future manifestation of the divine
courtroom in all of rabbinic literature, b. Avodah Zarah 2a-3b is not only a
depiction of the future trial that awaits the nations of the world, but it is
also a sustained argument for the justice of God.[85] This presentation, just
like those presentations of the divine courtroom found in other types of
literature, uses the divine courtroom as a way to interrogate the justice of
God, in which the reader is expected to be the ultimate judge. Though it is
God who is seated as judge at the heavenly tribunal, the courtroom scenario is once again rotated so that it is clear that God is really the defendant
and the reader is seated in the ultimate judicial position.

Tractate Avodah Zarah of the Babylonian Talmud starts with an exposition of the word אידיהן in the mishnah, which prohibits engaging in business transactions with idolaters on the three days preceding אידיהן (m.
Avodah Zarah 1:1). Rab and Samuel differ on whether the mishnah should
be quoted as אידיהן, their festivals, or עדיהן, their witnessing. The editor explains that both can be supported by Scripture, since Scripture says "Let
them bring their witnesses that they may be justified" (Isa 43:9). However,
at this the editor questions whether the verse does not truly refer to Israel,
quoting R. Joshua b. Levi: "But does the verse, *Let them bring their witnesses that they may be justified,* refer to idolaters at all? It surely refers to
Israel; as R Joshua b. Levi said: All the good deeds which Israel does in
this world will bear testimony unto them in the world to come, as it is said:
*Let* them *bring their witnesses that they may be justified* – that is Israel;
*And let* them *hear and say: It is truth* – these are the idolaters" (b. Avodah
Zarah 2a). This tradition, attributed to R. Joshua b. Levi, recognizes the
forensic valence of Isa 43:9, and uses the full verse to flesh out an entire
courtroom process, in which Israel brings forth its witnesses before the
idolaters, who have no choice but to pronounce a verdict in favor of Israel.

---

[85] The most recent analysis of this tractate is by Jeffrey Rubenstein in his book *Talmudic
Stories: Narrative Art, Composition, and Culture* (Baltimore: Johns Hopkins, 1999). Rubenstein engages in a thoughtful analysis of the art of this narrative, which he calls a "homiletical
story," which brings out many important aspects of the text. My analysis differs from that of
Rubenstein, as will become evident.

An alternate verse is adduced to support the read of עדייהן, but the editor[86] keeps the conversation focused on this *agon*, in which Israel – and God – are vindicated before the idolaters, inserting here a tradition of R. Hanina b. Papa:

R. Hanina b. Papa – some say R. Simlai – interpreted: In the future, the Holy One, blessed be He, will take a sefer Torah in His bosom and say: whoever busied himself with this, let him come and take his reward (שכרו).' Immediately all the idolaters will gather together in confusion, as it is said: *All the nations are gathered together* (Isa 43:9). The Holy One, blessed be He, will say to them: 'Don't come before me with confusion, but every nation should come in with its scribes;' as it is said, *and let the peoples be gathered together,*' (Isa 43:8) and the word *le'om* means kingdom, as it is said, *and one kingdom shall be stronger than the other kingdom* (Gen 25:23). (How can there be confusion in the presence of the Holy One, blessed be He? Rather it is that they should not be not confused, and so hear what He says to them).[87]

This passage from Isaiah, brought in to explicate a particular read of the Mishnah, becomes the occasion for what is possibly the fullest presentation of the future trial of the nations, in which the nations are put to shame. The verse from Isaiah, and indeed the whole pericope of Isaiah 43, is a key structuring feature of the narrative, providing the background for the following presentation of this trial that continues for two full folios. Isaiah 43, part of the "Streitgespräch" (Disputation) category discussed previously, is an example of the *rîb*-pattern:

All the peoples gather together and the nations assemble. Who amongst them has proclaimed this and informed us of the previous events? Let them bring their witnesses and be justified and they will hear and say 'it is true.' You are my witnesses, declares YHWH, my servant, whom I have chosen in order that you may know and believe in me, and understand that I am He; no god was formed before me, and none after. I, I am YHWH and there is no savior besides me. I spoke, I saved, I made known, no foreign god. You are my witnesses, declares the Lord, and I am God. (Isa 43:9-12)

Here God invites the nations to come and present the evidence that they and their gods foretold the current and previous events. But immediately YHWH then calls upon Israel to act as his witnesses, because the *rîb* presented here is one in which the nations are accusing God and God is defending himself. God is not really calling the nations to trial; what he is

---

[86] Rubenstein has convincingly argued that the editor has inserted this narrative here deliberately in order to provide a fitting introduction to the theological questions posed by the Mishna and discussed in the rest of the tractate. Cf. Rubenstein, *Talmudic Stories*, 237.

[87] At least two strains of tradition are found in this *sugya*: the narrative, preserved in Hebrew, and the editorial comments, preserved in Aramaic. While the translation is my own, I follow the Soncino edition in setting off the Aramaic comments in parentheses. Rubenstein suggests that we should understand the Aramaic comments as "a series of talmudic footnotes separated from the main text not by placement near the bottom margin but by translation into a different language." Rubenstein, *Talmudic Stories*, 214.

doing is defending himself from their charges. This is an elaborate apologetic strategy. But before whom? It is difficult to suggest that it is Israel, because in the very next verse God calls Israel as a witness for him. Jeffrey Rubenstein, in his discussion of this rabbinic story, notes that "if Israel supply the witnesses they cannot be the audience as well. As we shall see, the homilist plays upon this confusion of who testifies for whom, upon the different ways of interpreting the scene."[88] Rubenstein is not correct. The tractate, like the author of Isaiah, does something deliberate here with regard to the witnesses. But if you understand what is really going on in the *rib*-pattern, and at play in these courtroom scenes, as I have explored previous chapters, there really is no confusion: God is calling Israel as a witness in his trial before the readers, who sit in judgment on his case. There is a separation between the Israel in the story and those who *read* the story. The author of Isaiah knows this and makes use of this, defending God before the readers. This, as I will demonstrate, is exactly what is going on in this rabbinic *sugya*.

The next part of the tractate explicitly locates us in the divine courtroom. Each nation comes in to plead their case before God, beginning with Rome:

> Thereupon Rome will enter first before Him. (Why first? Because they are the most important. From where do we know of their importance? It is written: *And he shall devour the whole earth and shall tread it down and break it in pieces* (Dan 7:23). R. Johanan says this is Rome, whose power is known to the whole world. And from where do we know that the most important comes forward first? Because R. Hisda said: When a king and a community come together, the king enters the tribunal first, as it is said: *To execute the judgment of his servant and his people Israel* (I Kings 8:59).[89] Why? You could say, because it is not the way of the world that a king shall wait without; or you may say before the anger is roused.)[90]

This mention of the tribunal brings the background of Isaiah 43 into the foreground. In what follows, each nation presents their case before God, trying to show that what they have done is related to the study of Torah, and thus worthy of a reward.[91] Rome claims, for example, that the only

---

[88] Rubenstein, *Talmudic Stories*, 224.

[89] Understanding the order being a plea on behalf of the servant (the king) first, and then the people.

[90] In other words, that the king tries to soften up the judge by pleading on behalf of the people, so that the people will not incur the full wrath of the judge.

[91] Rubenstein correctly notes that the Isaiah text does not present the arguments of the nations, and suggests that "The biblical neglect of the arguments of the nations is the point of departure of the homilist. He fills in the gaps in the text, imagining how a full transcript of the trial would read." Rubenstein, *Talmudic Stories*, 224. What he fails to grasp is that the arguments of the nations presented by the homilist are not designed simply as a hypothetical, rather they are designed to answer serious questions about God's justice posed by readers, questions which can be found in the comments of other rabbinic sages throughout the wide

reason she built many marketplaces, bathhouses, and accumulated so much gold and silver was "in order that Israel be able to busy itself with the Torah" (b. Avodah Zarah 2b). God calls them out on this claim, explaining that they have done everything for their own self-desires and interests, and not for Israel at all. When Rome slinks off, Persia tries the same tactic, explaining that the only reason she built bridges and waged wars was so Israel could occupy themselves with Torah. God shuts them down as well, explaining that *He* is the man of war (Ex 15:3), and asking whether any of them had busied themselves with *this*, i.e., the Torah.[92]

The rest of the nations try a different tactic:

> The nations will say to him: 'Master of the Universe, have you given us anything, and we declined to accept it? (But how can they say that, as it is written, *The Lord came from Sinai and rose from Seir over them, He shined forth from Mount Paran* (Deut 33:2)? And it is also written, *God came from Teman* (Hab 3:3). Why did he go to Seir, and why did he go to Mount Paran? R. Johanan says: We learn from this that the Holy One, blessed be He, went around to every nation and language and they did not receive it [i.e. the Torah] until he came to Israel who received it. But they will say: 'Did we accept it and fail to observe it?' And to this the obvious rejoinder is: 'Then why did you not accept it?' But they will say: 'Master of the Universe, did you suspend the mountain over us like a roof, like you did to Israel, as it says, *and they stood under the mountain*' (Ex 19:17)?)

These nations go on the offensive, defending themselves by making accusations, not against Israel, but against *God*. They question God, as if it is God who is in the dock, as to whether or not he ever offered them the Torah. They are making an argument that since God never gave them the Torah, it is not fair that they should now be punished for not observing it. They are accusing God of both the charge of partiality, in only offering the Torah to Israel, and also of applying an unfair standard of judgment, in then making that exclusive Torah the criteria for reward.[93] The editor here

---

corpus of rabbinic literature. "The nations" are not really bringing these arguments, rather the author is bringing forth these arguments to interrogate God on issues of justice and hopefully to put these objections to rest.

[92] When they slink off as well, defeated, the later editor asks why Persia would have tried this tactic if it failed with Rome, and explains that the Persians thought to themselves that they would have better luck since Rome destroyed the temple but the Persians built it.

[93] Rubenstein has not understood the way this trial operates on a literary level. He correctly notes that the issue on hand in this trial differs from that of Isaiah, in which the main issue is the identity of the true God. But then he notes that "for the rabbinic homilist this is no longer the issue. When God ushers in the world to come his reality cannot be doubted. The nations do not come to demonstrate the power of their gods, but to present their merits before the God of Israel." Rubenstein, *Talmudic Stories*, 226. That is true in terms of the scenario presupposed, but not in terms of the literary scenario – on a literary level, there has been no advent of the messiah. Rubenstein neglects to think about how the text functions. For the readers, there may not be questions about who is God, but there are still questions related to the operation of God's justice in history, questions which this tractate attempts to answer. By

breaks in to answer this charge with two verses as well as a comment from R. Johanan. This indicates how seriously the editor took this anticipated charge and how much he wanted to prove that it was a false one. By doing so, the editor is defending God – because God is in the dock – before the reader. It is not an accident that the nations become the accusers here. What Rubenstein calls a "role reversal"[94] is actually a "role reveal" – this is actually what is happening, literarily, once one takes into account the literary courtroom and the way it rotates the roles of the participants. This is an attempt to prove to the reader that these charges are baseless, and God is unimpeachable on this issue. There is no explicit verse in the Bible that suggests that God ever offered the Torah to any other nation, but the editor finds the proof in these verses that suggest that the presence of God shone on other nations, suggesting that there was no other reason for God to shine over other nations if not to offer the torah. This is then buttressed by appeal to the authority of R. Johanan, who transmits the aggadah, although it is not accompanied by Scriptural citation.

The nations have an answer for this as well, suggesting that Israel was given an unfair advantage to see how important the Torah was by the theophany that accompanied its presentation, and they were not. While this is an important charge on its own, its effect here is that the nations are presented as admitting that yes, they had an opportunity to receive the Torah, and they did not accept it, thus contradicting their previous statements and revealing their charges to be lies. The nations' own words thus provide for the editor of this passage additional proof that God is unimpeachable on this count. Their additional charge is then answered by God, who will assert that "there are seven commandments which you did accept. Did you keep them?" Scriptural passages are then adduced to prove that the nations did not even keep the seven Noahite commandments.

Commenting on the tactics here, Rubenstein explains that "the nations somehow become the judge of the fairness of God's standards, and God – at least temporarily – allows himself to be relegated to defendant. For a moment the story permits the illusion that the nations stand on a par with God and may question him as equals."[95] Rubenstein is not correct – the

---

neglecting the role of the reader in this courtroom, Rubenstein's analysis, though often insightful, fails fully to grasp the scope of the trial.

[94] Rubenstein, *Talmudic Stories*, 229.

[95] Rubenstein, *Talmudic Stories*, 229. Rubenstein notes that traditional commentators are bothered by this role reversal, quoting *Hiddushei hage'onim*: "These matters require explanation. How can God, who is witness and judge, debate (*lefalpel 'atsmo*) with the nations," to which Rubenstein explains that "this reaction fails to appreciate the satirical and humorous tone." Rubenstein, *Talmudic Stories*, 384 n. 32. Rubenstein's analysis is not correct here. There is not necessarily a satirical or humorous tone present in this sugya, at least not until the very end, with the nations's disastrous attempt to observe the commandment of sukkot.

nations are not acting as judge; they are revealing themselves in their true literary rôle as prosecutors, while God reveals himself as the true defendant. It is not the case that *God* allows *himself* to be relegated to defendant, it is that the author has put God on the defensive in order ultimately to vindicate him from serious charges. There is no illusion that the nations are God's equals; quite the contrary, their charges are revealed as baseless. But their charges are taken seriously, because they are serious concerns held by rabbinic readers.

The charges are not finished. Once again the nations go on the offensive, this time against Israel, and by extension against God, since God seems willing to reward Israel:

The nations will then say, 'Master of the Universe, have those who accepted her observed her?' The Holy One, blessed be He, will reply, 'I bear witness for them [אני מעיד בהם] that they observed the Torah.' They will say before him, 'O Master of the Universe, can a father bear witness for his son? For it is written, *Israel is My son, My firstborn* (Ex 4:22).' Then will the Holy One, blessed be He, say: 'Heaven and Earth will bear witness that Israel has observed the entire Torah.' But they will say 'Master of the Universe, Heaven and Earth are biased witnesses, for it is said, *If not for My covenant with day and with night. I should not have appointed the ordinances of Heaven and Earth.*' (Jer 33:25)[96]

We should note that the nations of the world are capable of quoting Scripture in support of their arguments, and are also capable of reading Scripture slightly against the grain to prove their points, just as the rabbis. These nations are not straw men for the editor to quickly shut down; rather, their objections are taken seriously, because the editor knows that he needs to persuade the reader that none of their charges hold water. This charge, that Israel has not upheld the Torah, is a serious one, so serious that God offers here to be a witness for Israel. Rubenstein suggests that "this charge seems totally out of place, for the issue is whether the nations deserve a reward or not."[97] But that is not really the issue in the literary trial; the real issue is whether or not God is just.[98] The trial of the nations is a vehicle for the author to explore this real question. The reason that this charge is so serious is because it is not a charge against Israel at all, it is a charge against God. The implication is that if Israel has not fulfilled the whole Torah, God has a responsibility to punish them perhaps to a greater extent than the nations, and certainly not to reward them! The nations anticipate that God is going to reward Israel, and is here accusing God of acting unjustly in this manner. They object to God bearing witness for Israel

---

[96] cf. the use of this verse in the same vein at Esther Rabbah 7:13.

[97] Rubenstein, *Talmudic Stories*, 230.

[98] Rubenstein does note that something else seems to be going on, but he thinks that "the trial is as much of the merit of Israel − of the life of Torah − as of the shortcomings of the nations." Rubenstein, *Talmudic Stories*, 230. The trial is not actually about Israel either; it is about God.

because of their close relationship, like that of a father to a son, and they object to heaven and earth being witnesses because they believe they are biased, using an out-of-context verse from Jeremiah to support their claims. Rubenstein sees in this a humorous note, because "the more they argue their own case, the more they emphasize the world-sustaining powers of Torah and the supremacy of Israel. The legal technicalities function as devices which enable the story to adduce additional evidence for Israel without concluding the trial. Yet legal testimony remains to be found; the suspense is not what the outcome will be, but how it will be demonstrated."[99] I would argue that these are not legal technicalities; they are real concerns about the equity of the divine courtroom and the way witnesses function therein. And the author is not interested in adducing evidence for Israel, the author is interested in adducing evidence for God.

For this reason, after a couple of editorial comments with regard to the creation of heaven and earth, the trial narrative continues with God's response to these objections, in which God proposes alternate witnesses:

Then the Holy One, blessed be He, will say, 'Some of you shall come and testify on behalf of Israel, that they observed the entire Torah. Nimrod will come and testify for Abraham, that he did not worship idols; Laban will come and testify for Jacob, that theft could not be reckoned to him; Potiphar's wife will come and testify for Joseph, that immorality could not be reckoned to him; Nebuchadnezzar will come and testify for Hananiah, Mishael and Azariah, that they did not bow down to an image; Darius will come and testify for Daniel, that he did not nullify prayer;[100] Bildad the Shuhite, and Zophar the Naamathite, and Eliphaz the Temanite (and Elihu the son of Barachel the Buzite) will come and testify for Israel, that they have observed the whole Torah; as it is said, *Let them bring their witnesses, that they may be justified* (Isa 43:9).

Here God offers another set of witnesses, from amongst the peoples of the nations themselves, who will come in and testify on Israel's behalf. All of these witnesses represent people who in the past had *accused* Israel, which makes them such effective witnesses here. God here makes the nations confront the fact that he can call witnesses from amongst their own, witnesses that they cannot possibly accuse of partiality or of having too close a relationship with Israel.

Commenting on this passage, Rubenstein notes the recurrence of this signal verse from Isaiah, arguing that "Where Isaiah summoned the nations to bring witnesses on their own behalf and vindicate their gods, the homiletical story interprets the ambiguous pronouns such that the nations produce witnesses on behalf of God and vindicate Israel; they confess that what God asserted – that Israel fulfilled the Torah – is true. This turn completes the dramatic inversion of the biblical paradigm in which Israel serve

---

[99] Rubenstein, *Talmudic Stories*, 230.

[100] i.e., by directing it to Darius instead of God.

as witnesses for God. In the rabbinic version of the trial first God, then the nations, witness that Israel fulfilled the Torah."[101] This is correct, but it is not the only way in which this verse functions here. Understanding the author's full literary strategy, the second half of this clause may refer to the verdict anticipated by the reader – that after all these nations bring forth their charges, and all the witnesses speak, "they" (i.e. the readers) may say 'It is true' – i.e., pronounce a proper verdict on the issue of God's justice. Everyone is thus included in the "they" of Isa 43:9: the nations, the forced witnesses, and the ultimate judges, the readers themselves.

God gets the final word here; this effectively shuts down the nations's arguments, as they stop presenting an offensive סניגוריא and instead plea for mercy, asking God to offer them the Torah again so that they can accept it (b. Avodah Zarah 3a). Though God refuses to do so, he does allow them to go practice the "easy" commandment of Sukkot. The editor breaks in with a question here – why does he give them this chance? – and the response is that "The Holy One, blessed be He, does not come to his creatures with tyranny (בטרוניא)." Even when the nations have no defense, insists the editor, God still gives them an opportunity to perform commandments, to observe the Torah, and thus to receive a reward. The nations then show themselves as being unable literally to take the summer heat, trampling down their booths and heading inside.[102] This provokes God to laughter, as it says, "the one who sits in heaven laughs" (Ps 2:4; b. Avodah Zarah 3b). This verse, which effectively closes this narrative, may have been brought in not only because it is an example of God laughing, but because the imagery of God sitting suggests enthronement, and God sitting on his throne is part of the standard imagery of the divine courtroom. Indeed, an alternate tradition that is preserved on this same folio, attributed to R. Judah in the name of Rav, suggests that this day can be divided into four segments of three hours, and "during the second three He sits and judges the whole world, and when He sees that the entire world is liable (נתחייב), He gets up from the throne of justice and sits on the throne of mercy."[103]

This section, too, in which God gives the nations the opportunity to observe a commandment, is part of the way in which the author uses the courtroom imagery to vindicate God and acquit God of any charges of injustice that people might throw at him. By demonstrating not only that God

---

[101] Rubenstein, *Talmudic Stories*, 231.

[102] Rubenstein presents an excellent analysis of why the commandment to build sukkot is the one presented here, cf. *Talmudic Stories*, 233-234.

[103] This idea that God has two thrones, one throne of justice and one of mercy, can be found elsewhere in Rabbinic literature. For example, in b. Hag 14a the tradition is attributed to R. Akiba, trying to argue that the two thrones in Daniel 7 refer to God's two thrones, one of justice and one of mercy, and not to two powers in heaven. See the discussion in Segal, *Two Powers in Heaven*, 47.

is able to answer all the charges and reveal their baselessness, but also that despite liability he will still show mercy, even to idolatrous nations, the author is attempting to convince the reader to pronounce the correct verdict on God. Though this narrative seems to trace from third-century Palestine,[104] the editorial insertions here demonstrate that even in the period of the stammaim, the courtroom imagery is still being used in this way, and the true judicial power is vested in the reader.

# G. Conclusion

While early Christian literature wrestled with the challenges posed by the Pauline anthropology, Rabbinic literature had no such tension to overcome, and it is in Rabbinic literature that the scenes and thematics of the divine courtroom reach new heights, culminating in the tour de force presentation of the trial at the end of days in the Babylonian Talmud. The divine courtroom is a consistent presence throughout the rabbinic literature in all its genres. Technical legal vocabulary develops to describe what will take place at trial. Elijah emerges to teach the people of Israel how to stand a defense (*snegoria*) before God successfully. The doctrine of merits emerges and develops. God is pictured at the *Bet Din Gadol*, the Great Court. Elaborate descriptions of the ultimate trial of the people of Israel in toto emerge in the Talmud. The legalities of justice and mercy and the roles of the Attribute of Mercy and the Attribute of Justice (practically hypostasized as deities in themselves) in legal context become standard points of discussion. Particularly important for the rabbis is the nature of intercession and petitionary prayer, as well as the type of arguments one can use at the divine courtroom when standing trial. These fanciful descriptions serve a pedagogical purpose for the rabbis, teaching others about the necessity of torah study, and serving to promote a high anthropology entirely opposite from that which one finds in the Christian sources.

Throughout all this literature, from the early comments of Pappias to the extended presentation of b. *Avoda Zara*, we have a sustained tradition of the use of the courtroom imagery both to question and to attempt to vindicate God. Pappias, like his contemporary Marcion of Sinope, uses the courtroom imagery to bring up essential concerns regarding God's justice, concerns with are echoed throughout the wide corpus of Rabbinic literature. The author of the talmudic Sugya uses the imagery to attempt to prove to his readers that God is unimpeachable with regard to this very is-

---

[104] Cf. Louis Jacobs, "Israel and the Nations: A Literary Analysis of a Talmudic Sugya" *Tel-Aviv Review* 2 (1989) 372-383, 381.

sue. Though the way in which the Rabbis imagine the courtroom is different from their Christian counterparts, this use of the divine courtroom scenes is a point of contact between both traditions.

Chapter 9

# Conclusion

In this monograph I have argued that throughout all of these different literary corpora one consistent use of the divine courtroom is as a way to try
God in the court of the reader. In these scenes, authors ask their readers to
make concrete decisions on the equity and propriety of the process unfolding before them. This literary strategy is both sophisticated and
straightforward. It reflects an understanding of the mindset of the reader
not solely as passive but as an active participant in the hearing or reading
of a text. It assumes that the reader is intelligent and has a propensity to
think critically about the text and imagery being deployed. It also assumes
that the reader will not automatically "trust" the characters in the narratives, or even the author behind the text. They will be able to see that
"something else" is being tried or needs evaluation beyond the plain sense
of the plot. This literary strategy understands the readers as empowered
individuals, expecting them to be part of the proceedings and thus inviting
them to do so. Ancient readers were not lemmings, willing to follow narra-
tors blindly without question or reaction. On the contrary, this explication
of the discursive dynamic present in these divine courtroom texts reveals
the incisive and inquisitive minds of both ancient authors and audiences.

Since they expected their readers to take a critical and thus judicial
posture towards what was transpiring before them, ancient authors explicitly directed their readers towards the verdicts they wanted them to hand
down. Far from being neutral chroniclers, these authors designed their trial
scenes in order to procure the verdicts they desired, whether it be by having characters in the text stand in for the desired reader response, as in the
book of Revelation, or by having characters in the text ask the questions it
assumes the reader will be formulating, as in the *Apocalypse of Peter*. The
author greatly participates in ensuring that their audience will come to the
conclusion they so desire. To put it in the terms of modern reader-
response theory, the authors of these texts do not grant the reader full au-
tonomy; they have directed the reader the entire time.[1]

---

[1] This understanding of what is occurring in the divine courtroom scenes would follow
Michael Riffaterre rather than Stanley Fish, for example, in terms of recognizing the priority
of the text rather than the priority of the reader.

However, readers do not always follow the text's directions, however manifold. Readers such as Marcion of Sinope, and the Pseudo-Clementine re-interpreter of the *Apocalypse of Peter* took a look at the process unfolding before them and made critical and negative judgments on that which they saw, deciding that the "justice" displayed in the texts was in some way deficient or not appropriate for a benevolent God. Part of what motivates this type of negative verdict is the lived experience of courtrooms in the ancient world, from the failure of kings to execute justice to the elaborate and fear-producing apparatus of the Roman imperial judicial system. If readers's experiences of courtrooms have been overwhelmingly negative, and associated with the manifestation of *injustice* rather than justice, it is not difficult to see why some ancient readers would have associated God's courtroom with the same possibilities and problems. As we have seen, some ancient authors, in fact, deliberately play on these expected presuppositions regarding courtrooms in antiquity in order to beg the question from their readers. Too often modern scholars have ignored this aspect of the courtroom scenes, instead assuming that the authors of divine courtroom scenes presented scenes of total justice and expected the readers to come with these same expectations. On the contrary, authors took their readers's predispositions into account when structuring their literary presentations of the divine courtroom, and used these courtroom scenes as explicit conveyors or vehicles for serious conversation and reflection on divine justice.

By no means does this conversation end with late Antiquity. It hardly needs to be said that images of the divine courtroom, particularly in terms of the last judgment, were popular features of medieval art and literature, from the Autun tympanum to the thirteenth-century *Dies Irae* to the Sistene Chapel.[2] Baun has amply demonstrated that the medieval *Apocalypse of the Theotokos* and *Apocalypse of Anastasia* include significant divine courtroom scenes, and use judicial imagery as central components of their works.[3] However, Brandon notes that these depictions steadily decline after the rise of Protestantism, suggesting that "Humanitarian feelings steadily rendered Christians uncomfortable about the apparent contradiction between the idea of a God of love and a vengeful Judge, who finally condemns the majority of his creatures to eternal torment."[4] In other words, Brandon is suggesting that ultimately readers handed down such negative verdicts on the depictions of God in the divine courtroom that the imagery itself was abandoned, or at least sidelined.

---

[2] For overview and discussion, see Brandon, *Judgment of the Dead*, 118-140.

[3] cf. Baun, *Tales from another Byzantium*.

[4] Brandon, *Judgment of the Dead*, 133.

It is interesting to note that Dante's *Divine Comedy* does not contain a courtroom scene. The text is so imbued with the notion of justice that Virgil chides the pilgrim for feeling pity for the tormented, as to do so is to suggest that their punishment is somehow opposed to justice (*Inferno* XX, 27-30, *inter alia*).[5] In Dante's distinctive poetics of *contrapasso*, each of the tormented is revealed to be suffering a punishment particular to his crime. Yet the sentences have already been determined long before the start of the journey; the pilgrim does not witness the judgment being rendered. The reader is thus given no opportunity to sit as judge over God's justice, as a courtroom scene so often provoked. And just as in the *Apocalypse of Peter*, when the reader might feel tempted to pass judgment by feeling pity for those in torment and wishing for their respite, they receive explicit admonition not to do so. And the most obvious way by which they would hand down a verdict – by sitting in judgment over the divine forensic process – is completely denied to them by the structure of the text.

In the Jewish tradition, the courtroom imagery also persists throughout the medieval period, perhaps most strikingly in the extensive *piyyutim* that form the Yom Kippur liturgy, depicting God standing trial over humanity every year. Throughout Yom Kippur, Jews are encouraged to view themselves as standing, helpless and pitiful, before the sovereign judgment-seat of God, who sentences them for the upcoming year. The beautiful medieval *Unetaneh Tokef* prayer expresses the solemnity and the anxiety of the forensic situation, suggesting that even the heavenly hosts fear, for they cannot count on being cleared in the court. Medieval rabbinic midrash continues to use the imagery of the divine courtroom to bring up essential questions about God and his judicial process, and to provoke its audiences to fear and trembling. The Midrash on Psalms repeatedly attempts to convince the reader that the upcoming judgment will be conducted according to the strictest standards of justice, even so far as to portray Habakkuk retracting the charges that he leveled against God (Mid. Ps. 90:7), or to insist that those who accuse God of conducting the trials unfairly will be publicly shamed (Mid. Ps. 1:22).

Upon concluding his exhaustive survey of the motif of divine judgment in ancient religions, J. Gwyn Griffiths comments: "What is very clear in the whole field of divine judgment is the way in which man has attributed to God the human activities through which man seeks to achieve justice."[6] I suggested in the introduction that one partial explanation for this persistent move, which has continued up to and including our contemporary world, is that courtrooms are Janus-faced, places both extraordinary and

---

[5] Obviously there are echoes here of the harsh words Jesus has for Peter in the *Apocalypse of Peter*.

[6] Griffiths, *The Divine Verdict*, 348.

ordinary, capturing both the ideal of perfect justice as well as the reality of imperfect justice. When applied to God, or to some form of thinking about a post-mortem judicial process, the use of courtroom imagery captures a certain sense of unease, apprehension about what is to come. Will one face the Deuteronomistic YHWH, predictable and operating according to clearly articulated criteria? Or will one face the unpredictable YHWH of Exodus 6, reaching out to strike, or the *Deus Absconditus* of Job? By applying the realia of human experience to God, and imaging God in this way, authors provoke just as many questions as they answer. It is no wonder that the *psychostasia* is, in one medieval artistic representation, depicted as a toothy deity, ready to consume. Courtrooms, though easily recognizable and identifiable, are terrifying.

In modern literature, the most obvious depiction of the judicial process as a hazy, insurmountable catch-22 is that of Josef K. in *The Trial*. Though certainly the details of the bureaucratic nightmare are particular to Kafka's own milieu, it is the same fear that stands behind Jesus's warning in the Sermon on the Mount: "settle matters with your adversary quickly when you meet him in the road, lest the adversary hand you over to the judge and the judge to the guard, and you be thrown in prison. Truly I tell you, you will not get out of there until you have paid back the last quadran" (Matt 5:24). What stands behind this instruction is the recognition of the serious danger of the legal system, how one circumstance can lead to another and spiral out of one's control. The disorientation, unease, sense of powerlessness, and weight of consequences that are felt by Josef K. and the reader along with him, as the narrator follows his perspective, are all emotions that are associated with courtrooms in the ancient world as well, and stand behind this type of warning. Ancient authors like Plato, Lucian, Matthew, and Marcion of Sinope well understood the presuppositions their readers would bring to the table, and took these into account when shaping their texts. I hope that this monograph has demonstrated how seriously ancient authors took their readers, building in implied arguments to sway them one way or another, knowing that they would not just follow the trials they presented as passive observers but as active participants, judging everything presented before them, as including the character of God himself, and the standards by which he executes justice.

# Bibliography

Adkins, Arthur. *Merit and Responsibility: A Study in Greek Values.* Oxford: Clarendon Press, 1960.

Afzal, Cameron. "Wheels of Time in the Apocalypse of Jesus Christ" in April DeConick, ed. *Paradise Now: Essays on Early Jewish and Christian Mysticism.* Atlanta: SBL, 2006, 195-210.

Albinus, Lars. "The *Katabasis* of Er. Plato's Use of Myths, exemplified by the Myth of Er" in Erik Nis Ostenfeld, ed. *Essays on Plato's Republic.* Aarhus: Aarhus University Press, 1998, 91-105.

Allen, Danielle. *The World of Prometheus: The Politics of Punishing in Democratic Athens.* Princeton: Princeton University Press, 2000.

Allen, R. E. *The Dialogues of Plato 1.* New Haven: Yale University Press, 1984.

Allison, Dale C. *The Testament of Abraham.* Berlin; New York: Walter de Gruyter, 2003.

–. "Job in the Testament of Abraham," *JSP 12* (2001) 131-147.

Alter, Robert. "The Voice from the Whirlwind," *Commentary* 77 (1984) 33-41.

Aronen, Jaako. "Marianus' Vision in the Acts of Marianus and Jacobus: An Analysis of Style, Structure and Generic Composition," *Wiener Studien* 18 (1984) 169-186.

Assman, Jan. *Death and Salvation in Ancient Egypt.* Ithaca: Cornell University Press, 2001.

Aune, David. *Revelation 1-5.* Word Biblical Commentary 52a; Dallas: Word Books, 1997.

–. *Revelation 6-16.*Word Biblical Commentary 52b; Nashville: Thomas Nelson, 1998.

–. *Revelation 17-22.* Word Biblical Commentary 52c; Nashville: Thomas Nelson, 1998.

Bablitz, Leanne. *Actors and Audience in the Roman Courtroom.* London: Routledge, 2007.

Barrick, W. Boyd and John R. Spencer, eds. *In the Shelter of Elyon.* JSOT Supp 31; Sheffield: Sheffield Academic, 1984.

Balentine, Samuel. "Prayers for Justice in the Old Testament: Theodicy and Theology," *CBQ* 51 (1989) 597-616.

Baracchi, Claudia. *Of Myth, Life, and War in Plato's Republic.* Bloomington: Indiana University Press, 2002.

Barnes, Timothy David. *Tertullian: A Historical and Literary Study.* Oxford: Clarendon Press, 1971.

Bassler, Jouette. *Divine Impartiality: Paul and a Theological Axiom.* SBL Dissertation Series 59; Atlanta: Scholars Press, 1982.

Bauckham, Richard. "Judgment in the Book of Revelation," *Ex Auditu* 20 (2004) 1-24.

–. *The Fate of the Dead: Studies on Jewish and Christian Apocalypses.* Supplements to Novum Testamentum 93; Boston: E. J. Brill, 1998.

–. "The Apocalypse of Peter: A Jewish Christian Apocalypse from the Time of Bar Kokhba," *Apocrypha* 5 (1990), 7-111.

Baun, Jane. *Tales from another Byzantium: Celestial Journey and Local Community in the Medeival Greek Apocrypha.* Cambridge: Cambridge University Press, 2007.

Beavis, Mary Ann. "The Trial Before the Sanhedrin (Mark 14:53-65): Reader Response and Greco-Roman Readers," *CBQ* 49 (1987), 581-96.

Behm, J. "παράκλητος," *ThWb* 5 (1954), 798-812

Bensly, Robert L., ed. *The Fourth Book of Ezra, the Latin Version Edited from the MSS.* T & S 3.2; Cambridge: The University Press, 1895.

Bernstein, Alan. *The Formation of Hell.* Ithaca: Cornell University Press, 1993.

Betz, Hans Dieter. *The Sermon on the Mount.* Hermeneia; Minneapolis: Fortress Press, 1995.

−. *2 Corinthians 8 and 9.* Hermeneia; Philadelphia: Fortress Press, 1985.

−. *Der Apostel Paulus und die sokratische Tradition: eine exegetische Untersuchung zu seiner Apologie 2 Korinther 10-13.* Beiträge zur historischen Theologie 45; Tübingen: J.C.B. Mohr, 1972.

Betz, Otto. *Der Paraklet.* Leiden: Brill, 1963.

Black, Matthew. *The Book of Enoch or 1 Enoch.* Studia in Veteris Testamenti pseudepigrapha 7; Leiden: E. J. Brill, 1985.

Blank, Sheldon. "Men against God: The Promethean element of Biblical prayer," *JBL* 72 (1953), 1-13.

Blickman, Daniel R. "Styx and the Justice of Zeus in Hesiod's *Theogony*," *Phoenix* 41 (1987) 341-355.

Bonner, Robert J. *Lawyers and Litigants in Ancient Athens: The Genesis of the Legal Profession* Chicago: University of Chicago Press, 1927.

Bornkamm, Gunter, G. Barth, and H. J. Held, eds., *Tradition and Interpretation in Matthew.* London: SCM, 1963.

Bowersock, G. W. *Martyrdom and Rome.* Cambridge: Cambridge University Press, 1995.

Box, G. H. *The Testament of Abraham: Translated from the Greek Text with Introduction and Notes.* TED Series 2. London: SPCK, 1927.

Boyarin, Daniel. *Intertextuality and the Reading of Midrash.* Eugene, OR: Wipf and Stock, 1990.

Boyle, Marjorie O'Rourke. "Covenant lawsuit of the prophet Amos: 3:1-4:13," *VT* 21 (1971) 338-362.

Brandon, S. G. F. "The Proleptic Aspect of the Iconography of the Egyptian 'Judgment of the Dead,'" *Ex Orbe Religionum* 21 (1972), 16-25.

−. *The Trial of Jesus of Nazareth.* New York: Stein and Day, 1968.

−. *History, Time and Deity: A Historical and Comparative Study of the Conception of Time in Religious Thought and Practice.* New York: Barnes & Noble, inc., 1965.

−. *The Judgment of the Dead: The Idea of Life after Death in the Major Religions.* New York: Char es Scribner's Sons, 1967.

Branham, R. Bracht. *Unruly Eloquence: Lucian and the Comedy of Traditions.* Cambridge: Harvard University Press, 1989.

Breech, Earl. "These Fragments I have Shored Against My Ruins: The Form and Function of 4 Ezra," *JBL* 92 (1973), 267-274.

Bremmer, Jan N. and István Czachesz, eds. *The Visio Pauli and the Gnostic Apocalypse of Paul.* Leuven: Peeters, 2007.

−. "Contextualizing Heaven in Third-Century North Africa," in Ra'anan S. Boustan and Annette Yoshiko Reed, *Heavenly Realms and Earthly Realities in Late Antique Religions.* Cambridge: Cambridge University Press, 2004.

−. and István Czachesz, eds. *The Apocalypse of Peter.* Leuven: Peeters, 2003.

–. *The Rise and Fall of the Afterlife*. New York: Routledge, 2002.

Brenner, J. M. Th. P.J. van den Hout, and R. Peters, eds. *Hidden Futures: Death and Immortality in Ancient Egypt, Anatolia, the Classical, Biblical and Arabic-Islamic World*. Amsterdam: Amsterdam University Press, 1994.

Brisson, Luc. *Plato the Myth Maker*. Chicago: University of Chicago, 1998.

Brown, Raymond *The Death of the Messiah*. 2 vols.; New York: Doubleday, 1996.

–. *The Gospel According to John i-xii*. AB; New York: Doubleday, 1966.

–."The Paraclete in the Fourth Gospel," *NTS* 13 (1966-67), 113-132.

Bruckner, James K. *Implied Law in the Abraham Narrative*. JSOT Supp Series 335; Sheffield: Sheffield Academic, 2001.

Brueggeman, Walter. "Theodicy in a Social Dimension," *JSOT* 33 (1985) 3-25.

Brunner, H. "Die Rolle von Tür und Tor im Alten Ägypten," *Symbolon* 6 (1982), 37-59.

Budge, E. A. Wallis. *The Egyptian Heaven and Hell*. La Salle, IL: Open Court, 1974.

–. Wallis, trans. *The Book of the Dead: The Chapters of Coming Forth by Day*. London: Kegan Paul, Trench, Trübner & Co, LTD, 1898.

Burkhert, Walter. *Greek Religion*. Cambrige: Harvard University Press, 1985.

Bultmann, Rudolf. *The Theology of the New Testament*. Trans. Kendrick Grobel; New York: Charles Scribner's Sons, 1955.

Burnett, Fred W. "Prolegomenon to Reading Matthew's Eschatological Discourse: Redundancy and the Education of the Reader in Matthew," *Semeia* 31 (1985) 91-109.

Carson, D. A. Peter T. O'Brien, and Mark A. Seifrid, *Justification and Variegated Nomism I: The Complexities of Second Temple Judaism*. Tübingen: Mohr Siebeck, 2001.

–., Peter T. O'Brien, and Mark A. Seifrid, eds. *Justification and Variegated Nomism II: The Paradoxes of Paul*. Tübingen: Mohr Siebeck, 2001.

Carson, D. A. "The Function of the Paraclete in John 16:7-11," *JBL* 98 (1979), 547-566.

Castelli, Elizabeth A. *Martyrdom and Memory: Early Christian Culture Making*. New York: Columbia, 2004.

Charles, R. H. *The Book of Enoch*. Oxford: Clarendon Press, 1893.

–. *The Ascension of Isaiah*. London: A and C Black, 1900.

Charlesworth, James, ed. *The Messiah: Developments in Earliest Judaism and Christianity*. Minneapolis: Fortress, 1992.

–, ed. *The Old Testament Pseudepigrapha*. 2 vols; Garden City, NY: Doubleday, 1983-1985.

Chazon, E. Glickler. "Moses' Struggle for His Soul: A Prototype for the *Testament of Abraham*, the *Greek Apocalypse of Ezra*, and the *Apocalypse of Sedrach*," *Second Century* 5 (1985-86) 151-64.

Cherette, Blaine. *The Theme of Recompense in Matthew's Gospel*. JSNT Supp Series 79; Sheffield: Sheffield Academic, 1992.

Chilton, Bruce and Craig Evans, eds. *The Missions of James, Peter, and Paul: Tensions in Early Christianity*. Leiden: Brill, 2005.

Clay, Jenny Strauss. *Hesiod's Cosmos*. Cambridge: Cambridge University Press, 2003.

Collins, John J. *The Apocalyptic Imagination*. Second ed; Grand Rapids, MI: Eerdmans, 1998.

Costa, Desmond. *Lucian: Selected Dialogues*. Oxford: Oxford University Press, 2005.

Couroyer, Bernard. "De la measure dont vous measurez il vous sera measuré," *Revue Biblique* 77 (1970), 366-370.

Crenshaw, James L. "The Sojourner has Come to Play the Judge: Theodicy on Trial," in Tod Linafelt and Timothy K. Beal, eds., *God in the Fray: A Tribute to Walter Brueggeman*. Minneapolis: Fortress, 1998, 83-92.

Crenshaw, James. L. "Popular Questioning of the Justice of God in Ancient Israel" *ZAW* 82 (1970) 380-395.

Crook, J. A *Legal Advocacy in the Roman World.* Ithaca: Cornell University Press, 1995.

Crook, John. *Law and Life of Rome.* Ithaca, NY: Cornell University Press, 1967.

Cross, Frank Moore. *Canaanite Myth and Hebrew Epic.* Cambridge: Harvard University Press, 1973.

–. "The Council of Yahweh in Second Isaiah," *JNES* 12 (1953) 274-277.

Dahl, Nils Alstrup. "The Johannine Church and History" in William Klassen and Graydon F. Snyder, eds. *Current Issues in New Testament Interpretation.* New York: Harper and Brothers, 1962, 124-142.

Daley, Brian E. *The Hope of the Early Church: A Handbook of Patristic Eschatology.* Cambridge: Cambridge University Press, 1991.

Dam, Cornel us van. *The Urim and Thummim: A Means of Revelation in Ancient Israel.* Winona Lake, IN: Eisenbrauns, 1997.

de' Cavalieri P. Franchi. "La Passio ss. Mariani et Iacobi" *ST* 3 (1900), 47-61.

de la Potterie, Ignace. *The Hour of Jesus: The Passion and the Resurrection of Jesus according to John.* Slough: St. Paul Publications, 1989.

–. "Jésus roi et juge d'après Jean 19:13," *Biblica* 41 (1960), 217-247.

Delcor, M. *Le Testament d'Abraham: introduction, traduction du texte grec et commentaire de la recension greque longue suivi de la traduction des testaments d'Abraham, d'Isaac et de Jacob d'après les versions orientales.* SVTP 2. Leiden: E.J. Brill, 1973.

–. "De l'origine de quelques traditions contenues dans le Testament d'Abraham," *Proceedings of the Fifth World Congress of Jewish Studies,* ed. P. Peli. Jerusalem: World Union of Jewish Studies, 1969. Vol 1, 192-200.

DeRoche, Michael. "Yahweh's *RÎB* against Israel: A Reassessment of the So-Called 'Prophetic Lawsuit' in the Preexilic Prophets," *JBL* 102 (1983), 563-574.

Dick, Michael Brennan. "The Legal Metaphor in Job 31," *CBQ* 41 (1979), 37-50.

Dochhorn, Jan. "Abel and the Three Stages of Postmortal Judgement: A Text-Critical and Redaction-Critical Study of the Christian Elements in *Testament of Abraham* A 13:2-8," in Ian H. Henderson and Gerbern S. Oegema, eds. *The Changing Face of Judaism, Christianity, and Other Greco-Roman Religions in Antiquity.* Munich: Gütersloher Verlagshaus, 2006, 398-415.

Dodds, E. R. *Gorgias.* Oxford: Clarendon Press, 1959.

Donohue, John R. *Are You the Christ? The Trial Narrative in the Gospel of Mark.* SBL Dissertation Series 10; Missoula, MT: SBL, 1973.

Donfried, Karl Paul. "Justification and Last Judgment in Paul," *Interpretation* 30 (1976), 140-152.

Droge, Arthur J. and James D. Tabor, *A Noble Death: Suicide and Martyrdom among Christians and Jews in Antiquity.* San Francisco: HarperSanFrancisco, 1992.

Dunn, Geoffrey. *Tertullian.* London: Routledge, 2004.

Dunn, James. *Romans 1-8.* Word Biblical Commentary 38a; Dallas: Word, 1998.

Edmonds, Radcliffe III. *Myths of the Underworld Journey: Plato, Aristophanes, and The 'Orphic' Gold Tablets.* Cambridge: Cambridge University Press, 2004.

Esler, Philip F. "The Social Function of 4 Ezra," *JSNT* 53 (1994) 99-123.

Evans, Ernest. *Tertullian: Adversus Marcionem.* Oxford: Clarendon Press, 1972.

Filson, Floyd. *St. Paul's Conception of Recompense.* Leipzig: J. C. Hinrichs'sche Buchhandlung, 1931.

Finley, John H. Jr. *Pindar and Aeschylus.* Martin Classical Lectures 14; Cambridge: Harvard University Press, 1955.

Fishbane, Michael. *Biblical Myth and Rabbinic Mythmaking.* Oxford: Oxford University Press, 2003.
–. *The Exegetical Imagination: On Jewish Thought and Theology.* Cambridge: Harvard University Press, 1998.
–. *Biblical Interpretation in Ancient Israel.* Oxford: Clarendon Press, 1985.
Fishburne, Charles W. "I Corinthians III.10-15 and the Testament of Abraham," *NTS* 17 (1970), 109-115.
Fitzgerald, William. "Pindar's Second Olympian," *Helios* 10 (1983) 49-70.
Fitzmyer, Joseph A. *Romans.* AB 33; New York: Doubleday, 1993.
–. "Further Light on Melchizedek from Qumran Cave 11," *JBL* 86 (1967), 25-41.
Ford, J. Massyngberde. *Revelation.* Anchor Bible; New York: Doubleday, 1975.
Frye, J. B. "Legal Language and the Book of Job." PhD. Diss.University of London, 1973.
Frymer-Kensky, Tikva. "The End of the World and the Limits of Biblical Ecology" in Adela Yarbro Collins and Margaret Mitchell, eds., *Antiquity and Humanity: Essays on Ancient Religion and Philosophy.*Tübingen: Mohr Siebeck, 2001, 15-26.
–. "The Strange Case of the Suspected Sotah (Num 5:11-31)," *VT* 34 (1984), 11-26.
–. *The Judicial Ordeal in the Ancient Near East.* PhD Diss., Yale University, 1977.
Fullerton, Kemplar. "On Job, chapters 9 and 10," *JBL* 53 (1934) 321-349.
Fussi, Alessandra. "The Myth of the Last Judgment in the Gorgias," *Review of Metaphysics* 54 (2001): 529-552.
Gagarin, Michael. "The Poetry of Justice: Hesiod and the Origins of Greek Law," *Ramus* 21 (1992) 61-78.
Gamble, Harry. *Books and Readers in the Early Church: A History of Early Christian Texts.* New Haven: Yale University Press, 1995.
Gantz, Timothy. *Early Greek Myth: A Guide to Literary and Artistic Sources.* Baltimore: Johns Hopkins, 1993.
Garland, Robert. *The Greek Way of Death.* Ithaca: Cornell University Press, 2001.
Gaster, Moshe. "Hebrew Visions of Hell and Paradise," *JRAS* 25 (1893) 571-611.
Gathercole, Simon. "The Doctrine of Justification in Paul and Beyond: Some Proposals," in Bruce L. McCormack, ed., *Justification in Perspective.* Grand Rapids, MI: BakerAcademic, 2006, 219-242.
Gebhart, Oscar von. *Das Evangelium und die Apokalypse des Petrus.* Leipzig: J. C. Hinrichs, 1893.
Gelberg, Sarah. *To Whom it May Concern: Aristotle's Theory of Audience.* MA Thesis; Illinois State University, May 1999.
Gemser, B. "The Rîb- or Controversy-Pattern in Hebrew Mentality" in M. Noth and D. Winton Thomas, eds., *Wisdom in Israel and in the Ancient Near East.* Supplements to VT 3; Leiden: Brill, 1955. 120-137.
Georgiadou, Aristoula and David H. J. Larmour, *Lucian's Science Fiction Novel True Histories.* Mnemosyne 179; Leiden: Brill, 1998.
Giblin, C. H. "John's Narration of the Hearing before Pilate," *Biblica* 67 (1986), 221-239.
Gilmour, Michael. "Delighting in the Sufferings of Others: Early Christian *Schadenfreude* and the Function of the *Apocalypse of Peter,*" *BBR* 16 (2006) 129-139.
Girard, René. *Violence and the Sacred.* Baltimore: Johns Hopkins, 1977.
Goldin, Judah. "On Honi the Circle Drawer: A Demanding Prayer," in Barry Eichler and Jeffrey Tigay, eds. *Studies in Midrash and Related Literature.* Philadelphia: Jewish Publication Society, 1988, 331-335.

Good, Edwin. *In Turns of Tempest: A Reading of Job*. Stanford: Stanford University Press, 1990.

Gordon, Cyrus. "*'Elohim* in its Reputed Meaning of *Rulers, Judges,*" *JBL* 54 (1935), 139-144.

–. "The Legal Background of Hebrew Thought and Literature." M.A. thesis, University of Pennsylvania, 1928.

Grant, Robert M. *Irenaeus of Lyons*. New York: Routledge, 1997.

Gray, S. *The Least of My Brothers: Matthew 25:31-40: A History of Interpretation*. SBL Diss. Series 114; Atlanta: Scholars Press, 1989.

Grieb, A. Katherine. *The Story of Romans: A Narrative Defense of God's Righteousness*. Louisville WJK, 2002.

Griffiths, J. Gwyn. *The Divine Verdict: A Study of Divine Judgment in the Ancient Religions*. Leiden: Brill, 1991.

Gruenwald, Ithamar. *Apocalyptic and Merkabah Mysticism*. Leiden: Brill, 1980.

Gunkel, Herman and J. Begrich, *Einleitung in die Psalmen: Die Gattungen der religiösen Lyrik Israels*. Göttingen: Vandenhoeck and Ruprecht, 1933.

Haenchen, Ernst. "History and Interpretation in the Johannine Passion Narrative," *Interpretation* 24 (1970) 198-219.

Halperin, David. *The Faces of the Chariot: Early Jewish Responses to Ezekiel's Vision*. Tübingen: Mohr Siebeck, 1988.

Hannah, Darryl D. "The Throne of His Glory: The Divine Throne and Heavenly Mediators in Revelation and the Similitudes of Enoch" *ZNW* 96 (2003), 68-96.

Hansen, M. H. *The Athenian Democracy in the Age of Demosthenes*. Oxford: Blackwell, 1991.

Hanson, A. T. *The New Interpretation of Scripture*. London: SPCK, 1980.

Harnack, Adolf von. *Bruchstücke des Evangeliums und der Apokalypse des Petrus*. Texte und Untersuchungen zur Geschichte der altchristlichen Literatur 9; Leipzig: J. C. Hinrichs, 1893.

Harrington, Daniel J. "Wisdom and Apocalyptic in 4QInstruction and 4 Ezra" in F. García Martínez, ed. *Wisdom and Apocalypticism in the Dead Sea Scrolls and in the Biblical Tradition*. Leuven: Leuven University Press, 2003, 343-355.

Harrison, J. R. "In Quest of the Third Heaven: Paul & His Apocalypic Imitators," *VC* 58 (2004) 24-55.

Harvey, Julien. *Le plaidoyer prophétique contre Israël après la rupture de l'alliance*. Paris: Desclee de Brouwer, 1967.

–. "Le 'Rîb-Pattern,' réquisitoire prophétique sur la rupture de l'alliance," *Biblica* 43 (1962) 172-196.

Hay, David M. and E. Elizabeth Johnson, eds. *Pauline Theology III: Romans*. Atlanta: Society of Biblical Literature, 2002.

Heil, John Paul. "The Double Meaning of the Narrative of Universal Judgment in Matthew 25.31-46," *JSNT* 69 (1998) 3-14.

–. "The Fifth Seal (Rev 6, 9-11) as a Key to the Book of Revelation," *Biblica* 74 (1993) 220-243.

Heinemann, J. *Prayer in the Talmud*. Studia Judaica IX; Berlin and New York: Walter de Gruyter, 1997.

Henderson, Jeffrey. "The *Dēmos* and Comic Competition," in John J. Winkler and Froma I. Zeitlin, eds. *Nothing to do with Dionysus? Athenian Drama in its Social Context*. Princeton: Princeton University Press, 1990, 271-313.

Hengel, Martin. *The Pre-Christian Paul*. London: SCM, 1991.

Himmelfarb, Martha. "Torah, Testimony, and Heavenly Tablets: The Claim to Authority of the *Book of Jubilees*" in Benjamin G. Wright, ed. *A Multiform Heritage: Studies on Early Judaism and Christianity in Honor of Robert A. Kraft.* Atlanta: Scholars Press, 1999, 19-30.

–. *Ascent to Heaven in Jewish and Christian Apocalypses.* New York: Oxford University Press, 1993.

–. "The Experience of the Visionary and Genre in the Ascension of Isaiah 6-11 and the Apocalypse of Paul" *Semeia* 36 (1986) 97-111.

–. *Tours of Hell: An Apocalyptic Form in Jewish and Christian Literature.* Philadelphia: University of Pennsylvania Press, 1983.

Hogan Karina Martin, *Theologies in Conflict in 4 Ezra: Wisdom Debate and Apocalyptic Solution.* Phd Diss. University of Chicago, 2002.

Holladay, William, "Jeremiah's lawsuit with God: a study in suffering and meaning," *Interpretation* 17 (1963) 280-287.

Hooker, Morna D. and S. G. Wilson, eds. *Paul and Paulinism.* London: SPCK, 1982.

Huffmon, Herbert. "Covenant lawsuit in the Prophets," *JBL* 78 (1959), 285-295.

Hurtado, L. W. "Revelation 4-5 in the Light of Jewish Apocalyptic Analogies," *JSNT* 25 (1985) 105-124.

Jacobs, Louis. "Israel and the Nations: A Literary Analysis of a Talmudic Sugya," *Tel-Aviv Review* 2 (1989) 372-383.

Jacobsen, Thorkild. "Primitive Democracy in Ancient Mesopotamia" *JNES* 2 (1943) 159-172.

James, Montague Rhodes. "The Rainer Fragment of the Apocalypse of Peter," *JTS* 32 (1931), 270-279.

–. *The Testament of Abraham: The Greek text now first edited with an introduction and notes.* T&S 2.2; Cambridge: The University Press, 1892.

Johannson, Nils. *Parakletoi : Vorstellungen von Fürsprechern für die Menschen vor Gott in der alttestamentlichen Religion, im Spätjudentum und Urchristentum.* Lund: Gleerupska Universitetsbokhandeln, 1940.

Johnston, George. *The Spirit-Paraclete in the Gospel of John.* Cambridge: Cambridge University Press, 1970.

Jones, A. H. M. *The Criminal Courts of the Roman Republic and Principate.* Totowa, NJ: Rowman and Littlefield Publishers, 1972.

Juel, Donald. *Messiah and Temple: The Trial of Jesus in the Gospel of Mark.* Missoula, MT: Scholars, 1977.

Kadushin, Max. *A Conceptual Approach to the Mekhilta.* New York: Jewish Theological Seminary, 1969.

–. *Organic Thinking: A Study in Rabbinic Thought.* New York: Jewish Theological Seminary, 1938.

Käsemann, Ernst. *Commentary on Romans.* Trans. Geoffrey W. Bromiley; London: SCM Press, 1982.

–. *New Testament Questions of Today.* Philadelphia: Fortress Press, 1967.

Kirk, J. R. Daniel. *Unlocking Romans: Resurrection and the Justification of God.* Grand Rapids, MI: William B. Eerdmans, 2008.

Kohler, K. "The Pre-Talmudic Haggada II C: The Apocalypse of Abraham and its Kindred," *JQR* 7 (1895), 581-606.

Köstenberger, Andreas. "'What is Truth?' Pilate's Question in its Johannine and larger Biblical Context," *JETS* 48 (2005) 33-62.

Laney, J. Carl. "The role of the prophets in God's case against Israel" *Bibliotheca Sacra* 138 (1981), 313-325.

Laytner, Anson. *Arguing with God: A Jewish Tradition*. Northvale, NJ: Jason Aronson, 1990.

Lieberman, Saul. "Some Aspects of After Life in Rabbinic Literature" in *Essays in Greco-Roman and related Talmudic Literature*. New York: Ktav, 1977, 387-424.

—. *Texts and Studies*. New York: KTAV, 1974.

Limburg, James. "Root ריב and the prophetic lawsuit speeches," *JBL* 88 (1969) 291-304.

Lincoln, Andrew T. *Truth on Trial: The Lawsuit Motif in the Fourth Gospel*. Peabody, MA: Hendrickson, 2000.

Lincoln, Bruce. *Theorizing Myth: Narrative, Ideology, and Scholarship*. Chicago: University of Chicago, 1999.

Linders, Barnabas. "ΔΙΚΑΙΟΣΥΝΗ in Jn. 16.8 and 10,'" in C. M. Tuckett, ed., *Essays on John*. Studiorum Novi Testamenti Auxilia 17; Leuven: Leuven University Press, 1992. 21-31.

Lipsius, R. A. and Bonnet, M, eds. *Acta Apostolorum Apocrypha*. 2 vols; Hildesheim; New York: G. Olms, 1972.

Lloyd, Michael. *The Agon in Euripides*. Oxford: Clarendon Press, 1992.

Lloyd-Jones, Hugh. *The Justice of Zeus*. Rev ed; Berkeley: University of California Press, 1983.

Longenecker, Bruce W. "Locating 4 Ezra: A Consideration of its Social Setting and Functions" *JSJPHR* 28 (1997), 271-293.

—. *Eschatology and the Covenant: A Comparison of 4 Ezra and Romans 1-11*. JSNT Supp Series 57; Sheffield: Sheffield Academic, 1991.

Ludlow, Jared. *Abraham Meets Death: Narrative Humor in the Testament of Abraham*. JSOP Supp Series 41; Sheffield: Sheffield Academic Press, 2002.

Luz, Ulrich. *Matthew 1-7*. Hermeneia; Minneapolis: Fortress, 2007.

—. *Matthew 21-28*. Hermeneia; Minneapolis: Fortress, 2005.

—. *Matthew 8-20*. Minneapolis: Fortress, 2001.

Lytton, Timothy D. "'Shall not the Judge of the Earth Deal Justly?' Accountability, Compassion and Judicial Authority in the Biblical Story of Sodom and Gomorrah," *Journal of Law and Religion* 18 (2002), 31-55.

MacDowell, Douglas. *The Law in Classical Athens*. Ithaca, NY: Cornell University Press, 1978.

Magdalene, F Rachel. *On the Scales of Righteousness: Neo-Babylonian Trial Law and the Book of Job*. Brown Judaic Studies 348; Providence: Brown University, 2007.

Maier, Harry O. "Staging the Gaze: Early Christian Apocalypses and Narrative Self-Representation," *HTR* 90 (1997) 131-154.

Marguerat, Daniel. *Le Jugement dans l'Évangile de Matthieu*. Geneva: Labor et Fides, 1995.

Marmorstein, Arthur. *The Old Rabbinical Doctrine of God*. London: Oxford University Press, 1927.

—. *The Doctrine of Merits in Old Rabbinical Literature*. London: Oxford University Press, 1920

Martyn, J. Louis. *Theological Issues in the Letters of Paul*. Nashville: Abingdon Press, 1997.

May, Gerhard. "Marcion in Contemporary Views: Results and Open Questions, " *Second Century* 6 (1987) 129-152.

McCurdy, G.E. "Platonic Orphism in the Testament of Abraham," *JBL* 61 (1942), 213-26.

Mealy, J. Webb. *After the Thousand Years: Resurrection and Judgment in Revelation 20*. JSNTSS 70; Sheffield: Sheffield Academic, 1992.

Meeks, Wayne. *The Prophet-King: Moses Traditions and the Johannine Christology.* Supplements to Novum Testamentum 14; Leiden: E. J. Brill, 1967.

Mendenhall, George E. *Law and Covenant in Israel and the Ancient Near East.* Pittsburgh: The Biblical Colloquium, 1955.

Merry, W. Walter and James Riddell, *Homer's Odyssey.* Oxford: Clarendon Press, 1886.

Metzger, Ernst. *Litigation in Roman Law.* Oxford: Oxford University Press, 2005.

–. *A New Outline of the Roman Civil Trial.* Oxford: Clarendon Press, 1997.

Mikalson, Jon D. *Honor Thy Gods: Popular Religion in Greek Tragedy.* Chapel Hill: University of North Carolina Press, 1991.

Miller, Merrill P. "Function of Isa 61:1-2 in 11Q *Melchizedek,*" *JBL* 88 (1969), 467-469.

Miller, Patricia Cox. *Dreams in Late Antiquity: Studies in the Imagination of a Culture.* Princeton: Princeton University Press, 1994.

Möllendorff, Peter von. *Auf der Suche nach der verlogenen Wahrheit: Lukians Wahre Geschichten.* Tübingen: Narr, 2000.

Moo, Douglas. *The Epistle to the Romans.* NICNT; Grand Rapids, MI: Eerdmans, 1996.

Moore, George Foote. *Judaism in the First Centuries of the Christian Era: The Age of Tannaim.* Vols 2 and 3; Peabody, MA: Hendrickson, 1997.

–. "Intermediaries in Jewish Theology – Memra, Shekinah, Metatron," *HTR* 15 (1922) 41-85.

Most, Glenn W. *Hesiod I.* LCL; Cambridge: Harvard University Press, 2006.

Mowinckel, Sigmund. "Die Vorstellung des Spätjudentums vom heiligen Geist also Fürsprecher und der johanneische Paraklet," *ZNTW* 32 (1933), 97-130.

Munoa, Phillip B. III. *Four Powers in Heaven: The Interpretation of Daniel 7 in the Testament of Abraham.* Sheffield: Sheffield Academic Press, 1998.

Musarillo, Herbert. *The Acts of the Christian Martyrs.* Oxford: Clarendon Press, 1972.

Newman, Carey C. James R. Davila, and Gladys S. Lewis, eds. *The Jewish Roots of Christological Monotheism.* Leiden: Brill, 1999.

Nickelsburg, George W. E. *Resurrection, Immortality, and Eternal Life in Intertestamental Judaism and Early Christianity.* Expanded ed.; HTS 56; Cambridge: Harvard University Press, 2006.

–. *1 Enoch 1.* Hermeneia; Minneapolis: Fortress Press, 2001.

–., ed. *Studies in the Testament of Abraham.* Septuagint and Cognate Studies 6; Missoula, MT: Scholars Press, 1976.

Nielsen, Kirsten. *Yahweh as Prosecutor and Judge: An investigation of the prophetic lawsuit.* JSOT Supplement Series 9; Sheffield: Sheffield Academic Press, 1978.

Nisetich, Frank. *Pindar and Homer.* Baltimore: Johns Hopkins, 1989.

Nitzan, Bilha. "Post-Biblical *Rib* Pattern Admonitions in 4Q302/303a and 4Q381 69, 76-77," in Michael E. Stone and Esther Chazon, eds., *Biblical Perspectives: Early Use and Interpretation of the Bible in Light of the Dead Sea Scrolls.* Leiden: Brill, 1998, 159-174.

Osborn, Eric. *Tertullian, First Theologian of the West.* Cambridge: Cambridge University Press, 1997.

Otting, Mary-Dean. *Heavenly Journeys: A Study of the Motif in Hellenistic Jewish Literature.* Frankfurt am Main: Verlag Peter Lang, 1984.

Pannenberg, Wolfhart. "Constructive and Critical Functions of Christian Eschatology," *HTR* 77 (1984) 119-139.

Paul, Shalom. "Heavenly Tablets and the Book of Life," *Journal of the Ancient Near Eastern Society of Columbia University* 5 (1973) 345-354.

Pearson, Birger A. "Melchizedek in Early Judaism, Christianity, and Gnosticism," in Michael Stone and Theodore Birgen, eds. *Biblical Figures Outside the Bible*. Harrisburg: Trinity Press, 1998, 176-202.

–. "Enoch in Egypt," in Randall A. Argall, Beverly A. Bow, and Rodney A. Werline, eds. *For a Later Generation: The Transformation of Tradition in Israel, Early Judaism, and Early Christianity*. Harrisburg, PA: Trinity Press International, 2000, 216-231.

Penchansky, David and Paul L. Redditt, eds. *Shall Not the Judge of all the Earth do what is Right? Studies on the Nature of God in Tribute to James L. Crenshaw*. Winona Lake, IN: Eisenbrauns, 2000.

Penna, Romano. "The Meaning of πάρεσις in Romans 3:25c and the Pauline Thought on the Divine Acquital," in Michael Bachmann, ed., *Lutherische und Neue Paulusperspektive*. Tübingen: Mohr Siebeck, 2005, 251-274.

Perdue, Leo G. and W. Clark Gilpin, eds. *The Voice from the Whirlwind: Interpreting the Book of Job*. Nashville: Abingdon Press, 1992.

Pesch, Rudolf. *The Trial of Jesus Continues*. Trans. Doris Glen Wagner; Allison Park, PA: Pickwick, 1996.

Pond, Eugene. "The Background and Timing of the Judgment of the Sheep and Goats," *Bibliotheca Sacra* 159 (2002), 201-220.

Pope, Marvin. *Job*. AB; New York: Doubleday, 1965.

Portmann, John. *When Bad Things Happen To Other People*. London: Routledge, 2000.

Powell, Jonathan and Jeremy Paterson, eds. *Cicero the Advocate*. Oxford: Oxford University Press, 2004.

Preiss, Théo, "Justification in Johannine Thought,' in *Life in Christ*. Trans. Harold Knight. Studies in Biblical Theology 13; Chicago: Alec R. Allenson, 1954, 9-31.

Race, William H. *Pindar I*. LCL; Cambridge: Harvard University Press, 1997.

Rankin, David. "Was Tertullian a Jurist?" *Studia Patristica* 31 (1997), 335-342.

–. *Tertullian and the Church*. Cambridge: Cambridge University Press, 1995.

Relihan, Joel C. *Ancient Menippean Satire*. Baltimore: Johns Hopkins, 1993.

Ricouer, Paul. *Essays on Biblical Interpretation*. ed. Lewis S. Mudge; Philadelphia: Fortress, 1980.

Robinson, H. Wheeler. "The Council of Yahweh," *JTS* 45 (1944), 151-157.

Roberts, J. J. M. "Yahweh's Summons to Job: The Exploitation of a Legal Metaphor," *Restoration Quarterly* 16 (1973), 159-65.

Rod, David. "Judgment as an Element of Audience Response in Aristotle's *Poetics*," *Theatre Annual* 36 (1981) 1-19.

Roetzel, Calvin. *Judgment in the Community: A Study of the Relationship between Eschatology and Ecclesiology in Paul*. Leiden: Brill, 1972.

Rohde, Erwin. *Psyche: The Cult of Souls and Belief in Immortality among the Greeks*. New York: Harcourt, Brace & Co., 1925.

Rowland, Christopher. *The Open Heaven: A Study of Apocalyptic in Judaism and Early Christianity*. New York: Crossroad, 1982.

Rubenstein, Jeffrey. *The Culture of the Babylonian Talmud*. Baltimore: Johns Hopkins University Press, 2003.

–. *Talmudic Stories: Narrative Art, Composition, and Culture*. Baltimore: Johns Hopkins University Press, 1999.

Rubinstein, Lene. *Litigation and Cooperation: Supporting Speakers in the Courts of Classical Athens*. Stuttgart: Franz Steiner Verlag, 2000.

Russell, Daniel C. "Misunderstanding the Myth in the Gorgias," *SJPh* 39 (2001), 557-574.

Rutler, George. *The Impatience of Job*. Illinois: Sherwood Sudgen & Co., 1981.

Sanders, E. P. *Paul and Palestinian Judaism*. Minneapolis: Fortress Press, 1976.

Sayler, Gwendolyn B. *Have the Promises Failed? A Literary Analysis of 2 Baruch*. SBL Dissertation Series 72; Chico, CA: Scholars Press, 1984.

Scafuro, Adele. *The Forensic Stage: Settling Disputes in Graeco-Roman New Comedy*. Cambridge: Cambridge University Press, 1997.

Schechter, Solomon. *Aspects of Rabbinic Theology*. Trans. L. Finkelstein; Woodstock, VT: Jewish Lights, 1993.

Scheindlin, Raymond. *The Book of Job*. New York: W.W. Norton & Co, 1998.

Schnackenburg, Rudolf. *The Gospel According to St. John I*. Trans Kevin Smyth; New York: Herder and Herder, 1968.

–. *The Gospel According to St. John II*. New York: Seabury Press, 1980.

–. *The Gospel According to John III*. New York: Crossroad, 1982.

Schneemelcher, Wilhelm, ed. *New Testament Apocrypha*. 2 vols. Louisville: Westminster/John Knox Press, 1991-1992.

Schökel, Luis Alonso. "Towards a Dramatic Reading of the Book of Job," *Semeia* 7 (1977), 45-61.

Scholnick, Sylvia Huberman. "Poetry in the Courtroom: Job 38-41" in Elaine R. Follis, ed. *Directions in Biblical Hebrew Poetry*. JSOT Supp 40; Sheffield: University of Sheffield, 1987, 185-204.

–. "The Meaning of *Mišpat* in the Book of Job," *JBL* 101 (1982), 521-529.

–. "Lawsuit Drama in the Book of Job." PhD. Diss. Brandeis University, 1975.

Schreiner, Thomas. "Did Paul Believe in Justification by Works? Another Look at Romans 2," *BBR* 3 (1993) 131-158.

Schwartz, Saundra. *Courtroom Scenes in the Ancient Greek Novels*. Phd. Diss. Columbia University, 1998.

Schüssler Fiorenza, Elisabeth. *The Book of Revelation: Justice and Judgment*. Minneapolis: Fortress Press, 1998.

Segal, Alan. *Two Powers in Heaven: Early Rabbinic Reports about Christianity and Gnosticism*. Leiden: Brill, 1977.

Segal, Erich, ed. *Greek Tragedy: Modern Essays in Criticism*. New York: Harper and Row, 1983.

Segal, Michael. *The Book of Jubilees: Rewritten Bible, Redaction, Ideology and Theodicy*. Leiden: Brill, 2007.

Senior, Donald. *The Passion Narrative According to Matthew: A Redactional Study*. Leuven: Peeters, 1975.

Shaw, Brent. "Judicial Nightmares and Christian Memory," *JECS* 11 (2003) 533-563.

Silverstein, Theodore and Anthony Hilhorst, *Apocalypse of Paul: A New Critical Edition of Three Long Latin Versions*. Geneva: Patrick Cramer, 1997.

Sim, David C. *Apocalyptic Eschatology in the Gospel of Matthew*. Cambridge: Cambridge University Press, 1996.

Sisson, Jonathan Paige. "Intercession and the Denial of Peace in 1 Enoch 12-16," *HAR* 11 (1987) 371-386.

Sloyan, Gerard S. *Jesus on Trial: A Study of the Gospels*. Second Edition; Minneapolis: Fortress, 2006.

Smalley, Stephen S. "The Paraclete: Pneumatology in the Johannine Gospel and Apocalypse," in R. A. Culpepper and C. Clifton Black, eds. *Exploring the Gospel of John: In Honor of D. Moody Smith*. Louisville, KY: Westminster John Knox Press, 1996, 289-300.

Smyth, H. W. *Aeschylus I*. LCL; Cambridge: Harvard University Press, 1922.

Snodgrass, Klyne R. "Justification by Grace – To the Doers: An Analysis of the Place of Romans 2 in the Theology of Paul," *NTS* 32 (1986) 72-93.

Sourvinou-Inwood, Christiane. "Crime and Punishment: Tityos, Tantalos and Sisyphos in *Odyssey* 11," *BICS* 33 (1986) 37-58.

Steindorff, Georg. *Die Apokalypse des Elias, eine unbekannte Apokalypse und Bruchstücke der Sophonias-Apokalypse.* Texte und Untersuchungen zur Geschichte der altchristlichen Literatur 17.3a; Leipzig: J. C. Hinrichs, 1899.

Stern, David. "*Imitatio Hominis*: Anthropomorphism and the Character(s) of God in Rabbinic Literature," *Prooftexts* 12 (1992), 151-174.

–. *Parables in Midrash: Narrative and Exegesis in Rabbinic Literature.* Cambridge, MA: Harvard University Press, 1991.

–. "Rhetoric and Midrash: The Case of the Mashal," *Prooftexts* 1 (1981) 261-291.

Stone, Michael. E. *Fourth Ezra.* Hermeneia; Minneapolis: Fortress, 1990.

–. *Features of the Eschatology of IV Ezra.* Atlanta: Scholars Press, 1989.

–. "The Way of the Most High and the Injustice of God in 4 Ezra," in R. van den Broek, T. Baarda, and J. Mansfeld, eds. *Knowledge of God between Alexander and Constantine.* Leiden: Brill, 1989, 132-42.

–. "Coherence and Inconsistency in the Apocalypses: The Case of 'the End' in 4 Ezra," *JBL* 102 (1983) 229-43.

–. "The Metamorphosis of Ezra: Jewish Apocalypse and Medieval Vision," *JTS* NS 33 (1982), 1-18.

–. *The Testament of Abraham: The Greek Recensions.* T&T 2: Ps. Series 2. Missoula: SBL, 1972.

Synofzik, E. *Die Gerichts- und Vergeltungsaussagen bei Paulus, Eine traditionsgeschichtliche Untersuchung.* Göttingen: Vandenhoek & Ruprecht, 1977.

Thompson, A. L. *Responsibility for Evil in the Theodicy of IV Ezra.* SBLDS 29; Missoula, MT: Scholars Press, 1977.

Tiller, Patrick A. *A Commentary on the Animal Apocalypse of 1 Enoch.* Atlanta: Scholars, 1993.

Tischendorff, Constantin von. *Apocalypses apocryphae Mosis, Esdrae, Pauli, Johannis, item Mariae dormito.* Lipsiae: Herm. Mendelsohn, 1866.

Tonstad, Sigve K. *Saving God's Reputation: The Theological Function of* Pistis Iesou *in the Cosmic Narratives of Revelation.* New York: T & T Clark, 2006.

Tsagarakis, Odysseus. "*Odyssey* 11: The Question of the Sources," in Øivind Andersen and Matthew Dickie, eds. *Homer's World: Fiction, Tradition, Reality.* Bergen: Norwegian Institute at Athens, 1995, 123-132.

Tyson, Joseph B. *Marcion and Luke-Acts: A Defining Struggle.* Columbia, SC: University of South Carolina Press, 2006.

Turner, Nigel. "The Testament of Abraham: Problems in Biblical Greek," *NTS* 1 (1955), 219-23.

Urbach, Ephraim E. *The Sages, their Concepts and Beliefs.* Jerusalem: Magnes Press, 1979.

VanderKam, James C. *The Book of Jubilees.* Sheffield: Sheffield Academic, 2001.

–. *Enoch and the Growth of an Apocalyptic Tradition.* CBQ Monograph Series 16; Washington, DC: Catholic University of America, 1984.

– and William Adler, eds. *The Jewish Apocalyptic Heritage in Early Christianity* . Minneapolis: Fortress Press, 1996.

VanLandingham, Chris. *Judgment & Justification in Early Judaism and the Apostle Paul.* Peabody, MA: Hendrickson, 2006.

Vermeule, Emily. *Aspects of Death in Early Greek Art and Poetry.* Berkeley: University of California Press, 1979.

Vernant, Jean-Pierre and Pierre Vidal-Naquet, *Myth and Tragedy in Ancient Greece.* New York: Zone, 1988.

Visser, A. J. "A Bird's-Eye View of Ancient Christian Eschatology," *Numen* 14 (1967) 4-22.

Ward, Roy Bowen. "Abraham Traditions in Early Christianity," *SCS* 2 (1972), 165-179.

Ward, S. P. *Penology and Eschatology in Plato's Myths.* Studies in the History of Philosophy 65; Lewiston: Edwin Mellen Press, 2002.

Water, Rick van de. "Michael or Yhwh? Toward Identifying Melchizedek in 11Q13," *JSOP* 16 (2006), 75-86.

Watson, Nigel M. "Justified by Faith, judged by Works – an Antinomy?" *NTS* 29 (1983), 209-221.

Weinfeld, Moshe. *Social Justice in Ancient Israel.* Minneapolis: Fortress Press, 1995.

–. "Ancient Near Eastern patterns in prophetic literature," *VT* 27 (1977) 178-195.

Weiss, Dov. "Between Values and Theology: The Case of Salvation through Children in Rabbinic Thought – Part 1," *Milin Havivin* 3 (2007), 1-15.

Wengst, Klaus. "Aspects of the Last Judgment in the Gospel According to Matthew" in Henning Graf Reventlow, ed. *Eschatology in the Bible and in Jewish and Christian Tradition.* JSOT Supp 243; Sheffield: Sheffield Academic, 1997) 233-245.

Westermann, Claus. *Basic Forms of Prophetic Speech.* Philadelphia: Westminster, 1967.

Willett, Tom W. *Eschatology in the Theodicies of 2 Baruch and 4 Ezra.* JsoP Supp Series 4; Sheffield: Sheffield Academic, 1989.

Wilson, Alistair. *"When will These Things Happen?"* A Study of Jesus as Judge in Matthew 21-25. Waynesboro, GA: Paternoster, 2004.

Wilson, Stephen G. *Related Strangers: Jews and Christians 70-170 CE.* Minneapolis: Fortress, 1995.

Wischmeyer, Oda. "Römer 2.1-24 als Teil der Gerichtsrede des Paulus gegen die Menschheit," *NTS* 52 (2006), 356-376.

Wise, Jennifer. *Dionysus Writes: The Invention of Theatre in Ancient Greek.* Ithaca: Cornell University Press, 1998.

Wolde, Ellen van, ed. *Job's God.* London: SCM, 2004.

Wright, George E. "The Lawsuit of God: A Form-Critical Study of Deuteronomy 32," in Bernhard Anderson and Walter Harrelson, eds. *Israel's Prophetic Heritage.* New York: Harper & Brothers, 1962, 26-67.

Wright, N. T. *What St. Paul Really Said.* Grand Rapids, MI: William B. Eerdmans, 1997.

Würthwein, Ernst. "Der Ursprung der prophetischen Gerichtsrede," *Wort und Existenz: Studien zum Alten Testament.* Göttingen: Vandenhoeck & Ruprecht, 1970, 120-24.

Yinger, Kent. *Paul, Judaism, and Judgment according to Deeds.* Cambridge: Cambridge University Press, 1999.

Zakovitch, Yair. "Psalm 82 and Biblical Exegesis" in Chaim Cohen, Avi Hurwitz, and Shalom Paul, eds. *Sefer Moshe: The Moshe Weinfeld Jubilee Volume.* Winona Lake, IN: Eisenbrauns, 2004, 213-228.

Ziolkowski, Theodore. *The Mirror of Justice: Literary Reflections of Legal Crises.* Princeton: Princeton University Press, 1997.

# Index of Ancient Sources

## I. Old Testament and Apocrypha

# II. New Testament

# III. Pseudepigrapha and Apocrypha

# IV. Other Ancient Works

## A. Greco Roman Works

# B. Rabbinic Works

# C. Other Works

# Index of Modern Authors

# Index of Subjects

# Wissenschaftliche Untersuchungen zum Neuen Testament

*Alphabetical Index of the First and Second Series*

*Bennema, Cornelis:* The Power of Saving Wisdom. 2002. *Vol. II/148.*

*Bergman, Jan:* see *Kieffer, René*

*Bergmeier, Roland:* Das Gesetz im Römerbrief und andere Studien zum Neuen Testament. 2000. *Vol. 121.*

*Bernett, Monika:* Der Kaiserkult in Judäa unter den Herodiern und Römern. 2007. *Vol. 203.*

*Betz, Otto:* Jesus, der Messias Israels. 1987. *Vol. 42.*

– Jesus, der Herr der Kirche. 1990. *Vol. 52.*

*Beyschlag, Karlmann:* Simon Magus und die christliche Gnosis. 1974. *Vol. 16.*

*Bieringer, Reimund:* see *Koester, Craig.*

*Bittner, Wolfgang J.:* Jesu Zeichen im Johannesevangelium. 1987. *Vol. II/26.*

*Bjerkelund, Carl J.:* Tauta Egeneto. 1987. *Vol. 40.*

*Blackburn, Barry Lee:* Theios Aner and the Markan Miracle Traditions. 1991. *Vol. II/40.*

*Blanton IV, Thomas R.:* Constructing a New Covenant. 2007. *Vol. II/233.*

*Bock, Darrell L.:* Blasphemy and Exaltation in Judaism and the Final Examination of Jesus. 1998. *Vol. II/106.*

– and *Robert L. Webb* (Ed.): Key Events in the Life of the Historical Jesus. 2009. *Vol. 247.*

*Bockmuehl, Markus:* The Remembered Peter. 2010. *Vol. 262.*

– Revelation and Mystery in Ancient Judaism and Pauline Christianity. 1990. *Vol. II/36.*

*Bøe, Sverre:* Cross-Bearing in Luke. 2010. *Vol. II/278.*

– Gog and Magog. 2001. *Vol. II/135.*

*Böhlig, Alexander:* Gnosis und Synkretismus. Vol. 1 1989. *Vol. 47* – Vol. 2 1989. *Vol. 48.*

*Böhm, Martina:* Samarien und die Samaritai bei Lukas. 1999. *Vol. II/111.*

*Börstinghaus, Jens:* Sturmfahrt und Schiffbruch. 2010. *Vol. II/274.*

*Böttrich, Christfried:* Weltweisheit – Menschheitsethik – Urkult. 1992. *Vol. II/50.*

– and *Herzer, Jens* (Ed.): Josephus und das Neue Testament. 2007. *Vol. 209.*

*Bolyki, János:* Jesu Tischgemeinschaften. 1997. *Vol. II/96.*

*Bosman, Philip:* Conscience in Philo and Paul. 2003. *Vol. II/166.*

*Bovon, François:* New Testament and Christian Apocrypha. 2009. *Vol. 237.*

– Studies in Early Christianity. 2003. *Vol. 161.*

*Brändl, Martin:* Der Agon bei Paulus. 2006. *Vol. II/222.*

*Braun, Heike:* Geschichte des Gottesvolkes und christliche Identität. 2010. *Vol. II/279.*

*Breytenbach, Cilliers:* see *Frey, Jörg.*

*Brocke, Christoph vom:* Thessaloniki – Stadt des Kassander und Gemeinde des Paulus. 2001. *Vol. II/125.*

*Brunson, Andrew:* Psalm 118 in the Gospel of John. 2003. *Vol. II/158.*

*Büchli, Jörg:* Der Poimandres – ein paganisiertes Evangelium. 1987. *Vol. II/27.*

*Bühner, Jan A.:* Der Gesandte und sein Weg im 4. Evangelium. 1977. *Vol. II/2.*

*Burchard, Christoph:* Untersuchungen zu Joseph und Aseneth. 1965. *Vol. 8.*

– Studien zur Theologie, Sprache und Umwelt des Neuen Testaments. Ed. by D. Sänger. 1998. *Vol. 107.*

*Burnett, Richard:* Karl Barth's Theological Exegesis. 2001. *Vol. II/145.*

*Byron, John:* Slavery Metaphors in Early Judaism and Pauline Christianity. 2003. *Vol. II/162.*

*Byrskog, Samuel:* Story as History – History as Story. 2000. *Vol. 123.*

*Cancik, Hubert* (Ed.): Markus-Philologie. 1984. *Vol. 33.*

*Capes, David B.:* Old Testament Yaweh Texts in Paul's Christology. 1992. *Vol. II/47.*

*Caragounis, Chrys C.:* The Development of Greek and the New Testament. 2004. *Vol. 167.*

– The Son of Man. 1986. *Vol. 38.*

– see *Fridrichsen, Anton.*

*Carleton Paget, James:* The Epistle of Barnabas. 1994. *Vol. II/64.*

– Jews, Christians and Jewish Christians in Antiquity. 2010. *Vol. 251.*

*Carson, D.A., O'Brien, Peter T.* and *Mark Seifrid* (Ed.): Justification and Variegated Nomism. Vol. 1: The Complexities of Second Temple Judaism. 2001. *Vol. II/140.* Vol. 2: The Paradoxes of Paul. 2004. *Vol. II/181.*

*Chae, Young Sam:* Jesus as the Eschatological Davidic Shepherd. 2006. *Vol. II/216.*

*Chapman, David W.:* Ancient Jewish and Christian Perceptions of Crucifixion. 2008. *Vol. II/244.*

*Chester, Andrew:* Messiah and Exaltation. 2007. *Vol. 207.*

*Chibici-Revneanu, Nicole:* Die Herrlichkeit des Verherrlichten. 2007. *Vol. II/231.*

*Ciampa, Roy E.:* The Presence and Function of Scripture in Galatians 1 and 2. 1998. *Vol. II/102.*

*Classen, Carl Joachim:* Rhetorical Criticsm of the New Testament. 2000. *Vol. 128.*

*Colpe, Carsten:* Griechen – Byzantiner – Semiten – Muslime. 2008. *Vol. 221.*

- Iranier – Aramäer – Hebräer – Hellenen. 2003. *Vol. 154.*

*Cook, John G.* Roman Attitudes Towards the Christians. 2010. *Vol. 261.*

*Coote, Robert B.* (Ed.): see *Weissenrieder, Annette.*

*Coppins, Wayne:* The Interpretation of Freedom in the Letters of Paul. 2009. *Vol. II/261.*

*Crump, David:* Jesus the Intercessor. 1992. *Vol. II/49.*

*Dahl, Nils Alstrup:* Studies in Ephesians. 2000. *Vol. 131.*

*Daise, Michael A.:* Feasts in John. 2007. *Vol. II/229*

*Deines, Roland:* Die Gerechtigkeit der Tora im Reich des Messias. 2004. *Vol. 177.*
- Jüdische Steingefäße und pharisäische Frömmigkeit. 1993. *Vol. II/52.*
- Die Pharisäer. 1997. *Vol. 101.*

*Deines, Roland* and *Karl-Wilhelm Niebuhr* (Ed.): Philo und das Neue Testament. 2004. *Vol. 172.*

*Dennis, John A.:* Jesus' Death and the Gathering of True Israel. 2006. *Vol. 217.*

*Dettwiler, Andreas* and *Jean Zumstein* (Ed.): Kreuzestheologie im Neuen Testament. 2002. *Vol. 151.*

*Dickson, John P.:* Mission-Commitment in Ancient Judaism and in the Pauline Communities. 2003. *Vol. II/159.*

*Dietzfelbinger, Christian:* Der Abschied des Kommenden. 1997. *Vol. 95.*

*Dimitrov, Ivan Z., James D.G. Dunn, Ulrich Luz* and *Karl-Wilhelm Niebuhr* (Ed.): Das Alte Testament als christliche Bibel in orthodoxer und westlicher Sicht. 2004. *Vol. 174.*

*Dobbeler, Axel von:* Glaube als Teilhabe. 1987. *Vol. II/22.*

*Docherty, Susan E.:* The Use of the Old Testament in Hebrews. 2009. *Vol. II/260.*

*Downs, David J.:* The Offering of the Gentiles. 2008. *Vol. II/248.*

*Dryden, J. de Waal:* Theology and Ethics in 1 Peter. 2006. *Vol. II/209.*

*Dübbers, Michael:* Christologie und Existenz im Kolosserbrief. 2005. *Vol. II/191.*

*Dunn, James D.G.:* The New Perspective on Paul. 2005. *Vol. 185.*

*Dunn, James D.G.* (Ed.): Jews and Christians. 1992. *Vol. 66.*
- Paul and the Mosaic Law. 1996. *Vol. 89.*
- see *Dimitrov, Ivan Z.*

-, *Hans Klein, Ulrich Luz,* and *Vasile Mihoc* (Ed.): Auslegung der Bibel in orthodoxer und westlicher Perspektive. 2000. *Vol. 130.*

*Ebel, Eva:* Die Attraktivität früher christlicher Gemeinden. 2004. *Vol. II/178.*

*Ebertz, Michael N.:* Das Charisma des Gekreuzigten. 1987. *Vol. 45.*

*Eckstein, Hans-Joachim:* Der Begriff Syneidesis bei Paulus. 1983. *Vol. II/10.*
- Verheißung und Gesetz. 1996. *Vol. 86.*

*Ego, Beate:* Im Himmel wie auf Erden. 1989. *Vol. II/34.*

*Ego, Beate, Armin Lange* and *Peter Pilhofer* (Ed.): Gemeinde ohne Tempel – Community without Temple. 1999. *Vol. 118.*
- and *Helmut Merkel* (Ed.): Religiöses Lernen in der biblischen, frühjüdischen und frühchristlichen Überlieferung. 2005. *Vol. 180.*

*Eisele, Wilfried:* Welcher Thomas? 2010. *Vol. 259.*

*Eisen, Ute E.:* see *Paulsen, Henning.*

*Elledge, C.D.:* Life after Death in Early Judaism. 2006. *Vol. II/208.*

*Ellis, E. Earle:* Prophecy and Hermeneutic in Early Christianity. 1978. *Vol. 18.*
- The Old Testament in Early Christianity. 1991. *Vol. 54.*

*Elmer, Ian J.:* Paul, Jerusalem and the Judaisers. 2009. *Vol. II/258.*

*Endo, Masanobu:* Creation and Christology. 2002. *Vol. 149.*

*Ennulat, Andreas:* Die 'Minor Agreements'. 1994. *Vol. II/62.*

*Ensor, Peter W.:* Jesus and His 'Works'. 1996. *Vol. II/85.*

*Eskola, Timo:* Messiah and the Throne. 2001. *Vol. II/142.*
- Theodicy and Predestination in Pauline Soteriology. 1998. *Vol. II/100.*

*Farelly, Nicolas:* The Disciples in the Fourth Gospel. 2010. *Vol. II/290.*

*Fatehi, Mehrdad:* The Spirit's Relation to the Risen Lord in Paul. 2000. *Vol. II/128.*

*Feldmeier, Reinhard:* Die Krisis des Gottessohnes. 1987. *Vol. II/21.*
- Die Christen als Fremde. 1992. *Vol. 64.*

*Feldmeier, Reinhard* and *Ulrich Heckel* (Ed.): Die Heiden. 1994. *Vol. 70.*

*Finnern, Sönke:* Narratologie und biblische Exegese. 2010. *Vol. II/285.*

*Fletcher-Louis, Crispin H.T.:* Luke-Acts: Angels, Christology and Soteriology. 1997. *Vol. II/94.*

*Förster, Niclas:* Marcus Magus. 1999. *Vol. 114.*

*Forbes, Christopher Brian:* Prophecy and Inspired Speech in Early Christianity and its Hellenistic Environment. 1995. *Vol. II/75.*

*Fornberg, Tord:* see *Fridrichsen, Anton.*

*Fossum, Jarl E.:* The Name of God and the Angel of the Lord. 1985. *Vol. 36.*

*Foster, Paul:* Community, Law and Mission in Matthew's Gospel. *Vol. II/177.*

*Fotopoulos, John:* Food Offered to Idols in Roman Corinth. 2003. *Vol. II/151.*

*Frank, Nicole:* Der Kolosserbrief im Kontext des paulinischen Erbes. 2009. *Vol. II/271.*

*Frenschkowski, Marco:* Offenbarung und Epiphanie. Vol. 1 1995. *Vol. II/79* – Vol. 2 1997. *Vol. II/80.*

*Frey, Jörg:* Eugen Drewermann und die biblische Exegese. 1995. *Vol. II/71.*

– Die johanneische Eschatologie. Vol. I. 1997. *Vol. 96.* – Vol. II. 1998. *Vol. 110.* – Vol. III. 2000. *Vol. 117.*

*Frey, Jörg* and *Cilliers Breytenbach* (Ed.): Aufgabe und Durchführung einer Theologie des Neuen Testaments. 2007. *Vol. 205.*

– *Jens Herzer, Martina Janßen* and *Clare K. Rothschild* (Ed.): Pseudepigraphie und Verfasserfiktion in frühchristlichen Briefen. 2009. *Vol. 246.*

– *Stefan Krauter* and *Hermann Lichtenberger* (Ed.): Heil und Geschichte. 2009. *Vol. 248.*

– and *Udo Schnelle (Ed.):* Kontexte des Johannesevangeliums. 2004. *Vol. 175.*

– and *Jens Schröter* (Ed.): Deutungen des Todes Jesu im Neuen Testament. 2005. *Vol. 181.*

– Jesus in apokryphen Evangelienüberlieferungen. 2010. *Vol. 254.*

–, *Jan G. van der Watt,* and *Ruben Zimmermann* (Ed.): Imagery in the Gospel of John. 2006. *Vol. 200.*

*Freyne, Sean:* Galilee and Gospel. 2000. *Vol. 125.*

*Fridrichsen, Anton:* Exegetical Writings. Edited by C.C. Caragounis and T. Fornberg. 1994. *Vol. 76.*

*Gadenz, Pablo T.:* Called from the Jews and from the Gentiles. 2009. *Vol. II/267.*

*Gäbel, Georg:* Die Kulttheologie des Hebräerbriefes. 2006. *Vol. II/212.*

*Gäckle, Volker:* Die Starken und die Schwachen in Korinth und in Rom. 2005. *Vol. 200.*

*Garlington, Don B.:* 'The Obedience of Faith'. 1991. *Vol. II/38.*

– Faith, Obedience, and Perseverance. 1994. *Vol. 79.*

*Garnet, Paul:* Salvation and Atonement in the Qumran Scrolls. 1977. *Vol. II/3.*

*Gemünden, Petra von* (Ed.): see *Weissenrieder, Annette.*

*Gese, Michael:* Das Vermächtnis des Apostels. 1997. *Vol. II/99.*

*Gheorghita, Radu:* The Role of the Septuagint in Hebrews. 2003. *Vol. II/160.*

*Gordley, Matthew E.:* The Colossian Hymn in Context. 2007. *Vol. II/228.*

*Gräbe, Petrus J.:* The Power of God in Paul's Letters. 2000, ²2008. *Vol. II/123.*

*Gräßer, Erich:* Der Alte Bund im Neuen. 1985. *Vol. 35.*

– Forschungen zur Apostelgeschichte. 2001. *Vol. 137.*

*Grappe, Christian* (Ed.): Le Repas de Dieu / Das Mahl Gottes. 2004. *Vol. 169.*

*Gray, Timothy C.:* The Temple in the Gospel of Mark. 2008. *Vol. II/242.*

*Green, Joel B.:* The Death of Jesus. 1988. *Vol. II/33.*

*Gregg, Brian Han:* The Historical Jesus and the Final Judgment Sayings in Q. 2005. *Vol. II/207.*

*Gregory, Andrew:* The Reception of Luke and Acts in the Period before Irenaeus. 2003. *Vol. II/169.*

*Grindheim, Sigurd:* The Crux of Election. 2005. *Vol. II/202.*

*Gundry, Robert H.:* The Old is Better. 2005. *Vol. 178.*

*Gundry Volf, Judith M.:* Paul and Perseverance. 1990. *Vol. II/37.*

*Häußer, Detlef:* Christusbekenntnis und Jesusüberlieferung bei Paulus. 2006. *Vol. 210.*

*Hafemann, Scott J.:* Suffering and the Spirit. 1986. *Vol. II/19.*

– Paul, Moses, and the History of Israel. 1995. *Vol. 81.*

*Hahn, Ferdinand:* Studien zum Neuen Testament.
Vol. I: Grundsatzfragen, Jesusforschung, Evangelien. 2006. *Vol. 191.*
Vol. II: Bekenntnisbildung und Theologie in urchristlicher Zeit. 2006. *Vol. 192.*

*Hahn, Johannes (Ed.):* Zerstörungen des Jerusalemer Tempels. 2002. *Vol. 147.*

*Hamid-Khani, Saeed:* Relevation and Concealment of Christ. 2000. *Vol. II/120.*

*Hannah, Darrel D.:* Michael and Christ. 1999. *Vol. II/109.*

*Hardin, Justin K.:* Galatians and the Imperial Cult? 2007. *Vol. II /237.*

*Harrison; James R.:* Paul's Language of Grace in Its Graeco-Roman Context. 2003. *Vol. II/172.*

*Hartman, Lars:* Text-Centered New Testament Studies. Ed. von D. Hellholm. 1997. *Vol. 102.*

*Hartog, Paul:* Polycarp and the New Testament. 2001. *Vol. II/134.*

*Hays, Christopher M.:* Luke's Wealth Ethics. 2010. *Vol. 275.*

*Heckel, Theo K.:* Der Innere Mensch. 1993. *Vol. II/53.*

– Vom Evangelium des Markus zum vier-
gestaltigen Evangelium. 1999. *Vol. 120.*
*Heckel, Ulrich:* Kraft in Schwachheit. 1993.
*Vol. II/56.*
– Der Segen im Neuen Testament. 2002.
*Vol. 150.*
– see *Feldmeier, Reinhard.*
– see *Hengel, Martin.*
*Heemstra, Marius:* The Fiscus Judaicus and the
Parting of the Ways. 2010. *Vol. II/277.*
*Heiligenthal, Roman:* Werke als Zeichen. 1983.
*Vol. II/9.*
*Heininger, Bernhard:* Die Inkulturation des
Christentums. 2010. *Vol. 255.*
*Heliso, Desta:* Pistis and the Righteous One.
2007. *Vol. II/235.*
*Hellholm, D.:* see *Hartman, Lars.*
*Hemer, Colin J.:* The Book of Acts in the Setting
of Hellenistic History. 1989. *Vol. 49.*
*Hengel, Martin:* Jesus und die Evangelien.
Kleine Schriften V. 2007. *Vol. 211.*
– Die johanneische Frage. 1993. *Vol. 67.*
– Judaica et Hellenistica. Kleine Schriften I.
1996. *Vol. 90.*
– Judaica, Hellenistica et Christiana. Kleine
Schriften II. 1999. *Vol. 109.*
– Judentum und Hellenismus. 1969, ³1988.
*Vol. 10.*
– Paulus und Jakobus. Kleine Schriften III.
2002. *Vol. 141.*
– Studien zur Christologie. Kleine Schriften
IV. 2006. *Vol. 201.*
– Studien zum Urchristentum. Kleine Schrif-
ten VI. 2008. *Vol. 234.*
– Theologische, historische und biographische
Skizzen. Kleine Schriften VII. 2010.
*Vol. 253.*
– and *Anna Maria Schwemer:* Paulus zwi-
schen Damaskus und Antiochien. 1998.
*Vol. 108.*
– Der messianische Anspruch Jesu und die
Anfänge der Christologie. 2001. *Vol. 138.*
– Die vier Evangelien und das eine Evange-
lium von Jesus Christus. 2008. *Vol. 224.*
*Hengel, Martin* and *Ulrich Heckel* (Ed.): Paulus
und das antike Judentum. 1991. *Vol. 58.*
– and *Hermut Löhr* (Ed.): Schriftauslegung
im antiken Judentum und im Urchristentum.
1994. *Vol. 73.*
– and *Anna Maria Schwemer* (Ed.): Königs-
herrschaft Gottes und himmlischer Kult.
1991. *Vol. 55.*
– Die Septuaginta. 1994. *Vol. 72.*
–, *Siegfried Mittmann* and *Anna Maria
Schwemer* (Ed.): La Cité de Dieu / Die Stadt
Gottes. 2000. *Vol. 129.*

*Hentschel, Anni:* Diakonia im Neuen Testament.
2007. *Vol. 226.*
*Hernández Jr., Juan:* Scribal Habits and Theo-
logical Influence in the Apocalypse. 2006.
*Vol. II/218.*
*Herrenbrück, Fritz:* Jesus und die Zöllner. 1990.
*Vol. II/41.*
*Herzer, Jens:* Paulus oder Petrus? 1998.
*Vol. 103.*
– see *Böttrich, Christfried.*
– see *Frey, Jörg.*
*Hill, Charles E.:* From the Lost Teaching of
Polycarp. 2005. *Vol. 186.*
*Hoegen-Rohls, Christina:* Der nachösterliche
Johannes. 1996. *Vol. II/84.*
*Hoffmann, Matthias Reinhard:* The Destroyer
and the Lamb. 2005. *Vol. II/203.*
*Hofius, Otfried:* Katapausis. 1970. *Vol. 11.*
– Der Vorhang vor dem Thron Gottes. 1972.
*Vol. 14.*
– Der Christushymnus Philipper 2,6–11.
1976, ²1991. *Vol. 17.*
– Paulusstudien. 1989, ²1994. *Vol. 51.*
– Neutestamentliche Studien. 2000. *Vol. 132.*
– Paulusstudien II. 2002. *Vol. 143.*
– Exegetische Studien. 2008. *Vol. 223.*
– and *Hans-Christian Kammler:* Johannes-
studien. 1996. *Vol. 88.*
*Holloway, Paul A.:* Coping with Prejudice.
2009. *Vol. 244.*
*Holmberg, Bengt* (Ed.): Exploring Early Chris-
tian Identity. 2008. *Vol. 226.*
– and *Mikael Winninge* (Ed.): Identity Forma-
tion in the New Testament. 2008. *Vol. 227.*
*Holtz, Traugott:* Geschichte und Theologie des
Urchristentums. 1991. *Vol. 57.*
*Hommel, Hildebrecht:* Sebasmata.
Vol. 1 1983. *Vol. 31.*
Vol. 2 1984. *Vol. 32.*
*Horbury, William:* Herodian Judaism and New
Testament Study. 2006. *Vol. 193.*
*Horn, Friedrich Wilhelm* and *Ruben Zim-
mermann* (Ed.): Jenseits von Indikativ und
Imperativ. Vol. 1. 2009. *Vol. 238.*
*Horst, Pieter W. van der:* Jews and Christians
in Their Graeco-Roman Context. 2006.
*Vol. 196.*
*Hultgård, Anders* and *Stig Norin* (Ed): Le Jour
de Dieu / Der Tag Gottes. 2009. *Vol. 245.*
*Hvalvik, Reidar:* The Struggle for Scripture and
Covenant. 1996. *Vol. II/82.*
*Jackson, Ryan:* New Creation in Paul's Letters.
2010. *Vol. II/272.*
*Janßen, Martina:* see *Frey, Jörg.*
*Jauhiainen, Marko:* The Use of Zechariah in
Revelation. 2005. *Vol. II/199.*

*Jensen, Morten H.:* Herod Antipas in Galilee. 2006; ²2010. *Vol. II/215.*

*Johns, Loren L.:* The Lamb Christology of the Apocalypse of John. 2003. *Vol. II/167.*

*Jossa, Giorgio:* Jews or Christians? 2006. *Vol. 202.*

*Joubert, Stephan:* Paul as Benefactor. 2000. *Vol. II/124.*

*Judge, E. A.:* The First Christians in the Roman World. 2008. *Vol. 229.*

*Jungbauer, Harry:* „Ehre Vater und Mutter". 2002. *Vol. II/146.*

*Kähler, Christoph:* Jesu Gleichnisse als Poesie und Therapie. 1995. *Vol. 78.*

*Kamlah, Ehrhard:* Die Form der katalogischen Paränese im Neuen Testament. 1964. *Vol. 7.*

*Kammler, Hans-Christian:* Christologie und Eschatologie. 2000. *Vol. 126.*

– Kreuz und Weisheit. 2003. *Vol. 159.*

– see *Hofius, Otfried.*

*Karakolis, Christos:* see *Alexeev, Anatoly A.*

*Karrer, Martin* und *Wolfgang Kraus* (Ed.): Die Septuaginta – Texte, Kontexte, Lebenswelten. 2008. *Vol. 219.*

– see *Kraus, Wolfgang.*

*Kelhoffer, James A.:* The Diet of John the Baptist. 2005. *Vol. 176.*

– Miracle and Mission. 1999. *Vol. II/112.*

*Kelley, Nicole:* Knowledge and Religious Authority in the Pseudo-Clementines. 2006. *Vol. II/213.*

*Kennedy, Joel:* The Recapitulation of Israel. 2008. *Vol. II/257.*

*Kensky, Meira Z.:* Trying Man, Trying God. 2010. *Vol. II/289.*

*Kieffer, René* and *Jan Bergman* (Ed.): La Main de Dieu / Die Hand Gottes. 1997. *Vol. 94.*

*Kierspel, Lars:* The Jews and the World in the Fourth Gospel. 2006. *Vol. 220.*

*Kim, Seyoon:* The Origin of Paul's Gospel. 1981, ²1984. *Vol. II/4.*

– Paul and the New Perspective. 2002. *Vol. 140.*

– "The 'Son of Man'" as the Son of God. 1983. *Vol. 30.*

*Klauck, Hans-Josef:* Religion und Gesellschaft im frühen Christentum. 2003. *Vol. 152.*

*Klein, Hans, Vasile Mihoc* und *Karl-Wilhelm Niebuhr* (Ed.): Das Gebet im Neuen Testament. Vierte, europäische orthodox-westliche Exegetenkonferenz in Sambata de Sus, 4. – 8. August 2007. 2009. Vol. 249.

– see Dunn, James D.G.

*Kleinknecht, Karl Th.:* Der leidende Gerechtfertigte. 1984, ²1988. *Vol. II/13.*

*Klinghardt, Matthias:* Gesetz und Volk Gottes. 1988. *Vol. II/32.*

*Kloppenborg, John S.:* The Tenants in the Vineyard. 2006, student edition 2010. *Vol. 195.*

*Koch, Michael:* Drachenkampf und Sonnenfrau. 2004. *Vol. II/184.*

*Koch, Stefan:* Rechtliche Regelung von Konflikten im frühen Christentum. 2004. *Vol. II/174.*

*Köhler, Wolf-Dietrich:* Rezeption des Matthäusevangeliums in der Zeit vor Irenäus. 1987. *Vol. II/24.*

*Köhn, Andreas:* Der Neutestamentler Ernst Lohmeyer. 2004. *Vol. II/180.*

*Koester, Craig* and *Reimund Bieringer* (Ed.): The Resurrection of Jesus in the Gospel of John. 2008. *Vol. 222.*

*Konradt, Matthias:* Israel, Kirche und die Völker im Matthäusevangelium. 2007. *Vol. 215.*

*Kooten, George H. van:* Cosmic Christology in Paul and the Pauline School. 2003. *Vol. II/171.*

– Paul's Anthropology in Context. 2008. *Vol. 232.*

*Korn, Manfred:* Die Geschichte Jesu in veränderter Zeit. 1993. *Vol. II/51.*

*Koskenniemi, Erkki:* Apollonios von Tyana in der neutestamentlichen Exegese. 1994. *Vol. II/61.*

– The Old Testament Miracle-Workers in Early Judaism. 2005. *Vol. II/206.*

*Kraus, Thomas J.:* Sprache, Stil und historischer Ort des zweiten Petrusbriefes. 2001. *Vol. II/136.*

*Kraus, Wolfgang:* Das Volk Gottes. 1996. *Vol. 85.*

– see *Karrer, Martin.*

– see *Walter, Nikolaus.*

– and *Martin Karrer* (Hrsg.): Die Septuaginta – Texte, Theologien, Einflüsse. 2010. *Bd. 252.*

– and *Karl-Wilhelm Niebuhr* (Ed.): Frühjudentum und Neues Testament im Horizont Biblischer Theologie. 2003. *Vol. 162.*

*Krauter, Stefan:* Studien zu Röm 13,1-7. 2009. *Vol. 243.*

– see *Frey, Jörg.*

*Kreplin, Matthias:* Das Selbstverständnis Jesu. 2001. *Vol. II/141.*

*Kuhn, Karl G.:* Achtzehngebet und Vaterunser und der Reim. 1950. *Vol. 1.*

*Kvalbein, Hans:* see *Ådna, Jostein.*

*Kwon, Yon-Gyong:* Eschatology in Galatians. 2004. *Vol. II/183.*

*Laansma, Jon:* I Will Give You Rest. 1997. *Vol. II/98.*

*Labahn, Michael:* Offenbarung in Zeichen und Wort. 2000. *Vol. II/117.*

*Lambers-Petry, Doris:* see *Tomson, Peter J.*

*Lange, Armin:* see *Ego, Beate.*

*Lampe, Peter:* Die stadtrömischen Christen in den ersten beiden Jahrhunderten. 1987, ²1989. *Vol. II/18.*

*Landmesser, Christof:* Wahrheit als Grundbegriff neutestamentlicher Wissenschaft. 1999. *Vol. 113.*

– Jüngerberufung und Zuwendung zu Gott. 2000. *Vol. 133.*

*Lau, Andrew:* Manifest in Flesh. 1996. *Vol. II/86.*

*Lawrence, Louise:* An Ethnography of the Gospel of Matthew. 2003. *Vol. II/165.*

*Lee, Aquila H.I.:* From Messiah to Preexistent Son. 2005. *Vol. II/192.*

*Lee, Pilchan:* The New Jerusalem in the Book of Relevation. 2000. *Vol. II/129.*

*Lee, Sang M.:* The Cosmic Drama of Salvation. 2010. *Vol. II/276.*

*Lee, Simon S.:* Jesus' Transfiguration and the Believers' Transformation. 2009. *Vol. II/265.*

*Lichtenberger, Hermann:* Das Ich Adams und das Ich der Menschheit. 2004. *Vol. 164.*

– see *Avemarie, Friedrich.*

– see *Frey, Jörg.*

*Lierman, John:* The New Testament Moses. 2004. *Vol. II/173.*

– (Ed.): Challenging Perspectives on the Gospel of John. 2006. *Vol. II/219.*

*Lieu, Samuel N.C.:* Manichaeism in the Later Roman Empire and Medieval China. ²1992. *Vol. 63.*

*Lindemann, Andreas:* Die Evangelien und die Apostelgeschichte. 2009. *Vol. 241.*

*Lincicum, David:* Paul and the Early Jewish Encounter with Deuteronomy. 2010. *Vol. II/284.*

*Lindgård, Fredrik:* Paul's Line of Thought in 2 Corinthians 4:16–5:10. 2004. *Vol. II/189.*

*Loader, William R.G.:* Jesus' Attitude Towards the Law. 1997. *Vol. II/97.*

*Löhr, Gebhard:* Verherrlichung Gottes durch Philosophie. 1997. *Vol. 97.*

*Löhr, Hermut:* Studien zum frühchristlichen und frühjüdischen Gebet. 2003. *Vol. 160.*

– see *Hengel, Martin.*

*Löhr, Winrich Alfried:* Basilides und seine Schule. 1995. *Vol. 83.*

*Lorenzen, Stefanie:* Das paulinische Eikon-Konzept. 2008. *Vol. II/250.*

*Luomanen, Petri:* Entering the Kingdom of Heaven. 1998. *Vol. II/101.*

*Luz, Ulrich:* see *Alexeev, Anatoly A.*

– see *Dunn, James D.G.*

*Mackay, Ian D.:* John's Raltionship with Mark. 2004. *Vol. II/182.*

*Mackie, Scott D.:* Eschatology and Exhortation in the Epistle to the Hebrews. 2006. *Vol. II/223.*

*Magda, Ksenija:* Paul's Territoriality and Mission Strategy. 2009. *Vol. II/266.*

*Maier, Gerhard:* Mensch und freier Wille. 1971. *Vol. 12.*

– Die Johannesoffenbarung und die Kirche. 1981. *Vol. 25.*

*Markschies, Christoph:* Valentinus Gnosticus? 1992. *Vol. 65.*

*Marshall, Jonathan:* Jesus, Patrons, and Benefactors. 2009. *Vol. II/259.*

*Marshall, Peter:* Enmity in Corinth: Social Conventions in Paul's Relations with the Corinthians. 1987. *Vol. II/23.*

*Martin, Dale B.:* see *Zangenberg, Jürgen.*

*Mayer, Annemarie:* Sprache der Einheit im Epheserbrief und in der Ökumene. 2002. *Vol. II/150.*

*Mayordomo, Moisés:* Argumentiert Paulus logisch? 2005. *Vol. 188.*

*McDonough, Sean M.:* YHWH at Patmos: Rev. 1:4 in its Hellenistic and Early Jewish Setting. 1999. *Vol. II/107.*

*McDowell, Markus:* Prayers of Jewish Women. 2006. *Vol. II/211.*

*McGlynn, Moyna:* Divine Judgement and Divine Benevolence in the Book of Wisdom. 2001. *Vol. II/139.*

*Meade, David G.:* Pseudonymity and Canon. 1986. *Vol. 39.*

*Meadors, Edward P.:* Jesus the Messianic Herald of Salvation. 1995. *Vol. II/72.*

*Meißner, Stefan:* Die Heimholung des Ketzers. 1996. *Vol. II/87.*

*Mell, Ulrich:* Die „anderen" Winzer. 1994. *Vol. 77.*

– see *Sänger, Dieter.*

*Mengel, Berthold:* Studien zum Philipperbrief. 1982. *Vol. II/8.*

*Merkel, Helmut:* Die Widersprüche zwischen den Evangelien. 1971. *Vol. 13.*

– see *Ego, Beate.*

*Merklein, Helmut:* Studien zu Jesus und Paulus. Vol. 1 1987. *Vol. 43.* – Vol. 2 1998. *Vol. 105.*

*Merkt, Andreas:* see *Nicklas, Tobias*

*Metzdorf, Christina:* Die Tempelaktion Jesu. 2003. *Vol. II/168.*

*Metzler, Karin:* Der griechische Begriff des Verzeihens. 1991. *Vol. II/44.*

*Metzner, Rainer:* Die Rezeption des Matthäusevangeliums im 1. Petrusbrief. 1995. *Vol. II/74.*

– Das Verständnis der Sünde im Johannesevangelium. 2000. *Vol. 122.*

*Mihoc, Vasile:* see *Dunn, James D.G.*

– see *Klein, Hans.*
*Mineshige, Kiyoshi:* Besitzverzicht und Almosen bei Lukas. 2003. *Vol. II/163.*
*Mittmann, Siegfried:* see *Hengel, Martin.*
*Mittmann-Richert, Ulrike:* Magnifikat und Benediktus. *1996. Vol. II/90.*
– Der Sühnetod des Gottesknechts. 2008. *Vol. 220.*
*Miura, Yuzuru:* David in Luke-Acts. 2007. *Vol. II/232.*
*Moll, Sebastian:* The Arch-Heretic Marcion. 2010. *Vol. 250.*
*Morales, Rodrigo J.:* The Spirit and the Restorat. 2010. *Vol. 282.*
*Mournet, Terence C.:* Oral Tradition and Literary Dependency. 2005. *Vol. II/195.*
*Mußner, Franz:* Jesus von Nazareth im Umfeld Israels und der Urkirche. Ed. von M. Theobald. 1998. *Vol. 111.*
*Mutschler, Bernhard:* Das Corpus Johanneum bei Irenäus von Lyon. 2005. *Vol. 189.*
– Glaube in den Pastoralbriefen. 2010. *Vol. 256.*
*Myers, Susan E.:* Spirit Epicleses in the Acts of Thomas. 2010. *Vol. 281.*
*Nguyen, V. Henry T.:* Christian Identity in Corinth. 2008. *Vol. II/243.*
*Nicklas, Tobias, Andreas Merkt* und *Joseph Verheyden* (Ed.): Gelitten – Gestorben – Auferstanden. 2010. *Vol. II/273.*
– see *Verheyden, Joseph*
*Niebuhr, Karl-Wilhelm:* Gesetz and Paränese. 1987. *Vol. II/28.*
– Heidenapostel aus Israel. 1992. *Vol. 62.*
– see *Deines, Roland.*
– see *Dimitrov, Ivan Z.*
– see *Klein, Hans.*
– see *Kraus, Wolfgang.*
*Nielsen, Anders E.:* "Until it is Fullfilled". 2000. *Vol. II/126.*
*Nielsen, Jesper Tang:* Die kognitive Dimension des Kreuzes. 2009. *Vol. II/263.*
*Nissen, Andreas:* Gott und der Nächste im antiken Judentum. 1974. *Vol. 15.*
*Noack, Christian:* Gottesbewußtsein. 2000. *Vol. II/116.*
*Noormann, Rolf:* Irenäus als Paulusinterpret. 1994. *Vol. II/66.*
*Norin, Stig:* see *Hultgård, Anders.*
*Novakovic, Lidija:* Messiah, the Healer of the Sick. 2003. *Vol. II/170.*
*Obermann, Andreas:* Die christologische Erfüllung der Schrift im Johannesevangelium. 1996. *Vol. II/83.*
*Öhler, Markus:* Barnabas. 2003. *Vol. 156.*
– see *Becker, Michael.*

*Okure, Teresa:* The Johannine Approach to Mission. 1988. *Vol. II/31.*
*Onuki, Takashi:* Heil und Erlösung. 2004. *Vol. 165.*
*Oropeza, B. J.:* Paul and Apostasy. 2000. *Vol. II/115.*
*Ostmeyer, Karl-Heinrich:* Kommunikation mit Gott und Christus. 2006. *Vol. 197.*
– Taufe und Typos. 2000. *Vol. II/118.*
*Pao, David W.:* Acts and the Isaianic New Exodus. 2000. *Vol. II/130.*
*Park, Eung Chun:* The Mission Discourse in Matthew's Interpretation. 1995. *Vol. II/81.*
*Park, Joseph S.:* Conceptions of Afterlife in Jewish Insriptions. 2000. *Vol. II/121.*
*Parsenios, George L.:* Rhetoric and Drama in the Johannine Lawsuit Motif. 2010. *Vol. 258.*
*Pate, C. Marvin:* The Reverse of the Curse. 2000. *Vol. II/114.*
*Paulsen, Henning:* Studien zur Literatur und Geschichte des frühen Christentums. Ed. von Ute E. Eisen. 1997. *Vol. 99.*
*Pearce, Sarah J.K.:* The Land of the Body. 2007. *Vol. 208.*
*Peres, Imre:* Griechische Grabinschriften und neutestamentliche Eschatologie. 2003. *Vol. 157.*
*Perry, Peter S.:* The Rhetoric of Digressions. 2009. *Vol. II/268.*
*Philip, Finny:* The Origins of Pauline Pneumatology. 2005. *Vol. II/194.*
*Philonenko, Marc* (Ed.): Le Trône de Dieu. 1993. *Vol. 69.*
*Pilhofer, Peter:* Presbyteron Kreitton. 1990. *Vol. II/39.*
– Philippi. Vol. 1 1995. *Vol. 87.* – Vol. 2 ²2009. *Vol. 119.*
– Die frühen Christen und ihre Welt. 2002. *Vol. 145.*
– see *Becker, Eve-Marie.*
– see *Ego, Beate.*
*Pitre, Brant:* Jesus, the Tribulation, and the End of the Exile. 2005. *Vol. II/204.*
*Plümacher, Eckhard:* Geschichte und Geschichten. 2004. *Vol. 170.*
*Pöhlmann, Wolfgang:* Der Verlorene Sohn und das Haus. 1993. *Vol. 68.*
*Poirier, John C.:* The Tongues of Angels. 2010. *Vol. II/287.*
*Pokorný, Petr* and *Josef B. Souček:* Bibelauslegung als Theologie. 1997. *Vol. 100.*
– and *Jan Roskovec* (Ed.): Philosophical Hermeneutics and Biblical Exegesis. 2002. *Vol. 153.*
*Popkes, Enno Edzard:* Das Menschenbild des Thomasevangeliums. 2007. *Vol. 206.*

– Die Theologie der Liebe Gottes in den johanneischen Schriften. 2005. *Vol. II/197.*

*Porter, Stanley E.:* The Paul of Acts. 1999. *Vol. 115.*

*Prieur, Alexander:* Die Verkündigung der Gottesherrschaft. 1996. *Vol. II/89.*

*Probst, Hermann:* Paulus und der Brief. 1991. *Vol. II/45.*

*Puig i Tàrrech, Armand:* Jesus: An Uncommon Journey. 2010. *Vol. II/288.*

*Rabens, Volker:* The Holy Spirit and Ethics in Paul. 2010 *Vol. II/283.*

*Räisänen, Heikki:* Paul and the Law. 1983, ²1987. *Vol. 29.*

*Rehkopf, Friedrich:* Die lukanische Sonderquelle. 1959. *Vol. 5.*

*Rein, Matthias:* Die Heilung des Blindgeborenen (Joh 9). 1995. *Vol. II/73.*

*Reinmuth, Eckart:* Pseudo-Philo und Lukas. 1994. *Vol. 74.*

*Reiser, Marius:* Bibelkritik und Auslegung der Heiligen Schrift. 2007. *Vol. 217.*

– Syntax und Stil des Markusevangeliums. 1984. *Vol. II/11.*

*Reynolds, Benjamin E.:* The Apocalyptic Son of Man in the Gospel of John. 2008. *Vol. II/249.*

*Rhodes, James N.:* The Epistle of Barnabas and the Deuteronomic Tradition. 2004. *Vol. II/188.*

*Richards, E. Randolph:* The Secretary in the Letters of Paul. 1991. *Vol. II/42.*

*Riesner, Rainer:* Jesus als Lehrer. 1981, ³1988. *Vol. II/7.*

– Die Frühzeit des Apostels Paulus. 1994. *Vol. 71.*

*Rissi, Mathias:* Die Theologie des Hebräerbriefs. 1987. *Vol. 41.*

*Röcker, Fritz W.:* Belial und Katechon. 2009. *Vol. II/262.*

*Röhser, Günter:* Metaphorik und Personifikation der Sünde. 1987. *Vol. II/25.*

*Rose, Christian:* Theologie als Erzählung im Markusevangelium. 2007. *Vol. II/236.*

– Die Wolke der Zeugen. 1994. *Vol. II/60.*

*Roskovec, Jan:* see *Pokorný, Petr.*

*Rothschild, Clare K.:* Baptist Traditions and Q. 2005. *Vol. 190.*

– Hebrews as Pseudepigraphon. 2009. *Vol. 235.*

– Luke Acts and the Rhetoric of History. 2004. *Vol. II/175.*

– see *Frey, Jörg.*

*Rüegger, Hans-Ulrich:* Verstehen, was Markus erzählt. 2002. *Vol. II/155.*

*Rüger, Hans Peter:* Die Weisheitsschrift aus der Kairoer Geniza. 1991. *Vol. 53.*

*Sänger, Dieter:* Antikes Judentum und die Mysterien. 1980. *Vol. II/5.*

– Die Verkündigung des Gekreuzigten und Israel. 1994. *Vol. 75.*

– see *Burchard, Christoph*

– and *Ulrich Mell* (Ed.): Paulus und Johannes. 2006. *Vol. 198.*

*Salier, Willis Hedley:* The Rhetorical Impact of the Semeia in the Gospel of John. 2004. *Vol. II/186.*

*Salzmann, Jorg Christian:* Lehren und Ermahnen. 1994. *Vol. II/59.*

*Sandnes, Karl Olav:* Paul – One of the Prophets? 1991. *Vol. II/43.*

*Sato, Migaku:* Q und Prophetie. 1988. *Vol. II/29.*

*Schäfer, Ruth:* Paulus bis zum Apostelkonzil. 2004. *Vol. II/179.*

*Schaper, Joachim:* Eschatology in the Greek Psalter. 1995. *Vol. II/76.*

*Schimanowski, Gottfried:* Die himmlische Liturgie in der Apokalypse des Johannes. 2002. *Vol. II/154.*

– Weisheit und Messias. 1985. *Vol. II/17.*

*Schlichting, Günter:* Ein jüdisches Leben Jesu. 1982. *Vol. 24.*

*Schließer, Benjamin:* Abraham's Faith in Romans 4. 2007. *Vol. II/224.*

*Schnabel, Eckhard J.:* Law and Wisdom from Ben Sira to Paul. 1985. *Vol. II/16.*

*Schnelle, Udo:* see *Frey, Jörg.*

*Schröter, Jens:* Von Jesus zum Neuen Testament. 2007. *Vol. 204.*

– see *Frey, Jörg.*

*Schutter, William L.:* Hermeneutic and Composition in I Peter. 1989. *Vol. II/30.*

*Schwartz, Daniel R.:* Studies in the Jewish Background of Christianity. 1992. *Vol. 60.*

*Schwemer, Anna Maria:* see *Hengel, Martin*

*Scott, Ian W.:* Implicit Epistemology in the Letters of Paul. 2005. *Vol. II/205.*

*Scott, James M.:* Adoption as Sons of God. 1992. *Vol. II/48.*

– Paul and the Nations. 1995. *Vol. 84.*

*Shi, Wenhua:* Paul's Message of the Cross as Body Language. 2008. *Vol. II/254.*

*Shum, Shiu-Lun:* Paul's Use of Isaiah in Romans. 2002. *Vol. II/156.*

*Siegert, Folker:* Drei hellenistisch-jüdische Predigten. Teil I 1980. *Vol. 20* – Teil II 1992. *Vol. 61.*

– Nag-Hammadi-Register. 1982. *Vol. 26.*

– Argumentation bei Paulus. 1985. *Vol. 34.*

– Philon von Alexandrien. 1988. *Vol. 46.*

*Simon, Marcel:* Le christianisme antique et son contexte religieux I/II. 1981. *Vol. 23.*

*Smit, Peter-Ben:* Fellowship and Food in the Kingdom. 2008. *Vol. II/234.*

*Snodgrass, Klyne:* The Parable of the Wicked Tenants. 1983. *Vol. 27.*

*Söding, Thomas:* Das Wort vom Kreuz. 1997. *Vol. 93.*
- see *Thüsing, Wilhelm.*

*Sommer, Urs:* Die Passionsgeschichte des Markusevangeliums. 1993. *Vol. II/58.*

*Sorensen, Eric:* Possession and Exorcism in the New Testament and Early Christianity. 2002. *Vol. II/157.*

*Souček, Josef B.:* see *Pokorný, Petr.*

*Southall, David J.:* Rediscovering Righteousness in Romans. 2008. *Vol. 240.*

*Spangenberg, Volker:* Herrlichkeit des Neuen Bundes. 1993. *Vol. II/55.*

*Spanje, T.E. van:* Inconsistency in Paul? 1999. *Vol. II/110.*

*Speyer, Wolfgang:* Frühes Christentum im antiken Strahlungsfeld. Vol. I: 1989. *Vol. 50.*
- Vol. II: 1999. *Vol. 116.*
- Vol. III: 2007. *Vol. 213.*

*Spittler, Janet E.:* Animals in the Apocryphal Acts of the Apostles. 2008. *Vol. II/247.*

*Sprinkle, Preston:* Law and Life. 2008. *Vol. II/241.*

*Stadelmann, Helge:* Ben Sira als Schriftgelehrter. 1980. *Vol. II/6.*

*Stein, Hans Joachim:* Frühchristliche Mahlfeiern. 2008. *Vol. II/255.*

*Stenschke, Christoph W.:* Luke's Portrait of Gentiles Prior to Their Coming to Faith. *Vol. II/108.*

*Sterck-Degueldre, Jean-Pierre:* Eine Frau namens Lydia. 2004. *Vol. II/176.*

*Stettler, Christian:* Der Kolosserhymnus. 2000. *Vol. II/131.*

*Stettler, Hanna:* Die Christologie der Pastoralbriefe. 1998. *Vol. II/105.*

*Stökl Ben Ezra, Daniel:* The Impact of Yom Kippur on Early Christianity. 2003. *Vol. 163.*

*Strobel, August:* Die Stunde der Wahrheit. 1980. *Vol. 21.*

*Stroumsa, Guy G.:* Barbarian Philosophy. 1999. *Vol. 112.*

*Stuckenbruck, Loren T.:* Angel Veneration and Christology. 1995. *Vol. II/70.*
- , *Stephen C. Barton* and *Benjamin G. Wold* (Ed.): Memory in the Bible and Antiquity. 2007. *Vol. 212.*

*Stuhlmacher, Peter* (Ed.): Das Evangelium und die Evangelien. 1983. *Vol. 28.*
- Biblische Theologie und Evangelium. 2002. *Vol. 146.*

*Sung, Chong-Hyon:* Vergebung der Sünden. 1993. *Vol. II/57.*

*Svendsen, Stefan N.:* Allegory Transformed. 2009. *Vol. II/269.*

*Tajra, Harry W.:* The Trial of St. Paul. 1989. *Vol. II/35.*
- The Martyrdom of St.Paul. 1994. *Vol. II/67.*

*Tellbe, Mikael:* Christ-Believers in Ephesus. 2009. *Vol. 242.*

*Theißen, Gerd:* Studien zur Soziologie des Urchristentums. 1979, ³1989. *Vol. 19.*

*Theobald, Michael:* Studien zum Römerbrief. 2001. *Vol. 136.*

*Theobald, Michael:* see *Mußner, Franz.*

*Thornton, Claus-Jürgen:* Der Zeuge des Zeugen. 1991. *Vol. 56.*

*Thüsing, Wilhelm:* Studien zur neutestamentlichen Theologie. Ed. von Thomas Söding. 1995. *Vol. 82.*

*Thurén, Lauri:* Derhethorizing Paul. 2000. *Vol. 124.*

*Thyen, Hartwig:* Studien zum Corpus Iohanneum. 2007. *Vol. 214.*

*Tibbs, Clint:* Religious Experience of the Pneuma. 2007. *Vol. II/230.*

*Toit, David S. du:* Theios Anthropos. 1997. *Vol. II/91.*

*Tolmie, D. Francois:* Persuading the Galatians. 2005. *Vol. II/190.*

*Tomson, Peter J.* and *Doris Lambers-Petry* (Ed.): The Image of the Judaeo-Christians in Ancient Jewish and Christian Literature. 2003. *Vol. 158.*

*Toney, Carl N.:* Paul's Inclusive Ethic. 2008. *Vol. II/252.*

*Trebilco, Paul:* The Early Christians in Ephesus from Paul to Ignatius. 2004. *Vol. 166.*

*Treloar, Geoffrey R.:* Lightfoot the Historian. 1998. *Vol. II/103.*

*Troftgruben, Troy M.: A Conclusion Unhindered.* 2010. *Vol. II/280.*

*Tsuji, Manabu:* Glaube zwischen Vollkommenheit und Verweltlichung. 1997. *Vol. II/93.*

*Twelftree, Graham H.:* Jesus the Exorcist. 1993. *Vol. II/54.*

*Ulrichs, Karl Friedrich:* Christusglaube. 2007. *Vol. II/227.*

*Urban, Christina:* Das Menschenbild nach dem Johannesevangelium. 2001. *Vol. II/137.*

*Vahrenhorst, Martin:* Kultische Sprache in den Paulusbriefen. 2008. *Vol. 230.*

*Vegge, Ivar:* 2 Corinthians – a Letter about Reconciliation. 2008. *Vol. II/239.*

*Verheyden, Joseph, Korinna Zamfir* and *Tobias Nicklas* (Ed.): Prophets and Prophecy in Jewish and Early Christian Literature. 2010. *Vol. II/286.*
- see *Nicklas, Tobias*

*Visotzky, Burton L.:* Fathers of the World. 1995. *Vol. 80.*

*Vollenweider, Samuel:* Horizonte neutestamentlicher Christologie. 2002. *Vol. 144.*

*Vos, Johan S.:* Die Kunst der Argumentation bei Paulus. 2002. *Vol. 149.*

*Waaler, Erik:* The *Shema* and The First Commandment in First Corinthians. 2008. *Vol. II/253.*

*Wagener, Ulrike:* Die Ordnung des „Hauses Gottes". 1994. *Vol. II/65.*

*Wagner, J. Ross:* see *Wilk, Florian.*

*Wahlen, Clinton:* Jesus and the Impurity of Spirits in the Synoptic Gospels. 2004. *Vol. II/185.*

*Walker, Donald D.:* Paul's Offer of Leniency (2 Cor 10:1). 2002. *Vol. II/152.*

*Walter, Nikolaus:* Praeparatio Evangelica. Ed. von Wolfgang Kraus und Florian Wilk. 1997. *Vol. 98.*

*Wander, Bernd:* Gottesfürchtige und Sympathisanten. 1998. *Vol. 104.*

*Wardle, Timothy:* The Jerusalem Temple and Early Christian Identity. 2010. *Vol. II/291.*

*Wasserman, Emma:* The Death of the Soul in Romans 7. 2008. *Vol. 256.*

*Waters, Guy:* The End of Deuteronomy in the Epistles of Paul. 2006. *Vol. 221.*

*Watt, Jan G. van der:* see *Frey, Jörg*

*Watts, Rikki:* Isaiah's New Exodus and Mark. 1997. *Vol. II/88.*

*Webb, Robert L.:* see *Bock, Darrell L.*

*Wedderburn, A.J.M.:* Baptism and Resurrection. 1987. *Vol. 44.*

*Wegner, Uwe:* Der Hauptmann von Kafarnaum. 1985. *Vol. II/14.*

*Weiß, Hans-Friedrich:* Frühes Christentum und Gnosis. 2008. *Vol. 225.*

*Weissenrieder, Annette:* Images of Illness in the Gospel of Luke. 2003. *Vol. II/164.*

–, and *Robert B. Coote* (Ed.): The Interface of Orality and Writing. 2010. *Vol. 260.*

–, *Friederike Wendt* and *Petra von Gemünden* (Ed.): Picturing the New Testament. 2005. *Vol. II/193.*

*Welck, Christian:* Erzählte ‚Zeichen'. 1994. *Vol. II/69.*

*Wendt, Friederike* (Ed.): see *Weissenrieder, Annette.*

*Wiarda, Timothy:* Peter in the Gospels. 2000. *Vol. II/127.*

*Wifstrand, Albert:* Epochs and Styles. 2005. *Vol. 179.*

*Wilk, Florian* and *J. Ross Wagner* (Ed.): Between Gospel and Election. 2010. *Vol. 257.*

– see *Walter, Nikolaus.*

*Williams, Catrin H.:* I am He. 2000. *Vol. II/113.*

*Wilson, Todd A.:* The Curse of the Law and the Crisis in Galatia. 2007. *Vol. II/225.*

*Wilson, Walter T.:* Love without Pretense. 1991. *Vol. II/46.*

*Winn, Adam:* The Purpose of Mark's Gospel. 2008. *Vol. II/245.*

*Winninge, Mikael:* see *Holmberg, Bengt.*

*Wischmeyer, Oda:* Von Ben Sira zu Paulus. 2004. *Vol. 173.*

*Wisdom, Jeffrey:* Blessing for the Nations and the Curse of the Law. 2001. *Vol. II/133.*

*Witmer, Stephen E.:* Divine Instruction in Early Christianity. 2008. *Vol. II/246.*

*Wold, Benjamin G.:* Women, Men, and Angels. 2005. *Vol. II/2001.*

*Wolter, Michael:* Theologie und Ethos im frühen Christentum. 2009. *Vol. 236.*

– see *Stuckenbruck, Loren T.*

*Wright, Archie T.:* The Origin of Evil Spirits. 2005. *Vol. II/198.*

*Wucherpfennig, Ansgar:* Heracleon Philologus. 2002. *Vol. 142.*

*Yates, John W.:* The Spirit and Creation in Paul. 2008. *Vol. II/251.*

*Yeung, Maureen:* Faith in Jesus and Paul. 2002. *Vol. II/147.*

*Zamfir, Corinna:* see *Verheyden, Joseph*

*Zangenberg, Jürgen, Harold W. Attridge* and *Dale B. Martin* (Ed.): Religion, Ethnicity and Identity in Ancient Galilee. 2007. *Vol. 210.*

*Zimmermann, Alfred E.:* Die urchristlichen Lehrer. 1984, ²1988. *Vol. II/12.*

*Zimmermann, Johannes:* Messianische Texte aus Qumran. 1998. *Vol. II/104.*

*Zimmermann, Ruben:* Christologie der Bilder im Johannesevangelium. 2004. *Vol. 171.*

– Geschlechtermetaphorik und Gottesverhältnis. 2001. *Vol. II/122.*

– (Ed.): Hermeneutik der Gleichnisse Jesu. 2008. *Vol. 231.*

– see *Frey, Jörg.*

– see *Horn, Friedrich Wilhelm.*

*Zugmann, Michael:* „Hellenisten" in der Apostelgeschichte. 2009. *Vol. II/264.*

*Zumstein, Jean:* see *Dettwiler, Andreas*

*Zwiep, Arie W.:* Judas and the Choice of Matthias. 2004. *Vol. II/187.*

*For a complete catalogue please write to the publisher*
*Mohr Siebeck • P.O. Box 2030 • D–72010 Tübingen/Germany*
*Up-to-date information on the internet at www.mohr.de*